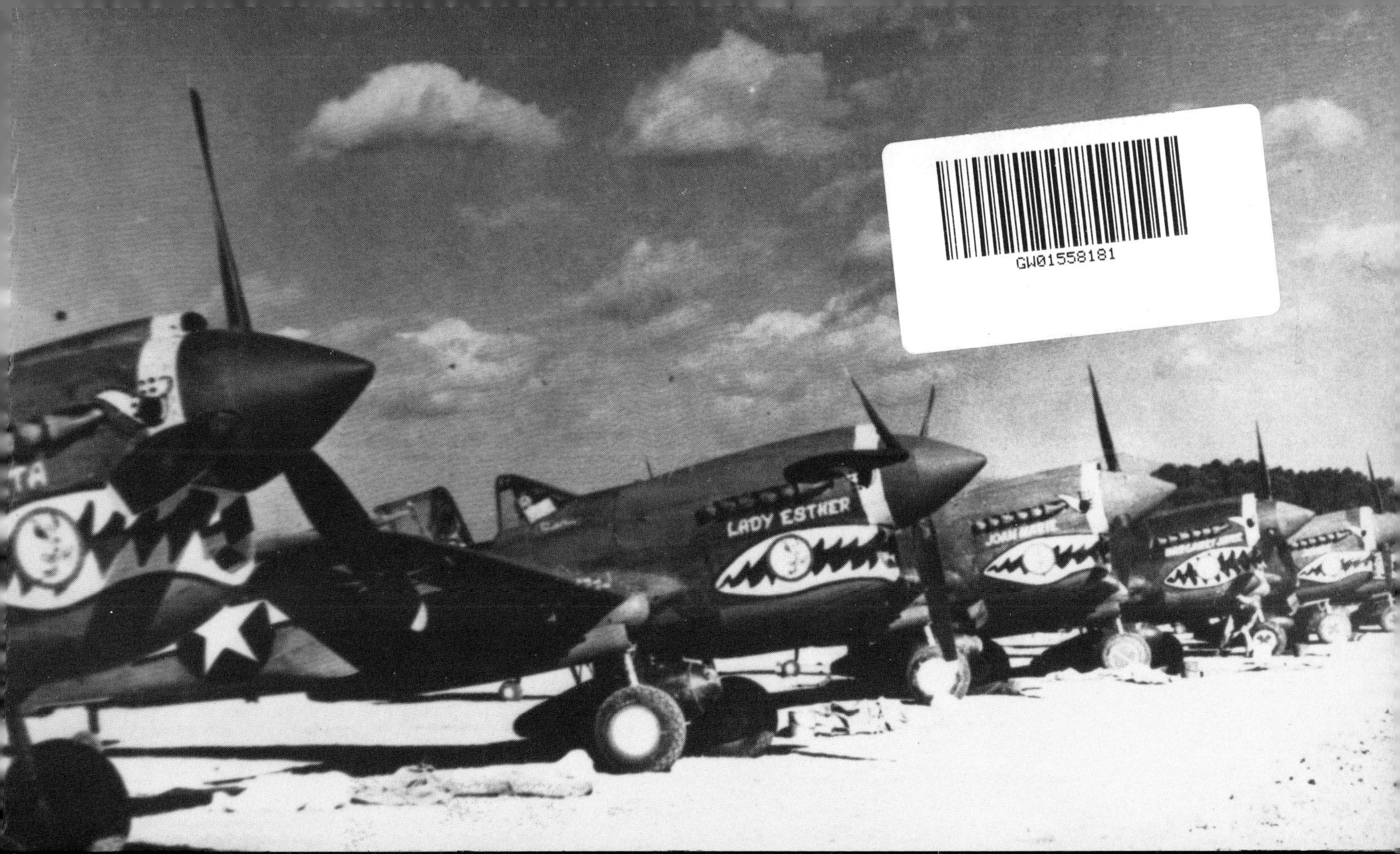
LADY ESTHER



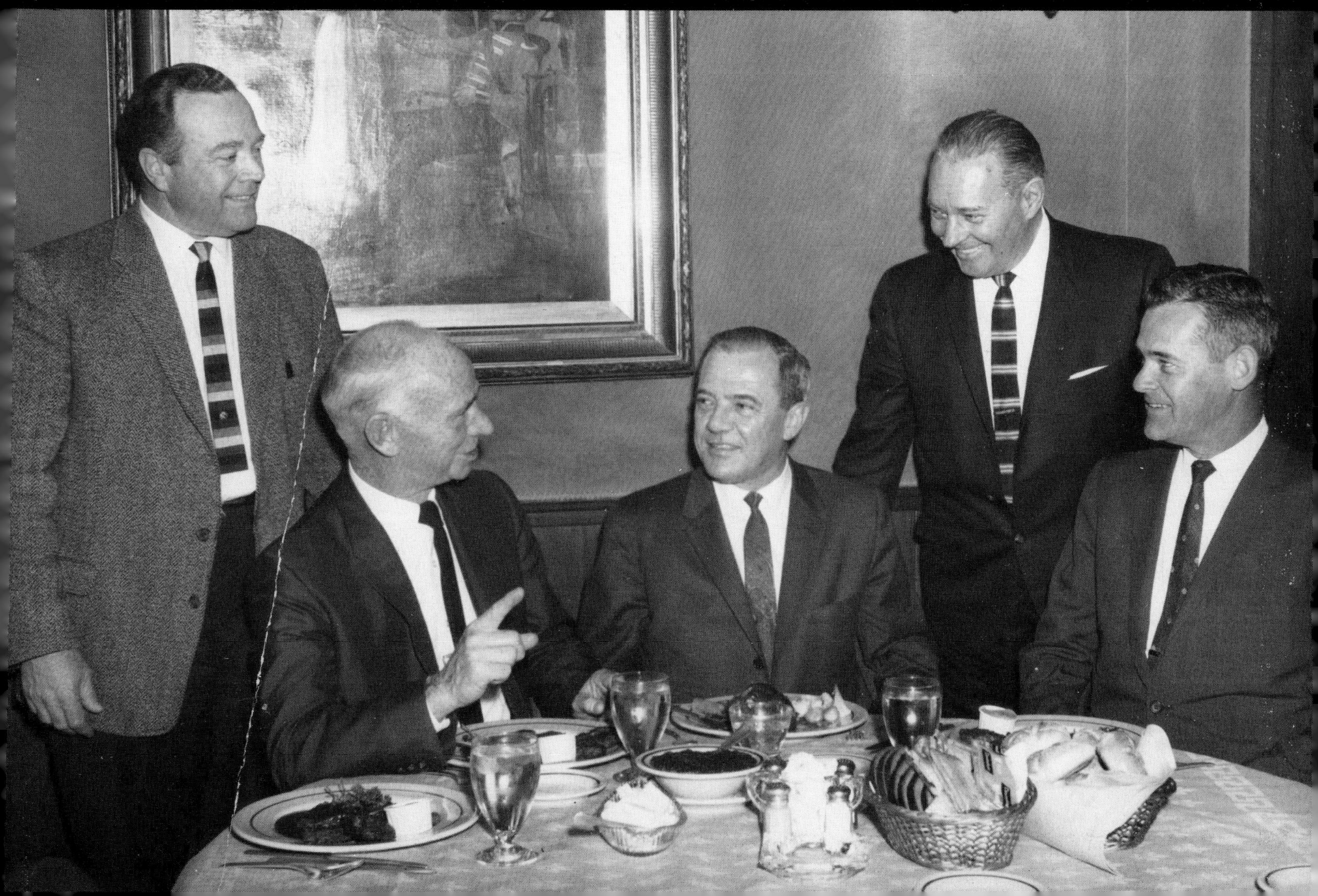

# Himalayan Rogue

## A PILOT'S ODYSSEY

TURNER PUBLISHING COMPANY

Paducah, Kentucky

TURNER PUBLISHING COMPANY
P.O. Box 3101, 412 Broadway
Paducah, Kentucky 42001
(502) 443-0121

Library of Congress Catalog Card No.: 94-60795
ISBN: 1-56311-149-7
First Printing: 1994
Second Printing: 1998

Printed in the USA. Limited edition: additional copies may be ordered directly
from the publisher.

_Front cover: Portrait painted by Peter J. Goutiere's sister, Geraldine Acomb, 1944._

# DEDICATION

This book is dedicated to my very brave son Christian and to my daughter Hannah. Also, to a very wonderful young man whom I don't really know: my first son, David.

To my Mum and Dad; may they now be together always. To my brothers and sisters: George, Christine, Vernon and Geraldine.

To my flying friends who are scattered in all parts of the world.

Lastly, to my very lovely wife Evelyn.

*His Majesty King Hussein and beautiful Queen Noor, Daughter of Najeeb Halaby, Ex-FAA Administrator.*

Dear Peter,                                      February 13, 1994

Thank you for your letter. I am glad you are well! I am surprised how well you remember our meeting (together with my uncle, His Highness the late Sharif Nasser) nearly forty years ago, in 1955, in the Jordan Valley. I would be happy to participate in your autobiography. This is not a liberty you have taken at all, but an honour and pleasure for me, and I look forward to reading it and seeing the pictures with great interest this summer, God willing.

If I have understood your letter correctly, you also wanted me to write a few words about aviation. I am in fact pleased to do this, because as you know I have always loved to fly and have spent many, many hours over more than four decades in many different cockpits, from my first solo flight in a twin engine Dove to intercontinental journeys in 747s. I have also thought deeply about flight, and been priviledged to witness, as you yourself have, the history of aviation unfold before my eyes in any ever-astonishing way.

I once wrote in a book, when I was younger, that what appeals to me most about flying is the freedom and space it physically and mentally affords me. However, I now realize that there is even more to flight than beauty of light and air. Indeed, flight epitomizes not only the true vocation of man, but also the very predicament of the modern world. For whilst our duty as human beings is to detach ourselves from the pettiness, meanness and ugliness of the world, and soar in the tranquillity and serenity of self-trascendence, nevertheless we must beware of the dangers of getting above ourselves — as in the myth of the flight of Icarus — and of the danger of flying too near the sun of pride and arrogance.

Moreover, the ever-progressing development of airplanes from simple, humanly-manageable flying crafts to machines now almost too complex for their pilots, reflects the technological march of progress of our world wherein on the one hand machinery is constantly improving and making life safer and better, and on the other hand the human being himself is in danger of being forgotten, quantified and smothered. In short, flight epitomizes the very exhilaration, beauty and danger of life itself, and for that reason a life spent in aviation is a life truly fulfilled.

May I take this opportunity to wish you also a healthy and prosperous 1994, from myself and Queen Noor,

As ever,

Your friend.

# CONTENTS

# SPELLINGS AND MEANINGS
## of Foreign names and Places

A

Abidjan: Ivory coast, W.Africa
Abyssinia: now known as Ethiopia
Acare Lane: red-light district, Calcutta
Accra: Ghana, once British Gold Coast, West Africa
Agra: where Taj Mahal is located, India
Aiapata: Naini-Tal District, India
"Ak-dum-Jaldi": Hindi for "hurry up"
Akyab, town on Arakan Coast, Burma
Aldrovandi Apartments: Rome, Italy
Almira: a wooden cupboard used for hanging clothes
Almorah: a hill station in the Himalayas
Amra Hotel: Amman Jordan
Amritser: town northwest of Delhi, India
Ankara: capitol of Turkey
Ankush: iron instrument to control an elephant
Annapurna: mountain range, Nepal
Aquaba: seaport for Jordan
Aroostook County: Maine
Asmara: Eriteria, Ethiopia
Assam Valley: India
Ayah: Indian maid servant
Ayesha: Maharani of Jaipur

B

Bacchapra: house in Monhyr where my father died, India
Baksheesh: alms
Ballijan: airfield in Assam Valley, India
Ballygunge: suburb of Calcutta
Baluchas: natives of northwest Pakistan
Balurghat: Village north of Calcutta
Bangladesh: country north of Calcutta, once E. Pakistan
Bara-Banki: District where my father captured dacoits, India
Barakpore: suburb of Calcutta
Basha: Hindi for hut
Basra: seaport for Iraq
Basti: my mother's birth place, India
Bereilly: railway junction to Naini-Tal
Betmari: a town in Lebanon
Bhaiya: in Hindi means brother
Bhasti: Indian that carries water in large goat skin
Bhim-Tal: hill station in Himalayas, India
Bhindu and Cahu Singh: employed by Cooch Behar
Bhowali: hill station in Himalayas, India
Bihar Province: India

Bijnor Jungles: once famous for tigers; India
"Billy-ke-pas-dhum-Hai?": Hindi for, "Has a cat got an ass!"
"Boo-Hao": Chinese for Bad
Borghese Park: Rome, Italy
Brahmaputra River: flows through Assam Valley, India
Bunia: an Indian merchant
Burrah: in Hindi means large or big

C

Calcutta: old capital of India
Catapult: slingshot
Chabua: U.S. Airbase in the Assam Valley, India
Chandernagore: once a French possession just north of Calcutta
Chaprassi: Indian messenger
Charpoy: bed, cot
Chaukadar: Indian watchman
Chenault: Commander of Flying Tigers (AVG) in China
Chengtu: U.S. Airbase in China
Chittagong: city on southeast coast of Bangladesh
Chiu-Lung-Po: auxiliary airport CNAC used in China
Chota-Hazari: small breakfast
Chowringhee Street: one of the well known streets in Calcutta
Chukar: Himalayan hill partridge
Constantinople: old name for Istanbul, Turkey
Cooch Behar: Maharajah estate north of Calcutta

D

Dacca or Dhaka: capital of Bangladesh
Dak: mail
Dak bungalow: rest house
Dalhousie Square: area and street in Calcutta
Damongo: a town in north west Ghana
Dandi: a sedan chair carried by coolies
Darjeeling: hill station in Himalayas; famous for its tea
Darzi: tailor
Delamayah: a country club in south Lebanon
Delhi: Old and New, capital of India
Dhoti: Indian loin cloth or sarong
Digboi Mountain: north Assam
Dinjan Airport: CNAC base of operation
Drigh Road: airport road to Karachi from airport, Pakistan

E

El Fasha: airport in west Sudan, Africa
El Genina: airport in west Sudan, Africa

8

F
Firppo's Restaurant: in Calcutta
Fiumicino Airport: Rome's old airport, Italy
Fort Hertz Airport: in north Burma
Fort Lamy: town in central Africa
Freetown: Sierra Leone, Africa

G
Gadhafi or Khadafy: ruler of Libya
"Gandhi-ji-ki-jai": in praise of the Hindu leader
Garrum-gussal: hot bath
Gat-Ramon Hotel: old hotel in Palestine (Israel)
Gavrillo Princip: Bosnian assassin
Ghooral: Himalayan mountain goat
Ghora-Ghari: horse and carriage in India
Ghurka: Nepalese military man
Godown: a storage place
Goula River: Naini-Tal Dist. India
Guatam Narayan: relative of Cooch Behar
Gura: U.S. base in Eriteria, Ethiopia
Gymkhana: a club or sports place

H
Haile Selassie: Once an emperor of Ethiopia
Haldwani: railway station on way to Naini-Tal
Hamadryad: king cobra
Hami: airport in Gobi Desert, China
Hanif: our servant in Monghyr, India
Han-Kau: Airport in China
Heliopolis: residential area of Cairo, Egypt
Himalayas: mountain range north India
Hindustan Building: in Calcutta
Hotz Hotel: in Agra, India
Huakong Valley: in north Burma
Humayan: Mogul Emperor of India in 15th Century

I
Irriwaddy: river in Burma
Isfahan: old capital of Persia, now Iran

J
Jahangir: Mogul Emperor of India
Jaipur: a Maharajah state in eastern India
"Jaldi-karo": "hurry up" or "make haste"
Jalebi: Indian sweet that looks like a pretzel
Jalpaiguri: airport in north India
Jasma: my little friend in Bhim-Tal, India
Jebu-Marra Mountain: a check point near El-Genina, Africa
Jiwani: fishing village west coast of Pakistan
Jodhpur: Maharajah states in west India
Joelicote: a hill station on way to Naini-Tal, India

K
Kaduna: a city in Nigeria
Kaichi: scissors
Kaladungi: town near Naini-Tal, India
Kaleege: a breed of pheasant in Himalayas
Kano: city in north Nigeria
Karachi: seaport in Pakistan
Karayia Road: Redlight Dist. in Calcutta
Karnani Estate and Mansions: apartment buildings in Calcutta
Kasauli: hill station in Himalayas
Katchigaon: forest station in Assam
Kathadin: Mountain in Maine
Kathgodam: railway terminus near Naini-Tal, India
Kenduskeag Stream: in Bangor, Maine

Khabbar: news
Khabbardar: "watch out"
Kailas Mountain: mountain near Bhim-Tal, India
Khaldi Airport: main airport for Lebanon
Khansama: a cook
Khartoum: capital of the Sudan on Nile River
Khas-Khas Tati: certain type of roots fixed on latice and placed on doors and windows for cooling homes in India
Khud: steep cliff
Khyber Pass: certain area on the NorthWest Frontier of India
Kingwan Airport: U.S. Airbase in Shanghai, China
Kukri: a Ghurka war knife of Nepal
Kulfi: type of Indian icecream
Kumaon: area in Naini-Tal where I lived
Kumasi: town in Ghana
Kunming: city in China we flew supplies to
Kweilin: a city in China on the Li River

L
Lagos: major port for Nigeria
Lal-Kuwa: a railway stop on way to Naini-Tal, India
Lalmanirhat: a U.S. airbase in north India
Lanchow: city in west China
Landour: hill station near Mussoorie
Langur: silvered furred monkey of Himalayas
Lathi: Indian watchman's stave
Likiang Mountain: mountain check point on way to Suifu
Lissanevitch: Boris our friend of the 300 Club, Calcutta
LoPchu: tea estate in Darjeeling
Lunghwa Airport: CNAC's air base in Shanghai

M
Machan: Hindi for a platform in a tree for hunting
Machhapuchhara Mountain: in Pokhara Nepal
Macwahoc: a town in northern Maine
Mahout: Indian elephant driver
Mahseer: a game fish of India; carp family
Maidan: Indian park or playground
Maiduguri: a town in northern Nigeria
Mali: Hindi for a gardener
Marrakech: a city in Morocco
Masalchi: Indian dishwasher boy
Masera Island: off the coast of Oman
Mattyr: Indian sweeper boy
Mekong River: crossing the Hump
"Mio-piko-ma": Chinese for, "Has a cat got an ass?"
Millinocket: a town in north Maine
Minigonka Mountain: in China, crossing the Hump
Mishmi Hills: in north Assam, India
Mohabir: a rich friend of mine in Calcutta
Monghyr: the town where my father died, India
Mooseluek Lake: in northern Maine
Moti-Mahal Restuarant: means "pearl-palace," in Delhi
Mount Kanchenjunga: third tallest mountain in Himalayas
Mumtaz: wife of Mogul emperor Shah Jahan, the builder of the Taj Mahal
Murgia: Hindi for died or dead
Musa: name of banana boat I worked as a sailor
Mussoorie: a hill station in India, where my mother lived
Myitkyina: a town occupied by Japs in Burma

N
Naini-Tal: a hill station in Himalayas where I went to school
Nullah: drain; narrow ravine
Nyere: town in Kenya where Jim Corbett, writer of the "Maneaters of Kamaon," died

P

Pagliacci: from the Opera
Pak-Dundi: Hindi for a jungle pathway
Panagarh: a town just west of Calcutta
Paochi: a town in China
Paoshan: a village in southwest China
Patna: a town on the Ganges River
Pattan-Din: a Dacoiti leader captured by my father
Patu: a cloth hat
Peepal tree: sacred to Hindus in India
Peshawar: a town in northwest frontier, Pakistan
Pheneel: a tar product used in India as a disenfectant
Pilibit Jungle: where mum and dad went hunting, India
Pilkhana: a place where tame elephants corraled
Poezavara, Ramond and Paulette: friends from F. Lamy
Pokhara: town in west Nepal
Pottschmidt (Pottie): check pilot for CNAC
Powalgarh: a village where Corbett shot the Maneating tiger
Prithi Singh: a prince friend of Jaipur, and polo player
Pugri: turban worn by indians
Punkah Wallah: the man who pulled the large fan with rope
Purdah: a Moslem woman's seclusion or robe, worn over the head

Q

Qutab-Minar: old monument built by Moguls near Delhi

R

Raimona: a forest village in Assam where I hunted tigers
Rajkamar: a prince of the State
Rani-Bargh: a village on the way to Naini-Tal
Ranikhet: a hill station in Himalayas
Rawalpindi: a town in north Pakistan
Ringal: stunted hill bamboo

S

Sadhu: holy man
Sadya: a village in north Assam, used as Army base
Sais: horse groomer
Salween River: divides Burma and China
Sanopah: small airfield on island in Chungking
Sari: a fine cotton cloth worn by Indian women
Sat-Tal: a lake area and a place for our picnics
Sepoy: Indian soldier during the British rule
Shah Abbas: Persian ruler in 18th century
Shah Jahan: a Mogul Emperor, built Taj Mahal
Shaitan: Hindi for devil
Shakari: Hindi for guide and hunter
Shepherd: Our landlord in Bhowali
Shikaras: flat boats used on Dahl Lake, Kashmir
Shillong Hills: hill station in Assam, India
Shimbuang: a town in north Burma
Simla: hill station in Himalayas
Sirinagar: capital of Kashmir
Solinski, Sigmond: CNAC mechanic, of DC-2 1/2 fame
Sookerting (Dum-Duma): a U.S. air base in north Assam
Suhrawardy, H.: a high political figure in Calcutta
Suifu Airport: in China
Suklo: our servant and bearer, with CNAC, Assam
Sunda Bunds: the delta area south of Calcutta
Suprabum: a town in north Burma
"Swalik Hills": jungles famous for tigers

T

Takaradi: a town in west Ghana
Tal: Hindi for lake
Tamale: a town in north Ghana
Terai jungles: in foothills of Himalayas
Tirchakhet: village near Bhowali, India
Tolligunge: a suburb of Calcutta

W

Wadi Sedna: village and landing field in Sudan
Wallah: man, person
Watchung Hills: in New Jersey
Whiteaway & Laidlaw: clothing store in Calcutta

Y

Yangtze River: in China
Yunani: U.S. Air Force base in China, near Lake Tali

# A FEW NOTES FOR THE READER

First, I would like to inform the reader that I am no professional writer. I have simply written my life story as the events came to me. When I started writing and documenting my experiences, I felt I should hold nothing back. I knew I had to write with rather a brash open mindedness, that admitted no double meaning. I have included my various intimacies and love affairs. I hope you're not shocked.

Though my childhood memories have been vivid enough, it still becomes difficult to associate dates and events as they took place during the early years. My "jack-o-lantern" memory started functioning at about the age of four. Events before that are strictly from stories my mother used to tell us; therefore, some of the dates I have given for my experiences may not be too accurate, but the events are true. In later years I lost my valuable flight log, due to the bloody Lebanese war that erupted in 1975. I lost other valuable documents at the same time. Since I had no log book to give accurate dates of events that took place, especially during my flying with CNAC, I have tried my best to be as accurate as possible. Should the reader find errors, I apologize for the mistakes. Again, I must state, the events and experiences are true.

As for the names of people I have mentioned in my life story, it will be noted that in some instances I have used only their first names, for reasons of my own. The little girl Jasma was a real person; I never did know her last name. She probably married a local villager in Bhim-Tal area. The hill women mature at an early age and marry when reaching the age of twelve to fourteen. I shall always remember that funny little pig-tailed girl.

Since this book is specifically about myself and my adventures through life, I would like to state that there were five children in our family, I being the youngest. I have mentioned them during my early years in India. My sister Christine went on to become a well known writer from Maine. I have not read all her books; I recall one, *Indigo*, which became a best seller. She also wrote about the Goutieres and her life in India. My sister Geraldine, who is an accomplished artist, has also decided to write about her childhood. It is difficult to say how the stories may be told. I am certain there will be a great deal of over-lapping, such as the incident of the leopard and our dog Bob.

The early years in Maine and America were wonder years and a drastic change for me. Though I adjusted quickly, I never lost my love for India. It was my brother-in-law Robert Weston that encouraged my love for the outdoors. Sylvia, too, was a great inspiration and a wonderful friend. My fondness for her has lasted all through the years.

The adventures in aviation were unexpected and changed my life style. I have written extensively about my flying experiences, mainly the WWII years and flying the "Hump." The Hump was that large spur of the Himalayan range that stretched across the north end of the Assam Valley of India, then turned south to divide Burma and China. The peaks rose from twelve to nineteen thousand feet. Further north they rose to twenty-four thousand feet. There were many of us that flew the same area. All had stories to tell. Some of my CNAC colleagues have written their episodes in various magazines and books. I have mentioned quite a few names of my flying friends and explained the twists of fate that brought us together. Calcutta was a melting pot of uniforms and developed into a great social center.

My time off from flying the Hump, was spent in Calcutta where most of us had small apartments. It was here that I met such wonderful friends as the Maharajah of Cooch Behar, Jaipur, Prithi Singh and Boris who ran the famed 300 Club. They have all departed this world while still fairly young. What I wouldn't give for one last hell of a party at the 300 Club on old Theatre Road with all those wonderful people.

Some of my CNAC friends have written or are in the process of writing their adventures of the "Hump." Once again, this probably will bring about some over-lapping of stories. It cannot be helped.

In reference to tigers and tiger shooting (hunting), people have said to me, "How cruel to shoot those magnificent animals that are going extinct." True. But, when born and brought up in the land of the tiger, with generations of families who have been hunters, it becomes a part of you. It is in your blood from the time you have your first catapult (sling shot). Tiger hunting goes back to the time of Alexander the Great, and the Great Moguls who ruled India during the sixteenth and seventeenth and eighteenth centuries. There has always been a great number of tigers whose habitat ranged from Persia, throughout India, Burma, Siam, Malaya and north to Siberia. Their numbers were in excess of sixty thousand in India alone.

From the time the British Raj came to India in the eighteenth century till the independence of India in 1947, there were about fifty thousand tigers in the land. It is stated in documentaries and magazines that the British and the Maharajahs had a lot to do with the depletion of the striped cats; that they organized large hunting parties with hundreds of beaters and elephants to flush the animals out. True, there were many such arranged safaris by the Maharajahs and British Government officials. Yes, through the years several thousand large cats were probably shot. Yet, in spite of all that hunting, it was no more than a "pee in the ocean." The safaris were well organized and regulated. Permits were issued for shooting in certain blocks of land. No my friends, it wasn't the British sportsman, or the great Maharajahs that made the tigers and leopards endangered species; nor was it a cruel sport as reported. It would never compare with the destruction of the American buffalo (bison) in the years of Buffalo Bill and the sportsmen that came from Europe to see how many they could kill for fun. Then there is the slaughter of the baby seals in the Arctic for their fine fur. The hunters walk up to the helpless seal pups, and club them to death. Talk about cruel; it's the most degrading sight to witness on TV.

The real cause, not only the endangering of the big cats, but all fauna and flora, is locally inspired. How? Though the United States Government prohibits importation of skins, feathers, ivory and antlers, it is still a flourishing business in Europe and the Far East—China, Taiwan. Tiger and leopard (especially the snow leopard) skins bring a small fortune, also the bones and other parts for sale as rheumatic cures. Because of this demand, the Indians are out slaughtering tigers by any means possible. One common method is poisoning, then trapping. Most Indians today are able to buy shotguns imported from Russia. These people are out hunting the year round, regardless of the season. Due to their meager salaries, many of the forest officers are doing the poaching. On a trip to Delhi on FAA business, I was informed by a Pan American official that the Indian customs had seized a shipment of forty tiger skins on a major airline destined for Europe. This took place in 1980.

Another of the major problems is the denuding of the jungles and habitat of the animals. Coal, charcoal and gas are too expensive for the majority of the poor Indians to use for their cooking. the cheapest fuel is wood. This comes from the lush Terai jungles. Many areas I knew as a kid, the Naini-Tal District and the once lovely pine and silver oak forests are more than fifty percent gone. By the turn of the century it will be all gone. The government is making a futile attempt to stop this cutting down of forests, but it will take a lot of manpower.

I have written my life story as I remembered it. I have not encroached on other people's experiences intentionally. If there are incidents that run parallel with what I have written it is purely coincidental. Other authors have used some of my experiences when I have mentioned them at parties, such as when I caught a Haji cooking rice in the toilet of the aircraft while we were on a flight to Jeddah.

As far as profanity is concerned: yes, I have used it openly. Sometimes when one is terribly upset and frustrated, it becomes difficult to bite one's tongue and say nothing. In these instances I have sworn mainly at myself. In no way has it been directed at any particular individual. It may also be noticed that some of the time I have taken my frustration out on the whiskey bottle. I have done so to dull the mind and try to forget. I would like the reader to know I am not an alchoholic nor a sex maniac!

One more note. I've always thought a great deal of PanAmerican Airways. When I commuted by train between New Jersey and New York in the 1930s, I sometimes would read about PanAm's pioneering flights to South America and across the Pacific to such places as Manila and Hong Kong. I was excited and envious of the pilots that flew the Clipper flying-boats to those distant places. I would half dream away the time thinking of those exotic islands in the Pacific. I would wake suddenly when the old commuter train came to a jolting stop at the Jersey City station.

Not in my wildest dreams did I think one day I would wear PanAmerican wings and insignias of PanAmerican Africa as a pilot, or for CNAC, which was an affiliate of PanAm.

After deregulation was introduced by Congress, the major airlines, like PanAm, felt the struggle to keep alive because of the influx of fly-by-night operators that took to the air. In time it would catch up with PanAm. By the early 1980s PanAm appeared to be in its death throes. The final blow was struck on December 21, 1988, when PanAm flight #103 was bombed out of the sky over Lockerbie, Scotland. It would not be long from that date when Pan American Airways finally folded its wings. So ended one of the finest U.S. Flag carriers of the world.

I hope you enjoy reading this book as much as I did putting it together

*A CNAC Plane crossing the Hump. Picture taken by CNAC Captain Jim Dalby.*

# THE HIMALAYAN ROGUE
## A Pilot's Odyssey

### by
### PETER J. deM GOUTIERE

## PHASE ONE: 1914 - 1928

In the year 1914 two major events took place: the first event of significance, and staggering to the world, was the Great War, or World War One. It was to rattle thrones of monarchs and destroy empires. What lit the fuse to this event? On June 28 Archduke Ferdinand and his wife Sofia, while on a state visit to Serbia, were assassinated by a twit of a Serb named Gavrillo Princip. This incident sparked the outbreak of the war between Germany and the allies.

After the war, many geographical and political changes took place. One was the end of the Ottoman Empire with Constantinople as its capital. It became Turkey with Ankara as the capital. Palestine and Trans-Jordan were created. Palestine, Egypt and Trans-Jordan were mandated to England, while Syria and Lebanon were to France.

Though England had a secure foothold in India since the Sepoy Mutiny of 1857, her roots in the colony were now stronger. The devastated countries and cities of WWI needed industrial products to rebuild themselves. England was in a position to supply quantities of raw materials such as lumber (teak and mahogany) and steel from India and Burma, rubber form Malaya. There was also a great demand for oil. England was able to supply this from Iraq and Kuwait that she controlled. Pipe lines were laid across the Arabian desert to Haifa in Palestine, and also across Syria to Sidon and Tripoli in Lebanon. England's colonies spanned the world. It was well known that the "Sun never set on English Soil." Trade routes picked up from England to the Middle and Far East countries. Better and faster steamships were introduced. It became necessary for England to send civil servants to her far flung lands. It encouraged young British men to go overseas. In time, these people would become frequent travellers to distant lands and return home on furloughs (leave). One of the favored steamship lines was the Peninsular and Orient Company, commonly known as P&O. The travellers became well experienced; so, to avoid the hot sun, they would book passage in advance. The idea was to assure cabins on the port side going out and starboard coming home; hence the word POSH was coined (Port Out-Starboard Home).

A new industry came into being: Aviation. England's Imperial Airways had inaugurated air routes from England across the Mediterranean, Middle East to Karachi, on to the Far East to Calcutta, Rangoon, Hong Kong and Singapore and even Australia. The airline operated mainly Sunderland flying boats. Pan American Airways had started flying mail between Key West, Florida and Havana, Cuba early in 1927. They were soon carrying passengers and further extended their routes through the Caribbean Islands to Central America. In a few years PanAm would cover most countries in Central and South America. It too operated flying boats built by Martin and Sikorsky and later Boeing.

As I mentioned earlier, this book really is about me, the second great event of 1914. I, Peter Joffre deM Goutiere, was born on September 28, 1914 in Aligarh, India. My middle name, Joffre, is from my Godfather, General Joffre of France, who previously commanded French troops in China and Africa. He was appointed Chief of Staff in 1914 for the allied forces in WWI.

The city of Aligarh is primarily a Muslim city, located between Delhi and Arga (Taj Majal). I am not certain about our genealogy. My grandfather, Antione de Goutiere, came to India shortly before the Indian (Sepoy) mutiny of 1857. According to records, it was somewhere around 1833 when he became an Indigo planter in the Bihar Province. He had to become a British subject to be a planter in India. My father, George Henry deM Goutiere, was born in 1869 near the sacred city of Benares on the

*My Grandfather, Antoine Goutiere, born in Bordeaux, France. Came to India in 1833 as Indigo planter.*

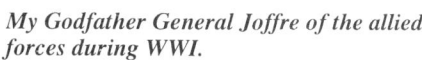

*My Godfather General Joffre of the allied forces during WWI.*

*Mum and Dad on their wedding day 1897.*

Ganges River. My Grandfather on my mother's side was General Russell Wintle, of the British Imperial Army. General and Helen Wintle were my grandparents. I, as so many thousands of other children, was known as a "war baby;" like all those born in British colonies, our bringing up was different from the normal life as is known in America and the Western countries.

India is divided into many provinces, such as Bihar and Bengal. My world was in the United Province. It encompassed such areas as Delhi, Aligarh, Agra, Cawnpore, Lucknow and many of the hill stations in the foot hills of the Himalayas, like Simla, Mussoorie and Naini-Tal. All these cities and towns were part of our Goutiere lives; mainly due to my father being Superintendent of British Imperial Police for the United Province. His career in the police was very exciting as relayed to us by my mother. She mentioned once how we got the two silver bowls that were shining on our mantle-piece over the fire place. In those days, as now, many parts of India and the U.P were infested with bandits known as Dacoits. During the years of 1907 and 1908, a famous Dacoiti leader by the name of Pattan-Din had eluded capture for years. The government had desperately tried to capture the bandit without luck. They finally asked my father to try and see what he could do to apprehend Pattan-Din and his bandits. It took the better part of a year, but my father finally was able to capture the bandit and a lot of his followers that were operating in the Bara Banki District. For his daring, he was awarded two silver bowls. Now, after so many years my brother Vernon has one and I cherish the other.

Because of the intense heat that scorches the plains of India during the summer months, from March through September, many of the families travel up to the hill stations. The stations are scattered the full length of the Himalayan range, from Kashmir and Murree in the Northwest, to Darjeeling in

the east. The Darjeeling station, which is famous for its tea estates, normally have families that come from the Provinces of Bihar and Bengal. The train service travels from Calcutta north to the bottom of the hills to a town called Siliguri. Around 1880 the British had constructed a miniature train service that is capable of ascending all the way from Siliguri to Darjeeling, an altitude of a little over seven thousand feet. The train, though small, still has to manipulate sharp, hairpin turns; one of the famous turns is known as Choonbatty Loop. There is another train service from Delhi to Dehra-Dun which is half way up to Mussoorie station. Not till the end of WWI were travelers able to reach the hill stations without stress. Many of the railroads could only take travelers to the bottom of the hills. Most roads were dirt and very treacherous. From the end of the train terminal at the foothills it was necessary to traverse the rest of the way by horse back or dandies (sedan chairs), canvas chairs carried by four coolies. Other rugged individuals walked. This was to be a yearly exodus from the plains. Schools were built at these stations. Instead of having school break in summer, as in the States and England, it is given during the winter months.

At the end of February the school children start on their way up. At the end of November they traipse back to their homes in the plains for Christmas. The journey can take several days. Some kids do so on their own at the early age of nine or ten. Normally, they meet other school chums and travel together. Though I was not one of the school age children at the end of WWI, I was caught up in the mad evacuation. For the most part, none of the outlying towns had electrical power. Places such as Delhi and Calcutta did. This enabled the offices to have overhead fans. The Hill Stations, such as Simla and Naini-Tal, had electricity. The other smaller towns in the plains and the hills did not have the luxury of electrical power and relied on other rural and makeshift means for keeping cool in the hot weather. One was the old type punkah (fan). It consisted of a large wooden beam or pole that was horizonatally suspended from the ceiling, on which was nailed a heavy frilly cloth, about two feet long. From the center of the beam, a long rope was attached and lead through a hole in the wall to the verandah. Here a man called a punkah-wallah, would sit on the verandah and pull on the rope, which gave the punkah a gentle swinging motion: this undulation, though slow, did create sufficient breeze for the whole room.

Another system that we had in the plains during the hot weather was called khas-khas tati. Khas-khas was a weed or root taken from the dry river beds; it was then woven on bamboo latis frames. These were placed against the doors and window. A water man, known as a "bhisti" (a-la Kipling's Gunga-din), had the job of sprinkling the khas-khas tatis with water. The ever present winds would blow through the matted screens and cause a cooled breeze and aromatic scent from the khas-khas.

Ever since I could remember, around the age of four, the train journeys that we would take going up to the mountains were hectic, noisy, and utterly chaotic. At each station where the train stopped, the various venders (box-wallahs could be seen and heard the whole length of the platform. The favorite call of some vendors I remember was "char-guram-char" (hot tea, hot tea). The cigarette-wallah would call "pan-beree-cigarette" (beetlenut-reffers-cigarettes); the other callers would be for ice water, fruit and toys, each having his distinctive cry. There were the ever present railway baggage coolies dressed in dirty red shirts and khaki pants. They wore brass arm plates to show they were the official baggage carriers. The coolies usually singled out the first and second class compartments and fought for the priviledge of carrying your luggage from one part of the station to the other, or out to the street. Their reward would be a few annas. One anna would be worth two American pennies. The rail journey was not too uncomfortable. The first and second class cabins appeared spacious. They were about 4 to 6 berths, with toilet and a couple of overhead electric fans. The meals were ordered ahead to the next station by telegraph and served hot on arrival. The caterers were a company called Spencers. The family luggage was not just a couple of suit cases, but consisted of bedrolls (bistras) and three or four large tin chests, padlocked. It would take at least three coolies to carry the heavy loads on their heads. Passengers who could not afford such luxurious travel would go third class, almost like cattle-cars with benches. The others would travel by road. The main road was the famous Grand Trunk Road which stretched from Calcutta all the way to Rawalpindi and Peshawar in the Northwest Frontier, made famous by Rudyard Kipling's story *Kim*. This was part of my world that I was brought up in as a child.

From infancy till about the age of four, the Ayahs (Indian nurse-maids) looked after the Raj children like all of us Goutieres were brought up. The Ayahs favorite little nursery chant or rhyme to us (how could I forget it; every child in India was lulled to sleep by it) was "Nini Baba Nini, Muckan-roti Cheeni; Roti, Muckan Hogya; Hamara Baba So-gya;" in English: "Sleep Baby Sleep; Bread, butter and sugar; when the Bread and Butter is Finished, the Baby will Sleep." Most English and European children born in India, as ourselves, learn to speak Hindi (Hinustani) before speaking English. The Ayahs took complete charge of the Babas almost from the time of birth. This gave the lady of the house free time to go gossiping at the club, have bridge parties, and go shopping in the bazaars. Early evenings would see a group of Ayahs on the Maidan (park). They would cluster together and gossip about their Memsahibs while the children played nearby, or lolled in their prams.

At the age of four, I began to remember this crazy life quite vividly. It was so exciting for me. I remembered so much of the childhood events that took place, which I shall relate later on From the time of my birth in 1914, it was my mother who told us stories and little incidents about myself and my brothers and sisters. After hearing some of these stories, I wonder sometimes how we ever survived.

There were many children who were not so fortunate. Disease and various illnesses took their toll; not to mention snake bites. One of the interesting stories my mother told was when she had sat me on the potty in the bathroom and left the door ajar. Soon, she heard me chuckling to myself and using the word, "Bui, Bui." "Bui" in Hindi means bug, insect or any creepy-crawly. When she came back to the toilet, she found me trying to drag myself along the floor, still sitting on the pot. She looked towards where I was headed and saw a karaite, a small, deadly poisonous snake jammed in the door. My Mum said she grabbed me, pot and all, making a fast exit and called one of the servants to kill the snake.

Another interesting story, was when my father had to leave on a trip, as he had received news (Khabar) of some dacoiti (bandits) activity about eighty to ninety miles from Aligarh. My mother was at that time pregnant with me. There were no cars or jeeps. In this case my father and his orderly had to go on horseback. They had travelled to the rumored area in a few days and had no further news of the dacoitis, One evening after having checked the country side, my Dad and the Orderly camped by an old Peepal tree (a sacred Hindu tree) miles from nowhere. After a meager meal and enjoying a cigarette by the fire late in the evening, a figure appeared out of the darkness from behind the tree and sat near them. My father offered the Indian a cigarette, which was politely refused. The individual then began to talk; he told Dad that he had become a proud father of a baby boy born that day. A few minutes later he got up and disappeared behind the tree. My Dad and his Orderly discussed the remark and wondered how he could possibly have known of my birth some ninety miles away. The next morning they both went in the direction the man had gone the previous evening. There was nothing behind the tree except a Moslem grave. When my father arrived back to Aligarh, indeed he was surprised to see that a baby was born; it was me! He mentioned the incident to my mother, and they wondered about the man behind the Peepal tree.

Another time, Dad was holding court on the verandah of our home where he was trying a lot of hoodlums and dacoits. I was about a year old playing near by. Suddenly, one of the servants rushed out, grabbed and took me indoors. He told my mother that one of the prisoners was casting a spell on me. That night I developed convulsions and vomitting. There was no such thing as calling 911 in those days. There was no electricity or phone. A doctor was sent for by the Chaprassi (messenger boy). It was a couple of hours before a doctor showed up. A high fever developed and the doctor was puzzled. He was told of the incident that took place that morning. He just shook his head. I was

*Hardoi garden with Mango bargh and water tank in background.*

given some sort of medicine and was rolled up in a blanket to sweat out the fever. It was forty-eight hours before I showed any improvement. When the fever had subsided, I was like a skeleton; all my beautiful mop of curly blond hair had fallen out. Mum said my head looked like a billiard ball! It was several weeks before I fully recovered. Was it a spell? Who knows? India is a land of mysticism and the gully-gully wallahs.

India is full of medium and magicians. There is the famous rope trick. The magician shows the audience a long rope; he then takes one end and throws it up it the air. It stays up. He then has a small boy scale up the rope and the boy disappears. A moment later the boy runs out from the end of the room or somewhere in the audience. This trick is believed to be done by mass hypnotism.

In the year 1918 our family was living in the town of Hardoi, approximately one hundred and fifty miles east of Alligarh. Our house was a large stucco and brick building with a tiled roof. The front had a deep verandah. The front yard was gravel. A pathway lead from the yard through a flower garden to a mango grove called a "bargh." I remember in the early evening our gardener (mali) would water the flowers with a large watering can. There were no such things as sprinklers and hoses. There was a fair size water tank at the far side of the garden near the mango grove. It was necessary for the mali to fill the tank from the well behind the house; he did so with a small buffalo skin made into a pouch. It looked a bit like the bag of a Scottish bag-pipe, but much larger. The mali would spend hours filling the tank. He would then throw a lot of goat droppings and other manure in the water where it would soak till ready for watering. Then in the evening he would fill his watering can and water the flowers. My brother Vernon and sisters Christine and Geraldine were always eager to help. I was four years old then and

didn't want to be left out. I had been given a small watering can for the purpose. On two occasions I had shouted at the mali to fill my can full, and both times I managed to go head first into the tank. The mali had to haul me out dripping wet shrieking and crying. The others stood around laughing. I was carted off to the house, my shoes squishing and with hair and pockets full of goat turd. Somehow I continued to live.

My Mum once told us that when we were in Hardoi that she and Dad had seen a ghost. On one occasion, she said, when I was about three, she heard me talking to someone on the verandah; when she asked me who I was talking to, I said it was a nice old man sitting in our favorite long-sleeve chair. She figured it must have been the ghost friend. Mum stated that the man had been killed during the Mutiny of 1857 and thrown into an old well. I understand that quite a few people had seen the ghost, long before we came to Hardoi.

That summer was spent in Hardoi; no hill station for me. My brothers and Christine went up to Naini-Tal to school. Geraldine and I remained home. It was extremely hot by May, just before the monsoon season; I recall the brain-fever bird, which belongs to the Hawk-Cuckoo family, calling in the mango grove. At night our beds were placed out in the front yard, each with its mosquito netting, looking like cocoons. A watchman (chaukadar) with a long stave (lathi) would stay near us at night. The call of the jackals was always eerie and frightening. I was scared of the night and the jackals. We had a dog named Bob, a brown spaniel that I loved. When it was possible I would sneak him into my bed. The jackal cry, as we interpreted it, went like this: "One dead Hindu;" another jackal would reply, "Where, Where, Where?" The first would call again: "Here, Here, Here." I'd stick my head under the cover and curl up tight. When I would wake up early in the morning, it was because the peacocks were calling from the field. I loved their strange calls. The hot winds wasted little time in stirring up the dust-devils. I would try chasing them around the yard. During the heat of the day, the punkah-wallah pulled the big punkah and the bhisti would splash water of the khas-khas tattis. We would stay indoors till around five o'clock in the afternoon and then gather around for tea. I never knew why we all drank hot tea in the sizzling hot weather. I really didn't mind as long as I could have a piece of cake and perhaps fall into the tank!

By mid July the first rumble of thunder could be heard in the distance; then the southeast winds would blow steadily. In the distance the sky would start getting black with masses of billowing clouds that seemed to roll along the earth, shooing great mountains of dust in front. One could see flashes of lightning in the darkness of the clouds. It looked awesome and frightening. We would stand on the verandah and watch the approaching storm. This was the beginning of the monsoons, a Godsend for the animals that were thirsty from the dry season. Minutes before the dust and rain enveloped the country and Hardoi, the servants would shout to each other to gather up the verandah furniture and drag it into the house and start closing all windows and doors. I would get headup with excitement and run around with Bob the dog and get in everyone's way. The storm would strike with vengeance, the wind and rain rapping the house and windows. The storm would pass by in a few hours, leaving everything dripping wet. It was impossible to go out in the yard. The place was a quagmire of mud and large puddles of water. Swarms of flying termites with gossamer wings came out of the ground and took to the air. Bee-eater birds flocked around catching the termites in flight. The ground gave off a wonderful, damp, earthy smell. The temperature dropped several degrees, making it more bearable. Geraldine and I couldn't wait for the mud to dry up enough so that we could race to the mango grove to gather the mangoes that had fallen from the first onslaught of the monsoons. Yes, this would be the world I would never forget. It seems it was all just yesterday.

My father became quite sick; the doctors thought it was tuberculosis. This was one of the reasons we would go up to the hills where the climate was cooler and dry. He had given up his police service and was doing law work. After the monsoon season had finished in late September, early October, we were packed and on our way to the hill station of Bhowali in the Naini-Tal District. I was always excited when it came time to pack and to be going somewhere; especially the train ride. From Hardoi to Bereilly was great; the compartment seemed large and I got to sleep in the upper bunk. The clickety-clack of the wheels on the rails lulled me to sleep. It was about four in the morning when we arrived at the Bereilly station. We were all bleary-eyed, but the shouts and yells of the porters soon had us awake. Early morning tea at the Spencers' restaurant got us well set for the next leg of the trip on the narrow gauge rail that would take us to the foot hills. The last stop of the journey would be the station called Kathgodam. It took almost three hours. From there it was necessary to take a taxi up the mountain road, full of hairpin turns. Finally we arrived in Bhowali. The weather was cold and clear. Coolies had to carry the luggage up the last few hundred feet to our new home known as AppleCot. It belonged to the Estate of Mr. Shepherd. He owned several bungalows and a hotel. At the edge of his estate, and just above AppleCot, was another house known as Oak Lodge. Evidently we had stayed there once when I was quite small in 1917.

AppleCot had a living room and a dining room, separated by a wall, not completely across, so that one could pass between the two rooms without having to go around via the verandah. There were also two fireplaces, one on each side of the wall. This was the only heating we had for the winter months. On the north side of the bungalow there were two bedrooms, and on the southern side another two, smaller bedrooms; each with adjoining toilets. The full length of the house, on both sides, were verandahs. There were entrances to the cottage from a main door on the left of the dining room, and one of the left of the living room; the same on the other side of the bungalow. My father was not at all well and spent most of his time in bed. He had the larger room on the north side, where he spent his time painting butterflies. One of our hobbies as children, and grown-

*Some butterfly paintings done by Dad in Bhowali, 1918.*

*Applecot, Bhowali taken by me in 1971.*

ups, is collecting butterflies, but they didn't last long, even when naptha (moth balls) were put in the cases to protect them. So Dad's idea was to paint them, and being a good artist, he went to work so they would last forever. The real butterflies were pinned in groups on the plain door. Dad took heavy cardboard pieces and first painted them to look like wood paneling; then would paint the butterflies on these panels. Now I am proud to say that after more than seventy years, we still have that collection.

During those days in Bhowali there was little for me to do. I could not roam far from the compound. My older brothers and sister were in school. My sister Geraldine and I were the only ones around. I spent most of the time with our dog Bob playing in the yard. Geraldine had one of the small rooms on the south side, and I had the other. Like most nights, I was afraid of the dark; my mother would keep my door open so I could see her at the dining room table where she would knit and sew in the evening when we had gone to bed. There was no electricity; we only had lanterns and kerosene lamps. One evening, after dinner when Geraldine and I had gone to bed, I was lying on my cot and looking out towards where my mother was sitting at the table sewing. My father called her; she put her sewing on the table and went through one of the passages to see Dad. Bob was leashed to the dining room table leg. As soon as she had left, the opposite door to the far verandah opened, and in strolled a very large leopard. Whether he saw me or not, I don't know; but he was not interested in me, he was after Bob. Bob just lay there wagging his stubby tail. The leopard came over without hesitation and grabbed the dog by the back of the neck and broke the leash as he dragged Bob out. It was hard for me to realize what had happened; I was in shock. When I tried to call out, I was choked up with shock and fright. When my mother returned to her sewing, I desperately tried to shout to her, but was unable to make any sound. I must have whimpered and made some sort of noise and she came into my room. I was pointing and then was able to shout "Bob, Bob!" She looked and saw that he was gone and his leash was snapped off. It was then that she realized what had happened. She raced out of the same door that the leopard had gone and shouted to the servants. Mum explained to them what had happened; they all grabbed tin dishes and banged on pans and looked around for the leopard. No doubt the cat must have put a lot of distance between himself and AppleCot. I soon got my voice back and was petrified and shaken. Though I didn't scream or couldn't, I'm sure I piddled in the bed. The next morning we all went out, I wasn't allowed to go too far from the garden. People were combing the hillside behind the Shepherd's house, looking for any signs of Bob, which I was sure would be only the remains. Nothing was found and that ended one saga of my life. It was a little later in winter when my father was feeling better, that we returned to Hardoi. We settled down for the rest of the winter

*The Bacchapra House on Ganges River, 1921.*

and then received word from the Shepherds to say they had found Bob's collar further down behind the mountain.

In the year 1919 we did not return to Bhowali or Bhim-Tal; we went to another hill station called Mussoorie, where my mother lived as a child and where Geraldine was born. We stayed in a bungalow just outside of the town and higher up on the mountain; the place was called Landour. Also in the area were two schools, St. George's College and an American-run school called Woodstock. Further down from Landour was a very lovely large building on a knoll overlooking Dehra-Dun; this was my mother's home, called Whyte-Bank Castle. It was built by my grandfather, General Wintle. We spent a year in Landour. I don't remember too much about it, but there were children nearby that I played with. I remember in the summer and the monsoons, my brother Vernon, Geraldine and myself would look for butterflies. At the end of 1919 we left Mussoorie and instead of going to Hardoi, we wound up at a place called Monghyr in Bihar Province. Some friends of the family had given us the house to live in for awhile. It belonged to an English lady known as Katy Belair. I was coming up on my sixth birthday when we arrived. The house was called Bacchapra. It was a beautiful big building over looking the Ganges River on the south bank. The house was horseshoe shaped. A dirt road followed the river from the west and stopped just below the entrance. The verandah wrapped around three quarters of the horseshoe building. At each end were several bedrooms with old fashioned toilets. Inside the horseshoe area was a small garden. There was also a good sized water tank for the gardener to water the garden, same as we had in

Hardoi. From there the garden got lost in the wild shrubs and beyond to the rice fields. The front garden sloped down to the thorn hedge of babul (Momosa) trees. Beyond the trees was the wide bank of the Ganges River. The Ganges (Gunga) is the most sacred of all rivers for the Hindus. They cremate their dead on the river banks and our area was no exception.

We soon settled in our new home with my Dad having the last room on the north side, on the left wing of the house. The dining and sitting rooms were between the bedroom, sort of a divider. It was late November 1920 and Vernon had returned. Vernon, and I shared a room on the far right. One night we heard an awful noise on the verandah just outside our door. Vernon lit a lantern and he peeked around the door; I was close behind. There on the verandah were two or three jackals fighting over something, a real tug-of-war. Vernon chased the animals away, and a closer look revealed the leg of a human being. It undoubtedly was a leftover from a Hindu cremation. We went back, leaving everything the way it was. Next morning the servants were called and, being Hindus, disposed of the remains by taking them down to the river.

Whenever we took a walk, it was down along the river bank. Quite often we would see skulls and remains of humans scattered along the way. These cremations were done for all Hindus, the rich and the poor. The rich could afford to have large pyres to really do a good job. The poor could only afford to gather a few sticks, or perhaps some palm leaves; this would do no more that singe the body; it would then be deposited into the river. The body was then left to the crocodiles, the crows, the vultures and the ever present jackals. I got used to seeing these carcasses scattered about, and paid no attention.

The town of Monghyr is enclosed in an old fort. Around it is a moat that is about fifty yards wide and fifteen or so feet deep, but without water except during the rainy season. There is a bridge at the outskirts across the moat. At the front end of the bridge is a high gate on which is a clock-tower. The white community, always gathered at the Gymkhana Club, where we also belonged. Vernon, Christine and all their friends played tennis and badminton in the afternoons. I was still a small lad of six at this time, but I watched with eagerness to see my sister and brother play. One evening, after their tennis match, we were all sitting out on the lawn of the club having tea. It was either Vernon or Christine who handed me a bowl of something and said, "Be very careful before you eat it; it's quite hot. I think you should blow on it first." I patiently blew and blew and blew and finally told it should be cool enough to eat. I took a mouthful and got the surprise of my life, it was ice cold! I almost spat it out. It was my very first experience with ice cream.

It was Christmas 1920, the first one I could really remember and appreciate. The Monghyr Club held the festivities Christmas Eve. We were all invited and the youngsters sat up front in what was the dance hall. There was a large Christmas tree standing in the middle of the stage. There were various baubles and ornaments hanging from the branches. This was the first Christmas tree I had ever seen. Someone dressed as Father Christmas was standing by the tree. He would pick out a present from under it and call out a name for that youngster to collect his or her gift. When my name was called, I got scared but with Mum's coaxing, I was able to get up to the stage and receive my present. I brought it back to my mother. It was a huge locomotive engine made of wood painted red and green. I was thrilled and wanted to know who gave it. I was told it was Father Christmas. Next day, which was Christmas Day, I was happy to have some friends over to the house. We could ride the engine down the slope in front of the house to the thorny trees. One of my friends was a little red headed girl named Hilda McGee. I always stared at her because she was covered with freckles and her two front teeth seemed to protrude out.

I also had two other friends that I played with often, known as the Daws. I don't remember their first names. I believe Mr. Daw was the manager of a steamship company that plied along the Ganges River between Patna to the west and south to Monghyr and Calcutta. I spent a lot of time with the Daws. The two boys had tricycles; while they would be having lunch or were away they would let me ride their tricycles, which I enjoyed.

The time seemed to hurry by at Bacchapra, with the walks along the Ganges and the early evening at the club. I would ride with my brother Vernon on his bicycle, sitting on the cross-bar. It would be late on the way home

across the moat. I was always frightened because the jackals seemed to hang around the moat and the bridge; they would let out their eerie cries as we rode along. At home I would cover my head with the blanket so I wouldn't hear them. During the day I was most brave. My range for running around extended from the back garden further into the fields. In front of the house, I could venture down as far as the babul trees near the river. The crocodiles were known to come up the banks to the shade of the trees.

One day I heard my mother call me; I had been playing near the servant's quarters in the bank of the house. The area around the water tank was slippery; when I cut the corner on the dead run, I slipped and went head first into the tank. It was full, and I remember going to the bottom and back up to the other side. When I surfaced, I was able to pull myself onto the lip of the tank. The water was not very clean; the mali had filled it with the usual goat and cow droppings, as was done in Hardoi. It was great for the plants and flowers, but I didn't enjoy my share that I had gulped down. There was goat turd in my hair and pockets when I reached the verandah. I recall Dad calling to Mum if I had fallen in the tank again; she replied, "Yes."

It was now February 1921; when, one morning as Geraldine and I were playing near an old medler tree, mother called to us. We returned to the back garden where Mum met us and looked solemn. She placed her arms around Geraldine and me and said that Daddy had just died. We felt terribly sad. Christine and George worked in Monghyr and came immediately. I remember we all gathered in the living room. Vernon would not arrive for several days. I know I cried too. Dad's sickness had been emphysema.

I never really knew my father. I am certain my behind had been spanked by him on occasions. My brothers and sisters spoke fondly of Dad. He was strict, yet full of fun and jokes. He was a heavy smoker and enjoyed his whiskey pegs (shots). Dad was also a great sportsman, polo player and big game hunter. The funeral was held a couple of days later, but Geraldine and I did not attend. My father is buried in Monghyr.

We then moved from Bacchapra closer to the town and within the wall of the fort and the moat. The place we now had was called Slater Cottage. It was very pleasant and had a lot of space around it, but was very hot. The house was a square, ordinary type bungalow without punkahs (fans) of any kind. There were khas-khas tatis to put on the doors and windows. There was a servants quarters nearby. One of the servants was a young Muslim man by the name of Hanif. He was a fine fellow and I liked hanging around the kitchen when he was cooking and arranging meals.

I remember there was a guava tree by the kitchen which I was always trying to climb. I never was able to because the trunk was very smooth. One day Hanif lifted me onto one of the high branches and then walked away. When I found myself alone and unable to climb down, I started to cry. Hanif

came back and lifted me down and told me not to try climbing trees by myself, that I would get hurt. I liked Hanif; he was always patient with me, even when I interfered with his work.

In April the hot weather was on us. The brain-fever bird kept up its agitated calling; "brain-fever, brain-fever," during the hottest part of the day. I didn't mind it; in fact I liked the sound, though it got on many people's nerves. We played in the compound during the early mornings and late afternoons, when it was not quite so hot. One afternoon we heard a lot of noise coming from the city and it gradually grew into a roar. It was a devastating sound. Hanif came running to us and said for us to stay indoors, that there was trouble in the city of Monghyr. We learned that Ghandi and his followers were creating a lot of disturbance. All the Indians were against the British Raj. They wanted to rise up and massacre the whites in the country, the same thing they tried to do back in 1857. The cry was "Ghandi Jika-Jai." We stayed indoors while Hanif and the other servants in the neighborhood said not to worry, they would protect us. The rioting cries continued for a week. The nights were especially terrifying. This is when they would light large bonfires that lit up the sky. Eventually, the police were able to subdue the mobs. After things quieted down, it was decided that we should return to the hill station of Bhowali. Christine and George would stay a little longer for their work. Once again we were packed and off to the railroad station. Hanif would not accompany us on this trip and bid us farewell. The servants, when they appreciate and think a lot of the English like us, learn to love the kids and the family in general. They become a part of the family. Hanif was one that I think would give his life to protect us.

The train ride was always great. I had now been educated by Vernon on how to use a catapult (sling-shot). I would sit by the window of the compartment and try to plink at birds that were sitting on the telegraphs wires as we whizzed by. There were many stops on the way; this would give a chance to pick up some pebbles (ammo) for the next leg of the trip. Our destination at this time was Beirelley, the same junction that we used coming from Hardoi. Once more there was the hustle and bustle or porters getting all the luggage. We had a long wait for the narrow gauge train that would take us to Kathgodam at the foot of the hills. This portion of the ride was fascinating. As always, I enjoyed the noise and aroma of the stations. I'd beg Mum to buy the Indian sweets (which she rarely did).

We climbed aboard the smaller train that morning and were on our way. All the Indian trains were coal burners. When I would open the window, soot and dust always blew in. My ears and hair would be covered. At the end of each trip it would be necessary for me to have a good scrubbing.

In those early days the narrow gauge passed through dense jungle, commonly known at the Terai Jungles. The Terai was that area at the base of the Himalayas that stretched from the punjab in western India all the way to the foothills of Darjeeling in the east. The width of the jungle would vary about ten to fifteen miles. Here and there the forest had been cut away by roads, railroads, villages and rivers. However, it was still the natural habitat for various animals and birds, such as the sambhur, a large elk-like deer. There is the barking deer or kharkar, the chettal spotted deer. Then, of course, there are wild boars, leopards, tigers and elephants. The song birds and game birds are in abundance. I couldn't wait to sit by the window as the train pulled away from the station. It was so exciting to know that one would see a variety of game as the train chugged on its way. The wildlife was used to the sound of engines, except the leopards and tigers. These sneaky cats are usually nocturnal and stay in the dense jungle. They are known to prowl along the rail tracks at night.

The train makes a couple of stops on the way; one is at Lal-Kuwa (Red-Well) and another at Haldwani. A telegraph line is strung along parallels to the rail. It is possible to see many wonderful birds sitting on the wires. There were fork-tailed drongo, the blue winged rollers, doves, king-fishers and bee-eaters, and many other varieties too numerous to name; not to mention the exotic jungle fowl and peacock. By the time the train passed Haldwani, it was possible to get a glimpse of the foot hills through the morning haze. The ride was about three hours, arriving at Kathgodam about ten a.m. This gave the traveller a good start to make it to Naini-Tal by afternoon. My Dad would not be with us now and we all felt the emptiness and were sad. At Kathgodam we arranged a taxi to motor us up the winding, hair-pin turns to Naini and then down to Bhowali. The road, as it ascends, follows the Goula River and its gorge. What I loved was the sound of the hill birds. They were different from the ones in the plains. Once or twice we would see groups of the silver-furred langur monkeys, that had black faces, hands and feet. They could be seen sitting high in the trees, some along the roadside.

The taxi took us along the winding dirt road, which was slow and treacherous. We passed the first small village of Rani-Bargh. My mother had the driver stop at the next small town of Joelicote. I wasn't aware that was where we were to spend a few months. It was a surprise. At Joelicote we were met by a Mr. Michael Warrick. Joelicote is located halfway between Kathgodam and Naini. The reason for its being was basically as a Catholic Mission; secondly, as a way-station for the long journey up the mountain (this was before taxis and one had to travel by foot, dandy or horseback). In my time the road, with all its hair-pin runs, was not paved. Joelicote overlooks the Goula River and its deep valley. Part of the river originates in Naini-Tal and can be a raging torrent during the monsoon weather.

The man who met us, Michael Warrick, had quite a strange and interesting history, so I was told later. The best I can recall is

*Christine, Geraldine, myself and Eric Tompkins, 1922.*

Michael Warrick was really a woman, a Miss Warrick. Her brother, the real Michael Warrick, had been killed in WWI; through some juggling of papers and documents, she was able to show he was still alive and living in India. Any war pensions, etc., were sent to Warrick in India. Hence, we now have a Michael Warrick who greeted us. He or she, as the case might be, was established in Joelicote running the Catholic mission. The few pounds sterling he/she received would go a long way in India. As far as I was concerned at that time, he was still Mr. Warrick to me.

Vernon was back in school. Christine and George remained in Monghyr. It was my mother, Geraldine and myself that were shown our rooms at the mission. We were to be there for about four months. During that period I was introduced to the ABC's of reading and arithmetic. We also attended the little church every Sunday morning. One amusing thing that used to take place at church: the little Christianized Indian children, who came with their parents, wore pants that were slit up the back; this made it convenient when they had to go potty. They squatted where ever, without having to take their pants down. In church, when they kneeled down to say their prayers, rows of little brown bottoms would pop out. We used to giggle at the sight. The new life at the mission was something I was not sure I liked. I was more interested in running around the garden with the catapult. During this period my mother was already making arrangements for our move to Bhowali. The monsoons had arrived, as they do every year around July and there was constant rain which made it impossible to go outdoors very much. There was not much else to do except study my ABC's. Time seemed to drag on endlessly.

Finally, by the beginning of winter in November, we were packing again for our old home in Bhowali. We said goodbye to Mr. Warrick and took a taxi which stopped at the Shepherd Estate. The servants helped with the luggage up the slope to AppleCot. The servants were the landlord's. As we entered the little bungalow, everything came back to me. I recognized the big table where three years before, our dog Bob was grabbed and taken off by the leopard. The butterfly painting my Dad had done in the same house in 1918 were now hung on the walls. I just walked around the yard curiously.

We had not been there more than a few months when Christine and George arrived. They stayed in another cottage across from us called StrawberryCot. Yes, during the season Mr. Shepherd did grow strawberries there, that I used to steal! Another lady came to live with us, a Miss Jessie Murray, a friend of George's.

The winter months are cold in the hills and Bhowali; the two fire-places that were in AppleCot, came in handy. Everyone would sit around the roaring fire and tell stories. I would listen with great fascination of what was being told. There were other English families that had arrived in Bhowali. One of the families was the Tompkins. There were several children in the family; one was a boy about my age by the name of Eric. We became great pals and were always together. I remember one occasion when Eric and I were with Christine, George and the landlord's daughter, Doris Shepherd; we wound up at a little hotel at the bottom of the hill, below AppleCot. There were quite a few grown-ups gathered in one of the rooms that afternoon. While no one was looking, we thought, Eric and I snitched a cigarette from the table and went behind the hotel and started smoking. One of the male guests must have seen us take the cigarette, he came around the corner and caught us in the act. He laughed and said, if we wanted to smoke, to try a pack of his cigarettes. The cigarette pack was an Indian brand called "Kaichi," meaning scissor. There was a picture of red scissors on the pack. The man told us to be sure to drink

*Bhowali Bazaar*

water after smoking to get rid of the cigarette breath. Eric and I thanked him and did as he suggested. There were six cigarettes in the pack and we smoked them all. I think we were able to drink a couple of mouth fulls of water, when it hit us. I can remember this as though it was yesterday. We both got dizzy and started vomiting. We got terribly sick and cried our eyes out. Christine and Doris came to my rescue, while someone else carted Eric off to his home. Christine and Doris decided they better carry me up the hill to AppleCot. Half way up, they dropped me; I guess it was because they were laughing so much. I was sick for several days. It was like the voodoo guy in Hardoi who cast a spell on me; the cigarettes had done the same. One thing I learned from that experience: it cured me from ever wanting to smoke again. I haven't touched one since. I do, at this old age, light up a cigar once in awhile, but never inhale.

Not long after my smoking experience, it was announced that my brother George and Jessie were to be married. The ceremony was held in the garden of our home with Mr. Warrick as best man! Eric and I were dressed up in white suits. It was a great occasion and everyone seemed to be having a good time. Eric and I were sure not to indulge in any cigarettes, but we did make hogs of ourselves with the wedding cake.

I settled back to my routine of chasing birds with Eric. George and Jessie had gone to Naini-Tal for awhile and then took off for Australia.

At this time I think I should explain the geographic relationship of the three hill stations about which my young life revolved. Naini-Tal was the seat of the Governor-General for the United Province (UP). It was the Governor's summer residence. In Naini there are six European schools: St. Josephs College (Catholic) which is a boy's school and

a convent for the girls; a brother/sister affair. Then there is a Diocesan Boy School (DBS) called Sherwood and it sister school (DGS), Church of England, then the Methodist school called Philander Smith College (PSC) and its sister school called Wellsley.

"Tal" in Hindi means Lake. Naini Tal is the shape of a giant footprint, East and West. Government House, St. Josephs, the Convent, DBS, DGS and Wellsley are situated on one hill, on the south side of the lake. PSC is on the higher hill on the north side and overlooks the lake and the other schools and Gov. House. There are two bazaars. One on the east of the lake called Tali-Tal and the other and larger bazaar on the west called Muli-Tal. Tali-Tal is where the buses, taxies, dandys, etc., come up from Kathgodam and stop: a terminus area. Muli-Tal is the main shopping area with hotels. Also, at that end is the Naini Yacht Club. There are several restaurants and tea-rooms; the best one I remember is Valerios, for tea and dancing. The large playground at the west end, called the "Flats," is where all the hockey, football (soccer), and cricket matches are held. It is also a parade ground for such occasions as Armistice Day. There is a road (mall) that skirts the edge of the lake, with willow trees. It is about a mile and half in circumference.

At the edge of the Flats, midway between the two sides, is a cinema and adjacent to it, a Hindu Temple called "Naini." At the cinema the school kids were able to see such silent movies as "The Black Pirate" with Doug Fairbanks, Sr., and the famous "Sheik" movies with Rudolph Valentino.

What is interesting about the Flats is how it was formed. Most of the hills of the Himalayas are of shale composites. The rainy (monsoon) season causes many landslides throughout the mountain range. About 1880 such a landslide occurred on the north side of the lake, about the area of the Mali-Tal bazaar and the Yacht Club, the same side of the mountain as PSC. It was a devastating slide that filled the west end of the lake and sent a tidal wave the full length that washed out Tali-Tal bazaar. Scores of people were trapped and buried alive. Emergency rescue units of the British troops stationed near Kathgodam were rushed to Naini, to assist in the rescue operation. About two hundred troops were at work digging out the poor souls, when a second terrible slide came down and buried one hundred and twenty British troops. The government said there was little or no way to rescue these brave troops; instead, the whole rubble heap was then leveled out and made into the playground called the "Flats." It is in memory of the people buried there.

There is a pathway that starts near the temple and leads up the slope of the south mountain, where the five schools are located. Halfway up this pathway was a very large outcrop of rock that overhung the pathway. The rock mass is known as Smuggler's Rock. Some call it Victoria Rock. "Smuggler" sounds more interesting to me. Hindu legend has it that the goddess Naini (for whom the lake and temple are named) was standing on top of the rock combing her hair with a golden comb. The comb slipped from her hands and dropped into the lake far below. She was so overcome by shock, that she also fell into the lake and drowned. Because of this tragic ending, the gods decreed that henceforth, each year a human life would pay for Naini's death. True to form a person has drowned in the lake. Many years later, during a monsoon, Smuggler's Rock broke loose from the side of the mountain and tumbled into the lake. From that point on, whether or not a life is still taken by the lake, I cannot answer.

The road from Kathgodam forks at Tali-Tal terminus; the right hand turns down and traverses around the mountain below PSC. Also, a narrow dirt road starts at the same area and continues along the mountain a little higher than the motor road. This type of footpath in Hindi is called "pakdundi." The path slopes gradually downhill and continues for several miles till it joins again with the motor road at a junction where the Bhowali Sanatorium is located. The town of Bhowali is another mile further along. The main road divides again on entering the town, where there is another staging post privately owned by a Mr. Cotton.

He also owned a garage, restaurant and small hotel. At the Cotton garage the main road turns left to a hill station called Ranikhet twenty-two miles away. The right hand fork passes through the Bhowali bazaar and crosses a stream along the bottom of a hill to the Shepherd's estate and our old home of AppleCot. The dirt road divides again; the left continues to Almorah hill station. The right hand road passes through a gun-site type gorge from which one can witness a beautiful sight of a spacious valley descending down and disappearing in the distance. At the end of this valley, and on a clear day one can see Bhim-Tal shimmering in the distance. Like Naini-Tal, this lake is also wedged between two mountains. The beautiful valley is called Thirshakhet. Just before entering the gorge, on the left, is a splendid marble tomb built by a Muslim prince. It is a wonderful landmark the Goutieres will never forget; nor the spectacular view from the gorge toward Bhim-Tal. Behind Bhim-Tal is a sugarloaf mountain called Khailas. The real Khailas and sacred mountain is actually hidden in the far reaches of the Himalayas, somewhere northwest of Sadya in the Assam Valley. Since most Hindus cannot get to the real Khailas Mountain near Tibet, then they will have the mountain come to them.

Again, this was my world, and when I had grown a little older (8 years), I could appreciate the beautiful butterflies and birds. This was my world—spacious, wild and beautiful. The whole area or district of Naini-Tal was also known as Kumaon. Kumaon was made famous by a Major James Corbett. Major Corbett was born in Naini-Tal and spent most of his life here, and where he became a great naturalist and hunter. He stalked man-eating tigers on foot, tigers that had killed hundreds of native villagers in the Kumaon. He had shot several in the area where we lived in Bhim-Tal and Bhowali. Corbett wrote several books about his adventures and the love he had for India. A movie entitled "The Man-Eater of Kumaon" has been made. Later, another short documentary of Corbett was filmed on sight in India by National Geographic. For many years he and his sister Maggie lived in a little town at the bottom of the hills near Naini-Tal, known as Kaladungi. There is also a cemetery named after the town, halfway up to Naini-Tal from Kaladungi. My father and mother knew Corbett; in fact, it was my dad that encouraged Corbett to write about his hunting experiences. I met Corbett when I was small and we were in Bhowali. He came and had tea with us, when he was on his way back to Naini. I remember him telling Mum to be sure the children did not wander far from the house, that a man-eating tiger had been reported some twenty miles east of Bhim-Tal and had already killed about two hundred natives. It was believed the tiger had ventured from the Terai jungles of Nepal. Corbett later tracked the tiger down and shot it. At the time of Indian independence in 1947, Corbett and his sister Maggie left India to reside in Kenya, in the town just north of Nairobi called Nyeri. He and his sister died there in 1956.

Now that George and Jessie had left India, it was decided once more to make another move, this time from Bhowali to Bhim-Tal. All our bedding, pots, and pans were loaded onto the heads of several coolies. I was plunked into a dandy. The procession lead off down the hill from AppleCot, onto the main road and through the gunsight pass. It was a beautiful morning and I could see Bhim-Tal in the distance. A little ways down the road, I decided to get out of the dandy and walk. Now that I had graduated to a fairly good shot with the catapult, I kept myself occupied taking pot shots at birds, mainly red-vented bulbuls that sat on the lantana bushes along the sides of the road. The four miles, down hill did not seem to take long, or tiring. At the end of the valley, entering Bhim-Tal outskirts, is a flat area of about fifty acres, most of which is wheat fields and hedgerows of thorn plums. Here one could spot graceful black partridges and wild hares; jackals too, I'm afraid! At the end of the plain, another footpath makes a gradual climb up to the house on the left. This is the house we were to occupy. The altitude change from Bhowali is about 2000 feet lower.

The house was much larger and roomier than AppleCot; it had an upstairs as well. The house belonged to a Mr. Athem, a fine Anglo-Indian from Lahore (which is now in Pakistan). I shared an upstairs room with Vernon when he was back from school. I should mention that all these homes came furnished. In Bhowali Mr. Shepherd also furnished the servants. Here in Bhim-Tal Mum and Christine would arrange for the servants. Christine had a room above as well.

There was a large upstairs verandah that gave a great view of the lake. The lake is man made by a dam on the east side, about half the size of Naini-Tal, and is fairly shallow at this end. There is a road (mall) going around the edge of the lake. Our house is about a hundred feet up the side of the mountain on the north side. There is a spacious front yard of gravel. The grounds drop off into terraces down to the main road and mall. To the left of the yard is a double iron gate and a small path that also descends to the lake. At this point one can walk either way around the lake which is about a mile is circumference. From the back of the house the mountain rises abruptly to approximately five hundred feet. On the opposite side a small hill which is heavily wooded with silver oak and a pathway that runs the length of the hill. The east side leads to a small hotel run by two women, the DeKalbra sisters. The west side path goes to a man by the name of Mr. Jones. He owns the whole estates and the hill and is called the Jones' Estate. At the back of Jones place and the hill there is an area called Sat-Tal, meaning seven lakes. During the rainy season the lakes are noticeable. During the winter dry season just two of the larger lakes remain. The whole of the Sat-Tal area is lush with rain forests of silver oak, rhododendron trees and some bamboo. It is a natural habitat for wild life such as tigers, leopards, sambhurs, and wild boars. Varieties of orchids festoon the trees. Special permission had to be granted by Mr. Jones for any hunting.

On the east side of Bhim-Tal the water is deep; there is good fishing for the sporting mahseer, a carp like fish. They are known to weigh as much as fifty to seventy pounds. They are rather boney, but delicious eating.

At each end of the lake are two bazaars. These bazaars do not have any European-style shops, as does Naini. For real shopping one has to make out a list with the name of the shop and one of the servants is sent to Naini to do the shopping. He will go up one day and return the next. At the east end of Bhim-Tal lake is a hillock with a large building that was taken over and made into a summer hotel, called Peachy's Hotel.

After settling in, my mother and Christine arranged for the servant staff. It was to consist of a cook called a khansama, a bearer or man-servant, a masalchi who is the dishwasher and does other menial chores around the house and to run local errands. Then the sweeper called a mattyr; his job is to clean out the bathroom and toilets, look after the dogs if any and to sweep the rooms and verandahs. The mali or gardener usually is part of the owner's household. He is the person that looks after the garden and acts as a caretaker of the premises. In Bhim-Tal there were no English kids to play with, as there had been in Bhowali; in fact I never saw Eric Tompkins again. The only person to have as a chum was the masalchi boy who was twice my age; there was also the mali's daughter, Jasma, who was my age and tagged along behind me when I went chasing the hill birds. I made catapults for her and the masalchi

*Smugglers Rock, Naini-Tal. With Mum, and me with Eton collar and boater hat.*

from parts of inner tubes given to me by Mr. Cotton who owned the garage in Bhowali.

During the winter holidays Vernon had returned from school in Naini for three months. Remember, there was no electricity; lanterns and oil lamps were used in the evening. There was no ice box to keep perishable items. Milk was always boiled and put in the coolest part of the house. There was a pantry box called a hot-case. Most perishable things were stored in it. The case had four rather long legs and each leg would stand in a saucer of water, to keep ants from getting to the food. The door of the case was screened to keep the flies out. There were several fireplaces in the house. The one normally used was in the living room. During the winter months, the temperature would drop to near freezing, so the fire places were most welcome. Here my mother was in her glory. She would sit and tell us fascinating stories about hunting trips that she and Dad took, and of Dad catching dacoits, especially Pattan-Din. I used to be spellbound, and at this young age, I'd imagine myself with my mother and father on these trips. Perhaps in this manner I was to remember her stories so vividly. Since there was no radio or any other means for Mum to entertain us, her story-telling did the trick.

One cold winter night when we had first arrived in Bhim-Tal, and as we sat around the fire place in the living room, there was a rustling sound just outside the front door, then a scurrying sound and some animal appeared to be running madly around in the back of the house. Vernon raced to his room and got the shot gun and waited. The animal came back to the front door with more scratching. All our doors and windows had dead-bolt type locks. It took a few seconds before Christine could unlatch the bolt and get the door open just a crack, and Vernon ready with his gun. They saw a dog on the verandah. Christine opened the door wide enough for the dog to race in and it hid in

*PSC college in foreground, with St. Josephs on opposite hill.*

the corner of the room and the door was slammed shut. It was evident that a leopard was out there in the dark. There was no other sound except the dog whimpering and its hair bristling on its back. The dog was a mangy looking, half starved pariah dog from the bazaar. Scraps of meat and bread were brought and the dog ate ravenously. It was a black and tan female. We let her stay the night, thinking she would run off back to the bazaar in the morning. Wrong; she would not leave the house. It now appeared we had adopted a new member into the family. She was fed regularly and given a wash down with a solution of a strong disinfectant of pheneel made from coal-tar. It is used throughout India. The sweeper boy did the

honors of looking after her. The dog took on a new character and became healthy and clean. Her coat of black and tan was shiny and the mange effects soon disappeared. Christine decided a good name for the dog was Beatrice; or, Beatrice the Bitch. The sweeper, who looked after her, couldn't pronounce the name, so he called her Buchi. She became a most faithful animal and would accompany us on our afternoon walks. Beatrice was also a great watch dog. Once when a vendor came by selling vegetables, the man appeared drunk and was rude to my mother and Christine. While on the verandah, Christine did what was quite normal: she touched Beatrice behind the collar, and the dog made a leap at the vendor's throat. Luckily, the man was wearing a high-neck Kaftan type collar that most of these people do; it buttoned at the throat. He was knocked over backwards with Beatrice on him trying to bite his neck. Christine pulled her off before any harm was done. The vendor cried out at first, and when the shock was over, he became very apologetic. He was told to leave immediately. I think he was happy to get out of there.

Bhim-Tal, being a hill resort, often would receive a few English and European visitors who would come up from the plains to escape the heat in the summer or come in the winter to try their luck at hunting and fishing, and would stay at the two hotels I have mentioned. All us locals got to know who had arrived in Bhim-Tal. I think most of this gossip was passed along through the servants. On one occasion, a Major Goode, on leave from the British Army and staying at the DeKalbra Hotel, had come to do some big game shooting. Late one morning word came that there had been an accident near Sat-Tal. A few hours later a procession passed along the pathway that came from the Jones' area toward the hotel. The procession consisted of a few natives, the gun-bearer and a stretcher with a body covered with a sheet. It turned out to be Major Goode. Word

was, that while hunting, the gun had accidentally gone off while the gun-bearer was carrying it. There is a small cemetery just below the Jones' bungalow, in a wheat field. Bhim-Tal does not have a church, so I don't know who gave the last rites at the funeral when Major Goode was laid to rest.

My brother Vernon and I quite often went shooting in the same Sat-Tal area, but first we had to get permission from Mr. Jones. He never refused, but always advised Vernon he was only allowed to hunt mainly for wild boar, and not more than two kaleege (pheasants). One late afternoon I accompanied Vernon for wild boar, without any luck. On the way back, on one of the pakdundi paths, Vernon noticed a pheasant fly up into one of the oak trees. This is one of their roosting habits. I stayed on the path while he stalked and circled around a small hillock, where he could get close enough to the tree for a shot. I saw him come around the hill, take aim and fire. I expected a bird to fall. It did, with three more! He had shot four pheasants with one shot; most unusual. The next thing was, how to get by Mr. Jones' place without him knowing we had four pheasants. Vernon stuck two of them into his cartridge bag, and I carried two in the open. Our larder was always well stocked with game that Vernon shot. There was rabbit, pheasant, boar, partridge and barking deer. Vernon never shot in excess of what was needed in the way of food. Vernon had become my hero fast. He was an excellent shot with the gun and the catapult.

The lakes and rivers in India teemed with fish; the famous one I have mentioned earlier is the mahseer. Naini-Tal, Bhim-Tal and Sat-Tal were well known for the mahseer. One morning, there was a commotion and chatter in Christine's room upstairs. I was always nosey and wanted to know what went on. News had come that there was an American sahib (gentleman) staying at the DeKalbra Hotel. He was on holiday to do some hunting and fishing. The commotion upstairs being Christine had spotted the American at the wide end of the lake fishing from a boat. She was watching him from the window with binoculars. The next thing Christine did was to take the mirror from the wall and flash the sun onto him. Mum was trying to stop her, but she and Geraldine were enjoying their sport. The American appeared not to notice and kept on fishing, and later returned to his hotel. Late that afternoon, at tea time, when we were all on the upstairs verandah, the American sahib showed up. He seemed like a giant, about 6'4" and lean. He looked English the way he dressed in khaiki shorts and had a mustache. The moment he spoke, his American accent gave him away. Needless to say, he appeared angry. The first thing after introductions, he wanted to know who was shining the mirror at him while he was fishing. Christine (who was nineteen) acknowledged her prank and apologized. He was then invited to stay for tea. The American had introduced himself as a Robert Weston and came from Massachusetts. He had fought in WWI, and had come to India to do some

*Michael Warrick, Christine and me, at wedding, 1922.*

big game hunting and fishing; he had a job with a jute company in Calcutta. (Jute is a type of plant, the fiber of which is used to make cheap rope and gunny sacks.) Robert said he had some luck in shooting tiger in the northern part of Bengal and Assam. He asked about hunting in this area, and before Vernon could reply, Christine butted in and started telling about the different areas for some good shooting.

It was not long before Robert Weston became a regular caller, thanks to Christine's charm, I would guess. Christine was a great outdoor girl too. She was a pretty good shot and liked horseback riding and walking. For me, I couldn't understand much of what was going on with their grown-up conversations. I was only interested in chasing the bulbuls, butcher birds and hoopoes with my catapult and have Jasma tag along. One thing I did not know at the time; my mother and Christine had been whispering and discussing something concerning me, which I was to find out soon enough.

I was now eight and a half years old and enjoying my world of Bhim-Tal and tagging along with Vernon when he went hunting. One morning at breakfast the news was broken to me that I would be going to school in Naini-Tal the coming season, which would be March of 1923. My great, beautiful, never ending world seemed to collapse all of a sudden. I was trying to be brave and not cry, but my lower lip started quivering and large tears started forming. I would be attending DBS (Sherwood) and Geraldine would be at DGS. My mother said it won't be too bad because she would be teaching at Wellesley College close by. It was a sad morning when I had to say goodbye to my friends, Jasma and the masalchee. As for Beatrice, she could not go either; she was left on her own. They all stood at the gate while our procession of dandies and coolies with all our gear on their heads started off up the mountainside. I looked back and waved, with a heavy, empty feeling. The twelve-mile trek up to Naini-Tal was no easy task, everything uphill, and every step leading away from Bhim-Tal. If I recall correctly, Geraldine and I stayed with Mum that late afternoon, at her little apartment in Wellesley. It was located just a short distance up the hill from Tali-Tal. The following day, Geraldine was delivered to DGS, and then Mum escorted me to Sherwood, or DBS.

Six steps led up to the graveled playground; on the right hand side was a long building with a covered verandah. At the further end was a much larger building. All of this was in gray stone and red tin roofs. The whole place looked foreboding. As we stepped to the verandah, a very tall figure appeared through the doorway. He was dressed in a dark suit and wore a black cap and gown. He had fierce-looking eyes, and a prominent, hooked nose; I was terrified! Without hesitation, he said to my mother, "You must be Mrs. Goutiere, and this must be Master Peter." "Yes," she said. "Good, I am Mr. Dixon, the Principal of Sherwood." Mr. Dixon then called a servant, who took my belongings from the coolie. The saddest

*Me on the tricycle with the two Daw boys. . . .*

*and holding four pheasants. .*

day of may life, saying goodbye to my mother. I tried to be brave, but finally broke down. Mr. Dixon put his arm around my shoulder and escorted me off through the passage to a dormitory on the upper level. Here, I was introduced to quite a few fellows about my age, and some older who had just arrived earlier. It did not take long to adjust, but for the first few days, I was still withdrawn and did not know how to conduct myself. I did not have any English friends; one loses contact. In other words, being with natives for months on end, I was going native. Most of the boys discussed the winter holiday, and what they did. They talked about how they had been given BB guns for Christmas, and how they'd been out shooting. Other talked of learning to swim. It was a little while before I picked up courage and finally talked of having a catapult and chasing around Bhim-Tal. Then they told me it was against the rules to have a catapult (or catty, for short) in school; that I should hand it over to the lady in charge. The lady in charge, or matron, was a Miss Beverly. She was not only our governess but also part of the teaching staff for the kindergarten. (The schools use the word standard instead of grade.)

After all our little odds and ends had been put away, and the beds had been made, we sat around, continuing our conversations. The bell rang, and that meant we had to go down to supper. This was in the large building that I had mentioned earlier. We all had to stand in line on the verandah first and be accounted for; the new boys, like myself, were introduced. We were the last ones in; we traipsed in behind the others, and sat at long tables covered with oilcloth. Each one had his little place to sit, with knives and forks. We didn't have chairs, but there were long benches with no backs; here we sat while the bearers came in and brought us our evening meal. I don't remember what it was, but it wasn't very appetizing. I nibbled away,

and that was it. We returned to the dormitory and turned in for the night. I didn't do much sleeping. I was thinking of my mother, and all the past fun I'd been having; and of course, Bhim-Tal.

The next morning, bright and early, everything was done by the bell. It would ring and up we'd get, taking our towels, a piece of soap and a toothbrush; then race off through a covered passageway that led to the latrines. There was a little bowl with tepid water in which I had to first brush my teeth, then wash my face and hands and parts of my body as best I could; get on back to the dormitory, get dressed and line up again. Baths were on Saturdays. Everybody was

*Vernon, Christine and me on steps of old Bhim-Tal house early 1923.*

23

*Robert Weston at our home in Bhim-Tal 1923.*

segregated into various areas, and Miss Beverly took us to our classroom, where we settled down. This was my routine. The first few days were miserable; I didn't know what I was doing, but it was just conversation, mainly. I did hand my catapult over to Miss Beverly, who said I'd get it at the end of the year.

It was not long before I learned that there were various seasons for different sports. In this early springtime, everybody, on the weekend, would team up. I had two young brothers with me, Jack and Billy Watson. The sport at this time of the year was hunting for bird's eggs, to see who could collect the greatest amount and the rarest of eggs. What we did when we'd get them was to put two pinholes, one on each end, and then try to blow out the yolks. In this way, we could preserve the eggshells for quite a while. Some boys had pretty good collections. I didn't know the first thing about it, but I caught on and got in the swing of things.

Then, on Sundays, early in the morning, we all had to get into our very best clothes, which consisted of dark grey shorts, a dark blue blazer, and shirts with Buster Brown collars and bowties, and what was known as a boater's hat - a flat, straw hat, with a ribbon around it with the school colors, which were red, white and green. We then marched off; being the youngest and the smallest, we were the last to follow the parade as it wandered down the hill to a small, very pretty church, called St. Nicholas. It was of the Church of England. The smallest of us sat in the front rows, on one side. Then in came the girls school group, from DGS; there was Geraldine, I spied her. Way in the back, I could see my mother, too. After church, we

were allowed to mingle, and I of course got hold of Geraldine and my Mum. Those few minutes outside the church were just great. This was our regular Sunday routine.

When the spring was over, the next thing was the butterflies. This, I enjoyed, because I'd done it before with Geraldine and Vernon. We used to chase butterflies in Bhim-Tal and Bhowali, so this was no different; I had a lot of fun. We'd mount the butterflies on little cardboard boxes as best we could and let them dry out. It wasn't long before Jack, Billy Watson and myself had quite a good collection; we got along very well.

Then came the monsoons — the heavy rains and the thunderstorms, with mists; the clouds covered the school and the mountains. There was one big fog bank with rain, and it rained and rained and rained. All the roofs were corrugated tin, and it used to make an awful noise when that rain would come down. The monsoons would last for two and a half months - July, August, into September. The next season after the butterflies were the beetles. They came out during the monsoon. There were many kinds of beetles: bamboo beetles, stag, dumpy and rhino beetles. The cruel part of collecting beetles was how to preserve them. I found out soon enough. The guys would twist the beetle's head off; gouge out the insides and then fill them with melted wax. Stick a match in the soft wax and attach the thorax and head. It was cruel, but we all had these hobbies to keep going.

It was the end of September and the monsoon rains had just about come to an end. It was always a wonderful sight to see everything washed clean. My mother had sent a message to me: Christine and Robert were going to be married in the Methodist Church at TaliTal. The Sherwood boys would not attend, but the students from Philander Smith and Wellesley schools would; it was their church. It was a Saturday morning with a bright sun. I was with my mother and Geraldine, in my Buster Brown collar and Sunday best. Soon as it was over, I felt sad. I knew Christine and Robert would be leaving for America. I thought I would never see her again.

I guess young people get over their little problems in a hurry, when there is so much activity around the school. The hockey and football (soccer) had started. All three boys' schools would compete down at the Flats. Then there would be the final for the championships. There was also the kite flying. This could get exciting, because they would pair-off for kite-fighting. The first hundred yards of kite string was coated with a type of ground glass. The opponent would try and wrap his kite around your string and let his kite have more string, giving a scraping effect and hopefully cutting your string. By the time that season was over, one could see kites stuck in trees and telegraph wires all over Naini-Tal. When the final hockey matches were held on the flats, it gave us youngsters a chance to gather around and cheer for our school.

It didn't take long before the school year was coming to an end and for the kids to get ready for the exodus back down the mountain with everyone going in different directions, back to their homes. Evidently, though I didn't know it at the time, I was more fortunate; I had my mother nearby. A lot of these boys, like the Watsons, whose folks lived in Karachi, had a horrendous trip back home, at least three or four days.

A message came for me to get packed, that a dandy would meet me at school. But just before leaving that morning, one of the older fellows gave me a box. He said, "You are Geraldine's brother, are you not? Please give it to her." I don't remember the boy's name. I took the box and got into the dandy. The four coolies started off, down the same pathway, past Tali-Tal, around the mountain, all the way down toward and past the sanatorium; through the bazaar of Bhowali, through the pass where I saw Bhim-Tal. By the time I got halfway down, I was intrigued by the present, I decided to open the box up and have a look. My eyes bulged out, for there was a whole box of chocolates. Well, one should never give a little boy who hasn't seen any candy for nine months a box of chocolates to deliver to somebody else. Needless to say, I had to try them out. I tried one, it was pretty good; then I tried another one, to see what was inside, and some of the soft ones, I'd squeeze and all the gooey stuff would come out; so I'd have to eat them. By now, I had demolished half the box. After going through the pass and seeing Bhim-Tal shimmering away in the distance, I knew I was almost home. I got out of the dandy and decided to walk the rest of the way. I had my slingshot, or catapult back again and started my same old tricks of chasing the bulbuls and mynah birds, whatever I came across on the path. By the time I reached Bhim-Tal, most of the chocolates were gone. I think there were several left, and sheepishly I gave them to Geraldine. Needless to say, she was furious, and shouted and yelled and told my mother what a bad boy I was; but there was nothing that could be done. I had to pay for that with a stomach ache. She told me that when I went back to school next year, I'd have to explain it to the boy, and I'd have to pay him back out of my pocket money.

At Bhim-Tal, with the dandy and empty box of chocolates, who was there but Beatrice the Bitch. She'd been waiting, and she knew exactly when I was coming back. She was all skin and bones, for she'd been turned back to being a pariah dog while we were gone. But it wasn't long till she was back in shape and chasing around, happy to have us there. Of course, there was Jasma also, a little snotty-nosed kid, with a funny little frock on and pigtails, and there was the masalchee.

We were back home, and I'd forgotten all about school, all those horrible things up there that one had to go through and learn. The masalchee, Jasma and I started up and down the hillsides, chasing birds. At this time, Jasma had grown a little older and so had I. When I did shoot some birds, she decided she'd go and make curry for me. With a little charcoal fire, Jasma got some dishpans, and we cooked our bulbuls and mynah birds. Even though they were song birds, it tasted good, especially after the food we'd been eating up in school.

Another time, when Jasma and I were wandering around, she said, "I'll show you something that is very good eating." She took me to a little patch near a wheat field where there were little sprouts coming out of the earth. Jasma gathered up a handful and speared them with a stick, and roasted them over the fire; then told me to eat them. I don't know what it was, but it tasted very good, kind of nutty; we enjoyed that, and when we had a chance, we were always looking around for more.

One bright, sunny morning, I got up very, very early; that's when the birds were out. Jasma and I heard a partridge, up on the hillside, behind the house. Jasma said she knew where they probably were. We started up the pathway; there were many little pathways over the wheat fields and on the mountainside. We came up perhaps 3 or 400 feet up on the hill, away from everybody, and sure enough, there were two partridges. These were the black partridge; they're beautiful birds, but wary. I tried crawling through the fields in one of the areas where the partridges were, but when I got close they took off; I never got a chance to shoot. Both Jasma and I sat down near the edge of the field; we were pretty well tired out from that walk and stalking. As we talked, kid-talk, I guess maybe it was grownup talk, I don't know — but she was talking about girls and boys, all in Hindi. I guess it's true the world over; you show me yours, I'll show you mine, sort of thing; that's what it led to. At this point, I hadn't even thought about it. She lifted up her little dress and showed me what she had, and I was amazed, because I'd thought she had something like mine. Then I had to show her mine. We were discussing the difference, and she tried to explain it to me, and I couldn't believe what she was saying, but she said that was true, and if I wanted to experiment, she'd show me how. Well, it didn't take long before she started to show me, and it was quite an experiment. I felt strange about it, being so young and innocent, but evidently she wasn't quite as innocent. At least, she knew a lot more than I did. But it was a strange experience, I don't mind saying. We spent a lot of the morning in the wheat field, and trampled some of it down. My little whistle by now had become quite red and inflamed; yet I wasn't frightened. She said not to worry, that was normal, and it would be all right. Years later, I was to hear a song in America, called "I Learned About Women From Her;" actually a Kipling poem. Well, I think I learned an awful lot from Jasma!

We wandered back down the hill, and Jasma went to her little home, where she and her father and folks lived; and I snuck in through the back and into the bathroom to wash myself. I was still frightened, but in time, everything went back to normal; the redness and irritation seemed to disappear, and I had a funny feeling that I wanted to see Jasma again. The next day, she wasn't around, so I just went with the masalchee down by the lakeside, trying to get some water birds with the catapult.

That Christmas a messenger (messenger is the mailman. He is recognized by a khaki tunic and spear with small bells attached near the spearhead) arrived with a big package on his head, from the post office in Bhowali. When we opened it up, it was from Mr. Athem, to my mother and us. It contained a great big cooked ham, a large cake, and a couple of boxes of sweets. We couldn't believe it; it was just a wonderful Christmas. Even though we didn't have a Christmas tree, and there was nothing in the way of Christmas presents, we all knew it was Christmas and New Year's. My mother decided that on this Christmas day it would be wonderful to take a picnic lunch down to Sat-Tal. The hamper of sandwiches, the water, and all things necessary for a good picnic were packed. The trip was not that easy, for me anyway. It would be about three miles, halfway through the Jones' estate, down the other side of the mountain to Sat-Tal. At the bottom near the lake was a small cottage that was on stilts, with steps that went up to the top floor. I remember Vernon leading the way when we came to the steps. We saw blood on the steps, and he got his gun ready, saying, "There's something up there, it might be a wounded leopard." Vernon went up while we waited at the bottom. He looked around on the verandah and opened the door, and there was blood in there. He came out and said, "No, the animal, whatever it was, has been there and gone." But before that, he searched all over the little cottage and found nothing. The bearer brought the hamper up and set it out on the verandah which overlooked the lake. It was a wonderful picnic; I'll never forget it, we enjoyed it very much. We had part of the new ham that had been given by Mr. Athem, some of the cake, and lots of sandwiches. I went wandering around with my catapult and was told not to go too far, because we were in an area where there were a lot of wild animals. I remember seeing one tree; right up at the top was a clump of what looked like grass, but it turned out to be mistletoe. I took aim with the catapult and knocked off some of the little limbs of the mistletoe. I brought it too my mother, and she was quite happy. In late afternoon, everything was packed up and we headed home. The steep incline from the lake to the Jones' area was quite a trip. About halfway up, we decided to take a photograph of my brother, my mother and me, and Geraldine took the shot by a large oak tree overhanging the pathway. I still have the picture, and later on in the book, I will repeat and show you why this is important to me.

Next day, I was able to get some sweets away from my mother, because I wanted to give them to Jasma and to the masalchee. You must remember, these were the only friends I had. Jasma came out again; this time she didn't have her dirty old pinafore on, but had a very nice little dress. Again, we went experimenting up in the wheat fields. I'm certain her Dad must have known something was going on, because in that area, the wheat field was beaten down. The three months' holiday went fast. Before I knew it, we were all packing up and getting ready for the trek, with the dandies and the safari, the baggage on the peoples' heads; away we went. I turned and said goodbye to Jasma, the masalchee and Beatrice.

The same faces were back in Sherwood School. We were back to the routine, but for one thing: I asked Jack Watson where Billy was; he told me that Billy wouldn't be there anymore because that winter, while they were swimming at the beach in Karachi, Billy had drowned. It

*A hill girl like Jasma in Bhim-Tal. "I learned about women from her!"*

was sad to know a young friend had passed away.

I settled down to another year of learning my ABC's, chasing butterflies, catching beetles, learning to fly kites, learning to race at our track meets, and then going on down to the Flats. This time, I was happy to see my brother play on the A Team for PSC College, as the captain. I remember they won that match and the final; a large cup was presented to their team. I do know that I avoided the boy who gave me the chocolates; he never mentioned anything to me, either. I'm sure Geraldine didn't tell him.

We were to spend one more winter holiday in Bhim-Tal with my same friends, little Jasma, the masalchee, myself, and Beatrice. One sad note: one day when Beatrice was in the yard, she attacked my Mother, but didn't bite her. The dog was beaten off and collared by the sweeper. It was thought that perhaps during the time when we were up in school, she might have been bitten by a mad dog. There were a lot of rabid dogs and jackals around. Beatrice was tied up, and on close examination, she started to froth at the mouth; her eyes got red, which is an indication of rabies. I'll never forget: I got a piece of meat and scraps, Vernon got his gun, and I led Beatrice out through the double gate, about 100 yards or so to another area of the field. I put the scraps down and let Beatrice go for the food. I couldn't look, but I heard the bang of the shotgun, and I knew Beatrice was dead. We left her there and walked back. It was a sad, sad day.

That winter, Christine sent us some Christmas goodies; I got a sweater and socks; Vernon, Geraldine, and my Mom also received all kinds of clothes and nice presents. She sent pictures of where they'd settled in Bangor, Maine. The pictures were of the wintertime, with mountains of snow. In the Naini-Tal area, we did get some snow, but nothing like that!

In the winter of 1925-26, we moved from Bhim-Tal up to Bhowali. I was now 11 years old. I don't know why the move was made, but our new home was Bhowali. We didn't stay in AppleCot, but in another very nice home belonging to the Shepherds, known as Oak Lodge. From the Oak Lodge garden, one could look at the same view as we had from the gorge just below us. One could see the whole valley, and Bhim-Tal in the distance. The last Christmas in Bhim-Tal, my sister Christine had sent not only some nice sweaters, she had sent me a Mechano-Set, a very nice and interesting toy. I couldn't wait to get back to school to show it to my friends. At the school, we all got together in the dormitory in the evenings and played with this Mechano-Set, making cranes and cars and airplanes. About a month later, the Mechano-Set disappeared - stolen. Miss Beverly had reported it to Mr. Dixon, the Principal, and he called everybody together in the auditorium; he wanted that Mechano-Set re-

turned immediately, but nobody came forward. It was about three months later that it was found. The boy at first did not confess, but had taken it down to the bazaar and had sold it. It was returned, and eventually the boy, one of the senior boys, had to confess and return the money. He was expelled. There was a lot of thievery of small things that took place in school. They called it "flicking;" the boy was called a "flick." If something is "flicked away," it was stolen.

On another occasion, there had been an argument, and my friend Jack was beaten up by another boy; so I challenged the other fellow. There was a little area near the latrine, where all the fights took place. I had to roll up my sleeves and fight. I put up a good fight; both my eyes were blackened and so were his; it was more or less a draw. But that was not the end. When we showed up at class the next day, we were both punished. For punishment, we had to put out our hands, and the master, with his malacca cane (a very flexible cane) gave us three smacks on each hand, which really hurt. It made the palms of the hands all black and blue, both the other fellow's and mine. Our hands swelled up, and we had to put oil on and massage them before we could pick up a pen or pencil to write. This was the English system at school. The master had the right to punish the boys by caning. Most caning was done on the behind, but for this type of misdemeanor, you got the beating on your hands, and I don't mind telling you, it hurt, and worked!

At the end of this year, 1926, we vacationed again in Bhowali. I could look out from Oak Lodge and see Bhim-Tal in the distance. I never saw Jasma again, or the masalchee. I accompanied my brother Vernon on many of his hunting sprees, for pheasant and partridge, around the Bhowali area. I was constantly on the go, hunting the various types of birds. The higher up we went, the more different types of birds we saw. One of the pretty ones was known as the Rajalal; he was a red-breasted and black-crowned bird, about the size of a sparrow, with a longer tail; beautiful bird. The female was the yellow one, with the same sort of markings, yellow and light brown. She was called the PilaRani; pila is yellow in hindi, and Rani is queen; and Rajalal is red king. They were an elusive type of bird and difficult to shoot; they usually stayed high in the trees, and being small, they were a difficult target. I did manage, after a while, to bag one of each. I was then able to shoot parakeets, too.

This gave me a headband that I'd longed for, in our PSC school colors of red, yellow and green. Because the following year, I was going to be in PSC, Philander Smith College, where my brother was attending. So, very proudly, I put on the hatband of the feathers of these three birds. I had been changed from the 2nd standard to the 3rd. I made that jump, al-

though I don't think I should have, because it was very difficult for me. I joined in all the sports and started to play hockey, soccer, and cricket; also the hobbies of looking for birds' eggs and chasing butterflies. This kept us busy all the time. It was the end of this school term; in November word came that Vernon had received his visa to go to America; the Westons had arranged this. After Christmas and New Years, 1926, in Bhowali, he packed up his belongings, and we saw him off at Naini-Tal. I was heartbroken again. But he left in good spirits and was eager to be on his way. That left my mother, Geraldine and myself.

In 1927, it was just the three of us, back in Naini-Tal, and the winter holidays were back in Bhowali and Oak Lodge. We had two dogs - one was brown, a mongrel poodle, with curly hair, who was called Cocoa. He was my special pet. The other was a female, black and white, a fox terrier type, Geraldine's dog, called Nancy. I remember we had taken a walk along the road that goes up towards Almorah. Some dogs had been following us on the way back; we kept our two pretty close to our heels. After returning to the house, we let the dogs out for a few minutes. Out of the dark, a big ferocious dog attacked Cocoa and Nancy and a terrible fight ensued. Mr. Shepherd's son, Frank, came out and shot the dog. Our two were pretty well mauled, but we treated them with iodine. Of course, we were always worried about rabies. It wasn't long before we had forgotten about that, and the dogs were always playing around. Cocoa followed me when I went on my little shooting expeditions. One day we came back, and one of the servants' dogs in the area was playing in the yard. Cocoa attacked him, scuffled him around and bit him terrible. We got Cocoa off, and he attacked Nancy, Geraldine's dog. We realized that these two, Nancy and Cocoa, were probably rabid. To add to our problems, the dogs, as we played, always licked us and nipped us; so who knew? It was decided that the landlord's son, his wife, Ann, and sister Doris, and I had to got to a Pasteur Institute for treatment. The only Pasteur Institute close was at another hill station near Simla, called Kasauli. The thing I liked about that was the train ride, back down through that little narrow gauge to Bereilly, there to catch the train that would take us to the foothills, where we'd have to take a taxi up to Kasauli. We had with us the head of Cocoa, in a box, to make sure that the animal was rabid.

At our little hotel, we were notified that Cocoa definitely had rabies. For two weeks, we would stand in line and get two shots every day, in the tummy. After the first four or five days, my stomach became black and blue and painful. It took two weeks and 28 shots before we were allowed to leave. I was glad to get out of there, back on the train, and to forget the doctor and the needle. Back in Bhowali one morning, I wandered behind the landlord's house along the trail on the side of the mountain. As I came around the bend, about 100 yards away, I saw a beautiful leopard sitting on a rock. We looked at each other for a minute, then I backed away slowly. When out of sight, I ran to the landlord's house and told Frank Shepherd. He got his rifle, and we raced back, but the leopard was gone. We went to where he'd been sitting, and saw a lot of fur and the footprints of the leopard. Frank told me it was probably the son of the leopard that carried away my dog, Bob, in 1918.

Mum, Geraldine and I returned to PSC school, and everything was back to routine; daily school work and playing hard. One day, we were informed that the Assistant Principal, a Mr. Fleming, had passed away that night of a heart attack. There was a funeral service and then a procession that took us past Muli-Tal and down the pathway that went to Kaladungi, and there at the Kaladungi Cemetery, Mr. Fleming was put to rest.

At the end of the 1927 term, Mother was very excited. She called Geraldine and me in to tell us that we'd received visas for America.

*We are headed up to Naini-Tal from Bhim-Tal. Mum, Geraldine and me with catapult and walking stick.*

# PHASE TWO: 1928 — 1940

The Westons had arranged for my Mother, Geraldine, and myself to come to the States. We packed up once again, got all our things sorted out, and said teary goodbyes to all our friends in Naini-Tal and Bhowali. It was early March 1928 when we left, as we always did, from Tali-Tal by taxis and wound our way down the precipitous hairpin turns to Kathgodam. I could hear the call of the brain-fever bird. We took the little narrow gauge once more, through the forest (watching all the interesting game and the birds on the telegraph wires), till we came to Bareilly. There was the mad confusion, the sounds and smells, until we got on board and headed for Calcutta, where we were to spend about two weeks at the Grand Hotel. Here we went through the formalities at the American Consulate, making final arrangements to be on our way. Mum did find time for shopping at the New Market. Our next train was south through Madras, across Adam's Bridge, and then Colombo, Ceylon. This was all new to me; I'd never seen this part of India. I'd never seen much of the world as yet; I'd never been on a big boat, and I'd never seen an airplane. This was all going to be very exciting. Yet, I had mixed emotions.

In Colombo, we stayed in a mission home for about a week until our boat arrived. I think it was a P&O named The Ormonde. One morning, as we walked near the wharf, we could see the boat anchored in the bay a few hundred yards out. I think it was a two-stack affair. On the 4th of April, a little launch took us and some other passengers out for boarding. Though it was exciting, I had that terrible feeling of being lost. We climbed aboard and put our suitcases, trunks, and everything you could think of in our cabin. Our cabin had a porthole; it was on the starboard side (I think that was an accident); it certainly was not "posh." We came on deck and looked around to see if we could find our deck chairs. Yes, there they were, with our three names on them, and right next to them was another one with the name of Wintle. My mother was so surprised, because Wintle was her maiden name. We were introduced around to all our other passengers by the purser, and most of them had been traveling all of the way from Australia and Singapore. My mother couldn't wait to meet Wintle. We were to sail late that evening, and when we heard the rumble of the engines and the anchor being lifted, the boat started to move. I looked back once more and saw the lights of Colombo, and I wanted to cry. I didn't know where the boat was going to take us; I didn't know anything about America, except what my friend said: "You'll see nothing but gangsters when you get there."

We had a light supper and went down to our cabin and bed. The next stop would be Aden. After the first two or three days, everything was going fine, that is until we got some rough weather. I felt as though I'd been smoking cigarettes! I started to get sick and vomit; it was terrible! It made no difference whether I lay down or stood up; it was just there, even the dry heaves. It stayed with me until we arrived at Aden. From Aden, it got better. Going through the Red Sea was hot, and we spent most of the time on deck. We passed through the Suez Canal, which was very interesting, and saw the camels and people in caravans going along the shore. Then we arrived at Port Said. We were there a whole day and night and allowed off to wander around in the bazaar. It reminded me somewhat of India, but yet it had a difference: the customs, the red-fezzed people, the vendors and the gully-gully wallah, doing his tricks. From Port Said, the next stop was Naples. After two days, I was sick again and wanted to jump overboard. Everything was wrong.

When the weather cleared, they showed us a movie. I don't remember the title, but it was a Western, one of Tom Mix's movies. We all sat and enjoyed that; I made friends with one young fellow. We even had some fancy dress parties. My friend and I won first and second place, when I dressed up as an Arab, and I was presented a small dowh boat. As we steamed into Naples Harbor, we could see the volcano Vesuvius. It had a plume of smoke coming from the crater. My mother was telling us about Vesuvius and the eruption and about Pompeii and the destruction it created back in the year 79 AD. The boat anchored out in the bay, and the next morning, we were taken ashore by launch. It was so nice to get ashore and on to terra firma. We walked around the promenade, saw many sights and people. We had lunch down near the quay; I'll never forget it — it was my first attempt at spaghetti. Actually, if I remember, it was the flat spaghetti, which is called linguini. I enjoyed trying to eat it, getting a lot all over me. The Italians sitting next to us were laughing at us. We enjoyed our two days in Naples.

The next stop was to Touloune, in France. Here was civilization the likes of which I'd never seen — a lot of electricity, a

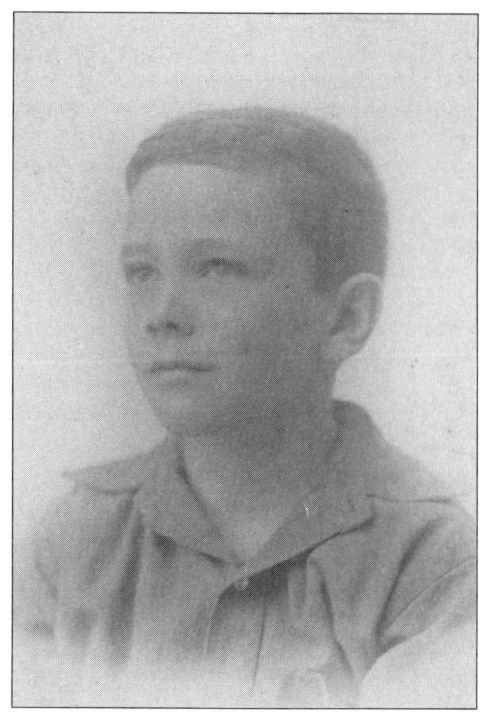

*My passport picture, 1928.*

lot of automobiles, and my first airplane. I saw it fly over the boat, and I stretched my neck and wondered and looked; it was a beautiful sight. We stayed in Touloune for another couple of days. Then on to Southampton. At Southampton, we took the train to London, and stayed in Kensington. Kensington is the old haunt of my mother's, where she stayed many times as a child. I was happy here; everybody spoke English. I got my first real haircut in a proper barber shop. We went to see some silent movies; I remember seeing Rudolph Valentino again in those Sheik movies, and the movie *Wings*, about airplanes. In the daytime, I'd sit on the balcony and watch all the cars. I started to distinguish Rolls-Royce from Rovers, etc. Mum took us walking around in Kensington Gardens; it was beautiful - in spring.

Two weeks later, we took the train to Liverpool, where we took our final boat ride, on the White Star Line. The name of the boat was The Celtic. This was about a 5 or 6 day trip; for the most part, I was sick, terribly seasick. Then, early one morning, the sun was just coming up from our stern, I looked out and could see in the distance what was Boston Harbor. There were the stark, brick buildings, with the sun glinting on the windows and the haze all over the city. My heart sank; I was looking for mountains and saw nothing but flatness. We came in close, and eventually the boat made its way into the wharf. There to greet us were Christine, Vernon and Robert. The car ride through the city to Cambridge was fantastic. I have never seen so much traffic.

We stayed with the Westons in Cambridge for a few days, where I met my first friend, Andy Dana, before the trip to Bangor, Maine. Geraldine and my mother stayed with the Westons. It was I who went with Christine and Robert, by train, to Bangor. It was the middle of May, the weather was beautiful and everything was green and lush. It looked great to me, but at no time had I forgotten what I'd left behind. I had stored a vivid image in the back of my mind of my world of Bhowali, Bhim-Tal and Naini-Tal. The train ride from Boston to Bangor, Maine was uninteresting. Though the seats were comfortable, I was not impressed with the pullman-type cars; I preferred our old Indian trains, where one had the compartment to oneself, where I could open the window and take potshots at birds that sat on the telegraph wires. I also loved our Indian stations, with all the noise and smells. The quick introduction to the American stations, where everything seemed so orderly, with no bedrolls and suitcases piled on the platforms, or in the middle of our compartment. People sat so quietly, reading newspapers or magazines. No, I just didn't go for the American train ride. I still wore my English-style shorts, with knee socks, my hat was the old Indian one that they called a putu hat (made of coarse wool). I had my bird feathers stuck in the band, and the old catapult in my pants pocket. When we got off the train at Bangor, a porter arrived with our trunks and suitcases. As we walked to the car park, everyone stared

*Christine with Kim as pup; taken in Bangor, Maine 1926.*

at me with curiosity; I tried not to notice them.

I took it all in, the new sights and the river nearby, Robert said it was the Penobscot River. Robert Weston led me towards the car, which looked grand. He said it was a Model T Touring Ford. Christine went with a friend who came to meet us; I think his name was Mr. Hinckley. I was not impressed with his car, called a Packard. I didn't know one American car from another. The Ford was impressive, because the roof folded back, and the wind would blow on you when you drove. We traveled through the main streets of Bangor and I liked it. It was not so noisy with traffic, as in Boston. I noticed a stream that ran through the town, and Robert called it the Kenduskeag Stream. He said a lot of the lakes and waterways were named after the American Indians that once lived in this area. The buildings were not very high, and were mostly brick. There were streetcars in the middle of the road; they were making clanking sounds, and when they turned corners, I noticed sparks coming out of the arms that rolled on wires overhead. I figured these streetcars were trains; they reminded me a little of our narrow-gauge trains that ran through the Terai Jungle.

After passing through the city, we motored up a steep incline, and turned right. The street was called Division Street. Robert turned into a long driveway and parked in front of a white building. "This is it," he said. I enjoyed the ride very much; it reminded me also of the Indian taxis that took us up to Naini-Tal. They, too, were open. During the drive, Robert said they had a hunting dog (setter) named Kim. I asked if the picture of a puppy that Christine had sent to us in Bhowali was him; it was. When Robert opened the door of the house and let Kim out, the dog bounded out and jumped all over him. He quieted down and came over to me.

I was a bit scared, for Kim was rather a big animal. After a few sniffs around my dirty knees, he wagged his tail and gave a friendly, growling bark; we were friends.

Robert then suggested I unload my things and carry them in. It was not until then that I realized there were no servants around. Christine and Mr. Hinckley arrived as I carried my belongings. Christine showed me the way up the stairs, all the way to the third floor, which she called the attic. One section had been converted to a nice bedroom, with a window looking out to the front of the house. After everything was deposited, I was shown the toilet on the second floor and the rest of the house. The toilet didn't remind me at all of the one we had in India, where the sweeper had to take the refuse out and dump it over the hillside. This one had a nice china bowl, and a long chain which you would pull, giving it a gushing, swirling sound, and everything disappeared.

The house had a fireplace in the living room (which we would have called a drawing room), just as our own had in India. The kitchen was large. The cook stove was a black iron affair, that used coal for cooking, and a large tall box affair she said was the icebox - this was all new to me. The first evening we had supper, which Christine cooked, and then came the washing of the dishes. It was a rude awakening when I learned I was now the masalchee-wallah, and the houseboy! At nine o'clock, I went up to my new room and bed. For awhile, I lay there, my mind racing in different directions, most of all to Bhowali and Bhim-Tal. I missed it so much. I was gradually falling asleep, when I heard footsteps coming up the stairs. They stopped at my door, which was open. I thought it was Kim, so I waited. He would take a few steps and stop. I pretended to be asleep. He was soon at the foot of my bed. First he put one paw on the bed, then

*In Bangor with Kim and my still wearing
English shorts 1928.*

the other; the next moment, Kim had crawled onto the bed. From there, he edged his way up, closer to me. I reached over and stroked his head and ears. Kim gently wagged his feathery tail, which banged against the iron bedpost. It was not long before we were fast asleep; my best friend and myself.

Very early the next morning, I was awake, with Kim nearby. I could hear strange birds chirping outside. There was no chota hazari (small breakfast) here. Christine bustled around the kitchen; there was the smell of bacon and coffee. I didn't drink coffee, never had tasted it; it was tea for me, and a glass of orange juice. I was interested to wait for the rest of the breakfast. Robert and I were served two eggs each, in their shells. I watched Robert put a piece of toast on the plate, take each egg, crack the shell, and scoop out the inside onto the toast, without breaking the yolk. The eggs were perfectly soft-boiled. He then broke the yolks with a knife and fork and smeared it all over the rest of the toast. Then, English-style, knife in right hand, fork in left, he ate. I never had eaten eggs this way. In India, the bearers always served the toast in an upright rack, so they would be separate and dry. The eggs were placed in an egg cup. I used to smack the top with the back of a teaspoon and cut the end off. Salt and pepper was usually put in little piles in the corner of the plate. I would then dig into the egg with the spoon, touch the bottom part of the spoon to the salt and pepper, and take a mouthful with a bit of toast. It was not uncommon in India to hear the cook early in the morning scraping the burnt edges off the toast, since toast was usually made over an open fire, speared with a fork. Our life in the hill area was something like what the Americans call camp-style. I tried copying Robert; however, the yolks broke. I ate my American-style eggs, and I have to admit, I enjoyed my breakfast, with the bacon. I did not enjoy my masalchee work, however. Though the school season would be coming to a close in six weeks, it was decided I should attend a few classes to get my feet wet, and to learn the American-style systems.

I was taken to a small private school on Hammond Street that overlooked a part of downtown Bangor. Yes, I still wore my Indian shorts. It was a "posh" school! I think it was called Summerset. I was placed in about the 5th grade level, and introduced to the class by the principal. I was introduced as a boy from India. The class was half-filled with girls, who kept peeking at my knees and giggling. The lady teacher, after the introduction, asked if I would tell the class a little bit about my life in India. It was a big order, and I was bashful. I finally was able to stand before the group and talk for a while. I talked about the leopard, about the jackals on our verandahs; then about the school systems, how it was reverse season to the U.S.A., and of chasing birds and butterflies, etc. I said I would bring a few bird feathers and beetles the next day. After class break, a group cornered me and asked many questions. They expected me to be black, that there were no schools in India, and where actually was India and Naini-Tal? I was surprised that these school kids didn't know much about that part of the world. In our classes in Naini-Tal and at DBS and PSC, we were taught a great deal about America. One of my new classmates was a boy named Jim Wilson, the son of the Mayor of Bangor, and another fellow called Dick, or Richard Dunn.

The next day, I did bring the feathers and beetles, and showed them to the class. I showed the catapult, and explained it was not a toy and could do considerable damage, and that we were not allowed to have them in our Indian schools. However, boys did, illegally. If caught, you could expect a whipping with a good flexible malacca cane. After the first few days, I lost a lot of my shyness, and was able to get along with the girls and guys. The Wilson boy invited me to his home, where I met the Mayor. They were interested in my stories of India.

As time went on, I was envious of all my friends with their bicycles. I remember in Bhowali, I tried making a scooter with the help of Mr. Frank Shepherd. It was very makeshift, but kept me happy. Dick Dunn, realizing my enthusiasm for wanting to learn how to ride a bike, let me have his at times. One afternoon, on my own, I finally mastered the balancing act of bicycle riding. After school came to end for summer, Dick came to the house and asked my sister and Robert if I could work the month of July with him. The job was delivering sample cornflakes all around the city of Bangor and Brewer and towns nearby. It paid about $2.00 a day. There were four of us. Dick showed up with the others and a man with a large van. Street by street and door to door, we made our way. I remember on one occasion, we were delivering the samples in a raggedy neighborhood, when Dick and I were chided and teased by a group of boys. They tried to take away our samples and make fun of me and my shorts. The man with the van was waiting in another area. I told them to leave us along. The more we did this, the more they chided. I got out my catapult and told them to be off or I'd hit them. They laughed, so I started whacking them on their legs and behinds with marbles that I shot from my catapult. Finally, with screams and yells, they ran off. Dick marveled at my accuracy. I became a hero when this got around. The rest of the work went by without incident, and I was paid $42.00. It was the first time I was to see so much money.

Christine was always a great sport, and helped. It was agreed that I could now buy a bicycle, and still have a few dollars left over. She took me to a sporting shop in the center of town, called Dakin's Sporting Goods. The owner was a Mr. Shep Hurd, who took us around and displayed all the new, shiny bicycles. They were too expensive for me. He said there were quite a few second-hand ones downstairs. In looking them over, I chose one that I liked. It was a brown one, with a tool kit, pump and a light; it was $28.00. The deal was made, and I had my first bike ever! Gone were all the memories of Bhowali and Bhimtal; all I could think of was riding the bike. I wanted to ride it home, but Christine didn't want me riding in the downtown areas. "Too dangerous," she said. "You'll get run over." so, it was loaded into the back seat of the car, and driven home. I showed it to Robert, who thought it was a good bicycle, but there was too much gadgetry on it. He thought that the light and tool box ought to come off. "No way!" I thought. I circled around the driveway a few times, getting the hang of it; it was delightful.

All that afternoon was spent cleaning the spokes and rims, wiping down the frame, and oiling the sprockets and chain. I could barely sleep that night. I was totally happy. The next day, Dick Dunn came over, and I let him ride the bike; he thought it rode well. Christine and Robert agreed I could go around the local streets, until I got used to the traffic and could find my way around. Dick said he would see to it that all went well. Dick was a year older. We rode up and down Kenduskeag Avenue, where a lot of my friends lived. I stopped and talked with a lot of them, showing off my new purchase.

The summer had gone fast. I had my introduction to the Fourth of July celebrations, and Robert made certain I knew how to use the manual lawn mower. It was late August when a bespectacled gentleman showed up in an open car, with a boy about 2 years old, his son. The gentleman's name was Horace Chapman. Mr. Chapman owned one of the major hotels in town, called the Bangor House. He had a large, round-shaped disc of straw in the back seat of his car. He said it was an archery target. I helped get it out and set it up on a stand at the far end of the lawn. We had a big lawn — I should know, since I had to mow it. He then produced a bow and a quiver full of arrows. I was impressed; this was the first time I'd ever seen this sort of equipment. I'd seen pictures of archery equipment, but not first-hand. The lawn was about 100 feet square. That distance, plus another 30 feet across the driveway, gave Horace Chapman at least 30-40 yards. He strung the bow, and standing at right angles of the target, started shooting arrows. The target was about four feet across, and on it was stuck an oilcloth with white, black, blue and red circles, with a gold center. He shot six arrows; they all hit in various parts of the target. He explained how to keep score. The gold was 9 points, the red was 7, the blue was 5, the black was 3 and the white was 1. Horace shot several rounds, and then asked if I would like to try my luck. Robert suggested I stand close to the target; he didn't want arrows flying into the neighbors' yard. When I was handed the bow, I unconsciously held it with my right hand, the same way I did my catapult. He said I was holding it left-handed, but to me it felt natural. Horace showed me how to notch the arrow with the odd-colored cockfeather on the outside. I pulled back on the string with the left hand, and the bow tilted, just the way I use my catapult. The arrow hit the target, at about the 12 o'clock position, on the blue ring. Horace Chapman let out a yell of glee. He definitely had a Maine twang accent! I had to borrow his arm-guard, because the bowstring slapped against my forearm. The next several arrows hit the target, with one bullseye, and the others in the red. He couldn't believe that I had never pulled a bow before. That evening, Robert said I did pretty well, and Mr. Chapman was most pleased.

The very next day, Mr. Chapman arrived at the house. He presented me with a bow and a quiver of arrows. Horace said they were his wife's, but she never was interested in archery. He felt I would have more use for them; I sure did! My goodness, I thought to myself; these American people were really friendly. That weekend, I joined Mr. Chapman and his friends. It would not be too long before I would know all of them. Horace told them I was a natural at age 14. I had not yet tried the new bow given me, but when I did, it was much lighter in weight and in pull. The first couple of arrows fell short of the target, about 40 yards away. I soon got the range and could pelt the target easily.

One of the men drew my attention. His name was Howard Peavey. He was rough talking, with a gravelly voice, a great person, with a shock of grey hair. I later learned it was his father who had invented the Peavey, a long-handled affair with a loose metal catch at the end. Lumberjacks use them for hauling, catching and pulling the logs around, and turning them over. I enjoyed his rough, carefree talk. He was just a great man.

September had arrived, and the fall season. This was the first time I had ever seen all the trees turn such pretty colors of yellow, bronze and red. With it came time to return to school. I did not return to the private one that I had gone to when I first arrived in Bangor, and met my friends, Dick Dunn and Jim Wilson. This was a fairly large grade school, quite a distance from home. It was called Mary Snow School. Now that I knew my way around on the bicycle, it was

agreed that I could take it to school. I was placed in the 7th grade. As usual, I arrived in my shorts and received snickers and giggles. All went well for the first couple of weeks, till one of the bully boys from school made fun of my clothes and prodded me for a fight. I never was a coward, nor was I a fighter, and I always tried to avoid this sort of nastiness. There was no way out of this one, with the kids gathering around. I figured he was about a year older than I, and bigger. I thought I'd get it over with, one way or the other; it was the other. I put up a pretty good fight; however, he got the best of me, and I wound up with a black eye and a bloody nose. All I was able to do was give him a thick lip and bloodied mouth. After school, he came over to me when I went to get my bike. He wanted to shake and be friends. He said he expected me to back off and run. He was surprised that I took up his challenge. We shook hands, and I said I would have liked to back off, but I was brought up not to be a coward. We were friends for the rest of the school year.

A lot of subjects we were being taught came easy to me, even though I was not that sharp at school in India. At PSC, for instance, we started Latin and French in the 4th grade; we also had algebra. By the 5th grade, we continued our languages and algebra and were introduced to general physics. The Three R's were from the first grade; geography covered mainly India and England in general. We covered the rest of the world, too.

I knew pretty much what the 48 States were, and the first thirteen colonies. My problem was being able to concentrate in class; my mind wandered a great deal, and to come halfway around the world and to be dropped into a classroom so completely different had me confused. Homework was something new that I'd never had before, as well as recesses and changing classrooms every so often. By the end of September, hunting season had started, and this was a little different to me, too.

Robert was most meticulous about hunting. Always, the night before, he'd have the shotguns cleaned and ready. His gun and Christine's were 20 bore Parkers. I was always eager to help. As for Kim the setter, he was beside himself, whining and barking; he sensed the coming events. There were cartridges of proper sizes and game bags. The first of the season was for shooting woodcock and partridge. The partridge actually are ruffled grouse. This was my first shooting experience in America. I was as excited as Kim. Robert and Christine had a particular hunting friend, a gentleman named Ruel Kimball. Mr. Kimball arrived early in the morning, and we were ready. Christine went with Mr. Kimball, while Robert, Kim and I went in the Ford. On the way, Robert explained how woodcock were hunted. Kim was a trained hunting dog. He had a small bell on his collar, and when Kim found the scent, he was supposed to stand still and point. When we didn't hear the bell, we knew he was pointing.

*My first long pants.*

I wasn't too sure where we were going. I think it was way up the Kenduskeag Stream. Robert steered off the main dirt road (most roads in Maine at that time were dirt) and onto a narrower lane. We got out, but not Kim. He barked and yapped and wanted to go hunting. When everyone was ready, Robert took charge and got Kim from the back seat. He had his leash on, which Robert held tight. We started along a footpath, what we used to call pak-dundi in India, up a small incline, then along a ridge. The trees were white; Robert said they were white birch. It was here that Kim was released. In a second he was off down the hill and into the alders, with the bell tinkling. I could see flashes of white as Kim raced about. Soon, he was out of sight. Robert shouted for him, but it was no good. In the distance, we heard a rumbling sound, and Christine told me it was a partridge. It was several minutes more before Kim came dashing through the alders to us. He was wet and mucky, with a yard of pink tongue flapping from his mouth. He got a scolding and was leashed. We continued a little further, and Kim was released once more. This time, he was a little more docile. Kim ranged the left side of the ridge and soon came to a stop and was pointing down at the alders. Christine and Mr. Kimball approached from the rear. Kim took a few steps forward and stopped, Robert saying, "Steady, steady." With the two guns close up to him, Kim made a dash into the alders; a flurry, and out flew a woodcock. It made a whistling sound as it flew. Shots were fired, and the bird fell. Kim was on it, and brought the bird to Robert. I looked the bird over and commented that it looked like the ones that

Vernon used to shoot in Bhim-Tal. Robert agreed, except, he said, these didn't have the painter feathers on the wings. (The painter's feathers were two small feathers located on the front of each wing. Artists can use these feathers for delicate painting, such as miniatures.) I pulled a few of the pretty dark and rust-colored feathers and placed them in my hat. Kim behaved himself and worked well, but he was a mess!

When the morning shoot was over we returned to the cars. I arranged a number of stones for a fireplace, while Robert and Mr. Kimball gathered dry wood, and Robert peeled some birch bark from the trees. This was all piled in the fireplace and lit. I was surprised to see the bark ignite so fast; it reminded me of the resin I used to pick up in the pine forest in Bhowali. A stout alder limb was cut, and a prong made at the slender end. Robert dug it deep into the earth and hung a kettle of water over the fire from it. Soon we had our tea. It was not the way I used to have tea with milk and sugar, just plain black. In time, I would get used to it. Kim was given his food. I thought back to 1924 and 1925 when we had Christmas picnics in Sat-Tal. There we had no fire, but bottles of prepared tea and the bearer doing all the serving. So many things were happening to me in America. I was trying hard to catch up, with all this outing and shooting; hunting had always been my favorite sport.

Almost every week found me raking the fallen leaves off the immense lawn. Kim was no help. I would have a large pile, and he would come dashing in through the pile and scatter them. Sometimes, he would just roll in them, and I'd cover him up. Kim was almost human. Here I was in Bangor, as the masalchee, and now the mali, or gardener. If my friends back there only knew, especially Jasma, what I was now doing, they would laugh.

As the days rolled by, it got colder, yet Robert always took me hunting. By mid-November, there was heavy frost on the ground and ice on the puddles. It was very much like the winters in Naini-Tal. I wore my gloves, sweaters, and wool cap like the other, but still wore shorts. The kids in school couldn't believe it. I continued my archery with Mr. Chapman and other archery members. Just before Thanksgiving, which had been explained to me at school by the teacher, a visitor drove in. He was a Mr. Duncan Dana, from Marblehead, Massachusetts, Robert's brother-in-law, Andy's father. Duncan Dana, I was informed, was the grandson of Dana the author of "Two Years Before the Mast," and whose father owned the New York Sun News Paper Co. He had come to do some duck-shooting with Robert. Duncan was also a great archer. He was a tall individual, rawboned and bald, a great person, and I liked him immediately. During the conversation that evening, Robert mentioned my archery enthusiasm. He thought that was great, and stated that he had an idea. On his drive up, coming through the town of Waterville, which is about 60 miles southwest of Bangor, he saw signs about an

archery tournament and turkey shoot. He had inquired, and the date was Sunday before Thanksgiving. Horace was contacted, and arrangements were made to participate, including me, and that we would have to borrow someone's archery equipment for Duncan. Early Sunday morning, Mr. Dana and I met at the Bangor House with Horace and a few of the archers. Duncan was given some archery equipment from a member that was not going.

We arrived where the event was taking place. Duncan and Horace discussed, with the Waterville archery members, that I be allowed to participate, because I was still a junior at 14; that I should use the junior range on the 50, 40 or 30 yard level, while the regular American round for the adults would be 60, 50 and 40 yards, and that my score should be handed in with the regulars. It was agreed. One or two locals were not quite certain, but consented; they eyed me suspiciously, short pants and all. The team leader of the Waterville group was a man named Jack Egan. He was the manual trainer for Waterville High School; he seemed like a fine guy. It was a beautiful day, clear and crisp, flags flying and a great array of targets stretched across a wide field; each with a number above it. Duncan paid the fee and signed me in. I think I was assigned target #12, at one end. There were two other junior fellows that joined me. They were from the high school and being tutored by Mr. Egan. When all the scores were handed in to the ladies who tabulated them, the winner was, of course, me! Yes, I had won the turkey! Duncan and Horace were tickled that I had won. I was presented with the large, live turkey. We put him in the trunk and drove back to Bangor. I couldn't wait to tell Christine and Robert the exciting news. Duncan had other ideas, he said to be very quiet. It was late evening when we arrived home. Duncan took the turkey out of the trunk, opened the front door and let the turkey loose in the hallway. It was as though an explosion had taken place. The turkey gobbled and flapped into the living room where Christine and Robert sat. When Kim saw the bird, he was after it; that's when all hell broke loose! Kim was chasing the turkey which jumped, flew and gobbled; and Kim barked. The two went through the living room, the dining room, knocking over things, then into the kitchen and back. Glassware and plates crashed, and pictures fell from the walls. Robert was cussin' Duncan; Christine was shouting and laughing, with all of us trying to catch the elusive bird. It turned into utter bedlam! I don't think Duncan expected quite the shambles that occurred in those few minutes. When the turkey was finally captured and Kim leashed, the dog's mouth was full of feathers. It was a while before everything quieted and some sort of order was restored. It took some time to clean up the feathers and turkey crap. I took the turkey down into the cellar and tied him up for the night. Duncan and I would attend to the killing of the bird later and prepare it for the forthcoming Thanksgiving dinner. Duncan apologized

to Robert for the havoc created. My getting to know America and the Americans was coming along in the most delightful way for a young kid like me from a distant land.

Thanksgiving Day arrived and Christine did a wonderful job cooking the turkey dinner with all the trimmings. One of the vegetables she served, I became curious about. It resembled long sprouts and tasted a bit familiar. Christine noticed me and asked if anything was wrong. I then remembered and said, "I know this funny sprout; Jasma and I had cooked something like this on sticks, back in Bhim-Tal." Christine called it asparagus. It all came back to me when Jasma had showed me the shoots coming out of the ground at the edge of the wheat field just below our house. Golly! All of a sudden, that seemed so long ago.

Duncan and Robert did some of their duck hunting, and I was back in school. Duncan stayed a couple of days longer and then returned to Marblehead. Before leaving, it was decided that all of us would come to his home for the Christmas holidays.

In mid-December, the first real snowstorm came. It actually was a blizzard and it arrived with a vengeance. I watched through the window as the snow piled up. The next morning, there was no way I could get to school. Robert and I spent all morning shovelling snow off the driveway. The driveway was more than a hundred feet long, and this was my first experience at snow shovelling. The first few feet of digging was fun; after that it was all hard work and tiring. Again, it was hard to believe, but there I was in my shorts. As the neighbors and the landlord, a Mr. Prentiss, stared at me, the snowplows finally came by and cleared Division Street. Kim loved the snow. I made snowballs that I threw in the air, and Kim would catch them. I chased him all over the yard. Some of my friends and Dick Dunn showed up with sleds and a toboggan. They were going to show me how to sled and use the toboggan. The Kenduskeag Stream had long since frozen solid. Now, with the snow, it made a great place to sled; down the steep bank and onto the frozen stream. Yet, they couldn't believe that I still wore shorts. Some of the girls rubbed snow on my knees. I think they enjoyed it; I know I did. However, Christine and Robert realized that I should transfer into long trousers. That weekend, I was marched off to a local store (Freeses), where I tried on long pants. They were terrible; they itched my knees, but that was that.

I made my debut in school, dressed in my first long pants. The class clapped when I walked in; well, that was something! Christmas holidays arrived, and we drove down to Marblehead to Duncan Dana's home. The house was located right on the water's edge, overlooking a large bay. It was a beautiful location. I met the rest of the family — Mrs. Nancy Dana, who was Robert's sister, and their three children: Andy, who was my age or a year younger; Anstis, a couple of years younger; and the youngest boy, Duncan, Jr. They called him "Dunkie." I shared Andy's bedroom.

Christmas preparations got under way. We got involved in the tree decoration. This was the first Christmas since I left Monghyr in 1921; it was now 1928. The Monghyr tree was tall, but very simple. This one had so much on it, one could hardly see the tree - electric lights, tinsel and baubles were glistening. Then heaps of presents started piling around it. Andy said we had to put our stockings either at the foot of our bed or by the fireplace downstairs. It turned out to be the fireplace. Andy and I spent some of our time downtown, looking at all the decorated shops and streets. There was Father Christmas, jingling a bell and what appeared to me, begging; almost the same idea as beggars I'd seen in the bazaars back in India. I told Andy, and he tried to explain the difference between begging and charity; I wasn't sure I understood. Anyway, we continued sightseeing, and I was amazed at the glitter and Christmas music wherever we turned; I enjoyed every minute.

The meals at the Dana's were sumptuous. I enjoyed the breakfast - for the first time, I had American pancakes and waffles. It took a couple of times to be able to eat bacon, sausages and syrup all together. But I never drank the coffee.

Christmas Eve was celebrated and other relatives of the Weston Family arrived. I had already met some when we arrived off the boat and stayed with Robert Weston's family, his Mum and Dad. Andy called Mr. Weston, Sr., "Old Man Weston." He was short and thin, and slightly bent over; he was bespectacled and had a thick, droopy mustache. Mr. Weston wore a dark blue-black cape that tied in front around his neck, and from nowhere he always produced a large, green bag, which contained several umpal type pipes, pipe cleaners, and tobacco; all sorts of gadgetry. He always had a pipe in his mouth, whether lit or not, and drool would trickle down to the bottom of the bowl and drop off. The edges of his grey mustache were brownish, from the pipe; Andy said it was soup! My mother had also arrived with my sister Geraldine, who'd been attending the Art Academy in Boston.

Andy and I talked for quite a spell. He said the first thing in the morning, we'd look into our stockings that hung at the fireplace. When everyone had assembled at the tree, his Dad, Duncan, would present the Christmas gifts. Again, I could never remember such an occasion, only that at the Monghyr club, so long ago. It was quite a while before I could sleep; the chatter of people talking downstairs, dishes being cleaned, with supper being rid of, and the preparations for the next day's Christmas dinner.

Morning came with a rush. Andy, Anstis, and Dunkie were already up and thumping down the stairs. It didn't take long for me to wash, dress, and join the group by the fireplace. Andy and the others had not bothered to wash or dress; they were still in their night attire. Andy presented me with my Christmas stocking; it was full. I pulled out one gift at a time, all kinds of trinkets, candy,

*The old house in Bangor. My window at top. Picture taken in 1993.*

nuts, oranges, and at the very bottom was a shiny coin. I thought it was a new penny; Andy and the others each had one. Andy asked me if I knew what it was; I said it was a penny. They laughed and said, no it's not, it was a five dollar gold piece! *Five dollar!* My eyes almost bulged out with surprise. Andy and Anstis said it was from the Old Man.

Christine, Robert and Nancy were already in the kitchen, fixing coffee, tea, orange juice, etc. I settled with my tea. Pancakes were in order for breakfast. I could barely eat; neither could the others. It took forever for breakfast to be finished. We helped to clean the table, wash and put away the things. Duncan told his kids to get upstairs and clean up before anything else. They were quick to do so.

The moment had arrived, and with all the relations, Duncan was deliberately slow in handing out gifts, especially to the kids. Of all the gifts that were being presented, among such things as ties, handkerchiefs, socks, etc, I was given one by Duncan that was long and heavy. He winked as I received it. The fancy wrapping was quickly off, and there was a gun case. Inside was a double-barreled, 12-gauge shotgun; I was absolutely dumbfounded. Though it was a well used one that had belonged to Duncan, it was the most beautiful gift one could ever imagine. I raced over and hugged Duncan, as though he were my father. I showed it to Christine and Robert. As I unwrapped another interesting package, it turned out to be a single shot .22 rifle from Christine and Robert. I just couldn't believe this was happening to me. How lucky can a young boy from India be. I was reminded to take great care of the guns, the same as Robert did with his. You bet I would! My mother was there, and it was wonderful to see her. My eldest brother and his wife Jessie had left Majorca, Spain and were in Winnipeg, Canada. They had three boys; Mark, Justin and Tony. The fourth boy, Peter, would be born in November, 1929. Vernon was working as a purser for the

United Fruit Company, that plied between New York and Central America. The boats also carried bananas from Honduras and Guatemala. He, too, was unable to be with us this Christmas. It was such a wonderful occasion, and Christmas had its meaning.

The next moment, it seemed, we were on our way back to Bangor. I couldn't believe that the holidays had come and gone so quickly. It was a long drive back, as the roads were slippery with snow and ice, besides, the Ford would not go more than 30 to 40 miles per hour! Robert had put chains on the rear wheels that kept up an incessant clackety-clang, all the way. It was cold sitting in the back, even though I was wrapped up in blankets. There is a wonderful landmark in Bangor; it is a very large water tank that is situated on top of a hill in town. At night, it is lit up with a halo of lights around the top. It was a welcome sight after that long drive from Marblehead. We soon had all our things brought in, and I carried my precious belongings upstairs. I assembled the gun and placed it beside my bed with the .22 rifle. I was soon asleep with Kim . I remember he sniffed at the guns and wagged his tail.

Winter in Maine, I found, could be long and cold, and no bicycling because of the snow; I walked to school instead. On occasions, Robert did drive me to school when the weather was foul. On the days off, he introduced me to rabbit hunting with the .22 rifle. The northern hares were unusual; they turned white in the winter, for camouflage. Robert would track them, and the rabbits always would hop and run in a large circles (counter-clockwise). I would wait at the spot where the rabbit had first jumped, and as Robert circled, the hare would come back near to the spot where I was waiting. Once in a while, I would miss with the rifle and get Robert annoyed after all the tracking he had done! The rabbits we shot became my job to dress and get ready for Christine to cook. She made a delicious stew from them; with hind quarter and back only.

*The model "T" Ford I learned to drive on Phillips lake in winter 1928/29, Maine.*

Robert insisted that I not use the shot gun, it was not sporting for rabbit shooting.

Andy Dana came up for a visit that winter and brought his .22 rifle. Robert, because he loved the outdoors and hunting, would take us. Once we had a thaw and all the snow melted. The rabbits were now caught in their white coats with no snow. I had my .22, and Robert always used his .22 Colt pistol and was an excellent shot with it. It was difficult to flush the rabbits; they would stay hidden in the thickets. In spite of our poor shooting, Andy and I managed to shoot two.

While Andy was still visiting with us, Mr. Prentiss, the person for whom Robert worked (Prentiss and Carlisle), decided to take us all ice fishing, which was to be another new experience for me. He drove the very large Cadillac touring car right out on the lake. The lake was called Peshaw Pond. It was cold and windy. We were able to get way out in the middle of the lake where the fish were supposed to be. I watched as Robert and Mr. Prentiss dug large holes in the ice; the ice being about two feet thick. It took a lot of chopping and hacking with icepicks or chisels about six feet long. They then set the bait, attached to a steel wire, with a red flag at the end. When the fish took the bait, the flag would spring up. This was quite a sport. There were about six holes that were dug. I had to run around and keep scooping out the holes, because they kept freezing over. The fish that we were trying for were pickerel; big, bony, ugly looking fish like a northern pike. Before the day was up and we were half frozen, we had a pretty good catch of fish. This was all very interesting for me; driving on a frozen lake and catching fish through the ice. Where we drove onto the lake I noticed several men cutting large blocks of ice and piling them up in stacks. I asked what that was for? Robert said that ice is used in ice boxes to keep things cold. The truck I saw had Getchell's Ice Co. written

on it. It was Getchell's that delivered ice for our ice box.

On another cold winter weekend, Christine mentioned that a lot of their friends were going out to Phillips Lake to go ski-jorring. This sport meant driving on the frozen lake and towing someone at the back of the car on skis, with a long rope. At camp there was a lot of excitement and talk about how this was going to take place and who would go first. I don't remember who went first or last; I do remember Christine driving the Ford with someone being towed at the back. It looked like fun, but I was not up to it. Everyone was back in the camp and there was a roaring fire in the fireplace. They seemed to be enjoying themselves telling jokes and drinking. I didn't understand much about prohibition, and it didn't seem to affect anyone here. Next morning, I asked Christine if I could learn to drive on the ice. One of the guests said he would take me out and show me in the Ford. After a few stalls and skidding of the wheels, I slowly got the hang of it; with the Model T, there were no gears to change. I couldn't go wrong on a big frozen lake. The guy finally got out and said to keep driving and; make big figure-eight turns and then try backing up. I caught on quickly and was then allowed to take some of the people on the ski-jorring twirls. I thought this was great and hoped the weekend would last longer. But good things seem to come to an end fast. It was over, and we returned home. It was not long after that, I was able to get my driver's license. I didn't have to take a test. Christine wrote to Augusta, the Capital, and asked that I be issued a license, by bluffing my age as 16! Low and behold, I received one in a short time.

The winter months were long, but spring finally arrived early in May '29. With it came a lot of slush from the melting snow. By the middle of the month, there was a light tinge of green reflected along the countryside.

Birds arrived from faraway places. The first harbingers were the crows and robins. The next outdoor sport was the fishing season. It was Robert that would introduce me to trout fishing. The trout were wily critters, but Robert was an excellent fisherman. He gave me an old rod to use. I would first have to go out in the backyard and dig up a can of worms. Lots of the streams would wind through heavy alder clumps. Robert instructed me how to sneak up to the banks and cast the line so it would drift down. I found it difficult to fight my way through the alders and not get my rod and line tangled up in the branches. I used to get frustrated at the alders and the line. By the end of May, when the weather was turning warmer, we were pestered with mosquitoes, black flies, and mingies. The mingies could go through any gauze or mosquito netting and were called "no-see-ems." The black flies didn't just sting, they took a hunk right out of your skin. In another month, out came the horse and moose flies. The moose flies were deadly. I don't recall such hungry insects in India. Robert had some kind of stuff called "fly-dope," horrible smelling; you'd have to rub it all on the back of your neck, your ears, and on your arms. It did keep the mosquitoes and flies away for awhile, but you had to keep repeating the method, or else they would finally get to you.

Another area for fishing which became quite famous for salmon was a mile up the river from Bangor, where a dam had been built. This was for the Hydro-Electric Plant across from Brewer. Both cities enjoyed that electrical power. At the dam, on the Brewer side, was a fishing club called the Salmon Pool. The salmon came up the Penobscot River to spawn. It took a while for them to find the sluiceway to get over the dam. It was a natural for fishing. There were thirty or more residents who fished here; each had his boat. It normally would take one person to row against the current, while the other would flycast for the salmon. The season opened when the ice broke up and left the river clear. This could be the middle or end of April, or early May. To get to the club, one drove across the Bangor-Brewer Bridge, then the road known as Main Street, going north, following the river to the dam and the clubhouse. The tradition was that the first salmon caught at the club was always presented to the President of the United States at the White House. This tradition was started in 1923.

I used to accompany Robert and Christine to the pool, when I wasn't at school. Though I wasn't allowed to fish, I enjoyed watching them, and once in a while I would take my bow and arrow along and practice in the large field which was part of the club. The catches were not that often, but when one was caught, it created a lot of excitement. Robert would possibly catch at least three or four during the season.

When the summer did finally arrive, Dick Dunn and another friend, Earl Ruland, and I would cycle out into the country with the .22 rifle and try to shoot woodchucks.

Woodchucks were difficult to approach, as they usually lived in the middle of a field. We had to stalk on our bellies to try and get close enough for a shot. On other occasions, the Hinkleys, who enjoyed picnics and outings, would come by on weekends and ask us to go hiking in some of the mountain areas. We went once on a trip to Bar Harbor. It was a beautiful place by the sea. The Hinkleys and Robert arranged that we climb a couple mountains. One was called Mt. Cadillac and the other was Green Mountain. They were both rather high and the tops were barren. It was a rocky climb; however, there were trails and markings. When we climbed to the top of Cadillac, there was a magnificent view; one could see in all directions.

A year or so later, the trail up Cadillac was made into a motor road. One could then drive to the top. Later that summer Christine mentioned that we were moving to a new home. It was on a hill overlooking the Salmon Pool Club, on the Brewer side of the Penobscot River. We went to see the new home in the process of being renovated. It was a beautiful, large, double-storied brick building. A long gravel driveway led up the hill to a circle roundabout, with a well in the center. The well had a green cover over it. To get water, you had to lower a bucket and wind it up with a handle. Workers were already hammering away. Christine said it was going to be called the Salmon Pool Farm.

At the end of August 1929, we moved in. Kim and I went exploring. There was a lot of land that stretched far back of the house. There was a small stream at the further end with a lot of open fields. At the end were alders and white birch, and pine trees. It was a great place for partridge, I thought. This move to Brewer meant I would have to change schools once more. I met my next door neighbor, who came over and introduced himself as Clyde Bennett. He was a fairly tall, blond fellow. We discussed the school I would attend. Clyde said it would be quite a hike every day, about a mile, but not to worry, for a small school bus would pick me up at the bottom of the drive. I was entered in at the 8th grade. Clyde was a freshman in high school. He was musically inclined, and played the clarinet in the school band. I did not adapt well in the school. My grades were not startling, and Robert gave no support to help me with homework. My room was a large one, over the garage, with windows on three sides. During the snowy periods, I could not ride my bike, but was able to take the bus, just as Clyde had said.

Before our move to Brewer, Robert turned in the Model T for a new 1929 Touring Ford, with manual gear-shift, dark blue, with attachable side curtains; it was kept in the garage. Late that September, Robert thought it would be okay for me to explore the back woods and see if I could find partridge, that I could take my shotgun to try it out. Christine joined me. The first time was not with Kim, since hunting season had not officially opened. We skirted the right side of the fields, along the alders, and I saw a pathway that led in a little ways and followed

parallel to the field. I took this and could see Christine walking along in the field. A good distance ahead, I heard a rustle and saw a bird, perhaps a partridge, flying into a small crabapple tree. I stalked slowly toward it; when I was closer, sure enough, I could see a partridge sitting quietly on a branch. I took aim and fired; the bird fell. This was the first shot I had fired with the gun, and it had quite a kick. I walked over and picked up my kill, still fluttering. Christine shouted to know what had happened. I cut across to the field where she was and showed her my prize. She was elated, and when Robert saw what a fine specimen the partridge was, he thought it should be mounted. He had a great collection of other game birds mounted in his living room and dining room.

There was a lot of hunting on the weekend and holidays. Robert set up a clay pigeon skeet shooting apparatus for practice. I learned to shoot pretty well. One Fall Saturday, Robert and I went duck hunting to Peshaw Pond, where we did our ice fishing. Robert set a blind in the marsh, right at the edge of the lake, and put some wooden decoys nearby. It was an overcast morning, and we managed to shoot about four or five golden-eyed ducks.

Robert then spotted a deer on the far side of the lake, about 1/4 mile away, walking along the edge of the lake. Robert rowed like hell, and he could row very well; he was once a member of the Harvard Rowing Team. He figured the wind and direction the deer was headed. There was a point of land that came between us, and when we neared the shore, Robert briefed me on what was to be done. We always carried a few loads of buckshot for such occasions. I was dropped off, and Robert rowed further away, South, and hid in some weeds. I started off at a trot, and had already earmarked the area where the deer would be. I then slowed down and crept forward. I came to a tall fir tree and hid behind some rocks and waited. It was not long before I saw the deer. It was a large doe. I waited till I was sure it was in range, then raised up and fired at its neck. It dropped in its tracks. Robert was so business-like, and always had things figured out; he never said "Good shot," or "Well done." He gave me the hunting knife and explained how to gut the deer. I thought I knew, having watched the cook do the same thing to our goats and sheep in India. I did exactly as Robert explained. We then put a lot of grass in the animal's cavity, and covered it up in the back seat of the car. We were supposed to report the killed deer to a game station or warden, but the season was not open yet! We got home and strung the deer up in the woodshed. It had been a great shooting season; I had been able to shoot woodcock, partridge and snipe; now the deer.

Winter arrived with more snow and a lot of shoveling. I got interested in making my own archery equipment. Christine and Robert gave me a Stanley Tool Kit to use for woodwork. I was able to make a fairly good work bench to help with my work. Mr. Chapman told me that in the coming year

*Horace Chapman with salmon.*

there was going to be several state-wide archery tournaments in different parts of the state; we would probably be practicing at the YMCA that winter. He also asked Robert if the archery team could use a section of the field in the back for an archery range. Robert thought it would be nice to have the archers use the fields. I practiced with my fellow archers at the YMCA and spent a lot of time making arrows for the coming season. I learned that the arrows should be balanced and weigh the same.

By the end of winter, I was ready for the archery tournaments, come what may. The first one, informal, was held at our place. I got the lawnmower and cut the grass around the areas where the targets would be, and that was a rough job. In those days all the mowers were manual; you pushed them! None of this today, motor driven easy mowers. Mr. Chapman, Howard Peavey and a few other members gave a helping hand. I dug trenches across the back of the targets to prevent arrows from sliding under the grass and getting lost. Next Sunday, the archery team arrived for the tournament.

I was informed that I would no longer be allowed the junior range, as I was now too good. I was proud to think I was regarded as a man at the age of fifteen! I met several new members. One was a Mr. Daniel I. Gould from Bangor. They all called him "D.I." He brought along a young man by the name of Everett McNinch. I think he was his handyman. Also new to me was Mr. Robins and his son Winston, from Brewer.

There were three different competitions: American round, York round and Clout shoot. The American round is the standard 60, 50 and 40 yard. The clout was new. This was a target mapped out flat on the ground 180 yard distance. The target was about fifty feet across with the same scoring pattern. At the bullseye, there was a pole and flag — like a golf hole. Not only did the archer have to judge the distance, he had to allow for wind drift, since the arrows had to be lofted quite high in their trajectory. I didn't come close to winning, but enjoyed meeting the new archers.

Horace and some of the members later asked Robert for another favor; they wanted to put an archery golf course that would encompass more of the fields in back. No cutting down of trees or any destruction to the property, though. It was agreed. It didn't take long for Horace and Winston Robins to show up that next weekend, ready to lay out the course. I helped the best I could. Once the nine holes had been laid out, I went to work with the trusty lawnmower! There was a neighbor down the street who gladly brought his hay cutting apparatus to make the fairways. He could keep the hay. Instead of a hole, we used a four inch wire hoop painted white and placed at the base of each pin. It all looked neat, and the three of us couldn't wait to try it out.

The next archery meet was to be held in Pittsfield, Maine; halfway between Bangor and Waterville. All of us met at the Bangor House and then drove to Pittsfield. I went with Horace and Winston. We arrived at the Pittsfield Inn around 8 a.m. Folks were gathering at the coffee shop. I sat at a table with Horace and Winston and some archers from Waterville, including Jack Egan from the turkey shoot day. I saw Everett McNinch enter, so I excused myself and went over and sat with him in a corner. We had a cup of tea together while other folks came in. In a few minutes, two girls walked in, a brunette and a blonde. They were fairly tall. The brunette was rather on the husky side and wore glasses. The blonde was just plain beautiful. I asked Everett if by chance he knew them. He grinned and said that they were D.I. Gould's daughters. I said "Oh, my gosh!" He said the brunette's name was Phyllis and the blonde was Sylvia. Then Everett said that they had driven down with him and were attending the University of Maine. They would be competing in the tournament, and Sylvia would be presenting the prizes after the meet. I thought to myself that I had to come up with at least one prize, so she would have to present it to me. It wasn't any sexy feeling; it was just a plain, warm friendly feeling that came over me. After all, I was 15, and Sylvia, I figured, must be at least 18 or 19.

By now, quite a few archers had arrived, and a hubbub ensued. D.I. sauntered in and looked around. He saw his daughters and went over to them. It wasn't long before D.I. saw us and brought his daughters over. All of a sudden. I felt weak and nervous when they approached. After introducing us, D.I. left and went over to Horace's table. When we sat down, Sylvia plunked herself next to me. It was not only the fact that Sylvia looked beautiful, it was her expression and her mannerisms and outgoing way. When she talked, there was a twinkle in her eyes. I just plain liked her! Everett didn't waste any time tell-

ing them that I was a Hindu from India. I must have turned a hundred shades of red. Sylvia noticed, and took over. She asked interesting questions about the country, especially about the schools, the life there and what I did. It was not long before she had me cooled down and talking quite freely. Time had flown, and we were called to the archery range. Sylvia stayed with me all the way, then went over to her target. At parting, she said, "It's gonna be lunch together!" That was fine by me!

I shot arrows like a boy possessed, especially in the York Meet, at the 100 yard distance. I checked the wind and allowed the drift, and more so for the Clout, at 180 yards. I had some pretty good scores and could hardly wait for lunch. Sylvia got hold of me and returned to the coffee shop. She informed me she did not wish to sit with the others; I was flattered.

I couldn't believe this, but what embarrassed me was I barely had enough cash for one hamburger, let alone two; and iced tea for her and hot tea for me. I think she sensed this, so Sylvia said to be sure to order apple pie and ice cream, that her Dad would pick up the bill. I was confused at first; though I had eaten apple pie, I never had it with ice cream. I told her this, and she laughed. Then for D.I. to pick up the bill, gosh! I wished to be somewhat more grown up, and say that I would take care of it, but I couldn't. She was so matter-of-fact, so easy to talk and get along with. She didn't want any other conversation except India, mainly the hills and my life.

When the whole tournament was over, the participants were asked to assemble in the main dining room for dinner and then the presentations. Again, Sylvia insisted I sit near her. This time Everett and Phyllis were with us. Mr. Egan made a ceremonial speech, and said that D.I. Gould would call the names of the winners when the meal was ended. Sylvia would hand out the trophies. I won 3rd in the American Round, 4th in the York and 1st in the Clout. I came forward for each, and on every occasion, when Sylvia presented the award, she would wink at me. I remember the trophies; 1st was a gold ribbon with the title of the round and date. I received one gold, one blue for third and one black for fourth.

After all the ceremonies were over and everyone was saying goodbye, the four of us were filing out and Sylvia asked how I was getting back to Bangor. I said, "with Horace Chapman," and with a twinkle in her eyes and a delightful smile, she said that would be no fun; "Why not ride with us in Tinkle Bell?" That was the name she gave the Plymouth. Before I could open my mouth, she went over to Horace and said, "Mr. Chapman, we're taking Peter back with us. Do you mind?" Horace chuckled and said it was all right. Sylvia was not made up with perfumes and a lot of lipstick; she was natural and wholesome. There were some electrical shocks going through me, I know that. Tinkle Bell was a 1930 Plymouth Roadster, with a canvas top. It was a two-seater, with

what she called a "rumble seat" in the back. There were two spare tires, one for each front fender, and they had mirrors; it was a greenish-blue color, with wire spoke wheels. Sylvia asked if I had ever ridden in a rumble seat. I shook my head and said, "No." She said, "Well, you're just about to; and Everett, you can drive."

Everett and Phyllis sat up front, Sylvia and I climbed into the rear. All their archery equipment was given to D.I. to take home, but Sylvia arranged my archery gear on one side of the rumble seat. There was barely enough room as it was. Now, with the bow stuck in one corner, we were really crammed together. I tried to be the English boy I thought I was, but when Sylvia linked her arm with mine and got close, I could feel her supple body against me. Then she asked Phyllis to hand over the blanket which they had up front. (Phyllis was called "Phyl.") The summer evenings in Maine are cold and damp, but she managed the blanket around us, and shouted to Everett, "Let's go!" We finally got underway, and once we were, Sylvia seemed to get even closer, if that was possible. It was about then that the heavens fell in on me and hell fell apart. I developed the hardest and hurtingest erection imaginable. What the heck; I was a healthy, strong young fellow, and the devil and nature had taken over. I tried to maneuver my behind so as to envelop the protrusion that was trying to explode through the trousers. All I could do was scooch down and try to hide it. I was glad that it was dark and nothing could be seen. It was good that Sylvia wanted to talk; however, I was unable to control the evidence; it stayed with me almost all the way. The next problem was how to hide it when I got out of the car! Perhaps I should have had English baggy tweed pants on! I would face that problem when the time came. Aside from the ill-comfort, the ride back was wonderful. The night was clear, stars out and the wind was blowing our hair. She was wonderful to be with. She talked a little of herself, that her Mum was living in Massachusetts, and she was at the University of Maine, studying to be a teacher. I had mentioned my butterfly collection in India, that I brought to the States. Sylvia said she was studying zoology; which dealt with birds, beetles, etc. Before I could stop myself, I said that she could have my collection for school. She said she would come by next week and pick it up. I suggested a little archery as well, and she said that would be fine. I learned she would be 20 in October - egad, five years older than me! My love for Sylvia was on a warm and friendly basis, and not about sex. It is hard to truly explain the feeling of a 15 year old. Perhaps people would call it puppy love, or some sort of infatuation; I don't know.

The next day, I was in my room when the Plymouth pulled up. Robert answered the door, and I heard Sylvia introduce herself. I came down the back stairs and through the kitchen, where we gathered, and she asked me if she could see the butterflies and beetles that I had spoken of before. I asked if it would be okay for Sylvia to come upstairs to my room. Christine said, "Sure, but don't do anything that I wouldn't do!" Christine and Sylvia laughed; I was upset. The room was a mess, with wood shavings and sawdust everywhere. She thought I had a great room, big and bright, which it was. She sat on the bed while I got the cardboard boxes out. Sylvia was excited with the collection. She asked the names, and I was stuck. All I could do was give the colloquial names that we used in school, like the dumpy beetle, the stag and the rhino and the crocodile, bamboo, etc.; the feathers as well. When I told her she could have them, she said no - to think of all the chasing in the far-off hinterlands and bringing them all the way to the United States. When I insisted, she came up with an idea: she said she would accept them under the condition that they be kept at the University of Maine, at the zoological classes, and donate them there in my name. It was agreed.

We practiced archery for a while, and then Sylvia wanted to know about the archery/golf, so off we went. I gave her some tips on the archery, and then on the golf course. We followed the course all the way, and at the far end of the course and to the last field, near where I had shot my first partridge. We were walking along the edge of the alders when she spotted a whole patch of wild strawberries. As mentioned, Sylvia was natural, wore simple clothes and no makeup; her legs were bare and tanned; her shoes were dirty, white tennis shoes, with a hole where her big toe always tried to protrude, and very cute. We gathered handfuls of strawberries and ate them there. She picked one, and before I knew it, squeezed it on my face and laughed. This started it! I rubbed some on her forehead, then her knees. We laughed and fought with the berries. When finished, we looked like two naughty kids who had been into the jam. I remember her hair shining very blonde and fine when I touched it. It was strange; I never thought back about Jasma and my experiments, in the wheat fields in Bhim-Tal; this was a completely different situation with Sylvia. There was no thought on any animal sex experimenting; it was just plain, wholesome fun, and love for a lovely person, a little older and wiser than me.

When we arrived back, Christine saw the mess that we were in, and asked Sylvia to come on in and use her bathroom to get cleaned up; I went up to my room and did the same. Christine had also arranged that Sylvia stay for a quick bite before leaving. I felt good that she would stay, because I wanted to show off all the trophies and the wonderful game room that Robert had. I showed the antelope heads on the wall that he had shot in India, and two lovely tiger skins that were on the floor. She was shown a lot of our Indian photographs, of our hill stations, including Bhowali, Bhim-Tal and Naini-Tal. I think she enjoyed the visit. I hoped so, as much as I enjoyed having the opportunity to show these things to her. She left late that evening and took the collections

of butterflies, beetles and the feathers for school. It was the last I would see of my souvenirs from India. It was nine years later, when I enrolled at the University of Maine and attended the same zoological classes, that I saw some of my collection there. To myself, I thanked Sylvia.

I saw Sylvia often that summer, and we rode together a lot in the rumble seat, coming and going to archery tournaments. There were times when all of us would take trips to Phillips Lake; part of the lake was also known as Lucerne. This is where I learned to drive. The rest of the summer holidays seemed to hurry by, almost before it had started. My world seemed to revolve around Sylvia. There were several other archery tournaments that we attended, and by now I was exceptionally good and collected quite a few trophies.

Summer was over, and the leaves were turning their fall colors. Yet, I was sad to know that school was upon us, and another year was about to come to an end. I was now 16. I enrolled at Brewer High School, and Sylvia was back at the University of Maine. Horace sometimes invited me out to his camp that he had in Green Lake. It was a wonderful spot, on a point of land. This was where I really learned to swim. Horace let me use his canoe; it was fashioned after the old Indian canoe. These canoes were quite famous, known as the Old Town Canoes. They were manufactured in a little town called Old Town, just adjacent to Orono, Maine, where the University is. I had a great time with Horace. We would often take our bows and arrows and climb up the mountains, looking for porcupines. These were usually quite easy to spot and to shoot. The state had bounties on them, because they were quite destructive and caused a lot of damage to the forest; we would get about 25¢ for each porcupine. I was quite happy to know that I would be getting a reward.

I may have excelled in archery, fishing and hunting, but my school grades were pathetic; only just passing. One thing, life around the Salmon Pool Farm was never dull. There was always something to do when I came home from school, chores of one kind or another; to chop wood, all types of chores that young people are requested to do. I was growing taller and stronger.

One afternoon when I came back from school, Christine informed me that she and Robert had bought two baby pigs, and that we'd have to put a fence around one area of an alder clump, not to far away. This we did, with chicken wire. They were fed all our garbage and other refuse, plus special odds and ends that we picked up for them at the market. They grew to be enormous, and Christine had named them "Frankie and Johnny," after the song.

As it got cooler in the fall and the first frost came, it was decided that Frankie and Johnny would have to be slaughtered. A Mr. Neilly, a nearby neighbor, a big, rotund individual, whose wife had passed away some years before, said he would be glad to do the honors. Robert and I roped the two hogs and

led them across the field to Mr. Neilly's place. It reminded me a little bit of when I led Beatrice, our dog, across the field and tied her up, where Vernon had to shoot her. Mr. Neilly butchered the two hogs, and told us to come and collect the meat. Christine and I got woozy stomachs, and figured we could not eat Frankie and Johnny. Mr. Neilly then said he would take his share, and gave the rest to our neighbors, such as the Bennetts, the Ginns and the Blanchards.

One Saturday morning, after doing some chores, I heard an airplane flying low overhead. Then it swooped again and flew right over our home. Christine and Robert came rushing out to see what was going on. The aircraft, a red one, came over our house for the third time, and landed on the field where we had our archery range. The pilot taxied the aircraft and brought it right into our driveway. It was Duncan Dana! What excitement! It was the first time I'd seen an airplane at such close range. He said it was a British-made Gypsy Moth, and that the wings could be folded. Duncan had come up to do some bird hunting with Robert. He stayed a few days. Before departure back to Marblehead, Duncan said he would have to take the airplane over to the main airport in Bangor, which at that time was known as Godfrey Field, for gas. The next morning, he asked me to go along for the ride. I was scared; however, no cowardice now! I sat in the rear open cockpit while the Duncan took off from the archery field. For a moment, on the banking turn, after we were airborne, I was lost. I had no idea where we were or in what direction we were going; not until we had leveled out, and I saw the Penobscot River below us, then the city of Bangor, and of course, the famous, ever-present white water tower. It was only minutes till we landed at Godfrey Airport. the gas was put in, and we were off again. This time, I was aware of my position by seeing the tower, the river, and the dam. I spotted our house on the hill, and we landed back in the backyard. I could hardly wait to tell my friends, back at school, and when I did, they were in disbelief that an airplane had landed in our backyard.

The next week, Duncan departed for Marblehead and took Christine with him. But somewhere along the way back, they landed on a small farm field, and wound up in a fence, tearing up the airplane. Christine thought that he'd misjudged the distance from the road, and hit the fence. It ripped the wings and broke off the propeller. They had to go back to Marblehead by bus and train. So that was quite an experience in itself.

Another wonderful gentleman from Bangor who came to see us quite often was a person by the name of Waldo Pierce. He was a frequent visitor. He drove a funny looking car called a Franklin. It was also a touring car, but the front end looked something like the head of a pickerel fish. Waldo would show up at odd hours, his beard and unruly hair blowing in the breeze. He always looked as though he had slept in his clothes, but what a fine person he was. He came one fine morn-

*My first ride in an airplane, Dana's Gypsy Moth.*

*Waldo Pierce with wife Alzera and baby Gabriel.*

ing with all his paint brushes and a large box of oil paints. Everyone had to get out of the kitchen while he decided to paint a large mural on the cupboards above the sink. It was a scene of the Salmon Pool Farm. I think it is still there. When Waldo came in the evening, he would usually bring a lot of large T-bone steaks and never less than two quarts of wonderful ice cream. One quart was especially for me, usually strawberry. He enjoyed watching me dig in, and I finished the whole lot. If one little bit was left, I used to sneak over and give it to Kim, who was always eager to enjoy some. Of course, Robert made certain he got the bones for the dogs as well. I would gorge myself until I was almost sick. Waldo was full of war stories, because he, Robert and Duncan were in the First World War together. He loved France and spoke

French fluently, always with the same sort of accent and waving of his arms. He learned his art techniques during the same period, and spent a lot of time painting, French-style. Even when he talked, his gestures and mannerisms were French. He told us he made friends with a man called Ernest Hemingway. Waldo said that he and Mr. Hemingway had spent some time in Key West, and that he had movies that they took when they were in Key West, Florida; another time he'd bring them over.

Christine was busy writing her books and her novels, and I was busy working on my bows and arrows. It was after Christmas that Horace Chapman called and asked if I'd go with he and a friend bobcat hunting with bows. That following weekend, Horace arrived with another gentleman, whose last name was Jordan; he was a game warden in our area. We went to Green Lake and drove the full length, which is more than 20 miles long. At the other end, we stopped the car. Mr. Jordan had two hound dogs with him. We started through the woods on snowshoes and had gone quite a while before we struck some tracks. He said they were bobcat and let the dogs go. They gave a wailing kind of bark and were gone, but we could still hear them in the distance. Eventually we came to the dogs, where they had treed the bobcat. Horace told me to take the first shot. It was an easy one; the cat was not more than 20 to 30 feet away. I pulled back on the bow and took aim; the arrow went through the cat right behind the shoulder. It no sooner dropped to the ground when the two dogs were on him. Mr Jordan pulled them off, and there was my first bobcat. What was also interesting; I would receive a bounty of $15.00 for it. We hunted the rest of the day, but no more signs of cats. It was late by the time we returned to the car and eventually home. I was eager to show Robert and Christine my trophy. I asked Horace if he would like to have the pelt of the bob-

cat, since I would take the bounty. He thought that it was a fair exchange.

Not long after the Christmas of 1930 and the New Year, my friend Dick Dunn from Bangor showed up in his Chevy car. He had graduated from the old bicycle days. He wanted me to go rabbit shooting that afternoon. We drove to a place behind Phillips Lake where Robert and I had done some woodcock hunting that fall. Dick had a shotgun, and I brought along the .22 rifle. We shot four rabbits; I think Dick did most of the shooting with the shotgun and got three. It was late in the evening when Dick drove me home. Christine was waiting for us and suggested that if we had any game, to let Dick Dunn have it. I thanked him for the outing and went into the kitchen where it was warm. Christine turned to me and said that Duncan Dana had been killed in a hunting accident in Marblehead. He had been outside the Bay in his dory, duck hunting. A severe, unexpected storm came up and capsized the boat. Duncan was a strong swimmer; however, due to the intensity of the storm and the icy waters and heavy seas rolling in, he really didn't have a chance and was dashed against the rocks. An extensive search was arranged. It would be more than twenty four hours before a local fisherman found the body washed up on an island. Christine and Robert made immediate plans for travel to Marblehead for the funeral services. I would have to take care of the house while they were away for the next two weeks at least. Robert said I could use the Ford for school. It was also agreed that Clyde Bennett could stay with me. None the less, I was terribly upset to know that Duncan Dana was dead.

Time seemed to pass quickly, and at the end of two weeks, I picked up Christine and Robert from the Bangor Station. Back at the house, Christine presented me with all of Duncan's archery equipment. Mrs. Dana thought it appropriate that I should have it. I was happy to have this equipment and to think that it had belonged to Duncan. I would keep the bows and arrows safely. His hunting bow was exceptionally strong. I knew I would have to do a lot of exercises and become stronger to be able to pull a 28 inch arrow with it. The pull of the bow must have been about 75 pounds.

The rest of the harsh, Maine winter finally started to taper off with a lot of slush and melting snow. The first harbingers of spring arrived: the pesky crows. Robert had bought a stuffed, horned owl from Parks Taxidermist in Bangor. We then rigged a board on a long pole and nailed the owl to it. The owl sat up in the air about ten feet. We made a blind nearby and sat and waited with our shot guns ready. It didn't take long for the first crows to come flying at the owl. Robert took first shot and knocked down a crow. The pesky critters came from all directions and were not afraid of the shooting. By eleven that morning our shoulders were sore from shooting and we had quite a lot of dead crows lying around. I know the farmers would be happy to learn that we had dispensed with these marauders. They raise heck in the corn fields. From that point on I would take Clyde and Dick Dunn crow shooting, which was good practice.

It was not long before the snow had gone and the magic painter had tinged the trees and fields a pale green; then all the wild flowers came into bloom. It was a pretty sight in the back fields. When school was over, Robert told me he had a summer job for me. He and another member of the Prentiss and Carlisle Company were going north to a town called Macwahoc in Aroostook County, to do some surveying. Robert said my job was to help mark off each chain (66 feet) length as Robert and the other man stretched each chain out. They would also have to hack their way through the underbrush with axes, and every so often, chip away some bark on large trees. My second chore was to follow along with a large size paint can and paint over the places they had cut the bark, with yellow paint. The job would be for the month of July, and I would receive $2.00 a day, including weekends. I knew it would give me a great opportunity to see the real Maine woods and learn about the outdoors.

We arrived in Macwahoc, which was a small town; what one calls a one-horse town. It would be our base of operation. Some of the time would be spent away from the town, deep in the woods. Here Robert and the other gentleman would cut down small saplings and trim them into poles. They would then place the poles into sort of A-type frames and cover them with boughs. I was to cut hemlock boughs and place them on the ground as matting. In the evenings, a fire would be lit in front of the "lean-to," and it became quite pleasant and warm. Robert's cooking was not the greatest, but it was enjoyed. The only things that bothered me during the whole month were the dang mosquitoes, horse and moose flies, and the mingies, "no-see-ems." They even seemed to like the fly-dope I used. I enjoyed my month's work in the woods, and I learned an awful lot from Robert and the other gentleman.

In August, I was still able to practice and participate at a couple of archery tournaments. One big one was held at the Augusta Airport. The airfield is located on a flat-top hill or plateau. There was not much air traffic in those days; we more or less had the whole field to ourselves. When it came for the long distance shoot, I had brought along Duncan's hunting bow and had made some special sleek arrows for distance shooting. Each archer had to shoot three arrows. When we went to find out where the arrows had landed, I was happy to learn that two of my arrows had outdistanced the other archer's and I had first place. Another meet we had was at our field in Brewer. This was great because the tournament included the archery-golf. Sylvia was along, and it was always great to be with her. I was also able to take her to the movies and pay for her tickets out of the hard earned money from the Maine woods!

Toward the end of August, one of the older friends in the neighborhood, by the name of Archie Blanchard, approached me. He asked if I knew American type football. I

*Our House in Brewer, Maine, 1930.*

knew something about it. I said it resembled English rugby. "Great," he said; "How about trying out for the Brewer High football team?" I had never thought about it before. He thought I was big and heavy enough to play in the backfield. Archie said he would talk to the football coach, Dana Dogherty, and if I was interested, to see the coach right away, as he was assembling the players and getting ready for training. I talked to Christine and Robert that evening, they thought it would be a good experience. I weighed myself of Christine's scale and was 155 pounds naked. That Monday at school, I wandered into the coach's office near the gym and said I was interested in playing football for Brewer High. Dogherty looked me over and thought I would make a good fullback. After practicing with the team, he placed me on the first squad. I didn't know there would be so much practice and rehearsals every day, exercising and running, until the first Saturday and first game against a school from up north. Our team played well, and it took me a little while to get adjusted, but I was able to make a touchdown; that was a real thrill. The following weekend, we were to play our arch-rivals, Bangor High School. Again, we came on the field amid lots of cheering; this time the Bangor boys were a little more powerful than ours, and we were getting a drubbing of 12-0 at the first half. In the third quarter, a boy rammed into me with his helmet and broke my nose. I continued to play on until the end of the third quarter when I got hit again, and this time I felt as though my right ankle was broken. Evidently, it was a very bad sprain. I was carted off, and that was the end of my football for a while. By the time the ankle had healed and I could walk without a crutch, the football season was almost over. We didn't have face masks, nor a defense team or offense. The one team played both.

I was now interested in some airplane magazines that a friend from school had given me. I

*Point Pleasant beach, N.J.*

was looking at one of the advertisements, something about building miniature gliders out of balsa wood. I asked Christine if I could order some of these, to which she readily agreed. The package arrived, and I was happy to see that there was some work that took great care in modeling the gliders. I was able to put one together and I had it in the living room. The next morning, when I came down, I found the glider gone.

During this period, the fall of '31, things were deteriorating between Robert and myself; I wasn't sure what it was, perhaps it was some sort of jealousy. I was able to do my hunting and shooting exceptionally well. We had a skeet range on our property, and I was able to do very well and compete readily with him.

So, in the morning, while looking for my glider plane, I decided to look in the ashes of the fireplace, and I found it hidden underneath all the rubbish. I pulled it out. Christine saw me and wanted to know what was happening. I told her that I thought Robert had destroyed the glider and hidden it in the ashes. He admitted it and said he didn't like stuff littered around the living room floor. Well, we both got an earful from Christine; that was the end of the gliders.

I spent a lot of time away from the living room, entering the dining room only to eat, and spent the rest of the time in my room, pouting and making archery equipment. Then I got a letter from Sylvia. She was now teaching in a small town, about 100 miles north of Bangor, called Danforth. I wanted desperately to see her; I needed somebody to talk to, a friend at least. So I told a white lie to D.I. Gould, and was able to get "Tinkle Bell" from him. I had a few dollars, so I filled it up with gas and drove up to Danforth to see Sylvia. She was tickled to see me, and said that she would come back with me to Bangor. Then on Monday, she'd take the car back with her. I didn't know how to tell her that I'd taken the car under false pretenses. When I did, she was quite upset, but at the same time started to laugh. She said, "Well, that'll teach the old man something." I was shocked that she would talk like that about D.I., but I had a feeling now that she wasn't too happy with him. She said I should take her back to school, but I said no, we were already down that far, let's keep on going and let the chips fall where they may. We had a great trip. It was worth any punishment I was going to receive later. Sure enough, she dropped me off at the house and took off for her place in Bangor.

On Monday afternoon, I was called into D.I.'s office, and he gave me a long lecture about lying and taking people's cars like that. He had planned for me to drive up the following week and get Sylvia, but now that was out. I took it on the chin and said I was sorry, and left. Christine drove me home, and said things were really not good back there, and that Robert was really mad with me, and that things had deteriorated to a fare-thee-well. We had a long talk, and it was decided that I would leave Brewer and join my mother, Geraldine and Vernon in New York. This was now the end of November.

There was not much I could do about it; arrangements were made. Christine and Robert drove me to Boston, where we spent one night. The next morning, I was put on a train for New York, where Vernon would meet me at Grand Central Terminal. I was most unhappy to say goodbye to Christine and to Kim, and to know I was leaving Sylvia even further behind.

Vernon and I hopped in a cab and drove to an area near Brooklyn, which was called Sheepshead Bay. I didn't know it, but I believe that this is where a lot of mobsters hung out. Vernon had a small apartment that overlooked part of the bay. I was quite upset that there was nowhere to play; all the streets were off-limits to me. The only time we would go out was when Vernon was home, then we would walk around on the shore

road. On his last trip back, he decided we were going to look for a place further inland, in New Jersey. That weekend, we took a ferry boat to Jersey City, and a train that dropped us at a town called Westfield. Vernon had already been in contact with a real estate agent there. He took us around and showed a few homes for rent. Finally, Vernon and Mum chose a lovely little home just south of the main downtown area. The home came furnished.

Packing, taking taxis, ferries and trains, reminded me a bit like our safaris in India. Westfield was a lovely town, still rather rural and out from the city of New York. To me, it did not compare with the wide open spaces that I had grown to love in Maine, especially Bangor and Brewer, and all the friends I had made. Yet, I was happy to be with my mother again, and to see Vernon and Geraldine.

Arrangements were soon made for me to attend Westfield High School. I had now missed three weeks of school, and this would make six schools I had attended in my short lifetime. I arrived at the school early on a Monday morning and talked with the principal, a Mr. Frank Neubauer, and his supervisor, Mr. C. Philhower. I gave him my background and when all formalities were completed, he thought I should start out as a sophomore, as I did in Brewer. It was hard to adjust to a new way of life, new faces and a slightly different system. The school here seemed more advanced than what I had in Brewer. One young student took me around and introduced me to everybody in the different classes. I wasn't certain what I was going to take, other than the basic subjects. Instead of French, I took Spanish. I would sit and be completely lost as the teachers lectured. The areas where I didn't have any problems were English and History, but their mathematics and algebra were far advanced. Spanish was brand new, especially jumping in right in the middle of everything.

The first couple of days, I was bewildered. I had no one to talk to. The following week turned out a little different. Some of the boys came and talked with me and soon learned of my past, my love for sports and the traveling I had done; and my upbringing in India. Some of the students I made very good friends with, that lasted for many years; one of the senior boys, named Robert (Bob) Burge, and some other fellows, such as Robson Young, Frank Ketchum, Fred Van Horne, Demont Van Doran and Storey Lee. All of a sudden, I found myself really enjoying their company. They took charge and showed me the city, their homes, and their way of life. They helped me all they could, Robert Burge, especially. He made sure I came to his house a lot, and he brought my mother over to meet his folks. They were just great, wonderful German people.

This part of life was great, but the school was difficult, even more so than the trouble I had had in Brewer. It was so difficult, so far advanced, that my grades were down to D's and F's. The principal thought perhaps it was because of the change, because of so

much traveling, that in time I would settle down. Again, I got this bashful attitude where girls were concerned. These young ladies were much different from the ones up in Maine. The boys seemed to be more grown-up. Most of them had their own automobiles, or could use their folk's cars. We always wound up at somebody's house, where I started to learn to dance. This was brand new to me. I never did really conquer the art of dancing; I'm still very poor at it.

I started to bring some friends home to my place, and they met my mother and sister. Mum used to sit down in the evening and tell stories about her life in India, and about us. The young fellows and some of the girls enjoyed this. They enjoyed it so much, that at times they would rather do that than go out to movies or go dancing. My mother had a certain knack about the way she told stories; it was just fascinating, and most of these young people used to sit spellbound.

I adjusted pretty well to the life in Westfield. It was such a grownup place, so close to New York City. Early in the spring, a bunch of the guys invited me to go with them into New York City. We drove in, and for the first time, I saw the city and could look up at the skyscrapers. It was awe-inspiring. The movie we went to was at Radio City Music Hall; it was a matinee, and the movie was *King Kong*. It was quite exciting, but the stage show was really an eye-opener! It was the first time I could see all the chorus girls, about 50 or 60 of them, kicking their legs up.

With spring on its way, everybody was interested in the track meets. There was running and jumping and discus throwing. They asked me to try out for it. I tried discus throwing, but couldn't compete with some of the stronger guys. However, I went to all the track meets and participated.

One evening, in the spring of 1932, while listening to the radio news (I think the newscaster at that time was Lowell Thomas), it was announced that Charles and Anne Lindbergh's baby had been kidnapped. (The Lindberghs lived on an estate in New Jersey called Hopewell.) This was to give the news media all kinds of information, to last better than several years. The U.S. Treasury went off the gold standard, so that the $50,000 that the kidnappers wanted in bills was useless. Almost a year later, the news flashed that the FBI had apprehended a kidnap suspect, a man named Bruno Hauptman. He was a German immigrant who lived in the Bronx, New York. He had been caught at a gas station with some of the kidnap gold-certificate money. The sensational trial lasted years before Hauptman was convicted in 1936. He swore he was innocent, that a German friend named Fischer had asked him to keep a package till his return from Greece. The friend never did return, and one day Hauptman looked into the package and discovered it to be money, and decided to use some of it, not knowing that it was from the kidnappers. There were various arguments as to whether or not Hauptman actually was the kidnapper. He was convicted and got the electric chair in Trenton, New Jersey.

During school break, most of the people went their different ways, but Robert Burge always seemed to stand by and take me around. Before all that happened in spring, my brother Vernon came back from one of his trips to Central America, and decided we'd better have a car. He and I went into New York City, because that's where things were cheapest. We came up with a small 1929 Ford. It was something like "Tinkle Bell." It was a roadster, with a rumbleseat, black with red wire wheels. Being a pretty good driver at this point, Vernon and I drove back to Westfield; it was quite an experience. There were no super highways then; and we had to find our way through different streets. Though we got lost quite often, we found our way through the Holland Tunnel and the Pulaski Highway, then to Route 22 and on the way to Westfield. There was great excitement; we finally got the car licensed in Jersey, and I had my Maine license changed over to New Jersey.

The fun was yet to come — that was, to try to teach Vernon and Geraldine to drive! At that point, I said I hope I never have to go through that ordeal again. All four of us drove out in the country quite a lot, to a range of hills back of Westfield known as the Watchung Mountains. We drove there parked and walked through the forest on trails that were very pleasant.

On one occasion, Bob Burge and I drove all the way out to Mount Pleasant. It was a beach area on the Atlantic Coast. We went swimming and enjoyed it; that afternoon we slept on the beach. When I woke up, I was roasted; I got terribly sunburnt. Bob had to do most of the driving back. I was laid up, and my mother put oil on me; she eventually made a tub full of tea, and she said this was a good way of curing sunburn. I soaked in the tea for about an hour, and I have to admit, it really did help. It didn't take long before I was well and able to get around again.

Robson Young's folks had a camp down at Mount Pleasant. We spent a lot of time there on weekends. My friends coaxed me into trying out for football that fall, when we returned to school. I enjoyed being back in a football uniform, though I didn't make the first team; I was on the alternate or second team.

Other young men I met in school, besides those I've already mentioned, were Paul Hennell, who was actually Canadian, and a boy by the name of Gordon Kellogg. Gordon's nickname was "Piggie," because he had pigeon-toes. He was also muscle-bound; he loved weight-lifting and was very good in athletics, such as javelin throwing and the discus. Gordon came from a very wealthy family; Mr. Kellogg was General Manager of American Can Company in New York City. Gordon also had a brother named Bradley, who was going to a different school. I got to see them often, and they invited me to their homes once in a while.

I wasn't able to do much in the way of archery, because I'd left most of my things in Brewer. After the football sea-

*Log cabin we built at Ferguson Pond, Maine 1933.*

*Above and below left: Building a log cabin around Mooseluek Lake, Aroostook County, Maine.*

*Myself with two months of beard after building log cabins 1933. Picture by Waldo Pierce.*

son, the three of us — Robson Young, Bob Burge and myself — decided to drive up to Brewer for the weekend, in our little roadster. It was great, though cold. We made it up there by driving all night. The only major road, at that point, was Route 1. It was great being able to see Christine, Robert and Horace Chapman again. On the way back, I don't know what possessed us, but we decided to take some of the route signs, as we went through each state. We wound up with a load from New Hampshire, Connecticut, etc., down and through New York to New Jersey. They might still be in Robsons' attic, if he still lives at his old home on Euclid Ave.

The following spring, 1933, there were more athletics and more track meets, and the next thing you know, school was over. Gordon Kellogg and Bradley asked if I'd care to go up to Maine with them for the summer, that they'd done so before and liked Maine very much. Knowing that I was from there, they said it would be great if I would accompany them. With permission from my mother, it was okay to go.

With great excitement and anticipation, we drove up in one of the Kellogg's cars. I think it was what they called an Essex, rather a speedy car, and Gordon was a crazy driver. But we drove and we drove, all night again, till we got to Bangor, then over to Brewer, where they met Christine and Robert. I picked up my bows and arrows from them, and we started all the way up to a little town called Oxbow, Maine. There, we met a guide, an old friend of Kellogs by the name of Archie Archibald. We were able to slosh through some old dirt roads till we came to a log cabin. Here, we had to assemble a little canoe, all our backpacks and everything else with us, and start hiking up a tote road along the Mooseluek River. It was a 20-mile hike; at the end of it, we came to Mooseluek Lake. There was a small island on the lake that we paddled to. We had to make two trips, in order to get our belongings across. We put up a tent and went to work to clean the old log cabin and build it up again. It was a job; it took several weeks before we got it complete with new cedar shingle roofing. The architect of all this was Archibald. During this time, we did a lot of trout fishing, which was stupendous; they were very large and beautiful fish. Once in a while, we had to take a trip back down to Oxbow to pick up groceries for camp. Archie told us of another area where there was good fishing, and a good spot to build a log cabin. The trail from the northern part of Mooseluek Lake led us through a winding, slightly mountainous region till we came to a beautiful little lake, known as Ferguson Pond. We had the canoe with us; it took several trips, but this was a small pond, and it did not take long to paddle back and forth. We elected to build our camp on a grassy spot we found at the far end. It meant going into the forest and cutting down pine trees, trimming them down to the right size, notching them, and stacking them together to build the cabin. Between the logs, we got moss and chunked in the areas that were bare. For the shingles and doors, we found large, dead cedars. These were cut down, then using a splitting gadget, we were able to split a lot of the cedars into very fine shingles. The floors were done by chopping and sawing long lengths of pine. It had to be seasoned wood. This took several weeks, but in the end, the job was done. In between, we were able to have fun and still continue our fishing. Though not allowed, Archie shot a deer. The three of us let our hair and beards grow; what beard there was at the age of 18.

Towards the end of the summer, Mr. Kellogg, Sr. decided to pay us a visit. We all hiked down and picked him up in Oxboro. He was a fine gentleman, and he enjoyed the trip and the fishing very much.

Again, the summer months went very fast, because we had such a wonderful time. We kept busy building these cabins. Archie said he would use them in the wintertime, when he came trapping. It was hard to leave and say goodbye to Archie; we then went back to Westfield. I thanked the Kelloggs very, very much for allowing me to be a part of their summer.

I settled down. My mother was very surprised at my beard and long hair, and decided I'd better get to the barbershop before anything else; but not before a lot of pictures were taken. Finally, my mother told me that my brother Vernon was going to the University of California, to study to be a doctor. Perhaps I could cancel my going to school for awhile and go to work to help pay the bills. She said that Vernon had arranged for me to go to work as a sailor for the United Fruit Company. I didn't mind not going to school, but I did mind not being able to play football; the coach had told me I would be on the first team. I'd also miss my friends and lastly, the fact that I would probably get terribly seasick. I hadn't forgotten my voyage from India to Boston.

Well, the day came, and I went to New York and presented myself to the Captain. The name of the boat was the *Musa*. It was a small, one-funnel freighter, but it did have some cabins, for about 12 to 15 passengers. I checked in with the Bos'n, who showed me my bunk up front, where I met all the other sailors. They looked me over and said, "Huh! College kid, huh?" I said yes, and that this was my first experience. They said, "Well, we hope you can make it. The last fellow, in fact, the one whose position you've taken, was somebody like you, who climbed up the rigging and fell onto the deck and was killed." That was quite an introduction! Anyway, I checked in, and immediately was cleaning various parts of the cabins. Every morning, bright and early, whether we were at dock or out at sea, we had to holystone the teak decks. I was given a broomlike affair, with a big block of sandstone. I had to rub up and down the decks, smoothing it down; then washing it with salt water.

The first trip out was in September, I remember, and it was a beautiful day. We went through the harbor, down the East River, past Ellis Island and the Statue of Liberty, and out to sea. It seemed that we no sooner hit rough waters when I started feeling woozy and seasick. The sailors said, "No problem; go ahead and let it go, over the side, but be sure to do it on the leeward side." I obliged.

The trip took us down to Cuba. As soon as we got in the Gulf Stream, the boat seemed to stop rocking, and I got over my seasickness. I was kept busy, doing my chores. One of the chores I liked most was to be up front in the bow, midnight to 6:00 a.m., to observe for any other boats, or whatever there might be up ahead. There was a bell that I would ring, once for the port side, twice for the bow, and three times for the starboard. The nights down there were beautiful; the stars just seemed to hang down like chandeliers.

The port of call was Santiago de Cuba. The ship went through a channel affair, and it was very, very green and lush. In the middle of the channel was an island; I'll never forget it, with a red-roofed bungalow sitting right on top. I think it was something to do with customs. We skirted around and came to dock at Santiago. Right up front, on the side of a mountain, was a large bottle. It said "Bacardi Rum." There was so much to do; handling people's luggage, off and back on. We finally turned around and back out. The next port of call was Tela, Honduras. This is a beautiful city in Central America. Here, we did go ashore and went sightseeing; then back to work again. We were there two days, loading bananas.

The next stop, further down, was Port Barios, Guatemala. We were here two days, then turned around and headed non-stop back to New York. We were fully loaded, with several passengers and loads and loads of bananas! On the way up, I noticed that there were a lot of spiders; some people called them tarantulas. Actually bird spiders, they crawled all over the deck. They came out of the banana hands. The sailors told me not to worry about it, that further along, it would get a little cooler, and they would die and disappear. The first trip was not too difficult for me; I enjoyed it.

In New York, I had one week off and was able to go home and see my mother and Geraldine. I got the announcement that Geraldine was going to get married. She had met a tall, fine-looking gentleman by the name of Fred Acomb. I went back on the boat again, and was ready to go; this time it was not quite so pleasant. I kept getting seasick during the rough periods. The Gulf Stream was okay.

One morning, we were notified to look out for a special small boat that might be in our area. They said a prisoner had escaped from Devil's Island and was known to be somewhere in these waters. We got excited about it, and wanted to know what we would do if we did find the person. We never did find that escapee. Later in life, I read a book called *Papillon,* written by the same fellow, a Frenchman, who had escaped; they made a movie out of it, with Steve McQueen.

On this trip, we didn't stop at Santiago, but went straight to Porto Barios. When we docked there, the crew got leave and took me with them. They asked me if I ever had a girl before in my life. I had to say no; I didn't want them to know about Jasma. They said, "Well, we're going to get your ashes hauled for you." They took me to a tavern that they frequented in the city, called Mama Zeze's. It was a horrible little place, all squat and smelly; beer and rum were flowing. I remember sitting at a table with my friends and some girls. My friends started disappearing through the door with these girls. Pretty soon, old Mama herself came by; she must have weighed about 300 lbs. She sat near me and wanted me to be her lover for that night. I said no, I had other ideas. I inched my way around the table, and she kept shouting at me in Spanish to pay or do something, but I just backed out; got through the door, and ran like hell. I think I ran all the way, which must be about a mile, back to the ship. That was my last experience for wanting any Mama Zeze around me! When the guys returned back, they laughed and said they'd planned it that way.

On one of my trips back from Central America, with a load of the usual bananas, the other sailors and I had done our share of tying the ship to the dock. We relaxed for a short time and watched several large trucks back up to the loading ramp. Once the trucks were loaded, they headed up town. Some of the other fellows and myself heard a commotion and a police siren way up the street. Not knowing what it was all about, we went about our other chores. Later that evening while having our dinner in the bow of the ship, someone said the rumpus we heard had been one of the banana trucks smacking into one of the iron supports for the elevated railway. We howled with laughter when the guy told us what happened. The driver of the banana truck was driving along merrily when he felt something crawling up his pant leg. He knew what it was, and without stopping the truck he jumped out. There in the middle of the busy street and took off his pants in a hurry and started hollering about spiders! When the police arrived, he was all shook up. We figured it was one of the large banana spiders looking for a nice warm place to hide! Next morning, there was even a write up in the local paper.

Life on the boat was pretty good, except on the trip we hit a rather heavy storm. The deck cargo of coconuts started to shift. It was our job to re-tie it during the big blow. It was rough going; I twisted my ankle again, but not quite as bad as I did playing football. I was able to continue working. Even though I was enjoying the work, I was not cut out to be a sailor. I stayed with the United Fruit Company till the end of November; about 4 trips, and that was all. The seasickness was too much to take. I returned home and told my mother that I could not continue, that I would find another job or go back to school. The principal of Westfield High decided against my returning, since I had already missed three months.

There was the possibility of joining the Civil Conservation Corps (CCC). People were talking of depressions, bread lines and no jobs to be had. Roosevelt had created the CCC to help the unemployed. The CCC was doing odd jobs around the country, such as cleaning up the parks, looking after forests, and building roads. I went to apply and was told I had to get special permission, since I was not an American citizen. I talked to Mum about it; she said, "Why don't you write to President Roosevelt." She was serious. Oh well! What did I have to lose. I sat down and wrote the President and explained my situation. Believe it or not, an answer came back from his office in the White House, possibly from his secretary, but with his seal. It mentioned that I should take the letter to the CCC office near me; that I would be accepted. I hopped on the train the next morning for Elizabeth, NJ. Who got on the train but Mr. Kellogg, he was headed for New York. He asked me where I was going, and I told him the story. I showed him the letter, and he was tickled. However, he said, "No such thing. I don't want you doing any such thing. Get off at the next stop and go home; come and see me in the evening about 8 o'clock." I told my mother what had happened. She suggested that I better see Mr. Kellogg as he suggested. I presented myself to him that evening, and he ushered me into his home. He said, "Here's what I want you to do: to-

*With United Fruit Co. Puerto Barios, Guatamala 1933.*

morrow morning, meet me here and we will travel together to my office in New York. I'm going to set you up with a job. I don't know if it will be right now, but you will have a job." I told him I appreciated it very much, and I would try to work my best for him.

The next morning, punctually, I arrived at his doorstep, and we were off to the Big City. It's not an easy trip. The train makes several stops on the way to Jersey City; then the ferry ride across the Hudson River to downtown Manhattan and after a short walk to the subway, up to Grand Central Terminal, Graybar Building. This is where the main office for American Can Company was located. We had to take an elevator to the eleventh floor. I followed Mr. Kellogg to his private office. He then asked his secretary to call some of his staff to the office. I was introduced as a boy from India and that I would be working in his department. I went to work as an office boy in Mr. Kellogg's office.

I met one of the senior file clerks who, in turn, introduced me to the other members and secretaries; he then showed me the type of work I was expected to do. The young fellow that showed me my desk was named Herman Tobin, a good looking individual who loved outdoor sports. I stayed in the office all day and followed Herman around as he did his chores. That evening, Mr. Kellogg took me back to Westfield. I guess I was hired!

For tickets on the train, I bought a monthly pass which was about nine dollars; that included the ferry across the river. The subway was 10¢ as I recall. It didn't take long for me to adjust to the commuting life, plus the know-how in getting around in the office and meeting new friends. Bob Burge had finished high school and was attending Duke University. I still had my other Westfield friends like John Frye, Bob Young and Ketcham. Monty Van Doren and I hit it off well, because he loved hunting; also a student named Healy. His nickname was: Mayor of Picton! Monty showed me several places near his home where there were many

pheasants. I hadn't shot these before. They were the English pheasant and beautiful. I had my old shot gun that was given me by Duncan Dana. It was still doing well.

My life went on. I occasionally heard from my friends in Maine, from Clyde Bennett and some of the others, Mr. Chapman and Sylvia. I guess young people are not that good at corresponding. Geraldine announced her marriage to Fred Acomb, and they settled in Plainfield, New Jersey.

By 1934, most of my friends from Westfield High had gone to different colleges. Another friend I had was Gover Kookergy. He was a great outdoor person and loved hunting and archery. It was he who stirred up my interest once more in the sport. I went with him and entered a few archery meets in New Jersey, but without a lot of practice, as I did in Maine, I was not able to come up with any success. Gover and I spent many weekends roaming the countryside, trying to hunt pheasant and cottontailed rabbits with the bow. I don't recall having any success at this either.

Gover once introduced me to a friend, who was working in the backyard on an airplane or glider with another fellow. His name was Robert (Bob) Buck. It turned out that Bob was one of the youngest pilots in America at that time; he had flown solo across the U.S.A. at the age of 15. He was an accomplished pilot. I certainly was impressed. I remembered my flight with Duncan Dana and figured it took some kind of genius to fly an airplane.

The following year, Bob took a mutual friend of ours, a fellow named Robert Nixon, on a flight all the way to Yucatan, Mexico and back. Bob later went on to become Chief Pilot for TWA, and continued his flying career. In years to come I would meet Bob Buck again.

I had now settled into my routine commuting to New York City and Westfield. I received a letter once from Sylvia. She had given up her teaching in Maine, and was now in Boston. She asked if there was ever any chance of my coming up that way. Though my little Ford roadster was sadly in need of

*Puerto Barios, Guatamala 1933.*

repair, I took a chance one weekend and drove to Boston to see her. The Ford performed well, and it was good to see Sylvia after three long years. We had a great weekend. We rented a canoe and paddled up many of the tributaries of the Charles River and found a decent spot of shore for a picnic. She enjoyed getting away from the hustle and bustle of city life as much as I did. Sylvia once said that she actually was planning to go to Miami, Florida. She hoped to work and get a PHD in Psychology. I figured if anybody could do that, she would be a natural.

I was now 20 years of age, and I felt that my feeling for Sylvia was not really puppy love. I had a real love for her, and though I never told her, I felt she knew it. It was difficult at this point to tear myself away and head back to Jersey. The drive back seemed endless, but that was it.

As months went by, I tried to see my friends as much as possible. Since Geraldine had now settled in Plainfield, my mother decided it would be best if we moved there also. Once we had done so, my train ride and commuting to Jersey City became even longer. I enjoyed my work in the office and my friends at the American Can Company. Then Hennell came to work with us. There were no TVs in those days, and radio was the main news media. On one occasion, Mum, who enjoyed listening to the BBC on short wave, heard that a German zeppelin, the *Hindenburg*, had crashed and burned on a mooring at Lindenhurst, New Jersey; that wasn't too far from us. The news was sketchy, but it was believed that many passengers on board had perished. The next morning, the newspapers had headlines and pictures of the story giving the details. My Mom and I drove to Lindenhurst, but could not get near; the police would not allow anyone near the site. The ever-curious sightseers had jammed the roads. This was 1937. That was the last of the German dirigibles. They would have continued the building of this type of air transportation, provided they could use helium gas (non-flammable) for

their airships, but the U.S. had a monopoly on this. They would not give any to the Germans. That was the end of an era.

Later, when we saw the actual news in the movie, which used to be the Pathe News, the whole zeppelin was on fire, and it came crashing down, with a few passengers and ground handlers trying to run from the scene; many of them on fire. They couldn't make it; the dirigible crashed, a burning mass on top of them. It was a terrible, grisly sight to see.

Though I was unable to return to school, I was learning a great deal about the real world. I read a lot of magazines and newspapers, and kept up with daily, current events through the newspaper and radio. I read history, ancient, medieval, and U.S. I took evening classes for a short period, in shorthand and typing. The old Ford had finally given out, and I sold it for about $50.00. I wonder what it would be worth today? A small fortune, I imagine.

Once, at a party which we had at Demont Van Doran's, I met a charming, lovely, young lady. She was a tall, blonde girl, who in some ways reminded me of Sylvia. Her name was Barbara, and she was a fashion model for a well-known clothing store on 5th Avenue in New York. She lived in Westfield. I was able to see her by taking a train or a bus to Westfield.

About the time I met Barbara, I also received a letter from Sylvia. She was in Miami and had married a Serge Troube. I felt downhearted, but now that I'd met someone who reminded me of Sylvia, the wound healed partially.

I always enjoyed the train ride to Jersey City. The newspapers were so full of interesting news. A great deal of it concerned the gangster wars going on around the Chicago area. I remember my friends in India at the Naini-Tal school who just before I left said to watch out for the big gangsters in the U.S.A. How true it was! It was interesting to read about the terrible St. Valentine's Day massacre, when a whole lot of them were gunned down; and about Al Capone,

Baby-Face Nelson, and Dillinger and his capture and killing at the movie house in Chicago. Later, there was Pretty Boy Floyd. I used to chuckle to myself about those names, but the stories were anything but pretty. Though Prohibition was over, racketeering was still full blast. I wish I'd kept all those newspaper articles. It would be years later I would see some of them again, in the movies; like The Untouchables, and The FBI Story. Another movie, of course from true life, was the Bonnie and Clyde episode.

In the summer of 1936, Paul Hennell and I took our vacation and went to Maine by bus. We stayed with Christine and Robert. Clyde Bennett was on leave from his music conservatory in Boston. One day, Christine said we could use her Plymouth to drive up to Mount Kathadin; its the highest peak in Maine, a little over 5,000 feet. It was a great trip. We stayed at a farm in a town called Millinocket. The farm was owned by a Polish family; they had two teen-aged daughters. The three of us were invited to stay with them. During our stay, it was decided we should have a party. We bought a couple cases of beer for our share, while the father arranged a barbecue. The girls invited some other friends from the neighborhood. It turned out to be a hectic party, during which several cases of beer were consumed. When I woke up in the morning, I don't know what time it was; I was upstairs in the hayloft, and there were girls all around. Strange, the last time I was in the hay was with Jasma. I don't know about Clyde and Paul, but I was a bit worse for wear. We all had a hearty breakfast. The girls were dropped off at their homes, and we were on our way to Kathadin. I don't know how we made it, but we did get to the top.

Another time, when I had the old Ford, I was with Robert Burge and Herman Tobin when we left Westfield and drove straight through to Bangor; from there up to Mount Kathadin. During the trip, we had many flat tires, we became expert at fixing them. The tires, of course, had the old inner tubes. It was on the last leg of our trip, from Millinocket up to Kathadin, that we picked up a hitchhiker, in what appeared to be a military uniform. He said he was with the CCC, Civil Conservation Corps, that same outfit I was to join some years earlier. About 5 p.m., short about 3 miles of the camp which was near the trail we would take to climb Mount Kathadin, we got another flat. It was now pitch black, and no flashlight. Our hitchhiker said we could leave the car there and walk to the camp, have a meal, spend the night, and come back and fix the flat the next morning. It sounded good. So, we walked; the old perimeter dirt road was not easy, without any flashlight or any light at all. We had to look up at the stars and see the opening between the trees. Sometimes, we wandered off into the bushes, or hit a tree. However, we finally made the camp, exhausted. The CCC fellow went in to get the OK for us to stay. In a short time, he came back to tell us that we could not stay nor could we have any food. It was hard to believe that we were refused food and lodging. We asked to see the officer, and he refused to see us. There was nothing else to do but turn around and head back to the car. If getting to the camp was hard work, returning to the car was even worse! It started to rain, and it was not only difficult to see the niche in the trees, but to know where the road wound. We took it by turns to lead the way. The one in front held his hand out, and the other held the tail of the other's jacket; something like elephants holding the other's tail. The leader often banged into a tree, wandered off the road, or walked through puddles. We had no idea how far we had gone, until the leader banged into the car. Weary, tired, hungry, and highly teed-off at the CCC guy, for whom we had some choice words, the three of us huddled in the front seat while the rain kept pelting down.

I think we passed out, huddled close together. When we woke, the rain had let up; there was a gray, overcast sky. It took several minutes for us to get out and unwind, stretch, and try to get our muscles back into shape. Once this was done, we fixed the damned tire. It took a little while, but we got it done; our hands were cold and everything was miserable and wet. Our first thought was to turn around and head for Brewer, but, oh my goodness, we'd come all this way; we might just as well try and get to the mountain. Bob and Herman had not seen it. So instead, we drove back as far as Millinocket, which is about 20 miles away. Once there, we had the car checked, including the spare, had a good breakfast and cleaned up a bit. With some sandwiches, we got back on the trail.

The wind had picked up and driven some of the heavy clouds from around the mountain. We got a good look at the peak. The three of us climbed to the timberline, where it really got cold; our clothes were still wet. With a little more effort, we made it up to the top. After taking a few photographs, we headed back. The clouds started to roll back in and it got misty late that afternoon. Coming down was almost as difficult as going up. The rocks were slippery and wet; our knees felt like rubber. We were happy to see the car and no flat tires. The cold sandwiches were great! What we hadn't noticed before, around the corner from the trail were several lean-tos that had been built, possible by the CCC. We were able to get one cleaned up and start a fire with the matches that we brought from Millinocket.

It's surprising how warm a lean-to can get, with a fire going in front of it. With our jackets about us, it didn't take us long to fall asleep. Sometime during the night, Bob shouted and woke us up. We lit some matches, and discovered we had company. A large porcupine had decided to walk over Bob's coat, where he slept. It took a bit of maneuvering, but we finally were able to ease the critter out. The fire was spruced up again, and a few more branches placed in front. We were back to sleep with no more bother.

The next morning, we had a cold, icy rinse in a stream nearby. Once this was done, we headed back to Millinocket and another good breakfast. Do you know, we never saw any CCC guys out of that camp, all that time. What were they supposed to be doing? We thought they were there to clear trails, or fix roads, but none of them were around.

Back in New Jersey, we figured we'd had quite a trip. The following year, it was going to be even more exciting. Bob wanted us to go back to Maine; he loved it. Since Herman couldn't make it, we got a friend who was living in Maine, by the name of Bill Eldrige. He was a commercial artist who had been studying in Boston; he knew Sylvia as well.

The three of us started off in Bob's car. At Millinocket, we took another route. When we left the car, we had to walk about 5 or 6 miles up a trail to what was known as Chimney Pond. The reason it's called "Chimney" is because there's a crevice that goes from the pond all the way up to the top. It was late August, and the weather was fine. It was agreed that we would try to climb as many of the trails as we could, as long as the good weather held out. We went up one side and down the other. On one side was the Dudley Trail and the other one we had taken last year, the Hunt Trail. We came back up and planned to come down the Cathedral Trail, which is on the right side of the mountain. There's a large plateau between the Hunt Trail and where the Cathedral Trail starts down to Chimney Pond. Also, there is a small spring, named after the poet Thoreau. Bill and I stopped to have a rest and a drink from the spring. Bob was tired, but decided he would continue on, but there was a cloud bank moving in, and they can move in fast. We lost track of Bob just a few paces after he left us. Bill and I decided that we'd better get going too and catch up with Bob. There was no answer to our call, so we thought he must have started down the trail to Chimney Pond. When we got down, a warden had shown up and was brewing tea at the camp. We sat around, but still no signs of Bob Burge. The warden thought that Bob may have holed up in one of the caves, because of the fog and the weather moving in. It was getting late, and still no signs of him. I went down to the pond and shouted up the chimney, and all I got was the echo. We had flashlights, and Bill suggested we go on back up the trail. He said he would go on the left, Dudley Trail and come across the ridge, and for me to go up the Cathedral Trail. We would meet up there and see if we could find him. I started up the Cathedral Trail with the flashlight, and I kept calling and looking in various crevices.

These trails are almost straight up at right angles; I climbed slowly. It was no rosy pathway. Every so often, I'd stop and call his name. I looked into large caverns to see if he'd fallen in or gone to sleep.

*Skinny-dipping in Chimney Pond after climbing Mt. Kathadin 1936.*

On and on I climbed, but still no signs. It was now pitch dark. Luckily, there was no fog. It was quite a while that I waited for Bill at the spring, because his was a much longer and tedious climb than mine. We rested and were puzzled over what had happened. We examined the trail near the spring to see if we could have edged off in a lop-sided venture, but the trail was clearly marked, even at night. Here we were at the top of Kathadin, in the middle of the night, sitting on a rock, wondering what to do next. Bill and I trekked to the area where the deep crevice went all the way down into Chimney Pond. We shouted to the warden and flashed our lights. He finally responded in the same way, waving the flashlight from side to side, meaning no news. We did the same. There was not much else to do but get back to camp. It was well after 2 a.m. when we turned in for a much needed sleep.

The warden was up early, fussing with pots and pans, and making up the stove for breakfast. The sound of the fire crackling and the smell of bacon got us up. We decided we'd give Bob one more day to show up before alerting the rescue folks from Millinocket. It was only two years previous, if I recall, that a young lad, about the age of 10 or 12, was on Kathadin with his Dad. Again, the cloud banks and fog had covered the mountain, and it can do so in a matter of minutes. The boy was separated from his father, and wandered off in the wrong direction. He had gone down the mountain; it was to be two weeks later that he was found, some 50 miles away from Kathadin, half-starved but alive. He'd received a hero's welcome; even President Roosevelt presented him with a medal. Now we wondered if Bob had lost the trail and wandered off the same side of the mountain, the way the boy had done.

After a good rest, Bill and I decided to go back up the Cathedral Trail to where we

*On Kathadin with Clyde Bennett, Paul Hennell and myself standing.*

*Bob Burge climbing Kathadin and a short while later got lost for a few days, 1937.*

last saw Bob, see if there were any signs, footprints, that might indicate which direction he may have gone. Back at the Spring, Bill and I backtracked a ways, then looked for any scuff marks on the main trail; there was nothing. The main trail had been pretty well chewed up by our comings and goings and other people's expeditions. The plateau slopes off to the left, or the north side, before the main trail verges into the Cathedral Trail and descends to the Chimney Pond. We left the trail here and followed the plateau edge to the timberline and scrubbed spruce. We followed the timberline to the left, looking all the while for signs or any pathways that we felt Bob might have taken.

All that we noticed were a few deer tracks as we searched the plateau quite thoroughly. We finally decided there was no hope, we gave up and returned to camp. We were hot and sweaty, and rather tired, but then we decided to have a quick swim in the pond — skinnydip, that is. The water was no more than melted snow from the mountain. It was cold, but it was refreshing. The warden said he would return to Millinocket the next day and notify the head office of the forest rangers, and set up a rescue search party. They'd probably skirt down the plateau into the forest and swamps that lay at the foot of Kathadin, more or less the way the young boy had taken. He took off the next morning. We told him we would hold the fort.

That afternoon, two woodsmen showed up and said a couple of people, who had been picking blueberries some distance from their farm, had run into a guy who looked kind of beat up. He said his name was Bob Burge, and that he was on Kathadin and got lost in the fog. The folks had taken him to the forest rangers' office, and he waited for us to arrive. Bill and I were two happy souls! It didn't take long to pack our gear with Bob's, and with the two woodsmen in Bob's car, we hit the trail back to Millinocket. Bill and I arrived at the rangers' place late that evening. When we saw Bob, he was a sorry looking sight. He seemed happy and cheery, however. The local Millinocket newspapers printed the story the next day, and I think Bangor News did also. Bob said that when he realized he was off track and lost in the heavy fog, he was going to climb back up, but decided it would be better to keep going, downhill, following a stream whenever he could find one. He lived on blueberries and whatever other berries he could find. He finally came to a fair-sized stream and followed it; then an old tote road that he got onto. He said he was able to find shelter un-

der some trees at night and catch some sleep. He knew we would be worried, but there was very little he could do about it. Bob said the next morning, the third day, the old road took him to a field, where he heard voices. He soon came across people picking berries. He said it was the best sight ever. They got back to their farm and called the rangers' office and told them about Bob. It appeared that the rangers and the warden who had been at our camp were already in the process of arranging a search party. We stayed in town the next night, and the following morning, after a cleanup and some good food, the three of us headed back to Bangor. I know one thing: Bill and I decided that we were in no hurry to climb Kathadin the next day, or the next year, or the next few years! As for Bob, he said it was a good experience and how easy it was to get lost. That would be his last visit to Kathadin. He sure talked about it back in Westfield; again it was written up in the local newspapers.

Vacation was over, and I settled down to my commuting to the office. As time went on, I realized I was not likely to get ahead if I continued to be an office boy or file clerk. One day, a rumor had it that Mr. Kellogg was transferring to the Chicago office. This would be a sad blow. When I had a spare moment and a chance to see him in his office, I asked about the transfer. He acknowledged it, but it would be a while yet. I discussed my future with the Company, and he agreed that it would be difficult, without an education. I said I might try to get back to Brewer High School, then enter the University of Maine. Gordon, Jr. and Bradley Kellogg, his sons, had finished school and gone into farming in the Carolinas. I said I would contact my friend, Mr. Horace Chapman, at the Bangor House; perhaps I could get a job there and work my way through school. Mr. Kellogg said it would be great, but quite an undertaking.

I was now coming up on 23. I discussed all this with my mother. She was always agreeable with whatever I wanted to do. She was just a great, great lovely person, and I loved her very much. Mum said she would write to Christine, who was always the advisor. I wrote to Horace and also to the school principal of Brewer High School, Mr. Gordon. Anticipation always seemed to take so darned long!

One day, when I returned home from work, hot and sweaty from the train ride - in August, which can be **hot** - Mum said, "Look what I have for you." There were two letters the same day, from Mr. Chapman and Mr. Gordon. I hardly knew which one to open first; I think it was Horace's. He was delighted to think I would come back to Maine and school. Yes, he would find me a job at the hotel, with room and meals; to please let him know right away. The one from Brewer High School was also most responsive. Yes, Mr. Gordon remembered me; yes, I could enter as a junior, and to please confirm so that I could be enrolled when classes started in September. I was beside myself with eagerness to get going. Without worrying about what Christine or Robert thought, since I would not be staying there, I wrote back that I'd be on my way as soon as I was cleared to leave American Can Company. I showed Mr. Kellogg the letters that I'd received, and discussed it with him. He was very happy. He said it would be hard work, to earn my keep and study at the same time, and at my age. He called in his secretary and said to have me released in a week, and to have the cashier give me a whole month's salary - all of $75.00, which in those depression days was a lot of money. That Friday, Mr. Kellogg wished me well and good luck in the world and told me to keep in touch. He was just a great gentleman, and very much like a father to me. I knew I'd miss him. I said goodbye to everyone, and left.

That week, I had my reservations to go by boat - don't ask me why! I don't really know for sure, but it was a small steamship company; I think it was called The Colonial Steamship Company. It operated between New York City, Boston, and Portland, Maine. I cabled Horace and the principal of Brewer High that I was on my way. That weekend, I said goodbye to my Westfield friends, and Barbara.

The boat left late afternoon on Monday. I had a cabin to myself. It was a long evening as the boat made its way through Long Island Sound and headed for Cape Cod Canal. There were a few people on board, and I chatted with several groups. Amazingly, I didn't feel seasick. We made a stop of Boston, where most people got off. The next morning, we arrived at Portland. From there, I took a Greyhound Bus to Bangor and was dropped off right at the Bangor House.

It was great to be back. Mr. Chapman introduced me to some of the hotel staff, many of whom I already knew. He had one of the bellhops take me to where I was to stay. It was the top floor, where most of the staff had their rooms. It was a pleasant room, with a wash basin, and a big window, through which I could see the Bangor-Brewer Bridge and the Penobscot River. There was a small ferry service between downtown Bangor and South Brewer, called the BonTon. It only operated from spring through fall; the river was frozen the rest of the time. Horace gave me permission to have my meals in the main dining room. Some of the staff were put out about this; I enjoyed the favor. Horace said I probably would be doing odd jobs to start with. During the summer months, he wanted me to be the doorman, and to be fitted out for a uniform. He was also having a telephone system installed in the cocktail lounge, which was known as the Peacock Room. There would be a switchboard behind the bar, with telephones on each table. Patrons could call the next table, the room upstairs, or outside, or long distance, and call the bar to order their drinks. He thought it would be good if I'd check out on the switchboard and be the operator. The hours would normally be from 6 p.m. to 12 midnight. In the summer, I could finish the doorman duties and go right on into the switchboard. I was to receive $10.00

a week, plus whatever tips I could make. This was more than I expected.

Horace had a very old Cadillac that had been converted into a semi-truck. He said I could use this once in a while. I asked to use it to check in at the school and to see Christine and Robert. He said I could use it anytime. However, I would be expected to supply the gas. My New Jersey drivers license was okay for now.

The next morning, bright and early, I drove over to Brewer High School, which was open, and checked with Mr. Gordon. A lot of my old teachers were there from previous years. I was greeted like a long-lost friend. I think my friends, like Horace, were saying how great it was, and what courage I had to take it upon myself to return to school at the old age of 23. My classmates would be about 15 or 16 years old.

I talked with my old coach, Dana Doherty, and the first thing he wanted to know was, "How old are you? I could use you on the football team." "No way, coach." The age limit, I believe, was 18, and I was well past that. I said I'd like to help as far as any training was concerned, if needed. He said he would let me know.

I told Mr. Gordon what my working hours would be, and hoped the faculty would understand if I happened to nod off to sleep once in a while in the class; they understood.

I then drove up to the Salmon Pool Farm, to see Christine and Robert. Kim was the first to greet me, with his jumping and friendly bark. Christine agreed it was a good idea about schooling; perhaps later, my mother could come and live in Bangor. She also let it be know that I would not be expected to live here, as I once did. I understood, knowing Robert; I doubted that I really wanted to, though I still respected him.

Horace was staying at his summer place at Green Lake. His kids were still on summer vacation and wanted to stay at the camp. This left them without any babysitter. Horace asked if I'd mind babysitting till school started, which would be in about two weeks time. Green Lake is about 25 miles east of Bangor, on the way to Bar Harbor. I enjoyed the sojourn of babysitting. Actually, John (Junior) and Barbara were old enough to look after themselves. There were two or three other kids in the neighborhood that I also attended to. Everything was fine, except my cooking. This I had never done before. However, they didn't mind my experimenting. I'd take them on nature walks, as there were some nice trails. I didn't worry too much about them falling into the lake; they were good swimmers. I was also able to start up my archery again. Horace made sure of that.

All of us moved back to Bangor the weekend before school. I started my chores at the hotel. I did part night watchman duties, swept the lobby, polished the brass spittoons; they had them then, and they were well in use. I also ran the old elevator. It wasn't long before the telephone system was installed, and I took on that job permanently.

The first school day was something else. Mr. Gordon called a general assembly, and I

was introduced as an old school friend; that I would be attending regular classes. All kinds of whispering took place. I later learned that the young people thought I was a new teacher.

I soon got into the school routine and curriculum. Coach Doherty asked if I could, from time to time, help with football groups; that is, help drive them to various games. It wasn't always possible, but once in a while I did. During the week, there was not too much activity at the Peacock Room. This gave me a chance to do my homework. I normally walked to school, about a mile.

On Columbus Day, Oct. '37, when I was in my room studying before work, there was a great commotion, police sirens going, and a rat-a-tat-tat. I raced to the lobby in a hurry. Everyone seemed to be gathering there, even the pedestrians from the street. A police car had blocked the main thoroughfare that goes downtown. After the noise and dust had settled, word came that there had been a shoot-out in front of Dakin's Sporting Goods Shop, where I had bought my first bicycle. Several people had been shot. It appeared that some gangsters had come to Dakin's the previous week and asked Mr. Shep Hurd if he could arrange to obtain some heavy machine guns and automatic weapons. Shep Hurd was quite a person, and he tipped off the FBI. They were waiting for the gang to return to pick up the weapons, and were intercepted by the FBI agents. Instead of surrendering, they opened fire. One agent was killed, and I believe Al Brady, the gangster leader; one wounded, the other captured. That little incident rocked Bangor, Maine, publicity-wise. In those days, I doubt that many people knew where Bangor was, or even that it existed. Shep Hurd and Dakin's got a great boost in publicity. For a long time afterward, the shop showed off the bullet holes in the front windows. There is a plaque in front of Dakin's store where this all took place and the name of Al Brady.

Days later, when everything was back to normal, I stopped in at Dakins to see and say hello to Shep Hurd. I told him how I'd returned to finish school. He remembered me, and I congratulated him on the capture of the gangsters. He showed me where he stood when the FBI man, who acted as a salesman, had started firing. It must have been an exciting and anxious few moments. That episode was enough to keep Bangor talking for months to come.

School was coming along fine. Mr. Gordon said I did not have to report in every morning, just go straight to my classes when they were due; if none, I could leave. The young kids got used to me, and asked me to their homes, and to their small parties on weekends. I was surprised at the girls' forwardness and their attitudes. They tried to get me involved in various child's games of Post Office and various other sexy little games that they pursued with real animal furiousness! I was usually the target. I couldn't quite cooperate. If they had been the age of Barbara, that would have been something else! Yet, I'm sure Barbara would

*Plaque speaks for itself. Taken 1993.*

not have wasted time with games such as Post Office.

I met another fellow by the name of Bill LaLibertie. He was a couple years younger than myself and was also working his way through school. He worked at night in the foundry, up the street from the hotel. We became pretty good friends. I'd invite him to the bar and see that he could get a good free drink or two.

Horace always would see that I had time off to go bow and arrow hunting. Robert would also ask me to join him during bird-shooting season. I'd sold my old shotgun in Westfield to Storey Lee for a couple dollars, so Christine let me use her Parker shotgun.

Between going to school, acting as telephone operator, taking kids to football games, trying to stay away from Post Office games, bow and arrow hunting and bird-shooting, I was kept pretty busy for my first year back in Maine.

I kept in touch with many of my friends at the American Can Company, and in Westfield; Sylvia and Barbara, too. My mother came up from Plainfield and settled in a little apartment in Bangor. I would run over and see her as often as I possibly could. School was coming along fine; my grades were exceptionally good. My history teacher knew I was interested in becoming a history major in college, and he encouraged me to participate by taking over his class, and discussions. We would discuss world events, and here again, the world was topsy-turvy, with Europe on the march; Hitler and Mussolini flexing their muscles. They were known as the Axis. Hitler took over Austria and the Ruhr Valley; Mussolini wiped out Abyssinia, now known as Ethiopia, and moved into Libya. War clouds were gathering, as Winston Chrurchill had said. All the newspaper and magazine reading I had done during my commuting back and forth from New Jersey to New York was now of value. A Mr. Branden was the history teacher, and

he helped me in many ways with discussions about world politics. It was the medicine I needed to get me out of the inferiority complex I so often found myself in; it helped a lot.

One day, I talked with Mr. Gordon, and told him I needed to get into something in the way of public speaking, or drama, to wipe out this bashfulness. It wasn't long before Mr. Gordon called me into his office to meet the school's drama teacher, a Miss Helen Bremer. I remembered her as having been in high school when I first was in Brewer, in 1930-31. Helen was now teaching junior high, and dramatics for the high school.

Mr. Gordon left us to talk things over. She recommended I try out for the junior speaking contest. I became flustered and wanted to back out, but when Helen looked at me with those great big blue eyes and black hair which made her eyes seem even more blue, I wilted and said "What the heck; let's go with it." Helen selected several short stories for me to choose from; then she would coach me. The first short story I chose to talk on was called "A Message from Garcia." I studied it till I knew it backwards!

If I recall, there were preliminary try-outs for the contest. Helen was with me all the time and gave me confidence. As I tried to explain, I really didn't care about winning any contest; I just wanted to win confidence, to be able to stand in front of any audience and talk. My progress was good. I was able to speak without faltering, or knees shaking. The next big hurdle was the contest itself. Helen gave me some more short stories to choose from. She said that when she gave her recital, she used "The Highwayman," but I finally chose "The Telltale Heart" by Edgar Allan Poe. I studied the words and practiced.

Helen, on occasions, took me to her family's home on Holyoke street, where I met her folks. I had already met her younger sister, Anna, who was in school with me. The day arrived for the contest; all of a sudden, I

was scared. All the kids would be there with their parents. The moment arrived; Mr. Gordon called my name, and I got up and plowed through the recital. I don't recall making any mistakes, but when I sat down, my knees were weak and my mouth was dry. I didn't win first place, but did come in second. Most important, though, was that I now was able to stand in front of a sea of faces and give forth with any kind of lecture or talk. I had the confidence that I was looking for, thanks to a lovely person named Helen Bremer.

I had become interested in helping Helen with her drama classes and putting on class shows. I remember one show, a one-act play called, "The First Dress Suit." The students performed well; in fact, too damn well. They won the State contest for Brewer High, and Helen's group in the same play won other competitions. I was spending a lot of time with Helen, also participating in a couple of her plays. I was now being seen quite a lot with my drama teacher.

That summer, I had my doorman uniform and worked the front entrance to the hotel. As people came and went, I opened the big double doors; and when cars drove up, I'd open the car doors, help unload luggage, and call the bellhops to take the baggage into the hotel. I normally would drive the guest's car to the hotel garage around the corner, and give the owner his ticket later. For this, I would normally receive at least 50¢ to $1.00, which was good money for me. The piggybank would get filled in a hurry.

One morning, as I was walking up and down the sidewalk in front of the hotel, I noticed a black sedan parked across the street. It looked dilapidated and had mud all over it, with what appeared to be some spikes of grass on the roof. I continued my duties, and paid no more attention to the car. About an hour later, I noticed four people approach the car; I thought I recognized a couple of them. They were roughly dressed and unshaven. I went over to them; it was my friends from Westfield. Bob Burge (it was his car), John Frye, Frank Ketcham, and Robson Young. My goodness, what was going on? It was quite a reunion! The four of them had taken a vacation and driven up to Brunswick, Canada. On the way back, Bob was forced off the road by another car. There was an embankment that caused the old Dodge to roll over several times, down the slope; hence, the condition of the car, with grass growing off the roof and no windows.

I got them rooms at the hotel for at least a couple of days, and it was a wonderful two or three days before they departed. The car was fixed, and then they were on their way.

Our archery club had more or less ceased. There were no more tournaments, as before. The group was more occupied with their personal affairs and business. I usually would go bow hunting with Horace. I, too, was more occupied with my school activities. I was now seeing Helen a lot, and visited her at her home whenever chance permitted. Summer passed and I was into my senior year in high school.

Before long, I got engaged to Helen and felt happy about it. We planned to be married at the end of the school year, after graduation. The school kids were abuzz about the engagement and marriage.

In October of 1938, there was one heck of a storm that swept Maine; it was a hurricane. Power lines and trees were blown down, schools were closed, and the rivers were being flooded. When I came out of class and was outside on the way home, a familiar face appeared through the rain. It was Herman Tobin, from the American Can Company. He had just been married, and had come to Maine for his honeymoon. Here they were, in the storm. I brought them over to the hotel, before they continued on their way. It was good to see him and his new bride, Estelle. We talked about old times at the American Can Company, climbing Mount Kathadin, and of course, the CCC Camp. Mr. Kellogg had long gone to the Chicago Office, and a lot of changes had taken place.

Spring arrived, and soon after came graduation. It was a wonderful feeling to know I was to receive my high school diploma, and a great burden seemed to have been lifted off my shoulders; I was congratulated by so many of my friends, such as Horace and the old-timers from the archery club. It was a super feeling.

Helen and I were married that summer of 1939. The reception was at the Lucerne Country Club. After the ceremonies, Helen and I drove to Bar Harbor, where her aunt had a camp on one of the inlets. On the way, we were stopped by the police, who said there had been a terrible accident up ahead. We were told that a large van, with a farmer and his family on board, were on their way home from shopping. Among the items that they had bought was a bundle of dynamite. Somehow it detonated and blew the van and family to bits. As we drove by, we had to go slowly because of all the rubbernecking people. Literally, everything had been blown to bits - pieces of cloth and cushions hung all over the fence and were strewn over the field and the road; it was a ghastly mess. We hurried past to the camp, where a drink was in order.

When we returned to Brewer, Helen and I were given a room at her folks' house. It was on the ground floor, off from the kitchen. Mr. Bremer, Helen's Dad, had very nicely wallpapered the whole room, and we had varnished the floor. It was great and comfortable, so I did not stay at the Bangor House any more. I continued work there, however. Helen had to change schools, because Brewer High did not accept married teachers. Through friends, she was able to get a teaching job at an elementary school in a town called Veazie, halfway between Bangor and the University at Orono, located on the Penobscot River.

Between us, we had been able to save enough money to buy an old 1935 Plymouth sedan; the "Green Hornet," it was called. This was necessary to get to college daily.

Bill LaLibertie attended the University also, so we rode up together and helped with the gas. Another fellow joined my car pool, by the name of John Plummer. John was about five years older than us, a rather big individual, a real New Englander, a jovial, happy-go-lucky person. Our classes and commuting, with Helen being picked up and dropped off, became routine. Big John, as he was known, was always full of jokes and French-Canadian poems, most of which he concocted. He loved hunting, fishing, and bourbon whiskey straight. Bill continued his work at the foundry, and I at the Bangor House.

There were four people that worked in the Peacock Room as bartenders; Percy Morrow, Phil Osser, Harold Wassen, and Ken Upton. They rotated the bar shift and tending the tables. I took care of the telephone and orders that came through the telephone system, or the rooms. After closing, we would all pitch in and clean up the tables, stack the glasses, empty ashtrays, and do a general sweep-up of the carpet. On Fridays and Saturdays, after everything was cleaned and the bar was closed, the five of us would sit down and play a special game of cards that the guys called "High-Low-Jack-and-the-Game." It was a lot of fun, and didn't take too much intelligence. There was small betting included, and often I could make two or three dollars. This would go into our piggybank at home. Sometimes Bill LaLibertie would drop by after work on his way home and join us. I would then drop him off, since he lived in Brewer, not far from us.

On one of his excursions into the Peacock Room, Bill took me aside and asked me if I would like to learn to fly. Golly, I froze. "Who me? Fly? No, sir. I thank you though." "Why? Because, I get terribly seasick, and I can't imagine what would happen in a airplane." Then I thought of the flight I took with Duncan Dana; I wasn't dizzy or seasick then. However, this was more serious and scary. He begged me to think it over and let him know in a few days. I asked him to explain what it was all about. Bill said it was being done through the University of Maine, paid for by the U.S. Government. It was called the Civilian Pilot Training Program, or CPT. To start, they needed a minimum of ten applicants. He said if I'd join, it would help. Later, if I didn't care to pursue it, I could drop out. First there would be the ground school, to learn about the airplanes, the weather, and navigation. It would start by the end of November, in about three weeks time. He wasn't sure whether we would get college credits for it; there would be no flying till Spring. I said, "Okay, but don't tell Helen yet. If I definitely stay with it, I'll tell her."

The next Monday, I went with Bill to enroll. When the form was filled out, the man said, "Oh, man! You're not a citizen. You have to be a citizen to join the CPT." The same old song I had when I wanted to join the CCC! As it turned out, it had been a Government official, a Mr. Hinkley, who came up with the CCC, and he was now instrumental with the CPT! The first free moment

I had, I went to the Bangor Superior Court to apply for my citizenship. I had already had my first papers, or Papers of Intent, when I lived in Westfield, New Jersey. An appointment was made for November 9. That was the day I became a U.S. Citizen. I was now clear to join the CPT.

I asked Horace Chapman if I could have two nights off a week, as the CPT classes were to be held at night at the University. I thought it best to tell Helen what I was up to. She certainly was not happy about this new program of flying. I could not blame her at the time, for I was not even sure of what I was doing, other than the novelty of it. The ground school was interesting, yet difficult. It was also different from anything I had studied before. A lot of terminology sounded foreign, such as ailerons and dihydral, etc. The classes were for six months; at the end of which we were to receive a written exam by a Civil Aviation Officer, who would come from Portland, Maine. If we passed, we would then take the physical exam from a designated CAA doctor. The written exam consisted of questions with several answers; it was necessary to work the problem out first, especially in the navigational questions. Somehow, we passed, yet I wasn't certain I knew what I had studied - drift angles and pressure altitude, etc.

Then came the physical exam, which turned out to be a thorough and exhausting one. The first day, I had drops put in my eyes; after that, I couldn't see. Someone else had to drive. I had to pee in a bottle and crap in a can, jump up and down, race around the room in jockey shorts, then lie down while I was tested for blood pressure, with about two things going at once. I also had to have a thorough eye and ear exam; I guess this is why those drops were administered. The following was what the doc called a depth perception test. We had to stand about 15 or 20 feet at one end of the room, then I was shown two bars, which were on slides. It was up to me to try and jockey these two back in as close to an alignment as possible. The exam took a couple of days; it was about this time that I was beginning to get my eyesight back. The part that no one appreciated was when the doctor was sticking his big finger up the bum and twisting it around. I didn't know what to expect at first, but when it happened, I just about leaped off the table and up the side of the wall. He said it was necessary to check the prostate. Was I ever glad when the whole thing was over! I thought it was just going to be like sticking your tongue out and saying "Ahhhh!"

Well, one day the aircraft and the moment had arrived. It was a Saturday morning. We all came out to the Bangor Airport; it was the old Godfrey Field. It now had a nice long runway; I think the directions were 33° and 15° degrees, there was also a short runway at right angles to the major one. There was a hangar in the northeast corner of the field, with another small building attached. In front of the hangar, there were four or five yellow airplanes and several instructors. I don't recall how we got paired off with the instructors; I know I was assigned to an instructor named George Garey. George introduced himself and then led me over to one of the planes. It was a Piper Cub (J-3). It had two seats in tandem. George was most meticulous in his instructions and briefing. He started with the propeller, and then the engine, and so on, around the airplane to the tail. Then he explained the functions of the stick (Joy-stick) in the cockpit; there were two, one at each tandem seat. George explained how the controls worked, and how they were hooked up to the sticks, and what affect it had on the plane when you moved the stick in different directions. He showed me the two pedals on the floor and their use with the rudder. We spent about a half hour in briefing and instruction. Then he said we were ready to take off, that we would fly for about half an hour where he would demonstrate, in the air, the operation of the stick functions and the rudder, and for me not to touch anything, just watch the stick move and see how the plane reacted. There were also two throttles, one for each cockpit. I was getting rather fidgety, yet quite excited. I was told to climb into the back seat and fasten the seat belt around my waist. This was no easy maneuver; the cockpit was small, especially with a heavy jacket on, but George was patient and showed me the best way to enter the cockpit and to buckle the belt. Then he climbed into the front. Though a rather small individual, the whole view up front was obliterated. He settled in and fiddled with knobs and switches. He called a mechanic over to stand by to start. George called the word, "Contact!" and the guy gave a mighty heave on the two-bladed propeller, but it took two or three swings before the motor finally erupted with a roar; the propeller whirled. I also noticed two blocks of wood under the wheels, with a long rope. Once everything was operating, George said they were called "chocks." I sat back and tried to be relaxed. This whole ceremony was so different from the time I flew with Duncan Dana.

After a long taxi period, we finally took off. The two flap-type doors rattled and shook in the wind. I tried to observe what George was doing, at the same time looking for landmarks. George finally turned in his seat, and when he did, the plane seemed to move about, too. He had to shout fairly loud so I could hear him over the noise of the rattling and the wind and the motor. He pointed to the altimeter and said we were at 2000 feet, and showed me how the indicator operated. He then pointed to the airspeed indicator. The needle was in the area of about 60-65 mph. From here on, he moved the stick in different directions, and the airplane responded to it. He had me look straight ahead and observe the horizon, where the front panel was level with the outside horizon. There were two black iron tube bars that protruded from the front panel and angled up into the wing overhead. George now showed me how the plane was kept level, then a slight movement of the stick to the left and the aircraft banked to the left, a change in the hori-

zon took place. The bar showed an angle of the airplane in relation to the horizon. This he did several times, left and right, then he showed what happened by pushing the stick forward. The horizon got larger and the speed increased. He then pulled back on the stick, the horizon disappeared below the panel, and the speed decreased. He did this a few times. He showed me, by indicating and pushing the rudder pedals left and right, how the nose would turn left to right. The next thing George said was, "Okay, Pete; now you take hold of the stick. Hold it lightly by the black rubber handle. Hold it steady and keep the nose straight and the horizon level." I froze with my right hand on the stick, as instructed. "Good," he said, "now gently move the stick to the left," and I watched the nose and the horizon change as he had done; then to the right. He shouted, "Dip the nose," then "Lift the nose," and "Move the rudders." He said that was all okay. When I moved the stick left and right, I pressed the rudder pedals in the same directions. I always watched the horizon, the airspeed, and the altitude; trying to keep them constant. Then I asked him, "Am I flying the airplane?" He nodded. I couldn't believe it! The speed, altimeter, however, didn't stay constant. I imagine it must have been gyrating all over the place. However, George said it was good, and "I have it…" He swung the aircraft to the right and made a sharp nose down altitude. For the first time, my stomach seemed to come into my throat. George called back that time was up, and we were headed for the airport. He pointed ahead; I could see the strip of runway far ahead of us. He told me to hold the stick with him, and as he would make the landing, for me to follow through with the stick and rudder, but very gently. When I did so, my mind forgot about my squooshy stomach. I was at ease as the runway approached. He said to keep my hand on the stick and feet on the rudder while he landed, but don't try moving anything; just follow through. The runway seemed to come at us in a hurry. He pulled back on the stick, and I noticed him closing the throttle. The plane seemed to fall away and squooshed onto the runway.

I realized it was a whole new experience, and I knew I was going to like it. Bill was waiting for me, smiling. "How do you like it?" he asked. It was then I realized I could barely hear him; there seemed to be bubbles in my ears, like swimming. He said to try swallowing. I did, and eventually the ears popped. We drove back to town elated. Our flight instructions were mainly on weekends, and sometimes when there were no classes. It didn't take long to get the hang of flying; George was a good instructor, as I am sure the others were, too. After eight hours, George said I was ready to solo the last half-hour.

George stopped the airplane and got out, and said, "Okay, Peter; take it around. Also, remember the plane will be lighter." I got scared again, as I sat in the rear seat, with no instructor in front for confidence. I grinned, however, and taxied down to the end, turned

onto runway 33. I checked for other traffic, and gradually applied power. In about 100 yards, the plane seemed to leap into the air. Once I was up and away, I felt I ruled the world. I thought to myself, "Am I really up here, at 1000 feet, flying an airplane? The jungle-hillbilly boy from the Himalayas? Hey, Jasma; look at me now!" I said in Hindi, and laughed. I came around the pattern just as George had instructed, and I found myself on a final approach. As the runway came up to me, the threshold of the runway approached; I could see a figure standing off to one side. I knew it would be my instructor. As the white center line zipped under me, I gradually eased off the throttle. The airspeed dropped to around 50 mph, and I came back slowly on the stick. The plane seemed to hang in the air for a few seconds, and then, it squooshed onto the runway. It was not a hard landing; I made it. George ran up to me when I stopped. He reached in and congratulated me by shaking hands. He climbed back into the front and taxied back to the hangar.

Several of us soloed that day. We all went into town to celebrate. I couldn't wait to tell Horace Chapman and my friends, before returning to Brewer and Helen. I don't know how pleased she was about the solo. Things had not been going well since I started my flying. With the summer holidays, there was more time to take my flying lessons, and to get ready for my flight test for the Private Pilot License (PPL). It was on one of these training flights with George that a near incident/accident almost occurred, that shook both George and myself. We had been out doing various maneuvers and exercises, such as S-turns and pylon-8s. George said to finish it off with a 270° turn maneuver over the airport, at 2000 feet, and make a spot landing. This meant to come over the landing end of the runway at a heading of 330°, close the power or the throttle, make two spiral descending turns, proceed out to the base leg and final approach, to land within a certain area of the runway, without using any more power. The weather was clear. I came over the runway at 2000 feet. I made the two spiral turns, then the base leg and final. Everything was working out. I was allowing for the wind, as I noticed the windsock near the end of the runway. I came over the threshold at about 20 feet. At about that time, when I was about to cut the power and land, I heard a "tick" and a little shake and jar of the airplane. George looked out ahead as I concentrated on landing for the spot. I touched down just about where I should have. Then I saw two cars with flags, racing down and speeding to us on the runway. Instructor Percy Billings gave a signal by passing his finger across his throat, which meant to stop, or cut the engine, which George did. Percy looked in and asked if we'd noticed anything, if we were okay. We looked innocent enough and said everything was fine. He said, "Well, look behind you." There, about 50 feet behind us was another Cub, with little stubs of propeller rotating. We all got out, including the other pilot and instructor. We inspected our plane and found that the other plane's propeller had cut one of our longerons in two, with a gash in the fabric, and had just missed cutting the elevator cable as well. According to Percy and some of the bystanders who watched the two airplanes had approached the airport from the same direction, with the other aircraft about three to five feet below mine. We both executed the same maneuver, letter-perfect to each other. We remained at the five feet separation throughout the spiral turns, out to the base leg and final. Not until I initiated a nose-up attitude of the plane to flare, did my tail section hit the other propeller. Percy and the others could not signal us, as each one would think it was for him, and make a different maneuver; perhaps pull out and make a possible collision to occur at that higher altitude. They were hoping one of us would see the other and pull away. We didn't and hence continued to complete maneuver till almost touchdown. All of us were dumbfounded. From that day on, there was to be caution from all instructors and ourselves.

The great day arrived for our flight test and private licenses. Inspector Thomas came from Portland to administer the check rides. I had been so used to having George Garey with me, that I became nervous with a stranger in the cockpit. Inspector Thomas directed me and explained what maneuvers to do.

Throughout the flight, Thomas never opened his mouth, only to give instructions and hand signals; not till the end of the ride, when Thomas pulled back the power and said to make an emergency landing. George had always instructed me in these forced or emergency landing situations to have a field or a road picked out whenever flying, don't just pick any field. If the altitude is high enough, circle the aircraft, don't dive it, and look around for a good landing spot. Don't take your eye off it. Check the wind, by smoke, or trees swaying, or waves in the water. Thomas had given me the emergency while the airfield was behind us. We were at about 500 feet. I made my circle to check for a field, and noticed the Bangor Airport not too far. I headed for it, in a shallow glide. Having made this approach before, I knew I could make the airport. Mr. Thomas then pointed to a field below, but I wouldn't accept it. I came over the main runway at about 200 feet, circled right, turned onto a short final. I landed without any problems and taxied to the hangar. He said it was a good flight, but why didn't I take the field under us? I said with the rate of descent and the tailwind, we could make the airport. He said I'd made a good decision, because never change from what I have already decided to do. I said I might have taken another field if my altitude had been much lower. I received my license.

The permanent license finally arrived from the CAA head office in Washington. The number of my Private License was 9190-40; I guess the 40 stood for the year 1940. The first person to fly with me as a passenger was Horace Chapman. It was great to have him on board. We took off early on Saturday morning. He wanted to fly over Green

*Bangor "Godfrey" Airport where I learned to fly 1940. Later became Dow Air Force Base.*

Lake and see his summer home. We circled the airport and headed for Green Lake. It was an easy place to find because of the road that ran directly from Bangor to Green Lake, and to Bar Harbor. We had a good look at the house by circling it a couple of times. Then we flew back and landed. Any flying I wanted to do from here on, I had to pay for. I depleted my piggybank in short order. Helen would not go up with me at first, and I could hardly blame her. Toward the end of summer she took a trip with me. We flew down the Penobscot River to Bucksport and back.

Sometimes, if friends had a few dollars, I'd take them up. John Plummer was another one. I was able to build up quite a few extra hours this way. That fall, Bill got me aside one day and said that there was going to be a secondary course, which would start soon. It would be all aerobatics, in a bigger plane, called a Waco (UPF-7), a biplane with open cockpits. The planes arrived in December, and Percy Billings was my instructor. Percy had been a pilot in World War I and had seen action in France. He was an excellent pilot, but a little quick in temper; nonetheless, we got on well. The Waco was a big biplane. It had a radial engine, and it was blue with yellow wings and tail (Military colors).

We got into the heavy flying suits; I already had on my long-johns, and the temperature in Maine at that time was well below freezing, at least about 15° to 20° degrees Fahrenheit on the ground. I was given a leather helmet and goggles. It reminded me of the movies we had seen depicting World War I "Hells' Angels," and the movie *Wings*, all of which I loved. We had parachutes that acted as cushions that we could sit on. Percy had explained how to use the chutes, just in case!

Percy climbed the plane up to about 5000 feet, and did several steep turns to the left and the right; and the stalls, and I was following through with the stick. He then

*One of the Gullwing Stinsons we flew in the cross-country course. This one nicknamed "Grey Goose".*

said, "Okay; hold on, and don't touch anything." He dove the airplane and did a complete loop. I was really surprised and bewildered, and a for a second didn't know where I was. After a few more gyrations in the air, Percy asked if I was okay by shouting at me against the wind; I could barely hear him. Then he told me to go ahead and try to fly the airplane straight and level, then gradually to make some turns to the left and right, as I had done with the Piper Cub, nose up, nose down, etc. He told me to make some steep turns to the left and to the right, then to bring the airplane up to a stall position by just holding the stick back in my stomach. This I did until the airplane shuddered and shook and fell off to one side, usually the left, and started to dive. He told me to push the nose down and then build up speed and pull back on the stick. It wasn't long before I could fly the Waco. After a few more landings and a few more lessons, Percy told me to solo. This was another exciting day; I was happy about it. All went well. From that point on, most of my flying was solo. The only other instructions were various exciting maneuvers, such as slow rolls, snap rolls and spins. The group was given about 20 hours of flying in this machine, and I enjoyed every minute.

I was quite content to climb up to 5000 and do my maneuvers; then I always loved to roll the airplane onto its back and hang there, gliding down. I could see all the snow and white fields below. There was no rating for these maneuvers. The instructors would write off the aerobatic course in our logbooks.

Through all this, I was having problems with Helen and my home life. I knew very well she did not like my flying, but the flying bug had me. I knew flying was here to stay. Again, Bill came to me and said there were going to be some more courses coming up, but instead, he was going to join the Navy. I think it was Percy Billings who said that the flying was to take place in Waterville, Maine. This is where, if you recall, I had met Jack Egan during archery at the turkey shoot, some years ago. Most of the guys decided that they were going to finish the course (cross country) in Waterville. A decision had to be made whether or not I could continue college or flying; I couldn't do both. It was a tough decision, but I decided flying was what I would have to do: I could always come back to college.

*Willie "Babe" Wilder, Frank "Pete" Peterson, "Rob" Robertson, studying hard at Waterville cross-country course in 1941.*

*My good friend Sylvia.*

# PHASE THREE: 1941 — 1947

## When flying was dangerous and sex was safe

I drove to Waterville, where three of us took a small room in a private house. There was Pete Peterson, Rob Robertson, and myself. There was another fellow who later joined us, by the name of Willie Wilder. We met the person in charge of the school, by the name of Wes Marden. He introduced us to some of his instructors and explained the course. We were to study for our Commercial License(CPL), which would take about six weeks to two months. If we passed the written exam, then we would do some flying in the Piper Cub. After that, we would go into the Cross-Country Course. He pointed out two of his airplanes. He called them Gull-Wing Stinsons. They were high wing monoplanes, with about four seats. They were rugged looking airplanes; one was gray and one was red.

We settled down to the task of ground school and studying for our written test on the Commercial License. In between, we were doing some flying with our new instructors. It was just an extension of what we already had in the private pilot license course.

One day, Mr. Thomas arrived to administer the written exam, which we passed. The day came for my turn to fly with Mr. Thomas. He remembered me from the previous flight check for the Private License. I thought I did pretty well; he said I did, including all the emergency landings which he gave me. I now had to go to Boston to get a Restricted Radio-Telephone Operator's Permit. This was done through the Federal Communications Commission. Toward the end of July 1941, I took an exam to obtain permission to use radio communications in airplanes.

Back in Waterville, I started the cross-country training in the Gull-Wing Stinsons. There would be two of us, either with Wes Marden or another pilot, who would take the airplanes on cross-country flying. We covered a lot of territory. We made flights down to Boston, over to New Hampshire, Vermont and Connecticut, and back; sometimes north to parts of Maine and Presque Isle. We were then instructed about navigation and night flying. The Civil Aviation Administration

(CAA) had visual beacon lights between cities, which were stretched about 50 miles apart. One could follow these from one city to another. We also had what they called radio ranges. They were radios that would give out signals of A and N, and normally one tried to fly between the A and N, which was what they called the Nul. When we were on the nul or twilight zone, that meant we were right on course. These nuls were along the same airways, or where the lighted beacons went from city to city. On actual instruments, you would fly the nuls.

I enjoyed the course very much, even though we didn't fly these airplanes from the left seat; we could fly it from the right. But the main program was to teach us navigation and night flying. When the course was finished, we were told that we would go solo on our own cross-country flights using the Piper Cubs, which was the icing on the cake.

Three of us teamed up to go on our flight: Pete Peterson, Rob Robertson and myself. We were told there would be no night flying, since there were no navigational lights of any kind on the airplanes. It was strictly VFR, daylight hours only. We planned our course to go from Waterville, across New Hampshire and Connecticut, probably stopping at two stations, onto Haverstraw, N.Y.; down the Hudson River, to Flushing Airport, just outside of Manhattan. From there, we were going to return across the Long Island Sound to Putnam Field in Connecticut, then to Grafton, Massachusetts overnight, next day to Portsmouth, New Hampshire, and back to Waterville, completing the circuit.

Our flight, with the three of us flying together in formation, made the trip perfectly all the way down through Haverstraw and Flushing Airport. Though it was not on the schedule, we decided at the last minute to make a whirl around Manhattan and the East River. Then we continued back north to Putnam Field. At Putnam, the daylight started to wane; it looked like we might have to stay

*On Peshaw Pond with J-3 Cub. I watched my bartender friends ice fishing, 1941.*

there overnight. Finally, we said with any kind of luck, we could make Grafton. We took off for Grafton, which would be about another hour's flight.

We hadn't been up half an hour when there was very little twilight. It was like somebody putting a blanket over us; it became dark immediately. There we were, caught in the night, with no navigational lights. We tried, however, to continue on course, yet not knowing how close we were to each other. We could not read the compass, because there was no light for it. I had some matches; once in a while, I'd light a match and look at the compass. Between that, and being able to see the beacon lights, I continued on course. I was at about 2000 feet, when I noticed a runway lit up, right underneath. I said "This is it," and hoped that the other fellows had seen it as well.

I let down and circled the airport to see the wind direction. I saw a lighted windsock; it was limp. I elected to land on what I thought was the easiest side of the runway. I landed and taxiied up to a hangar. I was greeted by some people who asked me what I was doing. I told them what my program was, but I also said that there were two other fellows upstairs somewhere, and I'd like to make sure that they came in and landed. The airport manager kept the runway lights going and the rotation beacon on the tower, but no signs of Pete and Robbie. I thought, after another hour, that they would be out of gas, and should have landed someplace. I hoped that they were okay. The airport manager said he would notify the Highway Patrol and see if anybody had landed anywhere in the State. Not long after the alert was sent, they finally called us and said that a pilot landed at Boston Airport by the name of Peterson. I said, "That's great; we have one more still up there, somewhere." The news media always seem to grab these things. I don't know how they ferreted this news, but they had it, and the next morning, which happened to be Sunday, the newspapers said that there was a pilot by the name of Robertson missing somewhere in Massachusetts; hopefully, he had not crashed.

When I had landed at Grafton, I met a young pilot whose name was Robert, or Bob Burke. Bob suggested I go home and stay at his place that night; that we would find out about Robbie the next day. I spent the night at his house. At about 8 o'clock in the morning, we got a phone call; lo and behold, it was Robbie! He said "What's going on? I'm looking at the newspaper. It says that I'm lost. I'm not lost; I'm at home, in bed, reading the newspaper!" We said, "Well, how did you get there?" He said, "I had to land at Leominister Airport, which is a military base. Now I've got problems with getting the plane out." I notified Boston and the police, and told them the lost pilot was okay and was safe at home. Leominister was quite a distance away. Burke and I drove up and talked with Robbie and the officer in charge, to let the aircraft go. They decided that they would not give him any fuel; that he had enough to fly it over to Grafton. We then contacted Pete

*Our PanAfrica group (42-A), January 1942. At the PAA Air Ferries training base.*
*Front Row: Bart Hewitt, Ed Frankiewietz, Bob Burke, Tom Carroll, and Harry Bernard.*
*Back Row: Sam George, Bob Keel, Myself, Arnie Graff, Enos Kirkpatrick, Jack Kenny, Art Dorman, and P.C. Hill.*

and said that we would land there, then continue the flight to Waterville. I thanked Bob Burke and the airport manager at Grafton for helping us so much. At all times, we were in contact with Wes Marden in Waterville, though he was not too happy with our excursions; he was wishing us well. We landed at Boston and got a hold of Frank. The three of us then departed for Portsmouth, New Hampshire. Coming up on Portsmouth, we noticed a fog bank rolling in from the sea. It was nip and tuck whether we could make the airport before the fog rolled in. We didn't make it; the fog beat us to it. We had to divert and found a farmhouse with a lovely pasture, without any cows, and landed safely. The farmer came out and wanted to know what was happening. We told him our story. He said, "Oh, yeah; I heard about you people in the newspapers and the radio. We're happy to have you here. You can spend the night, and we'll get you some gas so you can take off tomorrow." We appreciated that very much, and spent the night with the farmer. The next morning, it was clear; the fog had lifted, and we were able to fly into Portsmouth Airport, refuel and head back to Waterville. What was to have been a two-day excursion, turned into three. I guess that's aviation all over the world, then and now.

Wes Marden greeted us and was happy to see that there were no scratches on his airplanes. We told him what had happened. He said, well, not to worry, but we'd have to write an extensive report for the CAA to know why we were flying without lights at night. We got our heads together and came up with some pretty good reports and excuses, which evidently Mr. Thomas bought.

Now the flying was over; it was late September. I said goodbye to all my friends, who went their separate ways. I went back to Brewer, to see what was going to develop next. I was interested in obtaining an instructor's license and studied for that. In the meantime, I spent a lot of time with some friends and instructors at the South Brewer Airport. We did a lot of "hanger talk," and I was gaining a lot of experience from listening to instructors' conversations. I met a Mr. Sailor who owned a Piper cub at Brewer Airport. He told me that I could fly the airplane whenever I wished, as long as I would fill it up with gas. It didn't take me long to round up a whole lot of people who were willing to pay for short flights around the city and up and down the Penobscot River. I enjoyed this, and was building up my flight time.

Winter comes early in Maine, with a lot of snowstorms. It had snowed here late in November, and I saw some of my friends from the Peacock Room. One weekend, they said they were going fishing at Peshaw Pond; I said I'd meet them there. I flew up and saw the little figures down below on the lake. I circled around and landed on the frozen lake. I watched them fish for about an hour. I then took off, gave them a buzz, and headed back to Brewer.

On another occasion, a tall, lanky, rawboned individual approached me, who was interested in learning to fly, but wasn't sure whether he would like to be in the air or not. Would I be willing to take him up, so he could get an idea? I don't remember his full name; I think it was Lewis. It was early in the morning when I elected to take him on his flight. I climbed to about 50 or 100 feet when the engine quit, stopped dead. Right ahead was a small, plowed, corn field, and I put it down safely. Some of the people at the airport got in their cars and raced over to see what the problem was. We examined the airplane, and figured it was carburetor ice, or ice that had formed in the fuel. One of my mistakes of that morning was that I forgot to drain what they called the fuel sump. Normally you do this, because overnight condensation and water will form. If it is not cleared, it will form into ice. This is evidently what had happened and caused fuel starvation to the engine.

We got the airplane started again, but I didn't take my passenger; I told him I'd meet him back at Brewer. I came back and landed. He was still eager, even more interested, especially to know that I was able to bring the airplane back safely, without an accident. We flew for about 30-40 minutes, and came back. He said he liked it very much, thanked me, and disappeared.

I mention some of these names, places and people because, later on in life, I was to meet them in different circumstances.

Sometimes, if there was no flying, I would meet John Plummer, and we would go deer hunting. We never got any, but it was good sport; good walking through the woods.

One Sunday morning, while I was in the hangar at Brewer Airport around the old pot-bellied stove, listening to the radio, the commentator came on and said, "Stand by for an important message from the White House." We listened intently. President Roosevelt came on and gave the famous speech to announce that Pearl Harbor had been bombed; December 7, 1941. Everybody seemed stunned. It took a little while to come to our senses; it was decided that we'd close the hangar and go home. I went back and talked to Helen. I said I'd go down and see if I could join the Air Force. She was not happy about that.

The next morning, Monday, bright and early, I was at the doorstep of the recruiting office. I went in and filled out the forms. They were happy to see that I had so much flying time (350 hours) and a Commercial License. They said that would be great; there'd be no problem. However, after the man, a Captain in charge, looked at the form, he said, "Oh Heck! We can't take you; it says here that you are 27 years of age, our age limit is 26 1/2. I'm sorry." I looked it over for myself and saw that I was nearly eight months over the age. I was downhearted and disappointed. I asked the captain if he couldn't back date the form to early March. "No way." I came back home and told Helen. I think she was happy. The next alternative was to try and get my instructor's license. Though I still worked at the Bangor House, I felt I should get a flying job of some kind, and I knew there were a few instructor's positions around the country. Mr. Thomas thought it was a good idea, too.

I studied an instructor's manual and then drove to Portland to sit for the exam. When the exam had been corrected I missed by one question. It meant I would have to study some more and come back in a month and try again. A few days later, one of my pilot friends phoned to say that if I was interested, Pan American Airways was hiring pilots to ferry U.S. Army Air Force fighter planes (P-40s) across Africa. He was a little vague; but the planes would be assembled in a place called Accra, West Africa. They would then be ferried across Africa, all the way up to Cairo, Egypt. They were to be delivered to our allies who were fighting the Germans in North Africa. It sounded exciting to me. The pilot said to call a Captain Brick Maxwell of Pan Am in New York City. He gave me the number to call. I reached Maxwell by phone. He reiterated that they were hiring pilots, and if I was interested, to come down and talk with him. I caught a train to New York and found my way to the forty-fourth floor of the Chrysler Building. It wasn't difficult to find, since I had worked in that area. The receptionist ushered me in to meet Captain Maxwell. After a brief discussion, I filled out a PAA form. He looked it over, and said I qualified and that his secretary would take it from there. I had to run to a photographer and have passport pictures taken. The next thing I knew, I was getting inoculation and vaccination shots for my trip to Africa, which consisted of smallpox, yellow fever, tetanus, typhoid, cholera and a whole lot of others that I can't even remember. By the time I'd finished, I was sick as a dog with fever. I called my friend, Robert Burge, who was married and living in Westfield. I took the same old subway, ferryboat, and the train to Westfield. He met me at the station, and I was just about able to make it to the apartment where they put me to bed. I think I was there for about two days, recovering.

Once again, I was on my feet and felt healthy enough to travel. I returned to the 44th floor of the Chrysler Building; I had to see how things were progressing. Maxwell said the passport was in process, and should be ready in a few days, for me to go on home. He would be in touch.

Just before Christmas, I received my passport, with a bunch of visas for Africa; also, an airline ticket, with a note that said that I should be at Newark Airport the first week of January, to report to the Air Ferries office at 119th Street in Miami. I said goodbye to everyone, especially Helen, who was always very staunch and very brave, but still not happy about my going.

At Newark Airport, I met two other pilots who were on their way. One was Tom Carroll, the other was Ross Menuex. The flight was in the evening; it was Eastern Airlines, DC-3, and we were informed that they'd made about two or three stops on the way down. It was an interesting flight at night, and arrived in Miami early in the morning. There was no one there to meet us, so we took a cab to the hotel in town. We were pretty well tired out. After a rest, we called the Air Ferries office at 119th Street. They said they would send a car to pick us up. The PanAm building was quite elaborate; it once was a country club (not to mention a hideout for Al Capone!). We were ushered in, bags and baggage. I met a whole group of young fellows that had already reported in, and was surprised to see Bobby Burke amongst them.

Bob took me into the barracks, where there were rows of beds, uppers and lowers; I believe I had an upper bunk. After I put my things away, he took me into the bar, where we met some more pilots. There were about thirty of us altogether. We were a day or two late for the classes. We were studying more advanced navigation and weather, along with Morse code. It was necessary to receive and send at least 12 words a minute. Our class was designated 42-A. The class studied navigation all the way up to what was called "dead reckoning." It was the next step before celestial, which I don't think we were going to have.

There was a local pub about a mile down 119th Street which was famous from "Ripley's Believe It or Not." The Bottle Cap Inn had been constructed completely of bottle caps. The owner, Joe Wiser, had hammered in thousands upon thousands of bottle caps that cover the ceiling, the walls, the floor, the bar, all the chairs and tables, and the john. It was a nice place, with a friendly atmosphere. The owner thanked us, because we were the best patrons he had. We were there most every evening after classes. This was one good way of getting to know friends; they were just a fine bunch.

When we did have a break from classes, I telephoned and got a hold of Sylvia; I wanted so much to see her again. She came by and picked me up. I met her husband, Serge, and their son, Richard, whom she called "Dickie." He was a little strap of a fellow, about 5 or 6 years old, blonde, and resembled his mother very much. I did see them once in a while, and it was so nice to be able to talk about the old times, the archery days in Maine. She was very excited, as was Serge, about my new adventure into aviation and my going to Africa.

Whenever our group had the opportunity and permission to use the PAA car, we would go to Miami Beach for relaxation and swimming. The days hurried by, with a lot of work and ground school. By the time we finished the exams, about two months had passed. We were informed that we would get instrument procedures training. They had two Link trainers, little blue boxes, like miniature stubby airplanes, with stubby yellow wings and tail.

Besides studying the regular weather information that was also necessary, we were taught about the weather in Equatorial Africa. We also learned about the Gold Coast, where we were going to be based. The area was later to become the country of Ghana. We learned about Nigeria and Lake Chad, the Sudan and Khartoum, the Nile, and Egypt. There were a lot of new geographic names that we were now becoming familiar with.

The Link trainers and instrument flying were a whole new concept of flight for me. It was an interesting course, and what was unique about these Link trainers was an apparatus which was hooked up to the trainer that would mark your flight on paper, like a robot pen following your course. The instructor could follow every move you made. There were rated turns, which were made by time only, and were called "timed turns." When making an approach to the airport, the whole flight was shown on the chart. At first, I found it a little difficult.

There was always a good side to all this training and hard work; it was when the airplanes always showed up and we had a chance to start flying. The planes assigned to our Pan-African group were AT-6s, military type advanced trainers. This would be the prelude to the P-40s, that we were scheduled to fly in Accra, Africa. The excitement and anticipation was killing, especially for us young fledgling pilots.

The AT-6s arrived at Opa Locka Airport. My instructor was a "Pete" Peteler. The AT-6 was an all metal, low-winged plane, with a 650 horsepower engine. It had two tandem cockpits, with plexiglass canopies overhead. Instructor Peteler climbed into the front cockpit, and I was in the rear. There was an intercom system by which he could communicate. We took off with a high-pitched whine and a roar. Peteler had been a skywriter in his career, and it seemed we were up to 5,000 feet in nothing flat.

He commenced with all types of aerobatics; vertical slow rolls, loops, and Cuban-8s. He was good and wanted me to know it. Pete then gave me the controls and let me do the normal turns and stalls. He said to follow him through on the landing. The next day, I was told to get into the front seat. Pete showed me how to start the engine and check all the necessary items before anything else. How to prime the engine and check the controls, use of the hydraulic brakes and the flaps, things I had not done before.

We eventually taxiied and took off. I could feel Peteler helping me on the controls. Once we were up to 5,000 feet he had me go through various maneuvers and use of the gear. I lowered the gear and flaps and stalled the plane. This was giving me the feel for landing the heavy plane. We did slow flight, with the gear and flaps down; I was getting the feel pretty well. We returned to Opa Locka for landing and takeoffs. The first couple of attempts were a bit hard and raggedy. Pete never let the aircraft get away from me. Gradually, I was getting the know-how; in a few more sessions, Pete let me solo. It felt great. From then on, it was all solo, except for other advanced maneuvers. I'd go up and perform some aerobatics, slow flight, and Cuban-8s. From the back seat, we were given practice in instrument flying, with the needle ball concept, same as the Link trainer.

My final test was the instrument portion, a triangular course. I received what winds we could from the ATC, chart the course and figure out our estimated time of arrival at each point on the triangle; shake and wiggle the airplane when we thought we were there. It was a good exercise and flight test. We were not allowed to use radio navigation. Four of us, as I recall, had done an exceptionally fine

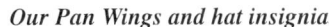
*Our Pan Wings and hat insignia.*

*Pan American clipper (B-314) type that flew us from Laguardia to West Africa in 1942.*

job. In fact, we were asked by the office chief if we would prefer to stay on in Miami, go on Pan-American Flying Clipper Boats and get celestial navigation. It was a great temptation, but we agreed to stick together. All of us were also given some night flying, using emergency type strips; in other words, only the left side of a runway would be lit up with smudge pots. On the first ride, I had a new instructor; the AT-6 was an old one that had not been used for quite a while. It had been in the hangar and had some work done on the skin under the fuselage area. There were no wheels on it at that time, and the brake drums evidently had become rusty.

We took off late in the evening for the training field at Homestead Airport. I circled the field and lined up for the final approach with the smudge pots burning distinctly on the left side of the runway. I touched down in a normal landing configuration; all was going well at the roll-out. As the aircraft started to slow, I planned to turn off about three-fourths down the runway. I braked the left brake, and it grabbed; it grabbed hard and started the plane to swing left. I automatically hit the right brake; it grabbed, and the next moment the AT-6 flipped over onto its back and skidded to a stop. I cut the ignition; the canopy was already open. I undid my safety belt, forgot

that I was upside down, and landed on my head and shoulders. After that quick shock, I looked to see how my instructor was; he was still in the back seat, all tangled up somehow and screaming for me to get him out. The instrument hood had flipped over and covered his canopy; it must have been real dark in there. The canopy was closed and couldn't be opened, because one end was on the ground. Several mechanics had raced out in a car and started bashing in the glass. Everyone was afraid of a flash fire as gas fumes and puddles of gas could be smelled and seen. It took a lot of people to pry the canopy open and get the pilot out. He was scared and angry; he shouted at me that I had caused the accident by slamming on the brakes at once, which caused the plane to flip over. It was later learned that the brakes had seized because of the rust on the brake drums; I was exonerated from blame for the accident. Other than a bent propeller and skin damage on the vertical tail, the plane was soon fixed and flying again.

Eventually, the course wound down and a big celebration was held at the Pan American facility. After the banquet, Juan Trippe, PAA President, gave a speech and presented us our diplomas and Pan American Wings. We were told we could return to our homes for farewells and a short visit, then report to LaGuardia Marine Terminal in mid-May, for our de-

*Enjoying my pipe at the CNAC bungalow, 1943.*

parture. The group boarded the train at Miami and headed north.

It was nice to be back home and relax. Helen was friendly and all seemed well. I met and talked with Horace, and also went over and saw George Garey and Percy Billings. We talked a lot. I told them about our experiences in the AT-6 and even the accident I had. Then I talked about going to Africa and the unknown. The news was full of the war: the Germans battling Russia; the Desert Fox, Rommel, on the prowl in Libya, on his way to Cairo; the war in the Pacific, and Doolittle's raid on Tokyo. My mother was worried and told me to be very careful. Christine and Robert were all for me and wished me well. Horace Chapman had given me a nice watch, and Robert presented me with a Smith & Wesson .38 revolver; a beautiful gun. Helen tried to be cheerful, but I could feel her worry. I explained I would not be fighting, only delivering planes to Cairo, not to worry. During our conversation, she said that she would very much like to have a baby. Well, we would try.

On leaving, I told Helen to be sure and let me know how everything was progressing. At this moment, I had a bad feeling about leaving, then I thought, "Oh, gosh; there were so many thousands of Americans and other allied people now caught up in the war, many dying, and some dead." I dispensed with the thought of staying home.

On arrival at the Marine Terminal in LaGuardia Airport, I met the gang from the Miami 42-A group. We converged in the lobby and chit-chatted. It was dark when the Pan American Clipper flight was called. The floodlights on the walkway were shining on the flying boat and made the plane look gigantic; but no question, it was an enormous airplane. It was a Boeing 314, Flying Boat, the latest in aviation flying machines. Besides the 30 of us pilots, there were quite a few other passengers, heading for South America and Africa; mostly maintenance personnel and engineers of Pan American.

We all looked dapper in our khaki drill uniforms, as we came on board and were ushered to our seats by cute stewardesses. I had a window seat that was under the wing and looked over what appeared to be a pontoon. I was informed it was called a sponson. We were welcomed on board and offered drinks. Finally a steward came by and gave a briefing on all the flotation gear and the emergency procedures. It was not long after that I heard the engines; there were four of them. The lines were let loose, same as our old steamship. I could feel the flying boat moving out. It seemed to taxi for quite a distance till it was announced that the clipper flight was ready for takeoff.

The engines roared into life, and the boat shuddered and shook, then surged forward. It took forever, or so it appeared, to build up speed. I could see water splashing up from the bow and over the pontoons. Gradually, I could feel the flying boat lifting off; then we were airborne. I tried to look back, and could just see some lights in the distance, possibly the coastline of Long Island. The ship seemed stable, with not much motion. It was dark outside; nothing could be seen. We were over water. The seat belt sign was turned off, and the pilot came on the speaker and introduced himself as Captain Pipinger, that we were headed for Bermuda.

The splashdown at Hamilton, Bermuda was in the wee small hours of the morning. We were half asleep and bleary-eyed from all the free scotch. It was nothing but hustle and bustle when the plane was tied up; people rushing aboard, baggage, boxes, and catering. We were soon airborne and headed for Port au Spain, Trinidad. The weather was clear at this time, and the sea was deep blue. We spotted a ship here and there, but not as much traffic as there would normally be in peacetime. I wondered if my old banana boat was there somewhere. Our height was a little over 5000 feet, when the Captain came down to meet us. I noticed his Pan American hat did not fit right. I learned that he had had an

operation some time ago; the frontal part of his skull had been removed, giving a caved-in look. But "Pip," as he was called, was a regular fellow, and said we could go up by turns to the flight deck and look around; we jumped at the chance. I was amazed at the size of the cockpit; also that we had to climb up a spiral staircase to get there. The yoke, or stick, protruded straight up from the floor. There was a separate place for the engineer and navigator, and all the engine instruments; I never saw so many! It was an enlightening experience to see the cockpit. The engineer explained to me that there were two doors, one on each side, and a crawlway that he could go through to inspect the engines on both sides; to see if there were any problems. He could even fix or change generators, etc., while in flight.

Late that day, we arrived at Port au Spain. The plane was docked and all passengers disembarked to spend the night at a hotel in town. It was a Pan Am hotel. How nice it was to get off and stretch our legs. Everyone was still weary; the flying boat was no fast ship. It cruised about 130 miles an hour. I loved the town, to see all the tropical plants and people who looked a lot like East Indians. The place had an English atmosphere; I almost felt at home. The hotel was no four-star affair, but it was comfortable; it was more like a hostel. There were ceiling fans in all the rooms. The bed I had was more of a cot, with mosquito netting.

The morning arrived with the chatter of birds and the noise of cars and carts. Everything appeared in a rush. We hustled off in a bus to the plane, and I don't remember even having breakfast; I'm sure we did. Soon, we were airborne. It was another beautiful morning, and the water was clear as crystal; an emerald green color. One could see the bottom as we skirted the shoreline. The next stop would be Belem in Brazil. After a few drinks and a good lunch, Captain Pip came on the intercom speaker and informed everyone that we were just about to cross the Equator into King Rex Realm, but it was getting rainy. At the right moment, the Captain gave the yoke a quick shake or a jerk; it felt like we were going over a bump. He then announced, "You have just crossed it." Shortly thereafter the Chief Purser came by with parchment-type forms and said this was a special certificate in our own indoctrination of Jupiter Rex Lord and Realm. I still have my certificate.

Belem is located partway up the inlet of the great Amazon River and its tributaries. The water was muddy, with a lot of flotsam. The buildings were drab and really weather-beaten. They appeared to be covered with mildew and moss. Everything was damp and dripping wet. It should be, because it rained most of the time. The hotel was no four-star hotel, either. It was very drab and all the beds and the whole room smelled of mildew and mustiness. We slept under mosquito netting. After dinner, we were told of a nightclub nearby that we should go and visit. There was a raspy band that blared out rhumba music. We ordered drinks at our table. Shortly, some girls came by to ask if we wished to dance. When the girls got close, there was a smell of heavy perfume. My girl said she would like to have another drink. While at the bar, she asked me if I wanted to sleep with her for about ten or fifteen dollars. She said she was good; that Errol Flynn had once slept with her! I then thought that he must have been real hard up! I said, "No, thank you," and I returned to the table. I was happy when we departed from Belem; it was really a place in decay.

The next stop was Natal, Brazil. This was the jumping off spot for West Africa. Everyone who was there normally had to buy the famous Natal mosquito boots. The people who sold them must have made a fortune. I didn't buy a pair, yet some of the guys did. Natal was a little more pleasant then Belem. All walks and types of pilots hobnobbed at the main hotel. Ferry pilots delivering bombers to the Russians in Teheran, passed this way. Others delivering planes and cargo flight to India and China were here. We stayed a few days in Natal; it was fun talking to ferry pilots. We learned a lot of the route that we would be taking. We talked about the P-40s; they didn't envy us one bit. They said pilots flying the medium bombers, such as the A-20 and B-26, were getting lost, and forced landings were happening all the way to Khartoum. We were beginning to have misgivings and apprehensions about the P-40 trips.

Our flight was called the next evening. It would be a night flight across the South Atlantic, so they could use celestial navigation. Not only that, it was reported that there were German submarines, U-boats, that would surface and take potshots at the aircraft flying overhead. We were satisfied that it was going to be nighttime. The Southern Cross, one of the constellations in the southern hemisphere, always came clear and majestic; it certainly looked like a cross. We all had a good sleep on this everlong crossing. The flight arrived at a place called Fish Lake. The Station Manager for Pan Am there said that he didn't know of any aircraft that was coming to pick up a group of P-40 pilots, to take to Accra. The only place he knew perhaps would be further up the line at Bathurst, another British possession.

So after refueling, we headed for Bathurst. Once we landed, we inquired about the planes that were coming to pick up the pilots. The British said they knew of no plane scheduled for us. Perhaps it could be at Bisseau, a Portuguese territory. By the time we floated into Bisseau, we were dog-tired and called it a day. The crew had done more than their share for that trip. It was a pleasant town, and I got to know a Customs official. With my little bit of Spanish and his Portuguese, we got along just fine. He invited me to dinner at a local restaurant; it was wonderful food, and the wine was superior. I said I wanted to buy a couple of bottles of wine; would it be possible? He said stand by and not to worry; he would get some. He called somebody to run over to a shop nearby; lo and behold, he came up with a case and had it taken to the hotel. The next

The "Camel's Dick", checkpoint that can be seen fifty miles away. Near El Genina, West Sudan.

morning, he saw us off. We headed for Freetown, Sierra Leone. Again, no one knew anything about a plane coming to pick up a bunch of pilots. If nothing else, we were getting a good look at West Africa!

We spent the night at an RAF Base at Freetown. Actually, the port is called Victoria. To show our appreciation for their hospitality, I broke out several bottles of Portuguese wine; it was appreciated. Our same crew, with Captain Pip and the cabin attendants, all one happy family, were lost in Africa. It was getting exasperating, but we were enjoying the sightseeing tour.

Word came that we were to go back to Monrovia. The next day, we were all bundled off for Monrovia. Here we found that there'd been two DC-3s that had been waiting for several days at the main base, Roberts Field. We finally had made it. Now that we'd gotten to know the crew so well, we hated to leave. We wished our hosts on the clipper ship and Captain Pip a safe journey home, and parted company. When all were accounted for and loaded like lost souls onto the DC-3s, we headed for Accra.

Accra Airport was quite active, with a variety of aircraft scattered about the airfield. There was only one runway, situated on a plateau overlooking part of the town and the ocean. Accra Gold Cost was also British territory, where all driving and familiarities of the British were noticeable.

After clearing the formalities, the group of us were taken by bus to our quarters, some distance from the field but still high on the plateau. There were several groups of barracks (Gifford Camp), low, one story buildings, but neatly built and clean. They were lettered alphabetically. Most of us were assigned to Barracks E, and some were in D. They were very clean and nice, but no air-conditioning. There were nice beds, with mosquito nettings. It was breezy and cool,

due to the sea. It was within walking distance of the mess hall, and the times of meals were posted on the doors. There were two assigned to a room, and Bobby Burke was my roommate.

After a rest and cleanup, we walked to the mess hall. Here, we met a bunch of other pilots in the group. I recognized Frank "Pete" Peterson, with whom I'd learned to fly in our original CPT in Maine. He said there were a few others from that group. It was like old home week, and we talked about the old days, the duck hunting that we had done together. The next morning, the houseboys assigned to our various barracks showed up. Bob and I were pleased with our houseboy. After breakfast, some of us were driven over to meet the Chief Pilot. I met Captain Kris Kristofferson, a tall, fine-looking fellow. His assistant was a Captain Cy Goyette. A scheduler was there, by the name of Bob Blair.

We asked questions about the routes, could we obtain maps, and any other news of when the P-40s would be coming our way. There was no news. We cooled off and got adjusted to our new quarters and way of life, even got used to the local Black Star Beer. There was a local pub downtown, called The Bucket of Blood. It certainly smelled like it. It was always crowded with all walks of life, mainly the British soldiers, or Tommies, as they were called. They were tough cookies; most of them having seen action in the desert.

There was a beach as well. The local villagers had fashioned makeshift surfboards to use. There was one problem with the surf; if you weren't a good swimmer, it could get you in trouble. There was an undertow that quite often developed when the tide was going out. The bottom of the sea was like cement; there was no getting a toehold. It would just draw you out. Several people had been drowned; it was treacherous. A couple of the

*Hotel in Teheran, Iran where PanAm Air ferries stayed 1942.*

*Myself, Kiwi and Jim Fox at entrance to Taj Mahal. January 1943.*

local villagers had elected to become lifeguards.

Village women came by with baskets of fruit on their heads, selling pineapples and bananas. The youths would shimmy up the palm trees that lined the beach. They would shake down green coconuts, and with a machete-like knife, chop off one end and hand you the nut to drink the coconut water.

After a week of this leisure-type living, we were curious about our future and P-40s. After a few days, we were called into a meeting with Kristofferson and the General Manager, General Kraigher. They informed us that the P-40 program was canceled. We would be incorporated into the DC-3 schedule and fly as co-pilots on routes across Africa and other parts of the Middle East. Our first flights would be as supernumerary crews. This would give us an idea of navigation and how the airplane handled, and the use of lowering the gear and flaps. This was better than sitting around and doing nothing.

My first assigned flight was, as most of these other flights, to Lagos, Nigeria, then to Kano, Northern Nigeria, to Maidugri, and to Sudan, El Genina, El Fasha, and the final stop would be Khartoum. From Khartoum, we would head north, up the Nile, to Cairo. From Cairo, across the Suez to Tel Aviv, Palestine, Basra, and Teheran. It was going to be a fascinating trip. All daylight hours, by pilot navigation only. There were no reliable radios, per se.

Our first night was spent at Maidugri; the second was at El Genina. It was here that I was introduced to the one and only friend, which was a giraffe. He always hobnobbed around the garden of our barracks. The manager showed us how, when the giraffe lowered his head, you put your arms around the front of his neck. Then he'd lift you up. You swung your legs around and slid down his neck onto his back. I didn't go for this, because it would be quite a drop if you happened to miss.

Our stop at Khartoum was actually Wadi Sedna. (Wadi in Arabic means creek, ravine, or stream.) Then we went to Cairo. Here, the Australians and the British soldiers were trying to sell captured German Lugers and paratrooper guns. We had our quarters in the outskirts called Heliopolis. It was a residential section, with its own airfield where we kept our airplanes. A local tram or streetcar would take us into Cairo proper. We did this and sampled a lot of the area, mainly a cafe area known as Groppie's, where they served drinks or ice cream. In fact, there were two Groppie's; there was Little Groppie's, which we found out was located in Heliopolis; the one that we visited was Big Groppie's, operated by Greeks.

We enjoyed our stay in Cairo. The next day, we flew across the Suez Canal. I recognized Port Said; my heart leaped. It was here that we had stopped so long ago, on our boat, the Ormonde in '28. We flew on across the Sinai Peninsula, up to Lydda Airport. We couldn't find the airport till we were right over it, the airfield had been so well camouflaged by the British. Lydda was the main airport for Tel Aviv. We checked in at the Gat-Ramon Hotel. The city was well blacked out; it was very difficult to find our way around. The next day, we did have time to go to the beach. We were so surprised to see all the people there, as though there was no war on at all. Everyone wore swimsuits, so we wouldn't know if they had uniforms. What was so fascinating, and an eye-opener, was that the girls were not bashful at all. No matter who was looking, they took off their clothes and put on their swimsuits, right in front of God and everybody!

Next day, the flight took us over Trans-Jordan and Amman, to Basra, Iraq. We overnighted there; it was terribly hot, and we had to stay at RAF barracks. We couldn't wait to get out of the place. No one wanted to move. We were happy to leave and headed for Teheran. It was necessary to climb pretty high to get over the range of mountains that separated Iraq from Iran. This was not too long a flight, but a very interesting one.

After crossing that range, there was the main valley of Iran. Far in the distance, there was another higher ridge of mountains; on the other side was the Caspian Sea. Teheran was nestled in on the side of the highest of the peaks. The mountain rises up to about 18,000 feet, and is quite normally covered with snow the year round. The airport elevation was about 3,000 feet. When we got out, we noticed how fresh and clean the air was. After Basra, this was very pleasant. I noticed a whole row of what looked like Air Force B-26 bombers. The station manager said that they were, but were now handed over to the Russians. They just come along and paint the Air Force star red. They will be gone by tomorrow, he said. We were here to pick up some of the ferry crews that had brought these planes all the way from Miami.

The station manager took us to a lovely hotel on the side of the hill, that had a pool. It was cool and relaxing for us to be sipping scotch and sodas. The streets seemed clean;

on the side of each street there were streams that ran from the mountains. The water ran very fast. It was used for drinking, washing, and whatever. Most shops were selling copperware and silver articles such as lighters, cigarette cases, vases and candlestick holders. Though cheap, I did not buy anything, just did a lot of window shopping and sight seeing. This was June '42.

After two days in Teheran, we got our passengers, about twenty of them, and headed back to Accra the way we had come. On the way, it was agreed that I could do a part of the flying, straight and level. Most of the airplanes had no autopilots. I was eager to get my hands on the yoke and navigate cross-country. By the time we got back to Accra, I was a pretty good hydraulic expert, meaning I could lower the flaps and the gear. The flaps were a bit tricky; I had to know just when to shut the hydraulic power, as the little flap indicator moved along a slide with increment markings.

The next flight took me along the West Africa coast, that stopped at most of the places that our flying clipper had a few weeks previously. We had to skirt and give a wide berth to some of the French possessions, such as the Ivory Coast, and Dakar, Senegal, since the French had capitulated to the Germans and were now known as the Vichy French.

The following week, it was the Cairo flight again, and I almost fell over when I found the Captain of the flight was Wilson York. Wilson was one of our CPT instructors in Bangor, when I first learned to fly. His folks owned the York Cabins in Maine. I was a regular co-pilot now, and no more supernumerary; I could fly the airplane.

The trip was the same routing as before. We overnighted again in Maidugri. The facilities at this station were most primitive. The latrine was about 100 yards from the camp. Early in the morning, before it was even daylight, I took a lantern and went to the biffy. I placed the lantern on the ground, about four or five feet from me, where I sat on a wooden commode. I'd been occupied there for a few minutes when, from the corner of my eye to the left, I thought I saw something move. I looked more closely near the shrubbery, lo and behold, out strode a monster tarantula! I would guess he was bigger than my hand - I mean, he was gigantic. He walked right up to the lantern, then around it. I thought I could see his eyes glisten. I forgot what I had come for, and just sat still. The spider then started to the right and disappeared behind the biffy. I was not going to wait to see what developed next; I grabbed my pants, the lantern, and ran for the barracks. Once there, I finished my paperwork in my room. I told Wilson and the airport man what I had seen, and the size of this tarantula. The airport manager said there were a lot of them around; they would not bite unless really molested. He also said that they can jump quite a distance. This really got me. I'd had visions of the darn thing jumping onto my lap while I was sitting on the pot. I'm not frightened of most animals, but all types of insects, especially spiders and

*Taj Mahal, Agra; with its dome shrouded in bamboo, 1943.*

*Myself, Kiwi Mueller, "Potty" Potschmidt, Jim Fox at Taj Mahal.*

scorpions, get me. As a child in India, I'd had my share of them. I guess I've always hated these creepy, crawly things.

We got away from Maidugri and landed at Khartoum. We overnighted there, and then on to Cairo. After cleanup, Wilson York and I headed for town via the tram. He knew of an Australian who would sell us some German arms, either Lugers or paratrooper guns. The sergeant took us out to his camp, which was quite a ways from town. After he rummaged around through all the paraphernalia in his tent, he finally pulled out two paratrooper guns. They were semi-automatic, with folding stocks and pistol grips. It looked like the pistol grips were of bakelite. The magazine held about 35 rounds of .9mm ammo. Wilson and I each bought one, with a whole lot of ammunition. Next day, with our new purchases tucked away in our rooms, we visited the Pyramids and Sphinx. After having studied about the ancient land in school, it was wonderful to have the opportunity to visit the site and see these wonders of the world in real life.

At Heliopolis it was a beautiful evening, with a bright moon overhead. When there is moonlight in the desert, it is possible to read a newspaper it is so very bright. We finished our meal and were relaxing about nine o'clock, when there was an air raid alarm. There was a mad rush, especially with the Egyptians; they really took off in all directions. There was not much we could do or anywhere we could go. Wilson wasn't with me, but another crew member was; it may have been Kirkpatrick. We decided to go upstairs, onto the roof, and see the action. We were on the roof when we heard bombs exploding around Cairo. Most of the searchlights were in that area. There were a few around the Heliopolis Airport; they were shining their lights like spears into the sky. Soon, from nowhere and from behind where we were, I heard a swishing sound. As we looked, two aircraft, which appeared to be fighter planes (you could almost see the Luftwaffe cross under the wings) dove for Heliopolis Airport. A few seconds later, we heard the bombs explode. Then we heard the roar of motors as they accelerated into the blackness of the sky. They never were spotted by the searchlights, and before we knew it, they were gone. Now dead silence, except for smoke and fire from where they had done their damage. All clear was given after

awhile, and we went downstairs. The Pan Am manager came in and said that we were pretty lucky; a lot of the airport had been damaged, but our plane had not been touched. However, we would not be leaving the next day, until the rubble and some of the potholes had been repaired.

We were allowed to go to the airfield and check our airplane; it was intact. Some of the others were completely demolished, and those that weren't had shrapnel holes. An ack-ack gun emplacement had been hit by the Luftwaffe. We were able to take off the next day for Khartoum.

After leaving Khartoum and heading for El Genina, Wilson and I were eager to try out our guns. We had no passengers; we had some cargo, mainly mailbags. Several windows on these aircraft had plug-type discs that could be taken out for ventilation. I got my gun and went back in the airplane and opened one of the ports. At my signal, Wilson hedgehopped along the desert. I aimed at passing bushes and trees. The gun erupted with rapid fire; I just held the trigger and let her go. There was very little kick, and I could see the sand flying where the bullets were hitting. It was some feeling to see how this gun reacted. Back in the cockpit, I told Wilson that it was a fine weapon. He said okay, that he wanted to try his. He got out of his seat and said for me to fly while he tried out his gun. I enjoyed the chance to sit in the left seat and fly low over the rushing landscape. I could hear the static of the gun. I knew he was enjoying its performance as well. He thought it was much more efficient than our tommyguns. The U.S. guns were heavy and not accurate, because of the violent kicking. This one barely moved when fired.

Wilson, after our conversation, must have noticed how pleased I was to be sitting there in the left. I was all set to get out, when he said, "Why not stay there and try landing it from the left?" Naturally, I was elated. Though Wilson followed me through pretty closely, I did make the landing at El Genina. It was a great feeling and gave me more confidence.

Genina, like most of the stopovers on this route, was still primitive, but not quite so much as Maidugri. All our stations had managers and ground support personnel. We told them about our guns, and that we'd like to go out and try hunting antelope. The manager took us out in the morning, and we cov-

*"The hump".*

ered quite a wide area, but saw nothing in the way of antelope or any warthogs. On the way back to camp, we spotted our friend, the giraffe. He said, "Don't shoot at that one."

On the way to Maidugri, Wilson said he wanted to stop at Fort Lamy, Lake Chad. It was a French occupied territory, but it was Free French. He understood that there was a fellow who sold Canadian Club for a couple dollars a bottle. We were welcomed, and yes, there was an Arab in town who had Canadian Club. Wilson and I shared a case and took off for Maidugri as soon as possible, because we had made an unauthorized stop.

Back in Accra, it was all routine again, as far as our life there was concerned. Most of the time was spent at the beach. I bought a bicycle and did see some of the country. By the end of August, the Italians were wiped out in the northern desert and Rommel had been routed.

The following trip that I was to take was with a new captain, whose name I can't remember. We went as far as Khartoum and were then supposed to return. I should mention that on the way, between Maidugri and Khartoum, there is a very large protrusion of giant rock structure. It could be seen or spotted from at least 50 miles away, a great check point to make sure you were on course. It was actually called Jebu Marra, and rose out of the desert to about 7000 feet. We called it "The Camel's Dick." We were on course for this final trip to Khartoum without any incident. We arrived at Wadi Sedna late that evening, and checked in. There were accidents that had taken place along the route; all flights were not that easy. One had taken off from Wadi Sedna early in the morning and had lost an engine, and crash landed just at the other end of the runway and skidded

off into the desert. No one was hurt. The First Officer, or co-pilot, on that flight was my friend, Tom Carroll. Another crew out of Kano for Genina got caught at night and were lost. There were no ground contacts, because one could see very little at night in the desert. There were no cities as we have over here to follow, or the 50-mile beacon lights. They had made a forced landing near a village in the Sudan, without injury. The copilot on that flight was my 42-A friend, Harry Bernard. These things kept us on our toes.

The manager of the Khartoum station that evening had informed the captain and me that our flight would be taking a side trip the next day; we were scheduled to pick up some passengers from Asmara, Eriteria, which is now Ethiopia. This was an interesting flight, about two hours due east from Khartoum. I could see and feel the change from the desert to the field of green, then the forests and the high mountains. The actual field we were to land at was called Gura; it is a little over 8000 feet altitude. It was a U.S. Military base. Pratt & Whitney had set up an engine overhaul and repairs shop for the B-24s. These were the B-24s that were being shot up out of the desert, and their raids into Europe and Italy. The laborers were mainly Italian prisoners of war, who had capitulated and were eager to work for the Americans. They were happy to be out of the war and, as they said, work for the Yankees.

The captain and I stayed at the Pratt & Whitney facility. One of the best treats was the restaurant, which had real home-style hamburgers and wonderful thick milkshakes. That evening, after supper, a Pratt & Whitney fellow asked if this was our first trip; it was. It was freezing cold, and we hadn't come

prepared. The guy said he had a treat for us. "Have you ever heard of the House of Mirrors?" (A whore house.) No, we hadn't. "I think there's another crew here from Pan Africa, who are already up there." The Pratt & Whitney guy explained, when he was driving, that the house was built by Mussolini for his officers before World War II, when the Italians were fighting Haile Selassie in Abyssinia, as it was called at that time. It was actually located in the city of Asmara, which also was the capitol of Eritria.

When we arrived, I noticed it was a posh place of ill repute, with Italian girls. My curiosity, more than anything, was aroused! The guy left us and said a cab would drop us back. We entered into the rather stately building, with large double doors. A charming, Italian woman greeted us. She must have been about 50 and was no doubt the Madam; certainly not like Madame Zeze's in Honduras. The main living room was elaborately furnished in dark red velvet, heavy upholstery. From nowhere, four or five young girls sauntered in. They wore long evening gowns with low necklines. It was quite obvious they wore nothing under the dresses. They were all Italian, and brunettes; very little English was spoken, and we were welcomed to sit down. One of the girls went to the bar and opened a bottle of champagne. It was cold and tasted good. After the drink, it was now or never; what were our intentions? They were quite attractive young ladies. The captain shrugged his shoulders and said, "Let's go." I didn't know whether he meant out or upstairs; I soon found out. He got up, selected a girl by the arm, and started up the stairs via the balcony and through some doors. So what was I to do? I followed suit. I chose a lovely young lady, who led the way. Her name was Marie. She opened the door to a room, which was one of several along a dimly lit corridor. The door was closed and locked behind us. One small light was on, near the big iron-framed bed. Marie then turned on a much brighter, overhead chandelier light, and I got the significance for the name "House of Mirrors." The whole ceiling was mirrored, so was the wall behind the bed. Wow! Marie then went over to a table, where she hand-cranked an old-style gramophone. The record was one possibly of Caruso, or someone like that. Then out of the cupboard, she took Italian red wine - could have been Dago Red, I don't know. Her English wasn't bad. She was looking forward, she said, to returning to Italy one day, when the war was over. She was sent over when she was very young, in 1937, and had not known much of any other kind of life. Marie wasn't sure if she had a family back in Milan or not, because when the war started, there was no more communication. She said that was basically the same with the other girls. Marie was about 28 years of age. I told her that hopefully the war would be over soon, and she could return to her people. The wine and the record soon finished; it was time to carry on with the job at hand. Marie knew just what to do. She stood up, reached around and unbuttoned her dress at the back; it must have gone all the way down to her behind. The next minute, the dress slipped off her shoulders, and she stood there nude. I went over and switched off the chandelier light. It didn't take long to settle down in the fluffy bed. Marie was a delight. Every once in a while, she had me on my back, so I could not help looking up at the mirror and the performance. It was a whole new experience, but was not really my cup of tea. I guess I was brought up to be old-fashioned. Marie complied with my wishes that we perform the act in the old-fashioned way; I hope the reader will know what that is! There was no rush about this night; in other words, no "wham, bam, thank you ma'am." If you cared for seconds, help yourself. It had been an awful long time since there had been any close relationship with a fair young lady; seconds were in order!

We lay there resting. I went over to the john and cleaned up. I was about to get dressed, and Marie stopped me. "No," she said, "you must come with me." She donned her robe, opened the door and led me by the hand down the hall, me bollicky bare! I expected people to come out from any one of the doors. "It's okay, it's okay," said Marie. At the end of the hall was a glass door. We entered a well lit room; there behind a table was an Italian, dressed in a white gown and a mouth mask. He looked like a physician about to operate. He welcomed me and said, "Put your friend here on the table." Marie pointed to my whistle. "Put it on the table," she said. There wasn't much left to put on the table, after all that exercise we had just been through. I obeyed, and the doctor (as I presume he was) had a bowl of warm water, and from it took a sponge and washed the whole caboodle. I was not allowed to assist; he seemed to be enjoying his work! All cleaned and dry, the doctor then smeared it over with some kind of salve. From a box, he took a small roll of gauze bandage. He wrapped up the whistle, with finesse, then tied a neat bow at the end. He patted it and said, "Be a good boy." At all times, Marie held my hand. I thanked him, and we walked back down the hall, with the bow wagging. I got dressed, and we took another glass of our wine and went downstairs. We sat around, chatting. My pilot came down. We joked a bit about the performance of the doctor. I told Marie that I was married, that my wife, Helen, was expecting a baby in a few months. She was excited for me and wished me well. We said goodbye, then a taxi was arranged and time came to leave. I felt a little sad, leaving the House of Mirrors and Marie. I hope she made it back to Milan and rejoined her family. I hope they all are very happy now. That was our first and last visit to Asmara.

Back in Accra, I decided to try out my paratrooper gun again. I took another friend, and we walked some distance behind our barracks. In a field, there were several large - and I mean large - anthills. Most of the earth in Accra and along that coast, in that country, is not earth or mud as we know it; it's laterite, a thick, red, composition type of earth. The anthills were constructed of this;

*At the Royal Calcutta Golf Club; enjoying a gin and ginger-beer, a speciality of the club.*

the ants build them into large pinnacles that stand about six or seven feet high. I chose one, and standing about thirty yards away, let off a burst of fire. The anthill erupted with flying laterite. My friend also had a go at it. It really was a fine gun, and knocked heck out of the anthill. We had riddled it pretty much, then walked over to see the damage. The mound that was left was alive with ants. I decided to retrieve a bullet or two, to see if it mushroomed or stayed whole, or what kind of damage it did to itself. I took a long stick and started digging away at a lot of the loose laterite. I had to stick it quite aways into the large cavity and saw a bullet. I was about to take the stick out and reach in with my hand for the bullet. Just then, a large claw came out and grabbed the stick. My reflex caused me to jerk the stick out, and still clinging to it as I pulled, out came an enormous scorpion! He was big and dark green, almost an iridescent sheen on his ribbed back. He was quite bristly and was trying to sting the stick with his tail. We got him on the ground, where he stood with tail cocked over, ready to do battle. I got a fair-sized piece of rock and struck him on the back, near his thorax. I broke the stick in two and carried this large insect, chopstick fashion, back to the verandah. Someone got a ruler, and the scorpion measured nearly ten inches. I took it to our clinic where the PA doctor got a jar and filled it with alcohol, and placed the scorpion in it. He kept it all the time I was in Accra. He said he was going to take the scorpion back to the United States, and keep it as a showpiece for people who were interested in insects. Needless to say, I didn't go back to the anthill to look for any more bullets.

I was on another flight, a special charter that took us to Kaduna, Nigeria. A B-26 on its ferry flight had crashed on the bank of the Niger River. The crew members were alive but were in the hospital with broken limbs. The airport in the area was bright green, with lush grass. We were allowed to land, after the cattle had been cleared form the field. The RAF had a small base there.

We spent the night, and visited the pilots in the hospital. Next morning, still in casts and bandages, they were placed on stretchers into our airplane. The stretchers were tied down well in the center of the airplane aisle. The tie downs were thoroughly inspected to make sure they could not break loose in any way during the flight, or in turbulence. One of the pilots said that both engines had quit while cruising at 7000 feet. The only place to land was the river bank.

When I got back to my room that afternoon, I noticed the lock on my trunk had been broken open. I pulled the trunk out from under the bed. I found that my paratrooper gun and my Smith & Wesson revolver were missing. I was angry and upset. I called the houseboy and asked who had been here while I was away. He didn't know; my roommate, Bobby Burke was on a trip. Someone must have known the place would be empty for a couple of days. I went to the Chief Pilot's office, Captain Kristofferson, and told him. There was little that could be done. I was terribly upset. I didn't think it would be the houseboy; it had to be someone from the camp who knew I had the weapons. On my next trip to Cairo, I might get another gun. As luck would have it, I did take another trip. This time, after we had left Khartoum, it was late in the afternoon. Halfway up, we were told that we were not going to be able to make it into Cairo, that we'd have to land at an auxiliary airport on the Nile, which was called Luxor Airport. Luxor was the famous place of the ancient Pharaohs, where the Valley of the Kings is located.

We got in late in the evening, and stayed at a place called "The Winter Palace Hotel." The bartender, Azziz, made the famous Azziz Gin Fizzes. I could barely wait to finish my meal to find out if there was a possibility of seeing some of the tombs of the Pharaohs, namely, Tutankhamen. Several people said yes, it could be arranged. The Captain and I soon were in a taxi that took us to the Nile. Then, by boat across the river; from there another taxi took us to the Valley of the

*In PanAm summer uniform, Karachi, India. Pakistan wasn't invented then.*

Kings. Though very quick, it was a trip I'll never forget. We were shown many of the tombs by fluorescent type of light that they burned. This was the only lighting system available at that time. We had no cameras, but were intrigued by all these deep underground tombs, with all the Hieroglyphics and various designs on the walls. We must have spent at least two hours looking around, and were very thankful, especially me, for having had this opportunity.

The next morning, we left early. In Cairo, I couldn't find the Australian who was selling the paratrooper guns, but I found another fellow who sold me a Luger. It was a fine weapon. I also had to buy some more ammunition. This was my last trip to Cairo.

In Accra, I got to know a lot of the South African Air Force personnel, who came to pick up Ventura bombers that were ferried over. They were a great group of pilots. We had a lot of fun with them. Parties were frequent in one or the other's barracks, with quantities of Black Star Beer. We exchanged mementos, badges, and wings.

Towards the end of September, Captain Kristofferson informed all crews that the United States Air Force was going to take over the Pan American operations, that the Pan Am pilots, all of us, could stay over and join the Air Force here, or we could return to Miami and be a part of Pan American Airways. It was about this time that we learned that the group here with Pan Am Africa were not part of Pan American's system or its seniority list. We all would have our little meetings and discuss what we should do. I had my own ideas. If the Air Force would take me now, well over the age of 26 1/2, then I should have a say. I would join as a Captain, in India, where I spoke the language. I talked to Captain Kris, who was very understanding, and told him I wanted a trip to India. He

said fine, that he would put me on the next flight to Karachi. That flight would not be for a couple weeks, about the end of September. A lot of my friends were packing up for Miami. Some said they would join TWA or Eastern, and a few would stay on with Pan Am and fight the seniority status.

More and more military crews started moving in with DC-3s having Air Force markings. I had my final birthday party with some of the gang and South African fellows. It was a good bash. I was now 28. One of the last Pan Am flights was set for Karachi, and I was placed on it. I packed my things, less the guns, but I did have my Luger, and said farewell to Captain Kristofferson, my friends, and the houseboy. In parting, I gave the houseboy my bicycle.

The route to Karachi was the same all the way to Khartoum, and at Khartoum, Captain Nasholds fell ill. It was necessary to find a replacement. It took a couple of days to do so. The pilot was an Air Force Second Lieutenant, and had just checked out on the DC-3. Between the two of us, we felt we could get the plane to Karachi.

I was excited about returning to India. It had been 14 years since we'd all sailed out of Colombo. I could already hear the brain-fever birds, and the vendors calling their wares at the railroad stations. I thought of eating all those Indian sweetmeats that I'd always known as a child, gilabees, gulab-jamons, and balushsis; I drooled. The moment came, we departed Khartoum for Aden. We climbed high; the new skipper was not familiar, but luckily, I had come this way once before. We passed over near Asmara to our left, and I thought of the House of Mirrors and Marie.

From 12,000 feet, we started our descent while we were over the Red Sea. We circled Aden, and I saw the port where we once anchored. At moments, I felt that it never happened, yet I knew it had; almost as though it had been yesterday. The airfield was a ways from the city; it was dry and dusty. The RAF were in control here and took good care of us. We stayed at their facility and enjoyed their pub and mess hall. The place was stifling hot, and the overhead fans did little to relieve the heat.

The next morning saw us on our way again. The early morning was sultry, the sea was an oily green, and there was very little breeze. The next stop was Masera Island, off the Oman coast. As the plane circled, I noticed there was not a tree or shrub to be seen. The runway was oil and sand, the windsock at midpoint. Thank goodness we were only stopping for fuel. The next leg, to Karachi, would be a long haul. As we parked, I noticed several military aircraft, mostly RAF Blenheim bombers. The person in charge was one of our old Pan Am pilots, who had joined the Air Force and was now based here. How anyone could stand the island, I don't know. I was happy when the tanks were full, and we were on our way again.

It was my leg to fly, and the new captain let me do so from the left seat. It would be great, coming back to India, flying an air-

plane. (I keep referring Karachi to India. Pakistan was not invented yet, and would not be until August 1947.) The course was due north along the Oman coast, then across the Gulf of Oman till we came to the coast of Iran and India, near the fishing village of Jiwani. Here we turned easterly. The coast was barren until we were approaching Karachi. I descended to 1500 feet, now I recognized some of the vegetation, especially the Babul trees, thorny little trees with feathery leaves. The airport was easily recognized by a tremendous, large building on the west side of the field. It was a black hangar built especially for a dirigible. After landing, a U.S. jeep with a "Follow Me" sign drove up and signaled us to follow him. We parked near the terminal. We did not go through any Customs or Immigration formalities. There was a great deal of activity at the terminal and ramp, military personnel and other uniformed people, too numerous to mention. It was exciting for me to pass through the terminal and have Indian porters carrying our bags. It could have been the old Bareilly station, when my folks and I were changing to the narrow gauge to go to Kathgodam.

There was a mad scramble outside, the taxi drivers pushing and shoving, vying for our services. Pan Am had a station wagon on hand to take us into town. I just stood, staring and listening to the noise and the babble of the Hindi, the crows and the mynah birds. There were circling hawks, which we call cheels. It's a falcon-type bird, turned scavenger through the generations. I was thinking of all the experiences that had happened to me since I left India in 1928, and now I'd returned. Had all that really happened? Did I once live in America, and Maine? Was there archery? Did I know of Horace Chapman, or a Sylvia? Did I live in Westfield? Did I play football? Did I go to Central America, and climb all those times on Mount Kathahdin, looking for Bob Burge? My mind was spinning as we took the road into town. It was Drigh Road. The Indian driver spoke broken English, and said that we were going to stay out at another section of town, near the sea, called Clifton.

When we approached the city of Karachi, I noticed more humanity, a lot of pariah dogs, swarms of crows. Now there were horse and buggies; I remembered them from long ago. We used to call them Ghora Gharis. We turned left at an intersection and headed across a wide open area of flats, and arrived at a residential area, where there were lovely European-style homes. The driver pulled up to one that was quite spacious. That was the Pan Am House, called "Green Briar." All luggage was taken out, and a bearer came and carried our things in. I was still half-dazed to think I was really back in my homeland, after fourteen years. There were other people there, mostly U.S. Military. I did not let anyone know at this time that I spoke Hindi - Urdu. I pretended to be a real Yankee.

The building was a mansion. The Captain and I had separate rooms. The bearer put my things down and tidied up the room.

He opened the windows and I felt a cool sea breeze. I didn't have any rupees or change to give as a tip; I said I would take care of him later. He salaamed and left. It was late afternoon, and the sun was starting its journey downhill into the sea. There were myriad birds, but no brainfever birds. I cleaned up, hung my clothes in an almira (a box-like closet), and came downstairs. There were a few fellows around the bar, with an Indian barkeep. I saw my Captain friend; we sipped a few beers. He said this was not for him; he thought the city dirty and terrible. He wanted, hopefully, to leave for Accra as soon as possible. I kept my secret, and he was due to leave within a couple of days, poor guy.

An American Lieutenant-Colonel came in, clean-cut, uniform of olive green jacket and pants called "pinks." It was the U.S. Air Force military dress uniform. He carried a swagger stick, a British officer's tradition. I noticed he wore regular Air Force wings on his left chest, and an RAF wing on his right; rather unusual, I thought. He ordered a scotch and soda. I excused myself from my Captain friend, and went over and introduced myself to the Colonel. He was the Commanding Officer of the Karachi Base. I changed my drink from beer to scotch and soda. He was easy to talk to, and he liked India. He had served with the RAF before joining the USAF. I don't remember his name. I was glad to have met the Colonel, as I intended to meet him later on. I needed someone to talk to in order to have a replacement as a co-pilot position for the return trip to Accra; as I planned to get off here. This was a good opportunity to approach the Colonel with the prospect of finding another pilot. He told me to come to the airport the next day, and he would check into the matter. He felt sure there would be someone available.

The dining hall was fairly large. I returned to my friend, and we had our dinner together. It felt good to sit and have a bearer serving the meals, to know that I would not have to get up and wash the dishes like a masalchee. I mentioned my plans to the Captain. He was not too surprised, but couldn't understand why I wanted to stay in India. "One of those things," I said. I'd be going to the airport in the morning, with the C.O., to locate my replacement. I slept like a log. I was awakened by a gentle knock on the door, early in the morning. I opened the door and there stood a bearer with a small tray of tea and toast. "Oh, my God!" I thought, "Chota Hazari!" When was the last time I'd had that? Seemed like a hundred years ago. I ushered him in, and he set the tray on a table. The tea served in India is like no where else. It has a special flavor, maybe because they use boiled buffalo milk. There was a little doily over the milk jar. It was of a mosquito-type gauze, with glass beads sewn all around it; the beads kept the gauze firmly over the top. I enjoyed the tea and toast, as I sat near the window, looking out towards the sea. It must have been near there somewhere where my school chum Billy Watson drowned in 1924.

I had breakfast with the C.O., and then left in his staff car. A short distance out of

*Kunming Lake*

*Kunming Lake and "Windy Hill".*

town, there was an RAF man, hitchhiking a ride to the airport. The C.O. had the driver stop and pick up the pilot. He sat in front with the driver. The C.O. asked his base, and he said he was based in Lahore, Punjab. When he turned to talk, I noticed his name tag; it was "F. Cotton." I asked if he was from India. He said he was; he was born in the Punjab. I asked if he had any relatives named Cotton in the Kumaon District, the town of Bhowali. He was surprised I knew the place. He said yes, Fred Cotton was a cousin. He had been there and stayed at their hotel. Small world, I thought. The C.O. was quick to pick this up and asked me how I knew about that town. I'd let the cat out of the bag. It was then I told the Colonel and the young pilot the story of myself and my childhood in India, mainly Bhowali, and knowing the Cottons. The RAF pilot was also intrigued to know that an American lived in India. The Colonel said he'd detected a slight English accent. Americans thought I had one, and yet the English said I had an American accent; I still don't know either way.

We dropped Pilot Cotton off at the terminal. As soon as the Colonel had finished with his morning visitors and paperwork, we sat down to talk. He asked if I'd consider joining the U.S. Air Force. I said I'd tried the day of Pearl Harbor, but was turned down because I was a few months too old. He said he'd see to it that I'd be made a Captain and fly routes in India. It sounded good and not as scary as flying to China. I said I'd consider it, and I'd let him know over a scotch and soda that evening.

While I was at the bar enjoying my scotch, a tall blond, good looking fellow strolled in. He wore a different type of uniform than the rest of the military around the bar. He introduced himself as Cliff Groh. He stated that he had been flying for the American Volunteer Group (AVG), in Burma and China, and had now transferred to China National Aviation Corporation (CNAC). He was on his way to the States to bring back a DC-3 for the company. Cliff asked me if I knew of any flight that may be headed for West Africa. He wanted to get to Miami as soon as possible. I said to stand by; I would talk to the Commanding Officer. I was able to get back to Cliff a little later and told him that I had phoned to the Colonel at the field. The Colonel said he would arrange things as soon as the next flight came through. He thought Cliff Groh could be placed on as an

extra crew. This put Cliff at ease. We then sat at the bar till dinner. During this interim, I had been talking to the bearers in Hindi. He was intrigued in the way I was gabbing with the locals. Curiosity got the best of him, and he asked, "How come you are able to speak the lingo so easily with these guys?" I thought this over for a moment, then looked Cliff in the eye and said; "Cliff, I have been here almost ten days now, and it has been easy to pick up!" He gave me a sly look and knew I was kidding. After a good laugh, I confessed to him that I had been born in India and told Cliff a little bit about my early life. He thought that was great and would come in handy.

When the next Pan Africa came in, the first officer was one of my friends from the Miami days, Tom Carroll. A fine young fellow with a lot of humor and laughs, everyone liked Tom. The flight would be returning in a couple of days, and I was able to get Cliff on the flight. I was glad I had some time with Cliff and discussed CNAC with him. Tom said he probably would be joining the Air Force in Accra when he got back from this trip. I wished him all the luck in the world. It would be years later before I would see Tom again.

It was now November 1942, and the weather was getting cooler and more pleasant. I spent some of the time visiting downtown Karachi. The main street in Karachi was known as Elephanstone Street. It had different types of shops. Some were quite European, with men's clothing and souvenirs. I would window shop from one end to the other.

One day, the C.O. said he needed a co-pilot for a flight to Calcutta and back. I jumped at the chance. The flight stopped at Agra, home of the Taj Mahal. When we arrived there, I was disturbed to notice that the whole beautiful dome of the Taj was covered in bamboo matting. Someone said it had been cracked by an earthquake, that it was being fixed. Another said it was camouflage. I believed the latter. (Agra was just a short distance from Aligarh, where I was born.)

The next day, after about a 3 1/2 hour flight, the flight landed at Dum-Dum Airport, Calcutta. This is where the famous Dum-Dum bullet got its name; they were first manufactured here, at Dum-Dum, during the mutiny in 1857. The taxi drive to Calcutta was a long, hazardous trip, on a two-way

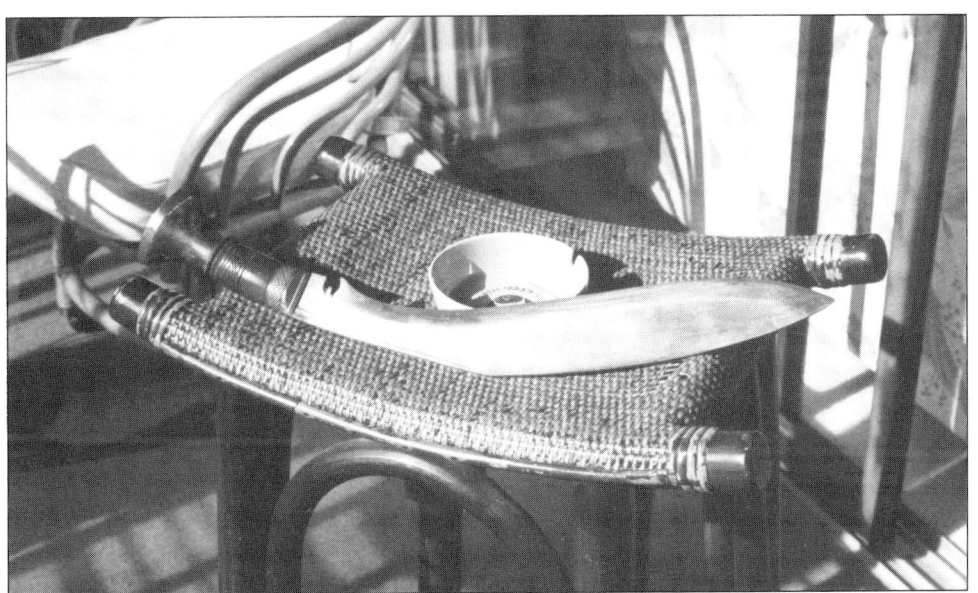

*The knife I traded from the PanAm agent for the steel trunk in Karachi, 1942.*

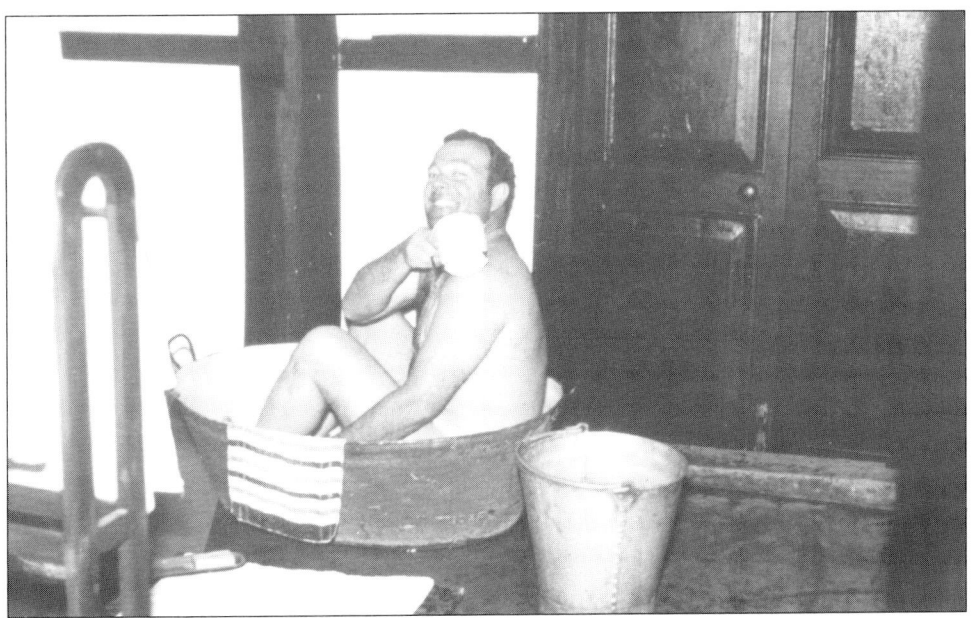

*A typical Indian bathroom and tub.*

road which is very narrow. Traffic was horrendous; that, and the cows, the buffaloes, goats, and the people, all trying to navigate on the same road, was something else. The closer we got to the city, the worse the traffic. We finally arrived at the Grand Hotel. I recognized it at once as the same hotel where we'd stayed in 1928, when we were arranging our visas with the U.S. Consulate. The streets were worse than Karachi; I had never seen so many beggars. I don't remember seeing that in 1928. It was probably due to the number of troops coming to Calcutta. At the new market I bought a genuine kukri knife. We had 24 hours, then back to Karachi, via Agra.

The weather was good; the flight wasn't far enough north that I could see the Ganges and perhaps get a glimpse of Monghyr, where my father died. Another time, perhaps. In Karachi, I showed the Kukri off at the bar.

Most of them that were sold at the shops were locally made, with artificial stones and beads, much smaller and poor imitations. This was the real genuine thing; nothing fancy, but good and sharp, that would probably cut a goat's head off with one swish. The Pan Am agent fell in love with it and wanted to know if I'd sell it to him. I said no, but I would consider a trade for that very fine steel trunk he had. It was a Pan Am trunk, used for carrying catering equipment and other things on the clippers; it was gray colored. A deal was made, and we swapped. I could get another knife, I thought, on the next trip.

The C.O. said there would be a flight to Chabua, Assam in the next couple of days that I could deadhead (extra crew). The U.S. Air Force crew and myself left in two days, and our first stop was Pelham Airport, Delhi. Delhi was fairly cold; it was right after Thanksgiving Day, early December, and we

checked in at the Taj Hotel in Old Delhi. It was more of a hostel than a hotel, because so many troops were coming and going. Beds were scattered all over the place; just pick one. Another crew came in and took their cots. I was surprised to see a full-fledged U.S. Colonel place his gear on a bed near me. He introduced himself as Colonel Doctor Flickinger. We hit it off right away. He was checking a lot of the military clinics, then was coming to Assam, probably Chabua; to be based there permanently. He was interested in hunting and hoped to someday shoot a tiger. I said he was going in the right direction, to eastern India.

The next day, the Colonel and I visited a couple of gun shops in Delhi. We were recommended to visit a famous gun place called Manton's, in Old Delhi. We saw quite a few guns, though nothing of interest to us. The ones they had were very expensive. That was our tour of shopping. That afternoon, the temperature warmed up, so we decided to visit a Mogul tomb, of one called Humayan, who was one of the emperor Moguls of the 16th century. The tomb is just outside of Delhi. While walking through the spacious, lovely gardens, I heard it for the first time; I stopped in my tracks and listened - it was the call of the brainfever bird. Doc asked what I had stopped for. I said, "Listen to that bird." It was in the distance, but clearly heard. We waited till it called, starting with a number of notes, getting louder and louder and more shrill at the end; it sounded as though it was clearly saying "brainfever, brainfever." I told the Doc about the bird that was called the brainfever bird, because of its call. He said it sounded weird. I said it was unusual for it to be calling now; normally, it called continuously during the hot weather, just before the break of the monsoons. Most people detested the cry, maybe because of the hot weather. I loved it; I grew up with the sound; my day was made. I felt at ease as it called several times. I felt I was in Monghyr, or in Khatgodam. It sent my mind back, all those years. How I wished my mother could hear the call now. We walked further, and the guide continued explaining about Humayan and the great Mogul Empire that once was.

Doc and I retired that evening after we had a few drinks. The next morning, I met the pilot who would be flying me to Chabua. At Pelham Airport, I followed him when he got his weather briefing. Most of the way would be clear, except nearing the Assam Valley and Shillong. There would be a lot of cloud coverage; Chabua would be clear. I looked at the route we'd be taking. We would be going along the Ganges till it met the Brahmaputra, then follow the Brahmaputra northeast to Assam, with the Shillong hills on the right; the great Himalayas and Darjeeling on the left. We would first pass near or perhaps over Patna and very close to Monghyr. I told the Captain if the weather was clear and there was a break, that possibly we could circle the area. I'd point it out. He said there would be no problem.

Passing over Patna, at about 7,000 feet on top of the overcast, there were a few breaks, but not enough. I think we had passed Monghyr. I searched and searched, but couldn't see any breaks. I was so disappointed not to see the town.

We turned and flew north, along the Brahmaputra where I could see the Shillong Hills on the right. In the distance to the left, the high mountains rose up into the sky. It was not long before we saw well-quilted tea estates, all along the valley. Soon, there was an open spot with a lot of buildings, which turned out to be the main base of the Air Force, Chabua. We circled and landed.

The crew taxiied up and stopped at the terminal, which was nothing more than a basha, a straw and bamboo hut. Everything was unloaded, including all my goods and chattels, my nice steel trunk, suitcases and boxes. I was led to one of the bashas where the crew would be staying. They gave me a cot and said that was it. The next morning at the mess, I asked somebody where the CNAC office was. The officer in charge said their place was an airfield called Dinjan. "I'll get a guy assigned to drive you over in a jeep, and talk to the people." The sergeant and I drove off through the tea estates. It was interesting to see a much different type of scenery and foliage than I was used to as a kid in United Province.

Dinjan was about 10 miles away. We came to a gate and a driveway, where I saw a "building on stilts," made of wood, probably teak and mahogany. In the front yard, there was a man and a girl playing badminton. I got out and the guy came over; I asked him if this was the CNAC bungalow. The man, a stocky fellow with a shock of black hair, came up to me and said yes, this was CNAC, and what could he do for me? I introduced myself. He said he was Captain Hugh Woods (Woody) and that was his wife, Mage. I said that I understood CNAC was looking for pilots. "I don't believe it," he said. "We've been sending people over to Pan Am looking for pilots, and here you come, walking out of the tea patches' in Assam, of all places." He laughed some more.

I thanked the sergeant who brought me over. I sat with Captain Woods and gave him a verbal resume of my flying experience. I said that I had about 300 hours as a co-pilot in the DC-3 with Pan Africa; my total was about 800 hours. When I said I spoke Hindi, he was pleased. Woody said he would write a letter to the Chief Pilot's office in Calcutta. They did the actual hiring, but he didn't see any problem; that I would be able to talk with a Chuck Sharp and William "Bill" MacDonald, or perhaps Frank Higgs. Woods explained CNAC and its background, that there were approximately 16 aircraft with old DC-3s from Pan American in the States. Two or three of them were being used as passenger planes based in Calcutta. A few of the pilots were in the States and would be returning early in 1943. Woody said a few of the pilots would be coming in this evening from Kunming, across the "Hump." It was called the "Hump"

*The CNAC bungalow in Dinjan, 1944. (Courtesy of Capt. Giff Bull [CNAC])*

because the route to China was over the spur of the Himalayas that ran north and south; the aircraft had to fly at least 15,000 to 18,000 feet. Further north, the mountains were even higher. He told me that there was a spare cot in one of the rooms upstairs in the bungalow where I could dump everything. A bearer came in and asked about the laundry. I asked his name; he said it was Suklo. I said I would have laundry for him in a few moments. Then I sprang it on him. I said in Hindi that I needed a hot bath. He gave the biggest grin ever. What I had said was "Garram-Gussal tier karro humarhwasta;" that is, "I need a hot bath for me." I could hear him telling the other servants out back the new sahib spoke excellent Hindi!

Throughout India, other than the large cities, most of the hot water for baths is prepared in large old kerosene tins, with the tops cut out and a heavy wire across the top for a handle. These are set on wood stoves. They normally turn pitch black from heat and soot. The bathrooms, as well, are rudimentary, with: a commode; an area set apart that holds a zinc tub that's just big enough for a grown person to scooch into, with knees up around his chin; a tin mug, always handy to pour water over oneself; a small rack with soap, usually carbolic; and another rack for towels. Suklo announced that my bath was ready, in Hindi. He watched my expression. I smiled and acknowledged. I enjoyed the tub; I splashed water and it felt good. Once I had finished and dried off, I stepped into my room; there Suklo had found my clothes and laid out new underwear, shirt, pants and socks. I chuckled; it was typical of a bearer.

I got dressed and wandered out to a fair-sized porch on the same upstairs level. It was late afternoon and the weather was cool; birds were everywhere. Suklo came out shortly with a tray of tea and what turned out to be cinnamon toast; it was great.

Woody and Mage normally would go out

to the Dinjan Airport in the afternoon to do some of the scheduling and meet the flights as they returned from the Hump trip. He would check the maintenance squawks and see that all planes arrived back safely, without any incident, then drive back with the crews. Woody and Mage had their own quarters somewhere else. The tea planters' bungalow had been leased from the people known as Proudfoot. They sere Scotch folks who managed the tea estate.

I enjoyed the tea. At dusk I heard a van approaching. It was a weapons carrier/military van. Six or seven pilots emerged from the van with their flight kits. They wore officers caps, leather jackets with Chinese flags on the backs, khaki uniforms and heavy boots; some of these were mosquito boots, perhaps from Natal. They came up the stairs and I introduced myself. They were all Americans. They howdied and went to their rooms to change. These were the Hump pilots; they looked seasoned. They called for Suklo. Each pilot came out to the verandah later and introduced themselves again. They looked my uniform over and asked where I had come from. I said I was from West Africa, that I was with Pan Africa and that it had folded. I was now interested in flying for CNAC. They said I'd be hired, since the company was short of pilots. Soon, Suklo brought out a bottle of gin and grapefruit juice; also some cut limes and soda. One of the fellows, who called himself Charles Sharkey asked me to have a drink with him. The booze here was usually bottles that belonged to the individuals, which they'd brought up from Calcutta. I poured a gin and looked at the label on the bottle, which read, "Carew's Distilled Gin" made in India. Sharkey barely looked old enough to have a drink, let alone fly an airplane across the Hump. He said he came from Lawrence, Massachusetts.

I met and remembered two of the other pilots; we will note why shortly. One was Skippy Lane, and the other was called "Pri," for Privencal. Sharkey said there should be a flight for Calcutta in a few days, to check the schedule that was always posted on the main door. Sharkey gave me a map to ponder over. It had a few routes to Kunming and Chungking.

I enjoyed relaxing at the bungalow and having my chota-hazari early in the morning, looking over the map and enjoying long walks along the pathways between the tea hedges. I even found my way down to the Brahmaputra River. I saw a tea pickers' village and chatted with some of the local villagers. I asked about the hunting possibilities in and around here. They said most of the shooting was across the river. The farmers there were pestered with deer, mainly sambhur, that loved eating their crops. Yes, there were tigers and leopards, too. Not much black partridge, but a lot of jungle fowl and duck. They all seemed interested in me and how an American was able to speak Hindi so fluently, almost like a native.

About the third day, I looked at the schedule; there was a flight to Calcutta, with me as extra crew. It was suggested I take all my gear and belongings with me, that it would be awhile before flying, and I would probably get a place to live in Calcutta. The pilot of this flight would be Charles Sharkey. Since the van was pretty crowded, Captain Woods took me out in the jeep. The distance to the field at Dinjan is about twelve miles on a very bumpy, dusty road. The airplanes were all camouflaged in olive drab, with a large black circle and white Chinese insignia or marking, which I understood to mean "Chung," or "National." Dinjan had one building at the south end of the ramp, which was our terminal and a local customs shack. The aircraft were lined up on the north side of the ramp, facing the building. CNAC crews, at this time, consisted of a U.S. Captain, a Chinese co-pilot, and a Chinese radioman. There were a few others deadheading to Calcutta that morning. None were as excited as me. I thanked Woody for the hospitality, and looked forward to seeing him again as a bona fide crew member. He was sure I would. It was not long before Sharkey had the aircraft loaded and airborne, headed south. I think the flight was a little more than three hours, that took us over the Shillong hills, along the plains of Bengal and the city of Dacca, which is now the capital of Bangladesh. Sharkey touched down neatly at Dum-Dum Airport and taxiied up to the CNAC Terminal. Everything was unloaded by the coolies employed by CNAC. I don't know how I missed not coming directly here when I came to Calcutta with the Air Force, a little over a month ago. Anyway, here I was, and Sharkey took me in to meet the CNAC Managers.

I met Chuck Sharp, a little fellow with a round baby face and a pleasant smile. He parted his hair almost in the middle. Sharkey didn't give me a chance; he said, "Chuck, here's a new pilot for ya." I gave him Captain Woods' letter, and Chuck smiled. Evidently Woody told him something about my wandering into CNAC compound from the

tea bushes. Captain Frank Higgs joined us. Higgs was about my size, lean and dark-complected, rather hairy, with heavy eyebrows that met in the middle above his eyes. His eyeteeth were a bit prominent, but very white against his dark skin. He smoked a pipe.

They asked about my flying career. I told them about CPT and Pan Am Air Ferries training, about Pan Africa and the DC-3s, and the time I had in them. Chuck's Chinese secretary placed a form in front of me, and I was told to fill it out. It seems that in the aviation business, one is always filling out one type of form or another. After Chuck and Frank Higgs had looked over the form contract, they shook my hand and welcomed me to CNAC. Sharkey did, too; he was waiting to take me to town. We were going to stay at the Grand Hotel, which I already knew. Chuck also arranged for me to get some money. My salary was to be $400.00 a month as a co-pilot or junior captain, until I checked out as a full-fledged captain. Then I would receive a base pay of $800.00 a month, and after 70 hours of flying, I would receive $20.00 an hour. The average flying for a captain was around 120 hours per month. Every year, I'd get a raise of $100.00, up to a maximum of $1200.00 per month base pay. In those times, it was a fortune. I picked up a packet of rupees, and Charles Sharkey and I headed for town.

The drive into the city was always a thriller. One never knew if it would be made. It never failed that there would be a traffic jam along the way, because a buffalo cart was making a u-turn on the road. It was not easy, since the carts had old-fashioned iron and wood wheels that had no turning capability. The arc was always wider than the road, so the cart driver usually had to back up a couple of times to complete the turn. There were two or three of these excursions, going one way or the other. A car dare not hit one of these carts, especially the oxen. You might have the whole neighborhood on you in a minute, with sticks and bricks at the windows. The oxen are sacred animals to the Hindus.

Fortunately, the winter season was now approaching, and the weather was cool. We got to the hotel and checked in. Due to the influx of military personnel and scarcity of hotels and rooms, we were lucky, because CNAC had an "in" with the management. CNAC steered a lot of business their way. Charles and I had to share a room, however.

It seemed I was always packing and unpacking my belongings; the story of my life. Now I was unpacked again. I kept the steel trunk locked. It contained my Luger. Charles and I came down to the ground floor, where there was a semi-open patio, with a fountain in the center and a few palm trees and bushes. Individual tables were scattered around. When the bearer appeared, I ordered gin and ginger beer, a taste for which I acquired in Delhi when I was with Doc Flickinger. We sat and enjoyed the drinks and atmosphere. It was hard to believe that, for all the sincerity, gentility, coolness and re-

finement, that just 20 or 25 yards away, down the foyer and out on the sidewalk, there was such poverty you could hardly believe; people begging, others lying on the sidewalk, covered only with burlap; and further down, a woman lying on the sidewalk menstruating, with flies and pariah dogs hovering near her. Even as a child, I had not seen this depravity. No one seemed to notice or care; they just walked on by as though nobody was there.

We stayed indoors; there was no reason to go anywhere else. We had our lunch in the hotel and went back upstairs to rest, the same as everyone else does in India, during the noon and afternoon hours. The ceiling fans were not necessary. I guess I must have dozed off, for when I woke and looked at my Horace Chapman watch, it was after four o'clock, and Charlie was in the biffy. The toilets at the hotels were a little more civilized: the johns flushed, but not until you pulled the chain a few times; there was a shower with hot water. We got cleaned up and came back down to the bar at 5:30 or thereabouts. That's when everything comes to life.

I changed my drink to scotch and soda, and Charlie asked if I liked Chinese food. I said I'd never had any. He said he knew a place that had excellent Chinese food, that I should get used to it, as I would be eating an awful lot of Chinese food when I started flying for CNAC. I noticed most of the beggars and starving humanity had disappeared off the streets in the evening. As we stepped out onto the sidewalk, we hailed a taxi. There was a blackout in the city; all cars had most of their headlights with the top half painted black. The cars looked as though they were half-asleep, as did the people. We wandered through a maze of little streets and big streets and dirty lanes, on and on. Finally, we came to Calcutta's Chinatown. We stopped at a two story building, fairly well lit in spite of the blackout. I saw the sign, the Nanking Restaurant. "This is it." The Sikh driver was paid. (Most of the drivers in these cities are large built Sikhs, with bright colored turbans and long beards tucked under their chins, and always wearing steel bracelets as part of their religion.)

A Chinese gentleman greeted us at the top of the stairs. He said he was the owner and his name was Peter Young. The floor was white tile and clean. The tables were all set with cloth napkins; in India, they called them serviettes. All restaurants and hotels used cloth napkins. I let Charles Sharkey do the ordering, and while we were waiting for the food, we indulged in more drinks. The food came in fancy bowls, decorated with Chinese artwork. Charles Sharkey said I had to eat with chopsticks. I said, "Why, when all the tables have knives and forks?" He said "You'd better learn the art of eating Chinese-style, or starve." Sharkey gave me my first lesson in eating Chinese food with chopsticks. My right thumb muscle and forefingers were sore after an hour of trying to eat with sticks, but damned if I'd give up! Finally, it worked, and I enjoyed the food. It was customary to spill and drop food all over the table. I had done my share. Peter Young said that the Chinese felt that if you did spill your food, it meant that you enjoyed the meal. I don't remember too much of the menu, or the names of the dishes, but some of them were exotic; such as shark's-fin soup, chicken fried rice, boneless roast duck, sweet and sour pork. They were all strange names to me; it was more than enough. A lot went to waste, and I thought of the poor beggars in front of the hotel.

One of the servants called us a taxi. (The taxis, by the way, in Calcutta, were old pre-war American-made Oaklands, touring cars, something like the old Ford of Christine and Robert's.) I had gorged on good food and felt bloated, but it was good. My thumb and fingers still ached from the use of chopsticks. We got back to our room, and it didn't take me long to fall asleep. I don't know what it is, perhaps due to some strange metabolism in me, but I have a horrible habit of waking up early in the morning, no matter what hour I go to bed. My average sleep is always about four to five hours. Whatever the reason, I was up at the crack of dawn the next day. I had my chota-hazari downstairs and was off for a brisk walk.

The Grand Hotel faces onto the Chowringee Street, probably one of the more notable streets of Calcutta. It's a wide thoroughfare; on the further side of it runs a tramway. Beyond that stretches a large open area called a Maidan. Maidan is a Hindi name for parade ground. In this case, it was a park or a commons. This one was about 1 1/2 to 1 3/4 miles long, and a little over a quarter of a mile wide. At the south end is the famous Victoria Memorial Building, built in memory of Queen Victoria. It is always prominent, in shining white marble. Chowringee runs all the way past it. On the north side is a very large water tank, perhaps a hundred square yards, and it is used for everything by the natives. There is also the area known as Dalhousie Square, which has most of the office buildings, including the Hindustan Building, later to be taken over by U.S. forces. Also on the maidan is a small Chinese pagoda and garden. On the further side, to the west of Chowringee Street, is Fort Williams. It overlooks the Hoogly River, which is a part of the Ganges. This is where all steamships dock.

There were few people about when I crossed Chowringhee and the tramway onto the grassy maidan. I walked about halfway diagonally across, almost headed toward the Victoria Memorial, when I was stopped by some British soldiers in one of their wagons. They informed me that the way I was traveling would be off-limits. I looked puzzled. I guess they must have noticed, because one of the fellows, who I recognized to be a RAF officer, said this place was an emergency RAF field. The main road on the maidan had been converted into a landing strip. I could now see some fighter planes parked in the distance on the far side, near the fort. I said I was out for my morning walk,

*Calcutta 300 Club on Theatre Road.*

and I was told I could do so by turning left and heading straight down towards the Victoria Memorial. This I did, and then back up the other side of the maidan. I could see now where the area of their field was. I could also see cricket patches where the RAF played, and hockey and soccer fields.

I made my way down the full length of the maidan, and walked about the Victoria Gardens. It was pleasant and cool, with the ever present chatter of birds and hawks. I crossed Chowringhi and walked up the sidewalk. I saw a large church on the maidan; it was called St. Paul's Cathedral. There were many shops in this part of the street; one famous one was the English Army and Navy Store; also Whiteaway and Laidelaw. I then crossed Lindsay Street and came to another famous spot, an old pre-war restaurant know as Firppo's.

I was back at the hotel; Sharkey was already in the midst of his breakfast when I joined him. He said he was going to look around Calcutta for an apartment. He had some addresses; would I care to join him? I had nothing better to do, so decided to drive around with him and get a look at some of the suburban areas. We came to a place called Tolligunge. We passed a racetrack and a golf course. I enjoyed the drive, especially in the open taxi. The streets in Calcutta are wide and well-shaded with trees, mostly peepul and banyan. There were also a number of the royal poinsettia; they're beautiful when in bloom. The addresses we were given for the apartments were not really very nice. We had covered a lot of territory that morning, and it was now midday. We gave up on the apartment hunt, and Charlie said he was going to take me to another hotel for lunch, where some of the other CNAC crews were staying. It was the Great Eastern Hotel, located at the north side of the maidan near Dalhousie Square.

The sidewalk that passed the hotel was wide and covered. It was swarming with beggars and people lying around on the sidewalk. We went in to the lobby, and on the left there were two billiard tables. Most people were standing around with large glasses of beer, chitchatting. Then Sharkey remembered something. He said, "Hey, wait a minute! Come with me, Pete. You'll need to get a few things for your uniform. You can't wear your Pan Africa insignia for CNAC." He led me back out to the sidewalk and turned right. About a block away, we

*Victoria Memorial, Calcutta.*

came to a jeweler's shop, with elaborate displays of goods in the windows. The place was called Hamilton's Jewelers. A well-dressed Indian gentleman asked if he could help us. Charlie said we wanted some silver CNAC wings, an embroidered CNAC hat insignia, and any CNAC patches for the jackets. The attendant didn't take long to obtain the items from a stock he had, in a drawer behind the counter. I think the wings (pure silver) were around 100 rupees ($30.00); the other items were much less. I didn't have any civilian clothes; only the khaki uniforms I'd had for Pan Africa. Charlie said I could get some clothes made later; possibly from Whiteaway & Laidelaw's or a Chinese shop that he knew. I took off my Pan Am wings and donned the new silver ones for CNAC.

We were at the bar, sipping our drinks, when a couple of CNAC pilots joined us. One was a Captain Snell. The reason I remember him is because he would be my captain later, when I started flying the "Hump." After a couple of beers, we went into the main dining room. The ceiling was very high, and the fans slowly revolved. On a stage at one end was a full orchestra, playing some very old tunes. They called it luncheon music. The waiters were dressed in their white outfits, with dark red cummerbunds, and the same color bound around their pugrees, or turbans, with brass hotel insignia.

I always enjoyed the local Indian food, and I ordered my favorite curry, as only these people know how to make. Though the food was hot, I enjoyed every mouthful. My mother always said to eat bread with your curry; it cuts out the hotness. Perhaps, but the beer went well with it. My American friends didn't go much for hot stuff. I followed the curry with their local ice cream, called kulfi. It was a good meal, and I was content.

I walked back to the Grand Hotel with Sharkey. I adjusted quickly to my return to India and its way of life. I did hear the brainfever bird call once in a while. Another bird that was there most of the time, in the midday, was the good old coppersmith, making his "tonk-tonk" call. It was quite a walk, but I didn't mind it; I was enjoying the sights and the sounds. We skirted around the tank and made our way across the top part of the maidan, and down Chowringee.

At the desk, I noticed a slip of paper in our keybox, behind the counter. Charlie

*Coolies relaxing in front of Great Eastern Hotel, Calcutta.*

*Looking down Chowringhi Street from Hindustan Building, Calcutta.*

*Near Dalhousie Square, Calcutta.*

asked the attendant for it. He read it and said, "It's for you, Pete. Captain Higgs wants you to fly locally with him tomorrow morning. It's evidently a test flight, and this will be a chance for some training." Sharkey was a bit disappointed; he was hoping I would accompany him to one of the famous back streets of Calcutta, Acare Lane or Karayia Road, where the prostitutes were. Margo, who was to become quite synonymous with Calcutta, is one of the more famous ones. It was once written in Time Magazine that there were two things you should visit when you come to India; one is the Taj Mahal, and the other is Margo. If you have to miss one, make sure it's the Taj Mahal! I thanked Charlie anyway, but I knew I would not have gone with him. I doubted they could compare with the House of Mirrors in Asmara.

Next morning, the car picked me up at 0700, for Dum-Dum Airport. There were a couple of Chinese people in the car, besides the Indian driver. They turned out to be mechanics. We talked all the way out. They were

interested in Africa and it's operations. I talked about Cairo, the air raid that I witnessed, and also buying a Luger pistol. They stopped me right there and asked if I still had the gun. I said yes. They informed me that if I could get it to Kunming, China, I could sell it for at least $2,000. I was amazed at how openly they talked about smuggling; of how you could get about $100 draft for a carton of American cigarettes. I asked what a draft was. It was good American money; a check made out on a reputable bank, back in the States. Actually, they stated that though the word "smuggling" was used, they felt that taking cigarettes and the like was not real contraband goods. The Chinese welcomed all such material, since the Japanese had cut off all modes of transportation, including the famous Burma Road. All seaports along the coast, such as Canton, and Shanghai were gone. I told these young fellows that I would see about the gun.

I met Captain Higgs at the office, and while he sipped coffee, I had tea. He said the plane would be ready shortly. It had had an engine change and propeller; because something had been written up about vibration, and a test flight was necessary. If all went well, we would then change seats, and he would like me to do a few takeoffs and landings; also an instrument approach or two. I was eager. When with Pan Africa, I had made many preflight inspections on the DC-3 and had talked with those mechanics in Accra about some of the aircraft systems. I thought I knew the DC-3 pretty well.

Frank Higgs did the preflight, while I accompanied him. One licensed mechanic came aboard with us. Higgs told the tower what our intentions would be. The tower said they would fit us into the traffic. We took off and climbed about 3000 feet eastward, toward the Sundabands. Frank and the mechanic went over the checklist. The plane flew smoothly; we did not notice any vibration. All engine instruments read in their normal parameters at different horsepower settings. If I recall, it was the right engine, the one off the co-pilot's side. When it came time to shut down the engine and restart it, Frank asked me to do it. I said I'd never shut down an engine before. Frank looked surprised, then laughed, He said, "OK; this is a good time to start learning." He explained it all to me, step by step: throttle closed, mixture cutoff, push the red button overhead and watch the prop blades turn to a feather position, then the fuel cutoff and the ignition. The reverse would apply when we restart the engine. It worked beautifully. The test flight was completed in about half an hour. Frank obtained a clearance to re-enter the traffic pattern for landings and then touch-and-go. The tower was a British fellow, who said, "Circuits-and-Bumps will be approved, pending traffic." I was now in the left seat, and I tried to act normal, but again, with a strange instructor, I became nervous. On the final approach, I almost forgot to call for the gear down. He said that in the actual world, when we're flying, the Chinese co-pilot would not do a thing for you unless you asked

them directly to do it. He said, "So don't always rely on them to automatically put gear or flaps for you." I came on in, a bit fast. The plane skipped and bounced. Frank had kept his feet on the floor and his hands in his lap; I actually had done it all by myself. In Pan Africa, the Captain was usually right there to see there were no mistakes. He trimmed the wheel and the props' fine pitch and the throttles forward. I kicked rudders too much, and the aircraft fishtailed down the runway, but once airborne, Frank Higgs said, "OK; keep her a little slower."

I noticed CNAC procedures were different from Pan Africa's. Frank said that he wanted the gear when we turned on final, and flaps at half position at 1000 feet, full flaps at 500 feet, and not more than 90 miles an hour. All our indicated air speeds were in miles per hour; knots were not introduced for a long time to come. The touchdown was a little more graceful. We made about four of five touch-and-goes, or "circuits and bumps."

For the hood (instrument) flying, Frank rolled up his jacket and stuck it up in the window in front of me. I looked over the approach for Dum-Dum and went on out to make a procedure turn and then back, for the non-directional approach. Those were the only kinds in India and China, if any at all. There was no range station. Secondly, what was difficult was the directional finder used on these planes; they were a manual-type loop, a small crank overhead between the pilot and co-pilot. This rotated a manual loop outside, above us. To know when you were crossing a bearing, a needle in the cockpit would flip from one side to the other; or if it was in a nul or "Right On" position the heading was correct, and it would be centered and give you a heading on the crank. The pilots called them "coffee-grinders."

I was able to gyrate the plane and crank, in a half-assed fashion, but somehow I got the plane lined up with the runway. At about 400 feet, Frank took his jacket away, and I found I was off to one side. I straightened out and landed. It was a full stop; we taxiied back to CNAC. I knew I'd had quite a workout, as I was sweating. "Okay, Pete," said Frank. "Be ready for your first flight after tomorrow. You and I are going on a passenger run to China. The crew bus will pick us up at about 6:30 in the morning. Bring a small suitcase or bag." I thanked Frank for this chance to fly and said I'd be ready at 6:30.

The CNAC jeep took me to the hotel. I had a bite to eat and went upstairs. Sharkey was there reading. I said I had quite a workout with Frank Higgs, and that I would be going with him on a trip to China in the next couple of days. Charlie told me to get a piece of paper and write some names down. The first stop would be Dinjan, DJN, and then Kunming, KMG, and Chungking, CKG, where I'd be overnighting; the next day possibly either Kwelin or Paochi and Lanchow. Whichever it was, it was going to be a hectic trip. Then on possibly to Hami in the Gobi Desert, back to Lanchow and then the return trip would be Chungking, Kunming, Dinjan and Calcutta. All I thought of now was that I hoped I could make it back before Christmas!

I told Sharkey I had to buy a small suitcase, and asked what to do with all this junk I had in the room? He said the hotel had a "godown" or storeroom. I went downstairs, and asked the man at the desk about buying a suitcase. He said there was a place not far in back of the hotel, off Lindsay Street. It was called the New Market. He said you could finds most anything there. I told Charlie I'd see him at the bar later. I found the market without difficulty. The hubbub and noise could have directed me, and true, there was everything. I asked various shopkeepers to direct me to where I could find suitcases. One corner of the market was loaded with every kind of suitcase, trunk and dealwood boxes. I was also told, as my memory served me correctly, not to accept the first price. One had to bargain; it was customary. I remembered how Mum used to do just that.

I found the size suitcase I figured would do; it could be called an overnight bag. At first the rascal wouldn't budge in his price. I guess he knew I was European, with the uniform. We talked a little more, but still he wouldn't budge. I shrugged my shoulder and walked away to another shop that had about the same thing. The seller, sometimes called a "bunia," was happy to sell me the case for a bit less than the first fellow. I was happy with the purchase, and headed back. I did take time out to wander around and see the different shops. Throughout the place, there was the aroma of incense. I eventually found my way out and back to the hotel.

Sharkey asked what I had in the way of warm clothes. "Very little," I said. "I have a sweater and a RAF jacket." (A kind of demi-size jacket, Eisenhower jacket, made of very heavy brown wool.) He said, "Better take it, 'cause you'll freeze your ass off in Kunming and Chungking, especially Lanchow. It's colder up there than a welldigger's ass." It was the first time I'd heard this expression. I was to learn many more.

I then called the house bearer, or room boy, and asked if he could get the CNAC badge sewn on to my hat, and the other one on to my jacket. He said there'd be no problem, and took off. He wasn't gone too long. Evidently, they had a person who does sewing for the hotel, called a darsi (tailor). He had it done, correctly. I didn't do much else the next day, and did my walks. I was running out of rupees, so I just window shopped. I packed everything I needed in my little suitcase, the rest I took to the man who handled the godown. I got to know one of the clerks who worked the desk; his name was Mr. Franklin. He was an Anglo-Indian, and a nice individual. I told him I'd return in about a week, and please save me a room. It was okay; he said, "A lot of you CNAC people are living here, we will look after you."

I guess Sharkey visited Acare Lane or Karayia Road! When I saw him in the morning, he looked as though he had been through the proverbial wringer. The crew bus came for me right on time, and we drove by and picked up Frank Higgs at his place. The apartment looked real swanky, the sign overhead read "Fountain Court." Frank looked really swagger in his uniform. There appeared to be no official type of uniform for CNAC. Frank had a bush jacket that appeared to be made of a good quality material, probably gabardine; the pants were "pinks," military type. This was a passenger flight. I was surprised to see that so many people were going to be traveling, mostly Chinese. We had a radio operator. This is necessary to inform our progress and obtain WX ahead. The plane did not have bucket seats, but was plush by stateside standards. The stewardess was a cute Chinese girl. We were airborne at 8:00 a.m. as scheduled.

After fueling at Dinjan, we went through customs; the customs fellow was an Anglo-Indian named Hogan. Once off the ground, I became interested in our course, and got a look at the famous "Hump." Frank said he would point out areas of interest and checkpoints for future use.

The weather during the winter is usually clear, but can also be a bitch. There were a few clouds, but it was mostly clear. Digboi Mountain was the first point, at about 8000 feet, on the "Huakung Valley" (sometimes called the "False Valley"). We then went over another small ridge to North Burma and Fort Hertz, but it was unreliable, because we never knew if the Japs had taken it or whether it was under Burmese British control. Sometimes a radio beacon would be placed there; that was how we would know. Often as not, it belonged to the Japs.

There was nothing but jungle, cut here and there by streams and rivers; to the north of the Burma Valley, the Himalayas reach right up high out of the steaming jungles. "Don't get caught up there," said Frank, because of the Mishmi tribes. He said they were reputed to be headhunters. The area was all unexplored. Then came the two rivers, the Iriwaddy Rivers. He said the first one was called the "Red," and the next would be the "White" River. Then the highest point of the mountains reached up to about 15,000 feet, snow-capped. We were heading about 110° degrees magnetic.

I asked about Jap activity, zero fighters, etc. "Yes, there were some around, but we always had to keep our eyes open for such activity. No planes had been shot down as yet, or any of the military." We climbed to a little over 16,000 feet, and through some broken clouds, we crossed the first high ridge. Then I saw a blue ribbon of river. Frank called it the "Blue" River, technically known as the Salween. We had oxygen masks, but I didn't use mine. Frank would use his, otherwise he kept it on his lap. I asked about the passengers. He said, "No problem; they'd probably pass out." The girl had an oxygen pack system to use for herself; if any passenger needed it, she would see that they could use hers.

Then the next ridge; it, too, was all snow-covered, and another river. He called

*Beggers and loafers sleeping in front of Great Eastern Hotel.*

this one the "Brown" River; it was actually the Mekong. I looked at the map and checked these rivers. I was very excited and certainly not afraid, enjoying every moment. There appeared to be no type of civilization here or around North Burma. Not till we passed the Mekong, did I see plowed fields and buildings in China. Frank pointed out a sugarloaf mountain up ahead, also snow-capped. He said that was Mount Tali, 14,000 feet. "Normally we don't fly over it because of some unusual, unstable air; go either left or right. He turned right and let down past the mountain. There was a large lake on the other side, which was called Lake Tali. I saw a large airfield ahead. It was Yunani, a U.S. Air Force base. We descended to about 12,000 feet. I still had not used oxygen. Another 45 minutes, a nobbed hill appeared ahead, with a slight gorge at its left. Frank pointed it out to me and said, you can see the water on the other side; that would be Kunming Lake. As we came through the gorge, Frank said the nobby hill on our right was called "Windy Hill." At the north end of the lake, two peninsula-like fingers jutted into the lake. Above it was a barren area. That was the airport. I could now make out buildings, as we approached. Frank Higgs pointed out the airport. People were working on a new runway. Frank called in, and it was strange to hear an American tower operator give landing instructions.

We landed to the south. The prevailing winds were from the lake. The airport elevation is a little over 6,000 feet. We taxiied back, and I watched hundreds of Chinese coolies working on the new runway. As we taxiied towards the CNAC Terminal on the west side of the field, I also noticed a whole row of P-40 fighters, all with the engine cowling and snouts painted like angry sharks, with mouths wide open and fierce eyes. They

*"Tut" Tutweiler with the oxygen mask in operation, 1943.*

*Sanopah Airport's cobblestone runway with bamboo Terminal Building. The airport goes underwater in monsoon weather. New terminal building has to be built every year after the rains.*

were the original Flying Tiger planes, now transferred to the 14th Air Force, commanded by the famous General Chennault. They retained the AVG logos.

It had been a bit rough over the mountains; some of the passengers had been sick. This we noticed when we came down the aisle. Frank led the way to the CNAC rest area. We had Chinese green tea and a few almond cookies. The stewardess had been good to us on the way, serving us sandwiches and drinks. I saw one of the ground personnel; he was not Chinese, but was a rather reddish-blonde haired fellow. It turned out that he was Polish, and his name was Ski (Skilensky). Frank introduced us. It wasn't long before we were airborne and over the Kunming Lake. We climbed out to the right and headed northerly for Chungking. Frank said never go easterly; the Japs were not too far away.

We headed north; the clouds built up, and we were able to stay on top, at about 11,000 feet. Here and there, peaks cut through the clouds. There were to be no radio beacons till reaching Chungking, over two hours away. Frank showed me the letdown procedure. The field we were to land at was an island in the middle of the Yangtze River, called Sanopah. The beacon was at the northeast side of the town, on a 3000 foot hill. To let down, one had to come over the station at 4500-5000 feet, lower the gear, chop the power and descend at 1000 feet per minute; hopefully to break out over the river

(Yangtze) at a wide bend beyond where there were rice paddies. He said that once you have the river or the rice paddies in sight, make a left turn back to the river and maintain at least 1000-1500 feet, never less. Half a mile from the end of the runway, which was 2000 feet long, made of cobblestones, there was a high tension wire that stretched across the river; when you crossed these wires, you chopped the power again, and descend with full flaps. Then pick up a guided line of white-washed stones that led to the threshold of the runway. As you cross the runway, make sure you're no more than 80 miles an hour, then you drop the airplane in, in a three-point position, and apply the brakes. There would be no room for error. The field was well below the city; the beacon was on the ridge, as was the city. There were small hillocks on the opposite side, and straight ahead of the island and the runway, the river made a bend to the left. At that side, and on that bend, was another high ridge of mountains, at least 3000 feet. So, there was no missed approach if the weather was down. If a missed approach was to be made, it was done at the high tension wires, or at least 1000 feet. The radioman said that the weather at this time was 2000 feet overcast, with two miles visibility. Forget the winds. I thought flying in Africa was something; even during the rainy season; this was a whole new experience coming up.

Frank flew just as he explained. We came over the station at a heading of about 350 degrees. I dropped the gear for him, and he chopped the power and pushed the nose down. It was here I felt my ass pucker up to bite the buttons off the cushions. I imagined the craggy mountains coming at me every second. Down we came, the altimeter unwinding from 5000 feet. Just as we were passing out of 2000 feet, I could see green fields as the cloud layer thinned out, then clear. Now it was visual, and Frank turned left, as I could see more hills to our right. He came around and intercepted the Yangtze River. He followed it at 1200 feet. I saw the wires ahead, and pointed. Frank nodded. Over the wire, he called for full flaps. Once this was done, he lowered the nose again, and we came down to about 400-500 feet. He picked up the white stones that led to the runway and touched down at the threshold, in a three point position. We rumbled and bumped over the cobblestones to the end; any further, we would have been in the water. He taxiied up to the bamboo shack that was the terminal and tower. The reason for this type of structure is that when the monsoon weather arrived, and all the snow up in the hills started to melt, the river becomes a raging torrent and swells well over its banks to at least ten feet, covering the runway and the island, and washing away the bamboo structures and the tower. During that period, another field a few miles away, to the northwest, is used. I never thought one day I'd be doing the same letdowns on my own.

This was a long day. I was tired and ready for the sack. But, oh no! I realized we now had to climb up the mountain, to get to

the city. There were some ferryboats, and a bridge built across from there to the mainland. Once on the mainland, I looked up and saw steps going all the way to the clouds and Heaven; there were 900 of them. Now I knew why Frank suggested a small suitcase! There were sedan-chairs that one could take; the coolies would carry you up. Frank and I elected to climb; it was a real exercise. We stopped a couple of times for breathers. At the top Frank hailed a couple of rickshaws. This was to be my first experience in a rickshaw. There were the rickshaws in Calcutta, which I had ridden; but not like this. I was surprised at the speed of the Chungking ones, especially when there was a downhill slope; there were several. When the rickshaw pullers would come to a slope, they would place themselves further back, towards the passenger. It gave more balance; the passenger would be the fulcrum. The puller would then stride out and be suspended for a couple of seconds, then the next step or leap, like an ostrich. Between strides, he may cover several yards at a time. It also became difficult traversing, because there was always the uphill on the other side. These guys were sturdy, muscular little fellows, especially their legs and thighs.

We soon arrived at a double-storied house overlooking the river. Frank paid for both the rickshaws with what he called "CN notes." I guess that meant China National. What I noticed about the ride through part of Chungking, was the musty odor and dampness, something like Belem, without the mildew, and not hot, but freezing cold. The weather was cloudy, with fog; this didn't help any. A Chinese houseboy greeted us. He reminded me of the old Charlie Chan movies, dressed in long, black, quilted coat, slippers, and black skullcap, and a pigtail. He had a pleasant grin when he saw Frank. The boy took both bags and ushered us in. It was warm inside; I appreciated it. A robust individual greeted Frank, and was introduced as Marty Gold, an American, evidently a businessman. There were several other people in the living room, around the fireplace. First the boy took us upstairs to a large, sparsely furnished room, in the center of which was an open brazier, with a few charcoals glowing. It did warm the room, but it was stuffy. There were twin beds, for Frank and myself. The host had offered his home to CNAC, and I don't know if there was a cost for this or not. We splashed water on our faces, then came down to meet his guests. Marty introduced us around. Frank knew most of the people. I recall there were only men present. The first person I met was a Mr. William Langhorne Bond. He was the President of CNAC. A tall, lean gentleman, with fair complexion and graying blonde hair, freckled, with very bright blue eyes, a bit rawboned, he resembled the actor Charlton Heston. He welcomed me to CNAC and Chungking. It seemed that Mr. Bond had joined CNAC many years previously. He had been a Pan American Representative, helping the Chinese with their fledgling airline; eventually he had given up his post with Pan Am to join CNAC.

I was introduced to a man by the name of Ted White. He was a reporter. The name was to really mean something years later. Another person, whose name I don't recall, was the manager of an oil company, I think Mobil Oil. CNAC was negotiating to use his bungalow across the river for CNAC. There was also an Englishman, with the Shell Company.

Frank told Mr. Bond I originally was from India and spoke the language. Mr. Bond said it would come in handy. He also said to Frank that he was planning to return with us on our way back to Calcutta. He would be there for Christmas. I enjoyed those people, who knew so much about China and India. I'm not sure if it was one of the English people or Mr. White who asked me about myself and how I arrived in India. I explained that my father was born there and was in the police service; that his father had been in the Indigo plantation years before, dating back to about 1830, the time also of the mutiny in 1857. I said I had a sister, a writer, by the name of Christine Weston, in Maine; that she had written several books. One of them, I said, was named Indigo. "Oh, yes," he said; "I know about her." I said I hadn't had a chance to read it yet, but it's about the time of my father and grandfather, as children in India.

I thought, here I am on my first trip to China, I meet people from all over and close to home, almost next door neighbors. The long day, and good food and whiskey, made me sleepy. I excused myself, and in moments, I was upstairs, fast asleep. I didn't even hear Frank come in. The houseboy had us up early with tea, then breakfast. No one else was moving. The houseboy got us rickshaws and once again, we were going up and down hills.

The weather was damp and cold; a heavy mist had dampened everything. The streets were dark and damp with moisture. It dripped from the eaves and the shrubbery. There were a lot of people. I think the reason for this was a lot of them had now become refugees from occupied territories that the Japs had taken over. It was also the new capital. They were just sitting around by little fires, trying to keep warm. There were no sidewalks. Everyone walked in the middle of the road; some had dilapidated bikes. There was not much glitter or color; everyone wore the same kind of quilted coats, down to their knees, with bare legs, sandals or cloth slippers, some barefoot. Everything was the same drab, dark gray color. The 900 steps down were not bad, but they were slippery. There was a light mist everywhere. One could just about see across the Yangtze, and the mountains on the other side; about 1/2 mile visibility.

The three of us sat in the bamboo terminal, sipping green tea. Frank was checking the passenger list and fuel. The weather and visibility were not that good. I had pretty

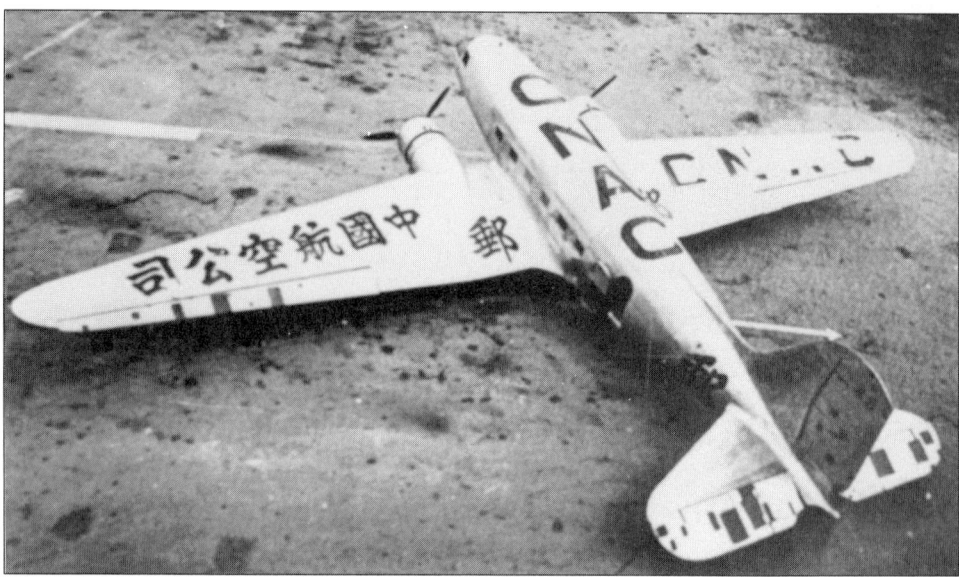

*The famous DC 2½ Ship #46.*

good eyesight, yet I couldn't see the high tension wires that stretched across the river. It was not long before the passengers were cleared to board. I found that each province in China, about 18 of them, was just like another country. The language differed, the type of food, no one trusted the other; they even fought each other. Therefore, everyone had to go through a clearance and customs. We were now ready. Frank got on board; I followed.

Though we landed one way, we would now take off the other: the way we had come, over the wire. Frank was matter of fact regarding the weather. He taxiied up to the very end and turned the aircraft around. I could swear that the tail-wheel was in the water. He held the brakes and gave both engines full power. I watched him check all the gauges; then he released the brakes. The old 3 rattled and bounced over the cobblestones. I thought we would roll right into the river ahead. At the very end, he hauled back on the yoke, and the airplane lifted off, hung in the air, slowly gaining speed as I raised the gear. The power stayed on till I could just see the wires pass under us. Frank then turned slightly to the left, following the river. It was only for a brief minute, then everything disappeared in the clouds. We finally adjusted climb power, and kept on, clawing for altitude. The plane climbed till we broke out on top around 7000-7500 feet. Frank Higgs relaxed and asked me to relieve him for a spell. I told him I thought that Chungking Airport left something to be desired. He said I'd get used to it.

The further north that we flew, the weather started clearing up. In about an hour, it was clear. Though there were patches of rice paddies or wheat fields along the way, it seemed to be getting more barren, with fewer trees. By the time we reached Lanchow on the yellow river, it was very barren and desert-like. Yet the Chinese had squared off every inch of land for crops. We flew over the city; Lanchow looked very much like a

Mexican town, all the homes squarish and made of adobe.

We went into the town by car and visited the CNAC office. Tea was brought out, along with the usual almond cookies. I noticed the people were a little different; they were more Mongolian-looking and Tibetan, I guess because Lanchow is very close to Mongolia. The airplane was ready, and we took off. This time we were on our way to Paoshi. This was a quick stop since no fueling was required. Fueling was normally done from large drums, and a hand-cranked pump, sometimes with a filter and sometimes without. Frank tried not to waste much time; passengers on and off. Once again, we headed for Chungking. The weather always appeared to be the same, rather marginal visibility in the morning, and better by afternoon. The sun dissipates some of the clouds and mist; not an awful lot, though. The radio officer handed us the weather; it was about the same as yesterday. Once we received the radio, Frank headed for the beacon. We were now in and out of clouds, where we maintained about 7000 feet till we passed over the beacon. He circled out and came back at 5000 and approached the beacon from the south. Once over the station, it was gear down, and we turned about 350 degrees and started our descent. I was still nervous. The rice paddies came up as we'd seen them before, at about 1500 feet. The left turn, then over the wires at 1200 feet, full flaps, the white stones, and onto the runway. Then again that slow climb up the stairs and the rickshaws to Marty Gold's. I was really pooped out.

That evening, the three of us went to a little wayside Chinese restaurant. The restaurant was dimly lit by candles and lanterns. There was very little oil for lamps or electricity in that part of town. The floor was very plain, hard mud here and there throughout the restaurant. The tables were oilcloth covered. I noticed spittoons near the tables. Bowls and chopsticks were brought to the three of us, and I was asked if I knew how to

*Relaxing at the hotel in Lanchow, China.*

*CNAC office at Lanchow Airport, 1943.*

use them. I said it just so happened that Sharkey had taught me how to use these instruments, back in Calcutta. We were given some hot, spicy soup, which was greatly welcomed because of the cold and dark, dank room. I heard a baby cry, some distance away. I saw the mother take the kid, carry it over to a spittoon nearby. She undid it's little pants and cracked it over the vessel, just like an egg; the yellow stream of crap spurted out. I pointed this out to my friends; they said, "Yes, you'll see a lot of that; that's what the spittoons are for." It was hard to believe, and I doubted that people back in the States would believe me when I returned, if I returned!

All kinds of dishes were brought, with sticky boiled rice. A couple of dark green, quart-sized bottles were placed on the table, without labels. I was told it was the local hot rice wine. I guess there is a first for everything, like the poor guy who ate the first raw oyster. Oh well! Frank filled a glass for me, and we cheered. I was surprised; it was good and warming. I don't remember what all we had, but the food tasted good, as it did when I had it in Calcutta. Marty Gold paid the bill, and we

returned home. Again, I hit the sack and was fast asleep in moments.

I believe I mentioned earlier that I rose early in the mornings, regardless. This time, the houseboy had to shake the hell out of me to get me awake. I had a hard time getting myself into motion; by the time I reached the bottom of all those steps, I was awake. Mr. Bond came aboard and was given a little extra care by the stewardess. Frank took off in the same manner as before, and I watched every move closely. We didn't see the wires till they swished under us. We came on top at about the same altitude of 7500 feet, and headed for Kunming. The weather cleared, and we landed straight in, towards the south. Mr. Bond and Frank took off for town, while I stayed with our airplane and watched the fueling. The CNAC fellow came up with the weather. There were several CNAC planes parked nearby. The crews were standing and talking to the ground mechanics, and sipping tea. Sipping tea is a normal practice throughout China.

I wandered over and introduced myself. One of the pilots was Chinese, and he introduced himself by the name of George Huang. He was a rugged looking fellow with a great smile, and appeared to be an outgoing type. Another tall, lean individual I had seen on our way here, two days ago, introduced himself as Arnold Wier. He was the chief of maintenance and mechanics for Kunming and Dinjan. He said, "I understand you have Bondy on board." "That's right." "Well, be good to him; he's our boss." "I think Frank is doing a pretty good job of that." ("Bondy" was the nickname for Mr. Bond.)

George Huang spoke with an American accent. He asked how I was getting along. I said this was my first trip and introduction to China. He asked how I liked Chungking. I said that was a whole new experience; the let down separated the men from the boys, and right now, I was a boy! He laughed, and said, "Once you check out and get the hang of things, you won't find it difficult." He hoped we'd get together sometime in Calcutta. The cargo planes were serviced, and the guys took leave and departed for Dinjan.

The weather given was usually fairly reliable for the hump and Dinjan, since it was all reported by pilots in flight. Other than strong headwinds, there was not much other than cumulus clouds. Dinjan was reported clear, as is normal in the winter season.

Mr. Bond and Frank Higgs drove up in the CNAC jeep. I said all was ready, just waiting for passengers to go through formalities. We climbed on board, and Frank ushered me into the left seat. He said, "You've gotta get started sometime." As the passengers boarded, Frank showed me the map and indicated we would fly low to Yanani, check the weather and then go a bit south, where the spur of the Himalayan Mountains tapered down. Keep your eyes peeled for Japanese zeros. Direct course was about 290° degrees magnetic. After starting and thumbs up from Arnold Wier, I taxiied to the north end of the runway and took off. We climbed out over

the lake a short distance and turned right, climbing past Windy Hill on our left. It was turbulent, due to the thermal currents and the arid country. We leveled off at around 12,000 feet and crossed Yunani. Ahead, I could see the mountains looming up. I stayed at about 280° degree heading, south of Tali and the lake. As instructed, I climbed to 14,000, dodging low clouds. I told Frank that three other planes were ahead by about half an hour. "That's fine, but very little talking, please. Radio silence should be a must, since there may be Jap planes somewhere in our vicinity, monitoring our frequency."

We passed a village below, to our left; it was shown on the chart to be Paoshan. Coming up now on the Brown, or Mekong River, the mountains ahead were a bit higher. I climbed and looked for any kind of a pass—nothing. So I climbed on up to a little over 15,000-16,000 feet, and cleared them with room to spare. Mr. Bond came up to see how things were. He said most of the passengers had been airsick, and now, more or less passed out. Frank offered him his oxygen mask. I said I would not be using mine, so please take it. He did, after wiping it with his handkerchief. The oxygen masks, the old rudimentary types, were dark green rubber affairs that fit over the mouth and the bridge of the nose, with adjustable straps for the head. From the bottom hung a horrible looking green rubber sack, at the end of which was a smaller black plug; it looked like a tit. The sack reminded me of a douche bag. The plug was for releasing drool deposits.

The flight over the spur caused swells or currents of air that would lift the aircraft like an updraft, then down. Usually the down was on the leeward side. Frank told me to be careful of these. They could drag you down below the oncoming peaks, especially if your were on instruments. We cleared the last ridge, and I turned to about 300° degrees, towards the north end of the Burma valley, just in case any strange Jap may be in the area. I was all eyes over the sky; the green-carpeted jungle under us. The Irrawaddy Rivers, the White and the Red, came by. I had dropped back down to 10,000 feet; the roughness had smoothed out. The north side of the valley ended with abrupt high, snowcapped mountains.

After cruising along a while, I saw a grassy area; it was Fort Hertz. We crossed another lower spur, and into the Huakung Valley. We crossed it. Then Digbobi Mountain mushroomed up ahead, and over to the Assam Valley; the whole area being a patch quilt of tea estates. The dirt roads reminded me of Accra; they were reddish in color, but were not laterite. There were scattered buildings, with corrugated tin roofs.

I flew towards Dinjan, letting down to enter the downward leg of runway; I think it's about 35°. The runway was macadam and well-defined. The gear and flaps were all normal. I crossed the threshold with a wheel landing. Not too bad for a beginner! I had made my first round trip across the Hump, and then some, meaning that Chungking approach.

*Bob Jenkins and Ridge Hammell with Elmer the Bear, 1943.*

*Ridge with the bear, 1943.*

Captain Woods, "Woody," was there to meet the flight, with his wife, Mage. Mr. Bond, Woods, and Frank sat in the CNAC office; I guess discussing business. I stayed away. The other crews had already landed and departed for the tea bungalow. The trip to Calcutta from Dinjan was duck soup - clear, cool, and not a ripple. We flew down the valley of the Brahmaputra River, with the Shillong Hills to our left. At Calcutta, Mr. Bond was met by Chuck Sharp, and along with Frank, they departed. A crew car took the radio operator and myself to town. Frank said to enjoy Christmas '42, which was just around the corner.

I was happy to be back and relaxed at the Grand Hotel. Mr. Franklin had my boxes sent to my room. I didn't do much that evening; had a couple of drinks and a sandwich. Next morning, I had my small breakfast and my walk on the maidan. I asked the clerk about any gun stores in town. I was informed that there were several. The best one was called Manton's. I asked if that was the same Manton's that was in Old Delhi. He said it was the main office, and the one in Delhi is a branch. I took a taxi to the store, which was not very far from the Great Eastern Hotel; around and behind Dalhousie Square. I wandered in and was surprised to see such an array of fine looking guns and fishing tackle. A person, I guessed to be the salesman, came up to me and asked if he could help. He looked English; his accent, when he spoke, gave him away as Scottish. He was about 5'6" and stocky. His light, graying hair put him at about the age of 50. As most English and Scotts, he wore a long gray coat, customary for sales people. He introduced himself as Mr. Todd, and said he

was the manager of the store. We talked about shooting and types of weapons that would suit my pocketbook. I didn't know much about English guns. Mr. Todd was very good and explained them. I could see I was in an expensive store. Most of the weapons were made by Holland & Holland, and Wesley Richards; shotguns and rifles. None were less than about seven to ten thousand rupees, way over my head, and these were all used guns! I'd taken about an hour of his time, without a sale. We were to become very good friends.

I stopped at the Great Eastern for a beer, and perhaps a bite of lunch. At the bar was Pilot Snell and another pilot I recognized by sight but not by name. He was Jim Fox. After introductions, I said, "Jim, I do remember you. You were with Pan Am Ferries, weren't you?" "Yeah, I was a class behind you." (42-B). It was so good to see him. He was about six foot, very lean, with black hair. We got along well. He said that Chuck Sharp had been in the States looking for pilots, and that Brick Maxwell had asked the people at Air Ferries for pilots. Jim said he was one of the few that came out while I was still battling around in Africa and Cairo. He was hoping to check out soon. Jim said he was staying with a group of other fellows in a place called Ballingunge. One of the pilots - I think he was Danish - Charles Sunby, was renting a member of the Danish Embassy's bungalow, and should there be an extra bed sometime, he'd ask Sunby to let me join in. I'd like that, I thought.

I started to meet more of the CNAC pilots. The short name for CNAC, I learned, was C-NAK. I took another advance of rupees at the airport, to carry me through the holidays. I got a lot of Christmas cards and mailed them through our U.S. Army APO that we were privileged to use. However, we were notified that our mail was subject to censorship and could be opened. Do not say anything that might be of interest to the enemy. I had notified Helen of my new address, and where I was; also Mum, Geraldine, Christine, Horace and Sylvia.

A few more crews came down from Dinjan. One was Pilot Johnson, a Canadian; he now shared my room at the hotel. Sharkey had found a place on Rainy Park with another friend. Christmas arrived, but not quite so glamorous or glittering as Stateside. One could tell it was Christmas, however; a few wreaths were draped in store windows. The Grand Hotel displayed wreaths and colored ribbon paper stretched across the foyer and dining room areas. A fair sized paper type tree decorated the stage, where the band would play Christmas songs. All the beggars and others must have known it was Christmas; they swarmed about the entrance like flies.

The hotel was putting on a big party for the occasion that evening; it would be about 60 rupees ($20.00) each. Sharkey, Jim Fox, Johnson, one or two others I don't recall, and I joined in. We all had to pay in advance for reservations. As I spoke earlier, Calcutta was in a complete blackout, which was administered by the British military. Indoors, though,

the hotel was lit up like a Christmas tree, as it should. The servants were all dressed in clean, white caftan coats, with bright red and blue cummerbund waistbands with big polished brass insignias on the front; the same for their turbans. Some were barefoot, but most had sneakers. They hustled about, seeing that each item was arranged just right; the glasses, the flowers displayed on the tables, and candles. They must have been planning for well over a hundred guests.

We checked our table for six; it was CNAC boldly displayed. We gathered at the bar, and I had my scotch and soda. The hotels such as this were handling mainly military transient personnel. At the bar, therefore, was a mixed group from all over - the British, Australians, Canadians, Americans, and us (CNAC). It was quite a sight, this very night, all getting slowly sloshed. At the stroke of 8 o'clock, the major domo called us to our tables. Everyone gradually broke away from the bar with one last gulp; some carried their drinks with them. To the right, as we filed along, were two long tables. On them were beautiful, well-decorated, cooked turkeys and a pig; salads; the proverbial English plum puddings, with holly twigs decorated around. This was going to be some gala festivity, all right. We drooled as we paraded by.

Everyone got seated. Somehow, I don't know if it could have been timed so perfectly, the orchestra started playing Christmas carols. At the second note, without warning, there was one hell of a boom from outside, then another, and another. Military police were blowing whistles. "Air raid, air raid," someone shouted, and sirens screamed. "Lights out!" bedlam, screaming natives took off in all directions; the white clad servants vanished in a flash. Many of the military departed their tables in a hurry. Luckily, there had been candles on the tables, giving an eerie glow after the lights were out. In what seemed seconds, the hotel was deserted, leaving everything in limbo. Some of us stragglers peeked out onto Chowringhee, which was a sea of humanity. Several more bombs exploded in the area of the maidan. By then, oxcarts and taxis were all going every which way; it was utter chaos. I looked around inside, and I realized the hotel was ours. A few of the sensible military and ourselves turned back to the food on the tables. Someone said, "Let's help ourselves before it gets cold." One of the English types got the carving set and operated on the turkeys, as a professional. We all stood in line dutifully and filled our plates. Some smarter uniformed guys got to the bar and put whiskey bottles on our tables. The food was good, and we all had one helluva feed! The English poured more brandy on the plum pudding. Someone touched a match to it and there was a small explosion, but soon it settled down into a ghostly blue glow over the pudding. The orchestra had left their instruments almost in mid-air. People got up; one gentleman played the piano and another beat on the drums. I thought they were all very, very good. We gathered around and tried to sing Christmas carols. One voice said, "This is the best air raid ever!" Another said, "Jolly good show, you Nip bastards!" I guess there were probably 15 or 20 of us. What a wonderful time was had by all. I don't remember how long all of this lasted, but we were just one happy family.

All of a sudden, the dining room light came on and caught us enjoying the piano and drums near the stage. It was Mr. Franklin who appeared on the scene. He looked very dignified and serious in his tuxedo, yet a bit dazed when he saw the remnants of the food on the tables. We ushered him in and insisted he join the group in drink and festivities, no he couldn't, he said he was on duty. We said "Duty for what? Everything is chaos, just join us." The servants never did return that evening. We got old Frankie pretty well into his cups and a good hearty meal. We told him it was on us. It was a fantastic party. Yes, we had paid for it. Some people couldn't make it home. It was decided to arrange rooms at the hotel. Franklin was not to take names, just move in fellows. So that was it.

When I woke the next morning, there were two other bodies on the floor and Johnson was still asleep in the other bed. I got to the bathroom and did my rituals undisturbed.

The other two guests on the floor were British First Leftenants. I got them up and said they were welcome to use my razor which was straight-edged. I had learned to shave in Brewer by using Robert's straight-edged razors. They wouldn't try that; they took quick showers and tried to look respectable, then realized they had better get back to their base, or maybe get into trouble, even though it was their Boxing-Day holiday. With many thanks they departed.

I ventured downstairs around eleven a.m. and ran into Fox and Sharkey. We looked around the dining hall and didn't realize we had done so much damage. There were broken glasses and bottles strewn on the floor. Bits of food and turkey bones also scattered around. I peeked outside and Chowringee was getting back to normal. Cars and taxis were abandoned on the maidan. There were more than usual amount of Military Police parading the street. There were not many beggars to be seen, and no looting! I asked an MP about the raid; he first looked me over before saying that the docks had been hit; one bomb on the maidan, with no serious damage. He thought a couple dropped near the Hoogly River hitting a ship. There was no other damage. Back at the bar, the bartender looked sad. He said the place had been looted; we didn't tell him the truth. However, a group of us chipped in and presented the man with a big baksheesh. This cheered him up. He was told he was not to blame and to serve us some luke warm beer. This took that terrible night-before taste away, like the sweepings from Chowringhee that stuck in our throats. We agreed it had been a great Christmas party, not to be forgotten in a hurry.

We went out and hailed a taxi. The CNAC guys were learning there was a new

fellow who spoke the lingo, and liked to have him around to interpret. Jim asked me to come on over and spend the day at his place. We dropped Sharkey off and Johnson and I went along with Jim. I never stopped loving the open taxi rides along the roads of Calcutta. There was the ever-present "tonk-tonk" of the coppersmith bird, and the occasional brainfever bird; he was always there somewhere. The crows and the mynah birds, too. I was loving the new way of life in the old country I knew as a boy.

We arrived at the neat brick-tiled bungalow, enclosed by a large high wall. The wall, like most walls in India around a house or compound, was rounded on the top, and embedded on the rounded surface were hundred of pieces of broken and chipped glass; glass of all shapes from broken bottles and plates or whatever. This is a protection from most anything climbing over. To look at one of these walls at a certain angle of light reminds one of looking through a kaleidoscope. The place was not much different from most homes; a large living room-cum-dining room to one side, with two medium sized bedrooms on each wing, and adjoining bathrooms. At the back of the living room opened onto a verandah. There were three or four steps to the lawn, again enclosed by the same wall and glass chips. I was pooped and plopped onto the sofa, and wished for some tea and a couple of aspro, which is another version of the English aspirin, only a little stronger.

Jim's bearer wasted little time in brewing up a pot of tea, with a couple of aspro on the tray. I had these, and it did the trick. We stayed and had a simple dinner that evening. The aspro was having its effect. The head was not aching. We were back at the hubbub, and I was eager to have a decent sleep at the Grand. I was up walking around the maidan route the next day. I saw a group of natives filling in a large crater; it must have been the bomb crater. The Statesman newspaper did not say much about any damage. It did say it disrupted the Christmas gatherings, and had the major streets of Calcutta impossible to travel. The good news was that an RAF fighter bomber equipped with the latest radar had taken off and intercepted the three Jap bombers and shot a couple of them down in the area of the Sundabans. The pilot had received a decoration for his efforts.

Johnson had to report back to Dinjan for his flying, so I was left by myself. Christmas over, hangover over, I was itching to get back to flying. The schedule was usually tacked on the Great Eastern board, near the bar, where most crews hung out. The next day, I wandered over, perhaps to meet some new faces. A group were huddled around the bar. I went over to join them. From the schedule, I learned that Snell had gone with Johnson to Dinjan. George Huang was present and greeted me. I met several others, but don't remember their names at this time. George asked me if I'd ever met Skippy Lane or Privencal, "Pri." I said yes, I'd met them when I first arrived at Dinjan, a few weeks ago. I asked why. He said, "I guess

you haven't heard." As George told the story, it seemed that the two fellows, Lane and Privencal, were having a booze-up on Christmas Eve at the tea bungalow, after their trip. Evidently they were feeling no pain. They discussed hunting and target-shooting with pistols. Pri said he used to test pistols for, I think, the Colt Co., and became a pretty good shot. Skippy Lane piped up and said, "Okay Pri, let's see how good you are. I'll bet you ten rupees you couldn't hit my foot." It may have been about 15 feet away. Pri took out his pistol and promptly drilled a hole right through Skippy Lane's left foot. That ended their party and any nonsense about whether Pri could shoot or not. Suklo, the servant, came running in after hearing the shot, and Skippy was writhing on the floor in agony. As I recall from the story, a local doctor was brought in to administer first aid; it was supposed to have been an accident. Well, it was possible. Skip and Privencal were flown to Calcutta. Skip was in the hospital, and Pri in Langhorne Bond's office. Pri was fired and sent home. Skippy came out of the hospital with a cast. After hearing this, a group of us went to see him at his apartment. He admitted that he had bet Pri he couldn't hit his foot. There was no question Pri had been with some gun company, possibly Colt, and was a professional with a pistol. We all signed Skippy's plaster cast and wished him well. That was to be the end of his CNAC career.

I stayed at the hotel and continued my walks and learned different parts of the city, such as the Strand, which was well known in the early 19th century. Christmas was history with 1943 around the corner. I saw Mr. Franklin, the receptionist, who suggested I go to the Hawaiian Club, just behind the hotel, for New Year's Eve. There would be a lot of young people there and dancing. I thanked him and toyed with the idea. That Eve, I could not find any of the CNAC guys, so after a nice dinner at the hotel, I wandered off to the Hawaiian Club, as suggested. It was packed with civilians, military, and girls. I went to the bar and ordered my scotch and soda. It wasn't a very big place; a bit stuffy from smokers. A live band of locals was blaring out favorite tunes of the 30's; one of them I think was called "Dearly Beloved." There was no one there that I knew as I had my drink, with one elbow on the bar, like all the other flies. I watched the milling crowd of dancers. I learned one thing in these months in India, that the ice in one's drink melted quickly. Secondly, once melted, it left a lot of sediment and crap at the bottom of the glass. I finished my drink before the ice melted. Still, there would be junk at the bottom. Touch wood, up to now I hadn't been sick with any of the known Karachi-crud, or Delhi-belly, or the Calcutta-drizzles, commonly known as diarrhea. The ice was made from Hooghley River water. The remains of cremated Hindus are washed away there. No doubt a lot of sediment is dead Hindus!

Indian bartenders were precise, almost stingy with serving drinks, mainly whiskey. There were two measurements, the chota peg and the burrah peg, meaning one small and one big, one finger or two. They would pour them according to the shot glasses; not a drop extra, perhaps a drop less. This is because good whiskey was hard to come by. I remember my bartender friends at the Peacock Room; they seldom were so accurate. If a shot glass was used, they made certain that another half-shot spilled over into the glass, even the most expensive brands. Anyway, this was war. I had not come to India just to drink. One will recognize, however, that I was enjoying my booze with all the other fellows.

I was at the Hawaian bar for some time; my elbow was tiring. I had tipped a bearer to find me a place to sit. In time, I was led to a place for two. I was happy to find a place and rest my behind. This was turning out to be nothing like the X-Mas-do that I had witnessed. I sat with a new drink to see what the New Year would bring. It was now about 11 p.m., when I felt that somebody was staring at me. I just sat watching the sediment settle at the bottom of my glass. The feeling of a stare was always there. I looked around the hall, and at a table between myself and the bar, there was a group of English soldiers and girls, all enjoying the evening. One of the girls, was sitting at the end of the table, facing her friends. I tried not to notice, but out of the corner of my eye, I saw she would look at me and stare. I looked quickly at her, she didn't look away. She looked blondish and fair, with big, wide, blue, beguiling eyes. She smiled. I motioned if she would dance; she nodded. When the opportunity presented itself, I went over. I didn't want the whole British Army to pummel the hell out of me, right then and there. They barely noticed as I came over. She got up, looking pert as we started our dance. She said her name was Allison. Evidently already prepared, she gave me a slip of paper and said she couldn't dance too much. She was awfully cute; I figured perhaps 18 years of age. I settled back with my drink and read the note. It said: "My name is Allison," and she gave me the phone number. She lived in Karnani Mansions, and said for me to call her the next afternoon, if I wished. The band played "Auld Lang Syne," and those favorite songs, into the new year; 1943 was born. Everybody wished everyone a Happy New Year. I edged my way over to Allison and kissed her on the cheek. I said, "I'll call tomorrow at four." She said that would be fine. Her eyes were certainly beguiling; they reminded me a little bit of Lauren Bacall. From now on, everybody was cheering, the balloons were bursting, and English-type crackers popped, and there were sparklers. What a war! It was a Happy New Year.

I slept fitfully, I guess waiting for 4 p.m. I called the number Allison gave, and she answered the phone and said would I come over for tea? A taxi dropped me at Karnani Mansions on Park St. There was no elevator or lift. I think it was possibly the third floor. I knocked, and Allison opened the door. She looked as she did last evening, only now in a short skirt and sandals and very cute. I came in and was introduced to her mother and fa-

ther. He was a sergeant in the British military. Tea was served; it was nice being able to sit with her folks and talk. They were interested in my background, when they learned I was originally born in India and became an American flying into China. After tea and all the polite chitchat, Allison winked at me and a nod to take off out of there. She told her folks we would walk about in the courtyard downstairs. We came out into the yard, and it was dark because of the blackout. She led me away from the walkway, off to one side. On another walkway, near some hibiscus hedges there was a metal bench. Here we sat, and for a while I was tongue tied. Allison spoke with a delicate tone of voice. She said her mother and dad were divorced. This was her step dad. Her dad was from Calcutta. We followed the normal way of men and women, with a gentle touch on the cheek and then a kiss. Allison and I met again and sometimes we went to the movies.

One day, Jimmy Fox came by and said he was taking a special flight to Agra, with Captain Pottschmidt; "Potty," he was called. He wanted me to go along. It was early the next day, in January, and of course I'd go. I called Allison and said I'd be gone a few days, and I would call again soon. The crew car picked me up with Fox. I met "Potty" for the first time. He smoked a cigarette with a holder. He said I could go along as an observer, and that was fine by me. There was George Huang, also, and a new fellow by the name of Kiwi Mueller; I wasn't sure of his title. The trip was normal, with Foxy getting a check. It was some kind of a special flight. We stayed at the Hotz Hotel, in Agra, and the next day, we all went and visited the Taj. It was still shrouded with a bamboo covering on the dome. The route both ways had us over Gaya, and not near the Ganges or Monghyr. It was a pleasant trip and nice to meet Potty and Kiwi. Everyone seemed to get along in CNAC.

On my return I contacted Allison. We were going to have tiffin, as the English call a lunch; we would have it at Firppo's. She looked great when she opened the door to her apartment. Instead of letting me come in, she ushered me out and closed the door behind us; she didn't want to waste time chit-chatting in the apartment. The restaurant was not very far, so we took a rickshaw. I don't know where these Indian rickshaw pullers get the strength to pull one person, let alone two people. They were skinny little fellows, and for just a few annas, they would haul you all over Calcutta.

Allison loved curry as much as I did. It turned out to be an enjoyable luncheon. She also spoke Hindi, and I learned that her birthday was the same day as mine, the 28th of September. She was not 18, but only 16! After a small coffee or demitasse, there came a moment of silence or suspense. It was then that we looked at each other and understood what we wanted for "afters." I asked Allison if she would care to venture over to the hotel. Her big green-blue eyes said "yes."

The Grand is a stone's throw from Firppo's. I retrieved my key, and we took the elevator up. We had planned to go to the movies later, but this was siesta time. I locked the door behind us; the room bearers always make a habit of wandering in when not wanted. I drew the curtains, and when I turned towards her, Al wrapped her arms around my neck, and we kissed. It didn't take long to send clothes flying in all directions, and once her dress was off, she had on funny looking panties; they were more like my boxer shorts of white cotton. Cute, I thought. The ever-present mosquito nettings were down, and it seemed to take forever to undo the tucks from under the mattress. Once complete, she crawled under the covers. I had to go around the other side and do the same. When I was under the covers with her, I found she had already discarded the shorts; seemed I was behind schedule - I had not gotten mine off yet. Now she was warm and smooth next to me. I almost exploded before I could venture further. I knew there would be some precautions before the act. Before Allison knew what happened, it was all over. I don't know how many times we rumbled and tumbled in bed, until there was a knock on the door. I looked at my watch; it was after 4 o'clock. The servant said he had brought afternoon tea. I told him to leave it outside.

We decided it was time to come up for air. I brought the tea in, and saw that the bearer, with great thought and consideration, had brought tea for two! It was good and well needed. I gave Allison first shot at the john. After all the ceremonies and the tea drinking, we took the elevator down. She said, "You know something?" "No." She said, "I'm going to call you Peter Rabbit!" It took me a second, we both laughed. I then said, "I hope it's not because of my big ears." "Oh, no," she said, "nothing to do with that." I don't remember the movie we saw; I may have slept, which I doubt, since most of the cinemas in India have built in bedbugs in the seats. You're going to get bitten, especially the girls, since they have the short skirts, and the bugs have an easy go at the backs of their legs and knees. This was no exception. Once in a while, you might even see a large rat running along the backs of the seats, going past people's heads.

I dropped Allison back at the Karnani, and rickshawed back to the hotel. I had a drink and something to eat, and back upstairs. I was expecting to return to a messed up bedroom, but no, the room bearers were pretty good. My bed had been made up, with the netting tucked back in under the mattress, new towels, and the tea tray gone. As you greet them, they say "Salaam," but never that mischievous look saying "You were a naughty boy." I saw Allison often, and we had our share of the rumble-tumbles. I liked her a lot. I told her I was married, and also an expectant father. She took it well, and knew that the war brought many strangers together. Even 16-year-old Allison was grown up in understanding the wily ways of men. She once said she hoped nothing ever happened to me in my risky flying, but should it, at least then she hoped she had given some pleasure to me.

The flights were posted, and I was finally placed on a schedule. This was the middle of January, when I had forgotten all about time. I informed Allison of my departure. The crew bus came by and picked me up, along with a few other crews. I deadheaded back up to Dinjan. I was scheduled next day with Pilot Snell. The plane number was ship 53. All CNAC fleet planes that date back before the war, had numbers as of their entry into service. All these aircraft, I might add, were mostly previous Pan Am DC-3s now converted to freighters, and were called C-53s. For conversion, the flooring was reinforced by heavy plywood. They could also be used as passenger, but only side rows, or bucket seats. They did not have any superchargers (two-stage blowers) as they were called, for the engines to go to higher altitudes; except one, and that was ship #48. Maintenance in Calcutta had successfully induced chargers for the two engines. The levers to operate these were the lock levers for the carburetor-ice heaters. The planes also lacked proper deicing equipment, or boots, for the leading edge of the wings; propeller deicing sometimes was negligent. For cabin and cockpit heating, we had the old steam heaters. The reservoir was located near the radio operator's chair; it never worked. Once in a while, when it did, it usually blew up at high altitudes. Some of the planes had conventional magnetic compasses, located up front above the glare shields, near the instrument panel. A few had the old boat-type compasses, the large one, placed just rear of the pedestal on the floor. Some aircraft did not have artificial horizons, only the old needle ball system. They had two red warning lights at the instrument panel for the low fuel pressure indicators. Some of the autopilots worked, others didn't. Most aircraft had the manual or left-right directional finders for radio navigation. These planes weighed about 2000 pounds. less than the C-47s that were to come. The C-47s were constructed for cargo; they had heavy metal flooring, with proper tiedown mechanisms, and bucket seats, all weather operations for deicing and autopilots, automatic directional finders, and artificial horizons and paddle-bladed propellers, and two stage blowers for high altitudes. Ships 60 or better were equipped with a lot of this. 50 series did not have many of these goodies.

Some of the old C-53s once had Wright engines; they were to be converted to Pratt & Whitney - 1830s. Another interesting note concerning ship 46: Just before Pearl Harbor and the U.S. entry into the war, the Japanese were fighting the Chinese and had already taken most of the northeastern part of China and the strategic parts such as Shanghai, and all the seaports. CNAC was still operating as a civil airline, and had a lot of Chinese writing on their airplanes to distinguish them and to let others know that they were civilian planes. Captain Hugh Woods had taken ship 46 to Suifu, commonly known

as Iping, just west of Chungking and on the Yangtze River. The plane was being loaded with passengers when a Japanese bomber dropped a load of bombs. They blew the right wing off, some of the shrapnel had hit the fuselage, but nobody was injured. There was no way that this airplane could be fixed. An enterprising young, American mechanic by the name of Sigmund Solinski, who was based in Hong Kong, suggested that CNAC fly a DC-2 wing up to Suifu. That wing would fit on the DC-3. They first thought him nuts, but other experts felt it could work. How the hell to get the wing all the way from Hong Kong to Suifu? Solinski, enterprising as he was, said "Sling it under the belly of another DC-3, and fly it there." Solinski drew up the method of how to sling the wing under the fuselage. Simply plug up and streamline the butt end, and place that end facing forward. Sol supervised the placing of the DC-2 wing under the aircraft. He went with the flight to Suifu; I believe Hal Sweet was the pilot. Sol and the mechanics attached the wing to the DC-3 and once done, it looked a bit odd and out of shape. Pictures were taken before its flight and also when the wing had been blown off. It was to become one of the most famous and legendary pictures of Douglas Aircraft Company. It was called the DC-2-1/2. Captain Hal Sweet flew it back to Hong Kong without any difficulty. A lot of improvising had been done at times, in that part of the world, to keep planes in the air.

I met a pilot by the name of Robert "Moose" Moss, a fine looking person. I don't get the significance for calling him "Moose." He was from Doe Run, Georgia and had the accent to prove it. I met others, like Bill Bartling. Once while Bill was practicing touch-and-goes at Ballyjan Airport, Bill lost his engines and flew into a clump of bamboo and lived. Bart was a person who could recite you all the scores and games and home runs of the baseball greats from year one. I might take an extra moment to add that a few of the pilots who came to C-NAK, such as Moose Moss, came from the famed Flying Tigers, the American Volunteer Group (AVG) put together and operated by Colonel Claire Chennault. The collapse of the Burma Road and of Burma saw the end of the short, glamorous career of the mercenary pilots of the AVG. There were other AVG pilots I would meet.

The next morning, at the bungalow, I heard the damndest sound. Once I came to, it was music and everyone was stirring. I found out that Suklo was instructed to wake the people up by playing a record on the one and only gramophone. This record was "Under Blue Canadian Skies." While everyone got ready, Suklo was getting the breakfast. A couple of crew buses, weapons carriers, took us out to Dinjan Field. Thanks to Frank Higgs, this was not to be a total loss for me on a regular cargo flight, or any mystery about the hump. The round trip to Kunming and back went well. It was good to be on the schedule again. Another flight from Calcutta arrived, and I was so surprised to see a couple of old familiar faces; here came Sam Anglin

and Ray Hauptman, from the old Pan Africa days. They had returned to the States and decided to join CNAC; here they were. We made regular flights, and had Suklo sandwiches and tea at Kunming, and be back at the bungalow, settle down on the verandah and have Suklo's cinnamon toast and tea.

Toward the end of February, I had completed about 30 round trips. On one of these trips with Snell, the radio operator handed me a message from Calcutta. It read: "The baby was born on 22 date, named David. Love, Helen." I was excited and told Snell perhaps we could celebrate when we got back to Dinjan. That's a good idea. I had a few bottles of Carew's Booze; I couldn't afford scotch. That evening, with some other pilots, I drank gin with grapefruit juice. I didn't care to have too many drinks, for tomorrow was another day over the hills. Woody said he would arrange my response to Helen. It was difficult to comprehend that I was a father to someone literally on the other side of the world. I had been so interested in myself and flying, and being back in India. At times, I felt I had never left India.

My flights continued, and I was progressing with my flying experience. On a day off, "Moose" Moss wanted me to go dove shooting with him. He had a Winchester shotgun. Also, Charlie Sunby said he would like to go. The three of us went out and walked down the road toward the river. Then up around the bank, till we got away from the tea hedges, to where some villagers had grown wheat and rice. There were a lot of mimosa bushes in the area. We spread out, with Moose in the middle. I could just make him out through the shrubs. A dove took off from nearby; I heard Moose shoot. Then I heard Charlie Sunby say, "Hey, Moose ! You shot the dove?" Moose came back and said, with his Georgia accent, "Has a cat got an ass?" When Charlie again said, "I thought you were shooting doves, not cats!" Dead silence. I started to laugh, and I couldn't stop. Here we were, in the wilds of Assam, one guy giving expressions in a Georgia accent, and another in a Danish accent, about cats! I got to Moose, and he saw me laughing. He said, "Did you hear all that?" I sure did. He had a funny way of laughing. He looked at me mischievously with his dark eyes, and said, "Pete, how would you say that in Hindi?" I thought for a minute; it was not the usual type of expression you would hear in Hindi. I said, "Well, has a cat got an ass?" We laughed for a while, then I said, "Billy-ka-pas thum-hai?" Moose held up the dove. I think Moose shot seven or eight. When we got back, he gave them to Suklo to be cooked.

At dinner, Moose told the story again, and asked me to interpret it as "Billy-ka-pas thum-hai?" Everyone learned the saying in Indian. Before the war was over, pilots said it all the way to Natal. George Huang added to it in Chinese, calling it "Mio-peko-ma."

The next few days, I did my flying with Moose. Suklo had given him the cooked doves in a bag, and we enjoyed them when we flew across the hump. The beginning of

*Fox's plane; #53. Picture taken by Chennault's camera man, 14th Air Force, May 1943.*

March, crews changed. One of the pilots gave me a letter. It was from Allison. She was all upset, because her folks told her they were moving to Peshawar, near the Khyber Pass. That's about as far as you can get from Calcutta and still be in India. Well, keep flying and get checked out; that's what I was here for.

It was around the 10th or 11th of March. I was flying with Johnson. During the stopover at Kunming, the planes were being serviced and readied with the new loads on the flight back. I'd like to mention how critical it was to bring much needed fuel and oil to Chennault's fighting forces. Not only would we at CNAC haul in drums of gas across the mountains, we would drain some of the gas from our airplanes; at least 50 gallons, leaving just enough to return to Dinjan. While the gas was being drained, the crews sat around talking nonsense. On this particular day one of the pilots said he knew a route through the mountains, where you didn't have to climb more than 10,000-12,000 feet to get through. If we followed him, he would show us the way. His name was Pilot Welsh; his dad once built some small aircraft named after him. There was Sharkey in one plane and Jim Fox in ship 53, that I had first flown; Welsh, Sharkey, Fox, Johnson and I. It was easy going right past Yunani, at 10,000 feet. We skirted Paoshan and Sugar Loaf Tali Mountain. We crossed the Mekong River. A bit bumpy and though I was flying, I was able to take a few pictures of the three planes in formation ahead of us. We crossed the next ridge, to see the Blue River below. Up ahead I saw Welsh head for what looked like a deep cut pass, gunsight shape, with Sharkey right on his tail. I could see clouds and mist coming over the mountains, then snow pelting the windshield. I kept my eyes on Sharkey, since Welsh had gone through and Sharkey was entering the gap. Fox was no more than 500-700 feet ahead of us. The snow was blinding; I could barely see Fox's plane. I was losing the pass. Then I saw Jim Fox's left wing catch a tree, he cartwheeled in a cloud of snow. I looked at my airspeed, it was down to 90 miles an hour. The vertical indicator showed I was going down at least 500 feet a minute. I hit the power and mixtures forward, stuck the nose down with a right turn. The pass is formed by two ledges at the hill that traverse straight down the pass to the river. I found myself in this gulch, easing the plane along as though I were hedgehopping downhill. I saw the airspeed building up, but very slowly; the controls were slack. I was praying that Jim Fox was okay. Oh, my God, I was sure he wasn't. I saw the crash. It reminded me almost of a silent movie when I saw him in the clouds of snow. We kept on coming down and I could see the river coming up at us fast. I forgot about the power; it was almost up to 45 inches or more on the manifold pressure. The plane reached good maneuvering speed, then we turned up the river and were over on the other side; now I was climbing. This is what Frank Higgs had stated; don't get caught on the downside of the mountain, or you'll wind up in a downdraft. God, I sure was. I had just about turned downriver when I found myself on instruments, with heavy snow and high mountains on each side. I climbed straight ahead, going south; I could care less about the Japs at this time. At about 14,000 feet, I turned right, to a heading of 290 degrees, climbed to 16,000 feet and leveled out. During all this, Johnson and I had not spoken; if we had, I don't recall it. Now I felt a cold sweat; my mouth was dry. I turned and said, "I saw Foxy hit the hill." His eyes bulged out. "You're sure?" "Yes." It was like watching that silent movie, I told him. I was so interested in watching for Sharkey, the gap, and Fox, I forgot that I was in a downdraft too. We were lucky.

We flew through the weather for some time, until it broke and found ourselves coming up on the False Valley, the other side of Burma. We hadn't used oxygen either, just forgot it. I let on down and headed for Dinjan. Moisture gathered in the airplane; the yoke felt sticky and I felt tears coming down my face. I got a hankie and acted as though I was drying my hands on the yoke. I did my eyes as well. Johnson still couldn't believe what I told him.

At Dinjan, Woods was there to greet us. The others had landed and were waiting for the ride in. Woody asked if I had seen or heard of Foxy. I told him what had happened and what I saw; that he had hit the hill. I prayed I was wrong, but I knew I wasn't. Woods said to go on in; he would wait a little longer, just in case.

The next trip was with Moose Moss. I told him about Fox, because Foxy had not shown up. I said I would show Moose the airplane and exactly where it hit. It was a clear, cold morning; the storm had passed. We skirted the North Burma Valley and then south along the first ridge until I saw the pass ahead and to the left. Unconsciously, I said "There's Foxy's Pass." From then on, it was called "Foxy's Pass," as far as C-NAK was concerned. We flew right through the gap looking down, expecting to see the broken airplane; there was nothing, only snow everywhere. The timberline was well covered with it. I asked Moose to circle again. Though the danger of Japs was always present, we circled a couple of times to the exact same place. I scanned every inch of the ground and saw nothing, not even a silhouette. So we continued on to Kunming; I was mystified. Moose said he may have hit the further side and was able to stagger into the Burma Valley. Perhaps the Japs had picked him up, near Myitkyina.

At Kunming, Moose said, "Let's go visit the Old Man," meaning General Chennault whom he had known from the AVG days. I wanted to meet this legend anyway. He was at his office and welcomed Moose and myself. I was introduced to him. He looked quite handsome, in a rugged sort of way, almost stonefaced, with deep lines down his cheeks. He was tawny complected. We sat down and had coffee, which I was not used to. I told of my experience of seeing Fox hit the hill the previous day, but today there was no sign of the plane. Moose said he may have made it over the hill, after hitting the tree. Chennault thought it a slim possibility. If so, the Japs would undoubtedly have him. It would be some time before we would ever know. We spent an hour with the general. He was most hospitable and easy to talk to. He said if he heard anything, he would send a message. We took our leave and departed.

Flying back, I told Moose I would make another run on the pass. At 10,000 feet, we crossed Yunani and Paoshan and the rivers, the same as we'd done on that fateful day, towards the pass. At 11,000 feet, I flew along the ridge and pointed to the spot I said I saw Fox hit. We stared closely as we zipped through the pass, and I skirted north and around the valley; there were no signs. We made one circle, then went on our way back to Dinjan, most disappointed. We told Woody that there was no sign of the plane or life. He agreed with Moose that Fox had been captured by the Japs.

By the end of March, I checked out, along with Ray Hauptman and Dick Rossi. I had come a long ways to being a captain on a most notorious / famous operation, "flying the Hump." Mr. Bond sent us messages of congratulations. It was a wonderful feeling. It was also during March that pilots Joe Rosbert and Ridge Hammel of Pan American Africa were on a regular scheduled flight to Kunming on ship 58. They were reported missing; they never arrived at Kunming.

I stayed on in Dinjan to finish my time for April and May, before returning to Calcutta for a rest. Around mid-May, I had returned from Kunming when Woody showed up and said that Rosbert and Hammel had been found; they were alive and would be at the tea bungalow in the next couple of days. The sketchy report was that, due to severe weather, they elected to return to Dinjan with heavy icing; while they were on instruments at about 15,000 feet, they hit a glacier on a mountain and had come to a skidding halt. The radio operator was killed when his head hit the pedestal. They had traveled all that time, one with a broken ankle and the other with a sprained ankle. Both had been picked up by the Mishmi natives and escorted to a camp where a British geographic expedition were staying. Both still had their heads! The British took care of the two and had them evacuated to the tea estate near Digboi Mountain and would be with us soon. We were happy. I was hoping Fox would show up the same way.

Woody had picked up Hammel and Rosbert and brought them to the bungalow. What a sight! All bearded and gaunt. We listened to their fantastic tale; a miracle, if ever there was one. It was a long fantastic episode, but they would now go on to Calcutta and relax, then decide what their next move would be.

There were other amazing episodes, too. A war correspondent, on the way to Kunming in a military airplane with other passengers, was lost and forced to land in the North Burma jungles, not far from Digboi Mountain. They had been sighted; planes parachuted supplies to them, including CNAC. I heard that a doctor from Chabua had gone over with other Red Cross personnel, bailed out from the plane to rescue the group, and later the group walked out. The doctor was Doc Flickinger, whom I had met in Delhi. The war correspondent was Eric Sevareid. If miraculous and heroic performances were occurring in other parts of the war torn world, it was happening here over the Hump as well.

Before I had finished my flight time for the month of May, I was on a scheduled flight across the mountains one bright sunny morning. Moose Moss was ahead of me headed for Kunming. He was on a direct course and a little north. I had skirted the north valleys and had swung south to go through Fox's Pass. As I flew through, I saw it. I saw Fox's plane next to some trees at the timberline. The left wing seemed to have been buried. The fuselage was cracked open just rear of the main door and the nose section had been crumpled in. I broke silence and called Moose. I said I had spotted Fox's plane, to come over. He knew where to come, and flew to me; I showed him the airplane. He agreed that it was Fox's alright and said we should see the "Old Man" on arrival at Kunming. In the meantime, I had the radio operator send a message to Woody and to Calcutta. Moose and I went to General Chennault's headquarters and showed him on a chart where the lost aircraft was spotted. The General suggested that we take some pictures of it. He arranged to lend one of his photographers the next day. Sure enough, the next day when I returned, there was a sergeant standing near the CNAC ramp. He had a large camera strapped around his neck and a parachute. After introductions, I asked the guy what the chute was for; he retorted, "Just in case!" I showed the sergeant the map and where the aircraft went down. I told him to be sure and give me instructions as to where we should be to take the best shots. He would do so when we arrived at the scene. As I approached the pass, the photographer looked a bit nervous, but right now I was only interested in getting as many pictures as possible. At the pass, I pointed out Fox's plane and from that point on, he directed me in what areas to circle. On each pass through the gorge, the sergeant started clicking away with some kind of big fancy camera. We spent about thirty minutes gyrating around the plane. I didn't want to dilly dally too long, just in case it might attract the Zeros like my owl and crows in Brewer! Also, I didn't want to frighten the man by telling him about the Japs. I then headed for Dinjan. I explained the route and why I headed north. He became more fidgety until we were in Assam. At the CNAC bungalow, I comforted him with Carews Booze. The next morning, we headed back for Kunming.

We took the north course for the sergeant's benefit, and we passed Tali Mountain to our right. There I had him take a few pictures of the famous pagoda that sat on top of a 12,000 foot mountain. A zigzag travel path led all the way up from the base, possibly for water. That would have to be some climb with two buckets of water on a yoyo stick, a bamboo stave shaped like a bow. The trick, I noticed, was everytime a man took a step, the two ends heaved the two buckets of water upwards; at the spring of the bamboo, the man would make a long stride forward; but even up this zigzag pathway, must have been a horrendous task.

The sergeant asked casually, when descending to Kunming, "Do you guys really

*Joe Rosbert and Ridge Hammel on arrival back to DinJan after their crash and 6 week trip back to civilization 1943.*

enjoy flying the hump?" "I don't know about the others, but yes, I enjoy it very much. So far, I haven't had many scary flights, except when I almost followed Fox into the mountain." "How about the Japs?" he asked. "I've never seen one. I doubt if the zeros have the range to travel that far north, on the route we take. Besides, we keep a pretty close watch. Even if we see any resemblance to a group of planes - which turn out to be perhaps a flock of geese headed south; they do fly at that altitude - we would head for the green carpet below and hedge hop through various ravines." I told him about one Jap plane that used to come over Dinjan area at very high altitudes, a photographic plane, we figured. No one could get near him. The U.S. Air Force took a P-40 and stripped it down to the bare minimum weight. He made it up to 30,000 odd feet and waited. The Jap arrived on schedule in the afternoon, the P-40 shot him out of the sky. There was an emergency frequency to notify any activities in and around the ground areas where the Japs may come up from Thailand to Rangoon; in late evening, to Myitkyina or Bahmo, to make a strike and return. The P-40 squadron stationed near us were always on alert. "So you see, we feel quite comfortable about our flight." He just shook his head. I dropped him off at Kunming, and he said he would have the pictures for Chennault. If I wanted copies, the General would decide that. I thanked him.

I finished my May hours and was scheduled back to Calcutta. Ray Hauptman was also returning. On the way down, he said that Bob Jenkins had joined us and should be in Calcutta. It appeared a whole lot of the Pan Africa group were now joining CNAC. I thought it great. Ridge Hammel was also on the flight. We sat in back and talked. He was conjuring the idea of staying or returning to the States. I suggested that he go back and then, if he felt like it, to return; he wasn't sure. It seemed that Charlie Sunby had the Danish bungalow now, and had asked Hammel, Jenkins, Hauptman and myself to move in, provided we arranged for the extra beds. I was happy to be out of the hotel. There were a lot of used furniture stores around Calcutta. With the help of Sunby's bearer, we got the beds, with mosquito nets. None of the bungalows were air conditioned; they had high ceiling fans. Winter is short in Bengal. The temperatures started rising in May, hovering around 100-110 degrees, with high humidity. This really brings on the brainfever birds.

On the spur of the moment, I decided to visit Allison in Peshawar. I hitched a military flight to Delhi, then got on the Frontier Mail Railroad to Rawlpindi and Peshawar. The train was hot and dusty, but I enjoyed it in spite of the heat. I arrived the following afternoon. There were people known as Pathans, in baggy pants and long shirts known as kurtas, with a short type waistcoat and balucha sandals that squeaked when they walked. A taxi got me to the Gaines' bungalow; that was the family name. It took a bit of doing, but I found it.

Talk about a surprise! They were happy to see me; Allison had a little sister, a toddler, and a nondescript dog. They all welcomed me. It was stinking hot; there were khuskhus tattis in the doors and windows. It took me back to Hardoi, where we used them. There were a lot of military people in Peshawar and very little to do. Allison and I went for early morning walks, or late in the evening. She then said to me, "Peter, I have a secret to tell you. I'm pregnant." I said, "Oh, no! It couldn't have been me?" She said, "No." I said "Who was it?" She said, "It's a Canadian, in the Air Force, in Peshawar." She'd told him; he didn't know what to do. I asked if she planned to have the baby; she didn't want a baby. I asked if there was a doctor who could perform an abortion; she hadn't checked. I said I'd talk to the pilot, but she said no, she would work it out with him. We enjoyed each other's company that week. It was soon time to return. The bearer took my bag, and Allison came with me to the station. I found a cabin in a second-class compartment. There were several other people already in it. I had an old Kodak camera, which I gave Allison, as long as she promised to take a lot of pictures. She said she would, and we said our fond farewell. The train chugged out, as I waved goodbye. My train companions were an Indian, an Anglo-Indian, and a Frenchman.

One of the Indian gentlemen suggested we get a large basin or bucket and a block of ice to put in the center of the compartment. It was a good idea! It was at the next stop that the Indian arranged the pan and ice. It was only a few rupees, so I footed the bill. We got rolling and as the little electric fan burred, it became quite comfortable. Someone suggested cards, but half the group didn't know bridge or poker. They could play whist, but I couldn't, so that fizzled. I suggested some drinks. Someone had lemon crush; I had the gin, and the group chatted awhile. As the custom for food, a waiter at the station was given the orders at Lahore, to be picked up the meals at Amritser. There were now five of us, and we all got along just fine. The food was served at Amritser, same old Spencer's. We got a refill of ice for the pan, and we slept till we arrived at Delhi. I was awake and stepped on the platform. Two of our friends got off here; I wished them well. The noise and the confusion, the same old vendors calling "Pan-biri-cigarette," and "guram-char." All this came flashing back

from when I was a little boy. I stood and devoured all the sounds and smells of every kind.

I climbed back to find two other people had joined us. The train pulled out and gradually found its way onto the correct tracks for Calcutta. I opened my shuttered window and watched dawn slowly creep over the countryside and the wheat fields. It was all so beautiful. Every so often, I'd see a native going out into the fields near a gully with his brass lota, or urn. I knew he would squat and relieve himself, wash his genitals with the water and return home.

I looked back in the cabin and noticed one of the new travelers sitting opposite me. A suitcase under the bunk had a sticker with writing in white. The name was Nathan, the insignia in bold letters saying "DBS." I asked him if that meant Diocesan Boys School. Surprised, he said "Yes." He knew I was an American, but how did I know what that meant? I told him I had once attended that school, as a little boy, and remembered a boy named Nathan at the school. He said "That would be my eldest brother." He was in the military now. So this young fellow had graduated and was stationed in Delhi. The Frenchman was a professor at LaMartineer College in Lucknow, made famous by Kipling's "Kim." We stopped at Lucknow, and he departed. I said I'd come and visit him one day.

When we came to another station, a sign on the platform read, "Hardoi." I stepped onto the platform and walked around; it was exactly as I remembered it, almost 25 years ago. One of my friends took a picture of me. I just wanted to get off and go visit the house; maybe my old ghost friend would still be there. No way, I had no time. The whole train journey had been most nostalgic and wonderful. My travel companions were friendly. The DBS fellow would contact me and give me the Hardoi picture. The train gradually slowed to a stop back at the Howrah Station in Calcutta. We all said goodbye. I hailed a taxi and headed for Ballygunge. I arrived sweaty, sooty, hot and tired. The bearer made me a hot tub. My CNAC friends were there, and I told them of my trip. I lay in the bath and soaked a long time, with a gin and tonic by my side. I got most of the four day's soot collection out of my pores, with a big, black dark ring in the tub as proof.

The bearer had put out neat, fresh clothes. All refreshed, I joined the group out on the back verandah. They laughed, and I knew some mischief was astir. Pretty soon, Ridge Hammel came out from the back, and on a leash was a cute Himalayan black bear, with a white v-stripe on its chest. It was so cute, just like a teddy bear, and friendly. Ridge had a baby's bottle full of milk, and naturally the bear followed Ridge diligently. "Whose was it?" It was Ridge and Bob Jenkins'. They had bought it at the New Market, where, as I mentioned previously, one can buy most anything, even bears, tigers or leopards, or a suitcase. "What were they going to do with him?" "We don't know; probably take it to Dinjan," Ridge said.

"They were treating him pretty poorly when I got him at the market." Ridge had decided to stay on with CNAC.

We were all back doing our thing, and Bob Jenkins was assigned to me for training. It was great. We shared the flight legs over and back. On one of these trips, Bob introduced me to a game called "Battleships." You would make up two grids and place your battleships and cruisers and submarines in certain areas. He would do the same, and then each one would take a shot. You take a shot by calling a grid, like A-1 or B-5, and you'd mark it. If you hit, you had to report it, until you sink the whole Navy. We played this game on our trips across the mountains; it passed the time, even in bad weather. We were careful to keep our eyes peeled for any suspicious flecks in the sky. Even during heavy storms, we were alert. It was the season when storms developed rapidly, especially in the Burma and False Valleys. Quite often, we would head for the thunderstorms; once in one, it would take you up, as one pilot said, "like an Otis elevator." This helped give you the altitude that otherwise you spent in a long climb.

On another trip, I was with Captain Bob Angle, from Pan American. On some flights, our cargo was large ingots of tin from Kunming; each weighed about 100 pounds. They would be lined in rows on each side of the cabin, lashed down by rope. I was flying this particular leg back, with these tin bars on board. So did a lot of the other flights coming back that day: Welsh, the one who had given us the trip through the gorge originally; a fellow named Tutweiler, called "Tut;" and George Huang. When I was over the last ridge at the Salween into Burma, a whole line of heavy thunderstorms blocked our way. Bob looked anxiously at them. I did, too. I knew the other guys were up at altitude. There didn't seem to be any way around them. I told Bob I was going under them. I chopped the power and descended. I kept coming down till about 6000-7000 feet. I could see under the squalls, and heavy rain. I knew where I was; as we crossed the White and Red Rivers, the rain was heavy. For almost half an hour or so, we were in it; then it let up, and we were again in the open. I climbed back up to 12,000 feet and crossed into the False Valley and home. Bob said he was glad this was his last trip; he was going back to the States and Pan American. He asked if I wished to buy any of his clothes; we were about the same build. It was great since U.S. clothes were hard to come by.

At Dinjan, George Huang arrived, all shook up. He had gone into the thunderstorm; it had started to shoot him up in a hurry, and it was rough. He didn't like it, so made a 180 degree turn cut, and by the time he was out of the storm, he had popped out at nearly 23,000 feet. When he did, the tin bars just kept on going. The sudden stop at the top popped the rope like string, and when the bars came back down, they tore the hell out of his airplane. Not a bar was left. He said he was very lucky, but Welsh was not. Evidently, some of the bars that came back through cut Welsh's control cables, and he spun in; he was never found. It was then that we all complained to Woody about the sloppy tiedowns for the tin, and for the 50-gallon drums of gas we took to Kunming. It was not long before he procured large nettings like the Air Force were using. It certainly helped.

On a trip back from Kunming in June, Woody called me into Dinjan Office. He said the Calcutta Police wanted me for questioning. "Me? What for?" He didn't know. I hadn't done anything wrong that I knew of. I paid all my bills, had not been disorderly or drunk. Woody said, "Take the next flight to Calcutta. If there is a problem, check in with Chuck Sharp." I said I would. I took the flight to Calcutta and went straight to Chuck's office. "OK," he said, "call me if the police give you a hard time." I took a taxi and went to the police station in Lal Bazaar. An Englishman in civilian clothes and a couple of Indians in khaki police uniforms were there. I introduced myself and gave him my passport. The Englishman asked me to be seated. After looking the passport over, he handed it back. "Well," he said, "You're a pilot for CNAC." "Yes, Sir." "Tell me, did you take a trip recently to Peshawar and back?" "Yes, I did. I went to see some friends there." "Was one of them a Miss Allison Gaines?" I said yes. "Nothing has happened to her, has it?" At the same time, I thought of the abortion; perhaps she didn't make it. "Oh, heavens, no!" The Englishman then said, "When you left her, did you give her a large sum of money?" Again, I was surprised. I said, "No, I gave her a camera, as a gift. I told her to take a lot of pictures." "I see; no money?" "No." "The reason I'm asking these questions is because we received an urgent message from her mother, that she had run away from home. She thought Allison had come to Calcutta to see you, that you had given her the money to do so. This is why we sent for you." I felt a bit relieved and said, "No, there was no money; only the camera. It's not worth very much. Does her mother know where she went?" "No, Allison is in Calcutta. Her mother said she probably was here with you." I said, "I am a friend, but would not ask her to run away from home. First, she is a minor; secondly, I am spending a lot of my time flying to China." He said, "Well, Mr. Goutiere, I realize you are telling us the truth. You see, we found Allison at one of her friend's homes. She is anxious to see you." "Where will I find her?" "You don't have to; she's right here." A policeman went to another room and brought Allison out. She looked pale and wretched and ashamed. I went to her, and she cried. I said, "Why did you do this? Why?" She said, "I'll explain later." The English Chief said, "What do you plan to do?" I said, "Well, I can see that she gets back home safely." Allison shouted out that she didn't want to go back. I said, "OK, then I'll place her in a YWCA, and perhaps she can start secretarial school." That would be okay. It was agreed then that I would be responsible for her at the YWCA. The police

would notify her parents. I said I'd write them, as well. The police were sorry for the inconvenience. I thanked them very much, especially for finding Allison.

I took Allison back to Ballygunge for a spell, till she got over the fright. She confessed to me that she had sold the camera and had enough for a third-class ticket, which was one of those terrible excursions on a bench; there was no place to lie down, just sit for nearly four days, and eat chapatties (Indian bread). She was still pregnant. The Canadian fellow had left Peshawar. I got her into the YWCA, but no school, she said. She said she would contact her friends about an operation. I was scared, in case of a mishap. Allison learned that the fee would be around 300 rupees. I gave her the money and paid a month rent at the YWCA, with enough extra to live on. I told her to write her folks immediately; I would also. She promised and thanked me. I had to leave, to finish my hours for June.

I told Chuck Sharp all was okay. I got back up-country and did my flying for June, and also for July. The monsoons had arrived, which was a whole new experience in flight. From takeoff at Dinjan at 200 feet, you were on instruments; normally make a circle to overhead the field via radio station, then fly out at 110 degrees magnetic. The instrument flying was like silk. At altitude, you'd pick up some icing. There seemed to be a better range for reception of radio stations. Best of all, there was no worry about being jumped by Japs. Yunani station normally was good; so was Kunming. The letdown was to the north, turn down over the station towards the lake; it was simple. Kunming, in clear weather, would have occasional air raids and bombing by Japs. It was called a "Jingbau." It was also alerted on the field by a black or red ball alert, which was on a pole and hoisted like a flag. A coolie would hoist up the ball; black was precautionary, and red meant "get out." Get the plane off as best you could, and literally head for the hills!

It was believed that if you didn't bust your ass during the first six months of hump flying, you were not only lucky, but considered a veteran and a professional. I guess I squeaked into being a veteran. I had better than a eighty round trips. The weather seldom cleared up during the rains. I remembered this from my school days. Everything in the Dinjan bungalow turned green with mildew overnight. Guns had to be cleaned every day, or they'd rust. And, oh, yes, I did sell the Luger in Kunming earlier, as advised by the Chinese friend. I now obtained a Colt .45, from the Colonel Doc in Chabua; he said he had an extra.

There were more pilots every day, quite a few from old Pan Africa. One was Sam Belief, a co-pilot I flew with on my first trip from Accra to Teheran. I don't know why, but he became jealous and envious of my being here ahead of him and checked out; he would not fly with me. No matter. End of July flying, and I was back in Calcutta. I looked for Allison, but she had moved out of the Y, and had gone off with her friend,

named Molly. I was given an address, and I found Molly's place. She said that Allison's family had transferred back to Calcutta from Peshawar, and that Allison had gone back to live with them. I asked about the operation. Yes, it was a success, but she had not told her folks. They were living at a place on Ripon Street, not too far from the Grand Hotel. I tapped on the door, and Allison answered. She was surprised, almost as she was when I saw her in Peshawar. "Come on in!" They were on the ground floor level.

That evening, I took her to dinner at good old Firppo's. They had dancing every evening. She was well and seemed happy. She said she couldn't take the YWCA; they were too strict. She had moved in with Molly, and her family had moved back. She had the operation just in time; she had never told them. I asked if she was behaving herself. "Yes," she said. That Sunday, my friends at Sunby's bungalow were planning a special tiffin (luncheon). Ridge was going to stay and fly. I asked if I could bring Allison. Of course! There would be other girls there, too. There was quite a group, including Sharkey and his girlfriend, Ray and Bob brought girls over, and then, the bear: Elmer (that was what they had named her). It rained, so everyone was indoors. It was a good afternoon party; the food was great, with loads of beer and Carew's gin. After coffee and tea, people started disappearing. I led Allison into my room. It seemed a long time since we had been together. We soon fell asleep. We reneged our teatime, and stayed under the mosquito netting till dark. Allison beat me to the bath and then got dressed. I joined her and the others. Sandwiches and drinks were served. Allison and I were still full from lunch; a couple of drinks put us right. The party finally broke up.

We were all back to flying again. Several new planes, C-47s, had now arrived, brought back by Cliff Groh, another new AVG pilot by the name of Bus Loane, and Duke Hedman. It was nice to fly a plane with two-stage blowers and heaters, artificial horizon and automatic direction finders. However, they were heavier and slower to climb. Still, you didn't have to sit huddled in blankets watching the needle ball and using the coffee grinder. Another character arrived on the scene, a George Robertson; they called him Robbie. He talked a lot, and shone a gold tooth when he laughed. Guess who else arrived? It was Privincal. He was reinstated and back, with a new pistol. He and Robbie always argued as to who was the better shot.

Robbie had a .45 revolver. He said he could whip Pri, and Pri said, "Put your money where your mouth is, and let's find out." I don't think Robbie knew Pri's professional skills and background. He took a five of spades from an old deck and tacked it on a tree in a corner of the yard. We all stood on the upper verandah and watched the shootout, a hundred rupees a shot, nearest the spots. Robbie called the spade at the 2 o'clock position. He was chewing his tobacco. He spat a glob off to one side, took aim, and fired. Bark flew from the tree, several inches to the right of the card. Pri had his .38. I could see the way he stood and handled the gun, there would be no contest. Pri fired and nicked the card close to the spade, by about half and inch. One hundred rupees given to Pri. The next one was on the left, at the 11 o'clock position. Pri first, and he nailed it. Robbie spat and took aim. Again bark flew; another hundred rupees. On around counterclockwise. Robbie did a lot of chewing and spitting, but never came close to the target. Pri hit the rest of the spades. Robbie said, "I'll make you an I.O.U." One thing's for sure: Robbie never again argued Pri's expertise; I don't think Pri collected the rupees either.

The monsoons were not helping the Army pilots. If they could sit it out, they did. They were losing a lot of aircraft. It was suggested that the new Air Force pilots fly with us for a month, and gain some experience, before going on their own. The offer was refused. A General Tunner came on the scene and told the Air Force that there was no such thing as weather, to get going and fly, that C-NAK were flying the hell out of them. We had developed a CNAC song. The tune was from the original "Cannonball;" we called it the "CNAC Cannonball."

One verse was:

The Mountains they are rugged
The Army boys do say.
Army gets the medals,
And C-NAK gets the pay.

The main object, anyway, was to get the supplies to Chennault, whether it was medals or pay; we knew we were doing our share, each one about 120 hours a month. The RAF did send us a few officers for training. The one assigned to me was a Bob Murray from Jamaica. We flew together for a month.

I had a few days off in July, and I was back in Calcutta. I learned from a lot of CNAC fellows that Allison was cutting a swathe through the U.S. uniforms in town; I didn't believe it, but when I was with her, I asked her point-blank. Her answer was point black also. Yes, she was going out a lot, and why not? I was away several weeks, so you can't expect a girl to just sit at home for 24 hours a day. I guess she was right, and me being married. However, she would go with me when I was in town.

I saw George Huang and Rossi often. George asked if I'd like to join them on another special trip to Kashmir in September. You bet I would, and how! We would fly from mid-August to mid-September, one month straight; about 240 hours in monsoon weather. There would be about 200 hours actual instruments. Tutweiler would also join us. George Huang would bring his wife, Babs, and Mage would join us, too. Scheduling gave us the O.K. We started to fly our asses off, and it was rugged. We flew the 240 hours without becoming gibbering idiots. I don't know how.

On one of these trips, I had my old ship, #48, and I was coming back empty from Kunming. To get over some of this weather, I used the homemade blowers. I was able to get the airplane, believe it or not, up to almost 23,000 feet indicated. I just seemed to hover up there. We were doing well with true airspeed, even though we indicated about 95 miles an hour. I got the plane back into Dinjan from that trip, and all was well. On the return trip, it was Sam Anglin that was going to take ship #48, that would be the following morning. He took off, and was not heard of again; he never reached Kunming. A report came back to Woody that an Air Force pilot had been flying close to Sam Anglin when he saw the left engine catch fire. Sam evidently had gone as far as North Burma, when he turned around and was headed back. He was low, and so was the Air Force fellow, who was hovering right over him. He tried to contact Sam to bail out, but Sam was headed back to Dinjan, his left engine spewing flames. He didn't jump; he stayed with the airplane, and it wasn't many more minutes when the flames had eaten through the firewall into the wing. Then it blew up. That separated the wing, and Sam spun in. Another fine pilot lost. It was assumed that Sam did not know those carburetor—ice locks were for the blowers; he was very meticulous in going through his checklist before any takeoff. I'm sure he used those blowers thinking they were the locks for the deicing, because he probably checked the deicing equipment before takeoff. In high stage, it probably was what caused the fire. This is an assumption only, because the airplane had been flying beautifully the day before.

Our 240 hours were rugged. In the meantime, Babs and Mage had permission to enter the State of Kashmir, which was at that time governed by a Maharajah. Everything was now complete. We were in Calcutta, and our safari gear prepared. Babs and Mage were to mail our visas for Kashmir.

The four of us negotiated with the U.S. Air Force for a ride on one of their airplanes, at least as far as Delhi. The military was good at passing the buck. Someone said we would have to see General Stillwell. Stillwell?! My God, all we want is a ride to Delhi! I think George Huang said, OK, we'll do that. I don't remember where we wandered to, to find out about General Stillwell, but it was somewhere at Dum-Dum Airport. You know something? We did find him, and we did see him. We walked in and introduced ourselves. "Oh, yes; you are the pilots that are hauling all the goods across to Chennault, and I believe also you're hauling Chinese soldiers back so we can build the new road across North Burma, from the Digboi and Lido. You bet you can ride on a U.S. plane!" He called someone, and we had the OK. I couldn't resist it; I had a short-snorter in my wallet, that was started with a dollar bill back in Miami, and was signed by those who would join it and pay one dollar, or buy a drink. I got the short-snorter and asked the General if he would kindly sign it. It was a five rupee note that I attached to the dollar. He was happy to do so. We thanked him very much and were on our way the next day, on an Air Force C-47. The pilot was a young Warrant Officer. The flight was with a stop at Gaya, another Air Force base, more of a training field. We let down wandered around, and finally landed. We taxiied for a few minutes, then took off again, flew about, then landed one more time. The pilot came back and said, sheepishly, that he had landed at the wrong field, back there. Oh, what the hell; no problem, but let's get to Delhi!

At Delhi, we thanked our young fellow pilot. I remembered his face, rather a baby face; he was very young. We got on the train at Delhi, the same frontier mail I rode, going to Peshawar to see Allison. We had the compartment to ourselves; it was great. I had to show off a bit, though. On the train, I asked a coolie to bring a large pan and a block of ice; "Remember my last trip?" all in Hindu. With a big smile, he was gone. It did not take long. He arrived with the whole thing on his head, and placed it in the middle of the compartment. We all chipped in; the man received the biggest tip of his life. I felt we would need this on the way to Rawlpindi, where we would be getting off. Our meals were ordered in the usual way, the food tasted good. At Rawlpindi, we checked in at a Kashmir office for our permits to enter the Principality, but no luck. Babs and Mage must have missed somehow, there was no such pass. The man said, though, to go on to Murree; at that station, they would be rushed to us for sure. We all piled into the taxi - yep, same type as they had in Calcutta - and we started up the mountains, to the Hill Station of Murree. The scenery and climate changed - lovely pine trees, the first deodars, Cedars of Lebanon type firs. The air was cool and refreshing, after the train ride.

We checked at Murree office for Kashmir, but there were no passes. We then sat around and sampled the famous Murree beer. It was cold and hit the spot. As we were leaving town, we saw a Dandy, or sedan chair, with four coolies, carrying a pretty looking Red Cross girl. We stopped the taxi and waited. She was lovely, she was certainly not bashful. "Hi, there!" she said. We all "Hi'd" as well. Her name was Diana. She was on vacation going to Murree; her base was in Calcutta. She would be there, after her holidays. That was great! She was invited to a special birthday party, my 29th. We gave her the address in Ballygunge. The taxi halted at the border, and there was a local policeman guarding the road. I asked him about the passes for us. No, sir; there were none. George and Rossi devised a scheme; Rossi, Tut and I would walk up past the sentry, casually taking pictures, then go around the bend of the road and out of sight. George would hop in the cab and drive up and tell the guard he was going to pick us up and be right back. George said he tipped the guard a few rupees for letting us take photos.

We were on our way to Sirinagar, the capitol of Kashmir. We stopped on the way, further up, and enjoyed the sight of the Jelem River, racing down the gorge where there

*Pretty Red Cross girl comes by in mountain rickshaw to Murree.*

*The Kashmir guardhouse where we slipped through.*

*Our Red Cross girl at my birthday party (29), in Ballygunge, Calcutta.*

was a rope suspension bridge. We stopped there for photos and rest. Late that afternoon, we arrived and found an agent who had arranged our houseboat on Dal Lake. We asked about our passes. He had sent them long ago, but we told him we had not received them. How did we get through? We said that the guard at the gate down the road had felt sorry for us and let us go. Babs and Mage were excited to see us.

All of us were taken to the boat, though it was a bit grimy. I told the man there'd be no pay until the boat was cleaned up, with new sheets, towels etc. "Yes, yes, right away." He shouted, and then with yells, as Indians always do to get things moving. The taxi driver took leave.

There was a bearer and cook that went with the boat. When the bearer realized someone spoke Hindi he was all over us, getting whatever we needed. We needed a lot of things, like ice and tonic water. "Yes sir!" he shouted. "Ak Dum-jaldi; yes sahib," that meant, "Yes, right away fast, we'll have it." It was most pleasant to sit at the aft end of the boat and sip our drinks. It was a while before the cook had made dinner; not the

greatest, but we can eat anything when hungry. The scenery was beautiful. The lake was bright blue with the high mountains rising up in the back. No wonder the Mogul emperors loved it. It was a beautiful sight. Far in the distance you could see an old mogul bridge. Srinagar, the capital, was of prime interest and a resort for the Moguls. One of the famous Moguls was Jahangir, and the other was Shah Jahan who built the Taj Mahal for his wife, Mumtaz. In Kashmir, where they spent a lot of their time, they had built the Shalimar Gardens, which are famous the world over.

At the end of the day, when the meal was over, we were tired, and soon went to bed. Next morning, we were up with our chota hazari. We couldn't go wrong with that. George was up, and we'd taken an early walk, A regular breakfast was in progress. The shikaras started to arrive. These are boats paddled by two people, one in front and one in the rear. They are low in the water, with cushioned seats and a frilled overhead canopy. They came from all directions to take us sightseeing on the lake, or wherever we wished to go. If I recall, we took two for a start, to do a little sightseeing and then on to town. They started off as though they were competing in the English, Henley Regatta. I finally convinced the paddlers to take it easy; we wanted to look around. The paddlers were obedient and listened well to my Hindi. Tut, Dick and I were in one boat, and after paddling in a civilized manner, we'd be damned when our paddlers started chanting; the one in the rear "Scotch," the one in the front, "Soda!" With that rhythm, they went paddling along: "Scotch," "Soda," "Scotch," "Soda." Old Dick reeled with laughter and all of us joined in. The chant was taken up by the other boat as well. It was a beautiful scotch and soda morning as we glided through the clear water.

I was happy to see there were flocks of white-chested kingfishers, with grey-blue wings and backs; also the miniature ones, the little fellows, who could certainly dart over the water, from one perch to another. We were dropped off at the section of town of Sirinagar. Though most things were cheap, one could spend a fortune on so many wonderful items to buy, mainly the Kashmiri woolen goods. The most popular and expensive is called Pashmina wool, also called "ring shawls." The

shawl is so soft, it can be pulled easily through a wedding ring. There were silk scarves and other hand-embroidered items of interest, like table clothes and serviettes of all colors. Then carpets, of all shapes and designs. Babs and Mage "ooohed" and "aaahed" at everything. We were directed to a nice Kashmiri restaurant for late lunch. Kashmiri curry is a different style altogether, but still hot and very good. Some of the group preferred simple fried chicken. We then inquired about hunting. Oh, yes; this could be arranged, guns and all. The four of us decided to go. We enjoyed the day snipe shooting with great success. We gave the birds to our cook to have ready next day for lunch. We came back next noon for a good feast, but as the taxi dropped us off, a foul smell greeted us and we almost got sick. I raced in and asked the cook what he was doing. He said he was taught to cook game birds with all their insides. Our birds were cooked, guts and all, hence the strong vile aroma. "No way, you can throw those birds away." We diverted to a restaurant back in town.

The Shakari (hunting guide) said he could also arrange a big game hunt for us: bear hunting, if we wished. It would be a great distance further in the mountains, it would be necessary for tents; a real safari. We contemplated this and decided it would be a good trip, whether we got anything or not. It would be a chance to see more of Kashmir.

The day came. A bus would take us a small distance, then it was pony and pack horse. You should have seen the array and what was in the safari! Tents, chickens, goats, chamber pots, etc. George and I got a kick out of this. The horses were a Godsend to lead us up the steep zigzag slopes. Late afternoon found us at a lovely campsite near a roaring, clear, ice-cold stream. The porters pitched the tents and had meals cooking. If we never saw a bear, this trip was still worth it. Though the water was cold, the four of us were able to strip to our shorts and dunk in the pool; it was refreshing. That evening the food tasted good. Now let's go for the bear hunt.

The guide said that the animals came at night into the cornfields. He would arrange the michans, little platforms, in the trees, where we would sit and wait at night. The four of us walked for hours further up the mountain until we came to some villages and cornfields. Instead of michans, they had us sit on roofs of adobe-type huts. There was no moon; two of us sat on separate roofs, Rossi and I on one, and George and Tutweiler on the other. The guides had flashlights. We sat huddled, with shotguns loaded with ball cartridges. As night crept over us, it got very cold; we shivered. In about an hour the guide said he heard a bear coming into the fields just below us. Dick would shoot first. "Yes," he said, "it's here!" He flashed a light on a Himalayan bear. I could see the white V on its chest. It was facing about three-quarters in our direction, in a semi-sitting position. Dick shot, and I followed. The guide switched the flashlight to another section, and said the bear had run into the field. He was sure we had hit the beast. We would get him in the morning. We heard other shots, also. The guide called to the others, and for us all to meet. We gathered in the field, near where George and Tutweiler had shot at their bear. We looked around and saw the path back to camp. The man said there had been blood, and that we had hit the animals. We gathered at the hut, but decided we dare not follow at night, in case the wounded animals would attack. So we returned to camp. I somehow became skeptical, and told the others. The two guides were too confident that we had hit and wounded the bears. Why didn't they go down and look at the place where we shot? Something was fishy.

In the morning, we all climbed back up the pathway, the two guides ahead. At the cornfields, some stalks had been broken, bear tracks were visible, and there was blood and some black hair, at our field and at the others. The guides led us along the trail, and kept showing us tracks and numerous splotches of blood. The tracks turned off the main path, into the woods. They advised us not to follow, to stay back here. In about an hour, they were back and said the blood indicated a good hit, but too difficult to follow. They would put trackers on and get at least one bear later. At camp, we knew it had to be a hoax. Never mind; we were enjoying the scenery and the camp life. A couple of days more up there, and we were on our way back to Sirinagar sans bear. We talked to some English people we met, whom we had a picnic lunch with on one of the small islands on the lake. The subject of the bear shoot was brought up, and the Englishman laughed and said, "You fell for that? It's all arranged: the guides go ahead the night before, and with their cohorts, place a stuffed bear in the place where you can get a shot at it. The guide shines a light in another direction, while a man sneaks the stuffed animal away." We laughed, and figured we'd been had. Never mind; the trip to the higher hills was great.

Our vacation was now ending, and preparations for departure were made. It all wound up quickly! Back to Rawlpindi, and the train back to Delhi. This time, a British soldier got on as well, but he would be getting off at Lahore. We were talking about the scarcity of whiskey in Calcutta. The soldier's name was Sergeant Hogg, and he would be coming to Calcutta in a few days from Lahore. Lahore had loads of good whiskey. We, however, would not have time to race in and buy some; the train would be departing in about 45 minutes. Hogg said he would be happy to purchase as much as we wanted, and bring it to Calcutta when he came. The guy looked innocent enough, so the four of us chipped in about 1000 rupees for about two or three cases. As Mr. Hogg walked down the platform, and our train pulled out of Lahore, Rossi and George said, "There goes our 1200 rupees!" And how right they were. We called his regiment and asked about Sergeant Hogg; "never heard of him." We were had again! I think if the guy had shown

up, George would have mangled him, because George was strong as an ox.

We were in Calcutta in time to arrange my birthday party. Our cook out did himself, with a terrific buffet, without Sgt. Hogg's whiskey! Everyone contributed to the bar. About 30 pilots and girlfriends arrived. Not Allison. Sometime during the festivities, the bearer announced that a memsahib was outside. Ray Hauptman and I went to the door, and there stood Miss Red Cross herself, Diana. We'd invited her, back at Murree, but forgotten all about it. There she was, looking so very lovely. We brought her in and introduced her. She got in the swing of things in a hurry. People filtered in and out, mingled and danced. It was a great birthday party, and I was now 29.

By the wee small hours, people started to fall by the wayside, and others found their way home. I asked Diana if she wished me to take her home. No, she said, unless I wanted to get rid of her. Of course not! I'd much prefer it if she did stay. That was it; we wandered into my room to relax. When she was down to her skivvies, I flipped! She had on the same type of undershorts as Allison. I chuckled to myself and wondered if that was the vogue in Calcutta. It must have been near noon or so, before we unraveled. We both felt the effects of that night's party. But what a birthday present! I asked if her folks would have worried. No, they were understanding people. The bearer had somehow got Diana's clothes and cleaned and pressed them. She looked crisp and chic in her Red Cross uniform of light blue.

Some of the folks were out on the back verandah. Diana, Rossi, Hammel, Jenkins, Ray; we all joined in. It had been a great day. It's amazing how quickly and silently the servant can come in and clean up a terrible mess. We had beer and snacks to sober up. Then, the bear was shown, and we all played with the bear on the lawn. But the time came for me to take Diana home, without her getting into any trouble with her folks. I think someone had tried to get our friendly bear, Elmer, drunk; he looked rather groggy. Time had come for us to close shop and head back.

There was a lot of activity in Dinjan. We were now on a new route to Suifu, where ship 46 had once become a DC 2-1/2. Ridge Hammel had brought Elmer up to Dinjan, and he stole the show at the bungalow. Everyone loved Elmer. Cliff Groh took the little fellow under his wing. At dinner, we were introduced to the new route. Robbie, with his gold tooth grin and Georgia drawl said the Suifu run makes the Kunming route over the hump look like a "macadam road." Potty gave us all the briefing. There was supposed to be a radio station at the base of the mountain called Likiang, commonly known as "The Green Dragon." The mountain was 21,000 feet high. You had to make sure you flew around it to the right. You'd never make it from the left because of the severe winds and rugged peaks. Further to the north and on our left were The Three Sisters, also around 21,000 to 23,000 feet. Further along is the highest mountain of all, about 25,000

*Result of snipe hunt. I did not use the old flashlite and sack!!*

*Haircut on the houseboat in Kashmir.*

feet, called Minigonka. After passing Likiang, and two hours later, you'd pick up a rugged, jagged cliff, that looked exactly like the Rock of Gibraltar. From there it was safe to let down to about 12,000-13,000 feet, and hopefully pick up the Suifu beacon. The field was a big grass patch on the bend of the Yangtze River. Again, don't miss or pull up on instruments, because there's a high ridge on the opposite side of the river, in line with the runway. Suifu was never VFR; like Chungking, always overcast, foggy and damp. "Well, good luck fellows."

I had Mike Schroeder, another Pan Africa pilot, on my first flight and on several other of the flights, before my Kashmir holiday. He was assigned to me again on the Suifu schedule. I was happy to have an experienced pilot along. We climbed as high

*Tutweiler, Babs Huang, and Dick Rossi enjoying a shakara (gondola) on Dahl Lake, Kashmir.*

as one could get a DC-3, in and out of the clouds most of the way. Finally, I picked up Likiang radio and saw bits of the towering, craggy mountain. We skirted around it and got back on course for Suifu. The trip most of the way was overcast, but we were on top; there was Gibraltar sticking out from the white sea of clouds. After passing the rock, we were able to pick up Suifu radio. The let down was made, and we broke out at about 700 feet into fairly clear visibility. Markings were clearly made on the grassy field. We got out and stretched, had a drink of tea and a bit to eat. I could now get a good look at the terrain, the rough looking hills on the other side of the river. Suifu, I understand, is also famous for its fine Chinese silk. It had to be ordered, and the CNAC ground personnel would buy the silk for you. I kept that in mind. Also, a super-powerful drink that came in earthen jugs was made at Suifu, with heavy grease paper covering around the mouth, tied with thick oily string. Some of the fellows had brought several pots of this back to Dinjan, and we all tried it. It was rough; one had to be desperate to want to drink it. We gave it the name of "White Lightning." Only thing it was good for was for Suklo to light the fires with in the morning. It exploded when a match was touched anywhere near it.

Mike Schroeder made several more trips with me to Suifu, and the monsoons were now breaking up and clear weather was appreciated. We got a good look at Likiang, Minigonka, and Gibraltar. We always expected a letdown at Suifu. On one trip, Suifu was fairly socked in. We came over the station, circling on top. One pilot, Al Wright, said he was going to give it a try. We waited on top. Shortly, there was a dark patch of cloud spread over the further area. Just before that, another Chinese pilot said he was going in for an approach. Four of us circled

above. The grey-black smudge was still visible. Then another black smudge appeared. Suifu radio called and said he thought the planes had crashed at the other end of the field. The rest of us reported in and said we were going to Kunming instead. On arrival there, we learned that both planes had hit the cliff on the other end. The weather had been almost zero-zero when the guys tried to land. Then they tried to make a missed approach. I told Mike of the various downdrafts on the lee side of the mountains; don't ever forget them, and don't ever be caught in them, either! In clear weather, fly low to the north of the Burma Valley and watch for Japs. With loads of tin, stay away from the thunderstorms.

I flew a trip on the 12th of October to Kunming, and the weather was beautifully clear, new snow all over the mountains. It was the same on the way back, beautiful weather. On October 13th, I had the day off. I borrowed a gun and went green pigeon shooting. They're beautiful, bright green pigeons, and very hard to spot in the trees. I'd shot a few, and was back at the bungalow. Woody came driving up and called those of us who were there. He said, "Hey, fellas; the Japs struck in the valley, early this morning, Zeros all over the place. A whole lot of planes have been shot down. We've heard from most of our flights, but not from Mike Schroeder." We all jumped into the crew car and returned to the airport with Woody and waited. There was an Air Force squadron located at our field, called the 10th Troop Carriers. We all milled around, waiting for the flights and news. Far in the distance, we heard a screaming, shrill noise like a banshee. In came a C-47, on a straight in landing. It was one of the military troop carriers. We went over to greet the flight. The plane was riddled with holes; the props had holes through them. Inside, you could see rows and

stitched holes, up and down, on the top of the cabin. Good Lord! How did the pilot make it back? The two pilots and crew chief got out and stood against the fuselage. They asked for a smoke, and before the cigarette was lit, one of them fainted. He came to, and one of the troop carriers, Major Duke, took charge and got the guys drinks from the nearby mess. The captain finally was able to disclose the events, as best he could. As he stated:

The morning had been a very clear one. About forty-odd aircraft were up high, 16,000-18,000 feet, headed for Kunming. From nowhere, the Japs dove in at them; they were sitting ducks. In minutes, planes were spiraling in, some on fire. Before he could maneuver, bullets ripped into the plane while he dove for the ground. The pursuers left him when he was at tree height; he hedgehopped back. We then learned that Mike was one of the unlucky ones. He had been shot down, without a chance to escape. The other CNAC guys had flown low and north; they made it to Kunming safely. In all, 23 to 24 planes were downed that morning. I was sick, when I learned about Mike. I told Woody, that I'd talked to Mike and advised him how to fly in good weather. Why did he go way upstairs to 15-odd thousand feet, to be caught helpless? We were all saddened when we returned to the bungalow.

Woody came back and said, "As of now, all flying will be done strictly at night." This was a whole new experience. We did not know about night effects on our radios, but we soon learned, and found our radios were unreliable. Thankfully, the monsoons were over; for the most part the weather would be clear at night. I found I could just about have my instrument panel dimmed very low. I could see well at night, with the snowcapped mountains ahead. What the hell, I'd fly south over to Shimbuang and Suprabum at about 10,000 feet. I could see Foxy's Pass and skim across to Yunani and Tali, and then into Kunming. Amazingly enough, Kunming was always lit up, as though there was no war on; not much in the way of a blackout. On moonlit nights, it was an eerie, beautiful sight, clear as could be; I could see for miles.

But when weather did set in, flying was difficult. At the beginning, it became difficult to get used to the St. Elmo's Fire that shimmered on the propellers and windshield like the dance of the Valkyries. Thunderstorms lit up the skies for miles. I kept my cockpit lights on as bright as possible, so as not to be blinded by the bright flashes. The C-53 and C-47 took the storms well. I'd lower the gear and slow down to about 80-90 miles per hour. The plane would wallow like an old buffalo in the Calcutta mud. One night, when I had Jules Watson with me, the weather was clear for most of the trip, and then it started getting a little bit murky after Yunani. We arrived over Kunming, which was overcast, with heavy, low clouds. A ceiling of around 400 feet was reported. The top was around 10,000 feet. The radios worked fine, and I made my outbound leg.

Once inbound and into the clouds, the ADF needle would spin; at no time would it ever point. I'd pull up and try again, for at least three or four attempts, always the same spin. I thought of staying on top till over the station, drop the gear and flaps and descend on a southbound heading till I'd break out over the lake. From that altitude, I figured I might just go too far and hit Windy Hill, or hills to the left of the lake. Maybe it wasn't 400 feet. I told Jules to tell Kunming we couldn't make it; we would return to Dinjan. I think he was relieved I didn't try to gamble. Several planes had already crashed at Kunming, due to their own crazy-acting radios.

After a few hairy experiences, especially Suifu, it was agreed that our operation would now go into a 24-hour schedule, and we could select our trips. We could make 1-1/2 trips a day if we wished. This would finish our time sooner. Some nights, we'd wind up in Kunming and back to Dinjan the next day. Many flights were now hauling Chinese soldiers from Kunming to Dinjan, to help build the Stillwell-Lido road. It was to be built from Digboi and Lido area, through the False Valley, to Burma, Fort Hertz, into Shimbuang or Suprabum, and hopefully, to Myitkyina to drive the Japs out.

I picked up a load of soldiers one trip. As you may recall, there were only bucket seats on these planes, and sometimes no seatbelts. First, we had the group of soldiers, about 25 of them, go to the rear of the plane and relieve themselves. Then were marched into the plane and seated. I would take a long rope, tie it at one end, and loop through where the seat belt hinges should have been. The rope was passed over their laps, through these openings, on the way to the top near the cockpit. Here, a mighty heave, and then tie it down. These people were a happy-go-lucky crowd, always laughing and smiling. There were no stewardesses to handle them, nothing to eat. We figured they had their meal before flight. Airborne and on our way! I'd always level at 10,000 and pass my same old Paoshan route, hopefully through Foxy's Pass. This flight, I had to climb up through weather, to 16,000-17,000 feet; icy, cold and rough. I never dared go back to see how the people were. After about an hour, I burst out into the Burma Valley, which was clear. I couldn't sit up here as a sitting duck, so I cut the power and descended back down to 10,000 feet, then north over the Digboi and Dinjan. This trip, the troops had been roasted, frozen, blacked out, roasted again, rough-aired, and then finally on the ground in a little less than four hours. I opened the cockpit door slowly. They didn't look happy. Some said "Boo Hao," which means, "very bad." We undid the rope, and they almost fell out of their seats. Vomit was a slow stream from the top to the bottom, where it collected in a pool of thick slimy rice. U.S. 6x6 trucks were ready to take them on their long bumpy road to Lido. I was most cautious, climbing down from the cockpit to the end, because of the slippery goo. Once out, I felt sick myself. Thousands of these soldiers were brought in. Once they got their bearings and equilibrium

*The safari leads off with goats, chickens and commodes! Kashmir, 1943.*

back from the horrendous flights, they adjusted to the new climate. They got good G.I. food and living quarters, a hell of a lot better than they had in China. For this, they performed miracles in building the famous Lido Road. As we flew our trips, one could almost see the road progressing through the very harsh jungle terrain.

C-NAK still had more planes arriving; many more new pilots and faces. We were flying our butts off to Kunming and Suifu. At times I averaged around 140 hours per month. Our schedules were now being arranged from Calcutta, not by Woody. We still were awakened by Suklo's Canadian Blue Skies, and sometimes the Warsaw Concerto. Every time Robbie was with us, and as soon as the gramophone was shut off, he would shout out, "OK, fellas; drop your cocks and grab your socks!" Cliff would hustle down and feed Elmer, who was getting big now. I think it probably slept with Cliff.

One day, Cliff took Elmer on a flight across the hump. There was an Army plane ahead. Cliff strapped Elmer in the captain's seat, with Cliff's cap on. He pulled up alongside an Airforce plane. The First Officer looked over and appeared to leap out of his seat. One can imagine him looking over and seeing a black bear flying a CNAC C-47. That story went around for a while.

It was not all a bed of roses. We were losing planes here and there. I will not discuss all of them, only those that were of personal interest to me, such as Mike Schroeder, Foxy, and Sam Anglin.

By the end of November, I had around 170 round-trips, and approximately 1200 hours of hump flying. I guess I was seasoned in the ways of the treacherous flying.

I was back in Calcutta for Thanksgiving and I had joined the Royal Calcutta Golf Club. There was an A course and a B course, of 36 holes, which sported 54 water tank

hazards. Though I was not very good, I enjoyed playing. The foliage and the birds, especially the brainfever, were always there. On weekends and holidays, a bar was usually set up on the 5th and 10th holes of the A course, with a waiter present to serve you. You paid for drinks by the British chit system, no money. It was carried on the bill and presented at the end of each month. A Mr. Langston was the Club Manager, and very fine English individual. On days off, a few of us spent our time playing golf and enjoying the hospitality. After playing, the club's special drink was gin and ginger beer; it had to be a must. After a good shower, a bearer would wrap a large turkish towel around you and proceed to give you a thorough rubdown. This included a drying of feet and toes, even putting on your socks for you. What a life!

CNAC was also invited to join another club, the 300 Club on Theater Road. It was managed by a White Russian who had escaped from Odessa, Russia, at the time of the Revolution in 1917. His name was synonymous with the club as whiskey was to soda; Boris Lissanevitch was his name. We used to call him "Boris-the-son-of-a-bitch." The club was a coat and tie affair. Allison by this time had gone astray. She was chasing every uniform she could find, which wasn't difficult. By now, there were thousands of GIs in India, especially in Calcutta. It was a shame, as I thought she was a lovely young girl. I kept hearing stories of her from my friends. She even was involved with some of the CNAC guys. Even when I wanted to see her, she was off with a new uniform. I wanted to talk with her and try to straighten her out.

I started to frequent the 300 Club regularly. The atmosphere created by Boris and his White Russian colleagues was very pleasant, and the food was probably the best anywhere in India. Reservations were always necessary. In the winter months, the place was crowded. Boris made dinner arrangements out on the back lawn and open verandah. He had a live orchestra that was good. The mixture of patronage was interesting; there were British, Americans, and wealthy Indians. Most were in uniform. The Indian ladies came dressed in exotic saris, one of the most feminine dresses I have ever seen, and in a way quite sexy when worn tightly, with bare midriffs.

On one of those occasions when I was at the 300 Club by myself, I noticed a group of British army people talking at the bar. One of them was an Indian. He was tall and handsome, and looked very much like Stewart Granger. His uniform was black, with high caftan collar buttoned up, and there were silver shoulder epaulets with fringes and dark blue trousers with a dark red stripe down the side. The boots looked like patent leather, with spurs. He was a fascinating looking individual, and appeared to be enjoying his company with laughter. Boris had joined the group, in his tuxedo. Boris looked a lot like Peter Lorre of the movies, and talked somewhat like him, as well. Later, as the group went to their table and Boris was making his rounds, I cornered him and asked who that uniformed fellow was, the Indian. "Oh," said he, "that's the Maharajah of Cooch-Behar." Where is Cooch-Behar, I asked. "Well, it's due north of Calcutta, about 200 miles, at the foot of Darjeeling." I now had a good idea; I would look it up on the map. "I'll introduce you to him when there is a chance." "That will be fine." It did not come about that day, and I left shortly after. I was not that interested in meeting any Maharajahs; he just struck me as an interesting person.

A notice on the board at the club said there would be a special Thanksgiving Dinner 1943 for the Americans. Those who wished to attend would please leave their name and number in the party. I put my name plus three, hoping I could get Diana and perhaps one or two of the fellows from the house. I think it was Ridge Hammel who said he would join me. We couldn't get dates; our uniforms took the place of tuxedos. We arrived fairly early. I didn't come often to the club, as it was expensive. We enjoyed our drinks that early evening, and watched several people come in. I noticed on the board that Chuck Sharp and McDonald would be there, that would be great. One of the rooms had been set aside for the Thanksgiving dinner. Other guests were being seated, few came to the bar. Then here came Cooch-Behar, in another, more ordinary uniform, in khaki. Since it was only a weekday to him, he looked around and came to the bar and ordered a scotch and soda. He spoke good English. I couldn't resist it. I said, "I believe you are the Maharajah of Cooch-Behar. I was told by Boris." "Yes." Then I introduced myself and Ridge Hammel, and said that we were pilots with CNAC, flying the hump. "I've heard of you guys." We chatted; he bought us drinks. I said we were going to the Thanksgiving Dinner here. Cooch-Behar then suggested that we come and visit him

sometime. His principality was on our route to Dinjan; he had a small air field a few U.S. Air Force planes used for training. There was also good shooting. He said that whenever I wanted to, please let Boris know and he could phone. I really got interested and said I would. We parted and went to our table.

There were a few Americans who showed up in civvies, including Chuck and Mac. We exchanged good wishes, and set about with our own meal. I guess Boris knew the tradition, for everything was there, including cranberry sauce. He must have bribed someone to get it from the U.S. commissary, because the British didn't eat it with their turkeys. Boris came by, and was complimented on the dinner. I also said that we had met Cooch-Behar. "Good," he said; and to let him know if we wished to go for a visit. Boris said it was great shooting; lots of game. I'd let him know. We were going to fly soon, and hoped to have Christmas in Calcutta. Boris insisted we have Christmas dinner at the 300 Club; he'd make arrangements for a table.

I'd been sending money home, though not as much as I would have liked to ; there had been those loans to take care of, and living expenses. George Huang had said to me to hang on to CNAC, that I was one of the Chinese's fair-haired pilots. I would be welcomed to stay on with the company when the war ended, based in Shanghai, which sounded good to me. I wondered and hoped Helen would come over. I did my flying and returned to Calcutta.

When I got off the plane, Chuck Sharp came to me. He asked, "Have you been with Pan Am overseas, including Africa?" I said yes, "It's been almost two years." "How would you like a trip back to the States for a couple of months, then fly a C-47 back? Petach and Allen would be going around the end of February 1944." "I would appreciate that very much."

With that in mind, I went the next day and played golf, visited the club; this helped take my mind off flying. I flew my December schedule and was back in Calcutta for Christmas. Just before Christmas, who drives up a in a taxi, but Allison. "Hi," as though all is well. She was disturbed and mixed up; she thought she might be pregnant again, but wasn't sure. Who was it this time? She had no idea. I didn't know whether to give her a good spanking or tell her to get lost. She suggested a trip to Darjeeling for New Year's?" "Darjeeling!" I'd never thought of that. But first, I decided to have my Christmas at the 300 Club, and would let her know.

Boris' 300 Club Christmas was a gala event, nothing like the one a year ago at the Grand Hotel, when the Japanese came over. Boris always put on a good spread and a good show. The tables were lavishly decorated, including the English-type crackers. When the people pulled them, they made a small bang and a crack. The person who had the largest part of the bonbon would get either a headband or some little trinket. It was normally for kids. It was a great, successful party, and it was really a worthwhile Christ-

mas Dinner. The day after, which is British Boxing Day, I gathered up Allison, and we took the night train to Darjeeling. The train stopped at the foothills, at a town called Siliguri, equivalent to Khatgodam. However, there is a miniature train from Siliguri to Darjeeling, which I have mentioned earlier. We took the little train, and it was quite a ride, very slow, gradually winding its way up to 7000 feet plus, something like a caterpillar inching its way up a branch of a tree. The weather was freezing. A four-man rickshaw (two pushing and two pulling) took us from the station at Darjeeling to Mount Everest Hotel. The rickshaw fellows were a little different than the Chungking type; these were very slow. The ride was a very steep trip from the station to the hotel. Everyone seemed to be shivering except the pullers; they panted all the way. They have a habit of pretending to be overworked, looking for a bigger tip, or baksheesh.

We checked in at the hotel, which in the winter is not that crowded. We had a room facing towards the plains. It was a pleasant room, but still very cold. The whole place seemed to be what we call "cold-soaked." The fire was lit in the fireplace; you paid extra for the wood. Allison seemed more like herself now. We had our afternoon tea in the room; it was the only warm place. Rather nice, sipping tea where it originated from. On the train coming up, I recalled and pointed out to Allison two or three tea estates. It would be many years later that I would get to enjoy and always ask for a special brand from one of these tea estates, which is called Lopchu. It is not exported.

We wrapped up in sweaters and scarves, and decided to take a stroll close by. The air was crisp. There were several well marked walks that meandered from the hotel around the hills. Allison and I walked along one of these. It was so quiet and peaceful. Most of the cottages here had tin roofs; they resembled Switzerland. Every so often, we came to park-like benches, with wooden overhead roofs. I felt I could walk for miles. It was in Darjeeling that many of the Mt. Everest expeditions started from; now they start from Katmandu in Nepal, a much easier start-off point. There was not much twilight, as soon as the sun is down, darkness engulfs the mountains. Lights were coming on by the time we were back. We found the bar and ordered drinks. I wouldn't have to worry about the ice melting fast in these drinks, because they didn't really need any. I think Allison had her gin and tonic, and I reverted to scotch and soda. It was about then that dinner was announced. We ordered a third drink for our table. It was a fairly large dining room, and not all the tables were made up, the hotel staff cut almost in half. This was not the season for people to come to the hill stations. The little menu was typed on a card; it was no 300 Club menu. The soup was mostly lamb broth, and the meat was lamb with potatoes, and finished with some sort of blancmange pudding and coffee, which never interested me.

After the simple dinner, Allison and I wandered up to our room. Needless to say, it was cuddling weather, and I had thrown a couple of logs on the dying fire to perk it up. We lay in bed, catching our breath like the rickshaw pullers; the fire crackled and spat, casting strange dancing shadows on the walls. Except for the company, it felt like being home in Bhowali and Bhimtal. I could almost hear my Mum telling us some of her true exciting stories. I was brought back to reality by a nudge in my side. In the morning, I was awakened by a gentle knock on the door. I knew it would be the bearer with our early morning tea. I wore a blue flannel nightsuit, I remember, because I'd bought it from Bob Angle, before he left. There was one problem with it; it was a drawstring affair, and the fly had no buttons. As I walked, in my half-sleep, to answer the door, I think my whistle had popped out. I opened the door, the bearer looked me over, but without smiling or chuckles. He brought in the tea, put it on the table, salaamed, and walked out. Allison was now sitting up. She looked at me walking back and started to howl with laughter, pointing at me. I looked down, and said, "Something's got to be done about these pajamas."

Water had been set for our baths. We wandered back downstairs. I didn't feel much like any more breakfast, but another walk, because that's about all there is to do in Darjeeling, if you know what I mean. We bundled up and headed off to look for some new pathways and trails. There were many. We walked for a considerable time, then stopped at one of the places with a bench. I took out a jackknife, and carved our initials on one of the posts. I'm sure, if it hasn't burnt down or rotted away, our initials are still there.

For the next day, the clerk at the desk suggested we should visit a place called Tiger Hill; there we could witness the early morning sunrise on Mount Kanchenjunga, the third highest mountain in the world, a little over 28,000 feet. We could go by taxi, fourman rickshaw, walk, or by horseback. We decided to go by horseback. Our ponies would be ready at four a.m. in the morning. We were up at three and on our way at exactly four. It was terribly cold as we started our trip. It was still pitch black outside and was necessary for the horsemen (sices) to hold the reins and guide the ponies along the road. It reminded me a bit of the time my friends and I were walking along the trail at Mt. Kathadin. As we rode along on the horses, we were not able to see much; the ponies plodded along slowly mile after mile. Eventually, we came to an open area where I could just make out the trail and a plateau, as the early dawn began to creep up. The horses were stopped at the bottom of a high wooden, lookout station. Allison and I were happy to get off as our behinds were really getting sore. These mountain ponies are devilish animals and uncomfortable on

a long ride such as this. They would throw you off at any chance.

We walked up and down the trail for a few minutes to circulate our blood and to get warm. From nowhere, here comes a man bringing us two cups of hot tea; a most welcome sight. Al and I then climbed up on the platform and waited for the early sunrise to catch the peak of Kanchenjunga. We could clearly see the mountain about fifty miles away; it was a massive heap of snow and rock, all a silvery gray color. The weather was clear and very cold with little breeze. Tiger Hill is about ten thousand feet high. The first rays of sun came up from our right and its shafts of light caught the mountain peak and turned the silver gray mass into a beautiful dark pink, as the lower peaks were waiting their turn. The dark pink turned to a lighter shade and now the lower peaks were turning rose pink, and further down in the valley there were the grays and dark green. The scenery was spectacular! It certainly was worth the trip. Allison and I stood in awe as the pinks changed to yellow, then the dazzling whites of the snows. Even flying over the Hump was not so beautiful. Nothing could match this sight. Kachenjunga, though so distant, appeared to be close enough to throw a pebble onto the snow. The servant who had served us tea on our arrival, had now joined us with most of his head wrapped in a brown woolen scarf and said, "If you look beyond, you will see three peaks in the distance, far beyond Kanchenjunga; the one in the middle is Mount Everest. The close one is Makalu." Having read several accounts of the assaults on Everest and the lives lost on it, I was excited to see the majestic peak; even from this distance, which was about a hundred miles away.

It was a beautiful morning with the bright sun warming us. Allison and I walked further along the trail from the lookout. All this area was just above the timberline. We came to the edge of Tiger Hill plateau. Here it dropped away below us for thousands of feet. At the bottom, one could see the thin silver ribbon of a river as it snaked its way toward the plains where it probably emptied itself into the Ganges or Brahmaputra Rivers. It was so very hard for Allison and I to drag ourselves away from the spectacular scenery. We were told that on the way back, we could stop at a dairy farm called Kaventers. I remembered seeing a tea place in Darjeeling, when we walked there, called Kaventers. I guess it was a part of the same company. I also remember my mother telling us kids long ago about a place that she knew that was called Kaventers. They sold wonderful butter and delicious thick cream. The horse ride going back was more interesting. We could see the scenery and also notice the steep dropoffs on the left side of the trail; one slip and you and the horse could roll quite a distance, unless you came up against a tree. Most of the trees here were the beautiful silver oaks and rhododendron with heavy lichen and moss.

Halfway back we came to some buildings, and on the entrance of the gate, a sign read "Kaventers Dairy Company." An Englishman greeted us as we dismounted, and welcomed us to Kaventers. Al and I were shown some of the farm animals, mainly large hogs. They looked well-fed, enormous and pink; they looked like the morning at Kanchenjunga. I think the gentleman's name was Mr. Bee; he was the manager. We entered the main building; the room was not too spacious, but did have several tables laid out and a roaring fire in the fireplace. It was warm and pleasant. Al and I settled for tea, while the order would be eggs and bacon. The breakfast was great. Allison said she would like to have stayed on the rest of the day. I had to agree. I was thinking of that cold air outside; but the time had come, and after paying our bill and thanking Mr. Bee, we mounted our ponies and were on our way. The guide told us also, that further along, we would come to a Tibetan monastery or temple that had been there for many, many years. Sure enough, as we came around one of the bends, further to one side, there was a large, beautiful monastery. There were the prayer wheels outside, which we could turn, and many fluttering flags. The flags represented a lot of their prayers. We asked the head man, who looked like a Lama or high priest, if we could enter. "Yes," but we must first take off our shoes. We went in and looked around; it was dark and smelled of incense. When we came out, the man had one of his priest produce a large horn or trumpet-like affair, something like the Swiss people have up in the Alps. It was about a ten-foot trumpet which rested on the ground. It was quite an awesome sound, when the priest blew the trumpet. He was calling people to prayer, as our churchbells. It was very strange and beautiful. We thanked the Priest, then gave some rupees in their hands, for which they were grateful. We climbed our mounts and headed back to Darjeeling and the hotel. A bit sore from the ride, we were back at the hotel for a clean-up. Allison and I had walked all over Darjeeling and seen most places, even had tea and cakes at the little Kaventers Restaurant. At the bazaar one day, I spied a shop that had the Ghurka knives (Kukris). The usual bickering took place, but finally I bought a beautiful knife, the real thing, even nicer than the one I'd traded to the Pan Am guy for the steel trunk in Karachi. I was happy now and ready to return to Calcutta. The day came. This time, we had coolies carry our luggage, and we walked from Everest Hotel to the mini-railroad station. There was a lot of hubbub and noise, and people getting ready to descend down to Siliguri. Though the ride downhill was very pleasant, the miniature train was still slow and precarious. We stopped at the famous Loop. At Siliguri, we noticed the temperature change; it was warmer and damp, after the rarefied atmosphere of Darjeeling.

In Calcutta, when we arrived, I dropped Allison at her place on Ripon Street. The taxi took me off to Ballygunge. The bearer helped me unpack, and when we came to the blue flannel pajamas, I asked if he could get a couple of buttons sewed onto the fly; I didn't want another mishap. He said he could arrange that. The few day's rest in the hills had been good, and I was ready to go back to Dinjan for more flying. It was now 1944, and the Germans were being pushed back by the Russians, and North Africa was liberated. The Americans were slowly taking the Pacific Islands, one at a time, with considerable losses. The Japs still held fast in Malaya and Burma, and most of China. So we, the lifeline to China and Chennault, would continue with the supplies.

I had a new co-pilot when I arrived back in Dinjan. His name was Roy Farrell. I let him fly most of the trips of January, when he was with me. There were many characters that passed through our CNAC portals; some stayed, some made a faster exit. The military now had C-87s, which were B-24s converted into freighters. Also C-46s. However, the military were still losing a great number of aircraft. We heard that a major airline from the States also had received a contract to fly supplies across to China for six months. They were given C-87s to do the job. With a lot of hoopla, they would teach the CNAC and all the others how to deliver the goods. They also had a full complement of flight engineers and navigators. Well, to make a long story short, they lost several airplanes and lasted the six months and said anybody who would stay and fly out here was crazy, so let the CNAC guys do it. They wanted out in a hurry, and they were gone.

One individual that entered our CNAC company was a pilot by the name of Bennett; I don't remember his first name. He had made about three or four flights with us, each one with a different captain, and on each occasion, the flight wound up with some sort of difficulty, mainly engine troubles or not being able to make a letdown at Suifu. He had been nicknamed "Jinx" Bennett. Wouldn't you know, on the next flight, he was assigned to me! The flight was to Suifu, the ship number was 56. It didn't have any deicing equipment on board, or any kind of heating system; as I think I mentioned before, these ships were old C-53s. I had a talk with Jinx the evening before, and I discussed many things about this airplane. I said there was no heating system, that we'd better take a couple of blankets along. It looked like a clear day ahead, as we jolted and journeyed around on the trip to the airport. But you can never tell about the weather in this area, especially over the mountains. It can be clear one moment and then turn sour and miserable the next. It's always good to be prepared for the worst. The flight went well past Likiang Mountain, as we skirted around to the south of it, and then on our way till we could spot Gibraltar in the distance. I explained the route to Jinx. We were about 16,000-17,000 feet, and all bundled up in blankets, no autopilot. I used a part of the blanket over the yoke, as a glove, and flew manually. We took it by turns. As I said, the C-53s are light, so it was easy to handle. I explained the coffee grinder, or manual loop.

I told him always keep it in the null position. We arrived at Suifu station, on top of the usually socked-in weather. I circled overhead, and was in that holding area for nearly an hour, with no sign of the weather clearing for a letdown. As I mention, two airplanes who'd tried that before had smacked into a mountain down below. So, Ray Hauptmann and I decided to head for Kunming. We were carrying drums of fuel; so to me, it made no difference if we dumped them in Suifu or Kunming; they would be welcomed. It was late afternoon when we arrived at Kunming. The cargo was unloaded, and since we were not scheduled for Kunming that day, there was no return load for us, thank goodness. We checked the weather, and Dinjan was overcast, with a reported ceiling of 7000-8000 feet, but no rain, so I figured this should be an easy flight. It was dark as we passed Yunani, and I climbed to 17,000 feet and headed on a course of about 290 degrees. I could barely make out the Salween River up ahead, as stratos clouds sailed by. I was in and out of clouds, so I climbed up to 19,000 feet and a myriad of stars greeted me. There was just the two of us, no radio operator, but in a few minutes the stars disappeared, and I turned on the landing lights. I could see the reflections of clouds ahead and higher. Remember, I did have much in the way of deicing equipment, which is why I tried to steer clear of the clouds. I checked the approximate time I had passed the Blue River, or the Salween, and I had the manual loop in null. Another pilot, who was a veteran, by the name of Roy Leonard, once told me that in these old planes, keep your sliding side window open at least about half, even if you're half freezing to death. I don't know why, but I did just that. From 290 degrees heading, I thought I would turn left a little to 285, for Helen. There were no stars, and now and then it became a little bumpy. I turned on the lights and knew I was in heavy clouds. We stamped on the floor to warm our feet; they were really numb. I would guess at this time, and in the few minutes that followed, I was picking up a lot of ice. The controls started to feel heavy; prop ice was flying against the fuselage, making a loud bang every once in a while. This kept us awake and made Jinx jump. The airspeed dropped off, and I added a little more power, what little I could. At that altitude, usually the throttles were all the way forward, and the props were kept at about 1950 RPM; it did no good. I started getting St. Elmo's Fires, that played tricks on the propellers and also on the windshield. I turned on the cockpit lights bright as I could; there was no sense trying to look out at this time. The controls were really heavy, and I started to lose altitude. I turned further left to 280 degrees, this was for David. I revved the props to help throw off the ice, and I turned on the landing lights again; they barely shone at all. I looked out the open window and could make out that there was one hell of a load of ice on the wings, as reflected by the landing lights. I now got a little nervous, but didn't want Jinx excited. He was not aware of the situation. I

thought of Rosbert and Ridge Hammel, hitting the mountain just to the north of me. The winds, too, can play tricks, so I decided to turn still further south, to 270, for Sylvia and Mum. I was dropping now through 14,000 feet, and added max rated power without burning up the engines. The plane wouldn't hold altitude, and I think Jinx must have realized there was some kind of trouble. He asked if everything was okay, so I asked jokingly, "Have you ever had a load of ice on your airplane — and I do mean on the outside?" "No," he said. "Well, okay, take the controls and move the airplane." He tried and said, "Oh My God! The whole thing is frozen!" "Almost." I told him now to try to move the manual antenna; it was frozen. I then told him we undoubtedly had picked up a load of clear ice, back up there somewhere. I explained the difference, while the plane was still gradually losing altitude. I said that clear ice is like the ice-cubes in your refrigerator, and if your have metal ice-cube containers, they will just stick to the metal. Rime ice, I said, is the frosted icing in the lining of the refrigerator. They can be chipped off easily. The clear ice was probably caused by pre-cooled droplets of rain that were not frozen, even though the temperature was around 30-40 degrees Centigrade below zero, which we were. The sudden shock of the metal froze all the droplets, that's what stuck onto us, in large amounts, over and over again, possibly three or four tons, more than the airplane could hold. With a lot of nursing of the plane, it finally held at close to 12,000 feet, with a lot of power. I don't know what would have happened if we'd lost an engine about then; there'd be nowhere to got but down. Still I could not use too much meto power, or I'd burn up too much gas as well as the engines. The engines were behaving beautifully. I tried calling Dinjan, Chabua, and other bases; there was no response. I tried tuning frequencies for all the other stations, hoping I could pick up one, but there was nothing but static. I could not see out of the windshield; there must have been a foot of ice up front. I'd flown an hour since Salween, so I should have been picking up some sort of radio contact. Every once in a while I would squint out through the half-open window, but all I saw were clouds going by and snow. I didn't want to overshoot the Assam Valley, or I would wind up hitting Kanchenjunga Mountain. It was about another 10-15 minutes before I glanced out of the window again. I was checking all the gauges and heading when I thought I saw something flash by, and as I looked out again, I saw nothing. I was about to turn my attention back in when I definitely saw a light go past under me; then I saw another. I was breaking out somewhere. I cut the power, and the plane almost fell out from under me. I gave a little more power, as we broke through at about 9000 feet. We were in the Assam Valley, and after looking around, I saw an airport, which turned out to be Chabua, right ahead. I turned up north towards Dinjan, and at this altitude, the ice started melting. I could turn the coffee grinder now and talk to the tower, but the plane was still very heavy. I would have to come in at about 110 MPH with a wheel landing. I made it okay, and Woody was there to greet me. I opened the window as I cut the engines, and Woody shouted out, "Where did you collect all this ice?" Jinx and I climbed out, and I wanted to see this for myself. It was frightening; the whole contour of the leading edges of both wings, long lengths of thick ice dropped off; there must have been at least six to eight inches or more. There were some spots on the tail and from under the wing, and the windshield had a little. I said, "Too bad you didn't bring the whiskey, Woody!" I tried to be jovial for Jinx, but nothing doing; I saw him, he was shivering. Finally, he came out and said, "Woody, I just quit!" That was Jinx's last flight. I talked to Ray Hauptman, who had been ahead of me, and he hadn't picked up any ice.

By the end of February's flying, we were informed that Julius Petach, Ray Allen and myself were scheduled to Calcutta. From there, we were to head for the States via military airplane. This was good news, and I was ready to go back for a little leave. We packed our things and said "au revoir" to our friends. We hopped on a DC-3 that took us to Agra, then to Karachi. At Karachi, we climbed aboard a DC-4, the first I'd even seen. It was a monster airplane. Though bucket seats, we enjoyed it. We stopped at Cairo, and instead of the old route via Khartoum and across Central Africa. This time we traveled due west to Tobruk, on the North African Coast, as the Germans and Italians had been booted out. From Tobruk, we flew to Marrakech in Morocco. We were going to have a few days' rest here. Transport wheels took us to Casablanca, where we spent nearly a week waiting for our flight west. Casablanca was a great city, and I enjoyed it very much. I took long walks along the waterfront and saw the Atlantic. It seemed good, and I didn't see any Casbah, Peter Lorre or Humphrey Bogart.

Our flight was on another DC-4, that took us via Santa Maria, on the Azores, where we spent the night, then on to Gander, Newfoundland; from there to Boston. It would have been nice to have been able to get off and catch a train to Bangor, but we were informed we had to go all the way through to N.Y. and to report to the Pan American office. We arrived late in the afternoon at LaGuardia, and a limo took us to the Roosevelt Hotel in Manhattan. I called Christine, who was tickled to hear me. She gave me Helen's number, as she had moved to another address. It was nice to say hello to Helen too. She wanted to know why I was in New York, and not on a train to Bangor. I tried to explain, but sometimes these situations are difficult to put across. I, too, wasn't certain why I was in New York. I soon found out. The next day, when we reported to the PanAm office at LaGuardia, the first thing was to take a physical exam - the works, which was to last all day. Next, we were up on the 44th floor in the Chrysler Building, and a Mrs. Moffet, a pretty secretary, escorted us to meet Captain Maxwell. We were

to be interviewed, he told us, to look our best for the next day, to have our pictures taken, with possibly a writeup in the newspaper. First, we would receive a briefing as to what we could or could not say, in reference to our working and flying in and out of China, with the PanAm people and the press. They took our pictures, with us staring at a world globe. We were written up in the New York newspapers and the Washington Herald. This was all very hectic. I just wanted to hide someplace. Still PAA hung onto us for other briefings and preparing our flights back to India. I called Sylvia, who was divorced and living on Long Island. She said she would come and meet me, that I could stay with her and her mother in Bayside. Sylvia came by train, and she looked lovely as ever when we met at Grand Central Terminal. She was working at Grumman Aircraft factory, as a tower operator. I stayed at her place, which was also her mother's. Her son, Richard, was about 9. I remember him back in 1942, when we met in Miami. The car she had was a 1930 Model A Ford Sedan; she called it "Heliotrope," because of its color. I had given Pan American my phone here, since I was still on call. The first day or two, I just relaxed and enjoyed the peace and quiet as Sylvia had to work. I have mentioned before, Sylvia was a beautiful and wonderful friend; there never was at any time any familiarity between us. I confided in her about my life, how it had changed a lot; that I just couldn't go back and live a "stay-put" life in Maine, such as a 9-to-5 job. I felt that there would have to be a separation between Helen and I; I had that feeling. Sylvia said I'd have to talk it out with Helen; maybe I could get it resolved. It was only fair. Yes, I knew I'd have to. I knew my life was meant to be overseas, as a pilot; undoubtedly, with CNAC in China, after the war. I told Sylvia about my various affairs, especially with Allison. She thought that was understandable. She said I was a good-looking fellow and must have loads of girls. I said no, I didn't, but I could have, if I wished. I would not go chasing girls, not really.

The next day or two was also very relaxing. We then went back to the PanAm officer, and finally we got the clearance to leave. I took Northeast airlines up to Bangor, and I informed Helen and Christine I was on my way. When I arrived at Bangor, at the old Godfrey airport where I'd learned to fly, which was now known as Dow Air Force Base, there was not a soul there to meet me. I waited awhile, and when nobody showed up, I decided to take a taxi. The address that was given me was about a mile from the old Holyoke Street address, past the high school. I paid the taxi and found the number of the door; it was an upstairs apartment. I rang the bell and Helen opened the door; she greeted me at the top of the stairs. She looked great, and she was not at all dressed up for the greeting. There were big hugs and kisses, yet way inside, I felt guilty and almost a stranger. It had been almost two years since I had been back, and so much had happened, so much water had flowed down the

*Helen and David 1944.*

Penobscot River in these two years. Then Helen said, "Perhaps you'd like to see your son." I'd almost forgotten and was jolted back. Oh, my God! Yes, I wanted to see him! He was in his cot, asleep, with his little diapered bum up in the air. That was all I could see, but he looked damned cute. I dropped my things in the bedroom and came back to the living room. How does one start a conversation? What does one say? It had been so long. I could have used a drink, but it was too early. I guess we did all the preliminary little chitchat, I'm not sure, and I settled for tea. It was not long before David stirred, and Helen went in. She did all the necessary cleaning and powdering of his behind, as I watched. He was getting a full mop of curly brown hair; his big blue eyes stared at me, as if to say, "What the hell is this stranger doing in our house?" Probably right. Once he was all shining, Helen said, "Here; you hold him." I didn't know how; I don't think I had ever held a baby, especially one that was staring the hell out of me with those big blue orbs of his. I reached for him, and he shied off. Helen finally convinced him, I think, that I was his daddy. He allowed himself to be held by this stranger. Now David looked at me with those eyes about six inches from me. I understand babies can stare grownups down. He was winning, and he was heavy. He finally heaved and wanted out and cried for Mom. However, Helen was strict and made him understand I was going to have to hold him. I did my best, though my arms ached. David quieted down, and I walked him around the room. I finally sat him on the floor, and he took off for the kitchen, on all fours. He could waddle and walk, but preferred to crawl. The evening came around, and I was as ready for a drink as David was for his mush, or whatever it was he was eating. I watched him being fed in his highchair, as I sipped my drink. I talked to Christine. She would come by tomorrow or the next day, and we would see my mother too. After our meal, I played with David. I think he was getting used to me. A little later, he was tucked in his cot for the night. I started to tell Helen a little bit about my flying experiences in Africa and in India. I had a few pictures to show her, as well. The evening ended, and we decided to go to bed. I had to do the honorable thing. I don't remember when it was that I woke up; it was early, I know, and whether it was this particular morning or not, but it did happen.

*David and I at Christine's house Brewer, Maine, 1944.*

*David at Christine's place.*

David was crying and babbling. Helen said, "I think you ought to tend to him, so he'll get used to you." I don't know why she said this, but there must have been a method in her madness. I got up and wandered through the living room to David, and I smelled it: a strong stench of shit! I walked in, and the sight that greeted me is something I'd never seen before, not even Elmer the bear. I gasped, "Oh my god, no!" David was in his crib, standing up and holding the rail. He had his vest on, but the diaper was gone. He was literally covered with shit! From head to foot! His curly hair was caked; it was all over his face and arms. I looked around the room and somehow he was able

to plaster all the walls and window; it was on the floor, and in between all the rungs of the crib. I never saw so much crap scattered around in one room. How could somebody so little have so much crap in him? David stood there looking at me with his big blue eyes through a mask of shit. I could sense him saying, "OK, you son-of-a-bitch stranger; this ones for you!" We stared at each other for a minute. In spite of the mess, he looked cute, and I started to laugh. He joined in with shrieks of laughter, and his four teeth shown, even those were covered with crap! This brought Helen in, and she had to join in. She said David's crib was on wheels so he could jockey it about, and that's how he was able to cover the room and all the walls. If flying the Hump was a whole new experience, so was this! Where does one start to clean up such a mess? Helen was a trooper, and she knew, possibly from previous experiences.

What a little fellow! What a smell! Well, somehow Helen knew where to start and all I did was get in the way. I think she first cleaned David up by putting him in the tub. He got a good going over, and once dressed, he was handed to me to look after in the living room. She gave me the food, and I fed him. This got us out of the way while she went to work with mops and buckets. Helen had the place clean in short order. I hoped that this was not a daily occurrence. Though the room was clean, the odor seemed to linger on. Windows were opened, which helped, even though the weather was cold. Everything was nice and clean and tidy when Christine arrived. Helen told her of my introduction to David and domestic life; she had a good laugh. We picked up Mum, and we went back to the Salmon Pool Farm for lunch and to spend some time there. Robert came back from work, and it was great to see him. He never seemed to age, very distinguished and English-looking. I asked about Kim. Robert said that about a year ago, Kim was getting very old, about 16 years, and that is old for a dog. There was a severe thunderstorm passing over, and Kim whined to go out. Robert said he let him go, and that Kim walked right straight out into the back fields where we used to shoot archery, and he didn't return. Robert said he called him several times, but there was no response from Kim. The next morning, Robert went out to the fields and found Kim lying dead. It was the way I think he wanted it, but I felt sad. Robert buried Kim out there. He was my very first American friend.

I wandered through the house. I saw Waldo's paintings still on the kitchen cabinet. Somehow, of a sudden, it seemed alien: David, Helen, the surroundings, looking at the Salmon Pool. Mr. Bennett had died, so I went to see Mrs. Bennett, whom I loved. All my young friends had gone off in different directions, many to war. I asked about Dick Dunn; alcohol got him. He had been at a party out in Branch Pond and was canoeing back to his camp at night when the canoe tipped over and he drowned. I kept telling myself to snap out of it, get with it; have fun with

Helen and David. Let them enjoy you, too. Mum sat quietly taking everything in. It was so good to see her again. I told her all about seeing India; the train rides and the trip to Kashmir. No, I had not gone back to Naini-Tal yet; that I felt strange about going there; that I had written to Mr. Busher, the old principal from Philander Smith College. He was retired and living at Joelicote, and most of the PSC boys were at war, fighting somewhere; a lot of them in the Burma Campaign. He said that two of my chums from the school, Jim Davis, and Eric Gosh, who changed his name to Henderson, were with Customs in Calcutta. I had not contacted them. Also, that Miss Mooney, who used to teach the second grade and had quite a loud singing voice, was teaching in Calcutta. I had flown over Monghyr, but had not been able to see the old house, but I would one day. I could tell that she was homesick for India; God, I wished I could take her back with me, but it was not possible. She dreaded the thought of ever flying. I told Helen and Christine I needed to get a car so that Helen and I could get around. The old '36 Ford had been sold, since Helen didn't drive. Christine said she would drive me around and see about a car. She said that there was also gas rationing throughout the country, and how would I manage? I thought I could get some coupons, being attached to the military. I found an old '41 Buick sedan that I bought.

I went to Dow Air Force Base and met with the Commanding Officer, and he was happy to give me all the coupons I needed. I guess he and everybody else had read about my heroics across the Hump. I even gave some coupons to Christine. By now, with the news and publicity, I was receiving calls and letters from friends and strangers all over the states. Out of the blue, I got a call from Pete Peterson, my Pan Africa friend. He had returned and obtained a job with Northeast Airlines in Boston. We got together and had a fine reunion. I had to go and visit Horace Chapman at the Bangor House, and my friends who worked at the Peacock Room. It was old times again. I saw some of my instructors, like Percy Billings, and George Gary. I went to see Wes Marden, who had given us our crosscountry flying and commercial licenses. I was surprised when I learned he was under house arrest! Some financial mixup with the bank and the Coca-Cola plant he operated. I got permission to see him, and he looked a bit debauched. He figured he'd get it straightened out. We sat and chatted awhile, and then I wished him well. Helen, David and I went out to her Aunt Helen's summer camp near Bar Harbor, for a short spell. I was beginning to settle down and enjoy my new life. Different clubs and schools, like Brewer High, asked me to give talks. It was a delight to talk at Brewer High. Most of my teachers were still there, and I think they all enjoyed what I had to tell them about the Hump and Africa. I talked at the Kiwanis, Rotary, and also at the University of Maine.

One afternoon the doorbell rang, and when I answered it was my other friend, Bill

LaLibertie, in his Navy uniform. He looked just great, he had an attractive wife with him. What a surprise! Bill was his old self. He had been stationed on the aircraft carrier Yorktown, and had seen a lot of action in the Pacific. Bill had been decorated for his efforts. We took a few days and took Bill and his wife back to camp at Bar Harbor for a visit. Bill and I saw our instructors, and our bartenders at the Peacock House, two or three times. John Plummer was with the Seabees in the Pacific, building runways. Bill and his wife left, and said they were heading back to Miami, where he would be instructing for the Navy, probably at Opa Locka.

I was enjoying my stay and rest in Brewer. I loved David, and was becoming adept in changing his diapers. He was also learning fast on the use of the potty. We went to Helen's folks often, and how I loved their New England cooking. As April and May slipped away, it was getting time to take the next plane back to Calcutta. I called PanAm in New York, and Mrs. Moffet informed me that an Air Force crew had beat me to it, but I definitely would get the next C-47 and asked if I knew that Sharkey had shown up? He was home in Lawrence, Massachusetts. She gave me his number, so I called Charles. He said he'd hoped to be coming this way in mid-June, and that he would call when he was on his way. The next thing I knew, Sharkey did call in June. He showed up with, believe it or not, Mrs. Moffet and her husband. We then took a trip to Moosehead Lake, not far from Mt. Kathadin and Millinocket. Moosehead is famous for its beauty, its fishing, and summer camps. It's one of the biggest lakes in the state.

Back in Brewer, Sharkey asked if I would join him going up to Montreal; the Moffets would be returning to New York. Helen thought it fine, but she would not go, because of David. I thought then I could go from Montreal to Toronto, and visit my eldest brother, George, whom I hadn't seen since 1928 in London.

In May, I had talked to Helen about Calcutta and Allison, and the strange feelings about our future. It was not easy, and she was terribly upset. It was not just Allison or girls, it was our whole life, even before I went overseas, ever since I entered college and my work at the Bangor House, my late nights; something had gone wrong then. Having David, I hoped, would bring us together. As I looked at my life, the future in Maine, the terrible yearning for the carefree life, the danger and challenge of the Far East flying tugged at me, as much as it did when I looked at David and Helen. My life had changed so much the two years I had been gone, the flying and travel, seeing the world - I was now a world traveler. Above all, India had always been a great part of my life. I never for a minute had ever forgotten my childhood and the way of life it presented. I mentioned earlier, when I arrived back to my homeland after fifteen years, I felt I had never left. Now I realized how my mother must have felt, knowing she would not see her beloved India that I know she loved so much.

This part of my life, with Helen, should not have happened, but it did, and what was next? Perhaps pilots should never marry; I don't know.

Sharkey came by and picked me up early. I said bye to Helen and David, and headed for Montreal. We spent about a week together at the Mount Royal Hotel. From there, I took the train to Toronto to see my brother George. He looked exactly the same - very lean, a slightly crooked nose and a little bent in the shoulders. This was a wonderful get-together. It was sad to know that he had divorced Jessie, whom he had married in Applecot, Bhowali. She and the four boys lived in Vancouver and Victoria Island, British Columbia. George and I spent about ten days together. I was in touch with PanAm all the time. One morning, they informed me to report to a medical facility for a physical, and the required immunization shots. I said good-bye to my brother and took a train to Boston, then up to Maine. I had my physical at Dow Air Force Base, and the various immunization shots. I was able to have a little more time in Brewer with Helen and she would accompany me to Miami. I said my farewells. I was heartbroken when I hugged and said goodbye to David, who was getting used to me. He would stay with his grandparents and Christine.

At Miami, I checked in with PanAm CNAC people for the trip to Calcutta. The planes were delayed by a couple of weeks. Ray Hauptman was there to take one of the planes. He had just married in the interim. Then the four of us saw and visited various sights and a few nightclubs on the beach. We also met our crews. The pilot who would be with me was Gene Powers, Ray's was Sid Wilson. The navigators would accompany us for the South Atlantic crossing to Accra, West Africa. There they'd leave us, and deadhead back to navigate another trip. We met some of the old Pan Africa group, that were flying as First Officers now on Pan American, on the flying boats. A few were with Eastern Airlines; just like old home week. Bill LaLibertie showed up with his wife. We had quite a gathering. It was one party after another.

One day Ray and I ventured up to West Palm Beach to the Air Force Base to pick up our essentials for the flight. We took flight jackets, khaki clothing, etc., and I got another .45 pistol. I bought a 35 millimeter camera, much better than the old box-type affair that I had given to Allison. I picked up loads of film and printing paper, because film and printing paper were rare commodities in India. Also, whiskey. I loaded down with Scotch and Canadian Club, and I was told to pick up the rum at San Juan, Puerto Rico, which would be our first stop.

Helen and I had another discussion about the future. Perhaps divorce was the only answer. I was all screwed up inside, since I loved Helen and David, but knew our lives had now turned so different, mainly mine. I know I was the guilty one and the loser. Helen decided to return a few days early, before my departure. I saw her off at

*Sylvia and son Dickie in Long Island, 1944.*

the train for Bangor. I moved out of the downtown hotel, I think it was the Paramount, and moved to the MacFadden Deauville on the beach. I tried to get drunk the first night there and Sid Wilson was helping me; that's for sure! We started at the Nautilus Bar at 11 A.M., when it first opened. He ordered bourbon and I scotch. The bartender ordered us sandwiches, but we never left the bar except to relieve ourselves. At 7 P.M., we agreed it was time to eat a real meal. Where we went and what we ate, I'll never know! I don't even remember going to bed. When I did wake, almost at noon, I had a terrible hangover! Strangely, I didn't feel that bad, but could have felt better. We met back at the bar, and the same bartender was there. He looked at us in surprise. "Egad," he said; "you're both still alive! Do you guys know how much booze you consumed last night? You never got off your stools, and I expected that when you did, that you'd both fall flat on your faces. I don't know how you both walked through that revolving door! Did you know that the two of you drank the equivalent of a fifth of booze each? One bottle each?" No way, we couldn't have! He showed us the bill: there were 68 drinks run up on the National Cash Register. The bartender concocted a Bloody Mary for us, to sober up; it was on the house.

The drinks may have done the trick. I don't remember too much of that day. I was trying to forget, and I guess I did. The great time had arrived. I got the bartender to sell me two dozen of his bar glasses, with the sailboats and "Nautilus" written on them. I wanted to remember my stay at the McFadden-Deauville. I had them packed

*Charles Sharkey and me taken by PanAm for publicity, 1944.*

carefully. All the belongings were loaded aboard the C-47; I'm certain we were overloaded, especially when we filled the extra cabin tank for the ocean crossing. I knew the aircraft would be about 35,000 pounds for takeoff. The navigator met us, and after introduction and briefing, we took off from Miami, and as a salute to our bartender friend, I flew over the McFadden-Deauville Hotel, heading to San Juan. We overnighted there and then filled up with fuel and Bacardi Rum, for the next stop would be Georgetown, Guyana. Then to Belem, Brazil. I arranged with the navigator to let me know when we crossed the equator. I'd give a bump, and he would pour a cup of coffee over Gene Powers' head, as an initiation to the Jupiter Rex Realm. Right on Target, we did just that. I looked over at Gene after the coffee had been poured over him, and he had a silly, surprised look on his brown coffee face, as it trickled down from his black curly hair. "Happy Jupiter Rex, and congratulations for being introduced into the special realm," I said. I don't think he found it amusing at the time. He had to stay with the coffee mess over him the rest of the way to Belem.

Ray Hauptman and Sid had a passenger from Miami, going to Calcutta, a Mrs. Kitty Schilling, the wife of Eric Schilling, who was an AVG pilot now flying for CNAC. She was going over as a Link instructor for us. A pretty blonde.

I was happy when we departed Belem for Natal. On the way, our navigator said he would try out our drift sight over the Amazon jungles. He reported to me that something was wrong with it, he couldn't get a picture; it was just blank. He'd get it fixed at Natal, good old Natal. Same hotel, a lot more new faces, and the bootmaker was still mak-

ing his fortune. The drift sight was fixed, and the navigator had informed me the wrapping paper had not been taken off the lens! All was well, all tanks full including the cabin tank. I could feel the plane was overweight, almost like the night of the icing, across the Hump. Let's hope we don't lose an engine, or into the water we'd go. We made it out of Natal, but not too high; enough to cool off and hopefully out of range from the U-boats that were prowling the South Atlantic Ocean. The navigator gave me some OJT on the sextant and shooting sunlines for navigation. It passed the time. We arrived at Ascension Island right on time, with all the gooney-birds (they are related to the albatross).

The following day, we took off, and late in the afternoon, we arrived in Accra. It was hot and muggy, just the way I had left it, two years ago. It was more crowded and active. We stayed in the same area of the barracks as we had before. We visited all the sights and of course, the Bucket of Blood! We stayed a couple of days here, then said goodbye to the navigator. Ray had a compact 8 millimeter movie camera that he said I could use. We flew direct to Kano, Northern Nigeria. Not much change, only more U. S. personnel; the same old Nigerian blew the long trumpet that rested on the ground. It was to alert the workers on the runway that an aircraft was approaching or taking off. It was fun seeing the old places once more and me a little older and I hope, a little wiser. The next stop was Maidugri. I stayed close to the camp and didn't venture to the distant toilet, to see any more tarantulas.

From Maidugri, we flew across Lake Chad and on to El Genina. In the distance, I pointed out the Camel's Dick to Gene. We flew for quite a spell before reaching it. I circled the massive rock and took pictures. The giraffe was still at El Genina station, and

appeared content. Khartoum was hot and dry, with dust devils all around. We stayed at the old barracks at Wadi Sedna. I got rid of the extra cabin tank; it was a nuisance, and we did not need it. I had hoped the route into Karachi would be via Cairo and Tel Aviv; it was hoping a bit too much, as all flights to India normally now went via Aden. Next morning, we were off and up over the Ethiopian Mountains. As I passed Asmara, I wondered about Marie. She should be a rich girl by now and hoped she had returned to Milan.

I flew over Aden Harbor, and again thought of 1928 and my first trip from India. We stayed with the RAF, and the next day a quickie stop at Masera Island for fuel, then another long hop to Karachi. The long large black hangar for the dirigible that I remembered was still there, and a good landmark. We stayed at the Air Force barracks at the airport. The Commanding Officer with the RAF Wings had left. I took Gene into Karachi the next day and showed him around. The sounds and smells greeted me, plus the cacophony of the birds, the mynah birds and the crows and the cheels. I was home again. I had given Ray his camera back, but was getting used to my new 35 millimeter one. Karachi was left behind as we were off to Agra. Always a delight to see the Taj, even though it was shrouded with bamboo.

Our next final hop was to Calcutta. We were airborne late, and this time nothing, not even weather, would prevent me from flying over Monghyr. I got over the city of Patna on the Ganges, and then turned east and followed the river and dropped about 1500 feet. I told Gene what it was all about. He seemed as excited as me. The weather was fairly clear, and I had my camera ready. I knew exactly what I was looking for, and I knew the shape and location of the old Bacchapra house. I stayed over the river, wide and muddy from the monsoons. There were a lot of boats going in both directions. Then, I saw it! Bacchapra! standing majestically on the high bank of the river. I quickly turned south, so I could take pictures from the left window. I descended to 500 feet. The house looked beautiful, all by itself. The horseshoe shaped garden, the water tank I fell into; it was all there, and I could see it clearly. I let Gene fly. I was telling him about it as we circled: the jackals, and about my father. But the second time around, people came out of the house on the rear verandah, and I waved. They probably thought we must be lost. On the final pass, I came in low over the water and buzzed Bacchapra. I hated to leave. Golly, I hoped the pictures would turn out. It was late evening, and the sun was well down at the horizon when we landed at Dum Dum. A U. S. Air Force "Follow-Me" jeep directed us to their ramp. The U. S. Airforce thought it was one of their flights, since it still had the Air Force insignias. I said I was actually CNAC, so was the plane. He said, "Never mind; let's unload the things. CNAC can pick up the plane tomorrow." CNAC office was closed for the day. This was a break for us; the military don't have to go through customs. The sergeant escorted us through their gates to a taxi. It was going to take two taxis.

Ray had beaten us to Calcutta. I had stayed on an extra day at Karachi. I took Gene to Ballygunge. I would help him find a place later. In the meantime, the Japs were making an attempt to cut across northeast India and perhaps take Assam. They had moved almost up to Imphal. The British troops came to the rescue and turned them back. In Dinjan, I asked if Roy Farrell was there, and if so, I'd like to fly a couple of trips with him till I got the feel again. He was happy to oblige. It was on these trips that Roy said he was negotiating with an American to rent the fellow's apartment in town and would I join him and a new pilot by the name of Robert P. Miller, (RPM). He said it was a small apartment on the fourth floor. There was an elevator (lift). It sounded good, since Ballygunge was full of people, and Sunby would have to give it up anyway, since the Danish tenants would be returning. When we finished our August flying, I went with Roy to look over the place. It was small, but with two single beds in one bedroom, and another on a small porch, which would do. The deal was made. I returned to Ballygunge and picked up all my gear and whiskey. The new apartment had a bright window that looked over the maidan and Linsey Street. The place was called Humayan Court, I guess named after the great Mogul Emperor. It was close to all the shops - New Market, Firppos, the movies - and with it came a Muslim bearer. His name was Mohammed. His appearance was clean. He always wore a red fez cap, which is particular to the Egyptians and the Turks. He had terrible teeth, what there was of them. The apartment was furnished, except for an extra bed, which we had to buy. Mohammed's first order of the day was to hurry up and bring some ice and soda; Roy, Bob and I were going to celebrate our new home with freshly bought whiskey from Miami. Mohammed also graced our little table with freshly roasted peanuts, sprinkled with red hot pepper. It was a bit noisy, with the traffic on Chowringee Street. The cars and taxis blared their horns continuously, and as you may recall, the taxis have the special bulbous type horn on the side when depressed and made the honk, honk; they were called Calcutta horns. The cabs ran continuously; that and the jingle of the rickshaw bells. Yes, we would get used to it, I'm sure. I couldn't wait to take my photos to the Kodak shop on Park Street, which was also close by.

The next day, I walked into the Kodak shop, and a dapper, bespectacled Indian was at my service. I said I had several rolls of 35 millimeter, black and white for developing. He gave me a dejected look and said there was no paper (positive) for developing. An order had been placed six months ago, but nothing had come in from England yet. I handed him a package that I'd brought from Miami. When he opened the wrapping and saw the new positive printing paper that would do more than a thousand prints, his eyes popped through his spectacles. "Where did you find this?" I said I brought it from the States. It had my name on it, and I said that he could keep it for me, but no one else could use it. He would treasure it. So my pictures would be ready in a week. They came out well. I had the ones of Bacchapra enlarged, two prints each.

Back in the apartment, the three of us talked. Roy was a fair-haired member of the Royal Calcutta Golf Club, since he could master the course at par, which was about 74. He was good. R. P. Miller was the same for the Saturday, or English Club, a very elite club, which specialized in good tennis players. RPM was an extra fine player. I was already a member of the Royal Calcutta Club; I had a new set of clubs from Dakins, and was loaded with golf balls, a rare commodity in India. The three of us hit it off well. Roy and I played golf, and RPM tennis. We visited the 300 Club and got to know Boris very well. Mohammed learned our type of food, and our likes and dislikes.

Our time was up again, and we were back flying. The planes Ray and I had brought, #99 and #100, were already flying the Hump. Privencal had been killed in an accident in Kunming in bad weather. It was sad. After September flying, Roy was bubbling over at the apartment to tell me that a lot of WAC's, Women Army Corps people, had arrived in Calcutta, and that there was a problem. There were a few Captains and Colonels that wanted to date some of these girls, but were not allowed to, because the girls were sergeants and corporals. The officers, asked us to pick the girls up and bring them to our apartment; they would meet us there.

I said, "No." Roy said why not? "Well, where's our dates?" "Oh, yeah!" He decided to talk to the Colonel, and they arranged to have three extra girls for us. Sounds weird, but the girls arrived in a G. I. bus. I told Roy we would stand away and look them over. Five girls stood around, looking for someone. We figured they were the WAC's. Strangely enough, they were young and pretty. We sauntered over and introduced ourselves. It's not too far walking distance from the bus stop to our apartment. Mohammed was in his glory and efficient. He had ice and soda; the drinks and snacks on the table. He insisted on being barman as well. The Colonel and the Captain arrived. I noticed one girl called Ginny, red-haired, slightly freckle-faced and cute; she talked like a midwesterner, perhaps because she was from Omaha. But, we got along just great, and I guess Roy and Bob did, too. The WAC's were based at Barakpur, more commonly know as Hastings Mill, which was just outside of Calcutta, about twenty miles away. The bus picked them up at 11 PM and drove them back; they had to be back by midnight. We learned each other's schedules, and the girls became frequent callers. Allison at this time had run off and had a baby. At one stage, she said it was mine. I questioned her, and she agreed it could also have been one of several people. With the WAC's, it was just clean fun; we enjoyed their company.

One fine afternoon, Ginny and I were alone at the apartment. We had a few drinks, when Ginny said that she would like to have a bath. I got her a towel and poured the hot water. I said, "How would you like to have your back rubbed?" She said, "I'll call if I need it." I heard her splashing and giggling, then she called out, "OK, you can come in a scrub my back, but bring a drink with you." I poured each one of us a drink and went in. I'll be damned! There she was in the tub with all her clothes on! I thought it funny, so I took my shoes and socks off and joined her. We sat in the tub, enjoying our drinks. There we were when there was a rap on the door. I said, "Come in," and there was Roy and some other WAC's and a GI sergeant. Not feeling too much pain, I said, "Pour yourselves some drinks and join us." I think they drew up some chairs. I was introduced to a very beautiful WAC; I don't recall her name now. Her friend, the GI, was named Tony Martin, a good-looking fellow. Through a haze, he looked a bit familiar, but I wasn't sure. Finally, Ginny and I hopped out into the bedroom, and Mohammed got a change of clothes for me. Ginny had to put on some of mine, while Mohammed said he would fix Memsahib's uniform. Mohammed somehow cleaned, dried and pressed Ginny's uniform, like new. You might say from this the gang was formed. I don't remember all the names, but there was Ginny and Sylvia, Tony Martin's girl, Roy, Bob and myself. Tony, I finally learned from Ginny, was an actor-singer. Yes, now I remember him in a show or two. The problem with the Colonel and the Captain was that they were not allowed to date WAC's. Tony could but had nowhere to take his date. It looked like our apartment was going to be quite a place! Us CNAC bastards were the only ones who had it both ways; we could date the WAC's and take them out to most places. However, we could not take them to the 300 Club, as it was off limits to enlisted personnel, or the Golf Club.

One thing to remember: we flew damned hard over the worst route and terrain in the world, with many odds against us; mainly the weather and the Jap Zeros. The CNAC pilots had to use all the hat tricks they could devise to make it across to China and back. We lived hard, because we never knew when it may be our last trip. There were many that didn't make it. We just hoped they did live it up and had their fun and games, booze and the lot. It would have been a shame not to have lived a little before hanging up the wings. Our group of three; Roy, Bob and myself, was one of many groups in C-NAK. Some of the fellows preferred and wound up at Acare Lane and Kararia Road. One or two were known to shoot locks off the whore house doors at wee hours of the morning. They would crawl into bed with a floosey and not touch her. Some of the gals looked after the drunken sots, kept their wallets and passports, and sobered

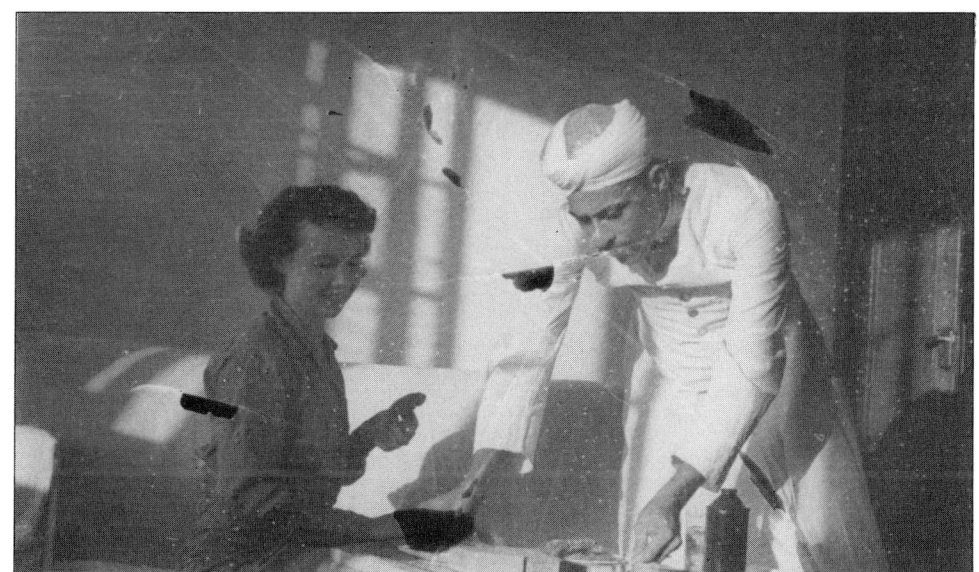

*Ginny in the apartment being served by Mohommed, 1944.*

them up the next day. The crew cars were known to come by and pick them up for their flights to Dinjan. A few guys preferred screwing the tea-pickers around Dinjan, right there in the tea patches! I guess it was a physical, chemical need that had to be taken care of. For me? I think I have mentioned how I took care of myself. I never visited the whore houses in India. There was no need to. If it came my way; that was it. Let me explain how it once came to me in a strange and unusual way. You probably won't believe what I am about to tell you, but here is what happened. The lid was off as far as the amount of flying that we could do per month. We could fly as much as we liked, as long as it didn't jeopardize safety to ourselves or airplanes.

It was in the middle of November, 1944, when I had finished making my trip and a half from Kunming, and wound up back in Dinjan. I was really worn out and tired that day; I hadn't shaved for a couple of days. Suklo had made me a hot tub, and I was relaxing and enjoying the steamy hot water and almost half asleep, when a message from the airport arrived. Suklo handed it to me. "Pete, a very special flight tonight to Kunming. You are the only pilot available, so please try to make it. A special for the Air Force." For the Air Force! I thought. That was a bit unusual. Oh well, if that was the case, I guess I had to go. Suklo made me a hot bowl of soup and toast while I dressed. I gulped it down and got started in the crew bus that jolted me back to the airport. I might add, the company was short of radio operators and co-pilots, all Chinese. We were now flying with either a radio man or co-pilot, but never the full complement. When I arrived to check in, I learned I would have a radio operator. The plane was a C-47 with all the good equipment on it. I asked the CNAC man at the desk what the special Air Force cargo was. He wasn't sure what it was. I went out to the plane and checked the cargo for myself. It was the usual load of 100 octane gas in fifty gal. drums well netted down. It was dark

when I thought I better make a check of the external of the aircraft (walkaround). I started out with my flashlight, when I noticed a group of people off to one side of the plane. One of them, an Air Force Captain, came over to me and asked if I was the pilot of this flight. "Yes, I am." Then another Captain joined in. They said there was a very special VIP to be flown to the Red Cross in Kunming and would I mind taking the passenger. I said there would be no problem. From the group they presented a cute blonde girl dressed in khaki fatigues. (This was turning out so much like the movies I had seen before). Lets say, I forgot her name! So this was the VIP. I could see the glint in the officer's eyes. I told them the girl was lucky, because I would arrange a first class seat right up in the cockpit; since I didn't have a co-pilot for the flight, only a radio operator. I shook hands and said farewell to the group. I helped the young lady up the stairs into the cabin. The Captain took her luggage and tossed it in after us. She had a leather jacket, and I told her she would need it as soon as we were airborne and to keep it handy. The three officers had kissed her *bon voyage*. The plane was dark and smelled of gas. I was glad she didn't smoke. The radio officer came aboard. I showed the girl where to sit. I strapped her into the right seat and explained about having to operate the cowl flaps for the engine cooling, which was on her side of the cockpit. After all was squared away, I started the engines. I was tired and hoped I wouldn't go to sleep going across the Hump. All-night flying in the plane alone! Thank goodness it was a C-47 with an auto-pilot. I saw the group and waved to them as we rolled out to taxi. It was pitch black outside, but once we were airborne I switched off the landing lights, the only light available, and what we could see, were the myriads of stars that looked so bright. I circled once for altitude, and headed for Digboi Mountain. The girl said she was from the Digboi area and that her folks were tea planters. I dimmed the fluorescent lights to almost out, and I

showed her a dark blob going past on her side. I said that was Digboi Mountain. About then the engines started to vibrate. I flashed the light and noticed the cowl flaps were still in the open position. I asked her to put them in a trail; she wasn't sure. I undid my seatbelt and reached over in front of her. I put my right hand on her shoulder as I leaned over with the left and set the cowl flaps. Before I could straighten out in my seat, she leaned forward and kissed me. I had not set up the auto-pilot as yet. I normally flew the airplane till cruise, and then used the auto-pilot, if I had one. This time, I didn't waste much time. We continued where she had left off. It was getting hot and heavy, with her wiggling about in her seat. I came up for air and attended to the flight. I didn't wish to slap into a hill at this stage. I had planned to level at my usual 11,000-12,000 feet, and head for Foxy's Pass, which was my route at night. I assessed what might develop, and decided to climb up at least to 16,000. Once there, I set everything in cruise and well trimmed. I then turned the auto-pilot on and double-checked that all was well. I didn't want the radio operator looking in on us and falling out of his chair, so I took our two jackets and strung them across the cockpit opening. All was cozy up front. We were ready to continue with nature's wily ways. Don't ask me how, but where there is a will, there's a way - even in the front seat of a Volkswagen bug which hadn't been invented yet! I slid my seat as far back as possible. The armrest moved away, and the girl came onto my lap, with all kinds of twists of arms and legs. If you think that was something, remember; we were at 16,000 feet, and at the best of times, one gasps for oxygen. We hadn't done that, and I think the girl was about to collapse over me. I fumbled around and got the oxygen mask for her to breathe 100%. We were in this position for quite a spell, when I realized I was getting lightheaded myself. I figured I needed the oxygen more than she did. I breathed on the mask like crazy; after all, I wasn't just sitting there with a pretty thing astride of me; I was doing my evening pushups too! In time, we had exhausted ourselves. Every once in a while, I had to peek over her shoulder to see if the plane was going in the right direction. These auto-pilots have a habit of precessing either to the left or right. If it went to the left, we'd be sitting on top of Likiang Mountain; or-the other way, we'd be over Rangoon, with the Japs. Everything behaved well. I checked the time: almost three hours since we took off. I figured another 30-40 minutes of comfort, and we should be approaching Kunming. The flight thus far had been smooth as silk. The only ripples were from us. It hadn't been more than ten minutes or so, when I looked off to the left and saw Kunming almost coming up under us. The strong prevailing winds had pushed us along fast. The only thing to do was to untangle ourselves from this comfortable position. The girl rearranged her fatigues somehow in that cramped cockpit without kicking any of the cockpit knobs or levers.

She got settled in her seat again, and I had her breathe her own oxygen on that side; I was doing the same. Here we were, way the heck up at 16-17,000 feet, and it was a long spiral down. I would not let down more than a thousand feet a minute; our ears popped like mad. I finally got the airplane around, called in and made my approach and landed. I taxiied into our CNAC ramp and was met by several of our mechanics and unloaders. The radio operator had a sheepish grin on his face. I guess he probably had been peeking over our makeshift curtain. I inquired about the Red Cross people who were supposed to be here to meet this flight. It was near one A.M. No one came or inquired. I got the baggage, and we went over to the CNAC hostel. CNAC had built a new section of the hostel, to cover many of our now-growing crews. The manager who handled the hostel was Walter "Pappy" Quinn. The place was quiet. I went to his room and woke him up. He loved his booze, but normally couldn't handle it. I got him up anyway and made sure he was well dressed. I said that I had a young lady with me. He figured it was one of the Chinese from the city, but when he saw the blonde, he woke up in a hurry. We needed something to eat and clean up. "Oh, yeah," he said, "I'll arrange that." The girl went into the john and decided to take a shower. In the meantime, Pappy and I looked for something to eat in the kitchen. We found canned soup and stale bread. It would do. A drink would help.

After the young lady had finished, I followed with my shower and a cleanup. I felt much better. We had some of Pappy's Carew's Booze, and then settled for some soup and bread. I asked Pappy Quinn about the Red Cross. He said they never move about after 8 o'clock. He said, "I can arrange a couple of cots, in one of the spare rooms." She said she needed sleep; I knew I did. I saw her climb into her bunk, and I did the same, and just passed out.

I don't know what time it was, whether day or night, or the following day; I lost track. As I woke and tried to move, her warm body was next to me. She was awake and whispered, "That was fun last night, up there in the airplane; but let's really enjoy it here, in bed." What a delight. She came out from the john again, the girl had discarded her fatigues and was now completely dressed in a woolen type dress, with beads around the collar. She looked very pretty that morning; (I guess it was morning: I'd lost track after all that flying). Actually, it was after 11 A.M., coming up on 12 o'clock.

We moved out to the living room, and there was Pappy, arranging schedules and meals. He said, "You guys finally surfaced!" "Yeah, and we're starving." He called one of the boys and arranged a good breakfast-cum-lunch. I was feeling pretty good, and Pappy said if we waited a few minutes, he would deliver us to the Red Cross, which was a ways from the field. After our meal, while on our way to the Red Cross, I asked the young lady what in the world was she doing, joining the Red Cross in China? "Oh,"

she said, "I forgot to mention it; I came to marry a Lieutenant in the Air Force." I was numb for a moment, then we all laughed, and I wished her all the happiness in the world. I never heard of her again. I know it sounds crazy, but it actually did happen, that dark, clear night across the Hump.

Within the 24 hours, I'd flown about 16 hours, with a little diversion on the side. My plane was still sitting there, waiting to be flown back to Dinjan. Pappy wished me a safe trip, and I left.

When I landed at Dinjan in the late afternoon, I saw Woody on arrival, and he asked if I'd gotten the passenger over safely to Kunming, because the Captain from the base was inquiring. I said she was safe and in good hands all the way, delivered to the Red Cross as per request.

When I got back to Calcutta at the end of November, I contacted Ginny. She asked if she could come over and bring Tony and his friend. I said of course; they didn't need invitations. Tony wondered about playing golf at the Royal Calcutta Club. Actually, he was not allowed, so I decided to fix that. Tony and I were about the same build. I dressed him up in a CNAC uniform, and off we went, since the girls didn't play. They were still welcome. We concocted CNAC stewardess uniforms for the girls. It was a great afternoon. I got extra wings and insignias for the girls and they played stewardesses for CNAC. It worked out well. Tony was always a lot of fun, and I could see how he was a showman. He was never pretentious, always a fun guy and one of us, just a great person.

Early one weekday, I was at the 300 Club on my own. In came Cooch-Behar, the Maharajah. He recognized me, and we had several drinks together. Boris always joined in with the CNAC crowd, whom he like very much. Cooch-Bahar asked if I'd join him for dinner, that there would be some of his friends, too. I met a few of these people before. They all loved their Scotch. I met a George Sen, Pearson Surita, and a Nepalese-looking individual called Mohabir. He was from Nepal and was related to the royal family. This was the beginning of a great friendship between Cooch-Behar, myself and his friends. They were fascinated to learn that I spoke Hindi, had lived in India before, and was a naturalized American. I was to meet many more of his friends. I was often invited to his residence in Alipore, which is about five miles south of Calcutta. He always asked when I was coming up to the Palace. I said, the first chance I could, I would be there.

It became known that there would be four of us to start checking out now on the C-46. It was Julius Petach, Ray Allen, Stuelke, and myself; we were to go to the Air Force Base at Dumduma, or Sookerating for training, and to report to Captain Jim Grace as soon as possible. The four of us reported to Grace's office the next day. He was a young fellow who said, "You mean, we're going to teach you guys how to fly?" "That's right." Some type of ground school would be started the next day; I think given by a Curtiss-Wright man, and Pratt &

Whitney engine representative. We sat through the classes, and found the lectures and ground school to be very good. This is the first schooling I'd ever had in any particular airplane. The DC-3 was just up and go; a sort of OJT and learn as you went along.

We were then assigned to aircraft with well-qualified Air Force pilots who had considerable time in C-46s, but not across the Hump! It was a new experience, getting into this monster, but it was a pleasure, with more sophisticated equipment. As the Air Force trained us on the C-46, we were training them too, on how to fly the Hump. On moonlit nights, I took my instructor across at 11,000 feet, all the way through Foxy's Pass. He was dumbfounded. He called it "The CNAC Scenic Route". We all had a good time with the Air Force people, especially after a flight, one had to have (battle rations). After every flight, we all had to go into the main headquarters office and partake of a couple of good slugs of whiskey; it would almost knock a guy on his butt.

Jim Grace was a good pilot and a very fine gentleman. We finished the course and felt we could now manhandle this big airplane. At Dinjan, we told Woody it was quite a plane, and hoped we would have them soon. Yes, he said, they would be on the way shortly.

I finished my flying for December and returned to Calcutta. I went to the gun shop, Manton's and saw Mr. Todd. He informed me he had a shotgun I might be interested in. It was an old English Westley Richards. It was about 1500 rupees, or $500.00. He said it was a good buy. The owner was going back to England. I bought it; a Christmas present to myself.

Our gang started arriving back at the apartment in Calcutta. I guess we were going to have our own Christmas party, and perhaps New Year's as well. Roy had some weird people that he wanted to invite; I wasn't too impressed. He asked a General Hackett, who was the base commander, and his Colonel friend, a dentist. Hackett, of course, at the last minute, couldn't come to the Christmas party, and that was just as well, because our WAC friends would be there, and Tony Martin. It was to be a gala event. Cooch-Behar and Boris were invited. Boris couldn't come because he was doing his own thing at the club. There was Mike Lothrope and his wife Molly. He was the Manager and part owner of the Magnolia Ice Cream Factory and parlors. Sharp shooter, Robbie showed up. I think Roy, who had a way of knowing the inner track, was able to scrounge a turkey through the U. S. military commissary, and Mohammed, though Muslim, arranged a suckling pig. Everything was laid on, including the firecrackers, that the British always had. We had a small artificial Christmas tree, as well. I wasn't sure how everyone would crowd into this small apartment; I just hoped no one would get too drunk and fall off the balcony.

The evening arrived, and our guests poured in. We met the bus and picked up our girls. I don't think Tony made it, either. Cooch-Behar did, and his brother, Raj

Kamar; they called him Digger - a good looking fellow, but couldn't hold his whiskey. Before the turkey or roast pig were to be served, most people were feeling little or no pain. I instructed Mohammed that when he served the pig, to be sure to have an apple in its mouth, a Western tradition. He understood, so he said. Then, after all the people were seated and things were going well, the moment had arrived, and whether it was because he was Muslim and didn't wish to touch the pork, or whatever, he didn't understand my English-Hindi which confused him, Mohammed entered, carrying the roast pig on a lovely tray, well-garnished, but we all froze, those who noticed; instead of an apple in the pig's mouth, the apple was in Mohammed's mouth! No one cracked a smile or said a thing. He placed the pig on the table and walked out. We chuckled at first, then went hilarious. I excused myself and went out. I told Mohammed to get rid of the apple in the garbage. I asked him why he had done that, and again I explained what I had intended for him to do. He then caught on and joined in the laughter. I guess that was to be one of our original ideas in serving a pig !

The meal was a great success, and Digger did finally pass out. Everyone had a whale of a time. The girls were allowed to stay till midnight, thanks to General Hackett. Oh, yes; no Jap raids that night.

New Year's was also another great wingding. The eggnogs were extra special. We got the cream and ice cream for the mixing from Magnolia, and good old Canadian Club and some Bacardi from San Juan, Puerto Rico. It was a super drink, and we had silver goblets that we bought from Hamilton's Jewelry Shop. That was New Year's celebrated into 1945. I saw Tony often, and on one occasion had an opportunity to introduce him to Cooch-Behar, and they, too, became fine friends. The war in Europe and Africa was long over; everything was in the process of the formation of the United Nations and straightening out the countries and who gets what. In the Pacific, the U. S. was now kicking the hell out of the Japs, but still at a great cost of life. Our war effort was still going strong. The Japs had Burma and Stillwell was doing very well with the Lido Road; it had progressed into Northern Burma. Our flying was at its zenith, but still lacking full complements of crews; either radio operator or co-pilot. The main task for them was to throw out the cargo in case of an engine failure at a critical part of the Hump. Most of the new Chinese co-pilots could not fly at all. On one occasion, I had one of them as a co-pilot when I took off from Kunming. The weather was warm. I gave the controls to the co-pilot while I wrestled to take off my sweater, which got tangled in my headset. I was still unraveling and grappling with it, and trying to pull it over my head, when I felt my ass getting light in the seat. The sound of the air rushing faster. I was able to untangle myself out of the sweater and as I looked out, I saw Kunming Lake coming at me fast. The guy had frozen

on the yoke and had pushed it down in a steep dive. I shouted at him in English, which he didn't understand. I pulled hard to get the yoke back; he had his elbows locked. I had to hit him and shove his head down. I finally wrestled the plane away, and pulled up about 200-300 feet from the water. It was the scare of my life! I looked at the fellow after I had got the plane back on course; I shook my head and he grinned. "Me no fly," he said. That's right. This was a C-53 and no autopilot. I hand flew it on to Dinjan and said, "Oh, what the heck!" CNAC had a new hostel also in Dinjan, because of the amount of new crews arriving. It was not far from the downwind leg for the north runway. I saw the white building, and gave it a good buzz job. Woody saw the plane dive and thought it was about the crash. I pulled up and headed for the runway and landed. I must have made Woody mad; that was two of us. When I arrived back at the barracks, he asked why I had done that buzz job. I said I was very angry; I was nearly killed because of a coolie for a co-pilot. I took it out with a buzz job. "I'm sorry," said Woody, "but you're grounded for a month". "Okay," I said, perhaps I had it coming. I returned to Calcutta to cool off.

I saw Boris at the 300 Club. "Guess what?" he said. "I'm arranging a big shoot at Cooch-Behar, elephants and everything; big game. Do you want to come along?" "It would be mainly CNAC guys". "You bet I would! When will it be?" He said the first week of February. I think it cost about 1500 rupees for two weeks. We would fly up in a CNAC plane that would drop us off at Cooch-Behar Field. "Sounds great. I have only a shotgun." He said "that's fine; we have other guns, also; the Boss'." He called Cooch-Behar the "Boss". I later learned to call Cooch-Behar "Bhaiya", which means brother. There would be quite a group. General Hackett would be there, for one, also General Bob Neyland, who later became Head Coach for Tennessee University. There was a Colonel Moffet, Roy Farrell, Moose Moss and Dick Rossi, MacDonald, and several others, with Doc Richards; our erstwhile doctor. The day came when we were offloaded at Cooch-Behar on a beautiful winter morning. When we entered the Cooch-Behar palace grounds, it was manicured to a fare-thee-well, utterly beautiful! The palace was an all-brick structure of two stories, that was long, with the main entrance at the center, and a large dome above it. A whitewashed verandah ran the full length, and on its walls were at least 50-70 staghorns of sambur and cheetal. The whole front of the grounds was enclosed by a high brick wall, and the inevitable broken glass on the top; a double iron gate at the entrance, with a long hundred yard or so driveway of red clay, and rows of cannon flowers on both sides. At the end of the drive, which stopped at the entrance, were two large cannons that guarded the front. There were large water tanks, also, in the center of the garden, common in most parts of Bengal and on our golf course; prevents flooding.

As we drove up to the palace entrance, Cooch-Behar greeted us. He was about 6'2", slim of waist, and wore his clothes fittingly close. The trousers appeared military cut and part cowboy. He always appeared immaculate, with a cheery smile and fine white teeth; a perfect gentleman and host. His personal palace secretary was a little fellow by the name of Caju Singh, who always wore grey flannels and blue blazer, with the Cooch-Behar crest. I could see he had a mischievous twinkle in his eyes. His wife, Bhindu, was a couple of inches taller than him. She was a charmer, and dressed always in an Indian sari, a lovely person. Digger was present also, sober, and looking great. It would take a few drinks, and he'd be on his way again. Sad to say, drinking would one day be his demise. There were three ADC's that we met, and another person who almost stole the show; she was an elderly lady, dressed in an all-white sari. She was French and had been hired by Cooch-Behar's father years ago, the late Majarajah. She was the governess for the now present Cooch-Behar and brother and sisters, later to be part of the main chef and maintained the kitchen, and accepted as being a part of the family. We were shown our rooms by Caju, and he called the lady Auntie. After I cleaned up, Roy and a few of us met in Bhaiya's informal smoking room, where there was a billiard table and a few easy chairs. One of the palace bearers, in his regalia, served drinks. The forthcoming shoot was discussed. Bhaiya said that two blocks had been reserved for our shooting. Each block would be about 15 or 20 square miles, just in Assam, and a corner of Cooch Behar. There were forest bungalows, plus some tents to take care of the guests.

Dinner was served in the palace dining room; it sure was palatial. The food was excellent, as supervised by Auntie. It had a French taste to it all. Bhaiya loved jokes, especially when Boris told them. He usually got them mixed up in his funny English-Russian accent. Bhaiya's pet expression was, when he started to laugh, he would say, "Oh, shut up", meaning that was a good joke. We then retreated back to the billiard room, for brandy and coffee. By one o'clock or so, we all crawled under our mosquito nettings and off to sleep.

The bearer had our chota-hazari by 7 A.M. I was up and did a stroll around the extensive gardens. There was also a small, Japanese-type garden on one side with a bridge across a waterway. When I got back to the palace, I noticed that Boris was already making arrangements for our trip. The elephants had departed to the campsite. After a sumptuous breakfast, we gathered at the rear of the palace with all our gear ready to get going. Cooch-Behar would not be coming with us at this time. He said, "Perhaps I can make it later."

We were aboard our truck, cars and jeep. It was about a 75 mile trip to camp. Most of the way was a dirt road and very dusty. Dust and all, I enjoyed the ride. I saw all the villages and the green fields well laid out. Our first camp was a place called Raimona. Roy and I were assigned a tent. I forgot to mention Roy and I had also brought along Mohammed, to do the odd jobs for us. He had our clothes laid out and ready, also a bath. We were dust-laden, but I couldn't waste any time taking a bath right now. While Roy was busy doing that, I asked where the elephants were being fed and cared for. There were about 25 or 30 of them. The mahouts or drivers for the elephants at their pilkhana (stable for elephants) were present. I sat and talked with them for nearly an hour. They were delighted I could converse with them. Each one said I should ride their elephant. I said I would love to, but I had to leave it up to Boris-sahib; he was running the safari. I didn't know then that one day, one of these lovely creatures would be given to me, or assigned to me, by the Maharajah himself, with a mahout.

It is not easy to climb on to an elephant and expect him to walk off while you bark out the instructions. The elephants won't budge. They are very alert, gentle and clever animals. But the mahout usually grows up with the animal; they become buddies, you might say, and almost live together. It is this combination that enables the elephant to do exactly what the mahout wants. However, an elephant, though gentle, can become very ferocious, and has been known to kill even his mahout, especially when they're in musth. That's the time of the year when they just about go crazy. They have two little holes right by the eyes that secrete musk; this is how you can tell that the elephant is going musth. Normally, at this time he is tethered or tied securely to a tree or some sort of pen that he can't get out of, till musth period (a part of their rutting season) wears off.

I finally returned to camp and cleaned up. I will relate a little further an inference of these wonderful animals, the elephants. The group gathered upstairs of the forest offices bungalow. It was built basically as ours in Dinjan. The upper platform, I think, was built that way for the monsoons, floods, and any prowling animals. We settled down to the business of evening drinks that Mohammed was happy to pass around. We were to do without the ice, but because of the coolness of the evenings, the soda and mixers were cold. The cook was retrieved from Cooch-Behar, and he was good.

The next morning, Boris informed us we would go "gooming." This amounts to a general shoot, all the elephants in a long line, walking slowly through the jungle. You may shoot at whatever comes up in front of you. We would be away from the actual tiger areas; however, one may lurk just where you least expect him. We were all ready next morning. The elephants arrived without a sound, as though they were wearing crepe soles. Some of the elephants wore strapped howdahs, a basket-like arrangement made mainly of wicker with one seat in front, and one in the rear, with a rack to hold the guns. If you stand up in one of these, your view might be from 12 to 13 feet high; one can have a grand view of the jungle around you.

Most of the jungle is tall; the grass is as high as an elephant's eye! Sometimes it's called "tiger grass" or "elephant grass," and it's very thick. Animals that inhabit these grassy areas have made types of paths or grass-like tunnels or warrens. They can travel quietly underneath, without being seen. It was through a lot of this terrain that we would have our general shoot. Each of us was assigned an elephant on a howdah. Like hunting dogs straining at the leash, eager for the hunt, so it appeared with these elephants. Once we climbed aboard, usually from the rear after the animal has squatted on its haunches, you grab a rope that fastens the howdah and pull yourself up. No one wanted to be old-maidish and get aboard by using the ladder. Once mounted, it didn't take long for the whole safari to move out in single file. As big as elephants are, they can move quite fast. Once off the dirt road, and a few miles from camp, the elephants strung out in a horizontal line, about a hundred feet apart, and the shoot started. I had my shotgun loaded with buckshot; in the pocket of my jacket, I had ball, or lethal, cartridges, and in another I had birdshot, for jungle fowl or partridge. Whatever game we shot would be used for the camp larder.

I could hear shots down the line, and the call of a hit and/or a miss. There were quite a few peacocks; one could hear them calling their eerie call. Several black partridge had flushed, but I was not ready for them. There was a rustle, and something darted away in the warrens. The mahout said it was a wild pig. There was a great expanse of high grass without much change in scenery or sight of any game. Then, too, the movement of the howdahs as the elephant walked, jounced you from side to side. One could never hope to hit anything when this was in motion, one had to stop still for a shot.

About an hour out, my mahout had moved out to one side and we drifted off on our own. We could hear the odd shooting. We came into an open area near some dead trees that had fallen, and stopped for a moment; our elephant reached around with his trunk and pulled up large clumps of grass. He would then lift his front foot and beat the grass onto it and knock all the mud off, then neatly fold it into his mouth. The mahout must have realized or sensed something. He signaled by slowly raising his left hand. From the left, I saw the grass move; then I noticed a set of horns, and the form of a deer, walking. It would cross at least about my 11 o'clock position. As the deer came into range, I fired; he dropped in his tracks. A multitude of birds took flight, and more peacocks called. The elephant, I then noticed, had stopped any movement when I was ready to shoot, and he was absolutely still. We moved over to the dead animal, and the mahout got off, and had the elephant get down on its four knees. I scrambled down the back and slid down the large rump, still holding the gun. The mahout joined me to inspect the trophy. It was a large swamp deer. Between the two of us, we lifted it onto the back of the elephant and tied it down. This completed, we

*French lady "Auntie" at the Cooch Behar Palace, 1945.*

were on our way. We heard another shot or two in the distance, and goomed in that general direction. If another deer came our way, I would not shoot; one was enough for the camp larder. I changed to birdshot, in case a jungle fowl or partridge flew up.

Our whole group rendezvoused near a fast-moving river; it was called the Sankosh River. It was clear, cold water; right out of the mountains, which were only a couple of miles away. Here, we had a picnic lunch, and instead of drinking beer and hard liquor, the British had invented from time past a drink called Shandy. This was a bottle of beer mixed with a bottle of lemonade, half and half, a pleasing drink without any alcoholic effects. After the picnic and enjoying the scenery and relaxation, we circled back the way we had come. Someone had shot a kharkar (barking deer), and several peacocks. Late that afternoon, we wandered back to camp. The game was taken away for meal preparation. Any of the game we didn't need, the mahouts would be glad to have. In the meantime, Boris arranged to have several small water buffaloes staked out in the heavy forest area as bait for tiger, and tigers there were. One could hear them call at night. One of the guides, or shakari, brought news, or khabbar (that's Hindi for news). He'd arrived that evening, to say there had been a kill, not too far off the dirt road that led to camp, approximately four or five miles away. There was great excitement, and Boris and General Hacket and General Neyland were discussing who would go with whom, and who would have what position. My mind kept rushing back to the evenings when my mother used to tell us kids stories by the fire, in Bhowali and Bhimtal, how she and my father, usually on Christmas shooting, for general game and tiger; the areas that they did most

*Maharani of Jaipur "Ayesha" and cousin Gautam, 1946.*

*At the Raimona, Assam shooting camp, 1945.*

of their shooting were the jungles of Pilibhit, Bijnor, and also the Swalik hills in United Province.

It was arranged that we would have our own howdahs. I would have one of Cooch-Behar's ADCs with me. The two Generals were to be given preference positions. The rest of us would be arranged after checking the site when we got there. The morning arrived, clear and chilly. The jungle fowl were crying like barnyard roosters; after all, these are the great-great-granddaddies of our domestic ones. The howdah elephants were there, all in a row. The other elephants had left with the No. 1 shakari (guide), for the kill area. He would recommend to Boris the likely place the tiger would break. I had a

little female elephant; she was spry and eager for the hunt. The group led off, with Boris leading while we got the dust. This was inevitable; it was very fine dust, from years of trampling.

It was noted that a tiger, after its kill, may or may not eat the buffalo at that moment, but he would lie up close, sometimes right next to it, or at least within a hundred yards or so. In this way, he would keep the vultures and jackals away. The shakari met the group by a ravine that cut across the road, and he pointed up to the right and said that the kill was about a mile up in that direction. We started up the right side of the ravine, which during the monsoon must be a roaring torrent. At the kill site, all the other elephants had gathered, and would do the beating to flush the tiger in our direction. There was also timbered Sal forest there. (The Sal trees are normally used for railroad ties.) The shakari said the tiger was probably across the dry ravine, in the tall grass. The elephants beat down on the grass and scrubs on this side of the ravine, giving the shooters at least one shot as the tiger charged through, across the ravine, which is about ten yards wide. Our elephants moved out of the way, while the others trampled and cleared a swathe along the bank for quite a distance. It was interesting to see how those elephants operated and stomped down all that grass. If there were any trees, they don't go around it; they push their forehead and trunk against it and gradually, with a lot of force, push it over and then with one foreleg would push it all the way down. The mahouts carry with them a two-foot implement that looks like a cudgel, but not really; it's a wooden handle with an iron top, and it had a hook at one end. It's called an "ankush." They use this in emergencies to hit the elephant hard on its head. You can hear this being done from a distance. It makes quite a loud "plonk" when he its the elephant. One feels like taking an aspirin for the poor beast! Normally, they don't have to hit them; they can go ahead and nudge the animal behind the ears, by using their feet. This is the way the elephants were guided and told what to do, also with the word "Thub, Thub!" I guess that means everything in general.

While all this was going on, the jungle sound was low, almost silent. Our elephants were then backed into the grass and vegetation, with only their heads protruding in the open. We of course perched much higher and had a good look at all our range. Secondly, each person was only allowed to shoot not more that 45 degrees in front of him; otherwise, a ricocheting bullet might hit a person or one of the animals if he shot too far to the right or left. Our elephants, once in position, had a habit of fidgeting about. They would reach around, pull down the vines and branches to chew on, or tufts of grass, which, as I mentioned, they would beat on their feet to knock off the mud. I loved watching them. The one the Colonel had took a heap of dust and heaved it over his head for a dust bath, spraying the mahout and the Colonel. Another habit would be to lean on one side for

a while, and then the other. This made the howdah pitch way over. I wondered how I could shoot if a tiger came running through. It seemed ages since the beaters had left. In the distance, I heard a beater, or probably the shakari, call out: "Khabbardar!" It means "watch out!" I got the Colonel's attention, and motioned to him to watch out. He was ready, with a Winchester lever-action rifle. I had my shotgun, with the lethal cartridges. Then the beaters saying "Thub-Thub" again. I heard a shot to our right. I was tense and ready. The Colonel was looking off to his right, up the ravine. I noticed my elephant had stopped moving and was dead still. Looking up the ravine from where the shot had been heard, I saw spears of grass move, about my one o'clock position, and in a second, out bounded the tiger, going like hell. It seemed to leap the shallow ravine; as it cleared, I fired. The tiger somersaulted and lay dead, between the Colonel's elephant and mine. The Colonel got so excited when he turned and saw stripes lying there, he just opened up and shot, shot after shot after shot, at the dead tiger. I shouted at him to stop, or else he would destroy the skin. At that moment, my mahout shouted at me to look to the left. A second tiger came by, at the 11 o'clock position. I pulled the first trigger, forgetting I had already shot the right barrel. I quickly realized my mistake and shot the left barrel. The second tiger somersaulted over and dropped. The Colonel couldn't shoot another dead tiger, because it was on the opposite side! I realize now, as I have seen it in the Maine woods, the Colonel had developed "buck fever," panicked, and emptied the gun at the dead tiger. I was now excited; as I reloaded the shotgun, my heart was pumping fast. Boris, the shakari, and the beaters arrived on the other side of the ravine. They cheered because the shoot was a success. General Hackett had fired prematurely, it seems, making the tigers change direction and come along the opposite side, towards us. The tigers were small, but heavily coated with their winter fur. The shakari said that he thought there was a third tiger, one that had turned back and gone further south in more open country, following the ravine. Off we went, to the area he indicated. We set up our positions. This time, I was stuck away from the others; my elephant enjoyed being left in peace and quiet. She munched on more grass; I could hear her stomach rumbling with all the grass and leaves she had been eating. Soon, she stopped and was still. The mahout raised his hand and pointed towards the right. I could see nothing. We were in an open field, with heavy grass about 100 feet away. From nowhere, the third tiger calmly walked along the edge of the grass, in full view. No one else was around; it was a clear shot. The tiger rolled over, got up, and started to run. I shot the second round, and the tiger dropped. Boris and all the others showed up and were surprised to see me with another dead tiger. Boris didn't look too happy; he wanted the Generals to have the shots. "I'm sorry," I said. The ADC with me that evening said,

"You know, Pete, tigers and animals in general are attracted to you; I've noticed this." I said perhaps, and then I thought, well, it could be. That evening, Boris said to the Colonel that one of the tigers was his. I asked how he decided that. He said the bullet was from his rifle. I asked if he checked for the ball cartridge. No, he hadn't. Well, never mind. I was happy that the Colonel got his tiger. There was a lot of shooting the following days, and the Generals finally got their tigers.

I had the shakari build a machan, or platform in the trees, over a prospective kill in the deep jungle. I asked one of the guys if he would like to join me, but no one was really interested. An elephant took me out late in the afternoon, and would pick me up at 8 P.M., unless there was a shot earlier. I made myself comfortable for the vigil. It was, just as my mother had always described the times she sat up in the machan with my father, waiting for tigers. The variety of birds and the jungle fowl, the peacock, kept calling. As darkness descended, everything gradually became quiet, almost eerie, with only the odd snort and movement of the buffalo. On several occasions, I heard a tiger call at some distance. There are many tigers in these jungles, which is a part of the Terai. None came near. Silently, hardly noticeable, the elephant loomed in the darkness. The mahout called. I stepped down from a branch onto the elephant's back. Just as silently, we returned back to camp.

One night, I told Roy we should go early in the morning and try for jungle fowl that came out near the farms for grain. We were up early the next morning and hopped into a jeep and took off to an area where we had seen the fowl before. Roy and I approached around the hedgerow on the one side, and the jungle on the other. I spotted a few of the jungle fowl near the wheatfields. From this point, we stalked along the edge on foot. We crept to a point opposite them, through the grass hedge. At a signal, we raised up and fired into the flock. When they took off in flights for the jungle, we fired the second barrel. As I recall, we bagged about six or seven. We were back in time for our chota-hazari.

I was enjoying every moment I was there; not just the hunting, but seeing the elephants and the villages. The elephants were like naughty boys in a strawberry patch. These elephants, as they would pass a village, would slyly move over to near the banana groves and pull up a whole tree, place it across their tusks and walk off. When the group would stop, the elephant would tear the banana tree apart and devour the inner succulent sections. Quite often, we would ride pad elephants, instead of the howdah. The pad was a large type of stuffed mattress, well strapped to the animal. I preferred the pad; it didn't have the jouncing around so much as the basket howdah. We started to do a lot of our own gooming on the pad elephants and returning late in the evenings. I'd lie on the pad and watch the stars; to heck

*Boris at jeep, Frank Meyers (CNAC) and Roy Farrell crossing on raft, 1945.*

with the rest of the world! I was lost in this one.

Late one afternoon on another day, Roy and I took the jeep and wandered along some of the cutout trails that were like the old tote roads in Maine. They served the same purpose. At the village of Katchigaon, where the next shooting would be and where the other bungalow was located, there was also a small lumber mill. Therefore, the trails are cut through these forests. It was here that Roy and I rode the jeep. Game quite often could be seen along the trails. As Roy and I were driving along slowly, Roy driving and me with the shotgun, loaded with buckshot, we came to a turn; and there on the left of the trail, not twenty feet away, was the largest bison I had ever seen. They are called gao. This fellow towered over us. His head was down as he stared fixedly. Maybe he thought the jeep was a female and he'd give it a screw. But whatever, he didn't move, and neither did we. Even if I'd had a rifle, I don't think I'd have shot it. The bison was an immense bull, quite black, with a white patch on his forehead and white ankles, or forelocks, as though he was wearing white bobbysox. He finally got our scent, and took off through the forest. As big as he was, he moved very fast. I told the folks back at camp, and Boris was excited; normally, they were not seen in this area. I hoped the big rascal lived a long, wonderful life!

I spent a few more days in Cooch-Behar, and I enjoyed the visit. We had become good friends. I thanked His Highness for the hospitality, and knew I would be back to see him.

In Calcutta, CNAC was getting C-46's, and our flying increased. One day, I was urgently called by Crew Scheduling to take a passenger flight from Calcutta, through China, on its regular service, the same schedule I had done three years before, with Frank

Higgs. The Captain was sick. I was to leave next morning. I got dressed up for this prestigious mission. The First Officer was a young fellow named Vincent Lu, a first class pilot. The flight progressed well. We came to Chungking letdown for the postage-stamp sized airport; no room for errors. The weather was as usual, always overcast, with a mile or so visibility. I braced myself and let her go: gear down, 1000 feet per minute descent; look for the river and the rice paddies, turn back to the river, over the power lines, flaps, and look for the white stones, just as before; then 80 miles an hour and touchdown. I did this as though I had done it all my life. Even Vincent said it was good. This time, it was not up the 900 steps. A coolie took our bags on a yoyo pole to the other side of the runway, where a motor launch took us across the swift-flowing river. We were going to stay at the petroleum bungalow on the other bank of the Yangtze. A Chinese houseboy by the name of Joe was there to meet us. It was a nice bungalow. Joe brought us tea, not English style, but green tea, without any of the fixings. Sometimes you might find a jasmine petal in the tea. There was Chinese food for dinner, with chopsticks. I had adapted well to the Chinese style of food and their customs. The only problem with this bungalow was the boat ride: it could get rough at times. I wasn't sure of the Chinese fellow who piloted the boat. I'm no fancy swimmer and these people will not try to rescue you, if you fall in. They believe that should someone save your life, you become that guy's property and his responsibility for life. They much prefer you drown or save yourself.

Next morning, we made it across with all the passengers ready at the field. I let my first officer takeoff, and we skimmed off the end of the runway and over the wires. We

*Result of tiger shoot and my first tiger. My bearer Mohamed holding camera.*

were on our way to Lanchow. At Lanchow, the manager informed me that I was scheduled for another airport which was not on our regular schedule. It was called something like Shangyi, somewhere in the Gobi Desert, then to Hami, and back to Chungking. Well, that was to be a long trip, but an interesting one. At Shangyi, there was a U. S. Navy weather station. You read it correct: a Navy station! It was a valuable weather station for the Pacific Theater of war. A movie was later made about the place, called *Destination Gobi*, starring Richard Widmark. The flight took us across the Great Wall of China. There was not much of it here; the construction was made of local stone and mud, which had crumbled due to time and weather; it was still impressive. The Great Wall is different in the various provinces and terrain it passes through. Up north, in the Peking area, it is still solid stone of granite, no deterioration or erosion. It stands in perfect condition and is a good tourist attraction. I have flown over the whole 1500 miles of it, a bit at a time, and could see the differences in structure.

The Navy personnel were happy, for CNAC delivers their mail. We chatted at the Shangyi office for a while. I said I'd be seeing them again. From Shangyi, we went on to Hami, where there was nothing except our operations station. There is a British expression that was apropos: "There is nothing but miles and miles of bloody fuck-all." Well, that fits that area. On that flight I saw a speck in the distance as we approached; it was a tree, the only blessed tree I'd seen till we arrived at Hami. Actually, it's in the Souchiang Province of China, a good check point like the "Camel's Dick" in Africa. The return was direct to Lanchow. The weather in Chungking was not too bad. We could make it before dark. Everything was great. At Chungking, I was informed that the flight

would stop and overnight at Kweilin. The approach next day into Kweilin was VFR. This gave me a good look at the terrain. It was entirely different from anything I had ever seen before in China. The rice paddies were bright green squares, as far as one could see. Amidst all of this were extremely high hills that jutted straight out of the ground, from 5 to 100 to 1000 feet or more, and the beautiful river (Li) with numerous bends throughout. The outcrops reminded me of the cypress butts or knees that protruded in the Florida Everglades, only of tremendous size, or like the kupchees that they have in South Africa, but more frequent. As I recall now, most Chinese art of the country seems to depict this type of scenery. The town was quaint and picturesque; the hotel was something else. We sat around for a while in the lobby, and after a fine Chinese dinner that Vincent had ordered, with the hot rice wine, I turned in for a good night's sleep. There was one electric light bulb that hung from the ceiling, right over the bed, with a long string, no shade. The string was the on and off switch. There were no curtains; black tarpaper was spread across the windows for the blackout. Once the light was out, I was almost asleep, when I thought I felt something bite me on the arm, then my neck, and the lower back. Then I felt I was being devoured. I got up and switched on the light; there was nothing. Maybe it was me, but I was still itching. Twice more this happened; I realized it had to be bedbugs, since I had welts all over my skin. I pulled the covers all the way down and saw nothing. I then carefully lifted the second pillow, near me; underneath was a red carpet of bugs! They must have been quick; by the time the light would be on, they'd skedaddle! I put the pillow back and went out and found a houseboy. I had him get a large can of Flit and squirter.

I explained the best I could. He pointed the squirt gun as I lifted the pillow. "Ah, ah," he said, and the guy sprayed the place. Bugs scattered in all directions, most of them died pronto. Before the boy left, I had him strip the bed down and squirt the whole frame and the room in general. Finally, after the war of the bugs, new sheets, and a big Chinese grin, I was able to fall asleep.

It was no time at all before I was awake. I was joined downstairs by Vincent. When I explained the situation to him, he said he had been through this ritual before, and he had his room bombarded before going to bed; he forgot to tell me. I wonder? We had eggs and steamed dumplings - I think he called them jaujas, or bauzias. But he said be careful how you pronounce it, because darbouzas means women's breasts!

I let Vincent do a lot of the flying; he was discouraged and disappointed that CNAC wouldn't check him out as a captain. If there was no chance, then he said the Chinese Air Force would accept him as a Colonel. The rest of the trip was routine, and I returned to Calcutta and had a few days off. Then Captain MacDonald said that I must have a quick check on the new C-46 that had arrived. I took the first flight to Dinjan with him. This done, I was happy to be checked out and flying the 46. At Dinjan, Mac got off, and I made my first trip to Kunming and back with the C-46. What a difference it was! The next C-46 flight was to be something else; it was all the way to Lanchow, non-stop. I had a American fellow with me, by the name of Christy Hanks. We looked the charts over to Lanchow via Suifu and/or Chungking. The weather looked perfect. I could see the snow peaks north of Assam Valley and Sookerating. I quickly drew a direct course from Dinjan to Lanchow. The course was about 30-35 degrees magnetic, with a distance of nearly 800 miles. It would be an uncharted course, and the first.

We had a pretty good load of cargo. It was a little strange to take off and head for the high range of mountains ahead of us. Our uncharted maps read most of the area had been "unsurveyed." The plane performed well, at a good rate of climb. I checked over Sadia and the sharp bend of the Brahmaputra River to my left. We cleared the lower hills at about 9,000-10,000 feet, and then saw passes we could explore. We were now approaching the high ridges, as we climbed through 15,000 feet. Below, I could see the dotted villages in the area and clear, small, round lakes or tarns. There was livestock there, too, possibly yaks. These places must have been around 12,000 feet. Not summer areas, as they appeared to be in pockets, and no way out unless they climbed over the high peaks. We got our machine up to 19,000 feet and leveled. To the far right, we finally identified the Three Sisters Mountains, and Minigonka, that was still farther south. I steered the airplane between several higher mountains that appeared to be around 23-odd thousand feet. The charts were not that far wrong; however, I added these and other peaks I could see onto my chart. The country was barren and very green, like parts of Switzerland, all high terrain. We finally made it across this unsurveyed expanse in about four hours. The mountains gave way to lower steppes and across the Yangtze River, with Chengtu far to our right, finally on into Lanchow. It was a good flight, about six hours, and we were happy to have done it. We saved quite a lot of time and fuel in doing so. The way back was not that easy. The afternoon clouds had built up around the peaks. However, with our revised charts, I was able to duck around and under the cloud level, to stay VFR at all times. It was a great experience and a successful flight. I appreciated having someone as capable as Christy with me.

When Ridge Hammel had recovered from his ordeal of hitting the glacier with Rosbert, and both of them finding their way back, I used to talk to Ridge, and he tried to explain basically where they had struck the glacier. It was with this in mind that on another clear day, coming back from Suifu, via Likiang Mountain, I went up north Burma Valley, to the 90 and 70 degree passes, to some high mountains at 16,000 feet. I skimmed these peaks as low as possible, though it was turbulent. I was tossed around like a leaf. Then I saw a flash that looked like a plane. I circled around and came back. I saw a plane lying on the side of the mountain. The winter snow had melted; but in the process, it had possibly dragged the aircraft further down the slope from where it had originally hit. It was not possible to get close enough to have a good look. I circled a few times and returned to Dinjan. I told Woody and Potschmidt that I had found Ship #58 of Rosbert and Hammel. Potty (who always smoked a cigarette with a long, silver cigarette holder, very distinguished looking) was quite excited. Potty had a complete range of photography equipment for his Leica camera. He suggested I use the Leica to take pictures of the plane, if the weather was clear. He briefed me pretty well on how to use the camera and the small telephoto lens. The next morning was clear, and I took off very early. This eliminated the turbulence, that would not be quite so strong. I was over the mountains and found the plane just as the sun came up over the peaks. I took about 10 or 12 shots at various angles. When I arrived back from Suifu, I gave the camera to Potty, and he said he would have the pictures developed. I told him I had positive printing paper at Kodaks in Calcutta. Great, then you get them done. On my return to Calcutta, I had the pictures developed. Several were not that good, but the others were clear. I gave them to Potty and Ridge, and kept one for myself.

In the midst of all this flying, there is always tragedy lurking in every mountain. As I have mentioned, CNAC had been short on qualified flight crews, sometimes flying with a co-pilot or a radio operator, but we didn't have the opportunity always to have both, as we used to in the beginning. We did prefer the radio operator to the co-pilots, who were not at all qualified other than to trim

*Returning with tiger I shot.*

*Roy and I after early morning jungle fowl shoot, 1945.*

the cowl flaps. They knew nothing about the gear and flap operations, let alone how to fly the airplane.

It was a clear night when Ridge took off with one of these copilots. He probably didn't know the co-pilot was incapable of flight, as I described. Ridge circled the airport after takeoff and was heading across the ridges at about 3 to 4,000 feet. A lot of us on the ground heard the roar and the whine of an airplane spin in. It was Ridge's airplane; he had spun in and was killed. I didn't wish to go to the site. Those who did

said that after the takeoff, it appeared that Ridge probably went back to the operator's seat to set up the radios, and let the inexperienced co-pilot fly the airplane. It was a dark night, and no horizon. The guy, I am sure, couldn't fly, let alone at night on instruments. It was a shock to me and a lot of his other friends. I finished my flying for that month; there was no room for sorrow, but just keep it to oneself, and this we all did.

I had finished my flying for May, and returned to Calcutta. My friend Ginny had

*CNAC planes parked at Sanopah airport, Chungking. Makeshift tower and terminal building, 1945.*

informed me that a group of her friends and herself were scheduled for R & R (Rest and Rehabilitation) to Darjeeling, with some of their GI boyfriends. She asked if I could escape and join them. I found a few of my CNAC friends, and we all agreed to join the mob for a few days in Darjeeling. We piled aboard the overnight train to Siliguri, then on to the fabulous hill station. The military had set aside a large bungalow for the R & R people. Instead of the Everest Hotel, we stayed at the hostel with the girls. I'll never forget one night, after a good robust party. We were tired and sleepy, especially at that altitude, when from one of the rooms came the sound of a GI belt buckle coming undone. The house was so quiet that the slightest jingle of anything, especially a belt buckle, could be heard. Then a voice that I recognized softly said, "These damn GI belts are sure giveaways!" Then howls of laughter and giggles from everyone. Next day we all visited Tiger Hill on horseback. This time, it was not clear; the early monsoons were moving in. But we did stop, on the way back, at Keventer's, and had a wonderful breakfast, and met Mr. Bee again. Ginny and I then hit on an idea to buy a uncooked ham from Keventer, and have Boris cook it at the 300 Club. Everyone chipped in, so we got two.

The holiday had been a great success, and we arrived back at Calcutta well rested. I took the hams to Boris; yes, he would have one cooked in beer, as only he knew how. I told Boris we planned a party. The problem was the 300 Club was off limits to the WAC's; secondly, we planned to invite Generals Hackett and Neyland. Boris said we could have it upstairs in his private quarters; it was not part of the 300 Club, even though it was the same building. We thought that was a good idea. The date was set for a Saturday. About six of the girls would make it. Roy, Lad Moore, and I picked up the girls,

all looking smart in their GI uniforms. We marched through the entrance of the 300 Club and up the stairs, and wouldn't you know, there at the bar were several WAC officers, who had command of the GI WAC's. They saw the parade up the stairs, and I could see the WAC Captains and Majors stare at us. Ginny said they had been recognized, and it looked like trouble. But Boris indicated this was not off limits, it was not a part of the club. The dinner was a great success; the ham was absolutely delicious, wine and all. Both Generals Hackett and Neyland enjoyed the company of the young ladies.

On Monday, I received a note from Ginny in Hastings Mill. All six girls had been called on the carpet by the WAC officers about their presence at the club. They insisted it was not a part of the club. "Like hell," they said; they were all put in the brig. The guys at the apartment thought it quite funny at the time, and were sure that they would be released in another day or so. It was believed that the reason they were in jail, if you want to put it that way, is because the WAC officers were not invited to the party; plain jealousy! Next morning, they were still in the brig and would be there for another week. We felt sympathetic and sorry, and got a hold of Boris, who also thought it funny, but decided he'd make a lunch of ham and chicken sandwiches. This and cold beer should cheer them up. So, Bob Miller, Roy and I drove to Barakpore, contacted one of the GIs that had been with us in Darjeeling, and in a roundabout way, got the food to the girls. The next day, we agreed that perhaps the Generals could help; we didn't want to do this, but as a last resort, thought we must. We went to see Cooch-Behar in Alipore. He suggested we all go see Boris. We wound up there for lunch and discussed the issue. I don't know which one, or maybe all three CNAC guys returned to Barakpore and talked to General

Hackett. At this time, he said he didn't know what had happened, but would look into the matter, as we had explained the night of the party that we were not a part of the 300 Club, and he agreed. The next day, the WAC's were released.

Our very first C-46 crashed into Digboi Mountain at night, with Captain Green. It was the only C-46 lost on the Hump operation. I made another passenger trip, from Calcutta, Chungking, Paoshi, and on to Lanchow. On the return, there was a great commotion. A VIP would be getting on for Chungking from Paochi. It turned out to be the Generalissimo Chiang-Kai-Shek's son. He had been shooting up north, and to prove that he had, he showed off a couple of long-tailed silver pheasants that he shot. I would love to have had one of those feathers; they were beautiful. The young Generalissimo was delivered safely to Chungking.

As our flights made it back and forth across the Hump, we could always see the Stillwell Road, how it was progressing rapidly. At one point, a whole lot of paratroopers, gliders, and military personnel were noted up near the Lido Road and Digboi. They then invaded North Burma and Shimbuang. These troops captured all of Northern Burma, the area of Shimbuang, and Myitkyina. This looked like the beginning of the end for the Japs. Some villages in Burma had been cut off from food and supplies for years, and the troop carriers were making rice-drop flights over the villages. We were asked to participate. This certainly was a diversion from our regular over-the-Hump flights. We lost one of our planes in the operation, through negligence. We were now landing and taking supplies to the front, to Myitkyina.

One evening, at our CNAC hostel, Bob Prescott, ex-AVG, had come into our hostel and said, "OK, you guys; as soon as the war is over, I want everyone to get ready and chip in $10,000 each, 'cause I'm going back to the States and start an airline, and I'm going to call it the 'Flying Tiger Airline.' It's going to be all cargo." A lot of the pilots did chip in; about 15 of them chipped in about 10,000 bucks and old Bob sat there with pieces of toilet paper or napkins, whatever he could find, writing out IOU's or saying that they now had 10,000 shares in the new airline. That cheered everyone up, but I couldn't quite see it, even if I had the $10,000.

The paratroopers moved out, and were on the way back from North Burma. One of the paratroopers, actually a glider pilot, showed up at our hostel; he was none other than Jackie Coogan! He entertained us with all sorts of stories of the invasion and his marriage to Betty Grable.

During one of the stays in Calcutta, I went to the 300 Club and was joined at our table by Cooch-Behar, (Bhaiya), and some other friends. While we were having our lunch, another gentleman came by in a Major's uniform. I didn't recognize him, but he looked familiar to me. Boris had all the tiger skins out front, airing, before they were to be shipped to a place called Van Ingin's, a taxidermist in the state of Mysore. After the Major approached, he was introduced as Melvyn Douglas. He was very pleasant, but not an easy-going fellow to talk to, as was our friend, Tony Martin. He wanted to know if he could take some pictures of the tigers that were stretched outside, being dried. It was fun meeting all these people, and to know what kind of personalities they had in real life. At the club, on her way through, we also met Paulette Goddard. She had been in Kunming and various parts of China to entertain the troops.

Calcutta had become a sea of uniforms, mainly U. S. The military had a large club of its own, known as the Karnani Estates. It was a stopover and a hostel. The ground floor had an enormous bar and restaurant. The place was normally packed with uniformed people; local girls were allowed, but not GI WAC's. The drinks and food were first-class, all Stateside stuff. They got the first pickings when the boats came in. The doorman, or bouncer, was a Major. We in CNAC were real bastards. We were, of course, civilians, mercenaries, earning General's pay with full military privileges. We were the only ones that could come and go to all these off-limits clubs, and still date GI WAC's. What a way to live!

With the uniforms came the hawkers, the decrepit types of beggars that you never see anywhere else in the world. There were more crows and pariah dogs, and rats and vermin of all kinds. The once spacious sidewalks were littered with homeless natives, begging, even the native girls. Of course, there was one of the old, well known favorites that always walked in the main street of Chowringee. Everybody had nicknamed her "Bare-ass Annie," and she paraded, caring less for being completely nude; she must have been about 25 years of age. There was also another who paraded up and down completely nude; he was nicknamed "Naked Ned." I guess he was completely mad, too, parading up and down Chowringee, bollicky-bare. His bondoon hung down almost to his knees, a fair gift for any female soul. I don't think he and Annie had ever met. That would have been an interesting sight! It was learned that not long afterwards, poor old Annie was run over and killed. It's a wonder they lasted that long. But who wouldn't go mad, between the heat, the begging, no food, and of course, the always present brainfever bird.

It was back in early 1943, when some enterprising, wealthy Indians had cornered the rice market in Bengal, and caused a famine, the likes of which could be written up in Time Magazine. People died like flies, all over the city. Police would come by in wagons and shake a cloth-draped figure; if it didn't move, he was dead. He was piled into the wagon and taken away. There were not just a few, or a hundred; there were thousands upon thousands who died of starvation during this siege of famine. The racketeers became multi-millionaires. The taxis came from everywhere; they were on 24 hours a day, tooting their famous Calcutta horns, which would squeak to give a rude sound a la Harpo Marx. This was Calcutta at the height of the war, no holds barred. Perhaps Annie had listened to the call of the brainfever bird, sometime long ago.

I'd made many friends in Calcutta, those of Cooch-Behar and the Americans that were representatives of steamship companies; of course, Mike Lothrope and his wife Molly, and Art Henningsen. Allison had gone her own way. She had moved away from her family and was living with an Anglo-Indian girl. Then Diana was mixed up with one of our pilots. One afternoon, Sharkey and I got together and decided to sit and have some ice cream at Magnolia's Cafeteria. While we were there, two cute Anglo-Indian girls walked in and sat next to our table. They must have been about 18 or 20 years of age. Sharkey and I finally invited them over. The normal chitchat went on for a while, and then suddenly, the two girls started talking in Hindi. I kicked Sharkey under the table. What their conversation amounted to was, one said to the other, "Which fellow do you like?" Then, "If these fellows ask us out tonight, should we go?" The other girl said, "Why not? They have money, they can take us to a nice restaurant for dinner, and dance." They discussed the clothes that they would wear. Then one said, "Well, suppose they ask us to their apartment?" "Well, I like my guy, and I'll go." "Do you mean you'll spend the night?" "Why not? It should be fun." "The uniforms are different than the GIs." "That's right, but they are Americans." "Okay, I'll go if you go, that is if they ask us." The conversation ended, and I thought, egad! I'd play along with their tune. I casually asked Sharkey what we were doing that night. "Nothing," I said, "Well, let's go to Firppo's. They have good music and good dancing there." "Yeah, that's a good idea." We asked the girls, and they looked at each other and said okay. That was the first step to the bedroom. We would meet here at 7:30. Ice cream finished, they left. Charles and I got a taxi to his apartment. Sharkey said, "What was all that about, kicking me under the table?" I told him the drift of the conversation. He laughed his head off. "We're gonna get laid tonight?" I said, "Well, could be." We laughed some more. We decided it would take place at Sharkey's flat. We spruced up a bit and had a couple drinks. Back at Magnolia's, we waited. The girls arrived, all prettied up. The one who told the other that her boyfriend looked cúte was mine. Firppo's was always a great gathering place, with nice menus and service. The band was something to be desired, but after a few drinks, it didn't matter that much. We danced till about midnight, and the moment of truth arrived. At the table, I asked Sharkey how the brandy was doing at his place. "Oh, I've been saving the Remy Martin for a special occasion." We asked the girls if they'd ever had real good brandy. They said not really, was it like scotch? A little, but you drank it in a little glass, small sips at a time. "No, I guess we haven't." "Well, how would you girls like to stop by for a drink then?" They looked at each other, and said "Why not?"

Sharkey's bearer had gone for the night, and as all bearers do, they get to know the habits of their masters. This one had left ice in a bucket and mixers on the table. Sharkey tuned up his record player, and he did have Remy Martin. We gave the girls little glasses, half full, just in case. After a few sips, theirs was gone. I was never a brandy drinker; I had my scotch. We pulled the rug to one side and danced on the smooth terrazzo floor. We took off our shoes and the floor was nice and cool. The girls did the same. Too much dancing, I thought; let's try the final step towards the bedroom. As prearranged with Sharkey, I knew my room. I got Sharkey's eye, and he nodded. I danced and steered the young lady, ever so gently, off the floor and into the bedroom, without a fuss from her. After the formalities of undressing, we climbed under the ever-present mosquito netting. It was next morning sometime, when the knock on the door came, and the bearer called "Sahib." "Ok," I said. The sun was bright through the windows, and on the porch, the bearer had arranged tea. It was around 10:30. Sharkey and his girl surfaced, and came out. The bearer brought more tea, then asked if we would like some breakfast, and/or what would everyone like? The normal would be fine for all; eggs, toast, and orange juice, or papaya, if he had it. I made a big slip here, maybe accidentally on purpose; I gave the bearer in perfect Hindi all the order, especially whatever the girls desired. He salaamed and left. For a moment, all went well, then dead silence. The girls looked at each other and then at me. "We heard you speak very good Hindi!" "Yes," I said; "why?" Her big brown eyes got even bigger. "You must have known what we were talking about yesterday, at Magnolia's!" "Oh, that! Well, yes, I guess I did." I wasn't sure if I was about to be showered with teacups and whatever was on the table. Then there was more dead silence. Finally, the girls looked at each other again and laughed out loud. Mine shook her finger at me and said, "You are a naughty boy!" We all joined in, and they decided to spend the rest of the day. We finally got them a taxi and parted all good friends. So this was our life.

We were back in Dinjan again. One day, we received word of another tragedy. This time it was our good friend George Huang who had bought the farm. He had hit a mountain in the Kunming area. The weather had been bad with fog and low clouds. He had tried to beat the weather, but had flown up a dead end canyon and crashed. Lots of my friends were folding early in life; when would it be my turn?

On another trip when I was returning from Kunming very early in the morning back in January of '44, I received word that all of Assam Valley was socked in with heavy ground fog. When I was over the False Valley nearing Digboi, I could hear excited voices over the radio saying; "I see one chute going down near the river." Then another saying, "I see three chutes coming down somewhere between Dinjan and Chabua". It sounded like an invasion to me. I finally got Dinjan radio and asked what was going on. I think it may have been Woody talking or one of the Army operators who was talking in general; saying that all airports had closed down due to heavy fog. I couldn't return to Kunming since I had drained out a lot of gas there, as well as the barrels of gas delivered. I had to continue and could probably hold for about thirty minutes at most. As I entered into the Assam area, sure enough, the whole place was a blanket of fog. Most of it was at tree level. I couldn't see any towns or roads; just trees sticking out here and there. I flew over Dinjan station and said I would circle overhead for about half an hour and would keep in touch. The radio man said I'd probably have to bail out as the Air Force pilots had just done. I understood that C-87s and C-46s had been set on auto-pilot to head for the high mountains west of Assam. I knew I would never bail out unless the plane was on fire.

What made the problem worse, there was a high overcast sky; this would not let the sun through to burn off the fog right away, and there was no wind. As I circled around the field, I drifted over toward our old Balijan field, which had now been converted into a fighter strip. I was about 1500 ft. and could just make out the outline of Balijan. I let down to 500 ft. and could make out the runway and some fighter planes at the north end. I thought I would give it a try. I would do the approach and keep an eye on the end of Balijan runway as best I could. I was able to line up some trees with the runway and continued on a visual approach. When I was skimming over the fog layer and watching the approaching trees, the runway disappeared. I knew as long as I kept my heading with the trees, that the runway would show soon after. I had the gear down and full flaps. I entered into the fog and was on instruments at about fifty feet. When I was above, I knew there was nothing ahead of me after I had passed the trees. I eased down to about thirty feet and could see below me, and there was the runway. I cut the power and wheel landed. I could make out the white center line of the runway just to my left and close. I couldn't see a thing up ahead. I held back on the yoke and started applying brakes as much as possible. I finally stopped somewhere on the runway. I opened the sliding window which is also part of the windshield. I could now make out the edges of the field and saw a taxi-way. I followed it for a short time till I saw a building just to the left and there were a line of P-40s parked near by. I shut down the engines and climbed out. A pilot greeted me and asked, "Where the hell did you come from?" I said, "Kunming!" "How the hell did you land in this zero, zero weather?" And when I looked around, he was right, one could barely see across the runway, let alone to the far end where I had just landed. I explained how I had been able to look straight down and could see the field and then lined up the runway with a bunch of trees on the approach. I followed the pilot into the shack

and met a group of pilots sitting around a stove sipping coffee. I asked to use the phone to call our operations in Dinjan to let them know I was at Balijan. I was happy to be down and even drink coffee with the fellows. It felt good. They asked if I had seen any of the pilots bailing out of planes; "No," but I was alert as I didn't want to fly into any of them or any pilotless planes. One of our other pilots tried to make it in to Sookerting in zero-zero wx. The plane landed short of the field and skidded into a stream. He had a load of Chinese soldiers on board. No injuries, except the pilot's ego. The Chinese were saying Boo-Ha-very bad!

There were rumors floating all over Calcutta and in Assam, that the Japs had just about had it; the war was almost over. I had now finished my July flying and had done some of the August flying too. So I was able to get on back to Calcutta for a rest. At the 300 Club, Boris mentioned that the Rajah of Bamra in central India wanted a group to come there for a shoot on his estate. A lot of CNAC gathered with Boris, the organizer! Our favorite, Chuck Sharp, the MacDonalds, Dick Rossi, Roy and another new Doctor for CNAC, Doc Hoye, were all there. A C-NAC plane dropped us off at the city of Raipur and would be back for us in a week. General Hackett and Neyland left word with CNAC in Calcutta, that if there was any interesting news, for them to send a plane immediately and drop us the information by chute. I guess they knew something we didn't. There was that atmosphere in the air that the war was coming to an end. The local news was full of the U. S. troops that were blasting the hell out of the Japs in the Pacific. In the meantime here we were in the middle of India doing big game hunting. The type of hunting here was different from what we had been used to in Cooch-Behar. Here there were no elephants. We stood on little platforms in the jungle and the Rajah used men as beaters to flush out the game. There were no tigers, mainly sambhur and other antelope. When a sambhur came our way, he was usually moving like the hinges of hell. It was strictly a snap shot with a rifle. No shotguns allowed; it would be unsporting. I had to agree. On one occasion at night, we sat in machans out near the rice fields and waited for the large bison, the same type of Gao that Roy and I had seen in Assam. Two nights out, a few bison showed up, but at a great distance. I tried a couple of shots, but no hits. I really didn't care.

One day at the palace, as we sat down and chatted, we heard a plane approaching. We ran out, and it was a CNAC aircraft. He came down low and dropped a packet with a small chute. Bearers ran out and brought it back to Generals Hackett and Neyland. Hackett, bespectacled and chubby, had the widest grin I ever saw. "Gentlemen," he said, "the war is over. The Japs have surrendered to MacArthur!" We whooped and hollered. The Rajah brought out his champagne, and we had several, then packed everything, as the plane had landed at Raipur and waited to take us back to Calcutta.

It was a strange and wonderful feeling. General Hackett and Neyland went their way, and we all followed Boris to the 300 Club. We had a great celebration. Bob Miller and Roy were making plans about returning to the States. So were many others. I, like a lot of the other people, kept on flying. The Jap threat in the skies was over, but not the mountains and the weather. We could now fly much lower, south of Foxy's Pass. Dinjan was slowly being evacuated. Prescott had collected his money and was on his way back to the States to start his freight airline. He was accompanied by many of the other AVG pilots, such as Cliff Groh and Duke Hedman.

We started a lot of flights into Chungking. The U. S. had promised a great deal of financial aid to Generalissimo, which Generalissimo wanted in gold bullion. A few of us were chosen to fly the precious cargo across to Chungking. We did this for a week. The bullion was in little barrels, like beer; armed guards around the planes, in Assam and in Calcutta. We were given graphs to give our position every thirty minutes. When the gold was delivered, there was quite a contrast of the security in India, compared to Chungking, at Chiulungpo Airport. We didn't carry cargo into the airport on the island of Sanhupa; it was too small, and C-46's normally would not make it. So, at this airport, which was now a military base, the coolies just rolled the barrels off and dropped them onto tires below. There they would put them on a truck and drive off; no security, nothing. The gold was to buy armament to battle Communism that already had started its movement with Mao Tse-Tung.

When I overnighted to Chungking in mid-September, I was informed I would be taking a Chinese group to Nanking, then on to Shanghai. I couldn't believe that this would be so soon. I was off early in the morning with my passengers. We made a stop at Hangkow. On arrival at Nanking, I was surprised and worried when I saw Jap officers in uniform. They were directing my plane to its parking spot. There, on both sides of the runway, were rows of Jap zeroes and two-engine bombers. I was the only foreign looking aircraft on the field. I was certainly worried. The Chinese crew said they would stay in the plane until they saw some Americans or friendly people. The Jap who had me turn the aircraft around and park knew what he was doing. "Well, here goes!" I said to myself. I came on out, leaving the crew and passenger inside. A jeep came down the runway, with a U. S. Captain and driver. "Hi! You're from Chungking?" I said "Yes." "OK. Then you have some souls on board." I said, "That's right." "Standby for the bus. The Jap came to me and bowed, Jap-style, and asked if we needed gas. No, I said, and found myself bowing, also. We waited for the bus, which was what appeared to be a Jap bus. It was driven by a Jap. Everyone was put on board, and headed for the terminal. This was mid-September. I got the weather and the clearance from the same Captain. I asked what would happen to the Jap planes. "Not sure," he said; "probably chop them up for dishpans." "Sure would like to have one as a memento." The Captain laughed. He said, "So would I!" I thanked him, and his driver drove me back to the plane the Jap still stood guard, then gave the usual bow as I approached. I did a slight one. I thought to myself, "Could it have been one of these damn Zeroes that shot my friend, Mike Schroeder out of the sky? Was that bastard pilot one of them? I would gladly put a bullet through him with my .45. I'd probably have to shoot a thousand of them, and still not get that bugger. Perhaps he's already dead. Let's hope so." I taxiied out, took off and headed for Shanghai.

It was a short flight, less than an hour. I saw the buildings rise up on the horizon, and the field northwest of the city. As I circled the field to make sure it was the right one, I noted a lot of military aircraft on it. I think the name of the airport was Kiangwan. I circled the field and landed. An American was operating the tower. I saw a CNAC DC-3 parked there; it was Chuck Sharp - he'd beaten me to it. He'd already arrived and was setting up operations. A "Follow Me" jeep came and escorted me to the terminal. Here, too, were Japs, walking around. I guess they were in a daze to learn that they had been defeated. An Air Force car took us to the Park Hotel. The hotel looked great. I checked in with the crew and contacted Chuck Sharp as soon as I had cleaned up. We met at the Cathay bar. One or two crew remembered their city; the others were from Hong Kong. Chuck said he was going to check into his old apartment and MacDonald's, would I like to join him the next day. I said that would be great. After a few drinks - Chuck loved his dry martinis, and I had my scotch; they were cheap - we had dinner at the roof restaurant. I couldn't believe how modern and well kept it was, in spite of the Jap occupation. The major-domo was a White Russian, and I was to learn through Chuck that there were thousands of Russians who had escaped the purge of the 1917 overthrow of the Russian Czar to China. The food and drinks were excellent. Chuck was reminiscing over his past in Shanghai, how great a city it was, and hoped it would stay that way now that the war was over. I could see he loved it, and couldn't wait to get settled. Chuck said that Shanghai was separated into several foreign sections, or quarters, such as the Russian Quarter, the British, the French, the American, German, etc. I said, well, Manhattan in New York was like that; they had the Jewish, the German, the Italian, and the Irish.

The next morning after breakfast, Chuck got a pedicab, a semi-rickshaw or three-wheeled tricycle. The driver sat up front, then there's a two-seater cab in the back. It was neat; the driver kept saying, "American good; ding hao, ding hao;" very good, very good. He took us down the Bund Drive, along the waterfront of the River Yangpo, where a few ships had already docked. On the left side, there appeared to be a racetrack, and in the middle of that was a golf course. All along the other side were the hotels and a YMCA. We soon crossed the river, through narrow

*Rosbert/Hammell plane they crashed and survived. I located this months later. Taken 1944.*

streets, then came to more open areas and nice wide streets and tall apartment buildings. We stopped at one of these, and Chuck paid the driver with CN. The guy wasn't sure, but took the money. Chuck talked to the manager, who took us up in a clean elevator to the apartment that Chuck said used to be his. He was happy to see it again, it was a fine apartment that he hoped to rent once more.

The following day, I returned to Chungking via Hankow. To my surprise, I was informed I would take more passengers back to Shanghai. The following day saw me winging my way back to Shanghai and the Park Hotel. I was at the bar by myself, when I noticed two young girls at a table. They looked like Europeans, or at least White Russians. One was blonde, and the other had light brown hair; very attractive, as most of these White Russian girls were. I asked the waiter if the girls would accept a drink from me. Definitely, and I joined them. They were most pleasant, and spoke fairly good English. I also learned that most of these people, not Chinese, spoke several languages. The two spoke Russian, Chinese, German, French, and English. The general theme in Shanghai and all over China was how grateful the people were to the Americans for their liberation. I enjoyed chatting with the girls. Not only were they pretty, they were intelligent. After a few drinks, I suggested dinner upstairs. One of them asked if I had tried the Russian food. No, I hadn't, other than Boris'. They knew of a nice place so, let's go! The three of us squeezed into another pedicab, and the driver wanted extra for that. It was OK by me, because I was in the middle. It was at the Russian Quarter,

where we were dropped off. I think the restaurant's name was Timochinko's. A live band played Russian music, mainly violins and accordion. The girls did the ordering. Before anything else, the waiter, in Russian costume, brought a carafe of vodka and three glasses. There was no label on the bottle. I'd never had vodka before, even at the 300 Club. The girls poured me a shot and said I had to toss it back. They watched with interest as I did. It hit me right between the eyes. I choked and gasped; my eyes ran with tears; I was in a state of shock for a few seconds. They laughed and said, "Now drink water," which I did quickly. I learned the stuff was 100 proof; my first lesson in Russian territory. I told the girls no more drinking like that; I wanted to enjoy life. We settled for wine. I don't remember all the food, but it was good. Later, after the meal, I dropped the girls off nearby and hoped to see them on my next trip.

In the morning, I thought of Boris and his White Russian friends, and decided to buy five large bottles of vodka to take back. In Calcutta, I presented the bottles to Boris. He had those Peter Lorre-type eyes, but when he saw the vodka, they bugged out. The one other White Russian fellow was the 300 Club major-domo or usher. I think his name was Dimitri. He was about 5'6" and a skinny little devil. He, too, was excited and did a Russian Cossack dance; then with a running jump, he somersaulted through an open window on the ground floor, right onto the lawn. We all laughed. Boris prepared hors d'oeuvres, and insisted I drink Russian style. I remembered the last attempt with the girls, but I did give it another try. This second attempt wasn't too bad, but two was enough. I later saw Ginny and Tony Martin. She was getting ready to move back to the States, as all the other girls. Some would go on to Shanghai; Tony Martin was going Stateside. He'd invited me up to Barakpore. He had some GI clothes that maybe I could use. I accompanied him to his camp the next day. He gave me some heavy woolen clothes, and a parka-like coat. I thanked and said goodbye, I was sorry to see him leave, but hoped I would meet him again.

Roy and Bob had gone. The owners of our apartment were returning, so I had to make other arrangements. I hunted around and found a fairly new downstairs apartment, not far from Cooch Behar's residence in Alipore. I talked Ray Hauptman into sharing it with me. The place was known as 24/3C Rajah Santosh Road. Also to join us was the Australian pilot, Sid Dekantzow. The premises of the building were walled in, with the glass pieces on top. All windows and doors had iron grating for security. It had two bedrooms, and a lovely backyard, with a lawn, but I had to rent furniture. A local tailor made the curtains. The bearer Mohammad (apple in the mouth fellow) came to work for us.

During the next few months, there was an extensive amount of flying. CNAC was moving everything to Shanghai by air. The C-46's were carrying three or four spare engines per flight. All the other spare parts, and whatever was possible, were carried by air. Some would go via Dinjan, some flights went direct; Calcutta-Northern Burma-Bhamo-Hankow-Shanghai. Passenger services picked up out of Chungking and all over China. I found myself based in Kunming for three weeks, hauling supplies to Hanoi and Haiphong in VietNam, or French Indochina at the time. I enjoyed the stopovers at Hanoi. It was quaint and different from the other countries. The people were smaller and wore strange costumes, especially the women, with their straw lampshade hats and long black pants with the plain white dress, slit up the sides to their waist. They all spoke French. The main hotel, WagonLitz, was a chain of hotels, pre-war. This one was known as the Grand Hotel. It was simple and rural-looking, with no air conditioning. A lot of the French that were interned there during the war were being evacuated. We did some of that, taking these people back via Kunming.

I got to Calcutta for Christmas and New Year's '46. We arranged a few good parties for the occasions. Boris and Cooch-Behar were always welcome guests. I was now meeting a great many more of Bhayia's friends. There were people like Wariz of Moshidabad. He was a dapper looking man with a thin, trimmed mustache. Then there was Mohabir from Nepal, and very wealthy. There was Pearson Surita, and George Sen, who could never hold his liquor. As these parties became more frequent, Mohammed came to me one day and suggested I hire a good cook. He brought a little man in one day; he stood about 5'5". He had the habit of putting one foot on the other, then the

other, back and forth. He was shy, but spoke pretty good English. I asked his name, and he repeated it as "Monti Domingo Rozario." I asked him what I should call him, and he said, "Please call me Cookie." He had been a cook at the 300 Club once. Cookie informed me that he could cook most anything, whether it be Russian, English, American, Greek, or Chinese, but his favorite specialty was pastries. "Curry and rice? Oh, yes, any kind." He was hired. In the midst of this, Sid Dekantzow asked, "Well, if you can do all these things, how about mixing gimlets? Can you mix drinks?" He said "Yes, sir; but what kind of gimlet do you want?" That really shook up Sid, because he didn't know there was more than one kind of gimlet. No questions about it; he was now our new man.

Then another pilot wanted to move in, but at this time, we felt we were crowded. Sid Dekantzow said he had a mahogany bar, over at his old apartment, he would bring it in a few days. Sid figured it would fit well on the verandah, which was enclosed with an iron mesh across it. The bar showed up and fitted perfectly.

The U. S. Military had decided to sell a lot of the surplus equipment such as jeeps, trucks, aircraft of all kinds. Sid and I bought an L-5, single engine observation plane. He arranged to have it kept at Alipore airport. We had fun flying it around. One day at the 300 Club, Boris suggested the three of us buy Cooch-Behar a small plane like ours, for Christmas. He was also arranging a Christmas get together at Cooch-Behar estate, and it would be a swell time to present the plane to him. There would be a lot of Bhaiya's friends along with some C-NAK people and military. Why not! I contacted a Major Pete Baldwin who was in charge of the sales. Most of the surplus was at an airport called Panagarh, eighty miles northwest of Calcutta. Pete recommended a Piper (J-3 cub), same as I first soloed in Bangor. The price was $600.00, still in a crate. That was perfect; the three, Sid, Boris and myself, chipped in. It was agreed I'd fly it up on Christmas Eve. Sid would fly the L-5 up with his girl friend Angela. The rest of the guests would be dropped off by a CNAC plane. Ginny and the WAC's were already headed back to the States.

Pete Baldwin sent a message to me at the 300 that the plane would be ready around one p.m. Christmas Eve. Moose Moss took my hunting gear with him to Cooch-Behar, and Boris had arranged for an English pilot friend of his to fly me to Panagarh in a Gypsy Moth. The weather was clear and cool, as Bengal usually is in the winter. I told the pilot the first ride I ever had in a plane was in a Gypsy Moth, back in 1930. "Good Lord, that ancient." I was not sure if he meant the plane or me! He dropped me off at the hangar, where I saw a couple of GIs puttering around the plane. It was the Cub alright. I spoke to one of the GIs, a Sergeant. He said it would be ready in about another hour; there was some difficulty sticking the wings on. I found a couple of crates to sit on and mulled over the route to Cooch-Behar. Though I

knew the route, I thought I'd check it for the J-3; since it flew low and slow. The distance is about two hundred miles, on a northeasterly heading. There would be little or no wind. I just figured time with no wind. ETA would be around three hours from the time I departed Panagarh. They kept fussing with the plane, and I was worried about time. As mentioned, there is no twilight here. Once the sun is down, night creeps in fast. This time of the year all villages and farmers in India burn the fields and pastures, which causes hellacious amounts of smoke that develops into smog.

The cub didn't have more than a hundred mile range, plus a few extra if one leaned out the engine to get that odd mile, and it didn't have any navigation lights and none in the cockpit. It would be necessary to land at some field on the way and fill her up again. I would not be able to make it to the U. S. base at Lalmanirhat. It was too far and would be dark. There was a place called Balurghat. It was a radio station but had no field. I could land on a dirt road or pasture. I asked the fellows if I could get a jerry can of gas to take along. "Sure thing." One of them found a five gallon can and filled it up. It was now three p.m. when the mechanics were wiping their hands to get grease off. I knew I'd be flying into the night after take-off from Balurghat. I also knew the Palace would be lit up. Bhaiya had lights that silhouetted the whole building, and it should be visible for at least twenty miles. Once there, I could find the field with no difficulty. The fellows put the jerry can in the back seat with my bottle of scotch. They wanted to know if I was going to test fly it first. I said I'd do that on the way. There was no time now. In fact, it was very late. I did a quick walk-around and gave the wings a good shaking to see nothing was loose. All looked ok. I climbed into the front and buckled in. It felt strange to sit in this little bug after flying DC-3s and C-46s. There was not much to check in this cockpit. The mechanic turned the prop for me, and the compression seemed good. Ignition on, he swirled the prop; it took on the second swing. All gauges - HA! Oil pressure came to life and settled in the green band. I waited a minute or two to see that the engine settled down. There was no radio; I just taxiied out to the middle of the long runway, checked the Magnito and took off. I think I zig-zagged all the way down and had the stick held taught in down attitude; I was waiting for the airspeed to build up to a hundred miles or more! I forgot that the cub usually takes off around fifty to sixty mph. I pulled back and the little thing leaped into the air. It was about three-fifteen p.m., when I was airborne. It took a couple of minutes for me to smooth out the flying; I was over-controlling the machine. I leveled at 1500 feet.

The flight was reminding me a lot of my solo, cross-country with my two friends back in '41. The weather was clear ahead, not a cloud in the sky. I could see fires were already going and smoke curling straight up. No wind. The sun was sinking off to my left and rear. I had now been flying for an hour; yet, it would be a while before reaching Balurghat. I had crossed the Ganges, which had taken nearly an hour. I added a little more power, since I still had about forty miles to go. The funny little gas indicator, out on the cowl was getting way down and barely bobbing. Five o'clock was on me, the sun had gone. I knew I'd have to put her down pretty darn quick or else. I saw an unmarked village off to my left. It did not show on the chart, but not far to where I wanted to go. I let down and circled an area that looked fairly flat. Then I saw what looked like a playground from about three hundred feet; I discovered it was a football field. I came in a little fast and kept well to the right of the goal posts. The plane floated a bit before settling, half way down. There were little heel brakes that I applied. She stopped before reaching the end. I turned the plane around and shut the engine off. Not too many natives were around at this time. A few came running over to see the airplane. I waited a few minutes for the engine to cool down before trying to pour fuel in the tank. I didn't want a fire at this stage, and I didn't have an extinguisher. I chatted with the natives. They wanted to know about the plane. I explained the controls, and tried to tell them about the compass and the chart I had. In about ten minutes I could see swarms of white dhotis racing toward me. Most natives wear white loin cloth (Dhotis). I decided to fill the tank and get going. I had the cap off, the jerry can had no nozzle. I curled my one and only chart as a funnel and poured in the five gallons, without spilling a drop. By now the crowd of more than a hundred natives were all around the plane, touching and wiggling the wings. I tried shooing them away. They wouldn't go. In the mob I noticed a man in uniform; he was a local policeman. He got his stave going and bashing a lot of the curious people to back off. I was going to have to crank the prop myself. It had been many years since I had done that. I would have to crank the prop from the right rear. I did set the parking brakes. With the right hand, I was able to swing the prop. Try as I may, the engine wouldn't take. I'd turn off the switch and rotate the prop the other way; perhaps it was flooded. The crowd was getting unruly; the police and one of two others tried to keep the crowd back. I was also worried that once I started her up, some idiot might run into the prop. If that happened; goodbye airplane and myself. They would tear the plane up and kill me. I kept up the routine of starting; finally after what seemed ages, the engine roared into life, with a multitude of cheering from the crowd. I climbed in and called the police to me and shouted to get the people off the field; he would try. I slipped him five rupees. He was a man possessed. He raced after all the natives, swinging the stave, a bamboo one about six feet long called a lathi. I taxiied to the other end of the field; when I turned around, the field was a sea of white. I waved for them to get out. No way. Okay, I gunned the engine and raced down the field, white dhotis were zipping past under the wing; I pulled her off at about forty miles per hour. I was safe again and gave the field a quick fly by. It was dark ahead, and I could barely see the little compass. I didn't have a flash light, only a couple boxes of matches that I used for my pipe. I'd light a match to check the compass heading. I climbed to twenty five hundred to have a better horizon and a chance to see the palace, hopefully ahead. There were fires burning as far as one could see, with smoke and haze. I could see a large glow off to my right; it would be the city of Lalminrhat. From there the distance was not more than forty miles. Though I could check the compass with a lighted match, it was not possible to see the fuel indicator outside the windshield; the reflection hampered that. I was judging everything by time.

How strange it was to figure the difference between this night flying compared to my solo cross-country in '41. Flying then over Connecticut and Massachusetts, it was almost like daylight; with myriad lights shining into the sky, one could see roads and little towns. Here it was all darkness, kerosene lamps and large bonfires as far as the eye could see. No radio communications, no static, no nothing; just the purr of the engine. It was cold with no way to keep warm. There, far in the distance, I thought I could just see a faint glow in the horizon ahead; perhaps it was my imagination. The little bug kept buzzing along; for how much longer, I don't know. The engine could quit any moment. It was coming up on an hour since I left the football field. The glow was becoming more discernible. Now I could make out the lights as only a blob. Another ten minutes, and I could see the palace silhouette clearly. I had made it. I came over the palace at about three hundred feet and aimed for the airport. I might add, there were no night facilities for the airport, not even smudge pots. CB airport was nothing more than a very large circular grass field, with a moat all around for drainage, and intermittent trees surrounding it. I flew over the city and now looked for the airport. Nothing in sight that resembled the field; nothing but bonfires everywhere and smog. I circled the area where I knew the field to be — nothing. I made the wider range of circles, still no field. I felt that my time was up in the air; the engine could quit any moment. I decided to set her down while I still had control. The only alternative, I felt, was to splash the plane into one of the numerous water tanks. The only way to tell if it was a tank, was to find a large dark square surrounded with trees. Most tanks were built in that fashion. I searched as I circled south of the town and saw just the square I knew would be a tank. In the winter they would only be about half full. If I slowed the plane to about fifty mph, and dumped it to one side of the tank, I wouldn't have too far to swim or wade to shore. I knew it would be a damn cold dunking. Here goes! I came over the trees as slow as possible; as I thought would be slow, since I was unable to read or see the airspeed indicator. Once past the trees, maybe fifty feet, I closed the throttle and drifted down into a dark hole and waited for the splash. I had floated a short distance when the cub fell out. I had no idea just how far I dropped, or how fast I may have been going, perhaps forty; the next moment the wheels hit ground with a pretty good wham. My God! I was on land, not water. I slammed on my heel brakes, and the plane stopped. I had no way of knowing where I was; only that it was south of the city. Cooch-Behar did have electricity, as the reader may have guessed. But there was nothing here. I sat for a couple minutes and shivered in the cold. I cut the engine and got out to stretch my legs. The only sound was the darn jackals calling. I decided to stay with the plane and let someone find me; besides, if a swarm of natives came around, they could damage the plane. I took the scotch from the back and got back in the cockpit to have a much needed drink or two. I thought how easy it was to get trapped into some silly situation as this. I thought I had learned my lesson in '41. For half an hour nothing happened; I got out and walked around for awhile. I noticed that the ground was not a plowed field; buy fairly even and grassy. The two drinks had warmed me up. Then I thought what a way to spend Christmas Eve.

Off in the distance, I heard a car driving along behind me and the trees. It seemed to be turning around back there; it revved up some more and was following a course parallel to my left and the large field I was on. I then could see headlights coming along behind the trees. The car or truck was cutting diagonally across my left. I stayed put, not knowing if there might be a tank or canal a little distance in front, to fall into. It surely would be the story of my life—falling into tanks! The vehicle came around the trees and was passing very close to where I was. I could see there was no water near me, so I ran toward the lights waving my arms. The car stopped and turned toward me. The bright lights were blinding for a minute. A door slammed shut and here came Bhaiya and Boris. Was I glad to see them. I looked behind at the plane; it was parked right next to a goal post. I had landed on another football field. Bhaiya said the plane would be ok for the night. He would place a guard with it. I grabbed my bottle of booze and a few odds and ends, and climbed into the front seat with Bhaiya. I explained the events since Panagarh. I saw Sid at the Palace. In his Australian accent, he couldn't figure out why I was not able to see the field. He and Moose had lit fires on the airport to show the way. I said that explains why; there were thousands of fires all over the area. Boris and the gang had already told Bhaiya that the plane was his Xmas present. "Oh Shut-up", were his words. I now enjoyed a good drink with soda. The field I had landed on was the local police football field. After being needled by Sid and Boris, I presented the ownership papers to CB.

The French Lady, Auntie, had put on a wonderful Christmas Eve dinner for the guests; plum-pudding et-al! Boris decided to give a speech which was hilarious, especially with the way his English came out. He now officially presented the airplane again to Bhaiya. All Bhaiya could say was "Oh Shut Up." We all clapped and wished Highness a wonderful Holiday Season with a super 1946. Bhaiya further said; "You mean that plane parked in front of the whore-house is mine?" Boris continued with "Hey, Boss, Pit (for Pete), Sid and Moose are going to teach you to fly it tomorrow morning; take it easy on the champagne tonight." It was near one a.m. when everyone called it a night and headed for their rooms.

Bhaiya had arranged for a lot of his horses to be saddled and ready for those who wished to go horseback riding next morning around eight a.m. It was a restless sleep for me. I guess the ferry flight of yesterday, with the anxious moments over Cooch-Behar and the party, had me pretty well beat. The bearer brought my "chota-hazri" about seven-thirty a.m. The noise of birds in the garden finally got me going. I sauntered into the living room around nine, where half the guests were in the middle of breakfast. When I finished, I asked one of the ADCs if he could arrange for me to be driven to the plane, so I could figure out a way to fly it out. I had a feeling it would not be an easy job. Perhaps we might have to take the wings off and tow it to the airport.

It was a lovely morning, cool and clear. Boris and Moose had gone snipe hunting. A few rubber-necking natives were on the field, but pretty well kept at a distance by the local police. I looked the Cub over carefully to see there was no damage. I drained the sump and saw I had very little gas in the tank. I had judged correctly last night. If I had circled a little longer, I'd have run out of gas; which meant it would have been a dead-stick landing at night. We drove to the far side of the field; the side I had approached from. As I looked back in the other direction, I was amazed to see that I had just missed the goal posts and gone under some telephone wires before landing. I guess sometimes the good Lord looks after drunken fools and pilots. I now had to figure out the take off. It would have to be from where I was. There were several jamon trees about 100 feet beyond the further goal posts and the road. I knew I could be airborne before reaching the posts, but wondered about the trees. They were about fifty to seventy feet high. At the lower left corner, there was an opening or gap between the trees. I think I could make it with a little side-slip. The ADC, two guards and myself hauled the plane back to the spot from where I'd planned to take off. First, I had the ADC fill the jerry can with fuel and to obtain a funnel as well. I then filled the tank with five gallons of fuel. The tank holds about ten to twelve U.S. gallons.

Once all was completed, one of the guards and myself hauled the little cub a few more feet back up a little incline; perhaps twenty feet more. Bhaiya had shown up. He had been busy getting some of his guests onto the ponies for their morning ride. He looked a bit concerned when I told him how I planned to take off. I said I got the plane in

here, it was my job to get it out. He was for having it towed out. I showed His Highness how to pull the prop through and then how to give the prop the final start. Be sure to stay back once started. I climbed in and gave him the signal for contact; he had to pull the prop several times before it started. I warmed up the engine for a few minutes. I was surprised how well the little engine behaved. I think it was a Continental manufacture. I had full power on for a few seconds then released the brakes; she raced down the field and picked up speed fast. I was airborne three-quarters of the way down; I then turned toward the gap in the trees. It looked as though I may make it over the top. In any case, I did a slight slip to make sure I didn't catch a wingtip. I was clear and climbed to a couple hundred feet. This time I had no difficulty finding the airport.

When Cooch-Behar arrived at the airport, I was busy filling the plane with gas and checking the oil. Everything was perfect. "Okay, Bhaiya," I said, "let's start this flying." He looked amazed that I was all set to teach him. "I'll give you the first few go-arounds, when Sid and Moose get here, they can carry on." CB would fly from the back seat as I once did. I was no instructor, but felt qualified to give a few lessons. I leveled at five hundred feet and had CB go through the motions and gyrations for straight and level, then turns and stalls. He seemed to catch on fast. Back at the airport, we did touch and go landings (circuits and bumps, as the British call them). We were flying, refueling, and flying some more. I asked CB if he was tired. No! "Let's do some more." I was hoping he would say yes. I was worn out. At twelve thirty we called it quits and headed for lunch. At the palace, we discussed the flying. Boris, Sid and Moose finally showed up. I told them we had done a lot of flying; that Bhaiya was doing a fine job. That afternoon, Moose and Sid took over. I think it was Moose who finally told Bhaiya to take it around himself - solo! There were many natives watching their Maharajah. When he took off by himself, there were many cheers and clapping of hands. He circled and landed. When he got out, he asked; "Now how do I go about making right turns?" It was so unexpected; there was silence for a minute, then we all laughed. Bhaiya got back in the plane and took off; this time he didn't stay in the traffic pattern, but disappeared into the blue. It was about forty minutes before he returned. The ADCs were getting fidgity and worried. When he taxiied in, we could see he was elated and happy to be flying solo. That was it! A day at the flying circus!

Christmas and New Year's week was a fun week at the Cooch Behar Estate. Bhaiya was off flying every moment he had a chance. The guests had a wonderful time relaxing and horseback riding. A couple tigers and a leopard were shot. The holiday was over and time had come to depart. The C-NAK plane picked us up for the return to Calcutta.

After the holidays, Boris informed us that he was organizing another shoot in the

same place as last year, in Raimona and Katchagaon, Assam; for us to try and get some of the fellows together. The safari would be in the middle of March. It didn't take much persuasion. Our two general friends would not be along this time; they had already departed for the States. It was to be a successful trip with everyone having a good time. One of the party had found a bunch of bats that were living in one of the outer buildings, and somehow placed them in a gunny sack. At night he let them loose in Doc Richard's room. Shouts and yells and cussing brought everyone to his room, bearers too. We thought maybe a leopard had sneaked in, but no; we opened the door, and a swarm of bats started flying out. Doc had hidden under the covers, spectacles and all! Doc was short of stature but tough and rugged; no one would ever want to tangle with him. Therefore no one confessed to the prank. Blackie Blackmore was lucky enough to shoot a tiger and was tickled pink. Moose Moss shot two. I'll never forget Moose; he was quite a character.

Moose and I were on an elephant, on another tiger shoot with the group of other hunters. We were all strung out in a line, waiting for the beating elephants to hopeful flush a tiger in our direction. Captain McDonald and his wife Peggy were on an elephant a little distance to the right, about a hundred feet or so. I think we were at the furthest end to the left. I was explaining to Moose about the behavior of elephants, how gentle they were. In a couple of minutes Moose tapped me on the shoulder and said, "Look over there," and pointed to Mac's elephant. The rascal elephant had extended his penis full length. It was at least a yard long and thick around as my leg. It then decided to get an erection, reaching almost to between its fore legs, and kept whamming against its belly. "Oh," Moose whispered, "golly, golly, look at that; lookee there! Ain't that somethin. Never seen nuthin' like that before. Well what ya know Pete?" I had to agree, I was surprised as Moose. Then I said, "Hey Moose; how would you like to sport something like that?" He didn't reply right away. Then he said, "You know something? I'd rather have one the size of a fly and be able to do it forty times a day; than to have one like that old guy over there, and only be able to do it once a year." That ended that conversation in a hurry. Mac and Peggy couldn't see what was going under them and just as well.

When I had a chance, after the shoot and before returning to Calcutta, I decided to stay a few extra days at Cooch Behar Palace, since there had always been an open invitation by Bhaiya. I was able to do some bird shooting locally. Cooch Behar also had several fine horses in his stable; which were once race horses, he now used them for pleasure on his estate. Bhaiya was a great polo player too. I had a chance to ride with him on several occasions early in the mornings. This was great relaxation and I learned to ride fairly well. But, like all good things, the time had come to say farewell and catch the evening train back to Calcutta.

On another occasion on layover in Calcutta, two of my CNAC friends showed up one afternoon with four American Red Cross girls. Mohammed and Cookie always enjoyed seeing company at the house. They hustled about arranging snacks and having the mixes ready on the bar. The group were enjoying themselves, the girls especially, since it was their first experience in this part of the world. They were interested to hear about flying in China and the "Hump" operation. One of the girls asked about India; she heard that I knew several Maharajahs. "Yes I do, why?" "I would sure love to meet one of them sometime." "I can arrange that, if you ever get the time off." She was a cute girl by the name of Edna. She then piped up and said, "How about this week end?" "Okay, I'll fly you up to meet the Maharajah of Cooch Behar; we can have lunch with him and be back by the evening. Its just a little over two hundred miles north of Calcutta." "Wow! You have a plane?" "Yes, a little one. If you can be ready by seven in the morning, I'll pick you up." The Red Cross had a place on Chowringee, a few blocks up from the Grand Hotel.

One cannot buy aviation petrol in India without a special coupons and especially aviation gas, without a Carnet. Sid DeKantzow and I didn't have this for our little L-5. For most part we used automobile gas, which had only about sixty-five percent octane and not good for high powered engines. The day before departure, which was Friday, I had my taxi driver friend arrange the gas. The L-5 had two tanks in the wing overhead. With the help of the driver I filled the tanks full. It was a cool morning in May of '46; but as the sun came boiling out of the bay of Bengal, it would be stinking hot. It always brought out mad dogs, Englishmen and the Brain Fever bird! Oh yes, and idiots like me! Cooch Behar had been notified I would be arriving with a female guest for lunch. Mohammed had arranged crackers and cheese, along with six cans of American beer which was not more than 3.2 percent. Edna was excited as I strapped her into the back seat of the plane. Our plane was always parked at the Alipore Airport, an ex-RAF base, just around the corner from where we lived. We were airborne at about seven a.m. I had the L-5 cruising at about 3000 ft and 105 mph. It was cool and clear above the haze level as we headed north. With any kind of luck, it should take around two and a half hours with very little wind. This was about the range of the L-5. The fuel tanks had separate gauges, one on each side of the cockpit, overhead. The last two gallons on each tank are indicated in red as a warning. By eight a.m. it was getting warm even at this altitude. I shouted back to Edna for a beer. It tasted good and refreshing. We finished a couple beers each and I could now see the palace up ahead. I started the let down at about nine a.m. I

*Taking group to Cooch Behar for Christmas hunt, 1945.*

checked the fuel quantity on the gauges, the needles were both just into the red warning marks. I figured I had enough to fly over the palace to let Bhaiya know that we had arrived, so he could send a car over to pick us up. At this moment I don't know what possessed me, I let down to two hundred feet over the palace and dropped a couple empty beer cans onto the roof. I was flying east to west. Once the empties were thrown out, I pulled up straight ahead and perhaps too sharply. As I did, the engine sputtered and quit at about two hundred feet. There was no time to fiddle with the engine to see what happened and try to start it again. It had to be fuel starvation when I pulled up with nearly empty tanks; that, poor fuel octane, and piss-poor judgment on my part. I shouted back to Edna to be sure she was strapped in and to be ready for an emergency landing. I looked for a place to set the plane down. If I went straight ahead, I probably would hit the wall that circles the estate. I had no alternative but to turn back toward the palace and try to dump it in one of the large water tanks in front of the building and the other side of the main driveway; beyond the tank were two tennis courts with their nets still stretched across them. I changed plans: instead of the tank, I would try for the courts; the net would act as resisters. Everything looked fine as I glided in with half flap. Just a bit fast coming over the tank I knew I had the clay court made. I now made the second, fatal error. I put down the rest of the flaps to slow me to just above stall speed as I was passing over the tank. The flap was too much and the plane stopped flying. We hit the lip of the tank about two feet low. It struck like an arrow into a straw target. Both wings flew off and skidded along the tennis courts. The engine also broke away and just flipped over the lip in front of me. I dragged myself out with the

seat still strapped to my butt. I looked at Edna; she appeared woozie with a big knot on her forehead. I pulled her out and we sat on the edge of the tank. I asked the inevitable question, "Are you alright?" "Yeah, I guess so; that was some landing!" She had whacked her head on the battery that is located in front of her. From the palace came Bhaiya, followed by a couple of his bearers carrying trays. On arrival I explained briefly what had happened. "Here, have a good swig of this." Bhaiya poured us a couple of hefty glasses of brandy from the tray. Edna appeared to be recovering, though the knot on her head had swelled considerably. She was talking normally and was happy to meet the Maharajah who was still in his night robe! After examining what was once an airplane, I decided it was beyond repair. It could be sold for junk and there was no insurance either. I was indebted to Sid for his half of the plane which I had to make good. Bhaiya arranged for a room so Edna could rest for a bit. Auntie would attend to her and arrange something to eat till lunch was served. I think a couple of aspro were given her with a cup of tea. In the meantime Bhaiya and I retired to his office to relax and for me to regroup. I was really angry with myself for doing such a stupid trick as that low flying around with a pint of gas in the tanks; the gauges too could have been wrong. I even had the shivers as an after shock. I realized also, that it could have been a heck of a lot worse; possibly fatal to either one or both of us. I had another stiff brandy to stop the jitters. Little Caju Singh, the Palace secretary, kept mumbling that the Boss (Bhaiya) should not fly his plane; he should get rid of it before there was another accident. "These little planes are not safe," he kept repeating. Edna had a good rest and decided to join the group for lunch. She wanted to know how we were to get back

*Blackie Blackmore, back to camera, "Moose" Moss, toasting George Sen, H.H. Cooch Behar peering around my right shoulder.*

*Sampans on the Yankzee River carrying loads of human manure!*

China Air Transport (CAT); a lot of the pilots were joining him. A great many of my flights were passenger flights. People were traveling in all directions. Flights were via Chungking, Hankow and Nanking and on to Peking. On one of these flights from Calcutta to CHK and SHA, lo and behold, who did I have for passengers? The last batch of WAC's and other US military personnel headed for Shanghai. Ginny was not one of them, but there were a couple of my jail-bird friends! We had a good flight all the way to Chunking via Bhamo, Burma. I watched the girls take the sedan chairs up the never ending steps to CHK city. I was able to meet them later for Chinese chow. I did the honorable thing by taking a couple of my C-NAK chums along. I think it was the same place where I had first ate with Frank Higgs and Marty Gold. The little restaurant was pretty crowded, perhaps due to so many transit passengers on their way to different parts of China. I was hoping some Chinese gal would come by with her baby and crack it over one of the spittoons, but it didn't happen. One of the girls asked what that terrible smell was. One of the fellows piped up and said, "That is shit." "What?" He said that's right, and explained that all human excrement was not wasted in China; that it was collected in honey-buckets and taken to one common area. Here it is bucketed onto barges and sampams on the river, then carried to different towns up and down the river for fertilizer. In fact, a couple of Chinese had cornered the market. They had become very rich, and were known as "King Shit," hence the expression. The girls thought we were joking, but that is fact; the smell is the proof. The rest of the meal I don't think they enjoyed. Next morning I met the WAC's at our little island airport and made sure they were all well tied down, as we used to do with the Chinese soldiers when we hauled them across the hump for Stillwell. I didn't explain the hairy letdown nor the same type of takeoff. At Shanghai, a military bus came by to pick them up. I hugged and kissed my friends goodbye. I'd probably not see them again. I checked in at the Park Hotel, then rendezvoused with one of my Russian girls; she was the blonde. We wined and dined at the same Russian restaurant, and yes she would accompany me back to the hotel for the rest of the night. I called her my Little Russian "Poopsik"! I don't really know its meaning, but it sounded cute.

Many of the CNAC pilots were being temporarily based at CNAC's stations, such as Shanghai, Chungking, Hong Kong, Calcutta and Kunming. We would check the news through the pilots and send letters via the crews, while I kept the 300 Club supplied with vodka! Through the news, I learned that quite a few of the pilots were now sending for their wives and families to join them in Shanghai. I thought it was great, so I wrote to Helen and asked if she would consider coming to the Far East with David. The answer was a flat No. I pondered this out and discussed it with Sid. He agreed she should

to Calcutta. I said we would have to take the evening train. I told Bhaiya we would have to notify her supervisor of the delay and that Edna would not be able to return till tomorrow morning. Caju suggested that he would contact Cooch Behar house in Alipore, the man there could contact the Red Cross. They would tell the Red Cross that the aircraft had mechanical difficulties—how true! This way they would not worry. We were able to laugh it off a bit. The evening train arrived at Cooch Behar station. Edna and I thanked Bhaiya for his hospitality and left. During the ride I kept putting ice-packs on her forehead. I was surprised how quickly the bump was receding. I drank a fair share of scotch during the trip. The accident was having an impact on me mentally. I saw Edna to her establishment

by late morning. She was sorry about the wrecked plane. I told her not to worry; that it was all my stupid fault.

One might think with all this gadding around Cooch Behar and going on tiger hunting safaris that I didn't have much time to do any flying. Not quite so. I did my regular flying and kept my schedule with the airline. We were all now flying about a hundred hours a month average. I did mine from Calcutta base, mainly to Shanghai and back. There were flight schedules that I took to various parts of China. I was getting to know China well and my seniority was now up within the first ten numbers, giving me a chance to choose my flights.

It was early 1946 when a lot of U.S. Air Force pilots joined CNAC. General Chennault was in the midst of starting an airline that was called come out and put me on the straight and narrow! Even in Calcutta would be great. I had seniority enough to be based either in Shanghai or Calcutta. I thought this would keep us together. I wrote Helen again to reconsider; that PanAmerican would arrange transportation, as they were doing with the other families. In response, I received another telegram that I should return to the States right away, or else. Well, I talked it over again with Sid. He said, it looks like she doesn't want to come over and that's final. I knew my life had been completely twisted around. A vagabond or Rogue perhaps; I could not see myself settled down in the States— not yet anyway. I wrote back that perhaps a divorce was the only answer. I had a good job and good money. All my friends were here and I loved the life in the Far East. One day in April the CNAC office contacted me in Calcutta, that the American Consulate in Shanghai would like me to stop by when I was in town. On my next trip to Shanghai, I stopped in to see them and talked with the Consul General. His secretary brought in a file as I sat there. He thumbed through a few papers and said, "You have a wife, Helen?" I said yes. "She asked if you would return to the States; If not, then she would like a divorce." I told the Consul my story, and that she did not wish to come to China, as some of the other families were doing. I had a fine job and good career with CNAC in China. The company would like me to stay on; I had worked hard for them and gained respect and seniority.

The company had DC-4s ordered and planned to operate to the States and Europe. I would be giving up a lot if I quit now. "Okay, I understand your situation. In that case, Pete, I have the divorce papers from her lawyer in Bangor." The name Bangor rushed through my head; did such a place exist, or was it just a dream: Horace Chapman, archery, Mount Katahdin, and all those great friends. What was going on in my mind? What had happened? I felt strange. The Consul showed me the papers, to read them carefully, and see if I agreed to the terms; then go ahead and sign on the dotted line. I felt cold and miserable, the terrible rogue that I was. I knew I was that, and selfish. I felt there was no way out; I had reached the point of no return in my life. I guess there are girls that may understand the ways of a pilot such as me, and be happy in that vagabond life. Perhaps if I kept my careless life, I might get a bullet between the eyes for trespassing in the wrong boudoir. If flying the Hump didn't get me, then some disgruntled "Shaitan" (Devil) would; "Kismet"—"that is fate." I picked up the pen and signed my life away. My mind knew what I was going through, but the hand was heavy and wavered. Finally I gritted my teeth and signed all the documents. It was done and I was miserable. I had thrown my life away. I then thanked the Consul General for his time and started out. The secretary, or assistant consul was showing me the way. She then touched my arm, and motioned me toward her desk; I followed her. She was a slightly built brunette with brown eyes. She said, "I couldn't help

*Marine Drive, Bombay where I did a lot of bicycling in 1946.*

noticing you at the Consul General's office; you looked worried and upset. I am sorry for what you must be going through." The secretary then introduced herself as Dorothy Wetzel. I thanked her and said I was okay, and would make it just fine. Then Dorothy said, "I think you could use a drink. How about meeting me at the bar in the Park Hotel?" She said she would be there in about an hour.

As we sat at the bar, me with my scotch, I was feeling a little more relaxed, and Dorothy was easy to talk to. She had just arrived in Shanghai by boat, and was staying at the hotel. She would be moving into a house allocated by the U.S. Embassy. Dorothy had very fine features and a trim figure; she wore clothes that did her figure justice. Her legs were shapely, with neat ankles and shoes that gave her legs a very attractive appearance. Her eyes were brown and gave her a pixie look. She put me at ease. After drinks, we had dinner at the roof restaurant. During our conversation, Dorothy mentioned that before the War she was based with the Consulate in Geneva, Switzerland, that it was her favorite spot. She had been born in Bartow, Florida. She and I had an interesting evening. I then dropped her off at her door and said goodnight. Dorothy knew I was based in Calcutta and made my flights to Shanghai via Chungking. She called me next afternoon to ask for a repeat of drinks and dinner. I apologized that I was to fly very early next day, but would take a raincheck when I returned.

On arrival at Chungking, I was informed that my schedule had been changed. Because of my seniority, I was told I was to take a high ranking Chinese to Nanking. This was now early May and for most part the weather would be cool and clear. At Sanhopah Airport I was introduced to a rather smallish man dressed in a dark olive, General's uniform. His name was General Tai-Li. He was the Generalissimo's right-hand man. I was informed I would be flying the General to many parts of China for

the next ten days to two weeks. I learned from the copilot and radio operator that the General was assigned by Chiang-Kai-Shek to earmark those who collaborated with the Japanese during their occupation. These people, if found guilty, would be shot. Tai-Li was not, as I would expect, to be a stern individual. He appeared simple and polite. He spoke very little English, so the copilot did the interpreting for us. After one of our flights wound up back in Nanking, it was revealed that I had just had a birthday a short time ago; thereupon the General insisted that there be a party that evening at the hotel. The Chinese love to have fire works for all occasions, even funerals. Naturally there was a great show of fire-works in front of the hotel before dinner. I had to sit next to the General at a sumptuous dinner as only the Chinese know how to give. It all went well with the hot rice wine. The General bestowed good wishes and a long life. I could sure use the wishes and long life in the crazy flying and hairy letdowns. By mid October I flew General Tai-Li back to Chungking. It was necessary to make a night approach and landing at Sanhopah Airport. There was a great hustle to get the field ready for a night landing. Smudge pots were lined up to identify the runway. There would be no way to check any rice paddies when I broke out; nor would I be able to see the high tension wires. Sure enough, I was informed of the usual overcast of about twenty-five hundred feet and fairly good visibility. I told the radio operator to inform the General that night landings there were not customary; this would be my first attempt. Tai-Li came into the cockpit to witness the approach and landing; this didn't help any. I broke out near 3000 ft. Though I couldn't see any rice paddies, I could just make out the Yantzee River. I descended to 1300 ft. and could distinguish some of the lights of the city on my left; in this manner I was able to follow the silhouette of the river, till I saw the smudge pots flickering in the distance. They looked bright in the darkness. All this time Tai-Li had his hand on my right shoulder; I guess an insurance to him that all would be well; to touch down and taxi in. When this was done, he called out "Ding-Hao, Ding-Hao." Before he deplaned, I suggested to the General that if he needed me for any further flights, to please contact our operations office in Shanghai; that I would be happy to fly him around again. Two months later the General took a Chinese Air Force plane on a trip and on an instrument approach to Nanking Airport, the plane slammed into a hill and killed all on board.

The next day I was back on my schedule, winging my way back to Calcutta; I had my load of vodka for the Club. I arrived early at the 300 Club and presented the bottles to Dmitri. He was all smiles, but didn't try the somersault through the window. Boris showed up all smiles too; then came another friend, Pearson Surita. We were at the bar having a drink, when in walked a U.S. Army captain with a heavyset gentleman in civvies and a beautiful young lady. The three sat at a table near by. Not too many people had arrived as yet. After a short time the pretty girl got up and went over to a slot machine in the foyer and was trying her luck. I excused myself from Boris and Pearson, and sauntered over to the machine next to hers. She asked if I was any good at the slot machines; "No I 'm not, and how are you doing?" I noted the bandit she was playing was taking all her rupees. I don't recall too well just what developed, or what went on; all I know, I was fascinated and could hardly take my eyes off her. I introduced myself, she said her name was Kiki, that the big fellow was her father. I invited Kiki over to meet Pearson and join us for a drink. She motioned to her dad that she was joining us. We had a couple of drinks. I noticed too that she was full of laughter and a very effervescent type of young lady. She told me she was born in Rangoon and all the family had evacuated from Burma when the Japs were moving in. She had finished her schooling in Darjeeling, and was glad that it was over. Kiki asked me if I would care to join she and her dad for dinner. How wonderful, and yes I would like to. Her Dad's name was Jack and he was full of fun and jokes. I liked him from the start. After dinner the captain suggested going over to the Karnani Estates for after dinner drinks. Karnani was where the US had its big night club. It was a POSH place with great American style food.

Kiki's last name was Voyantsis. We spent about an hour at the Officer's club, when Jack said he had to get along. He had a car and would drop me off. I said I lived in Alipore. By coincidence they lived nearby. It had been a swell evening and I hoped I would see Kiki again.

I did see her again, often, and met the rest of the family: her mother Mae, her brother John and little sister Penelope, nick named "Penny."

I found myself infatuated and falling in love. She spoke Hindi, loved curry dishes.

Before I knew it, we truly were in love. One day she mentioned her family was moving to Bombay; her dad was going to start a hotel there. That was bad news for me and a blow. I promised I would come to Bombay, whenever I had a break from flying.

When I returned to Shanghai, other wheels were turning that I was not aware of; I think Dorothy had her sights set on me. She had left a note for me at the hotel, to give her a call at the office. I called her one morning, and she mentioned the rain-check to have drinks. There I was at the bar waiting. Dorothy arrived looking pert as usual. After the drinks, she suggested having dinner at a Japanese restaurant she knew. We took the normal mode of transport, Pedicab! The place was different from any restaurant I had ever been in; first we had to sit on the floor, with cushions to bolster us up. The Japanese girls were dressed in their traditional costumes with the obi sash and a fancy bow in the back. It was interesting and I liked the atmosphere. How could all these people be so dainty, clean and polite, and yet so ruthless in war? I found it difficult to keep sitting and trying to eat in a cramped position; however, that was resolved when the girls had me sit on pillows, and all I had to do was to open my mouth and they fed me with the chopsticks. I felt, and probably looked, much like those baby robins in a nest, waiting for mother to bring another worm. The saki was the same as the Chinese hot rice wine, but served in miniature china cups. This, I thought, was great. I told Dorothy we would have to return another time.

At the hotel, I escorted Dorothy to her room. I started to say goodnight. Instead, she grabbed my arm and said, "No you don't! You're coming in here with me." She opened the door and ushered me into her room. Dorothy didn't waste any time; in two shakes of a duck's ass, she had undressed. She had a cute, sexy way of doing so. She tantalizingly crawled under the covers. Dorothy knew what she wanted, and how to go about it. It turned out to be quite a session. There would be repeat performances during the next few days.

The CNAC facility had now moved to Lunghwa Airport, which was once their old, prewar base. It did not have all the facilities as did the military Kingwan Airport, but it was closer to the city.

I reported to CNAC operations for my flight to Calcutta in a C-46 with a load of cargo and passengers. Most all passengers had to travel in the bucket-seat arrangement. C-NAK had not got around to plushing up their planes yet; only the two prewar DC-3s were plush. The route was normally via Hankow, Kunming, Bhamo in North Burma for fuel, and then Calcutta. The small terminal was crowed with Chinese passengers, causing loads of confusion; people scurried in all directions to catch a flight. As I made my way through the mob to our operations, I heard my name being called. It was Dorothy. I asked, "What in the world are you doing here so early in the morning?" "I'm going to Calcutta with you!" I said "What?

You?" "That's right. I have to go to the Consulate in Calcutta, to take some important papers to them." She had meant to tell me this before, but wasn't sure of the trip till the last minute. I had a strange feeling about this. There she was, at the spur of the moment ready to go. Thank goodness that Kiki was already in Bombay. I had mentioned Kiki to Dorothy. She knew I had a girl friend in Calcutta.

There was nothing I could do but fly my plane to Calcutta with Dorothy as a passenger. Calcutta was hot and humid; this didn't seem to phase Dorothy. She appeared to be enjoying the ride through some dingy parts of town, to Alipore. Actually, she seemed impressed. She thought it was great, with the wide streets and large, shady trees. I showed her a good time during the stay. We visited the U.S. Consulate, the same one my mother took us to in 1928 for visas to the States. Of course she had heard me talk about the 300 Club, so that was a must on our program. Dorothy met Boris and Cooch Behar and a lot of my other friends.

Before leaving for Shanghai, I arranged a couple of parties at the apartment. Dorothy seemed to enjoy my friends and Calcutta very much. I was hoping she would detest the pesky place! The time now came to return to Shanghai. I still felt that this trip was her own invention. I also realized how much Dorothy loved her sex; to a point one might call her "nympho." I don't really like the word, just because a gal likes a lot of sex. I guess it's a matter of opinion.

I spent most of June and July flying within China and then back on my schedule to Calcutta. It was hot and muggy with the monsoons. The Statesman newspaper in Calcutta was mentioning the independence of India. Negotiations were underway as to its rule, Muslim or Hindu. Mahatma Gandhi and Jinnah were trying to arrange a peaceable solution to the pending problem of Muslim and Hindu. A Mr. H. Suhrawardy (Muslim), a high official in the Muslim League of Calcutta, said that all would be well. I had no sooner returned to Shanghai when the Shanghai Herald was showing a front page of terrible riots taking place in Calcutta. Strictly Muslims and Hindus were having it out. First reports said a few hundred killed; then a few thousand. Curfews were imposed at night, and people would be shot by the military if caught on the streets after dark. CNAC flights were canceled to Calcutta temporarily. I was hoping that my friends were okay, especially Mohammed and Cookie. By mid August the riots and looting had been stopped by the military. I was now scheduled back on the Calcutta run. I had misgivings about returning there. The Herald had stated that well over 30,000 had been killed. I did want to return to see that all was well with the apartment and nothing looted, which was always the pattern in such political mixups. I sometimes believe they cause riots in order just to loot. At Dum-Dum I taxiied in and shut down the engines.

As I deplaned with the passengers, I could smell the stench of rotting flesh. The drive into town was not quiet as a couple of weeks before. There were upturned bullock carts and dead buffaloes; further along I saw carts laden with human bodies that were being hauled away. This is what greeted the crew and myself as we were nearing Calcutta. The hot August sun had bloated the bodies; dead women had their teats fully bloated out; the dead men lying in rows all had their throats cut, and their penises were bloated, stuck up in eternal erections. What a way to go! The area looked like an old asparagus patch. Hundreds of crows, vultures and pariah dogs were feasting on dead bodies. As we drove along, we held handkerchiefs to our nose and mouths. Chowringhee and the downtown streets had been cleaned up, with military and local police patrolling the streets.

There was little traffic or pedestrians, I guess because a curfew was imposed from sunset to sunrise.

The crew bus dropped me off at my apartment, Mohammed and Cookie were there to greet me; I was sure happy to know that they were well, and their families. Most of the rioting and killings had been in the northern section of Calcutta and not around Alipore, but it didn't go unscathed. I stayed in that day and got all the news from Mohammed and Cookie. It really had been hectic according to them. Next noon, I was able to take a cab to the 300 Club. I saw Boris, he said the riots had spoiled business considerably. He chuckled and said they had now devised curfew parties. That sounded a bit different. One could find out from the Club where and who would have a party at their home. I learned the next one would be at Waris Moshidabad, a couple days thence, on a Saturday. I thought I'd give it a try and brought along a bottle of vodka. Cooch Behar and Boris weren't there. The conversation was mainly about the riots; that the British and Indian troops had the situation under control and everything pretty well cleaned up. They said one poor sod lived in a drainage pipe for about a week, with a knife still in his back. They got him out and he lived to tell about it. After drinks and sandwiches, and folks had run out of conversation, people looked for corners here and there to lie down and wait till sun-up. It wasn't the most comfortable way to spend the night, but neither did one want to get shot.

I didn't care too much for their curfew parties; instead, I preferred to visit the club for lunch and wander home to a nice bed and early nights. Bhaiya was up at the palace on this trip so I missed seeing him. I had called Kiki several times, to make sure she was alright in Bombay. The family were staying at the Ritz Hotel, which was run by an Italian. She said her dad Jack was in the process of lining up a building near the Ritz on Church street. Once he had the place furnished and staffed, he planned to call it the Ambassador Hotel. I told Kiki I was hoping to get some time off in October, and would be over to see her.

In Shanghai, Dorothy was planning (conniving is more appropriate) to get me

*Blackie Blackmore on tiger hunt at Cooch Behar. He did get his tiger, 1946.*

very much involved with her, though I didn't know it at the time. When I checked in at the Park Hotel, she was there. Dorothy said she now had a house near the airport; to check out and come with her. She even had a jeep for transportation. I went with her not really knowing what her distant plans were. The house was very nice, with a fire place. An Amah (Chinese maid) went along with the house. Dorothy made certain the maid was an old hag!

I continued my flying regularly within China. I liked the flights to Peking because we had a chance to overnight. This gave me an opportunity to try out real Peking duck. The waiter would bring in a live duck, which you had to grab by its breast and give a squeeze. This way you understood it was a fine fat one! What I didn't know was these poor birds as soon as they were hatched, were nailed by their feet to a board and force fed. Anyway, the end result was great. The roast duck with the little pancakes and other trimmings was always done to perfection.

A lot of the pilots were leaving, or joining Chennault's CAT airline. Others were headed back to fly for Bob Prescot's Flying Tiger Airline. An accident that shook a lot of us up actually occurred back in January. It was my good friend Charles Sharkey. He was making a passenger flight in a DC-3 and on the let down had slammed into a mountain at Singtau, which was a US Navy controlled base. For reasons only known to them the Navy had moved their radio station. Sharkey had made the let down using the old procedure, where the station used to be. The new location and same frequency lead Charlie into the hill. What a helluva way to wind up. I felt really sad about it. We had been good friends and had a lot of good times together.

After returning to Chungking from one of my flights, I was informed by our operations I was to take a flight to Canton and Hong Kong. It would be my first trip to HKG. I had heard so much about the place from people like Chuck Sharp and MacDonald. I was given a let down chart for the two places. As I looked over the Hong Kong one, it resembled the Chungking one—hairy! and not easy. The procedure, as I recall, was to came over the beacon at about 4500 ft, gear down and descend easterly till you broke out over the sea. Once contact, make a 180 degree turn back for what they called the "Gap." It is a narrow stretch of sea between mainland Kawloon and Victoria Island. It sounds easy; but with low visibility and ceiling, plus rain, it can be a nightmare. Your behind starts puckering up. Sometimes its necessary to be as low as a couple hundred feet to stay contact with the windshield wipers swishing flat out. What you hope not to see is white breakers ahead. It means you are headed for the craggy rocks and mountain peaks. There is just time to make another quick 180 degree turn and pull up. You have missed the "Gap." If you have the guts, try it again. It would be three years later that my friend Charles Sundby on a let down with a DC-4 from Shanghai pressed his luck a bit too much. Perhaps he didn't see the breakers ahead; if he did, it was too late. One cannot swing a DC-4 around as easily as a DC-3. He hit the hill and killed all on board, including a VIP (Quentin Roosevelt). If you make it through the Gap, continue till a permanent check point comes up, which is the Peninsula Hotel off the right wing. Using the hotel as a pylon, turn right; this puts the plane on the base leg with a nub of a hill straight ahead. By now the runway should be in sight, to the right. Now fly between the hill and the large mountain on the left. Cross a major highway and land. Its time for a stiff drink and you have earned it. There was a joke going around, that whenever AirFrance came over the beacon, the captain would call for a shot of Cognac, "Before I makes zee let down!"

All this I was to learn later. Right now on my first trip to HKG I mulled over the letdown several times as I headed for Canton. I was flying on top of the overcast around 12000 ft with a load of pax in a DC-3. After four hours and a bit, I tried to tune in Canton station and was receiving only static. I tried HKG and still nothing. The radio officer was in contact with both stations on High Frequency. The reports said the cities were overcast. Canton had a ceiling of 2000 ft with good visibility; HKG was the same. I continued for another forty-five minutes, and noticed the tops of the clouds were sloping down gradually, I descended with them. There were no breaks in the overcast, it was solid. We checked again with the two stations, they reported their radio stations were operating normally, but I still could not pick up anything. I had now flown out my estimated arrival time (ETA) and continued. I had enough fuel for another 2 to 3 hours. I stayed on top for another half hour. The cloud tops and I had dropped down to about six thousand feet. I figured I must be over the China Sea some place, but where? I decided to descend through the overcast. I slowed the aircraft down to 90 mph, with the gear and half flap. I picked up moisture and a little rain. At 3000 ft and then to 2000 ft, there was still nothing. At 1500 ft there were breaks in the clouds and rice paddies under us. I reduced power and broke out over what turned out to be a large valley. Actually, it was a pocket in the mountains. The peaks ascended into the clouds. I turned the plane back the way I had come and a cold sweat came over me as I realized I must have skimmed over the mountains as I was letting down. I circled the valley and saw an opening that I could get through.

I put the plane back to cruise speed and headed for the opening. I came into a much larger valley and saw villages; beyond that I could see blue water: The China Sea. I got the charts out and found I was almost 100 miles north of course. Evidently some hellacious crosswinds had blown me off course; that, and damn poor navigation. I didn't' have to make the hairy HKG letdown, I had already done that and didn't know it! I stayed VFR and saw the "Gap." I followed the pattern shown on the letdown. I circled around the hotel and made my landing. It had been a harrowing experience. I took on more fuel and headed for Canton. I dropped off the passengers and returned to HKG VFR. I was not about to make any more crazy approaches today. The crew and I checked in at the Peninsula Hotel.

The Peninsula had always been the major hotel of Hong Kong; oddly enough, the Japanese General couldn't get used to this beautiful place and its wonderful architecture during the war years. He had constructed as Basha-type house (hut) on the mezzanine floor, that he himself would occupy. It was still there when the crew and I walked in, and we had a good look at it. The next day I ventured across to Victoria Island by the ferry service and walked around the shopping areas.

I was back at the hotel in time to meet some of my CNAC friends. Blackie Blackmore was one of them. The next day I took my flight back to Chungking. On the way I kept thinking of that crazy let down among the mountains, which gave me a chill. After a few days rest at Chunking I was winging my way to Calcutta. I was trying to forget the past events of a near mishap, and looking forward for a tall scotch and soda on my back porch. I taxiied in at DumDum Airport and checked our operations. There was a message for me from the US Consulate in Calcutta to please come and see them soon as possible. I immediately thought that Dorothy was up to something. I walked into the Consulate's office and was met by a very lovely lady by the name of Miss Casey. I handed her my passport and then got the rude awakening that it had expired in February '46. She explained that normally, naturalized citizens could only stay overseas for five years, and only three years in the country of their birth. This shook me up. What do I do next? Miss Casey informed me that since CNAC was part of PanAmerican, there would be no problem. Only if I was working for a foreign company would I have to return to the States immediately. She told me to get a couple of passport pictures and come back. I went to my Kodak friend on Park street and he did me up with a pretty good picture. Usually passport pictures are the most horrible looking things. It made people look like gangsters, a real mug shot! My new ones were great. The following day I presented them to the Consulate. Even Miss Casey had to agree that my man did a good job. I received my passport for another three years and was on my way.

It was now September in Shanghai, and I was busy doing my flying. I did stay at Dorothy's place, it saved a lot of hotel bills. After that months flying, I was informed that I was now entitled to home leave. CNAC informed me that Trans World Airlines (TWA) was starting its international operations into Bombay via Daharan, Saudia Arabia and Cairo. I was given a letter by Captain Sharp, to TWA office in Bombay for a courtesy ticket to New York. I didn't waste any time in returning to Calcutta. I told Mohammed and Cookie to look after things; that His Highness, Cooch Behar might be using the apartment during my absence. I might add that the furniture I had been leasing locally was now mine. The store I was renting from had been destroyed during the riots and the owners were killed. Sorry, what else could I do! I had a few days to settle my affairs and gave Mohammed and Cookie sufficient funds to keep going.

I didn't notify Kiki I was coming to Bombay; I wanted to surprise her. I caught an Air India flight direct to Bombay. Kiki's family were still at the Ritz Hotel. It was quite a ride from Santa Cruz Airport to downtown Bombay. I hadn't been there before. The nice part was driving through the Malabar-Hill area, with their palatial apartments and homes. The area is also famous for its Sunken Gardens and is well known for its poshness. The only gruesome part was the Parsi's "Tower of Silence." The Towers are where the Parsies place their dead on enclosed iron grates or racks, open to the elements; it is a round circular tower about a hundred feet high. The weather, the vultures and the heat take care of the remains. When decomposed, the rest fall through the grates, to be washed away through a space at the center of the floor below. The Parsies are the descendants of the ancient Persians who were fire worshipers, and known as Zoroastrists. They are the wealthy people of India. A Parsi by the name of J.D. Tata was the man who owned most of the steel mills, Air India, and many of the other large factories.

The taxi took me along the concourse that runs along the waters edge of Bombay Bay and is called Marine Drive. The driver dropped me at the door of the hotel. Here, one of the bearers came out and helped me with my baggage. It appeared to be a small hotel and cozy. At the desk I asked if Miss Kiki Voyantsis was here. "Yes, who is calling?" I told the clerk I wanted to keep it a surprise. "Please, just send for Kiki Memsahib." "Yes sir," the clerk said with a twist of his head, as they all do! I waited awhile, and out came Kiki from the elevator. It certainly was a surprise, and she looked pretty when she really opened those big brown eyes. I gave her a big hug and kiss. We returned to the desk and arranged for my room. It was a nice feeling to know that I would not be receiving any messages to go fly at some weird hour of the night or morning.

The October weather in Bombay can be most pleasant, with the monsoons finished and the cool sea breeze in the evenings. Her dad Jack was still busy arranging for his hotel, the Ambassador. When possible he would take us up to Juhu Beach which was near the airport. Sometimes we could use the car to tour around. Jack also had an old Italian friend visiting from Rangoon. His name was Angelo Lungi. He had spent most of his life in Burma. He turned out to be a lot of fun. Once in awhile Angelo and I would rent bicycles and cycle up and down Marine Drive early in the mornings. It was good exercise, and relaxing.

I tried finding out about TWA and its flights. No one was sure when they would start operating. Okay, I was in no hurry. Kiki and I visited the Taj Hotel once for lunch and dinner. Their food was delicious, especially fish and a special salad called Karanboi Salad. Kiki and I visited quite a few other places together. When Jack let us have the car, we would drive to Juhu Beach for picnics. It was quiet and nice. It seemed that time was flying and still no TWA, and it was time to return to Shanghai and flying. Before leaving Bombay, Kiki and I became engaged. She was worried that a marriage might not be feasible, since I was a divorced man and she was a Catholic. She felt she couldn't marry a divorced person. We would cross that bridge later. I then said goodbye and left for Calcutta and Shanghai.

Calcutta operations informed me that they had received word that the DC-4s would be arriving, for me to get back to Shanghai for training. I was also told that my friend Blackie Blackmore had been killed on an approach to Chungking. My friends seemed to be folding their wings one after another.

At the same time in October, it was reported that my friend Frank Higgs had also crashed into a hill and was killed. Milton Caniff, the cartoonist, made a eulogy for Frank "Dude Henek" Higgs in the Stars and Stripes military paper. It was hard to believe that these veteran pilots were making such fatal mistakes. Of course, I don't know why I had not bought the farm by now, with all the silly flying mistakes I was making.

In Shanghai I was greeted by some of my friends and Dorothy in her jeep. The next morning, over a cup of tea, I told Dorothy of my engagement to Kiki. She was upset to say the least, but that would not deter her efforts at any cost. One of my CNAC friends had it on good authority that Dorothy was mixed up with an Intelligence Agency. He called it the CIA. I wasn't sure what that was.

I visited Captain MacDonald's office the next day; he asked how would I like to fly Generalissimo Chiang-Kai-Shek's personal DC-4. "Wow! Yes, that would be great. But when?" "Right away." Mac said the plane had arrived and was based in Nanking. A couple days later I dead-headed to Nanking and was introduced to the crew that had flown the plane from the States. The captain of the DC-4, who was to give me flight instructions, was a fine fellow by the name of Guy "Tommy" Tomberlin. Tommy was a soft spoken, easy going individual; I felt we would get along well. After introductions to the crew, I was shown the Generalissimo's aircraft. It was really plush, with all modern conveniences: It had flushing toilets, a shower, foldout beds, tables, easy chairs, a modern galley with refrigerator, pure silver cutlery, and china, and crystal. After the inside of a C-46 with bucket-seats, this was some airplane! Tom and the flight engineer gave me some of the basics concerning the systems of the plane, including the avionics and flight characteristics. We then settled down to flight instructions. I was eager to get my hands on the monster to see how it flew. Tommy turned out to be a good instructor and had a lot of patience. He sure needed it with me. We flew several hours almost every day, for the next ten days.

I now had a little over fifteen hours and felt ready to check out. A couple other DC-4s arrived in Shanghai and CNAC crews were getting their training. Preparations were being made for the DC-4 service from Shanghai to Calcutta via Hong Kong. Tom and I sat in Nanking, with nowhere to fly, because the Generalissimo never did show

up; not even to have a look at his plane. We had been sitting around now for four weeks without any flights. We did fly the plane around locally, to make sure I could handle it. I called MacDonald and said if nothing was going to develop here that I would prefer to return to Shanghai and get back on my regular schedule. With the twenty odd hours in the 4, I felt I could officially check out and start flying the DC-4s on schedule. I appreciated the prestigious assignment, but with no flying and overtime, I'd rather give it up. Mac agreed and had more use for me there than twiddling my thumbs in Nanking.

Tomberlin and I returned to Shanghai. I was now supposed to check him out on the C-46. This was the agreement when the DC-4 pilots (ex-military) who joined CNAC had to go to the bottom of the seniority list. They would now have to fly the DC-3s and 46s. However Tom was not too happy with the arrangement. I could hardly blame him. Yet, us C-NAK pilots had done all the dirty work of flying the "Hump" for years and pioneered all the internal routes of China. We deserved the break.

Tomberlin and I took our first C-46 flight to Manila, via Formosa. We landed at Clark Air Force Base, outside of the city. A CNAC bus dropped us off at the Manila Hotel. The building still sported shell and bullet holes in the white concrete. The front pillars looked as they might collapse any minute. Not much reconstruction had been accomplished; most bombed areas were still evident. Once we entered the lobby, it looked in pretty good shape. After checking in, we gathered at the bar and noticed all types of uniformed personnel having their drinks, the uniforms were mainly USAF and Navy. I was enjoying my scotch, when a voice came across from the other end of the bar: "Pete! You old son-of-bitch, what are you doing here?" I looked across the bar, and there was the familiar face of my old PanAfrica friend, Phil Hill. For heaven's sake; after four long years of war, here we meet—fantastic! Phil came over and looked great in his Navy uniform. Then Tom piped up, "I know you Phil." It turned out they were on one of the islands during the war with the Japs. What a small world! We certainly had a wonderful get together that evening. We ate at the bar where Phil introduced me to eating Philippine "Sate," hors-doeuvre of meat bar-b-qued on small bamboo skewers. You had to dip the pieces of meat into hot, spicy, peanut sauce. It tasted good and we made our meal of the stuff. Phil had toyed with the idea of joining CNAC, but could not quite make up his mind. I tried twisting his arm, but I was not able to twist it enough! It was a swell evening and visit with Phil. I wished him well and hoped we would meet again real soon.

Quite a few DC-4 crews had now arrived in Shanghai and I was introduced to most of them. I welcomed them to the world of CNAC. Dorothy thought it great that we use her home to have several parties for the new pilots. Tommy Tomberlin appeared disenchanted with the set-up of having to fly

*Checking out on DC-4 Shanghai, 1946/47.*

C-46s around China. He finally quit and returned to the States. The last part of November till the twentieth of December had me flying my China routes, since the pilot roster appeared to be thinning out. Actually I was back in Shanghai on the 23rd of December, just in time for Christmas and New Year's. On Christmas Eve all pilots wanted to make their flights from around the FarEast back home to Shanghai. Some of them had their families there. Others were expecting their wives to arrive by boat any day. Besides, who wanted to be stuck in Chungking or Kunming over the holidays? I arranged a get-together with some of the DC-4 crews and old CNAC hands. Around five o'clock in the evening, I took the jeep to pick up the pilots from the Park Hotel and YMCA. I returned for the second group of guys at the hotel, when I noticed the weather was getting bad with heavy fog setting in. In fact, it was difficult driving; one could barely see ahead, and should one hit a pedicab, a mob of Chinese would turn on you.

I had a drink with the fellows at the Park Hotel before returning. It had now become a thick, peasoup fog as we heard a plane overhead. If Lunghwa Airport was as bad as it was here in town, the plane certainly could not land. By the time I arrived back at the house, the weather was zero-zero, no visibility at all. It now sounded as though there were several planes milling around upstairs. I wondered why the flights were allowed to take off for Shanghai in the first place. The crews surely must have received weather reports. CNAC and the Military gave out pretty good forecasts. We were happy to be on the ground, safe and sound, as this was no night to be flying. My new friends, Dorothy and I settled down for our Christmas Eve party. Dorothy had obtained a turkey through the U.S. commissary and the whiskey. Though one could buy a lot of American things in Shanghai, they were getting expensive. In the back of my mind, I kept thinking of those fellows up there, circling around trying to land. To me there was no way they could make it. The USAF did have a Ground Control Approach (GCA), a new radar operated system at their Kiangwan field. Once the planes departed such places as Hankow, the airport would shut down. Maybe Nanking was open. A few more drinks and I was forgetting the situation. I don't remember how I was able to get the fellows back to the hotel that night. I remember it was nigh impossible to drive, I had to creep along. The next morning was clear and the fog had burned off. The news was out on the radio and the local *Herald* paper: Several airplanes had crashed at both airports, trying to land in the fog. Many passengers and crew had been killed. I raced out to Lunghwa Airport to the operations office. There were a lot of grieving souls milling about. I got to operations which was crowded; all the VIPs were present; I found it difficult to get the attention of Captain MacDonald and Chuck Sharp. I finally talked to Mac. He said that Pilot Greenwood had run out of fuel above the field and almost made it in; unluckily he hit another aircraft that was parked on the field. All on board were killed. Greenwood's wife had arrived the day before. He must have tried to get back to meet her. One of our 46s had hit a pagoda on the final approach. Captain Preus survived, with major injuries, but most of his passengers died. A CATC DC-3, trying to land at Kiangwan, on the GCA, overshot and hit a house on the north side of the runway - all were killed, including a woman and child in the house. Captain Joe Michaels was one of the lucky ones; he made it in safely on the GCA in a C-46 and 50 passengers. It turned out to be a very sad Christmas week.

We all kept on flying our schedules no matter what the circumstances. Many of our friends had folded their wings.

Dorothy appeared not to be too shaken about my engagement to Kiki. She was using all her wily ways of a woman to get me away from Kiki. I stayed away as much as possible from the house and her. I was busy flying the DC-4s with a couple of the new pilots, mainly the Calcutta run with the hopes of checking out officially.

Our Chinese pilot licenses were based on the American CAA style. Instead of having the airplane type on the license, it gave horsepower only. Mine read 5600 hp for the DC-4. On one flight I took my C-NAK friends to my home in Alipore and had arranged that we take a week's leave. I don't remember all their names now; Joe Michaels was one of them who had safely landed his C-46 that foggy night in Shanghai. There was also Chuck Simms, our flight engineer. I was able to arrange with Cooch Behar for us to come up for a short hunting trip. I think the other captain was a Jack Burns.

On one of the shoots, in typical tiger grass, the elephants flushed a leopard. It was an elusive cat and was hard to corner. I had Joe and Chuck on a howdah elephant, the other pilot was with one of the ADCs; they too were on a howdah, and stationed across a dry stream from me. I had not planned to shoot anything; I wanted them to have the sport. I was on a pad elephant sitting behind the mahout. There was an open area in front of Michaels where I hoped the leopard would come out. The beating elephants came along slowly and the leopard emerged on their side of the stream, right in front of Joe and he didn't see it. I gave a light whistle to get Joe's attention. I pointed at the leopard.

I thought Joe would fall off the elephant when he saw the cat, he was so excited. By the time he tried to shoot the leopard bounded back into the grass. Joe took a shot and raised a lot of mud and dust behind its tail as it disappeared. The elephants chased it around to another area of tall grass. Again, we set up a beat with the fellows placed in likely spots. First, the elephants had trampled down long swathes in the grass about 10 feet wide. I stayed off to one side again. Right near me was one of those animal warrens, or tunnels. As mentioned I was on a pad elephant. I watched the beat progress and warned the guys to keep a sharp lookout, because the cat would be moving fast. When I thought the leopard would be coming their way, my mahout put up his hand, signaling that the leopard may be coming toward me. If it did, I was sure he would be coming along the tunnel. I had an old Cooch Behar paradox shotgun. Its a gun that has rifling at the last three or four inches of its barrels; one can use bird shot, or a special type ball cartridge that will travel like a rifle bullet when it passes through the rifling area. I was using these special cartridges. I saw grass move up ahead, so I leaned over to get a good shot if it came through that opening; it did, in a blur of spots. I fired. The animal somersaulted and spun around. I was ready with the second barrel when the leopard sprang about 10 feet off to my left and diagonally past the elephant.

In a split second my elephant turned to its right and bolted, leaving me treading air with the leopard. I shot the second barrel at the same time; I didn't know if I had hit it or not. I landed on top of the gun, about 10 feet below and was stunned for a moment. I woke up with my head ringing. I didn't move, but could feel that the gun was broken under me. I lay and played dead; I didn't know if the leopard was dead, wounded, or running like hell miles away. The elephant was long gone too. While I was thinking about these things I felt something touch the back of my shoulders. I knew if it was the leopard, I must not move. I knew I was in the position that my dog Bob was in Bhowali years ago; he must have been a brave little fellow who took his fate with grace. I should do the same, I thought. There was the touch again and a little more firm this time. Why didn't he get it over with? Then I heard a voice say, "Sahib, Sahib!" I slowly turned my head, as I had been lying face down. I saw the elephant standing over me; he had been nuzzling me with his trunk to check if I was dead. There was a shout, "Sahib is okay, he is okay!" The mahout gave the indication and signaled with his two hands to the side of his head and tilted, a sleeping sign saying "murgia (its dead)." Meaning the leopard. I asked "Where?" The mahout pointed just beyond me. I got up and there about five feet away lay the dead leopard hidden in the tall grass. I picked up the broken gun which was in two pieces. My ribs ached as if broken. I must have had the wind knocked out of me. I looked the

leopard over and figured it to be almost seven feet long and 160 pounds. My elephant squatted down. I patted its bristly forehead and trunk indicating I had forgiven him. I reached up with my left hand for the mahout to pull me up; when I did, a terrible pain shot through my left wrist and arm. I told the guy there was something wrong with my hand. When we headed back to the Palace I told Joe I was giving him the leopard because of the super job he did in landing the 46 at Shanghai during the zero-zero weather.

In spite of my hunting mishap, my friends and I had a wonderful visit at Cooch Behar. I checked in with the local doctor; he thought my left wrist was badly sprained. My wrist was bandaged up and placed in a sling. The sprain didn't give much trouble when I flew the C-46 or the 3; it sure did impede my flying the DC-4. The problem was trying to steer the plane while taxiing. It has a little steering wheel at the left of the cockpit; my left wrist couldn't cope with it.

In Shanghai I received a message that my sister Christine would be arriving in Calcutta, by boat, the latter part of March. I arranged my schedule to be there. She had planned to cover the independence of India around the end of July 1947. I was able to meet her and Robert at the docks, where five years ago the Japanese had bombed the place. They had a lot of luggage to clear customs, especially Robert's guns. They had planned to spend a year in India. It had been 24 years since they were last here. My number one taxi driver was on hand with another cohort to help take all the baggage and us back to Alipore. I made them comfortable at the apartment. In the short time I had, I took them to the 300 Club to meet Boris and my friends. Though Cooch Behar was not present, I arranged again for us to go hunting there at a later date. After a few days I was back doing my thing with C-NAK (flying, that is!). Christine had introduced me to a young American couple they had met on the boat coming over. Their names were Stan and Eleanor Healy. I arranged for them to stay at my place while they looked for an apartment. On my return to Calcutta I wasted little time in taking Christine and Robert to Cooch Behar.

We arrived by the night train and Bhaiya was there to greet us. My wrist was out of the sling, but it still ached. In fact, the two inner fingers started to curl up. Bhaiya had sent the elephants up to Kauchagoan, Assam to get ready for some hunting. Bhaiya now had another plane, an L-5, like the one I smashed up.

I flew Christine and Robert to Kauchagoan in the L-5 from the Palace. Bhaiya and a few of his friends arrived by jeep later in the afternoon. It was a swell get together at the old officer's bungalow. They loved Christine, especially when they saw how good a shot she was with the rifle. I know Robert was looking forward for a chance at a tiger. During the five days there was not a kill. Not a single bait (buffalo) was touched. It was unusual, since that area was noted for tigers. A few years ago the place was loaded with them. On one shoot, while gooming, we flushed a leopard. As the elephants plowed through the tall grass, the leopard emerged on a small hillock about fifty yards away. Robert got him with a single shot. The mahouts were as pleased as he was.

It was wonderful to have Christine and Robert with me and to meet my friends. We thanked Cooch Behar for a delightful visit. Christine promised to write a short story of the visit for the New Yorker magazine when she got back to the States. In Calcutta Mohammed was helping pack their things for the long trip to Delhi and arranging tickets for the train ride. I hated to see them leave; yet I had my flying to do as well. They planned to have Christmas in Naini-Tal and wished I might be able to join them. It sounded great, but I was not sure I could make it.

Back in Shanghai I learned that Captain Chuck Sharp, MacDonald and Woods had left for the States. Chuck and Mac went to PanAmerican, to fly in South America and Woody ventured into real estate in Miami, Florida. A Captain Allison, who once flew for the Airline before the war, took over as Chief of Operations. He put a new DC-4 pilot as Chief Pilot, a Jim McDevitt.

One day at the Park Hotel, who should I run into but my old room mate friend Roy Farrell. He knew I was around. He had checked at the American Consulate for something and ran into Dorothy. He told me so and gave me that dirty grin. At the bar Roy mentioned he had a DC-3 he bought in the States; filled it with all sorts of surplus material and was selling the stuff in Shanghai. He wanted to know if I would buy out his partner for five thousand dollars. At this time he had no idea what he planned to do. I couldn't see myself dumping that much loot into something that was not a sure thing. Our mutual friend Sid DeKantzow took Roy's offer. They operated the plane between Darwin, Australia, Hong Kong and Shanghai hauling freight. They were doing real well. One evening at the bar, they thought they should form a company; if so, what should they call it. Some bright person said, "Why don't you call it Cathay Pacific Airlines?" So that is how Hong Kong's major airline was born.

I was now pretty high on our seniority list; there were some old timers ahead of me; such as Charles Sunby, Gordon Poon and Dick Rossi. Some more pilots switched over to Chennault's CATC. The situation with CNAC was not that good; jealousies and grumbling. I didn't particularly get along with Allison; his name had nothing to do with it! Communist Mao was rattling his saber around the corner and people were fidgety. I was back in Calcutta with another pilot named Joe Hall. He was disgruntled with C-NAK too. At this time we were approached by some friends to join a local airline just starting up, called Orient Airways. They needed experienced pilots, especially with monsoon flying experience. Joe and I

sure had that. We arranged a meeting with the General Manager, a Captain Adam Richardson. We signed a contract to fly as captains. It would be easy, daylight flying between Calcutta, Akyab and Rangoon, Burma.

Joe was a tall, lanky pilot and slightly bucktoothed with a gravelly voice. He said he was engaged to a local girl. I asked who she was and Joe replied, "I'm sure you know her Pete; you must have met my girl." "I don't think so." "You mean you don't know 'Tits' Kennedy?" "Oh, yes, I think I do!" I did know her, a tall, good-looking gal, with a fair size set of knockers.

Shanghai was getting more and more like Calcutta used to be during the war, uniforms everywhere. Prices were sky-rocketing, the traffic noise increasing and the pedicab drivers getting rude and nasty. The local currency (CN) was worthless; it was just about necessary to take a wheel-barrow full to go shopping. More pilots were quitting CNAC and going into other adventures. Hank Smith and Eddie Quinn, the brother of Babs Huang, had joined and were flying for the Maharajah of Jamnagah in western India. Also with them was Jimmy Muff, a maintenance type. Jimmy was a unique character who sported a wooden leg, yet you would never know it. His claim to fame was that he held up his right sock with thumb tacks! Then there was our sharpshooting Robbie Robertson who married the famous Margo of Calcutta. On one of his trips to Chungking, he was caught smuggling contraband. He was about to be jailed, and still to be tried, when I found a way to smuggle him out. He and Margo wound up in Manila then back to Florida. My friend Jim "Indian Jim" Moore had taken off and found his way through Hanoi to Bangkok. As I say, my friends were scattering all over the globe seeking their fortunes.

Joe Hall did marry Miss Kennedy. I was in contact with Kiki, and told her I soon would be flying for a local company in Calcutta. She informed me that her mother planned to take the family to London; that Jack had opened his new Ambassador Hotel on Church street, not far from the Ritz. I hoped her mother would reconsider and let Kiki stay in Bombay till I had everything settled here.

Joe and I had said goodbye to CNAC, which made Dorothy unhappy. I was relieved that I had made the move. I couldn't have taken it longer in Shanghai with Dorothy; she was trying to be so dominating all the time. We couldn't get our India Pilot Licenses in Calcutta; it was necessary to go to Delhi and see the Director General of Civil Aviation (DGCA). I had a letter from Captain Richardson to the DGCA, to issue us Indian licenses based on our Chinese ones. We were introduced to an English gentleman in charge of licensing. Joe and I had our CNAC medicals that would be accepted. Though our Chinese licenses were in horsepower, they would accept them. All formalities were eventually attended to, though it took almost two weeks before we got the licenses in our

hands. The English guy was interested in our flying experiences, especially the "Hump." He was an ex-RAF pilot himself; medical had grounded him.

Joe and I returned to Calcutta, eager to start flying. Mohammed, my trusty servant, greeted me at the door, saying "Salaam Sahib. I have something of importance to tell you." "What is it Mohammed?" He looked worried and said to me, "Memsahib is here." "Memsahib? What Memsahib?" "Shanghai Memsahib. She came a week ago." Oh shit, no! It cannot be. What the hell was she doing here? Another ruse to the Consulate. I gave my things to Mohammed to take to my room and sauntered onto the back verandah and almost fell over. There stood Dorothy. "Hi," she said. "What in the world are you doing here?" "I quit the Consulate service and came here to live with you." I was speechless. I remember one of my pilot friend's remarks at the bar one day. He stated, "He who liveth by the sword, dieth by the sword." I was getting his message loud and clear. "You better have a drink," she suggested. "I don't need a drink, or you." I was getting mad and upset. I had never mentioned Dorothy to Kiki, and I didn't wish her to find out now. She had loads of Greek friends in Calcutta, and word gets around fast. What should I do? I told her she had to leave; to go to a hotel or the Consulate. I was so upset, I could hardly stand it. I went to my room, and found Dorothy had her things hung up in my closet. A whole lot of her cute shoes were in a row under the bed. I took all her things and threw them in the hall, slammed the door and locked it; then lay down. I could have killed her, I was so angry. I sat on the edge of the bed, moping and rubbing my bad wrist, which was beginning to ache. I noticed my two inner fingers wouldn't straighten out. I would have to see a doctor again, I thought. I lay down, and probably worried myself to sleep. A familiar knocking on the door woke me. It was Mohammed; he had tea ready. I opened the door, and Mohammed asked me if I wanted the tea in my room, or out on the verandah. I said I'd have it right here in my room. I guess I didn't have to explain it to Mohammed, he already knew my situation. I had my tea and cleaned up. (I forgot to mention that I had two black and tan miniature dacshund dogs, called Squirt and Puddles. Squirt was the father of Puddles; he was rightly named. They were well trained and cute.) I went out onto the back lawn and watched them play. It was stinking hot, even though the sun was going down. The garden crows were all around making a cacophony of noise; normally I would have enjoyed them; not now. Then came the brainfever bird doing his thing. This time he was getting to me; I could gladly have shot it! I headed back to the verandah and there was Dorothy waiting for me. She knew how to dress, and was looking crisp and fresh. "Are you talking to me now?" "I'm not sure," I said. "Let's have a drink and talk about it." I was not in the mood to talk, but thought a drink might help. Mohammed had put the ice bucket on the bar. He always seemed to be one jump ahead of me. I fixed myself a whopper of a scotch and soda, in one of my McFadden-Deuville glasses. My friends, the Healeys had moved to their new apartment, thank goodness. I don't think they would have enjoyed this atmosphere. The drink tasted good, so I poured another. I guess I was trying to steer clear of personal conversations. I telephoned Cooch Behar, to see if he was in town. He was expected back to Woodlands, Alipore in a few days. I called the 300 Club. Boris was no longer there; he had resigned and was planning to start a hotel and restaurant in Kathmandu, Nepal. He was also helping Bhaiya set up a distillery in Cooch Behar, to make vodka and gin where a few of his Russian friends went to work. A Mr. Harry Waters was now the new manager for the 300 Club. I made arrangements that evening. I guess I was simmering down. So it was the Club that evening with Dorothy. She could be a knockout when she wanted to be. Harry was an Englishman with a great sense of humor. During the evening and dinner, I sensed that Dorothy's mind was ticking away a mile a minute, conniving something. Back at the apartment she insisted on sharing my room. The only bed was not all that large. I didn't do much talking when we went to bed. It didn't take long to note that Dorothy didn't have on any nighty. I turned my back and tried to forget everything. She wasn't giving in, and tried jousting around with her little hedgehog at my back. Even if I had wanted to, I was too tired and full of scotch. Dorothy finally gave up and let me sleep.

Pearson Surita had given me Doctor Mookajee's phone number, whom I called for an appointment. He was Cooch Behar's doctor as well. I had met the doctor at the Club before. He had x-rays taken of the wrist and discovered that it was broken in several places. Doc said he would try to reset the little bones, but there was one that was completely twisted around, which was causing the fingers to curl up. He probably would have to remove it. I was ushered into his clinic, with Dorothy tagging along. Dr. Mookajee explained that if he removed the small bone, he would cut a few veins in the process; I would lose feeling in my left hand for a while, but not to worry; the blood would find a new route back to my fingers. It would probably travel around, down my ass, back up the left side and into the left hand and fingers. It would take about a year before any feeling would return. I told the Doc to be sure to save the little bone; I wanted it as a memento and would make it into a tietack one day. The operation was done, and the hand and arm put into a plaster cast. The terrible Calcutta heat caused prickly heat under the cast. The itching was driving me crazy. There was no way I could reach to scratch. However, Mohammed came to the rescue by obtaining a long knitting needle that enabled me to reach inside and scratch. The Doc had saved the bone for me. It was round and about the size of a marble. I placed it in a glass of whiskey, on the bar. Though my wrist was still in a cast, I was able to fly

the DC-3. The main route was from Calcutta-Chitagong-Akyab, and down to Rangoon. We would overnight at Rangoon, and hop-skip back to Calcutta next day.

Though I took Dorothy to the club and parties, I was having problems with her; she wouldn't leave. I kept recalling what the guy in Shanghai had said about the CIA. But what the heck did they want with me. I tried every way possible for her to return to Shanghai or the States. She wouldn't budge. Dorothy had a small .25 Beretta pistol, and kept threatening to shoot herself if I didn't change my mind about Kiki and marry her instead. I got disgusted and suggested, if she wanted to shoot herself, to get a room at the hotel, or do it out on the maidan. Then I got the feeling she may want to take me with her; that is, shoot me too. She wasn't making my flying any easier; nor were the monsoons.

The Arakan coast of Burma can be a bitch, and miserable from Chitagong on down. The radio beacons at Akyab and Chitagong were not at all reliable. During the rains, it would be instruments all the way and heavy rain. I knew too well, if you slammed into a 15,000 foot mountain on the Hump, you were dead. The same applied if you slam into a 100 foot hill, on the Arakan coast. On one occasion letting down at the Akyab station, I was on a final approach with gear and flaps; I was about to pass over the station, when the beacon went off the air. I called the tower and they replied that the radio station was still on. I continued the let down, sort of dead reckoning. I continued to about 300 feet when I broke out, I found the runway and landed. I told the operations the beacon was out, and if it was the same on the return next day, I would not land here. They promised to have it checked. On my return next day from Rangoon, the beacon was operating. I asked Akyab tower what the problem had been. I was informed that a large python had crawled into the generator area and short-circuited the whole thing; killed the snake too.

Joe and I were doing most of the monsoon flying; no one else seemed to be qualified. Dorothy had been here a month. Like an albatross around my neck. One morning at breakfast, she told me she had an idea; if I went along with it, she would then leave for the States. She would like to return to the State Department, but first she needed a marriage certificate; would I help her get one and sign it. I exploded, "You are crazy, out of your mind! No, I would not consider such a move." she said it wouldn't be a real one, a bogus. I had no idea what she was planning. Dorothy didn't know it then, but I had my own underground working for me: Mohammed. He mentioned to me that Dorothy had gone on two occasions to visit the neighboring town of Chandernagore, once a French colony. I knew the place, about thirty miles up the Hooghly River, and all the natives spoke French. I later learned that my Grandfather Goutiere once lived there. It seems that Dorothy had contacted a lawyer in that town and had made up a bogus marriage certificate. I asked her what was

going on. She confessed what she had done, and swore there was nothing legal about the document. I couldn't believe her. I took the so called bogus paper to Pearson's father, who was a lawyer (advocate), and a very fine gentleman. He dealt with divorce cases and marriage problems. I confided in him, and told him the story of Dorothy and what had transpired. He chuckled and said, "You young people! You let your cocks rule your heads, and see the trouble it gets you into!" I agreed. After looking the paper over, he said that if was bogus and of no value, though it had all sorts of seals and ribbons, and looked official. I said I wanted Dorothy out of my hair and the apartment. She was making a mess of my life and future. He said it was okay to go ahead and sign the thing; if I was sure she would leave after that. What a thought! After much deliberation and thought, and a few whiskeys, I signed the damned document, actually duplicates. I was going to keep one.

I contacted Stan Healy and asked if he could arrange a cabin on any boat leaving Calcutta soonest. Stan came up with one sailing in about ten days. I bought Dorothy a ticket on it. The ship was headed for Seattle via Colombo, Ceylon and Jakata, Indonesia. As she was getting ready, I asked Dorothy if she would deliver, or mail Blackmore's tiger that Blackie had shot and had been mounted by Van Ingen taxidermists. It was for his folks. They lived somewhere in the Seattle area. She promised to do so. The time had come that she would be leaving. It so happened that I was in Rangoon on that date. Mohammed would arrange to get her on board. In Rangoon that evening, I enjoyed myself eating hot kebabs and chapattees in a dirty area called Mogul Street. The place was lit by oil lamps. When I returned to the apartment the next afternoon, Mohammed and Cookie greeted me. I asked if Dorothy Memsahib had left. He nodded and said someone had come from the consulate and driven her to the boat. She had gone. A great weight seemed to have been lifted off my shoulders. I was ready for a drink and to relax; as there had been too much tension for the past several weeks. Then Mohammed continued, "Please, Master; come in and see this." I followed him and Cookie into the bedroom where he pointed to my Indian steel trunk which had been padlocked. I kept a lot of my valuables in it. There was about two thousand dollars in hundred dollar bills; solid 24k gold CNAC wings; some star rubies; sapphires that I had bought in Rangoon; a whole array of miniature carvings in soapstone, depicting statues in fornicating positions (it's a part of the Hindu temples in Karala State, at a place called Puri). Dorothy had evidently broken open the two locks and cleaned me out! I was so livid with rage, I felt like taking a flight to one of the ports where her boat would be stopping. Then I thought it might be Mohammed who may have done it; knowing the situation, I'd naturally blame Dorothy. I let the matter drop for now. I received a letter from Dorothy in Jakata. Among other things, she admitted taking all the goodies from the trunk, saying I owed it to her. When she finally arrived at Seattle, I found out she had not sent the tiger skin to the Blackmores. She was now in Chicago, shacking up with another CNAC fellow. I got the address and telegraphed that I would sic the police on her if she didn't send the tiger post-haste to the rightful owners. Dorothy finally did send the tiger to the Blackmores.

When the military pulled out of Calcutta, they left a vacuum; it was not long before the carpetbaggers started pouring in. Calcutta, as one probably knows, was once the capitol of India. At the turn of the century, the capitol was moved to Delhi.

The infamous "Black Hole" of Calcutta was so named by British soldiers at Calcutta's Fort William, which was located on the northwest perimeter of the Maidan. It was nothing more than a stone cell between 15 to 20 square feet and about 15 feet high with two, barred windows. It was used mainly as a punishment area. It had no facilities other than a tin pail in one corner. Something on the principal of the Sweat Boxes used in the Southern States after the Civil War.

What made the infamous "Black Hole" famous began with the capture of Ft. William and Calcutta early in the summer of 1756. The capture was by an Indian prince named Siraj-Daula from Murshidabad, north of Calcutta. After its capture, the prince rounded up about 145 to 150 English men, and crammed them into the cell. It was the hottest time of the year, just before the monsoons. The poor souls were kept there for about twenty-four hours. The next day, when the door of the cell was opened, barely 25 to 30 people were able to stagger out. The others had died of heat and dehydration.

There is nothing left of the sight. Somewhere in that area is a plaque in memory of those who died in the "Black Hole." I never was able to find it.

The British picked this flat swampy land and made it their major city, not for beauty but location, about 80 miles up the main tributary, or Hoogley River. The boats could travel up from the Bay of Bengal to this point. From here, boats could traverse up the main Ganges River. They could take the goods and passengers to places such as Patna, Benares, Alahabad, Lucknow and Delhi.

For Calcutta itself, the main function was commerce and the introduction of jute, a type of hemp used for rope and gunny sacks. (Otherwise who would want it?) The whole Bengal delta is only a few feet above sealevel; when the monsoons break toward the end of June, the rains come down like ropes. The streets flood in a few minutes. The only reliable mode of transport is the ghora-gari (horse and

*My friend Joe Michaels who was on the leopard hunt with me, 1947.*

buggy) and the rickshaw. The rickshaw-pullers keep going even when they're up to their axles and asses in water.

After the war Calcutta was taking on a new look. The 300 Club was humming, the Royal and Tolligunge golf clubs were full. Later model taxis were coming in to replace the old touring Oaklands. August saw the day of independence for India and Burma, the end of the British Raj. England was gone; Indians had the choice either to stay or go. Many, mainly Anglo-Indians, left for England or Australia. It was joyous for many people here, I felt happy for them; yet, I was sad, too. Because of the class distinction among the Hindus, it would greatly effect the people of the lower classes, such as the bearers. They never will be anything else. They will miss the Raj and the Europeans whom they serve. It was their choice; they made their beds, now they have to sleep in'em.

I called Kiki, now that Dorothy had gone, and asked about their trip to England. She said it was canceled, they would stay on in Bombay. I told her I would go to the Catholic church in Calcutta, to find out what procedures were necessary for our marriage and would let her know. I met with a Father Van der Velde and explained everything. He thought I may be Catholic, though not a very good one! I told him I was born in Aligarh. He would check with the churches for my name. He finally succeeded. I had been baptized a Catholic, in the town of Tundla, near Aligarh. "Yes, there would be no problem." I called and gave Kiki the good news. It was decided that Kiki and I would be married in the Catholic church in Calcutta by Van der Velde, early in September, 1947.

Kiki arrived and stayed with some of her Greek friends. On a trip to Rangoon I brought Angelo Lungi back

for the wedding. He had known Kiki since she was a baby. I contacted Ladd Moore, who was operating an airline in Burma; he was to be best man. Almost all the Calcutta friends said they would show up, even Marge Schaeffer. She had been portrayed in Milton Caniff's "Terry and the Pirates" as the Dragon Lady! Of course there would be Mohammed and Cookie, and my Sikh taxi driver. (His license number was #875.) Cooch Behar and Boris were in the States, cutting a swathe through Hollywood! It was a wonderful day, and a beautiful sermon by Father Van der Velde. Kiki's Greek friend sang "Ave Maria," a favorite of mine. Kiki looked extra beautiful as she walked down the aisle. Our reception was held at the 300 Club, since that is where we first met a year ago. It was quite a party with a lovely wedding cake and champagne.

Four of us rode back to the apartment in #875! Mohammed and Cookie were beside themselves with joy, with ear-to-ear grins to prove it. The two dogs barked, the garden crows crowed, and the brainfever bird made the distinctive call; this time I enjoyed him. One evening as a group of us were sitting at my bar in Alipore, I was showing my friends the bone that I was preserving from my left wrist. It was now quite shiny and smooth. Somehow, it slipped from fingers and landed on the tile floor. The bone made a couple of bounces and before I could retrieve it, Squirt, the little daschund, caught it, and with a couple of chomps with his jaw, swallowed the darn thing. I was mad and everyone else laughed. That was the end of my tie-tack!

Kiki and I did not take our honeymoon right away; perhaps in November or December, when I was entitled to take leave. On the first of December I went to the chief pilot's office to ask for leave. It was refused. I tried to reason with him; that Joe and I had done all the hard flying for the airline during the heavy monsoon weather, now that the good weather was here, the other pilots were eager to do the trips to Rangoon. Still he would not budge. "Okay, then," I said, "I resign." That was a shock for a moment, for both of us. Then he asked, "How about Joe Hall?" "Well, he just quit too!" I left in a huff, and went straight to Joe's apartment at Kanani Estates; the old U.S. Air Force Palace. Joe happened to be sitting at his little bar on the porch. He was a tall fellow, so his knees were almost under his chin as he sat on a low stool. After a pleasant chitchat about nothing, Joe asked if I got my leave. "No, Joe, it was refused." Then I said, "I told Jerry that I quit." "You did?" I said "Yep, and guess what?" "What?" "You just quit too!" Joe looked at me in surprise and said, "I did?" He was puzzled and then we both giggled. Joe set up two glasses. "This calls for a drink." He yelled at Jean to come out and celebrate. Jean was now pregnant and it was beginning to show. I returned to Alipore and told Kiki. She took the surprise well, God love her. Now we could take our honeymoon. Where do we go? I was thinking of Naini-Tal, where we could see Christine and Robert. Kiki said she would like to go to Darjeeling.

It was back to Darjeeling and the Everest Hotel. We took the overnight train to Shiliguri, then a taxi the rest of the way. Kiki pointed out where she went to school, but wanted to keep going. The weather was clear and cold. Little Caju Singh with his wife Bhindu were in Darjeeling also. They were great company and we met several times at the Gymkhana Club. I took Kiki by horseback to Tiger Hill and saw the sunrise on Kanchenjunga Mountain. On the return, we stopped at Keventor's for breakfast with Mr. Bee. We said some prayers at the Tibetan Monastery. It was a great holiday; time had hurried by, and it was time to return to Calcutta. I think we took the miniature train back down to Shiliguri; then the train to Howrah, Calcutta Station.

The Maharajah of Cooch Behar and Boris had returned from their trip in the States with a lot of interesting stories to tell. One evening at the 300 Club, I was talking to Bhaiya; when he casually asked what I planned to do, now that I was no longer with Orient Airways. I wasn't sure. I thought perhaps of returning to Shanghai and flying for Chennault's CATC. He once told me I would be welcome. At the moment I was happy to be in Calcutta with Kiki. Bhaiya then suggested I fly for him, as his personal pilot. There would be no fancy salary; he couldn't pay me more than his Prime Minister was getting. I could bring Joe Hall along also, till he found something else. "I don't have much in the way of airplanes. I'm entitled to a DC-3 from the government, sometime later." "Right now, we could possibly obtain a couple of surplus L-5s. Mohabir had a five place Fairchild-24, that we could also use." Cooch Behar Estate would pay for our apartments and local transportation.

Cooch Behar bought the two L-5s from the Panagar depot; he would keep the planes at Alipore Airport, close by. After talking it over with Kiki, we agreed I'd fly for Bhaiya. Joe and I signed the contract at Cooch Behar's place at Woodlands, Alipore.

*The leopard I shot when we were in mid-air!*

*My elephant that made the 180° turn and left me to meet the already airborn leopard!*

*My dog Squirt on bar stool, Calcutta,*

# PHASE FOUR: 1948-1951

Kiki and I took the night train up to Cooch Behar right after New Year's 1948. She loved the Palace and the grounds surrounding it. I introduced her to the elephants at the "pilkhanna," a sort of camp for the elephants. The mahouts were my friends, and happy to know I had my own Memsahib who spoke Hindi. I took Kiki on several local shoots with the elephants. The cast was off my wrist, which sported a two-inch long scar; just as the Doc said, there was no feeling, but I could move my fingers and hand normally. I could also play a little golf. Bhaiya one day told Joe and I that he had bought another plane, a Harvard (AT-6). It was at the Barrakpore airport, and would Joe and I check it out and bring it to Alipore. I don't know why he got it; it only could carry the pilot and one person in the back. The plane was brand new with about ten hours. I don't know about Joe, but I hadn't flown an AT-6 since Pan Africa days in 1942. It was almost a whole new experience for Joe and I; between the two of us, we finally checked ourselves out and enjoyed flying it again, after the little L-5.

At the palace there was all kinds of excitement; I asked the ADC what was going on. He said it was the Maharajah's Silver Jubilee coming up in a few days. His Highness Jaipur and his beautiful wife Ayesha, who was Cooch Behar's younger sister, would be arriving soon; along with many other notable guests. Another fine Prince arrived, by the name of Prithi Singh of Baria State. He was a handsome individual and a great polo player. I believe he played on the Jaipur polo team. Bhaiya too was no slouch at polo. The formal jubilee took place at the Palace Durbar Hall. This is where all the faithful business people and farmers of the estate came to pay their respects to their Maharajah. It was followed by a march-pass of the Cooch Behar elite. During a break in all the Pomp and Pageantry, H.H. Jaipur (everyone called him "Jai") and Bhaiya took me aside and asked if I would help Jai out and pinch-hit as his DC-3 pilot. The plane

was a plush one with long range tanks fitted in at the inside.

It seems the regular pilot was having problems with drugs, and was unreliable. If it was okay with H.H. Cooch Behar, I said, I'd be happy to oblige. In the meantime Joe and I did a lot of flying in the 6. We used it as though it was ours. (Two years later Jai's pilot committed suicide in London by sticking his head in a gas oven!)

Bhaiya organized several tiger hunts during the jubilee. To facilitate the transport to the distant shooting areas, it was agreed that I would fly some of the VIP guests in Mohabir's Fairchild-24. A couple of days before the shoot was to start, I drove with one of the ADCs named Nahru to the different areas where the actual hunts would be. I staked and marked out in dry wheat fields and other open areas for airstrips. This worked out just fine. It was nicer to fly to the remote spots and back without all that dust and bumpy ride in a jeep. However, toward the end of several excursions, I started developing difficulty with the engine; possibly a lot of dust was being sucked in through the carburetor. Someone had mentioned to the head villager, whose field we were using as an airstrip; that if a tiger was shot, I would take him up for as ride. Jai had shot the tiger, so I did my duty by taking the Zemindar for a hop. He wasn't at all scared, and enjoyed looking down at his village. When I dropped him off the other villagers, gave him a resounding welcome.

Though the engine appeared rough once or twice, I kept taking the guests back to Cooch Behar field. It was late in the evening when I made the last trip home with Jai and Ayesha on board. Ayesha in the back, Jai in front with me. About twenty minutes left to go at about 1500 ft. the engine acted up. It shook and sputtered; then roared into life. I nursed it along as best I could. From that point on, the darn thing would lose power and then roar again. In so doing I had lost quite a lot of altitude. I had a feeling I would not make the field which was about another ten minutes away. I told my very special passengers to get ready for a forced landing as I

*Boris pointing the way, with me in the Fairchild-24, ready to take guests to the hunting area, 1948.*

looked for any open space to set the plane down. No tanks in the vicinity!

I was able to hold about five-hundred feet, the engine stopped again. Ayesha thought this was great; she was actually enjoying the excitement. I was scared to death; here I was in the middle of nowhere in a crapped-out plane and the night closing in, with two of the world's richest and prominent people on board, ready to crash in the jungles of India. What a headline that would make. Ayesha kept giggling and commenting how exciting it was. I had now lost altitude to about 300 ft. and could just make out Cooch Behar field way ahead; yet it looked so very far away. I believe I mentioned before that the airport is surrounded on three sides with a moat for drainage. The engine quit once more, then revved up again I clawed for every foot of altitude the Good Lord would give me. I was hovering around 200 ft. and once more the damn thing died; the plane was coming down. I don't know if I was saying things like, "O shit! O shit! not now." I must have been saying something, 'cause both Jai and Ayesha were laughing. I assure you, there was nothing funny about this situation. At this low altitude I was committed to land straight ahead. I couldn't turn anywhere. I had yet to cross the moat. I told my VIPs to hold tight. I think by now Jai saw the seriousness of the situation. He had been in an airplane accident before. We skimmed over the moat with little to spare, and landed on the grassy turf. The engine had long quit and would not start. Cooch Behar's ground mechanic had heard the engine acting up on our approach. He was already racing out in a jeep to pick us up. Jai loved his champagne and martinis, which ever came first. He couldn't wait to have one to cheer himself up from the near mishap. We raced back to the palace and had our special drinks without delay.

The next day I was with the mechanic at the hangar. We deduced it must be dust being sucked into the engine. The fuel lines and carburetor were taken apart, cleaned and flushed thoroughly. It seemed to do the trick.

During the functions of the jubilee, I was kept busy flying Cooch Behar's VIPs back and forth from Calcutta and various other principalities in Jai's DC-3. It would be okay, except Cooch Behar and Jaipur, sometimes requested these flights be done at weird hours of the night or early morning, or in the middle of one of their parties, when I'd had more than enough to drink. It was not conducive to a long life.

In May of the same year, the Maharajah of Jaipur was to have a gala function of his own at the Jaipur Estate, almost a thousand miles west of Cooch Behar. His 18 year old daughter, Mickey, was to be married. Joe and I flew the AT-6 to Jaipur. Kiki was smart and flew with the others in the DC-3.

Rambargh Palace and the ever-so-beautiful, manicured gardens around the estate were out of this world. Joe was given a room in an adjoining building near the palace; no air conditioning. In May, the temperatures reach 110 in the shade. The servants always arranged to have the beds placed outside at night. As I had mine as a kid in Hardoi, long ago. Kiki and I were in another area. Maharajahs and princes from various parts of India arrived for the occasion. There were many European dignitaries as well. The palace was full, including the guest houses. There were continuos functions; some we could not attend. Early in the mornings, about 3 or 4 o'clock, it became difficult to sleep, because of the cacophony from the peacocks. Though wild, they roamed the gardens and strutted around near the beds outside. Joe said he almost leaped through the mosquito netting, the first time one of the birds let out a cry next to his bed. Drinks, food and music seemed to continue almost twenty-four hours a day. Most of the food was spicy, Indian curries that made you sweat. The scrambled eggs were loaded with hot green chilies.

The day before the wedding ceremony, all the ladies were allowed to visit Mickey in the secluded quarter (Purdah). Kiki was one of the lucky ones. The wedding ceremony started early in the morning, with a parade that seemed to go on forever. I did not attend it. I don't think Joe did either. Jai suggested we stay inside the palace where it was cool. I think Kiki decided to join the function with the others. At the end Jai came into the living room where I was sitting reading magazines. He wore a pale pink, long tunic to his knees and buttoned collar at the neck. The turban was also pink with a large jewelled emblem in front. He was soaking wet with perspiration, but still looked resplendent in his attire. Jai unbuckled his ceremonial sword and belt, placing them on the table along with the turban with its frontal decoration, a bejeweled badge, in the center of which was the largest darned emerald I had ever seen. H.H. casually said, "Pete, please look after these while I get a drink and change." The handle and scabbard of the sword were encrusted with precious stones. I asked Jai if I may try on the sword for size! "Go ahead." The belt and sword weighed a ton: How could he parade around with all that weight hanging from him? No wonder he was tuckered out! It certainly was a beautiful sword; must have been worth a small fortune.

One morning, one of the princesses (the wife of Prithi Singh) had decided to return to Baria, about 200 miles south of Jaipur. Joe was elected to the honors in the AT-6. By noon, there was no word of their arrival. Late that evening, word came that they were safe, but not without incident. Because of some sandstorms, Joe wandered off course and was lost. He set the plane down in an open field, and hit the only babul tree there. It damaged the left side and wrinkled the hydraulic lines. The two of them had to take an ox-cart to a nearby town, then a taxi the rest of the way. Joe called me and figured he could fly the machine back. Next day he arrived at Jaipur. We looked the plane over and straightened out some of the lines, with the help of Jai's mechanic. I flew it that afternoon. The gear retracted perfectly, but as I was starting down wind, the engine became terribly rough. I throttled back and landed the aircraft immediately. On the ground, it checked okay; that would be the last time we would fly the AT-6. Cooch Behar decided to give it to the Indian Air Force for spares.

During one of the afternoon functions, a more or less informal tea on the front of the palace, with dancing girls et.al., I was introduced to the Maharajah of Jodpur. He was a rotund individual, about six feet tall and must have weighed 350 pounds. He told us he had a couple of Bonanza aircraft that he flew. He invited Joe and I to come and fly. Jodhpur was about 100 miles south of Jaipur. I asked Bhaiya if we could go for a visit after the wedding ceremonies were over. This wedding, by the way, was written up in the Guinness Book of Records, I think, as the longest and most expensive ever.

It was after this that Joe and I took our leave and went to Jodhpur. Kiki didn't wish to come along. She stayed in Jaipur for a while longer, before returning to Calcutta.

Jodhpur Palace was a massive structure of sandstone. It resembled a fort. It was given over to the RAF during the war, as a training center. The grounds were not as green and immaculate as Jaipur. The interior, upstairs and down, was lavishly decorated, but again, lacked the Rambargh Palace warmth. It was cold, and I don't mean from the air conditioning. Something about the atmosphere: it just didn't seem like home. H.H. Jodhpur also had a DC-3 that was to be sent to him later on from Panagarh. He had a South African pilot who flew for him by the name of Godwin, whom I got to know quite well. The whole clan of Jodhpurs, from the Maharajah, to the youngest prince, were avid hunters. The only problem was, they liked to go at night by jeep and chase the black buck antelope. I didn't particularly go for this sport. At one side of the palace there was a man made lake, where in the evening we were invited to go swimming. There was a large platform or stationary type raft near the middle. A bearer would be rowed out and serve us drinks as we floated about near the raft.

On a clear, warm evening, the young prince, who had had a snootful of whiskey, was standing on the verandah of the palace that overlooked the lake. He had a .22 caliber rifle and started taking potshots around us. We all shouted at him to stop. The guy was drunk and crazy. Joe and I ducked behind the raft, even though it was a flimsy affair. After running out of bullets, he stopped. Later, the prince apologized, when I confronted him. H.H. said not to worry, that his brother was a good shot and had no intention of trying to hit us; I was not convinced of that.

Jodhpur, one day, cornered Joe and myself at his hunting lodge. He told us he was upset with the Indian Government taking over and demolishing all the maharajah principalities in India. He asked Joe and myself if we could locate at least a dozen bombers in Europe, with crews. He said he planned to bomb the hell out of New Delhi and a few military posts. I tried to be calm

*Taking head villager for a ride in the F-24 after a successful tiger hunt, 1948.*

as he spoke. I told Jodhpur that it was a tall order; Joe and I would have to think about it. "Take your time." Back in our room, I said to Joe, "I thought his brother crazy." Joe piped up, "I guess it runs in the family!" We had a good laugh. No way could we get involved in something like this. Our passports state that we cannot get involved in foreign politics. I saw H.H. next morning and told him that we appreciated the offer, but no, we could not be involved. He understood and said to forget it. He changed the subject and said, "Why don't you fly the Bonanza?" I went to the airport and talked to his South African pilot about the Bonanza. "Certainly, take the one in the hangar, its ready to go." He took a key off the rack and handed it to me. "What, no check out?" We walked around the machine; while doing so, the pilot explained the V-tail of the plane, how to start the engine; that was it. We pushed the plane out and pulled the prop through. I climbed in and checked the cockpit with the guy looking over my shoulder. Something like a car, I turned the key-ignition and that was all. The engine started up and the next moment I was taxiing out. I have to admit, it was an easy plane to fly. I played around at 1500 feet and came back and landed. It was a neat aircraft. I'd talk to Bhaiya about getting one. When I came back to the room, Joe had left for Calcutta. He had admitted to me before that he was scared of Jodhpur and wanted to get out. He had caught an Indian Airways flight that morning. I then flew some of H.H's guest to Bombay and to Delhi, in the Bonanza. The day I was to leave for Calcutta Jodhpur asked if I would fly his DC-3 back when it was ready. That would be fine, as long as I had Cooch Behar permission.

I was happy to be back home. I realized I had stayed away a little too long and hoped Kiki would forgive me. Next day I went over to see Bhaiya at Woodlands. I told him about the offer made by Jodhpur. He laughed. Yes, he wouldn't put it beyond the guy to try

something as crazy as that. One thing, he had the money to do it with. How the hell did he expect to fight the army. I thought him nuts. I also told Bhaiya that Jodhpur wanted me to fly his DC-3 back from Panagarh when it was ready. Bhaiya thought it okay, as long as I got paid for it.

When I spoke to Joe Hall, he told me he couldn't wait to get out of Jodhpur; the crazy guy might just try to knock us off for knowing his secret. I hadn't thought of that. We also figured, H.H. had invited us to Jodhpur, not just for fun and games, but to proposition us on his clandestine deal. Joe agreed. Anyway, I had left there as friends. I did not burn my bridges behind me.

Bhaiya came up with another interesting proposition. He wanted to start a freight airline as our friend Mohabir had done. Cooch Behar and Prithi Singh would put up the money; if we wanted a small share, that would be accepted. I contacted a CNAC friend who said he could obtain a DC-3 in Manila. The money was paid in rupees. Joe and I took off for the Philippines on Pan American Airways, that was now flying a service around the world. After the usual red tape we got a Philippine export permit to fly the plane back to Calcutta. We saw Roy Farell and Sid DeKantzow in Hong Kong. They were doing real well with Cathay Pacific Airlines. Bhaiya and Prithi were having difficulty forming the company. The plane sat at DumDum airport, without an import permit; politics as usual. Bhaiya, Joe and I went to Delhi to see what strings could be pulled. Nothing doing. I then received permission to bring the aircraft to newly formed East Pakistan. I flew it to Dacca the airport was known as Tezgaon, which was once used as an U.S. Airforce Base.

Through all this, Joe called to say Jean was going to the hospital and have her baby. He, Kiki and I went racing around to find baby things: A crib, and little pots and pans and bottles. The day arrived, and when Joe

came out of the hospital, he had a surprised look on his face; his front teeth were more out than usual. "Guess what? Jean just had twin boys!" Oh my gosh! We went racing around to do the same procedure again, buying a second lot of baby things. It was rather hilarious. We congregated at Joe's place to celebrate.

Not long after Joe's new additions, I received word that Jodhpur's DC-3 was ready at Panagarh. Joe was too tied up to go with me. I got a hold of Kiwi Muehler, who was now with Orient Airways, I think. He was able to break away for a few days to help me out by operating the gear and flaps. At Panagarh, I looked the plane over. It didn't appear that much had been done to it, except to be taken out of moth-balls and dust wiped off. I started up the engines, which appeared to run well. I tried all the hydraulics and flaps. After shut down, I checked the outside for oil and any hydraulic leaks. All was normal. Kiwi and I took off for Jodhpur, via Jaipur for refueling. At Jaipur we fill it up with gas and looked the plane over once more for leaks. It was late afternoon and hot when we departed Jaipur, and a short flight to Jodhpur, over a small ridge of barren hills. As I was flying over the hills, I realized my airspeed started to drop. I added a little more power, perhaps this was due to wind currents or thermos. I looked across the panel and noticed the gear light indicated down. Kiwi and I looked out of our windows and saw the gear had dropped down. Then I noticed that Kiwi had left the gear handle in the up position, instead of neutral. This probably allowed the fluid to leak out and the gear to drop. I figured we had about forty minutes to Jodhpur. I applied a bit more power to keep us above the hills. I must have been around 3000 feet. Just then, Kiwi noticed the oil quantity dropping on the right engine, then the temperature rising. A sure indication we were losing oil, not just a faulty gauge. I was about to feather the engine, when Kiwi shouted out, "Look, the left oil is going down too!" Egad! The left oil temperature was rising. I was losing both engines. No way could I make it to Jodhpur. Kiwi tried calling the tower without success. There was no football field to set her down! A few wheat fields were near a village. I figured I'd need more than that, with no flaps and perhaps no brakes. Up ahead I saw a large, long brown area, as I approached, it turned out to be a dried corn field, that had not been harvested. With no brakes, I felt the corn stalks would help slow the plane down. The gear was already down. I tried the flaps and there were none. There was air accumulated in the brake system; perhaps I'd have a smidgin of that. I was able to circle once and saw there was little or no wind. I approached over the village and landed. The moment the props hit the cornstalks, I was on instruments; cornstalks flew in all directions. But it worked; the plane slowed down and stopped in a very short distance. Kiwi and I got out and inspected the aircraft for damages; there were none. The plane had made a long swathe through the corn. People from the village came pouring out; their first time to see a large silver plane. The hydraulic tank was empty, as well as both oil tanks.

Kiwi and I decided to get back in the plane. The villagers might not be too happy when they noticed what had happened to their corn field. One individual came to the main door. He looked like the number one man. He was pleasantly surprised to know I converse with him in Hindi and explain what had happened. I also said I was sorry about the corn field. He gave a semi-toothless grin and was happy the plane had landed safely. Maybe we would let him have a look inside. Needless to say a whole line of raggedy villagers poured through the plane. I asked the head man where I could find a telephone. There was none around the area, perhaps I could find one at a railway station not too far away. It would be closed since there would be no trains till the next day and it was now getting dark. The head man (Zemindar) invited us to stay and have a meal that would be prepared in our honor; after all, its not every day that an iron-bird comes to the village to roost. The food was spicy hot curry. We had to eat with our hands. Both Kiwi and I had the experience of eating with our hands at various times in Calcutta. It is quite customary. We were given blankets, and the two of spent the night in the plane. Next morning, we walked the odd mile to the station with one of the villagers carrying our belongings. The Zemindar said he would look after the big bird. We bacheeshed (tipped) the old gentleman generously, and caught the train that took us to Jodhpur. Immediately Jodhpur was upset and thought we had done this on purpose. We explained that it was not the case why would we do something like that? I suggested that his pilot and the mechanic and I return to the aircraft, repair the leaks and fly it out. It took several days to change the lines and fix the leaks. Meantime, we had the villagers cut away all the corn stalks. The makeshift runway was about the length of the one we used to operate out of in Chungking. With enough fuel and the oil and hydraulic tank full, we were able to make a take off and land back at Jodhpur without any further incident.

Jodhpur couldn't be located. I tried several times to contact him, but no luck. When I returned to Calcutta I told Cooch Behar I couldn't find H.H. that all my flights were gratis. Bhaiya was mad and said he would write to Jodhpur and demand I be paid. I didn't want to make a scene and asked Bhaiya to let the matter drop.

Joe Hall got fed up with the whole thing. Now that he had a family to think of, he decided to return to Shanghai and fly for CATC or CNAC, what was left of it. We saw him off and wished him well. Bhaiya informed me there was no hope for starting the airline in India. He suggested I contact a friend of his in Dacca. He was the British Governor-General, who was in Dacca, acting as British representative to the newly formed East Pakistan Government. Bhaiya would give a letter to the Governor General, hopefully he could help by talking to the new Prime Minister, to get the airline started in that country. At Dacca I contacted the Governor General and handed him Bhaiya's letter. The gentleman was pleased to know that I too was a friend of Bhaiya's. He invited me to stay at his residence. He was most cooperative, and introduced me to the Prime Minister. The P.M. was also cooperative and immediately gave me a import license for the aircraft, which was already at the airport. When that was completed, I was asked by the P.M. if I could fly he and the Governor General around East Pakistan. They wished to visit a couple of the cities such as Chitagong and Sylhet. That was the least I could do to show my gratitude. The Prime Minister then contacted the Director of Civil Aviation (DGCA) in Karachi, and asked if some one could come over to license the plane. The assistant Director (a Britishman by the name of Bill Reed) came from Karachi to do the honors. He looked the plane over and gave it a temporary certificate (AP-AED). I would have to fly the plane to Karachi eventually, to have it inspected by an airworthiness man. At least I had my foot in the door.

I received permission to bring the aircraft back to Calcutta where there was better maintenance facilities. Mr. Reed had given a pretty good list of items that needed to be done first. It would take several months before it would be ready. In the meantime Bhaiya had bought a Bonanza. I went to Bombay to pick it up. It was a great little plane and I enjoyed flying it. I flew Bhaiya's mother, the Maharani of Cooch Behar on several flight between Calcutta and the Palace. She was a grand lady, whom I thought a lot of. At times after dinner at the palace, she always had her "paan" beetle-nut served to her in a silver tray. She never failed to offer me one. I got used to the flavor. One never swallowed the juice, or you would choke. First chance, I'd head outside to spit it out. I would later brush my teeth, to get rid of the red stuff that accompanied the beetle-nut.

Winter was with us again and Cooch Behar estate is hard to beat during that time. Bhaiya had assigned an elephant as my own, a little female, what else! Kiki and I spent most of the time at the palace. Christmas and New Years was another great occasion in Calcutta; I was doing quite a lot of flying for Cooch Behar. He always had many VIP friends that I would bring up from Calcutta. I would also take his guests on hunting safaris on the estate; a sort of white hunter, on my own elephant! One of them was Queen Elizabeth's jockey, Harry Carr. All the people that arrived had to go on tiger shoots. Bhaiya did accompany some of them. Normally he stayed at the palace while I wound up doing most of the safaris. My arm didn't have to be twisted. With Harry Carr, Bhaiya did go along. Harry shot a leopard and a large wild boar. I managed to get another leopard. This life was exciting and glamorous, however I knew I couldn't continue for long. I was not saving much in the way of money; more important was the passport difficulty. Being a second-class citizen. I only had one more year to go, before returning to the States.

Toward the end of January 1949 I was informed the plane was ready. I had two ex-USAF mechanics that worked on the DC-3. They new their airplanes and had done a great job. Mr. Reed had also given me a temporary pilot license to fly Pakistan aircraft. I could not find a first officer to go on the flight; so decided to take one of the mechanics, by the name of Jim Hopkins. Orient Airways had moved its head quarters to Karachi, and were using Convair-240s. Another outfit in Karachi was PakAir, an American company run by the name of TransOcean ran it. Their main office was in San Francisco. Kiki decided not to go with me on this flight. Perhaps she didn't trust the airplane and all the bad luck I had been having. I had notified Jodhpur once, that when I came through with Cooch Behar's plane, we would stop and help get his DC-3 in good shape. I had an idea he might sell it to us.

We landed at Jodhpur and taxiied to H.H.'s hangar. I saw his old DC-3 there. I talked to my friend, the South African pilot, and told him what I planned to do. He thought it a good idea and would have his people help work on the plane also. Jodhpur was nowhere around. I thought I would go and have a talk with him and see what he planned to do with his plane since he was not using it. It just sat in the hangar gathering dust. In the meantime the chief pilot gave the okay to start work on the 3. I spent a week trying to find H.H. He was everywhere, except where he was supposed to be; even at his hunting lodge. I took Hopkins, (Hoppie) along on some of the excursions into the wilderness. After ten days of traipsing around, I gave up. I told Jim to lets forget doing any more on the other aircraft. Lets pack up and head for Karachi. I told the two Indian mechanics to return to Calcutta. The next morning the chief pilot came to see me and said that His Highness was planning to impound our DC-3; that evidently, Joe Hall had borrowed some money from Jodhpur and not paid it back. I said that could not be so. I just don't believe that. It must have been a hoax to get our airplane. I thanked my friend for the information. I went to the Shell Company, and had enough fuel put in the tanks to take me to Karachi, via Ahmedabad, then I went to the tower and filed a flight plan for Bombay. I told Hoppie what I planned to do: Head toward Ahmedabad; cancel the flight plan and turn west for Pakistan. When Hopkins grinned he showed a gap in one of his front teeth, where a large filling had dropped out.

Hoppie and I started up the engines and called the tower. He gave us a taxi clearance to the north part of the field, for a south take-off; VFR via Ahmedabad. The airport was mainly gravel, with the runway strip down the middle. After taxiing halfway to the take-off area, the tower called and said to return to the ramp. Hoppie looked at me, I put my finger to my mouth, indicating to be quiet. We continued taxiing, and as I turned onto the runway, we saw a couple of jeeps and a car racing across the gravel towards the run-

*Left to right: Boris, H.H Cooch Behar, H.H. Ayesha, Meneka (C.B. sister) Prince Mohabir, H.H. Jaipur.*

way, about half way down. I called the tower and said, "I'm cleared for take off?" "Negative, Negative." was his answer. I replied, I do not read you too well; I understand I'm cleared to go." I poured the coal to the engines and barreled down the runway. Hoppie turned to me and said, "Aren't you going to check the mags?" "Yeah, later!" The vehicles were now on the runway to try and block the takeoff. I had about 80 mph as I approached them. It looked like they were not about to budge. I guess you could call it a game of "chicken". I was almost on them, when I shouted at Hoppie "Give me flaps, all you can." The plane ballooned up into the air; we were over the top of the vehicles. I must have cleared the lot by a few feet. I only hope the crazy prince was not with them, shooting up at us, as he did when we were at the lake. Hoppie got the flaps up and I settled down to cruise at 3000 ft. The auto-pilot didn't want to operate, so I had to hand fly it all the way. We made it to Ahmedabad without difficulty. I canceled the Bombay flight plan and made a new one for Karachi. We had our passports stamped at Ahmedabad and were on our way. Approaching Karachi, I could see the old black dirigible hangar in the distance; a welcome sight. The formalities of immigration and customs were normal. I felt relieved to be there. I remember Hoppie laughing as he recalled the situation about checking the mags.

We went to see Mr. Reed of the CAA whose office was in the Tower building. I was informed that he had been in an automobile accident, and was in the hospital at the RAF base in Muripur, about ten miles west of the airport. We were given permission to use a hangar just East of the Tower and got ourselves rooms at a cheap hotel at the field. Next day one of the CAA officers took us to the hospital to see Reed, who had his arm in a sling. I showed him the work done on the aircraft, more than was actually required. All the fuel and oil tanks had been

removed and pressurized for leaks, all control cables replaced and reset. He was impressed that we had done so much. However, I would have to wait till he returned to his office in about a week. Reed suggested I contact his deputy, a Pakistani named Mr. Ahmed. Mr. Reed also suggested that we use his apartment right there on the field. It was a long one story building on the right side of the main entrance to the airport. There were several of these buildings that were used by the USAF during the war. I remember staying in one when I was flying the CNAC plane back to Calcutta. Reed gave us the key and said his servant will take care of us. We were grateful for the apartment, and introduced ourselves to the bearer. I took Reed's room at the south side of the apartment. A hallway ran from the living room/dining room to the bedroom, where it became L-shaped and led to the only bathroom and a dead-end. The bearer arranged a bed in the wide hallway for Hoppie. I immediately started negotiations to form an airline with a letter given to me by the East Pakistan Prime Minister. As far as West Pakistan was concerned, East Pakistan, a thousand miles away, was another country, and the letter of introduction was of little value. Cooch Behar had some polo playing friends in Karachi; I'm afraid all they knew was polo. I finally met a General Khan, who introduced me to the Defense Minister, a Mr. Naquivi, a fine gentleman who also had been born in Aligarh. He didn't know much about starting an airline, but wished to use the plane as soon as possible, to haul supplies to an outpost called Gilget, across some more rugged Himalayan Mountains, near the country of Hanza and also near K-2, the second highest peak in the world. Since the partition of India, Kashmir had been annexed to India. Pakistan felt it should be theirs, because the population was predominantly Muslim. A confrontation and war between the two countries had erupted over Kashmir. I told the Defense Minister I would

do everything possible to have our plane permanently registered and a company formed. I doubted that I could just up and start flying charters for the Government. Besides, PakAir and Orient Airways would create a fuss. He understood, but please let him know soon as possible.

Most of the crew flying for PakAir were American, English and Australian, most of whom stayed at the Park Hotel in town. The hotel had a first class night club called the "Casino." It too was run by a White Russian, known as Artie, and he knew Boris very well.

One morning at our bungalow, a strange thing happened. It was around 7 o'clock and time for my "chota-hazari." The bearer brought the tray of tea and toast and set it on a small table next to my bed. The door was left open into my room, and facing the L-shaped hallway. I sat at the edge of the bed, pouring my tea, when I saw a figure walk past my door, barely ten feet away, headed for the toilet. It didn't look like Jim, and there was no one else that I knew of in the apartment. I sipped my tea and pondered this for a few minutes. I finished the tea and toast, yet the person had not returned from the John. I also remembered the individual was wearing a maroon night robe, his blue pajamas showing out from the bottom; he also wore black or dark maroon slippers. A towel was over his shoulder. He had black hair, neatly groomed. He appeared to be an American, about 25 to 30 years of age. It finally got the better of me, so I got up and went to the toilet. The door was open. I went in; there was no one there. It was the old style toilet with the zinc tub with a enamel wash basin and jug. The commode was the usual type, which had to be taken out daily by the sweeper to be cleaned. The door for the sweeper was bolted from the inside. The windows in the toilet had iron bars. It was not possible for any one to come in or go out, especially the person I saw. He would have to return along the passage past my room. I walked slowly back and thought about it. I then went to where Hopkins was sacked out, he was fast asleep. I woke him anyway and asked if he had been up and gone to the toilet a few minutes ago. No, he hadn't. I now checked the rest of the rooms; front door was also bolted from the inside. The bearer was in the kitchen, that would be the only other door open to the backyard. "No Sahib was here, only you and Hopkins sahib." I returned to my room and had another cup of tea and then got dressed.

When Hoppie and I sat down for breakfast, we discussed the apparition I had seen. Jim said the robe resembled the type worn by U.S. Military personnel and patients in hospitals. I went to see Bill Reed, still out at Muripur. He stated that some of the buildings were used as infirmaries for the troops. But he had not seen any strange sights, or apparitions while he had been living there. I know I did, and I wasn't drunk! Was it a ghost? Had some poor U.S. Officer died there in Karachi? I do not know, but the figure that I saw that morning was real; I'll not forget it. A ghost of a U.S. officer. I bet if I checked all the U.S. records, I might find out who that person was. In the meantime, I carried on with my work.

I went to see the assistant and acting CAA Chief, Mr. Ahmed, about the renewal of the Airworthiness Certificate. I was informed that the certificate could not be renewed till he did a further inspection, which meant I had to remove all the metal plates under the fuselage, that cover the four fuel tanks. I said that had been done in Calcutta. He could care less. There were literally thousands of screws that had to be removed . He wanted the oil tanks removed and pressurized. Three cylinder heads from each engine had to be removed, to inspect the engines. The propellers to be rebalanced, and all controls to go through a transiometer test. A gear retraction test. I sat near him and wrote down the list as the guy looked across the desk at me. I tried not to show my anger at this time; I told him I would see what could be done. A friend of Hopkins came to Karachi from Calcutta. He too, was an ex-USAF. mechanic. A first class individual, who said he would help me out. Jim had taken leave and returned to the States.

I helped Jack the best I could. It was no easy task. I talked to Mr. Reed about the hard time Ahmed was giving us, if there was anything he could do to rescind the individual's demands on the DC-3. There was nothing he could do to change Ahmed's orders. Consequently, the Air Force mechanic Jack, and I worked doggedly, tearing the DC-3 down, I was learning a great deal about the Gooney Bird, from the help I was giving.

The RAF also had a base of operation at a place called Drigh Airport. It was located on the main road between Karachi and the airport. A two way thoroughfare that accommodated trucks, cars, bicycles, camel carts, and sheep herders. The RAF base was about five miles down the road from the airport, toward town. For some whiskey, cigarettes and beer, they would gladly allow Jack and myself to use their prop shop to balance our propellers. The next question, was how the heck could we get the darn things from our hangar to the RAF? I finally devised a plan. The camel carts always came down the road at wee small hours of the morning, hauling fresh produce from the farms to Karachi market. The carts were actually fair sized flat-beds with regular automobile wheels, and usually pulled, slowly, by a couple of camels. Not without a great deal of bickering, was I able to hire one of these camel carts to haul our two props to Drigh Station. The deal was made for about ten dollars each way. Some years later, President Johnson invited one of these camel cart drivers to Washington and the White House. It turned the guy's life so far around; I believe he finally committed suicide! In that part of the world, don't try to change the way of life.

The trip with the props took the better part of the morning, with the two camels taking their own Pakistan time! The RAF personnel at the shop actually did the cleaning and balancing with a "chit" note saying the

*Entrance to Cooch Behar Palace, 1948.*

props were airworthy. Two days later we had the propellers back at the hangar. It was quicker than I thought.

While I had been busy with the plane, Mr. Reed had returned to his apartment. I moved into an apartment with an Australian pilot friend of mine, who I had known in Calcutta. He was now flying for PakAir. His name was Ray Gifford. The apartment was shared by another Australian, and an American. I hoped to be there only on a temporary basis. The place was spacious enough, with a large upstairs verandah and a nice front yard with a lot of shady trees.

Around ten a.m. on a Sunday morning, after a leisurely breakfast, Ray Gifford, Dan Beard and myself were relaxing on the verandah. Ray was still in his night pajamas, when a local barber came by and Ray decided to get his hair cut. It was necessary for the bearer to bring out a chair and a bedsheet. Ray plunked himself down and the barber started in. They have a way of snipping a bit of hair, then click the scissors a few times and then snip more hair. The scissors are usually dull and sometimes pull out a few hairs. Dan and I sat some distance away chitchatting. The barber had done a pretty good job on Ray. This included a shampoo and massage of the scalp and shoulders and it looked like Ray was falling asleep. About then, a snake charmer came by and stood at the gate and wanted to do his thing; like the cobra and mongoose fight. I heard Dan giggle, he asked me to find out how much the snake man wanted for a cobra. The guy said ten rupees ($2.00). Dan hurried down and gave the man the money. I was not sure what Dan was up to. He had the cobra by the head and the rest wrapped around his arm. It must have been about five feet long. All these reptiles have their fangs removed.

The barber saw Dan approach with the snake and disappeared into the apartment. Dan snuck up behind Ray, who was still lolling in the chair. Dan took the cobra, wrapped it around Ray's neck and formed a knot. I knew what was going to happen next and started down the steps toward the gate. I looked back and saw Ray frozen in an upright position, he and the hooded cobra staring at each other six inches apart. This would only be for a second. Then Ray grabbed the snake by its neck, trying to untangle himself from the sheet and the snake from his neck. I guess Ray must have been in a state of shock at the moment, for he had not uttered a word up to now. But the situation was something like a fast-burning fuse to a bundle of dynamite. I'll never know why the snake never took a whack at him. Perhaps he saw the deadly look in Ray's eyes and was frightened! Finally, Ray got the snake untangled and swirled it around and let it go. It whirled through the air from upstairs and lit about twenty yards away in the hibiscus hedge out front.

Gifford, still in his pajamas and bare feet, started after us. I have heard profanity often, but nothing as to compare what Ray was venting forth, especially in an Australian accent. He had a stick or club as he charged. The chase was all the way down one of the main streets into town, before he stopped from exhaustion. I known one thing, if he had ever caught one of us, we would be dead. The next thing was, how were we going to get home? We stayed away all day and wound up at the Park Hotel, where some other pilots were. When they heard the story they howled with laughter, but also thought the joke risky; like a heart attack. One of the fellows suggested to take back a stack of cold beer which Ray loved. By late afternoon the two of us snuck back to the apartment with half a dozen bottles of cold Murry beer. He was there and cooled off somewhat. Once the beer was served, Ray forgave us a little. To this day Ray thinks I was the culprit. Dan, though a pilot, was more of wheeler-dealer. He returned to Hong Kong and later to Australia, where he passed away some years later.

*Cooch Behar Palace, 1948.*

The American engineer, Jack, and I continued to work laboriously, and could see daylight at the other end of the tunnel. Ahmed came by once in awhile to see our progress and inspection areas we asked him to peek at. The cylinders and the steel plates were the most difficult, but we accomplished it. Buttoning up the areas was just as difficult. At the apartment I would relax as much as possible; I also lost a great deal of weight and looked trim.

One Saturday evening I was relaxing after another days work on the plane, another incident took place at the apartment that shook me up. As mentioned earlier, Dan Beard had left for Hong Kong. I was with Ray one evening, when in walked an American pilot by the name of Thomas who also flew for PakAir. I was not drinking, and hadn't since I started work on the plane. These two started on beer, and proceeded to get into their cups. The two of them were sitting at the dining table, I sat on a couch near by. Pilots can be the damndest people for arguing about petty little things, and be egotistical bastards as well. The American pilot, Thomas, was discussing flying DC-4s, he knew all about them. No one knew better than he how to fly a DC4. Ray who had flown them with Australian Air Force, had accumulated about 1200 hours on the 4s. They argued, each calling the other a liar. Then I noticed Ray turn pale and didn't speak. What I didn't know, was that the American had a pistol pointed at Ray's midsection. He threatened to shoot Ray if he kept disagreeing with whatever the stupid conversation was about. I went over to the table and talked the American out of the gun. He handed it to Ray who laid it on the table. They seemed to calm down and I suggested that I would get more beer. I took a horse and buggy to a nearby shop and got some more local beer. I realized later this was a mistake. The conversation reverted back to the DC-4s again, and who was the better pilot. The American picked up the pistol and again pointed it at Ray, both shouting at each other. Finally Ray

stood up and said, "Okay you bastard; go ahead and shoot!" The guy did. He opened up and started pumping lead into Gifford. I saw him crumple and fall to the floor. For a couple of seconds I was taken aback. I then jumped up and grabbed at the idiot and his gun, as more shots rang out. We wrestled over the gun. I finally connected a haymaker to the guy's chin, that knocked him back against the wall, about five feet away; this was when I lost the grip on his pistol hand. My momentum kept me coming towards him. He pointed the gun at me and fired; there was one loud "click". He looked surprised. I grabbed a chair and beat him over the head till he dropped the gun, which I kicked away to the other end of the room. I broke the chair over him till he was senseless. There was blood all over the place. At this point I thought I had killed the bastard. I got to Ray, as he moaned in pain. I didn't dare touch him, even though he appeared to be alive. He moved a bit and I was able to place a cushion under his head. He spoke and said he was dying, to please get a message to his Mum in Australia. The address book was in his bedroom. I consoled him, not to talk; I am sure he would be all right. Ray was on his back and I tried to see where he had been shot. I could see one leg had been shattered below the knee. I could also see blood oozing through his shirt around the waist. The upper part of the body looked all right. I told him to lay absolutely still, that I would find a doctor and the police.

I raced out and found a "ghora-gari", and told the driver to take me to the police station, "Ek-thum-chaldi!" (Right away, fast.). Down the street we went "clipity-clop." At the police station I talked with a police sergeant. He stated he couldn't leave or dispatch anyone, because they were short of police at this time. Only the Chief Of Police could give the order to go. And where was the Chief, I asked. "Home, I think." He gave me the address, and to make sure, I had him tell the Gari-wallah. We took off again, and found the Chief Inspector's house in darkness. I

shouted till a servant arrived from the back. He said that the Inspector and his wife were at the Gymkhana Club, this Saturday evening. The horse and buggy were getting a workout! I told the driver not to worry, he would be well rewarded.

At the Club, I found the Inspector, well sloshed! I told him the story, briefly. "Oh, my God!" he said. "Let's go." I paid off the gari-wallah with a generous tip, for which I received a big salaam. The Inspector had a car and driver, luckily. We stopped first at the police station to pick up the sergeant, and to call for an ambulance. We were on our way again. All this had taken a little over an hour. I figured both should be dead by now. At the apartment, we rushed up the stairs and into the dining room. There in the corner of the room were the two guys, sitting on the floor, with their backs against the wall. Ray and Thomas had their arms around each other, drinking beer! "I'll be go-to-hell," I said. "You sons-of-bitches are supposed to be dead!" "We're having our last beer, just in case." The Inspector sat at the table dumbfounded, looking at the blood everywhere. He wanted to know where the gun was. I looked around and found it under the cupboard and gave it to the Inspector. It was another half an hour before the ambulance arrived. Funny thing; with all the shooting and noise, no one came around to find out what was happening. I guess that's true in most places. No one wants to get involved.

The two fellows were put in the ambulance, while I went with the Inspector to the general hospital. Here they laid Ray on a cold marble slab, I guess where they put the dead bodies. A doctor cut his clothes to get them off, as the blood had coagulated to his skin. Ray lay shivering on the slab. An Orderly sponged Ray's body down with cold water; this made Ray shiver even more. Thomas, the son-of-a-bitch, was sitting at the other end, smoking, while his head was being bandaged. He was supposed to be dead. I could see several bullet holes in Ray. The one that hurt him most was the shattered leg with the shin bone sticking out. I suggested to the orderly to be gentle with the leg, so the lower part wouldn't flop about; this he did, but not too well. The orderly (or male nurse) looked at me and said, "How about Sahib?" "What about me?" I looked and saw my right hand and fingers were bleeding. It was the first time I had noticed it. He washed the blood off, and there were two marks where bullets had creased me, one on my right palm and the other on my left forefinger. He swabbed and bandaged them.

I returned to the police station in the morning and gave the Inspector a written statement. I asked about Pilot Thomas who did the shooting, did they have him in jail? No, Captain Gifford was not pressing charges. I said, "How about me? I was shot in the hands, see? I am all patched up." "No, Peter; you don't want to do that." It was all that paper work he was thinking about. "Okay, but one thing for sure: You will see that the Pakistan Government kicks him out." "Yes; he will leave very soon."

I saw Ray in the hospital, all bandaged and plaster on his leg. He appeared to be in pretty good spirits. Never a dull moment! I brought him some cigarettes to cheer him up.

I had to move again, this time to the Beach Luxury Hotel. The airplane, after so many hundreds of man-hours, was finally given a Certificate of Airworthiness and ready for a test flight. It had taken some doing. It never would have been possible, had it not been for my American friend Jack. Without his expertise, I would still be sitting on the ground in Karachi! His wife, who was with him all this time, was an invalid. Wherever they are, I hope the good Lord has been kind to them. On the check flight the plane flew beautifully.

The next item that raised its ugly head, the American Embassy here, informed me that my passport would be expiring the end of the year and could not be renewed. I would have to return to the States.

I contacted Kiki that I would be coming to Calcutta soon. I explained in my letter all that had happened, and that we would have to leave for the States towards the end of September, which would be in about three weeks. A CNAC mechanic had joined PanAmerican in Calcutta, a Bill Frost. He wanted to take over the apartment, the furniture and Cookie! This I agreed to.

In the meantime, Kiki's dad, Jack, had contacted his brother Harry, who owned a export-import company in Karachi. He asked to help me get the airline started. I decided to contact him on my return from Calcutta. It was wonderful to be in Calcutta, after the desert type weather of Karachi. Kiki looked great. Mohamed and Cookie had looked after her well. Bill took over the apartment and Kiki and I returned to Karachi. We met her uncle Harry one afternoon at his home. I explained the whole situation, and the part Cooch Behar had in the company. I said the airline's main reason was to fly the Haj, Muslim pilgrims to Jeddah, Saudi Arabia. He checked into it, and found that it had good possibilities and lucrative business.

Harry formed the company and we called it Crescent Air Transport. The DC-3, however, was still a cargo one. It would have to be converted to passengers. I hired two pilots to fly while I was in the States, arranging my passport difficulties. PakAir had a DC-3 in Karachi and asked me if I would ferry it to London for them. I agreed to do so as long as I could take Kiki as a passenger. It was an easy, day flying only trip. We spent several days in Rome. It was our first trip there. In London we were able to spend a whole week. This too was wonderful; I explained to Kiki all about the time I was in London back in 1928. We then caught a PanAm Clipper (Boeing Stratocruiser) to New York.

Kiki and I checked in at the St. Moritz hotel in Manhattan where I showed her around the city which I think she enjoyed. Next, we took the train to Plainfield, New Jersey and stayed with my sister Geraldine and her husband Fred. Geraldine thought Kiki was very lovely and asked to paint a portrait of her. It turned out to be a beautiful painting. In Plainfield we bought a second hand car and spent considerable time with my mother. It was so wonderful to see her and tell her all about India. Kiki and I then started our trip up to Lynn, Massachusetts. Her mother and the rest of her family had now moved there. Jack had another brother in the area by the name of George. He had an ice cream plant in Lynn. Jack was now looking after his hotel in Bombay.

After a short stay, I took Kiki up to Maine to visit Christine and Robert who had returned from India. It was wonderful to be in to Bangor and Brewer, to see so many of my old friends again. We had an evening with my gang from the Peacock Lounge. I think Helen had remarried to a man who worked with the State Department in the AID program. Christine and Robert had sold the Salmon Pool Farm and had moved to Castine on the coast. We spent about ten days with them before returning to Lynn.

I contacted Robbie, the sharpshooter of the Dinjan days. He was now living in Miami. I told him I had a company in Karachi and was looking for a good C-46. He suggested I come down and stay with him and Margo to look around while Kiki decided to stay with her mother in Lynn. I took a flight down and Robbie met me at the Miami airport. I must add here, for the past couple of years, I got the bug to read a loads of True Detective magazines that a friend had left me, in Calcutta. It was hard to believe that these grisly stories were true-life happenings. One comes to my mind now, of a guy in Texas who ran a cafeteria. He was always running ads for waitresses to work for him. One girl from Indiana had answered his ad, and taken the bus to Texas. She had worked there a couple of weeks, when she was propositioned by the owner. She would not give in to his charm, whereupon he killed her, dismembered the corpse and fed the remains to the pet alligators he had in a pond behind the house. He had done this to several other girls. The parents of this girl followed up on her disappearance and contacted the police. The FBI were called in, and contacted the cafeteria owner. When confronted, he drew a pistol and blew his brains out. After reading these terrible stories, I sometimes had nightmares. Who wouldn't?

Robbie and Margo had a ground floor apartment, just off Brickell Avenue, down town Miami. A spare room was given me that overlooked a courtyard of the complex. Robbie and I looked at several planes on the airport. Either they were too expensive, or were beat up. One evening, after chasing around, we had a bite to eat with the usual beer and chitchat about the old days of Dinjan and Calcutta. We turned in about 11 PM. I guess I had dozed off and was well asleep, when suddenly I was wide awake. I must have had one of those bad dreams, but wasn't sure. I thought it had been a shot fired. I was still sleepy and tried to get my thoughts together.

Robbie still had his hogleg revolver that he couldn't hit anything with; however, at close range, he might! I knew he and Margo had arguments and spats. I wondered if he had done the nasty deed. I got up and tiptoed to his room, their door was partly open. He and Margo were fast asleep. I returned to my room and lay down. I was thinking about what had awakened me. Then, in the distance, I heard a siren; maybe two. There are always sirens, at all hours of the day and night. The sound kept getting closer and closer. Before long, they were coming down Brickell Avenue. I sat up and listened. I could swear they were swinging into the driveway of the apartment complex. Sure enough, here they came, right into the yard with lights flashing. I saw lights being turned on in different apartments across the way. I quickly got dressed, and woke Robbie and Margo; that wasn't easy! They put on their robes and came to my room. We peered out of the window and saw several police and medics from the ambulance, searching the grounds with their flash lights. Robbie decided he better hide his gun, which wasn't licensed. One of the officers headed in our direction. He wouldn't be able to see us as I had my lights out. There was a row of bushes, under my window. As his light flashed near it, he and I spotted a body lying face down, just a few feet from my window. He was clad only in pajama bottoms with a gun in his hand. I called to the officer, "What happened?" He wasn't sure, but it appeared to be a suicide. The dead guy's wife had called the police; the policeman asked if I had heard the shot. "Ya, that's what woke me up." The guy's wife and a few others in their robes had gathered near the sprawled figure. We returned to the living room and I decided to have a shot of whiskey. I hoped it would help me sleep; it didn't work. I was up the rest of the night. I thought the morning would never arrive. When it did, I was bleary-eyed from lack of sleep. After breakfast I tried to get a little more sleep without success. I learned one thing: I would never read True Detective stories again.

We gave up on the airplane hunt. Robbie said that he and Margo were planning to drive up north to New Hampshire, to visit his folks and step son. They would like me to join them and would drop me off in Lynn. Robbie had a fire-engine, red Buick convertible, a four-holer, which gave it a sporty look. In 1949-50, there were no super-highways, such as turnpikes like R-95. It was Route-1 all the way. It starts at Key West and ends in East Canada. I was dropped off in Lynn, and they continued on their way north.

I was in touch with the State Department concerning my passport. The answer would always be, "We will let you know. Stand by." At Kiki's folk's home, I tried not to get in the way, just sit around and twiddle my thumbs. I would spend a lot of time at the Revere Beach Flying Club. Here I met a young fellow who was most interested in aviation. His name was Bob Kaye. He was always interested in hearing about flying in the Far East. I inquired about obtaining my Airline Transport Pi-

*H.H. Jaipur and H.H. Cooch Behar at Cooch Behar Jubelee, 1948.*

lot license (ATP). The manager said they could only give commercials and instrument rating. I decided to sit and try for the Instrument, for something to do. Bob sat in with me, I would try to help him all I could.

I noticed that Kiki was spending more time at home with her mother. I guess that was okay, since I went to the flying club a lot. I did so to stay out of people's hair. She was not interested in accompanying me on any trips I thought she would like. The one to Maine was the only one. One afternoon when I returned from the Flying Club, Kiki was upset and crying. I tried consoling her. She then told me that her mother wanted me to leave the house. If that was the situation I wanted Kiki to come with me. She said no; she planned to stay with her mother. There was no way I could convince her that she should go with me. I was upset and angry. I packed up my belongings and left. I went to see Bob Kaye, he suggested I stay at his house, till I had finished the Instrument course. I stayed a couple of weeks and finished the course. I talked to Kiki and said I had finished and planned to go to Plainfield and stay with my mother; that she should go with me. No, she was going to stay in Lynn with her mother. I thanked Bob and his folks for letting me stay with them. Next day I drove down to Plainfield. It was nice being with my mother. We would sit and talk a lot about our years in India. I know she missed her home country very much. I asked her about returning; though her eyes lit up, she would say no, there was nothing to go back to. All the people she knew had either died, or gone to different parts of the world, after partition. Her "brood" as she put it was now here on the American continent. I was the only vagabond and Rogue that was unsettled. I called Kiki once I was with Mum; still she would not budge. I called Bob Prescott of Flying Tigers, and asked if I could do some

flying for him, from the New York base. He said sure thing, and would be happy to have me. I explained it would only be for a short period. He said to contact the chief pilot in Newark Airport.

I had been flying for nearly two months when I received a letter from the State Department that I was cleared and could be issued a new passport. If I wished, I could obtain one in London. I didn't need a passport to enter England. I called Kiki to give her the good news. Fine, but she would not return with me to England. I had a feeling she was being influenced; it was just one of those feelings. I bought a PanAm ticket to London and checked in at Idlewild Airport (now JFK). I waited to board the Stratocruiser, the crew for the flight walked by. As they did, I recognized the captain. It was Captain Pippinger, the same pilot who had flown us Pan-Africa group to West Africa in the Boeing Clipper boat, back in early 1942. I called to him and introduced myself. He recalled the flight very well, going down the West African coast, looking for the right airport to drop us off. Once airborne, he said, I could come up to the cockpit for a visit. At the same time Captain Pip had me upgraded to First Class. I spent half the trip up in the cockpit talking about our experiences. The rest of the time was downstairs in the gondola bar and lounge. I enjoyed the trip, it was great. At the end of the flight, I thanked Captain Pip for a wonderful flight and hoped I would see him again. Not many years later, I heard he had fallen down in his house and banged the soft part of his head that killed him. I think I mentioned that Pip had an operation that had removed the frontal forehead skull.

Captain Don Brown, who flew the DC-3 (AP-AED) from Karachi to London, met me at Heathrow Terminal. He and the crew had rented a small apartment in London-Town, which was somewhere near Haymarket. The airplane was at an airport in central England and would not be ready for another ten days. Don was a good looking rascal, but could not hold his whiskey. He had all the English lasses falling all over themselves after him. When drunk, he couldn't produce. Being a good friend, I sometimes had to help him out!

I didn't waste much time in getting to the American Embassy, to obtain my new passport. It was a nice feeling, to know I was legal again. To kill time, Don and I joined the Astor Club. The place was known to entertain movie stars and other celebrities, such as Pearl Bailey. One evening I was there with one of Don's friends, when a group of people came in and sat near us. It turned out to be Bing Crosby, Jean Simmons, Trevor Howard and another young actress by the name of Glenis Johns. The girl I was with knew Trevor Howard and waved to him. The next moment, he came over and said we were invited to join Bing Crosby and company. Crosby, being a golf enthusiast, had been in Scotland attending the British Open Golf Tournament. He was scheduled to catch a PanAm flight next morning to New York. The group planned to stay right here to wile away the hours. I wondered if I might get stuck for some of the tab. I wasn't loaded with all that kind of money! It was turning out to

be a lovely evening. I had an opportunity to dance with Jean Simmons and Glenis Johns. Bing Crosby was curious about me and what I did. I spoke about China and India, and my friend the Maharajah of Cooch Behar. He said he had met Cooch Behar when he was in Hollywood in 1947. I asked Crosby if he had ever been to India and played golf at the Royal Calcutta Golf Club. He hadn't, but hoped one day to come to India and play golf. I said it would be a new experience. I said, for one thing, it was necessary to have a couple of boys down the fairway to watch over the golf balls, because the crows and hawks had a habit of swooping down and flying off with them. Even monkeys loped off with them. He thought it funny. The club closed at 3 a.m. From then on it was strictly a private party. Time came for the Crosby group to leave, he insisted that we all go out to see him off. Yes, he picked up the tab! There were a couple of cars with chauffeurs to drive us out. I don't know how those people can do it, I was dragging my behind all the way back. I was dropped off at the apartment and happy to crawl into bed. It was some evening! I told Don about it when I came to. He sure wished he could have been there.

Word came that our plane was finally ready. Don and I took the train up to Nottingham where it had been worked on. From there we flew it back to London. An agent known as Lambert Brothers got us some passengers and arranged our clearance to Karachi, day flying via Rome, Athens, Cyprus, Damascus, Bahrain, on to Karachi. Charter flights normally stopped at these stations, since there were never able to receive over-flight permission. only regular, schedule airlines had that privilege, such as PanAm, BOAC etc.

The next morning early, we departed for Rome. It was a clear, beautiful morning. The Alps were a wonderful shining white range of mountains. They reminded me of the Himalayas. We were at 14,000 ft. I told Don of this; he was not interested, as he gasped for breath! I told him to hang in there, we would be letting down over Italy shortly. The passengers and Don were relieved to have landed at Fiumicino Airport. The main airport, Leonardo de Vinci, had not been built. From Rome, we hop, skipped and jumped across the Mediterranean and Middle East to Karachi. We arrived late the following evening.

John Voyantsis, the son of Harry, was there to meet us. I had not met John before. He was youngish and bespectacled. He informed Don and myself that his father Harry had been taken ill and flown back to Lynn, Mass. He would be attended to by Jack's wife Mae and his brother George. John also informed us, that approval had come through for the purchase of a C-46. The Haj traffic had been arranged. We were scheduled to carry about five hundred Muslim pilgrims to Jeddah right away. since we would not be able to have the 46 for another month, John had leased a British "York" aircraft, to start the Haj. The DC-3 would also do it's share. I rested a few days and then boarded a PanAm flight back to New York. I went up to Lynn and saw Kiki. I told her she had to get ready, that we were going to Miami to pick up a C-46, to be ferried back to Karachi for the Haj. No, she said she would wait here in Lynn with her mother. I just couldn't understand what was going on. I stopped by to see my mother and Geraldine, before flying down to Miami.

The C-46 had been purchased through an outfit called Aerodex, a Miami base operator. The manager was a fellow named Ben Terry. I wanted to make certain the aircraft had proper interior, such as; good sound-proofing, 50 payloader seats and two toilet compartments in the rear. With cash in hand, people can work pretty fast. The plane was painted to my specifications, with a Pakistani flag on the tail. The registration number was AP-ADU. I contacted good old Robbie Robertson to fly for the company. He agreed. Through Ben Terry, I was able to contact two expert mechanics to maintain the aircraft in Karachi, and sometimes to fly as a crew chief on lengthy flights. One of the Mechanics was Demont Edwards, the second fellow, whom I shall never forget, was Jack Richards. Edwards took me over to meet Jack Richards, who was employed by Southern Air Transport. Jack was all gnarled and leathery, the back of his mousy colored hair stood up. He was freckled faced, and looked as though he could do with a strong disinfectant bath. He reminded me of "Alfalfa" from the "Our Gang" movies. Jack called me "Sir." I asked if he had a passport, or had been overseas. "No, I ain't got a passport, but I do have a dee-vorce decree." "Well, that's a step in the right direction!" "Yes, I would like to travel. Where 'ya goin'?" "Karachi." "Where's that?" "Over yonder about eight thousand miles." "Well, I ain't traveled that fer before, but sure lik'ta give it a try." "Jack, you're hired. Lets see how soon we can get you a passport." "Yes Sir!" We went down to the Post Office where they handled the forms etc. for passports. We picked up forms and had those horrible instant pictures taken. When it came to fill out forms, I realized Jack couldn't read or write. "Oh, Me!" Well, I did the filling out for him. I asked his age, he referred to his driver's license. "Where were you born?" "Key West." I said, "That's quite a ways south." He said, "Yeah. If it were any further south, Ma and Pa would have been treadin' water to have me!" I like Jack; he had a remark for everything, even though he was illiterate. I understood, though, he knew the Pratt & Whitney engines, and the C-46s, inside out, literally. The two fellows were hired, I put Demont (Dee) in charge of the supervision and getting the C-46 ready. It wasn't long before we were on our way to Washington, D.C. Here we were met by the VIPs of Aerodex. I had to have a little more work done on the toilets; they were a bit flimsy. Next stop was Boston. This time, Kiki was ready for travel, but did not appear happy to do so. I stopped at the hospital and saw George. He informed me that I couldn't see

*H.H. Cooch Behar, Harry Carr and self after morning shoot. Carr is Queen Elezabeth's jockey.*

Harry now, he was getting some special treatment and was doped up. I told George that, when possible, to say we wish him well; to have a speedy recovery, that we were looking forward to seeing him back in Karachi. I thought a lot of Harry, he had done so much to help me.

I had a short visit with my friend Bob Kaye. He mentioned that he might be hired by Eastern Airlines, probably on the "shuttle." I wished him great success. After all the goodbyes, we were on our way to Gander, New Foundland. Here, we checked the weather closely for our journey onto Bluey West, on the south coast of Greenland. The base was operated by the U.S. Military. At the briefing with Gander Operations Department, we were shown how to fly up the fjord. It would have to be VFR. At the end of the fjord was a large glacier, where a runway had been carved out. We were briefed that we would probably land straight in, even if it meant down wind, since the runway sloped uphill at a steep grade. The whole thing appeared to be like a dead end street. The takeoff would be the other way downhill. We had no extra fuel tanks on board. Once you had reached the point of no return (pnr), that was it. Gander was always in touch with Bluey, they knew when the long fjord was VFR. These conditions were usually early in the mornings. Robbie and I got our clearance early next morning and we were flying over a bright blue North Atlantic. We leveled out at 7500 ft. It was not long before we saw icebergs dotting the blue water. This was truly spectacular. After four and half hours flying we could see the craggy mountains and a gap where the fjord started. We entered the mouth of the fjord, it was a fantastic sight; high, green mountains on each side, with icebergs floating lazily along in the blue-green waters. We followed the inlet at 1500 ft. At the end we could see the glacier and black-topped quonset huts dot-

ting the side of the landing strip. I was in contact with the military tower and given permission to land. After touch down, I could see the steep uphill grade. It was not necessary to use the brakes. The military personnel handled us, and when they saw Kiki, they couldn't do enough. Though it was the beginning of September, it was freezing cold. A jeep took us to our quarters. After a clean up, we all sauntered over to a large, army PX. Here we were able to purchase, and stock up on items that we could use in Karachi.

It was nice to have Demont and Jack along, not only because they were first-class mechanics, but were jovial, easygoing rascals. We got along like a happy family. The other stops along the way were: Kyflavic Iceland, London, Fumaccino Italy, Athens, Damascus Syria, Bahrain and Karachi.

On arrival at Karachi, everyone but the band was there to greet us. There was a lot of baggage to clear through customs; they were most cooperative and let us through without too much hassle.

Rooms were arranged at the brand new Metropole Hotel, run by the Swiss. The Haj pilgrimage was well on its way. Most of the five hundred Muslims had been delivered to Jeddah by the British York and our little DC-3. It took a few days to finish all the formalities with the Civil Aviation authorities. The C-46 was then put to work immediately. There is no airport at Mecca, all the pilgrims usually travel by bus from Jeddah (seaport on the Red Sea.). Don, Robbie and I flew around the clock, hauling these souls back to Karachi. Then it happened, on a landing at Jeddah, Don dropped the C-46 in from quite a height, rupturing the seals on the main landing gear struts. Don had to fly the plane to Asmara, Eritria, House of Mirrors fame! It was the base for Air Djoubti airlines who operated C-46s. They were able to fix the gear, but we were to lose several days in the bargain. In the meantime we also ordered

*My Hajjis in flight to Jeddah, S.A., 1950.*

seals in the States, that were flown out by PanAm.

With the 46 out of commission, Robbie and I flew the DC-3. On one flight I was checking out a British captain. We overnighted at Jeddah. Our return flight would be about three o'clock in the morning. In those days, there was no specific area for the pilgrims to stay while waiting for their flights. Each agent marked off an area on the Tarmac (ramp) near where the planes were parked at night. Here, with all their goods and chattels, they would wait. Saudia was handling our flights. They had made out the flight plan, weather etc. and informed me that the passengers were on board ready to go. Another group of Hajjis were asleep just about two plane lengths away. It was still dark at that hour in the morning. The English pilot was in the left seat getting his check. He started up the engines; I guess one of the pilgrims from the sleeping group awakened and thought it was his flight getting ready to go. I could not see him, but when the other pilot did, it was too late. The man had picked up his bundles and came running to our flight. He did not see the propellers spinning in the dark. Consequently, he ran right into the prop on the left engine. He never knew what hit him. The pilot cut the engine immediately, but it was too late. The impact resembled a large plastic bag filled with wet napkins, garbage and shit, thrown into the spinning prop. It was a big splat; guts, bones, flesh and rags. went spinning in all directions. Our passengers were not aware of what had happened.

A good American friend of mine, who was technical manager of Saudian Arabian Airlines (Saudia), was handling us at the time, by the name of Jack Brown. He rushed out and saw the mess. Jack then got some of the helpers, possibly Pakistanis or Indians, Who poured water over the plane and swept up the mess in a hurry. People climbed all over the plane with ladders doing a pretty good job of cleaning. Jack said for us to get out, he would handle the situation with the authorities, and finish the cleanup. I thanked him and we taxiied out. I doubt if anyone else was aware of what had happened. They were all still groggy with sleep in the plane and the other groups sleeping on the ramp. The DC-3 didn't look too bad when we made the walk around in Bahrain. Back in Karachi, we had to report the incident to the DGCA. They would handle the situation with the Saudis. The flight had been in the English pilot's name. There was no problem as far as myself flying to Jeddah again to keep the flights on schedule between Karachi and Jeddah.

Don Brown brought the C-46 back from Asmara and was flying the Haj. I might add here: The Haj pilgrims come from all parts of Pakistan. Most of them are men; the women that go are wrapped up in "purdah," mainly a way of secluding Muslim women from public view. A purdah is a draped cotton garment worn over the entire body, from head to toe, with a small gause and two peepholes to see and breathe. These Hajjis carry just about all the life belongings. They expect to be gone anywhere from six weeks, to two months. They will have with them all sorts of pots and pans, kettles and oil lamps. They carry grain, rice and lentals; even chickens! The Hajjis will not eat during the day, they make up for it at night. This is probably a throwback from the ancient days when they traveled by camel or donkeys. It would take six to ten months to reach Mecca. Others come by boat.

On one of my flights from Jeddah, my Pakistani stewardess, came running to the cockpit and said the plane was on fire. The inevitable phrase was uttered, "Oh shit!" "Where?" I asked. She motioned to the rear of the plane. I had the copilot take over. I grabbed the fire extinguisher and went back to investigate. I followed the girl to the rear of the Aircraft, where I saw smoke coming out from under and around the door of one of the toilets. I opened the door and there squatted a Hajji, with a small brazier, or charcoal cooker, on top of the commode. He was nonchalantly fanning the coals. He was in the processing of cooking a pot of rice. All he was getting for his effort, was a lot of smoke. I told Daphne, to explain to the guy he was not allowed to do this. I also tried explaining in Hindi. I told the Hajii that there would be special Muslim food served to all of the passengers when we arrived in Bahrain. He said he wouldn't eat that food. That was too bad. I had Daphne take the disgruntled man back to his seat, while I dumped the rice and embers into the commode water. It all frizzled up in steam. I then gave a squirt of the extinguisher to make certain it was out. Back in Karachi I informed the DGCA people that some sort of check be made on the pilgrims. They should not be allowed to carry cooking utensils in the cabin; that there should be no kerosene oil in their lamps or stoves. They would check on this with the organization that sets up the Haj traffic every year. Well, I had done my bit for safety. I told my people to double check the passengers and their baggage thoroughly. If we saw a Hajji with a kerosene lamp or tin of it, it would be taken away. The lamp or stove would be drained and given back. Oil cans would not be allowed on the plane. The women travelers in "purdah" were also a nuisance. These gals would not go to the toilet as instructed. Instead, they would squat in the aisle of the plane and let it go. The urine would trickle down the aisle, snake fashion, all the way to the rear and form puddles. The stewardess had a heck of a time to get these people to the toilet. They had never seen or used the western type of toilets; they only knew the wide open wheat and corn fields, or the rural Indian contraption, which was a hole in the ground with two foot prints, one on each side of the hole. Even today, in modern Saudi Arabia they still use this style potty, which is nicely enameled with a garden hose to spray oneself after. The men passengers, who did use the toilet, did so by squatting on their haunches on top of the commode. Consequently, their business never hit its mark. One can't imagine the state of the aircraft after arrival at destination. There were the sweeper class that would clean the stinking mess. Special sweepers would be needed to clean the toilets and scrub the floors from one end to the other. Strong lotions of pheneel was used as a disinfectant. We would check below the flooring to see that urine was not corroding the control cables and other metals.

Living at the Metropole Hotel was getting to be expensive for the crews and apartments were difficult to find. There was a fleabag of a hotel called the Taj. How it carried a name like that, I will never know. It was livable and cheap. This is where we moved to. Don was happy sharing a place with Daphne. Robbie had a place at the airport.

One night there was a ferocious banging on our door. It was Don Brown and Daphne. "What's going on?" I mumbled in my half sleep. "Its Robbie. He has stolen our gold." "What gold?" "We'll explain it, if you will come with us to see Robbie at the field." On the way Don explained: He, Daphne and Robbie were bringing gold in from Bahrain. Evidently the exchange rate was worth the effort to smuggle. Robbie had been flying the DC-3 from Bahrain to Karachi, empty. The gold had been placed in the cabin, and on arrival that night, after landing, Robbie was supposed to taxi all the way to the end. While Robbie turned the plane around, Daphne was to toss the load out near the edge of the runway. After clearing customs, they would sneak out to that spot and pick up the loot. I might add, security at the field in those days was lax. Any one at that hour, like 4 a.m. in the morning could sneak onto the field. The only people who knew of their escapade, was Robbie, Daphne and Don. I confronted Robbie, he gave a very innocent look and said he knew nothing about it; or who had got ahead of them and swiped the gold. I told Robbie it was my airline and I didn't want it ruined because of smuggling.

Later, the same day the gold disappeared, an Arab agent of the smuggling group came to me with Don and Daphne. He informed me that he knew Robbie had the merchandise, if he didn't confess or say what happened to it, he would have Robbie's throat cut in two hours. If you know Arabs and Muslims (Calcutta riots!), that is their method of execution and retaliation for any wrong doing. This guy looked mean enough to do it. Don brought Robbie from the airport; I told him what the Arab man had told me. I could see Robbie was scared. He then said he didn't want any trouble and would borrow money from a friend in Calcutta. He swore he didn't have the gold. I don't remember the amount, but it must have been considerable. No one, I am sure, would lend that kind of money. However, that evening he came up with the money, less a few rupees. I saw to it that Don and Daphne gave this to their Arab friend. Soon as this was done, I had Robbie on the next PanAm flight to the States, which was in a couple days.

The successful movement of the Haj pilgrimage was completed by the end of October. PakAir was closing shop and taking their crews and equipment out. Orient was still operating schedule passenger service with their Convair 240s. It was agreed that Crescent Airline would handle the freight and special passenger or charter flights. John Voyantsis contracted a few cargo flights between Karachi, Lahore and Dacca East Pakistan, which is now Bangladesh. It was during this period that I had to let Don go. He appeared not interested in flying, I guess because there were no flights out of Bahrain!

*The C-46 (AP-ADU), 1950.*

I was able to hire another British pilot by the name of Bob Bithel. Though he had never flown a C-46, he was an experienced pilot, mainly on British type aircraft, and the DC-3s (Dakota) and had thousands of hours. This would give a break from some of the flying. It gave me more important things to attend to, to be with Kiki and some bird hunting! Jack and Bithel liked their beer. After a couple of pints of beer, Jack would start in on some of his jokes. It did not take long before everyone got to know Jack. Bob thought him quite a character, which he was.

Demont was an ardent hunter and had brought his shotgun from the States. I had my Westley Richards shotgun I had bought at Mantons in Calcutta, and had shot several tigers with. In Karachi I bought another nice English 20 gauge shotgun for Kiki. There was an area about fifty miles north of the airport. It was scrub jungle and a few villages that grew rice and wheat. Off the main road was a building called a "dak" bungalow. It was a government rest house; you paid about fifty cents a night to use it. Kiki, Demont, myself and a Anglo-Pakistani who worked for Crescent Airlines, Jerry Everson, would also accompany us. It felt great to get away from the noise and smog of Karachi, and all that flying. The whole area, for miles, was loaded with black partridge, sand-grouse and water-fowl. Jerry Everson, always brought his servant to do the cooking. He could come up with some fancy meals from the game we shot.

Harry Voyantsis had left Lynn and was in Athens recuperating. He never really recovered and passed away a few weeks later. We all felt sad about it. I needed him to run the company, his son John, was not cut out for the job and hired a couple Dutch people from KLM to run Crescent. Because of the arrangement I had made with Harry to manage the airline had been working well; he had made up some bogus Pakistani shareholders in Crescent. Still, the company was mine, and I in turn was responsible to Cooch Behar; this Harry knew. The Haj alone was a lucrative business. I figured the C-46 would be paid off in two years. When I asked John to let me check the accounts, to see how we made out on the last Haj; he couldn't then, because he had so much going on. He always had some excuse ready. I tried to figure out how we stood financially. It was necessary to advise Bhaiya of the situation. Harry knew of the initial monies from Cooch Behar and myself. John did not seem to care or understand about the setup. All he knew was what was black and white in his files, that I was not allowed to check. I had a strong suspicion that the Haj money was winding up in John's coffers for his export-import company. I also learned from the Dutchmen that the ground personnel were not being paid their regular salaries; nor the landing fees. The new Director of Civil Aviation was a Parsi, by the name of Mr. Karangia. He was a knowledgeable individual, and a straight forward person; I liked him from the start. I went to his office and explained about the landing fees; he said not to worry.

It was not long before Christmas rolled around, being short on C-46 pilots, I was doing considerable flying. Bob Bithel flew with me as I was trying to check him out. It was to be a quiet Christmas with not too much partying.

I remember once Demont mentioned how much Jack (who had now been nicknamed "Cactus Jack", perhaps it was due to his gnarled and windblown looks), loved small donkeys. He used to comment whenever he saw them roaming around in the countryside, on our hunting trips. So, early Christmas Eve, Demont and I took our driver to near one of our hunting spots. We spotted a baby donkey, and were able to buy it from a villager for about ten dollars. This was to be Jack's Christmas present. Very early Christmas morning, Kiki, Demont and myself sneaked into Cactus' room while he was still sleeping off the night before party. Kiki had tied a bright ribbon and an Xmas bell on

*"Cactus" Jack Richards cleaning off the windshield, Nicosia, Cyprus, 1951.*

the little fella, the donkey that is! We then placed the donkey on Jack's bed. It started to struggle and let out a couple of his "Hee-haws". This woke Cactus from that sound sleep. He couldn't focus his bleary, blood-shot eyes on the donkey, and mumbled what the hell was going on! Demont gave Jack a cold bottle of beer to get him surfaced; now he was able to see the animal, he couldn't believe it.

Cactus Jack was beside himself that Christmas day. Our driver raced off and found a sizable collar and lead for Jack's jack-ass! Jack took his present wherever he went; even to the airport. On New Year's day of 1951, we were all invited, along with the Embassy staff, to Ambassador Warren's for eggnog and brunch. Cactus had on his only dark blue suit and maroon shirt, he said it didn't show the dirt! We knew most of the staff, since we all belonged to the American Club of Karachi. The Ambassador's home was in Clifton. I recognized immediately that the residence was the same house that PanAmerican Africa used during my sojourn back in '42, where I traded my kukri knife for the PanAm steel trunk. Where many pilots rubbed shoulders during the war years; in those days it was called the Green Briar Mansion. When I entered the three or four steps onto the front verandah, and entered into the foyer, I felt nostalgic. I expected to see the Commanding Officer, a Colonel with Air Force and RAF wings to walk in. Almost nine years ago; where had they all gone?

Cactus Jack had brought his donkey along, and had the driver tethered it at the back to an old mimosa tree. In due course, Jack had his fill of beer, eggnog and gin; he was feeling no pain. He saw an elderly, good-looking lady, whom he grabbed by the arm and said, "Come with me honey; I want to show you the dang best Christmas present I've ever received." He took her to the back verandah, which was up stairs. Jack then put his arm around her waist, and pointed to the

little donkey. Cactus expounded on his present to the lady, how he looked after the animal, and it even slept in his bed! He did not know, or had forgotten, that the lady was the Ambassador's wife! She enjoyed the show and so did the Ambassador.

After couple more beers and eggnog, Cactus passed out. A group of us laid him out on a large, old Arab sea chest in the hall-way. We crossed his arms on his chest. Pho-tos were taken of Cactus, I sure wish I had one of them now. When the brunch was fin-ished, we had to carry Jack to the car and then put him to bed.

The charter flights between East and West Pakistan had slacked off. Around the end of February, John Voyantsis asked if the C-46 could carry freight in one direction and passengers back. "Yes, we could, that was the beauty of the payloader seats. He said that our agents, the Lambert Bros. in Lon-don, asked if we would do some freight char-ters for KLM, Amsterdam, Bangkok and Hong Kong. There were no return loads; we would have to scurry up return loads, possi-bly passengers, for the way back. John said he was trying to find agents in the Far East that would handle Crescent. John finally got Thai Airways in Bangkok with Hong Kong Aviation and Asian Airways in Hong Kong. At this time Demont Edwards had decided to return to the States. It was a great loss to see him go. I was left with Jack and an Irish lad by the name of Timothy Butler, whose accent you could cut with a knife. Tim was not too sharp on the C-46 and was teased a lot by Cactus and Bithel. Kiki decided to re-main in Karachi, while I took the flight with Bob, Jack and a new radio man named Tom Dutton. Actually he had once been in Orient Airways in Calcutta when I was with them. We picked up a few passengers to London; then empty to Amsterdam. It was the same routine: Bahrain, Damascus, Athens, Rome and London. Myself and the crew were in Amsterdam for three days and enjoyed the food.

KLM had our plane loaded and ready to go. It was nice to have professional people arrange weight and balance, clearances and good weather reports. They would be han-dling us all the way through to Hong Kong. Even first class catering for the crew. Wow!

Jack and Timothy checked the aircraft in Karachi. We were on our way to Calcutta. We had one night at the Calcutta Grand Ho-tel and a phone conversation with Bhaiya at his palace. I brought him up to date with the Company and John. KLM handled the cargo at Bangkok and Hong Kong. The trip went smoothly and the airplane ran like a sewing machine. Everyone along the line got to know Cactus Jack. Our agents in Hong Kong and Bangkok had arranged a mix load of passengers to Europe. Some were dropped off at Brussels and the rest in London. Though the flight took three nights and four days, the passengers enjoyed it. The people got to know each other, and good overnight stops along the way. Lambert Bros. car met us at Bovingdon Airport, not Heathrow. The car took the crew to a place called the Whites Hotel, in downtown London, on Bayswater Road. For a treat, I took the crew to the Astor Club. Some of the waiters working there re-membered me, especially the Bing Crosby wingding!

Before the next flight, Lambert Bros. had a going away party for one of its em-ployees. The bash was held at a floor above their main office. It was a large room void of any furniture, except for a table in the middle, on which sat a keg of beer! About 25 Lambertians and ourselves crowded around the table. The British don't normally drink their beer cold. There was no ice for cooling and made no difference too Cactus. In England, they call a pint of their warm beer, "wallop," and after a couple of those, Cactus was getting walloped. He started off with a few mild jokes, then came some real naughty ones. The English mob loved it; they would not leave Jack alone. With every joke he received an encore! They cornered him against the wall and he didn't have to move, because someone always kept his mug full of beer. He was performing well for his new found friends. One of the group piped up, "I say Cactus, don't you ever run out of jokes?" Jack replied, "Hell, man; these are only my pint size ones; you ain't heard my quart ones, yet!" That threw them into an uproar. We all stayed till the keg was empty.

The next day Lambert Bros. informed me that KLM had another load of the same. We took the plane to Schipol that evening. The next morning we were headed back to Karachi. After the usual check of the aircraft, we were on our way again; this time we took Tim Butler along, to help Jack, who had been working doggedly on these long flights.

In Bangkok we overnighted at a dumpy, weather beaten place called the South Pa-cific Hotel. The only redeeming feature was the bar. After a rest and cleanup, we all con-gregated there. The representative for Thai Airways, an American, also joined us. I don't know from where, but a bevy of pretty Thai girls showed up and joined the group. We all had a few drinks when a well-endowed gal came and sat near me. One of the girls in the bevy spoke up in fair English, "You no take that one; she wears falsies, like rubber!" The girl with the boobs jumped up and said, "No, no falsie." In a second she stripped to the waist and showed two fantastic titties. "See, see," she said, "no rubber, feel!" We agreed they were real. Feeling was believing! Everyone had a good laugh. Needless to say, the girl was not shooed away.

The flights between Bangkok and Hong Kong were always interesting. The route would take us southeast over Saigon, to avoid Cambodia; then northeast across Vietnam. We had to fly quite a ways out to sea and then north to Hong Kong. This was to avoid coming close to Hainan Island, which was very hostile and belonged to Communist China. The possibility of being forced down, or worse yet, being shot down was always a threat. This would lengthen our flight time considerably.

Hong Kong was always an exciting place to come to. Especially if you had to make that hairy letdown and approach through the gap first. We stayed at a small hotel off Nathan Road, on the mainland, just behind the Peninsula Hotel. The aircraft was handled by Hong Kong Aviation. Some of their Chinese mechanics, were once CNAC employees before China fell to Communist Mao. It was one of our senior Canadian Chinese pilots, Captain Gordan Poon whom I knew well, absconded with a CNAC Convair-340 and flew if from Hong Kong to Shanghai. I guess he figured on being a big shot in the eyes of Mao and their aviation Dept. It didn't work out that way. My CNAC friends with HKG aviation believed he wound up in jail and damned near died.

One of my C-NAK pilot friends was a guy named John Shumacher. He was born in China and spoke fluent Chinese. When he evacuated from China, he settled in Hong Kong and opened a first class tailor shop. When I would come to Hong Kong, I would always contact John. He and I played golf at a course not far from the Communist border. The 13th hole was just a five iron shot away from it. Soldiers could be seen patrolling along the high barbed wire fence on the other side.

One morning, Bob Bithell rapped on my door and informed me, with a silly grin on his face, that Cactus Jack was in jail on the island. He wasn't certain what it was all about. The Hong Kong police had tracked us down and wanted to confirm that Jack was employed by Crescent Air Transport. It was Bob they had talked with, he chuckled and wondered what the hell Cactus had gotten into. After breakfast we took the ferry to Victoria Island to find out. It was still fairly early as the ferry started its trip across. It was a pretty sight to see the Chinese junks sailing in the harbor. You knew you were in the Orient. Now they have ruined that traditional sight by putting motors in the junks. It was their unique sails that gave them that distinctive Oriental look.

A police officer at the wharf gave us directions to the main police station and jail

*Cactus and Demont Edwards all dressed up in Indian Saris Karachi, 1951.*

*Cactus Jack Richards all dressed up ready for a beer, Karachi, 1951.*

house. A police sergeant at the desk, took our names and information, then we waited.

An English police officer came out with a folder and escorted us to his office. We went through the question drill while the officer took notes. "Gentlemen," he started, "We have a Jack Richards, commonly known as 'Cactus Jack.'" Bob Bithell, in his English way, said, "Yes, I guess that's the bugger! What did he do this time?" "Well, if you gentlemen will sit down, I'll tell you what I know of the case, some of which has been related by your colleague. Last evening Cactus, I hope I am using the name correctly, was here in Victoria. He had been enjoying himself at some of the night spots. He evidently got himself pretty well sloshed! When he arrived at the ferry terminal, the last ferry for the night had already left. There he stood, not knowing what to do or how to get back. An English bloke with two Chinese ladies came by and, seeing Cactus Jack sitting on the dock, quite drunk, asked him if he needed any help. Jack had said, 'Ya, I need to get to the other side,' and the man replied, 'That's no problem, we have a boat right here, we will motor you across old boy.' The English bloke and his Chinese friends had a few drinks themselves. There was a small boat moored to the wharf. According to Cactus, they all got in and started to motor across. In the middle of the bay the bloke stopped the boat with no lights on it. The guy and the two girls took off all their clothes and jumped into the water for a swim. Cactus, sobered a bit from the sight, thought it was a good idea; so he took off all his clothes and joined them. They were enjoying themselves swimming around the boat, evidently playing hide and seek!; from nowhere, floodlights shone on them. The Harbour Police could see nothing but shiny, bareassed, white bottoms climbing back onto the little boat. They were escorted back to the wharf where they had started. The English bloke and the Chinese ladies were able to show their ID cards and were released, after paying a fine for no lights on the boat. Poor Cactus had no identifica-

tion; he said he left his passport at the hotel. The officer on duty thought it too late to call the hotel to find out. He also thought a good night's sleep in our jail would do him no harm!"

According to the police, Jack had charmed everyone at the station with his humor, no charges were going to placed against him. On the ferry ride back Jack had to tell us the story once more. At the hotel we made sure he had a hearty breakfast. It would be a long day tomorrow, to Bangkok, the round-about way.

On this particular trip, another American pilot friend joined us. He was one of the friends that hob-nobbed at the 300 Club in Calcutta. His name was Kyle Mitchell, a jovial, well-liked individual, and an excellent pilot. At Karachi I arranged a Pakistan license for Mitch. All was needed now was to check out Bob and Mitch, then I hoped I could relax, and check on what went on at John's office.

Kiki stayed on in Karachi while I made these long excursions to Europe and Hong Kong. We had dropped our passengers off at Amsterdam and the rest in London, and a few days to relax.

At the hotel (Whites), I learned that Tony Martin was in town, performing at the Palladium Theater. Mitch and I decided to see the show. I think Bob had gone off to his home some distance from London-Town. A place called Hull. I sent a message backstage, hopefully that he would be able to say "Hello." It did work, and he did remember me. It was great talking to Tony in between acts. He was doing well on the stage and in movies. Tony was married to the beautiful stage and screen actress, Cyd Charisse. She was with him and we were introduced. Tony mentioned that Cooch Behar would be in London later in the summer. I said it should be great, all of us being able to get together. I would be making another trip during the interim. During the next eastbound trip, I learned Kiki had some sort of female disorder and had decided to return to Lynn, Massachusetts.

Next evening, Mitch and I went to the Astor Club, where Pearl Bailey was performing. During intermission Mitch and I asked Miss Bailey to join us for a drink. She turned out to be swell person, we enjoyed talking with her for nearly half an hour. London is a place where everyone seems to meet everyone, especially from the theater world.

At another club called Le Rue, Mitch and I were enjoying the evening, having a drink and watching the show; there was a foursome sitting at an adjoining table. I recognized the two fellows, as part of Tony Martin's show from the Palladium. I commented to them how much we had enjoyed their show the other night. It was no sooner said, when Mitch and I were asked to join their group. However, we were planning to make it an early evening, so declined. One of the girls said we looked lonesome; why didn't we stop by at the Embassy Club on Old Bond Street. She was on the stage there, and would introduce us to some of the girls who were performing with her. Her name was Pam Davies. Well, for the heck of it, Mitch, Cactus Jack and I went to the Embassy Club next evening. During one of the intermissions, Pam met us at the piano bar. She handed us a menu, and on the cover were all the pictures of the girls. Pam pointed to herself and said, "Scratch that one off; pick from the others." It was some menu to choose from! I selected a cute face on the corner, and Pam said, "How about that? She's my roommate! She is 18, and her name is Maggie Miles, Margaret." Their performance came on again, and I easily picked out Maggie Miles. When the show was over, Pam and her three girls came over to our table. That's how I met Margaret. The reader will hear more about her through the rest of the book. I was able to take Margaret out to lunches a couple times before I left for my next trip to Hong Kong.

Though the war had been over for six years, England was still in the throes of rationing. It was not easy, just to run down to the grocery store and buy a bundle of whatever your needs might be. Such things as eggs and cheese were still rationed. Clothing too. From my Hong Kong trip I brought Margaret loads of nylons and fresh produce from Amsterdam. Customs were great and most cooperative. On each trip through Karachi I would stop off and see John and was given the same routine and excuses. At the Park hotel I met the Dutchman who was running the company. John had not told him that the company was mine. He certainly was surprised when I mentioned it to him. He now confided that John was not cooperating and was not giving him the necessary funds to meet all the bills; that the money was being used for other items in the export-import company, as I earlier suspected. The manager suggested I get rid of the bogus stock and get real bonafide Pakistanis into the company. This was easier said than done. Even-

tually, I came up with three individuals that were handling our Haj affairs and charters. They didn't have much cash at the time, but were willing to make a contract that would pay me back so much per month. At this point I wasn't sure. I wished that Harry were here. I was now disenchanted and losing patience.

On the next trip out of Hong Kong, the agent had a group of Catholic priests and missionaries who had been asked to leave China. They were to be taken to Brussels. I had a load of fifty religious refugees. They did not have a lot of baggage; they left China with what they had on their backs. The local Hong Kong press, Time and Life reporters were on hand to interview these people and to witness the departure. Life published their stories and pictures of our flight. We landed in Calcutta for a well earned rest, after twelve hours of flying. It was the crack of dawn Sunday when we took off from Calcutta and climbed above the haze level to about 6500 ft. After leveling off the stewardess came forward and stated that the priests were requesting whether they may hold a special church service on this flight. "Yes, tell them they may." "One thing more." the girl said, "they have a portable altar with them; they would like to have it set up just behind the cockpit door, and use their special candles." I told her it would be okay, as long as a fire extinguisher was kept handy, I'm sure they knew the delicacy of fire hazard. Should there be sudden rough air in flight, it would tip the candles. The gal said she would watch out. I also suggested the cockpit door be left open. I wanted to make certain that everything was right and no danger of fire. Two of the priests set the altar in the aisle near the cockpit. They had two candelabras, each holding three candles. They had on their robes and their crucifixes hung brightly from their necks. Bob was up front with me while Mitch relaxed in the back. I told him to take over the flight while I doubled checked the proceedings. It was something to behold! The weather was clear, a red sun came over from our back as we were flying westerly. Orange colored sun rays filtered through the passenger windows. The candles didn't seem to flicker while a priest gave the sermon in Latin. Time seemed to be suspended, as if the plane was on a sky-hook; the colors and hues became eerie, with the golden rays of light filtering in on these people of God, in their dark robes with golden chains and crucifixes. It was strangely beautiful. To think we were flying over a country of a completely different religious belief, and not too distant to the right was a cemetery where my father lay. If ever one was to believe in God, this was that moment.

At the end of prayers, a silver chalice was produced from a velvet bag, and then wine for communion. Bob and I were able to take turns watching the ceremony. At the end, the candles were neatly extinguished by an old fashion, silver snuffer. The altar was folded and taken to the rear. Bob and I sat back and watched the day brighten. As the weather got warmer, clouds, like cotton puffs, appeared on the horizon.

We spent the night at Karachi. We all stayed at the KLM hostel at the airport. Coming into Rome's Fiumicino Airport, there was great excitement in the back. The special passengers wanted to know if we intended staying in Rome overnight. When they knew we were, they were like little school boys. All the priests and missionaries were in huddles as the sight seeing they would do, especially St. Peters. As soon as I landed and the KLM bus arrived, I informed the group, that it would be a very late morning departure. Bob got off at Karachi and Mitch was with me on this leg, with the radio operator Tom Dutton and of course, Cactus Jack. Next morning we were bussed to the airport. Our passengers were beside themselves for having seen and prayed at St. Peter's. We finally delivered all our wonderful passengers at Brussels, safe and sound. I knew it would be a safe journey all the way: how else?

The Haj would be coming up by mid August and I had made another HKG trip. I was now returning from Hong Kong and decided to stay over in Karachi. Cactus could give the plane a good going over. I was able to meet with the Dutch gentleman again at the usual bar in the Park Hotel. He told me there may be a problem with the company not having paid its bills; the plane might be impounded. At this point, I was getting upset and angry at John. I didn't even wish to see him. All the new problems were building up at the back of my head, as Mitch and I flew back to London with our passengers. I was lucky to learn that Bhaiya and my friend Sid DeKantzow were still in London. We met at a favorite place of Cooch Behar, called the 49 Club. It too was run by a White Russian named Zigge. During our lunch I had a long talk with Bhaiya and Sid about John and the company. Sid suggested selling the C-46 and the DC-3. The 46 was here, a bird in the hand. The DC-3 would be hard to get out of Pakistan. I figured I could get about $110,000 for the C-46. That was the going market. However, I didn't have the papers to prove the plane or the company was mine. Bhaiya had the papers for the DC-3 in Cooch Behar. I had the 49% of the documents. I was sure Kiki's dad would vouch for us. "Who would buy the plane?" Bhaiya asked. I said I could get a hold of Aerodex in Washington, Joe Carnacero. They could arrange a sale. 46s were used all over the States and in South America. All that was happening with our 46 was a lot of wear and tear of a good aircraft and nothing to show for it. Most of the money was disappearing. John had a grip on the company, and I wasn't sure about having no-money-Pakistanis in the company. Bhaiya agreed with Sid, that we give it a try. My heart was pumping away, and I wasn't too happy about running off with the plane. I enjoyed working and the challenge; it was the fact I couldn't get any co-operation from John. I was busting my ass flying around the world for nothing. Secondly, I hated leaving my friends holding the bag. Bhaiya wasn't getting any returns for his investment. So, if he wanted to gamble, so be it. I told Bhaiya it would only be a fifty-

fifty chance that we could pull it off. I finished my lunch and told Bhaiya and Sid I was off to the hotel to call Washington and see what they had to say. I contacted Joe Carnicero and told him what I intended doing. He said not to do a thing until he got back to me after talking to his associates. I cooled my heels for an hour, when Joe called. They agreed the plane could be sold right away, if I would take $100,000. Next, they would discuss the circumstances under which the plane would be delivered. There would be no ownership papers with me. Joe said to hold tight, he would be having discussions with the Aerodex VPs and their lawyers. He would call me back again tomorrow. I received the second call the next afternoon; it sounded as though there were several people on the phone; I wasn't sure who I was talking with! The gist of it was: they had contacted a company in Havana, Cuba (still under strong man Batista), Don-Q Airlines, that wanted to buy the plane right away. Aerodex lawyers suggested I bring the C-46 to Miami; they would handle the ownership and other paperwork. First I wanted to make certain the Pakistan Government would not be involved. I didn't wish to be involved in any international incident. Not to worry, they would handle everything. All this info I was feeding back to Bhaiya, and he was more convinced to go ahead with the deal. Only thing I knew, once I committed my self, it meant I was burning my bridges behind me. Mitch could care less, but I told him over several drinks, I had mixed emotions. He even noticed the change in me and suggested we go back to Karachi for the Haj, then think things out. Actually Mitch was making good sense, but Sid and Bhaiya were all for the chance. I gritted my teeth and said we would go with their plan. I told Mitch to take the C46 to Amsterdam with Jack and wait further instructions. I mentioned to Washington that I probably would come via the South Atlantic. I had no deicing equipment on the aircraft and didn't wish to be stuck in Bluey West or Gander, because of weather.

I briefed Bhaiya on the deal and what Washington had come up with. Bhaiya said, "Pete let's give a try, I don't mind gambling. How do you feel about it? You are the one that is sticking your neck out." "Right Bhaiya, I don't mind, if I am blackballed from Pakistan, that's okay; but I do want to return to India some day." "I will talk to Jai, and make sure you will always have a visa for India." "In this game," I said, "you cannot trust anyone. I tried trusting my people in Karachi, it didn't work."

I contacted Mitch in Amsterdam and informed him to have Jack get a hold of KLM, and see if they can put a four hundred gallon tank in the cabin for a long range flight across the Atlantic, at least ten to twelve hours endurance.

All this had taken considerable time, almost two weeks. I was receiving frantic messages to bring the plane back to Karachi that the Haj would be starting shortly. I stalled them, by replying I was anticipating a load back. John kept saying to bring the

plane back empty if necessary. I kept in touch with Mitch and was having him push Jack in hurrying the installation of the cabin tank. This was being done by KLM. I told Mitch I had received about 3000 in sterling pounds. To find out if it could be changed to dollars there.

Everything seemed to have been done at the spur of the moment. Kiki had been taken ill, some sort of female complication and was already back in Lynn with her mother. I had left all my belongings back in Karachi; my nice clothes, guns, jeep station wagon and many other valuables. Well, these were material things and could be replaced. I was also closing the door behind me. In spite of many things, I liked Pakistan, I think because of the friends I had made there. I had locked myself out. Time would tell.

I said goodbye to Cooch Behar, and gave him the hand signal by showing my fingers crossed. It was difficult to say goodbye to Margaret. I was sure she would make her way up the ladder in show business some day.

I met Mitch and Jack at Schipol Airport and looked at the plane and the cabin installation. Jack and KLM had done a fine job, I hoped it worked when needed over water. Jack said he had arranged for U.S. Dollars in town as banks were now closed. We ate at the famous Five Fingers Restaurant, a unique place with wonderful cuisine. Jack's friend met us there and exchanged the sterling for dollars, almost $10,000. I had been informed in London that dollars were more practical to use than sterling in the countries where we would be stopping.

I made preparations to leave the following evening. The flight was planned via Marrakesh, Dakar, across the South Atlantic to Natal Brazil and keep going till we reached Puerto Rico. I inquired about buying a five-man life raft. KLM told me that the French had rafts at Dakar. Mitch and I had a long conversation with Schipol ATC. I told them what our plans were and would they cooperate? There would be no problem. I requested an IFR flight plan to Karachi, via the usual routes - Rome, Damascus etc.; that I would depart Schipol next morning. I asked ATC to give us a twenty-four head start, before sending Karachi the phony flight plan! Instead, we departed Schipol that evening for Marrakesh, Morocco and Dakar, Senegal. This gave us an opportunity to try out the gravity feed, fuel cabin tank. KLM had done a good job; everything worked well.

We arrived at Dakar a bit early than had planned; which gave us a few hours rest, before taking the all night, across the water hop. I obtained a 5-man life raft from AirFrance that would be sent back to them. Shell Company accepted our Crescent gas carnet (credit card) without out any fuss. All I was paying for, were landing fees and incidentals, at the other stops.

At 10 p.m. local time we received our clearance for our flight direct to Natal, a 10.5 hr flight plan. Now that I was committed, I was still worried that the Pakistan authorities might pop up here in Dakar, before our departure. I would breathe easier once air-

*Golfing in Kowloon, Hongkong near Communist border, 1951.*

borne. I advised our radio man to keep Dakar and Natal informed of our progress every hour. I gave the honor of the flight across to Mitch, and Cactus Jack took the right seat after takeoff, while I took a rest in the back. I suggested we level at 9500 ft to be above clouds as shown in the elaborate weather chart that had been handed us at Dakar. Then I rolled up in a blanket and dozed off. Jack had said the cabin tank was good for about four hours. He would switch to the cabin tank once we had leveled out. Somewhere, sometime, I felt and heard something strange. I woke and realized I was lightweight, the airplane appeared to be in a descent, the noise I thought I heard, was no noise at all. "Damn," I yelled, "the engines are not running!" I threw off the blanket and dashed for the cockpit, downhill! I saw a flashlight beam skimming around the instruments in the cockpit. All I could hear was, "Oh, shit! Oh, shit! Goddamnit! Jack, switch on the other tank! Switch on the other tank!" "I'm trying Mitch, I'm trying!" Jack finally had the flashlight on the fuel selectors on his right side. They were a couple of small red wheels that he was trying to turn. I shouted, "Turn them toward you Jack; toward you. You have them turned off!" Mitch was flying and headed down. He still had the artificial horizon, needle-ball, altitude and airspeed indicators. The cockpit had, with some of its own lights and the flashlight, enough light to fly by. For a few seconds there was mad confusion in the cockpit. There were hands and flashlight milling around, and me backseat driving. Jack finally managed to switch onto the main fuel tanks and as soon as the fuel flow started, there was one hell of a roar and whine of engines and propellers. The throttles had been left as they were previously, in the cruise position. The cockpit lights came on, and all gauges appeared to be adjusting. I reached over and closed the throttles to idle when I heard the roar of the engines. It took a few minutes before we regained our composure and no one spoke. The airplane had lost about fifteen hundred feet in the bargain. Soon we were back to our cruising level with a sigh of relief. Mitch spoke first. "God, Jack! I'm sure glad we didn't have to go in, there's a lot of water down there." Jack piped up, "Yeah, and that's only the top of it!" Leave it to Jack! We all laughed. What had happened: Jack and Mitch had turned on the cabin tank and switched off the regular wing tanks. The cabin tank was now gravity-feeding both engines, through the cross-feed system. There is a sight gauge, which showed they had approximately another 30-40 minutes of fuel remaining. However, what the gauge was actually showing, was back pressure, not real quantity. Jack had just checked the gauge and told Mitch he would switch over in about thirty minutes. He had just finished the words when both the engines quit.

We jollied each other, and had coffee and a couple of sandwiches. It had been a little more than four hours since take off. Now that I was wide awake, I told Mitch to go back for a rest and I would call him when ready for descent. I told Jack he could do the same. There was nothing to do up front, except watch the gauges. I dimmed the cockpit lights and adjusted the pilot seat to full recline position. The C-46 had wonderful pilot seats; better than a DC-4. I could have used that type of seat to a better advantage one night across the "hump"! I relaxed and thought of the past, and the repercussion when Pakistan finds out the plane is in the States, not Karachi. I would cross that hurdle when it came. I thought of the wonderful Calcutta days, my friends and the hunting in Cooch Behar. I wondered why I never visited NainiTal and Monghyr, the childhood haunts. I think I wanted to keep that as a special memory. It might not have been the same after all the years. I wasn't too sure of the real reason. I mulled away the hours and watched the constellation, Southern Cross swing down to the south west. Just like diamonds on black velvet at a jeweler display. Then I said to myself, "Thank you Pratt-Whitney for the purring R-2800 engines carrying us across the great expanse of water." I chuckled at Jack's remark; yes, there must be a lot of water down there, sharks too.

Natal was about three hour difference in time from Dakar. The ETA was around 0800 a.m., Saturday, Sept. 1, 1951. The autopilot kept wanting to precess to the right. I kept making the corrections every so often. Something to keep me awake. Tom had dozed off for a short spell, between his dots-n-dashes, Morse code. At about 0530, I turned on Natal Radio station, it came in loud and clear. The old "bird-dog" needle pointed straight head. I guess that's about as good navigation as could be expected, even if we had a navi-

gator. I spotted a white beacon light loom out below the distant horizon. It had to be the archipelago of Fernando Naranja, that showed on my chart. It was about 100 miles off the coast from Natal. I woke Mitch and gave him the seat to take us in while I took the co-pilot one. We landed exactly what the flight plan had given, 10 1/2 hours block to block. No navigational errors, except vertical!

Natal hadn't changed much. There was a bootmaker around, I doubt that it would be the same one, not too many sales. I think the original fellow had made his loot and gone. Probably has a highrise in Miami! I felt much relieved on this side of the Atlantic. We did not check into any hotel. We all had a well deserved breakfast at a restaurant nearby. A Brazilian Airline crew were also having a meal. The pilot came over and wanted to know if the plane was for sale; their company were looking for C-46s. I said this one was already sold. I paid the airport fees and restaurant with cash. Now, with our bellies full, a stretch and rest, we decided to push on. I wanted the operation over with and pay Bhaiya back; then start a new life. The next stop was Paramaribo, Dutch Guiana. When over some of the Brazilian jungles, we could all smell the jungle flowers, like jasmine and franjipani, our flight was at 7500 ft. The fresh air vent was wide open and was sucking in all that strong aroma of flowers. Next stop San Juan, Puerto Rico. It was Mitch's turn to fly. After passing along the coast line for Trinadad, Mitch looked over at me with a grin. "What's the matter?" "We have just run out of charts." "I thought we picked up enough maps for the whole trip." "I thought so too. Maybe they are in the back some place." Search as we may, there were no maps. "Hold everything," said Mitch. He pulled out a little pocket address book from his briefcase.

On the back page of his book was a six to eight inch square map of the world. It would take a magnifying glass to locate anything. He looked at the course and general direction of Trinidad. That is, if we followed along the coast line. If we got over Port-of-Spain, we could try various frequencies, and hopefully pick up their station; that was resolved when Tom Dutton contacted them. Sheepishly we asked the heading for San Juan from Trinidad and pertinent radio information. There was silence for a moment, then they came back with our request and asked if we were okay. Mitch told them we had run out charts.

We found San Juan, and landed safely! We were tired and happy to check in at a nearby hotel. After a good rest I telephoned Demont Edwards to get on over to San Juan; I had a ticket waiting for him in Miami. I then phoned the Washington people to let them know I had arrived safely in Puerto Rico. They told me not to be alarmed when a sheriff comes by and puts a sticker on the aircraft on

arrival in Miami; it is all part of the plan. We all talked to Demont when he arrived at our hotel. He knew the situation and said everything looked all right. Next day was Labor Day. I paid the landing fee and all other bills, and were on our way to Miami. The airport was deserted, but from under the bushes, one might say, here comes the sheriff of Dade County and sticks a big label on the door of the aircraft. We had parked the aircraft at Aerodex hangar, which was part of L.B. Smith Associates. At that time, it was located on 20th Street, which is now where the terminal building is. All of us got rooms at the Miami Airways Motel on N.W. 36th Street. The next day I visited Aerodex and met a Ben Terry. I don't remember the details, but was told to relax; there was nothing left for me to do. Washington office will keep us advised.

I rented a car for us and visited a few old friends. I called Sid Wilson from CNAC days. He was flying for National Airlines and was on a trip. I called his wife Betty and I suggested a get together soon.

The next morning, there was a call for me. It was the Federal Bureau of Investigation (FBI). Mitch, Jack, Tom and myself went downtown to their office, and were introduced to two young fellows by the name of Daily; they were brothers. They threw many questions at us, mainly me. I tried giving reasonable answers. They asked why did we bring to the States. I said to be completely serviced and repainted. "Why couldn't that be done in Karachi?" Jack replied, "Not possible, they didn't have the facilities." "Do you plan to sell the Aircraft?" "Well, not really; only if I could get a good price and pay off the lien." The Dailys asked if I was from Maine. I said I was, and went to the University of Maine for a couple years. It so happened that these two brothers had come from the University of Maine. What a coincidence. Through all the questions and conversation, I was given a clean bill of health.

I called Sid's home again, he was out on another flight. I decided to take Betty and Sid's brother out to dinner that evening. They knew a nice restaurant, the Lighthouse Harbor, run by a Greek! It was great to see Betty and to know Sid was doing well with National. It was a nice evening and good food. I paid the bill with one of the hundred-dollar bills. It seemed a long time before the waiter returned with the change. Instead, he showed up and said the manager would like a word with me. I approached the counter, and there stood a police officer. I asked if there was any problem. The manager stated, "This hundred-dollar bill looks as though it might be counterfeit." "Counterfeit? No way! I have spent almost $6000. along the way from Amsterdam, Holland and there has been no trouble." The officer took my name and motel. He said he would contact the Treasury Department, who would double check the bill. I was chagrined when Betty had to pay the bill. I apologized when they dropped me off at the Airways Motel.

At about 4 a.m. there was a loud knock on my door. I knew it could not be the bearer with my "chota hazri!" I opened the door, and there stood a couple of well-dressed individuals. They flashed their badges and said they were from the Treasury Department, T-men. "Come on in." The officer from the restaurant had given their office my name and motel that evening. They didn't waste any time. I retrieved the rest of the money from my wallet, a little over $2000, all in $100 bills. "Yep," one said, "they're all counterfeit." I said, "You haven't examined them all yet." They replied, "We can tell." I explained how I got the money, and where I had spent most of it. They laughingly said I should have spent it all in Brazil, because that's about all the kind of money they use there. The T-men took the money and gave me a receipt. They said I should come to the office later that morning. Here we go again! First the Sheriff, the FBI and now the T-men; what next? The three of us reported at the Treasury office, and were introduced to the Chief, a Mr. Marshall. It was another long session of questions. Jack couldn't remember the man's name who made the exchange. They said there was a gang doing a lot of counterfeiting in Europe, mainly Holland. If we could come up with a description, they would notify Interpol. We did the best we could to help. As we talked, Mr. Marshall's phone rang. It was San Juan Airport in Puerto Rico. They had just discovered the two hundred-dollar bills that I had paid them with were counterfeit. The San Juan airport manager insisted we be put in jail. Chief Marshall cooled the guy down and said I would send them a check right away. I said I would pay off all the money I had spent on the trip. He said "No, only those that call in." Even the Miami Bank had accepted one. I couldn't believe what was happening; what else could go wrong? I paid San Juan and Miami Bank. There was no back-lash from Morocco, Dakar or Brazil. Marshall had to agree, the $100 bills were good imitations.

I called Kiki in Lynn and asked her to come to Miami. First, she was terribly surprised what I had done. She would see about coming down later. Days turned into weeks without any news from Washington; it felt like the usual runaround. Ben Terry of Aerodex always kept his after office hours at the El Torro Bar on 79th Street Causeway. At one of the get togethers at the Bar. Ben informed us, that it had taken two weeks before Karachi knew what had happened to the C-46. Needless to say, all hell had broken lose. Bob Bithel and Don Brown were the only

souls that came to our rescue. Big headlines in the Karachi papers wrote, "American elopes with Pakistani airplane." Bob and Don retrieved our belongings; Kiki's Chinese chest, my guns and a few other belongings. The hotel servants had vandalized the trunks and made off with a lot of the clothes. Don shipped our things via PAA to Miami. To me, that was a miracle.

Kiki arrived in Miami, all upset, because her dad would not cooperate or help in any way. I guess he was getting his rupees out of India in some unknown manner, and didn't wish to have his name implicated. Slowly, I was being isolated.

At the El Torro Bar Ben Terry informed me that L.B. Smith's lawyer wanted me to come to Washington for a meeting. At last, things looked like they were beginning to move. I told the crew to sit tight with fingers crossed, I'd be in touch and to look after Kiki. The meeting was held in L.B's conference room where I met his lawyer. He was cool and wouldn't say much. He did tell me to keep quiet, he would do all the talking. He did tell me that a Pakistani would be present at the meeting. "Who was he?" He wasn't sure, but someone from Crescent. I cooled my heels and watched everyone enter. Then here came the Pakistani, it was Karashi, a person I regarded as a friend, and one of the guys I wanted in the company. He was scared and didn't want to sit near me or talk. Then a member of the State Dept. showed up. L.B's lawyer, after a lot of discussions, asked my role in the company. I previously mentioned, Cooch Behar didn't want his name involved because of India Pakistan trouble. I said it was my money that had bought the DC-3 to start the airline. Where were the receipts? I said in Karachi, with John Voyantsis.

I said I took the plane because it was mine and Mr. Karashi knew full well that it is and the whole story. His lawyer wouldn't let Karashi speak. Things were looking grim. I could feel that L.B.'s lawyer wasn't applying himself on my behalf. The State Department honcho appeared to be a high VIP; he was judge and jury. I don't know how legal that was. After nearly two hours of discussion, the bottom line was, that the plane either should go back to Karachi or be sold here. Crescent Air Transport would get the money. I was livid and angry, the VIP wouldn't listen to my reasoning and arguments. My so-called lawyer could care less. They wouldn't let Karashi speak, because he may spill the beans. I could see their game, and there was damned all I could about it. After the dust had settled, I spoke with Karashi. He knew the plane was mine, but said the people back there had offered him

*Some of the Priests/Missionary refugees from China on our flight from Hongkong to Europe, 1951.*

the company and other goodies. The plane would be sold.

But if he didn't speak the truth, he could not go back to Pakistan without going to jail. The plane was finally sold by Aerodex, and after everything was counted up, including my share of the DC-3, I wound up with enough to pay off the $9000 and all the crew salaries; I wanted to make sure they got a fair deal. As I told my friends, I had enough left over for a down payment on a Buick! Mitch went to work for a character company in Miami; Jack, I think, got his old job back with Southern Air Transport; while Sid Wilson helped me join National Airlines. So ended my saga; except, I learned a little later, that the State Department was playing "footsie" with the Pakistan Government to use the airport in Peshawar, in the north west frontier near the Khyber Pass, where I once visited Alison. They were going to operate their U-2 spy plane for flights across Russia. That is what cost us the money for Cooch Behar and myself. It was a shame I had to lose, not for myself, but for Cooch-Behar, because the State Department was going on some wild goose chase of spy flights across Russia, and eventually, as the news one day said, the Russians shot the airplane down and the pilot by the name of Powers was captured.

It was a sad letter that I had to write to Bhaiya, explaining the details. He took it very well.

# PHASE FIVE: 1952-1955

By January 1952, I was flying co-pilot for National on their Lode stars. It was humdrum flying; up and down and all over Florida. Sometimes we made flights to New Orleans, which was a little different; also flights from Tampa to Havana. Kiki and I had an apartment-style living for a while, until we were able to buy a small home in the southern part of Miami. Some of my old CNAC friends were living here: Hugh "Woody" Woods and Mage, from Dinjan; Chuck Sharpe was flying for PanAm. Quite a few of the mechanics were also with PanAm. Our Chief Radio Technician, Red Knight, and his wife. The one thing I found difficult to get used to was being furloughed quite regularly from National. It became necessary to join the Airline Pilots Association, ALPA. It was a good strong union, but I was not used to being told that I could not associate with this pilot or that pilot; I mustn't be seen with them. These were the scab pilots who came to work for National Airlines while the pilots were on strike. The thing was, I didn't know any of them, and didn't associate with them, anyway; however, when I flew with several, it was necessary to talk in the cockpit or at the motels where we stayed. Had I been involved in the strike, yes, I would have definitely joined in. In any case, I made many friends with a great number of the flight crews. They were a swell bunch of pilots.

I used to see Mitch every so often when we had some time off. He once mentioned about meeting a wealthy Haitian in Port-au-Prince, Haiti. The individual wanted to start a freight service from there to Miami; He said that PanAm was not doing enough to haul their cargo out of Haiti. So, with another CNAC friend, Austin Young, who had an old Twin Stinson (Bamboo Bomber), we flew to Haiti and met Mitch's friend who was most interested. I was willing to put up $4000 by leasing a C-46; it was the best I could do. The Haitian would form the company with Mitch and myself and would arrange all cargo flights, etc., that was agreed. Austin and I returned to Miami. (A few years later,

I think in 1959, Austin Young flew his Twin Cessna into Havana, just when Castro had come into power. The Cuban authorities took Austin into custody, saying he was a spy. After a quick trial he was found guilty and thrown in jail. My friend Hank Smith of CNAC sent me some Miami news clippings of the incident, and of how Austin escaped from the Cuban jail and found his way back to the states via the US Embassy. A few years later I met Austin in Miami and he told me more of the story and how Cuban jails are used for punishment. Around 1978 Austin Young died of cancer.)

I got a C-46 from a Brazilian company, the same people that would have bought my plane, in Natal. I should have sold it there, but I couldn't look into that crystal ball. I contacted Mitch and said it looked good. Now that we have a 46, let's get our ATP licenses. After passing our written tests, we ventured over to the CAA Flight Standards office, which was on 36th Street, in one of the motels not far from Miami Airways motel. A receptionist told us to go down the hall, where we'd find a CAA Inspector's office and guess who was sitting at the desk, none other than my very old friend Guy "Tommy" Tombelin, from Shanghai and Nanking. It was like old home week again. Yes, he would give Mitch and I a flight check, but first we would have to visit he and his wife, Gertie, in Coral Gables. Next day we flew around for our check flight, and Tom gave us our licenses. I returned to Port-au-Prince with a Hank Smith (Ex CNAC) and set about arranging flights, while our Haitian member was forming the company. The last signature was for the President, duVallier. Then a PanAm Convair 340 arrived, at Haiti with Juan Trippe on board. He had a meeting with the President and informed him the airport was built and operated by PanAm. They did not wish another company operating from that field, that was that. Our Haitian friend was angry that he was not allowed to form the airline. He gladly paid all the expenses that we had accrued in Haiti, the three weeks we were there. Another adventure shot,

thanks to Juan Trippe. He was the man who had pinned my PAA wings on me, back in 1942, now he was pinning one on my behind!

Kiki and I were enjoying Miami; there were so many CNAC friends around. On one occasion, CNAC people held a mini-reunion; I was amazed at how many CNAC characters show up. Another old fellow, named Sol Solenski, of the original CNAC group, who put together the famous DC-2 1/2, had retired and was running a liquor store in Coral Gables. It was almost like being back in Calcutta. I wrote a note to Margaret Miles, to see how she was making out with her acting career. I gave her my hotel in New York. I think we stayed at the Hudson Hotel. She answered that she had some bit parts in the cinemas, and would be in *South Pacific* with Mary Martin. Well, good for her, I thought. I then found myself writing quite often. I liked the young lady, but only as a friend, as I did Sylvia. Jim Hopkins, the same fellow who said, "Check your mags" at Jodpur Airport, on that must go takeoff, had arrived in Miami from Djibouti Airlines in Ethiopia. He hadn't changed, with his fussy hair and one

*Our C-46 that ran off the runway in Amman, Jordan, 1955.*

tooth missing. Jim spoke of the need for a charter company that could be set up in the Middle East, for the Haj traffic; that there was a great deal of Haj movement. Mitch, Jim and I sat and discussed how we could arrange this; I guess you could call us wheelers-and-dealers! Mitch and I felt we were persona-non-grata in Pakistan, but we would take our chances. I went to buy a bottle of scotch from Sol one morning, and happened to mention something about starting a deal for the Haj. Before I could say another word, he immediately informed me that he was interested, and wanted in before anybody else. He said having a store was like being in prison. His wife had a motel somewhere on SW 8th Street that she was happy with, and wouldn't leave. I told Sol I would see. Another National pilot who was interested was a fellow named Ralph Spurlock. He was tired of the furloughs, also, and wanted to join us. From this nucleus of people, we were able to put together a company, but we still had to have a foreign partner to really set it up. We had once met a Jordanian by the name of Munther Bilbasi at the Henry Hudson Hotel, a jovial young fellow who spoke very good English. He was now back in Amman, Jordan. Jim Hopkins said he would be willing to go over and discuss the possibilities of a company, while we would arrange leasing a plane from Miami. Hopkins was in Amman for about a month, with no word. Finally, we got a cable that Bilbasi had formed the company, and called it Jordan International Airlines, with His Majesty, King Hussein's blessing. Sol, Mitch and I scurried around, trying to lease a plane for the operation. No one wanted to lease a plane to go the troubled Middle East. One person finally did, by the name of Spillman, but his C-46 needed an engine change first. If we paid for that, the lease would be cheaper. Sol and I signed the deal. The contract was for a year, renewable. Sol had sold his liquor store and was ready to travel. Another individual I hired was a pilot by the name of Bob Strand. Bob had once flown for Saudi Airlines and Air Djibouti, but his problem was alcohol. Bob promised he was off the stuff and would do a good job of flying. His wife, Susie, was a gem of a girl. She was English, from Nairobi East Africa. I guess they had met when Bob flew there with Air Djibouti. I think she was rather apprehensive about going along but would do so, mainly to look after Bob, to see he toed a straight line and not do any drinking. I put Mitch in charge of the operation, and Sol the management. Ralph and I stayed behind, for the present. We would follow when we received word from Sol and Mitch. We gave them a good sendoff. Kiki took all this in stride, but did not appear to be overjoyed. The flight had arrived safely in Amman, and would be getting ready to operate shortly, for me to stand by. About two weeks later, a telegram arrived from Solinsky. It started with "Heart-break and tears," then went on to say that on taxiing out in Amman Airport, the plane was involved in an accident, so cancel my trip now. A letter followed, giving more details, and a

*Z. Solenski (Sol) with Jordanian police officer, Amman Jordan, 1955.*

picture. Bob Strand was taxiing, and at the end of the taxiway, there is a sharp right turn, before entering the runway, as at most airports. Evidently, Bob was taxiing too fast and had the tailwheel locked so he couldn't make the turn, and ran off the end and slipped down an incline. The only damage was one propeller, and his ego, as he was a personal friend of his majesty, King Hussein, who had come to see them off. There were no C-46 propellers in Jordan, the nearest one was in Cairo. Good old Solinsky to the rescue, and the number one improvisor, as had done with the DC-2 1/2. He was able to put a DC-3 propeller on the C46, Mitch and he ferried it to Cairo, where they installed a C-46 prop. While in Cairo, somehow they were able, or were talked into purchasing another old C-46 that someone had dug out of the sand, owned by an Italian named Giladini. He called himself "Doctor," like a lot of Italians do. After the dust and sand had been wiped off, a new paint job that covered the rusty spots, it looked pretty good, judging by the pictures they sent me. I received a message to come to Jordan. I told Ralph to hold off till the company was really on its feet. Kiki did not wish to come with me. I hitched a ride on Seaboard World Airlines to Frankfurt, then PanAm to Beirut on New Years Day 1955. I thought it would be fairly warm in Beirut, but when I got there, I had a rude awakening. It had been raining and near freezing. All I was wearing was a light sport shirt and linen slacks. I hopped a taxi that took me to the Capitol Hotel in town. Since they were expecting me, a room had been reserved. Around 10 PM I tried calling numbers that Sol had given but there were no answers. I was too tired, anyway, it could wait till tomorrow. The next morning, I was informed that one of the hotel managers knew Sol and Munther. He said they should be at the place called The Eagle Nest Restaurant, where they usually met around 9 or 10 in the morning. I should check with the

restaurant. A taxi took me up the hill to an area called Ras Beirut. The taxi guy spoke English, and was giving me a tour as we went along. When he finally had driven down one of the main streets, known as Rue Hamra, a nice shopping area; we swung down a narrow lane called Jeanne d'Arc, till we came smack against the University of Beirut, a lovely looking place, with gardens and tall cypress firs, and there was the Eagle's Nest. I gave the driver a fair tip for the tour. I noticed that almost all cabs here were black Mercedes. The waiter, dressed in black trousers, white long-sleeved shirt, and bowtie, ushered me in. I was the only one. I asked one of them about my people. "Oh, yes; you're Captain Peter!" "My goodness; how did you know that?" "Well, they talked about you, and you are coming to Lebanon. I'll take you to their apartment." He grabbed another cab. When we got to the end of Hamra Street, there was a small Mosque at one end, and an old apartment building beside it. I guessed that was it, because there we stopped. I got out and the waiter went back to the restaurant. I banged on the door at the ground floor apartment several times. Finally, a bleary-eyed Munther Bilbasi opened the door, still in his pajamas. "How come you guys are still in bed at this hour, when it's a work day?" "Hey!" said Munther. "Pete!" "Yeah." Then he shouted to Solenski to wake up. "Guess who's here?" I followed Munther in. Sol was out of bed, scratching his behind. When he saw me, he jumped up at me and started to hug and wrestle, with tears in his eyes, he was so happy to see me. I also met Munther's younger brother, Mothison who was with them. When everyone was dressed we walked down slowly, towards the restaurant, which was more or less known as the Jordanian International Airlines office. I asked about Mitch and Hopkins. Evidently, there was a feud going on between them. We all sat down, and I was starved; I'd had no breakfast. Munther ordered what he called

141

*Jim Hopkins (Hoppie) on left with two Jordanian employees for our Jordan International Airline, Jordan, 1955.*

"Mazee" sort of Arabic hors d'oeuvres; little dishes of various cooked vegetables in olive oil. This was eaten with Arabic flat bread, which reminded me a lot of our Indian chapatties, only a lot thicker, it was good. I still ordered fried eggs and bacon, and very fresh orange juice. Mitch and Hopkins showed up with another American, by the name of Bill Pierce. He was once with Djibouti Airlines in Asmara. It was nice to see Mitch and Jim. I questioned Mitch about the accident, and how it happened. He said Bob Strand wanted to fly on this particular trip because His Majesty was there to see them off, and they were friends. Bob had a few drinks the night before, which didn't help. Bob was taxiing fairly fast when he came to the 90 degree turn to the right. not only was he going fast, but he'd neglected to unlock the tailwheel. By the time Mitch got on the brakes and took over, it was too late; everything happened in a split second, and they rolled down the side. Luckily not more damage was done than the prop. That was the end of Bob. It was decided he'd better go back to the States. His wife Susan decided to stay on as our secretary. The airplanes we now supported were two C-46s. The one from Miami on lease had plush fitted seats. The other was all-cargo, it had bucket seats. Later Munther took me down town to meet the people who had arranged charters for the gulf states. The company's name was CAT - I'm not sure what that stood for. This was the office Munther and Sol were using for work. I then learned that the price for the charters to the Persian Gulf, mainly Doha, Qatar was hardly enough to pay for the fuel and crew, let alone maintenance and other airport expenses, and the airplane. The charters were full loads of fresh produce, from Lebanon, some from Amman, Jordan. Secondly, the flights had to touch down at Amman before going on to Doha.

I talked to Munther and Sol about this. Their argument was that these flights to the Gulf was to get our foot in the door. Once established, we would then get a better price. Secondly, our main objectives was the Haj. I was skeptical of this, but we would see. Mitch was taking the flights, with Jordanian First Officers. I planned to go with him on the next one down to Jordan, so that I could obtain a Jordanian pilot license. Munther was a great organizer, and said he would arrange everything. In the next few days, we were on our way to Amman. The weather in Beirut and in Jordan could get colder than a well-digger's rump. The flight was about 40 minutes to Amman. It was a clear day, and Mitch showed me points of interest, such as Mount Herman off to our right, most of it was all snow-covered. Off to the left was the Lebanese range of mountains, also snow-covered. The tallest of the range was about 10,000 feet, and is called the Cedars of Lebanon. The lesser lush valleys, with red-roofed homes and green fields, made it look very picturesque. We also crossed Bakka Valley, and a military field of Rayak, and way to the north, just visible, was the ancient ruins of Baal-Bek. We flew over Damascus, and headed south for Amman. At the southern tip of Syria, we flew over the Golan Heights, with the Sea of Galilee to the right, another ancient Roman ruin called Jerrash appeared ahead, still off to the right was the Jordan Valley, and Jordan River. Just visible on the horizon, was the Dead Sea. This was a flight through ancient history, you might say. Mitch now started his descent for Amman. The main runway at Marka Airport runs almost east and west, and is hidden in a valley. We landed to the west and taxiied off to the right at midpoint of the runway, to the terminal area. We went through Customs and Immigration, where the officers were most courteous. I noticed with interest that the police wore a British-looking pith helmet, with spikes on top, a very distinctive appearance - looked almost like the German Emperor's helmet. I was surprised to see that there were several DC-3s parked at the ramp. Some were marked Trans Jordan Airlines, and oth-

ers were marked Arab Airways. How could such a small country as Jordan sustain three airlines? Trans Jordan was American, operated by TransOcean, as they did Pak-Air and Air Djibouti. Arab Wings was a British operated company.

The city of Amman appeared to be very Arab-looking. It was rustic, all buildings were constructed of stone, also a few mosques. Amman has a great history, dating back to Christ, and of course, to the Crusaders. It was once occupied by ancient Romans, and Greeks who called Amman, Philadelphia. The hotel we went to stay in was the Philadelphia Hotel located downtown, near the grand Husseini Mosque, on Mahajareen Street. It was quaint and very cold. After having studied ancient history, then flown across these ancient lands in an hour, and seen all the wonderful ruins and the Biblical spots, such as the Sea of the Galilee and the Jordan River, all these hundreds of miles of country just steeped in history, I thought to myself, even though I stood in the hallway of a fairly modern building, I knew I was standing where "It" all began. After checking in, Munther advised us to get dressed up, that we would be having lunch, usually around 1:30, with His Majesty, King Hussein, and his uncle His Royal Highness Sharif Nasser, And a few other dignitaries from Parliament.

This had been the crossroads for many peoples, such as the Canaanites, the Egyptians, the Persians, the Greeks, Romans, Byzantines, Arabs, Crusaders, Turks, and Nabateans. They have all left their marks on the country, such as their religion, language, and architecture. There I was: a 20th Century invader, a Christian and now I was invited to an official gathering by His Majesty and His Highness, Sharif Nasser. We were taken to Sharif Nasser's palace, where this gathering was taking place. I was introduced to His Highness who spoke excellent English, and was a robust individual, light-skinned, with bluish eyes. A lot of the other guests had arrived, to whom I was introduced. Finally, everyone came to attention as a young person entered. It was His Majesty. I was then introduced to him by his uncle and Munther Bilbasi. There was a large living room, the furniture appeared to be overstuffed, Italian made. We sipped Arabic tea, served in a small glasses. It's very sweet, with mint leaves. The food was brought in and placed on a long dining table, a lot like the mazee I had in Beirut, with many dishes, such as stuffed grape leaves, slices of sheep tongue, hummus (chickpea paste and garlic), baba ganoush (made of eggplant); then there were olives and radishes and onions, tomatoes, and the famous Arabic salad, Tabbouleh. Being hungry, I started to dig in. Munther then said, "Don't eat too much. The main course is yet to come." His Majesty was cornered with some of his officers, I enjoyed talking to Sharif Nasser, who was an avid hunter; we had a lot in common. He said he would like to try tiger hunting one day. I said to give the word, and I'd arrange a trip to Cooch Behar. He was very excited and would like to go.

The main course for dinner arrived. There were two large circular trays, at least two feet in diameter. each tray had a mound of fancy cooked rice with roasted pine nuts, almonds, and fried onions. Stuck in the center of each pile of rice were cooked heads of two sheep, grinning at you, and clustered all around it were pieces of the lamb. Next to the trays were a couple of bowls of specially prepared yogurt, made into a sauce. This sauce is ladled onto the head, and all over the rest of the rice and meat. The dishes are called "Mansif." It is a very special, traditional food of the Bedouins. There were no knives and forks; it must be eaten by hand, but be careful: sometimes that food is fresh off the fire and can be very hot. It was this that we were about to indulge in; I noticed Munther signal something to Sharif Nasser, who nodded. I did not pay much attention. We stood in line, waiting to be served, when His Majesty stepped forward to one of the trays with a plate and started piling on the rice and meat. Then, with his fingers, he reached to the head of one of the lambs that was grinning, and plucked out one of its glazed, blue eyes and plunked that on the rice, as well. Egad! I thought. Is he going to eat the eye? His Majesty, without too much fanfare, came over to me and said, "Peter you are our guest of honor. I've given you this special plate," and then said, "Sathin," which I later learned was "bon appetit," or "good appetite." He then explained that I must eat the eye first, by squeezing a fistful of rice around it. Everyone in the room stopped talking and watched. I was embarrassed, and my mouth went dry. I could have used a scotch. "Thank you, Your Majesty. This is an honor." He gave that wide, straight smile, stood back and watched. I got a hold of the eye, and the damn thing looked right back at me. I quickly rolled a handful of rice around it, and with great effort, I stuck the lot into my mouth and tried to chew. The eye slid from one side of my mouth to the other. Then I carefully, with my tongue, cornered it on my right back grinder, and carefully chomped down. This time, I got it, it squished. I chewed frantically and got it down. Cheers and greetings that I had succeeded. I now knew what Munther had been up to, the rascal. It was after this that His Majesty came over and talked about flying, and wanted to know about the C46s in general. I soon found out he was a flying enthusiast, and a great pilot. I certainly enjoyed meeting him, His Royal Highness and the other Jordanians officials, as well. I can't say too much for the sheep's eye, though. Actually, there was no taste. The rice and yogurt sauce camouflaged it. the dinner feast was over, and very delicious.

The Jordanians are a friendly people. I knew I was going to enjoy being associated with them. The next trip came through. It had been a long time since I had flown the C46. We made the trip to Doha and back. It was agreed, mainly by Munther, that the air-

*Our C-46 in Amman, 1955.*

craft would stay in Beirut for better maintenance. The company was 51% Jordanian. This gave Munther a lot of say, administratively and we would handled the operations. Solinsky thought a great deal of Munther, and went along with whatever Munther said. I think Sol and the crew wanted to stay in Beirut; they could have their "ashes" hauled in that fun city. Beirut, as one individual stated, was "where intercourse had taken the place of the handshake!"

Munther was soon able to arrange most of the cargo at Beirut. We also took on two more local pilots to help. In spite of the small price Munther was accepting for the cargo flights, we were beginning to keep our heads above water. It still could have been better. The crews were not being paid a regular airline salary.

Munther finally found a decent three-bedroom apartment in Beirut, that was located in what was known as the ABC Building, at the corner of Rue Hamra and Jeanne d'Arc Street. It was a ground floor apartment, but we had to rent the furniture. The next door apartment was occupied by a beauty parlor, called Margaret Rose Salon. We got to know the owner, who was a Mrs. Margaret Sutton, and a Lebanese-Mexican girl name Ginny, who helped Margaret Rose. I was spending my time in between Beirut, and Amman. Munther and Sol would join me once in a while. On a stopover in Amman in February, the three of us were invited by His Majesty to be his guests at a Bedouin gathering that would take place across the Jordan River in Jericho Valley. Munther arranged rooms for us at the Winter Palace Hotel in Jericho. As we drove down from Amman and nearing the Jordan Valley, there were cement posts stating how far below sea level we were. The final one was about 1250 feet below sea level; Munther then took a detour and showed us the Dead Sea. We crossed the Alanbery Bridge, that spanned the Jordan River. It was very muddy and full, probably from the rains up north, and the

snow melting up in and around Mt. Herman. The entrance to the hotel was beautiful. The whole area was smothered in red and purple bougainvillea; it almost covered the front of the building. After checking in, we drove over to the ancient city of Jericho. Some American archaeologists were actively excavating the ruins. It was possible to note that there had been a number of cities, one built on the top of the other. The excavation showed about four, at that point. High above the ruins, on the cliffs behind the city, on the west side (part of what is now known as the West Bank), were a cluster of buildings tucked into the cliffs. They were Greek monasteries.

After lunch, we drove to the west side of the Dead Sea, where the Jordan government had built a hotel. The beach was charcoal color, because of the large amounts of lava deposits. Sol and I took off our shoes and socks and dunked our feet the Sea, to say that we had been in it, then returned to the hotel for drinks and dinner.

The Bedouin Gathering with His Majesty would start the next day. Almost every day was clear and beautiful. Munther took us to the campsite. A special one had been fixed up for the Royal party. The Bedouins had their tent city back on the East Bank of the River. His Majesty arrived, and we all sat nearby. Each tribe galloped up to His Majesty's tent on horseback, and fired off their rifles into the air, showing their faithfulness to him, There was also a part of the famed Arab Legion, formed by the ex-British officer, General Glubb. He was known as "Glubb Pasha." The Legion performed a march-by. There was the Desert Legion on camels. They looked resplendent, in their desert regalia, the camel saddles with long strands of colorful cloth tassels. This was quite a spectacle. Sol had his movie camera, and I hope he was getting good footage. His Majesty's magnificent Arabian, all-white stallion was brought forward, but HM didn't ride that day. It was saddled, with fancy tas-

*Beirut International Airport, Lebanon, 1955.*

sels denoting royalty. The Bedouin Tribes rode singly in two or threes, whole tribes, showing their riding skills. The finale was a charge by both sides in a sham war. This was something, as they charged head-on with rifles waving and firing. It resembled the real thing. All this was followed by the tribes playing of drums, groups of Bedouins and spectators, men only, clasping hands in circles, chanted and danced around. Some had knives, pistols, even cartons of cigarettes sticking out of their pockets; what a sight! It continued till late afternoon, and while all this performance was going on, the women-folk were busy scurrying around the tent areas, cooking up the traditional mansif that I have mentioned. Munther said some of the mansif meat was from small camels; maybe so. I knew one thing: I would not be receiving an eye of the sheep or the camel; I was alert!

The festivities were over late that evening, Munther, Sol and I headed back to Amman. I could have stayed and enjoyed another day here in the valley, where Christ was baptized and walked. I told Sol he'd better get the movie developed, so we all could have a look and perhaps get a copy. I don't know if he ever did; I know none of us ever saw the film, and none of us ever got a copy. It was a once in a lifetime occurrence for us.

Back in Amman, I settled back to making flights to the Gulf Area, and give Mitch a spell. Mitch did not appear to get along with Munther and Sol. He and Jim Hopkins seemed to pair off; I was caught in the middle. There appeared to be something amiss with pilots and most people involved in aviation. There were petty jealousies, gossip, how to screw you out of your job, your money, your girlfriend or wife. All this was fomenting in Lebanon with our company and the other local outfits. One of the pilots once said, "You can drink my whiskey, screw my women, but leave my money alone!" How true that is! Well, pretty good philosophy

anyway; if you don't have any money, then you possibly wouldn't have any whiskey, and no woman would want you, either!

By June, I had adapted pretty well to the Beirut way of life. It was a dreamy town on the Mediterranean; it was the Paris of the East, and a "Go-Go" place as well. But it took lots of money to enjoy the nightlife, which was 24 hours a day. As I said, pilots are a strange brood. In Lebanon, there was the Middle East Airlines, with mostly British and a few Lebanese pilots. There was an independent cargo outfit, called TransMediterranean Airlines (TMA). They used British Aircraft called Yorks, 4-engine aircraft. Then there was Air Libon, a 67% owned Air France company. They operated DC-3's and DC-4's. This constituted English, French, American, Lebanese, an assortment of Australian and South Africans, Spanish, Germans and Italians pilots. Each had their "cliques" and special get togethers. There was still some lingering animosity between the German pilots, the English and the French left over from WWII; pettiness again.

Our C-46's operated well, with very little maintenance. I had checked in with our CAA (which is now the FAA) office at the U.S. Embassy, to let the airworthiness people know about the N-registered C-46. They were not too interested and didn't bother us.

Beirut was becoming a most enjoyable place. The sights and shopping were great. Munther took us to many places of interest. The Roman Temple of Baal-Bek was one that I wanted to see most of all; it was a beautiful sight, those granite columns standing 100 feet up in the air. The rose colored granite had been transported all the way from the Aswan in southern Egypt. It is hard to imagine the thousands of slaves it must have taken to transport those monolithic stones along the river Nile, and possibly by sea, to Beirut, through Syria and then across vast stretches of land and mountains. It was awe-inspiring

to see this fantastic ruin. They had no doubt been through many earthquakes, raging battles, and the elements, and still standing.

On the drive back, we stopped at the Lebanese town of Zaleh. This was a gem of a place! It was located at the base of the mountain range that divides the lower lands and sea from the Bakka Valley. It's a little north of the major Beirut Damascus Highway. The town is famous for its Kasara Wine, made by monks in that area, and the fresh fruit and vegetables. Last but not the least are the quaint restaurants that are strung along the main Zaleh stream that splashes down from the high mountains. One or two restaurants straddle the stream. Most of them serve basically the same Lebanese-Arabic dishes, the breeze along the stream keeps the temperature cool. We chose one restaurant and Munther did the ordering. It made no difference; I knew whatever it was, it would be good. A complete mazee was first, all the little dishes that arrived covered the whole table. with it comes the Arab mountain bread: it is flat, whole wheat, made paper-thin, and about two feet in diameter. These are neatly folded, almost like napkins, and placed on the plates. You take one and tear off chunks to eat the mazee. For refreshments, one can order local or imported beer, all kinds of sodas, and the Kasara wine. Then there's Arak, which is a 100-proof alcoholic drink; it takes a special type to drink it; the base and flavor of Arak is anisette. All the restaurants have various brands, and whichever you decide on, will still knock you on your derriere. It comes in all sizes and shapes of fancy bottles, some of them without color or labels. It looks like gin or vodka. However, there's a special method in serving the drink. You pour in the Arak first, then the water, which turns milky; then the ice. Otherwise, it may curdle. You sip it slowly, and not on an empty stomach.

The main course, if you have any room after all the mazee, may be barbecued chicken or lamb, or fried fish. The dessert is fresh fruit, such as grapes or watermelon, apples and apricots, which they call "mish-mish." The meal and chitchat went into late afternoon. Munther didn't like to drive late. The drive is due west on the Damascus road, into the setting sun, and the highway is a narrow two way road. It is up and down hill, with hairpin turns. The Lebanese drivers are always eager to disobey the rules of the road. They drive fast and take their half of the road in the middle. Because of this, there are known to be some horrendous accidents, usually fatal. Munther was aware of this, and drove carefully.

Another interesting place was Biblos, just north of Beirut and Djouneh. Lebanon is the ancient country of Phoenicia. They were known as sailors and traders throughout the Mediterranean. Biblos is a miniature-sized town, the harbor almost enclosed, and was once their capitol. Some ruins still stand. Archaeologist found a burial site. This was evidently for one of the great Phoenician kings. The crypt was a large black granite stone. It still stands and contains all the remnants, and many artifacts. All these were in the Beirut Museum. There is a small amphitheater and a Crusader castle. So many wonderful sights in this small country!

At the northernmost city of Lebanon is Tripoli from there Munther took us up on a long winding motorway, to the Cedars of Lebanon, which is a ski resort and is about 10,000 feet at the top of a mountain. This whole range once had forests of beautiful cedars trees. The Romans, cut them down to build their vast fleet of ships, and to use for their houses and temples. The Ottoman Empire denuded the rest for use of their railroads and fuel. There are just a few trees left, enough to be counted on two hands.

By June, I had settled pretty much to Beirut life. I did not do much in the way of nightclubbing, as some people back home thought. For one thing, I didn't have the money. I got to know some French folks who lived up the hill from Beirut, A place called Bietmari, a very quiet town, surrounded by pine forests. At the top of the mountain, there was once a Roman city; some of its ruins remain. A Roman Catholic church has been built over the ruins. This French couple often went excavating in and near the ruins. They showed me a few artifacts they had found. I got interested and went with them on occasions, But I never found a thing.

Munther came to me one day after one of my Doha trips, and said there was a special trip he wanted to me to take. There was a load of cargo for His Highness Sharif Nasser from Rome to Amman. He wanted to know if I could make it non-stop. I said yes, if the winds and general weather conditions were favorable. I had a Jordanian First Officer, Jim Hopkins, and Munther with me. At Rome we stayed at Hotel Boston. Munther arranged the loading of the cargo, which turned out to be guns and ammunition (I think for the Jordanian police)! Within a couple of days, we were airborne, at midnight.

Munther returned by an airline. The flight went well for most part. As we passed Athens, clouds started build up, we skirted to the south, and climbed to 11,000 feet we had no deicing equipment, and no heat. We remained up there for quite awhile, By the time we passed Cyprus, the fuel was down more than I would have liked. When we were approaching Beirut, I decided we'd better get more fuel, I canceled the flight plan for Amman and landed at Beirut. I told Customs we were destined for Amman, we only needed fuel. However, they insisted they look at the cargo manifest. Their eyes popped when they discovered the load was guns and ammo. I called Munther to take over and straighten out the matter. I was too tired now to continue. It had taken Munther a couple of hours for the clearance and got the other pilot to finish the flight. I later learned that there was also a ruckus at Amman, when the load had arrived there, even though His Royal Highness was there to meet the flight.

I kept in touch with Spurlock and explained what was going on. I advised against

*Bedouins staging a mock battle for His Majesty King Hussein of Jordan, 1955.*

coming out, since I wasn't sure which way the airline would go. Out of nowhere, my good friend Jack Brown arrived in Beirut, he said that Jordan International had not been paying the lease on the Miami C-46, I cornered Munther and Sol, asked about the payments. Sure enough, a couple to three payments were overdue. Jack was willing to cooperate and try to get things worked out. He was representing Spillmans C-46. About a month later, however, it looked like the payments would not be met, I suggested the plane be flown back to Miami. Jack found a crew to ferry the plane. Sol went back also, disheartened.

Munther got another Lebanese man into the company; that was to be the beginning of the end. By August, I saw no hope. Mitch hung on and I threw in the towel, and was ready to return to Miami. I was in Beirut when one of the French/Lebanese friends asked if I would like to fly for the local airline, Air Liban; I was introduced to their Technical Manager, a Captain Lanata.

He was a little round-face individual, with a half burned cigarette always hanging out of his mouth. He didn't speak any English, even if he did, I don't think I'd understand it, since the cigarette was always interfering. Through a Lebanese employee named Suade, I gave a verbal resume of who I was and where I'd come from. I said I'd not flown a DC-3 for over five years but had about 6000 hours in the plane. "Never mind," Lanata said; he wanted me to fly right now, on a flight to Jerusalem. It was one of their scheduled routes. I knew Jerusalem Airport, and would give it a try. It was a morning flight with Lanata, the passengers were already loaded. I said I must first make my walk around of the airplane. He was astounded. "Walk around?" I said, "Yep." So I did my check, with the mechanic watching, I found two of the fuel tank sumps were not safety-wired, and made the mechanic safety them. I then climbed aboard into the left seat, with Lanata in the right, he still had that cigarette in his mouth. I looked around the cock-

pit, everything was written in French. The pilot who's place I'd taken, a Frenchman, spoke English pretty well. His name was Jacques Berje. Lanata was in a rush to get going. I think he was getting upset with me taking so long. I told Jacques Berje I had to familiarize myself, and for Lanata to be patient. He wanted to use a checklist. I made him wait while I did my visual check. He was surprised that I remembered so much, French or no French. We finally got started and taxiied out to runaway 21. The weather was good, so we went VFR. After take off I circled over the sea and back over Beirut and the mountains to Damascus, the route I'd always taken before. Lanata said to use the autopilot; I said no, I wanted to get used to the controls by hand-flying it. Jerusalem Airport was not that easy, because of the tricky crosswinds. I hope the reader understands that most of Jerusalem and all of the west Bank belonged to Jordan. It was not till the 1967 war Jordan lost that territory. I did get the plane down safely, We went into the small Terminal and had turkish coffee while Lanata smoked his cigarettes. Jacques Berje said Lanata was pleased with my flying and I did the same flight back, with one difference: on take off from Jerusalem, I made certain I did not fly over any Israeli territory. During these days, part of the old city was Israeli territory; the rest of the city belonged to Jordan.

The trip was routine. Lanata then turned to me and said, "Bon!" and gave a thumbs-up indication I was hired. It was now necessary for me to head to the office downtown to sign a contract and have a uniform made. I also obtained my Lebanese license, and got the medical from a Dr. Zabouni, CAA (FAA) designated examiner in Beirut. I'd written to Ralph, and explained the debacle of the company. I'd also told Kiki of the problems, she suggested I return to Miami. I was in the process of doing so, when I got the job with Air Liban. I planned to write her when I was certain this job was a secure one. I thought she would love Beirut.

*His Majesty's white stallion at bedouin gathering in Jerico, Jordan Feburary, 1955.*

I got my new uniform, my medical, and all pertinent papers accomplished to start flying for the company, As far as Capt. Lanata was concerned, I had my airplane and route check on the DC-3, and was now placed on Air Liban's schedule. The scheduled DC-3 flights were Beirut-Jerusalem-Beirut in the morning, then Beirut-Nicosia Cyprus-Beirut in the afternoon. This would be varied by flying Beirut-Alipo, the ancient capitol of Syria, then back to Beirut and Nicosia in the afternoon.

All that the Lebanese staff knew was that an American was flying for the company. Most of my crew were Lebanese, once in a while, I had an Italian or a Spaniard co-pilot. After getting my feet wet with the company and felt at home in the DC-3, I flew some midnight flights to Baghdad and Kuwait. It broke the usual Jerusalem-Nicosia monotony. I started meeting some of the crew members, mainly the German pilots. They were most friendly: Captain Steele, Captain Meyer, and Captain Bremer. It was Meyer who approached me one day and said he was leaving the company to join Lufthansa, in Frankfurt; he and Steele. He wondered if I would like to take over his little apartment, and furniture. I looked the apartment over, and made the deal; I was happy to have a small place to myself. I was tired of hotel life. The apartment was on the 5th floor penthouse, with an elevator. It had a large porch with a panoramic view of Ras Beirut, the mountains, and the Mediterranean. The place sported one bedroom, bathroom, a good size living room, and kitchen.

Mitch stayed on with Jordan International, and my old friend Ray Gifford joined Mitch. In the fall, around October, I had a caller: Jack Brown and his wife, Cora. Jack had been given a contract to organize the Saudi-Arabian Airforce in Jeddah. However, he wanted a place in Beirut for his wife. Capt. Steele had left for Frankfurt; his place was next to mine,

and was vacant, so Jack took it. How nice to have a friend around the corner. Beirut, it seemed, was beginning to gather my friends from around the world. Bob Bethel came to fly for Arab Airways, in Amman, old CNAC hands like Gibby Gibson showed up from Acapulco, Mexico; then there was Jim Moore, "Indian Jim," the elusive individual who disappeared via Hanoi and Bangkok. He must have done well, he planned to build a hotel off Rue Hamra in Ras Beirut; he was to call it the Commodore Hotel. Then there was Hank Lambert, who was flying for Aramco. Then Maupin and McEdwards. There were so many of the old CNAC gang, it was like old Calcutta days. We even had our own little reunion. Then, here came, Babs Huang, George Huang's wife who was now working for the United Nations, and was based in Amman, On top of all this, who flew in but none other than Cooch Behar himself. This was unreal! Word must have been getting around about Beirut being the Paris of the East.

Once I was informed that my job was secure, I sat down and wrote Kiki a long letter, to make plans to come to Beirut. I had arranged tickets on Air France. The response I received was on the cool side, with a little hint of negativity. On top of that, she informed me that she had been in a car accident and destroyed the Buick and someone's front porch. I wrote a couple more letters, and the response was cold and her final letter came, that she had no intention of coming to the Near East or Far East to be chief cook and bottle washer for me and my drunken friends. I wrote again, insisting that she come out; I didn't believed what she had written. I told her the tickets were still ready for her, all the way from Miami. This time, there was no uncertain terms in her tones: she wanted out, a divorce. I had hoped that Kiki could sell the house, and be happy in Beirut. No such thing. She was accusing me of chasing around with B-girls; I

wasn't. I was flying hard, with little time off, which I spent with my German friends, Moritz Bremer and his delightful wife, Inga. I felt someone was feeding Kiki a lot of misinformation. Kiki was adamant; the divorce papers arrived at the Embassy for me to sign. This time, there was no Dorothy to get involved with. After all the correspondence with Kiki, the terse replies and accusations about my behavior in Beirut, I felt she wanted out. I signed on the dotted line.

I went to my little penthouse, poured a healthy scotch and soda, sat down on the porch and stared out over the Mediterranean, that glittered and laughed at me. I sat silent and pondered to myself: was I really a dirty bastard? Should I have dropped everything and returned to Miami and picked up the pieces and started all over with National Airlines? Somehow, I wanted to return, but there appeared to be no future with the airline, with its furloughs. Here, I had all my friends, the country was beautiful, the flying was exciting, every flight was an international one. Perhaps I wasn't looking beyond my nose. I was trying to feel sorry for myself, but I don't think I was really being selfish. Perhaps I was muddled up. I loved America, and everything about it. I also felt the same about the Middle East and Far East. Especially when it is where you were born and raised, and to spend so many years flying in the same areas. One could say I was "torn between two worlds."

I went about my flying, and one day, Lanata asked me to go with him on the DC-4 to Cairo and back. I hadn't been in a DC-4 for quite a while. He wanted me to get some training for a future checkout. I accompanied him on the flight to Cairo and back. The second flight I took was to dead-head with Lanata on the DC-4 that left late Saturday afternoon, nonstop to Khartoum. From there, it was a night hop to Fort Lamy, Chad. The old days of Pan Africa and the Canadian Club came back to me. Lanata was surprised I knew this part of the world. Then we operated the flight from Ft. Lamy, to Kano, Lagos, Accra, Ghana, and the old places came rushing back; Coutenau and Abidjan, Ivory Coast. Here the crew had lunch at the airport restaurant. I was enjoying every minute. To the crew, I was explaining my Pan Africa days on the DC-3s, how we had to skirt around this country, as it was then German-Controlled under Vichy French. Lanata nodded, knowingly. I then learned he had been a prisoner-of-war with the Japs, in Hanoi. I told him that I was flying there, right after the war, with CNAC, from Kunming. Maybe our paths crossed somewhere. Lanata never appeared to smile much, more of a dead pan, but now he lit up, we got along just fine. That evening, about 8 p.m., we touched back at Fort Lamy. The next crew took over while Lanata and myself deadheaded back to Beirut, early in the morning. I was not tired when I got back to my apartment. I just sat on the porch and thought of the trip and the visits to all the old haunts that I knew in 1942, and especially Accra. It hadn't changed much. I felt drowsy and went into rest; I guess I fell asleep. I woke up with a start; it was cold, and I still had on my uniform. There was a knock on the door; it was Jack Brown. Jack was a tall, heavyset individual, with a crew haircut, and always wore a smile. He and his wife Cora invited me over to their apartment, across the hall. I took a quick shower, and changed to warmer clothes. It gets very cold in Lebanon in the winter months, especially in the evenings. Over drinks, I told them about my trip to Africa, how exciting it was to return to the old places I knew. It was after midnight before I got to sleep.

Most every day is beautiful, in this part of the world. The morning was bright and clear. I made my tea, and sat outside. I felt relaxed and content to be here. I guess my mind had been wandering over the past, probably because of my Africa trip. I was thinking of China, and CNAC, the days of Cooch Behar. My mind was bursting with myriad images of past events; all of a sudden I was back in London with Cactus and Mitch. I was thinking of those fun days, Then Margaret flashed in front of me again, I wondered if she had success in her theatrical world, whether she was married or not. I'd not written her for over a year-and-a-half. I remembered her as being very pretty, innocent and full of fun. I thought I might as well forget it; she must be married, or on her way to stardom. What the hell; there were so many pretty things right here in Beirut. Get to know a few and forget Margaret and Kiki!

That afternoon, I went over to see Moritz Bremer they had just moved to a new apartment. Inga now had a new baby boy. Moritz was a lot of fun and I think I wanted company, just to talk about some of the old days and the fun that we used to have. It turned out that Moritz and the other German pilots had been with the Luftwaffe, fighter pilots on Messerschmitts 109s, during WWII. He had shot down several B-17s, and had been in major dogfights with the RAF and USAF. Moritz and his buddies were the first to fly the German jet fighters, the 62s, he said that if Hitler had continued building these jet fighters, the Luftwaffe would have raised havoc with the bombers that were hitting Germany, and possibly could have knocked the bombing missions out. But Hitler didn't pursue this ultimate weapon. He was bound to make jet bombers. When defeat was in sight, Moritz and his friends gave up and crossed the line and surrendered to the Americans. When released, they went to Syria to train the Syrian Air Force, at Alipo. From there, they came to Beirut and joined Air Liban. They were great fellows. They spoke very good English, German, French, and some Arabic.

One morning I was busy writing letters to the states, when I got the urge to drop Margaret a line. It was just a casual note to say I was in Lebanon, flying, and had given up my position in Miami, that I was now divorced and wanted to know how she was doing after this long silence, and whether or not she was married. I mailed it to her old address, not knowing if she was still living there; it was an address in Kensington. I'd just about forgotten that I had written when one day I received a response from Margaret. Yes, she was surprised to hear from me, she was still getting along, and was no longer at the Embassy Club, but was doing a great deal of stage work, and on one occasion had a bit part in a movie called *Charley's Aunt* with Ray Bolger. The last paragraph was most interesting: Margaret said that she had a vacation coming up, and was planning to take her mother to Rome. Could we meet there? I checked with the chief pilot's office, and asked if I could have a week off, and possibly request a free ticket on Middle East Airlines that had just opened its schedule to Rome with Viscounts. Lanata okayed my request. I ripped off a cable, asking her the date of arrival, airline, etc. I was in Rome at Fiumicino Airport, when I met British European Airways (BEA) flight that came from Nice. As she walked off the flight, I recognized her immediately, more grown up and beautiful. I noticed her mother had not accompanied her; she had stayed in Nice. We met after she got through customs, there was so much to talk about. It was difficult to know where to start. First, she chewed me out for not writing. At that point, I said, I was trying to make a go of my life with Kiki, who did not wish me to write to other women, and rightly so, even with Sylvia, who happened to be a lifelong friend and someone I could always confide in and often did. She had become a Doctor of Psychology. I guess I was forgiven; Margaret didn't pursue the subject further. Instead, she asked about Lebanon and my work, and about Cooch Behar, whom she had met in London with me. Margaret had been studying singing, and was looking forward to being in *South Pacific* with Mary Martin. I thought that great for her. She would know as soon as she returned to London whether she'd get the part. Meantime, I had arranged rooms at the Hotel Boston, right off the upper end of the Via Veneto, in the heart of Rome. It was a wonderful week, and we covered just about everything that Rome had to offer, including Alfredo's with his golden spoon and fork, presented to him by Mary Pickford and Doug Fairbanks, Sr. The movie we enjoyed most was "Three Coins in a Fountain," and afterward we had to go and drop in a few coins ourselves. Before I knew what happened, the week seemed to vanish. The night before departure, Margaret wished that we spend it together in her room. She didn't have to persuade me.

Margaret's flight left the day before mine. I wish I could have tucked her into my suitcase and taken her with me to Beirut. I spent that evening at the downstairs restaurant called Tonnello's. They served fine Italian food, and good wine. The next morning I was on my way back to Beirut, but Rome had a fond spot in my heart.

# PHASE SIX: 1956-1962

I had no sooner arrived back when I was asked by Operations to take a special flight to Saigon. An Air France Constellation had lost an engine and was grounded there. Air Liban had a DC-3 cargo plane equipped especially for such operations. A spare engine was loaded aboard the DC-3, and the next day, I was on my way East. Again, it was like old times. I was a little worried about landing in Karachi. I had not been there since I absconded with my C-46 in 1951, this was now early 1956. At Karachi, I took time off to visit people concerned with Crescent Air Transport. They informed me that the company went out of business soon after I left. One of the Pakistanis said I should have taken the DC-3, as well. They knew the company was mine, and were sorry it didn't work out better.

We made the usual stops along the way, including Calcutta, and Bangkok, then Saigon. This was my first trip to the city, and it reminded me a bit of Hanoi, on a larger scale. Air France had put us up at the Hotel de Commerce, where we had a couple of days rest before heading back. I spent an extra day in Calcutta, and saw a few of my old friends. Cooch Behar was not there. I did see Boris, who was buying things for Kathmandu, Nepal, and some of the Russian friends. They never forgot all that good vodka I used to bring them from Shanghai. My old piano playing friend, Sonny Lobo, was still performing at the Princess Nightclub, run by the Grand Hotel. The rest of the journey was routine, before long, I was trucking on down the Airport of Beirut. At operations, I advised them of the trip, and was informed that Captain Lanata was pleased with it. I checked my mailbox and found a telegram. It was from Margaret; the message read: "Dear Peter: It's Leap Year, will you marry me? If not, please send pair of gloves, size 9." Signed: Margaret. I was treading on air.

On the way back to the apartment, I asked myself if I was doing the right thing, if I should say yes. Margaret was a city and theatrical person. How would she take to this roguish life of mine? Though we had discussed each other's lives in the short time we had been together in Rome, I knew she didn't really know me that well. Whatever argument I gave myself against marriage, it was overshadowed by the fact that she was a lovely person. Real issues were pushed aside in my mind. By the time I reached the apartment and had a scotch in my hand, I was already concocting a reply to Margaret's telegram. I sat at my little bar, which I was decorating with hotel labels from my travels, and roughed out a telegram to send to her. The answer was: "Dear Margaret: Sorry, there are no size 9 gloves in Beirut, so I'll have to marry you." More telegrams and letters swished back and forth. She wanted to know about the apartment, the size of the bed, the date set for her coming to Lebanon, and I arranged tickets on PanAm. I made certain the PanAm cabin crew, based in Beirut, would be on her flight to look after her. I visited the Episcopal Church and Church of England in Beirut, and was informed by the Minister that the church would gladly marry us. I don't know how I was able to keep flying and also check out on DC-4s with Lanata. However, it was accomplished.

Perhaps it was on one of our night flights to the Persian Gulf area. I'd taken off to the south with Lanata, to fly south overhead checkpoint Sidon, and make a 180 degree turn to the right, and come over Beirut BOD at 10,000 feet, then head for Damascus and the Gulf. The weather was nasty and rough, with thunderstorms. As I headed north towards BOD, a bolt of lightning struck the No. 1 engine and set it on fire. I was able to feather the prop and discharge the $CO_2$ immediately. The reflex actions were quick, by the time Lanata got the checklist, the fire was out. We came back in and landed at Beirut. Somehow, this impressed the old man, he said I was checked out, that I should take

*A mini CNAC reunion in Beirut, 1957.*

148

the delayed flight out early in the morning, after the engine had been checked safe to fly. Captain Lanata didn't go with me. I was happy to know I was on my own.

Time goes fast. The next thing I knew, Margaret had arrived on PanAm as prearranged, and had been well looked after by my PanAm crew. During the interim, I had purchased a secondhand German made Borgward car. It was a great to have wheels again, not spend all the money on taxis and depend on other people for transportation. Margaret looked beautiful as she walked through Customs. Though I knew Customs quite well, from all my comings and goings, they proved extra polite to Margaret, and let her through without any checking. I was aghast at the amount of things she had brought with her. She said the crew had helped get the extra baggage on board. There must have been a ton! It took two of the porters' cartloads to haul all the load to the parking area; in fact, I had to get a taxi to carry some of the load, which followed me to the apartment. Needless to say, I thanked the crew ever so much for their help, they were invited to the wedding that would take place towards the end of May 1956.

During the drive back to the apartment, Margaret was excited about all the strange sights she saw, such as donkeys, sheep on the streets and the continued honking of car horns. The main boulevard from the airport passed through a large grove of pine forests. I think they were planted at the time of the Ottoman Empire. Her eyes goggled at the sight of the beaches and the sea. She said in her English way that she hoped to "catch the sun," meaning to get a suntan. The taxi driver helped get the baggage up to the apartment by using the lift or elevator several times, I prayed it wouldn't quit, as the darn thing was temperamental. I thanked the driver for his extra service, and gave him a good tip. We were alone, except for the mountain of baggage in the middle of the main room. Margaret had a unique laugh of her own; she didn't laugh out loud. It was inward, as if she were inhaling excessively. It's hard to explain, but it was different. There she stood, with the mountain of stuff around, and her laugh. When she quieted down, I gave her a tour of our future home, which didn't take long. Margaret went around the few rooms, mentally redecorating them. She had several lamps and lampshades, a couple of curtains, and loads of towels and bedsheets, and myriad of other things for the kitchen and bathroom. First in order was to replace the old sheets of mine, with brand new ones from England.

Margaret admired the scenery from our balcony. She thought the apartment was small, and had several shortcomings, such as heat, but it was worth the difference. I truly hoped she would be happy, having now stepped into a completely different world, one that she had never experienced before. You write, you describe, and you send photographs of a habitat, but cannot give it the third or fourth dimension, which includes the noise and the smells.

*Christmas Bar-B-Q with a lot of help. Myself, Jim Moore, Maupin and Gibson. All CNAC in Lebanon, 1955.*

May 25th arrived, and we were married in the Episcopal Church of Beirut. Not too many people were present, just our immediate friends, and a couple from the PanAm cabin staff.

Margaret did not wear an elaborate wedding gown, but instead what she called a "tea-dress" with a large brimmed hat. She looked stunning. A reception followed at the Capitol Hotel, where everyone enjoyed kissing the bride. It was a wonderful day, and I wanted to forget the past. I had already been informed that I was to take my turn of duty on the trip down to Fort Lamy at Chad, that I would be based there for a month of June. I told Margaret she could stay here or come with me to Chad. There was no question about it; she was coming with me! The next week we spent getting hot weather safari clothes for her. A friend of mine, an American, had a Winchester rifle that I could use. Though Margaret had been staying with me prior to our marriage, there now seemed to be a new light in our life as man and wife. There was no way to pinpoint that change, but it was there. One thing I knew: I loved her even more, if that were possible. We soon had our safari paraphernalia all packed and ready to go. No matter what she wore, Margaret looked just grand. What else can an actress be? The flight left Saturday afternoon, and the DC-4 churned its way south, skirting widely past Israel and over the shores of Cairo, along the Nile and into Khartoum. My crew and I were deadheading, Margaret was a passenger. She was enjoying the new experience, and wondered if it would be the same at Fort Lamy, which is what I call the belly-button of Africa. I don't know how she could take to the presky hole, especially during the hottest months, I had my finger crossed.

From Khartoum, we headed west, the same old route of Pan Africa days, only this was at night. The flight touched down on schedule, around midnight. There was a great deal of activity off-loading. Everyone was speaking French. What didn't help matters much was the attraction of every kind of bug, beetle, and insect in creation, to the floodlights at the ramp. I thought I'd take Margaret off and let her have her first look at what was to be home for a month. It was quite a walk from the plane to the terminal, I watched her expression as the bugs and creepy-crawlies exploded as we stepped on them during the walk. At the terminal, we were greeted by my friend, Raymond Poezavara, a French man. He was the technician for the airport, for the French Government. I'd met Raymond on my previous flight. He was a hunter, and planned to take us on hunting trips. I'd brought him some cartridges for his shotgun, and loads of fresh vegetables and fruit. His eyes popped when he saw Margaret. The first Officer, a Lebanese, had wandered off to fetch the flight plan and weather. Raymond didn't speak a word of English. I could get along with my few words of French. There were bugs and beetles flying and crawling in the terminal, but Margaret appeared not to notice them. She was taken up with the hubbub of the people racing around. Raymond was all set to take Margaret back to the hotel. However, she wanted to continue the flight with me, We would see Raymond and his family the next day.

It was around 0200 in the morning when our flight was called. Raymond had managed to get the booty I brought him through Customs; they were French, also. He was happy, and we'd meet later. Though I had dead-headed to Fort Lamy, I was weary, and certainly not ready to make another full day of it, but it had to be. I looked at the weather over Kano and Lagos, our first two stops. It was usually overcast and rainy at this time of the year around Lagos and the West African Coast but the weather wasn't too bad. Margaret sat in the cockpit, after it became daylight, and I pointed out points of interest,

*Krak des Chevaliers, a well preserved Castle.*

*More of the ancient city of Baal-Bek, Lebanon.*

especially around Accra and Abidjan. At Abidjan we had lunch at the terminal restaurant as I had before with Lanata. It was run by the French, and the food was excellent. I tried to keep my Lebanese crew to refrain from drinking wine with their meal; however, this was a habit of the cockpit crews, drinking while on duty! This was something learned from the French pilots who flew for the company. As the French say, when they drink wine while on duty, it is nothing but French Coca-Cola! Margaret was intrigued by all this.

After lunch and a short rest we made our scheduled stops back to Fort Lamy. We touched down about 8:00 p.m. local time, and I was exhausted. I think I could have slept on a yogi bed, the one with spikes. The Hotel du Pac was anything but a 5-star affair. We had checked in that Sunday evening and were assigned a double room. We dumped all our belongings in the middle of what appeared to be the bedroom, but I didn't see any beds. The colored bellboy, who didn't

speak English, tried to inform us that all the beds were placed out in the courtyard, where it was cooler, as there was no air conditioning in the hotel. One of the crew members did all the explaining to us, Margaret decided, that she would unpack and arrange our clothes in the bedroom. I first got all the musty closets open. I had brought along bug spray and gave the place a good going over; I didn't want any of those large tarantulas crawling around my neck, or anywhere else. I left Margaret and joined the others at the bar. The crew drank their wine or pernoid, and I had my scotch. Margaret joined us shortly, but did not drink anything stronger than orange squash. We were very tired and headed for the beds that were strung out in rows in the courtyard. There must have been about 50 of them. Margaret and I first went to our room to clean up and change to our nightclothes. She started to snicker and giggle. "What's so funny?" I asked. "How are we going to arrange this? We're on our honeymoon!" Well, one thing for sure; we were not going to put on a sideshow for the hotel guests, knowing the French. One crew member was an Armenian fellow, a nice, tall guy who spoke pretty good English. I asked him which beds were which; he said he would find out. He came back with one of the managers, a French woman who was also giggling. It was fairly dark in the front yard where our beds were. However, she directed us to two single beds off to one side, and in broken English said these were ours. As I looked closely, the two single beds had been tied together, but still had separate mosquito nets over them. I also noticed they had decorated the bed posts on the mosquito nets with ribbons. Then the girl ran off, giggling. There was not much in the way of lighting, thank goodness, because this kept the flying insects away. I peeked under the bed with my flashlight and found a bell tied to the springs. We had a laugh over it. I finally got Margaret tucked away under the mosquito netting, and I crawled into mine. I was terribly tired; it was

only moments before I was sound asleep. Even if the environment were just so, I'm afraid my batteries were too run down at that point. Sorry, my French friends; no peep show tonight!

The early morning hours arrived quickly, and with them, the boiling sun over the horizon. We retreated to our room, not too far off and got ready for breakfast. No matter what Margaret wore, she always looked pert and cute. In her rough clothes, she was a delight. We walked into the small restaurant attached to the hotel; my crew was already there. We were invited to join them, but before doing so, I went over to the French lady who had ushered us to our beds last night. I took out the bell, rang it loudly, and plunked it on her table. I guess all the people were told of the trick, since there was a howl of laughter. It appeared now we were accepted as one of the clan. Most of the hotel guests were men; they all wanted us to join their tables. However, we stayed with our crew and enjoyed a leisurely, French-style brunch. A group of us took a short walk along the Chari River, just behind the hotel. This is the main river that runs through Chad from the lake. It was a very short walk, as the heat was getting intense. Margaret obtained a few postcards that she mailed off to her family. She said, "This will shock'em!" The cards were of African girls, all of whom were topless, with nothing but a G-string and a few beads!

That evening Raymond and his wife Paulette came over and insisted we join them for dinner. Remember, they spoke no English. I was able to understand the gist of the conversation. Margaret and I climbed in the back of the jeep and Raymond drove us to his place. They had a simple bungalow, and no air conditioning either, but did have several fans whirling.

The furnishings were comfortable. The servant brought ice and a large jug of French red wine, probably Beaujolais. The four of us sat at the table and stared at each other, waiting for some kind of conversation. Then their two children came barging in. They were two boys: Jean Francois and Ellan. Jean was about 15, and Ellan about 12. They spoke a little English, so we started from there. Raymond was interested in hunting. He and I and the boys discussed the possibilities. He brought out his rifle and shotgun for me to look at, and informed me that I had to get a license that he would arrange. Raymond arranged his work hours so he could take us hunting early in the mornings, before it got too hot. On one occasion I shot a reed buck in a fairly wooded area. Margaret had asked about snakes, and was told that there were some, but never seen, because, during the hot weather they lay in small caves, or hidden under grass or logs. As we sat on some rocks and drank water and ate a few crackers; from the corner of my eye I caught a movement at some distance in a tree. I slowly moved my sight past Margaret's shoulder, and looked in the direction that I had seen the movement, from the crotch of the tree, about 20 feet up, a large black snake appeared and started sliding down the main bole. I didn't wish to upset Margaret, because she had a mania about snakes. I casually took Raymond's rifle and pointed it at the sky and at the ground, and then aimed at the reptile, it was near the ground. I fired a shot at the snake, and it vanished. It was a large cobra. Margaret was not prepared for the shot, and asked in anger what I had meant by firing the rifle so close to her. I then broke down and said that I'd shot at a cobra. Raymond had seen it when I shot, he raced over to the tree, but there was no sign of it anywhere. When Margaret realized I was telling the truth, she was more furious. She realized that snakes were indeed around, it hadn't been long that she had gone to "spend a penny" behind one of these trees! We tried to cheer her up, that this was a rare incident, but she wouldn't have any of it. I got the silent treatment on our way back to the jeep. I noticed her peering in all directions as we drove.

I soon had my hunting license, and Raymond allowed me to use his jeep and extra gun for our friend to use. It was great, getting out early in the morning and seeing so much wildlife. I didn't shoot anything that moved; we chose the game mainly for our friends at the hotel, and Raymond. The houseboy took a share back to his village; nothing went to waste. Margaret got over her snake episode, even though I did get a dirty look, once in a while. Raymond and Paulette were most kind. They realized the predicament of the hotel and lack of privacy at night by having to sleep outside in the front yard. They insisted we have our lunches and dinner with them, which included the afternoon siesta in one of the boys' rooms. So our tete-a-tete was accomplished away from the hotel, to the chagrin of our hotel friends. Being with the Poezavaras, and able to go hunting, or just to see the wildlife, was wonderful, I knew Margaret was enjoying it. Otherwise, there would have been a terrible boredom, stuck at the hotel and nowhere to go. If Margaret had been teed off at me about the snake, I could hardly imagine how she would have felt by the second week, with nothing to do and no place to do it!

The Lebanese crew were happy. They had found a few Lebanese families living in Ft. Lamy. The Air Liban route from Beirut across Africa and its West Coast, was one of their most lucrative runs. There were hundreds of Lebanese families scattered across Africa and along the west coast. These people were in every conceivable business; their family ties were still in Lebanon. The airline was their link, perhaps a throwback from the ancient Phoenicians. One evening Margaret and I were invited, with the crew, to have a Lebanese dinner at home of one crew's friend. Considering Ft. Lamy, this family had a nice home. The dinner and drinks was outdoors in the backyard. The weather was clear and hot with brilliant stars overhead.

Though most of the Lebanese spoke some English, French and Arabic was the native tongue. The chatter was in Arabic, we felt we might be back in Lebanon. The food was Lebanese with Toubuleh, Homos and

*Margaret visiting Tivoli Gardens outside of Rome, Italy, 1955.*

*Margaret and my wedding in Beirut, Lebanon 1956. With our friends the Neffs.*

Mazza-Mansaf with the traditional drink of Arak. Other Lebanese arrived and wound up with quite a gathering. Margaret became the center of attraction which she enjoyed. When there was a chance, I asked some of the guests, if they ever knew of an Iraqui or perhaps a Jordanian, who once, long ago back in 1942, had business here in Ft. Lamy, and wound up with a near boat load of Canadian Club whiskey. The guy had a hard time trying to sell it off. For a second there was a surprised silence. "Yes," one said. "He is here still; you know him?" "Yes, in a way. Where could I find him?" "Don't worry; we'll get him for you." He shouted to his friend across the way and said I knew so and so, whatever the man's name was. "You were here in 1942?" they asked. "Yep, I was and I bought some of his whiskey." The host told his servant to run and fetch Mr. so and so. It would be some time before in walked Mr. Canadian Club himself. The conversation stopped

and I was confronted with him, I greeted the gentleman in Arabic; "Masal khair," which, I think means "Good Evening." He responded and that was about as far as I could go with that! I would never have recognized CC after fourteen years. We sat and talked in English about the Canadian Club. He laughed and said, "Yes, I remember the whiskey well. It had not been what I had ordered. It had mixed up and was a big mistake. It was necessary to sell the stuff for whatever I could get." "It was a great break for us," I said. "Many of us PanAfrica pilots stopped by for a case of two." He remembered it well and thanks to the pilots he was able to dispose of a good amount of it. It was another great evening, and the four week stay in Fort Lamy rolled by quickly. Margaret always accompanied me on the Sunday flights that I took to Abidjan. It was a relief to get away, and to enjoy the food at the airport restaurant. Raymond and Paulette Poezavara were

*Margaret and dead hyena-Chad, 1956.*

great company, we were sad to leave. The day arrived, when we got on board Air Liban flight and headed back to Beirut, the honeymoon in Chad was over. The Poezavaras were to remain everlasting friends. He has long since retired. The family now lives in the town of Blois, on the Loire River, famous for its wine.

Margaret and I settled back to a normal, routine life in the small penthouse apartment. Lebanon was a world of many types of people, very cosmopolitan. This gave Margaret the chance to meet and make friends. The Bremers were some of her favorite, and through them, we met another lovely German couple, by the name of Knemeyer, Lutz and Elizabeth. Lutz had the agency of the German car firm of Borgward, and they had two young boys, Joachim and Thomas. In November, Margaret had to return to England to finish her contract. I was going to miss her for the next few months. It would be the end of March of 1957 before she would return. During the interim, I did as much flying as I could, I was able to change my schedule with another pilot, and return to Fort Lamy for a month. The winter season there was much nicer. It was a few degrees cooler, and great hunting. I brought along a lot of goodies for the Poezavaras and a French English dictionary. This would help in our conversations. One evening the three of us, Paulette, Raymond and myself, sat around their table sipping Beaujolais wine and Raymond said to me, with a twinkle in his eye, "Peter, when I first saw Margaret, I knew we must have that lovely girl with us, to make sure, I let you have the jeep and the rifle!" And we all laughed. Then I said to Raymond, "You know, Raymond, it takes one Frenchman to understand another. You see, I wanted your jeep and your gun, so I brought my pretty wife along." "Ooh," he said, "You bastard!" and then we all had another great laugh. We clinked our wine glasses and that made our friendship even stronger.

The tour on this trip to Fort Lamy was fine. The weather was great, and Raymond got a lot of time off for hunting. How I wished Margaret had been with us this time; perhaps next winter. Time went fast and I was back in Beirut.

One day, in February 1957, I looked at my schedule and saw I was to take a DC-3 charter to a place called Ma-an, in Jordan. I'd never heard of it, so I asked our scheduler, Suade, what was all this about? He said it was to take a group of French tourists, going to visit the ancient city of Petra, I would be away for four days. I remember Munther Bilbaisi once having mentioned it when we were in Amman, some time ago. However, it didn't mean much at the time. I found a small tour book at a bookshop and took it to the apartment to brush up on where I was going. The flight was scheduled to depart on Friday morning. This gave me a couple of days to really study the history of Ma-an, and Petra. Other than Munther, I had never heard of the place. I believe it is mentioned in the Bible. After studying the history of Petra, I was excited to go. The city and its civilization came into being about 300 B.C., possibly by nomadic tribes from what is now Saudi Arabia and Yemen. Hidden in a cluster of high, rugged, craggy mountains was their city, and the beginning of the Nabatian civilization. The previous people, known as Dominites, were conquered by these nomads. Petra became the trade center where the caravans stopped on route from the Far East to Jaffa, Gaza, and to Jerusalem. They were never conquered by the Romans and the Judeans. Petra was ideally situated in the mountains, only one entrance, called a Siq, a narrow passage about 20 feet wide, with cliffs on its side, rising several hundred feet which was almost a mile long, winding passageway. The people carved large, decorative portals to the entrance for their tombs. The most famous of these is the one known as the Treasury. As you approach, usually on horseback, along this narrow passageway,

you can see the first part through a little niche. This is what I was reading; I couldn't wait to visit the site.

I packed some hiking clothes, boots, and a few rolls of film. According to the book I had, this would be a photographic dream.

The main water supply was originally from a spring, a mile further up the ravine, what is known in Arabic as a wadi. Before reaching the entrance of the Siq, the spring, as per the Bible, is where Moses is said to have smote the rock for water. The rock is still there, and the spring flows through it. Moses brother, Aaron, is buried on top of one of the mountains, not too far from the ancient city. It is also called the Rose City. After the final conquest of the Nabatians, not by armed forces, but by economic squeeze, the Romans took over in about the year 300 A.D. In the year 350, a severe earthquake ruined a part of it. The site was then evacuated, and the place lay abandoned ever since. Nomadic tribes lived here in small groups. The crusaders came in and built a castle at one end; it was later destroyed, but not before they had looted most of the tombs and whatever else they could find. Following them were the Ottomans, who did more of the same.

Around the year 1812, a Swiss by name of John Burckhardt, who learned Arabic, disguised as an Arab traveler came to the ancient capitol and took many notes and drawings of the whole ten-mile area of Petra. Later, in 1839, an Englishman, by the name of Roberts, entered the city. He was an artist, and made many paintings, which are now quite famous. He painted pictures of the tombs. These paintings are now in the museums. Copies can be bought in the gift shops in Jordan. Today it is recognized as one of the more unique ruined cities, and a "must" on most tourist attractions. It was to this site I was taking a group of French tourists on my first trip.

The DC-3 flight was obligated to land at Amman first, Here, everyone went through immigration and customs. We then flew to the town of Ma-an, about another 70 miles south, near the coast of Akaba. A bus at this point took us from there to Wadi-Mousa (Moses). At the bottom of the town is where we mounted little Arab horses and started on our way towards the Siq, or the narrow passage to Petra. Before reaching the entrance, there was evidence of Nabatian architecture, right at the beginning. The guide pointed out of the tombs that had been hacked out of the rocky mountains were actually, millions-of-year-old sandstone, that had once been under the sea. Even so, it was a marvel to try and figure out what kind of tools these individuals must have used, and the geometry and algebra that must have been involved. These were blocks at least 50-100 feet high. On the left was an even more gigantic carving, called the Obelisk Tomb, which was carved away from the mountain. This stood nearly 100 feet high. We were amazed at the workmanship. The gravel road led on further to a point where the road appeared to disappear. The guide said that this was the beginning of the Siq. We were then shown where the Romans had taken over Petra, in the year around 300 A.D., they had constructed an archway over the entrance of Petra. On the left, the Nabatians had carved a trough along the base of the cliff. This was a waterway, or viaduct, to the city. On the right and higher up were the remains of another waterway. It was a pipeline, cemented into the cliff, made of red clay. The road had once been of cobblestone, but now was washed away through the ages.

We started our journey along the Siq. At first it seemed eerie. The procession led by the guide was now in single file; it was that narrow. The cliffs on its side rose up 300-400 feet. Here and there, a bush or grass sprouted. Finally, the guide neared a narrow part of the Siq, and said to have our cameras ready, for what we would now see at the next bend should be classified as one of the wonders of the world. As I approached around the niche, after all the tourists had passed through and taken their pictures and gone on ahead, I gradually urged my pony forward, there through the niche, I beheld the fabulous sight that was famous to Jordan. In the early morning light, the edifice took on a pinkish-gray hue. The architecture carved out for this tomb stood out from the large flat rock. It must have been at least 150 feet high. No way can I possibly describe the carving; I just sat there and gaped. Here, this whole tomb was carved out of the side of a cliff, absolutely geometric perfect, hidden in this remote desert for centuries, and perfect, except for time and the elements. It had been carved for the world to see, like the Taj Mahal one thousand years later; as personal respect for one of the great Kings.

I dismounted at the entrance and entered the tomb itself. The inside, I noticed, showed the Nabatian's adeptness of their skill and how they must have struck the hammer and the chisel. There was no flaw in their work. It was remarkable to note that the architects and workers had to be perfect the first time; there was no room for errors. The eighty foot columns were absolutely perfect. From the tomb I walked the horse to the end of the Siq which entered into a large open space. The whole area was a mound of rubble where the city once stood. Part of a colonade and part of the main trough lead along the wadi. Toward the end is a large archway; beyond the gate is the ruins of the great temple. From the gate one can notice in all directions, nothing but many tombs cut out of the cliffs that surround the rubbled city. This was a bastion that invaders found hard to invade; not even the invincible Roman army could conquer.

It was at the very end of the main street that all the tourist tents were pitched. The tourist and the Air Liban crew would stay here for the next two days. That afternoon we were all on our own, so I went wondering through the tombs to look for artifacts. The Nabatian pottery was noted for its thinness, very delicate. One could see and pick up broken pottery at any place of the ruins. Bedouins came around trying to sell their

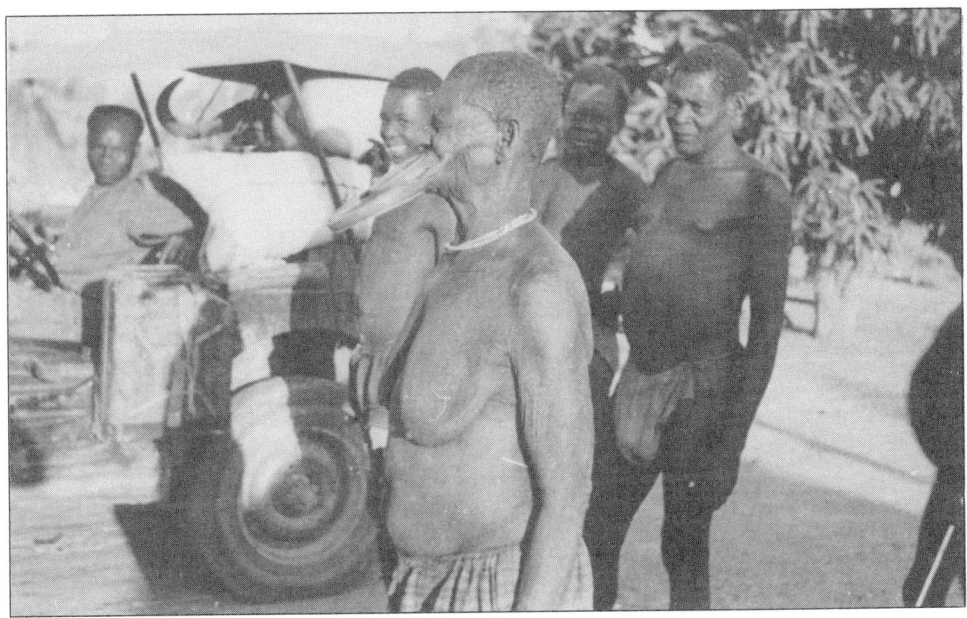

*Ubangi tribe woman.*

finds of pottery and old coins. We were warned not to purchase any artifacts here, as they were known to be fake. Secondly, it was against the law.

That evening, after a pot-lock supper, the Jordanian guide and some of the horse owners built a large camp fire for us to sit around. Some of our French tourists sat and sang French songs. Reflections from the fire cast great shadows on the nearby cliffs, while the tomb entrances gaped out at us, the intruders. The next day we were given a grand tour around Petra and most of the sights. The guide then lead the way across the ruins and up a myriad of steps which had been cut out of the rocks and sides of a mountain. It lead to what the guide called "The High Place." It certainly was, right on top of one of the mountains that over looked all of the ruined city below. We could also make out our cluster of tents at the far end. Then looking southerly, beyond the ancient city of Petra, was another high peak with a white dot which was Aaron's tomb. The "High Place" was a sacrificial place of the Nabatians. They usually sacrificed young virgins once a year to their god, or deity (Dushara) by name. After that exhilarating walk up the mountain, we returned to camp for lunch and a rest. I might add at this point, that there were no other lodging facilities in Petra. It would be a few years hence before a government hotel was built. After our rest, we were off on another hike; up another great flight of more carved steps. Another horrendous climb up the steps and along trails, we came to a magnificent carved out tomb, the guide called it the Monastery. Named so when Christianity came into being and was to be used as such by the Byzantines. Again, as the Treasury tomb this too was about 150 feet high. It was more of a yellowish sandstone; it did not have the pinkish hues, Yet it sure was inspiring. From the area of the Monastery one could look across to the Arabah Valley and Israel in the distance. On one occasion, when wandering

the area, I noticed many other steps carved in the mountains; some just seem to disappear into various cliffs and shrubbery. Our guide stated it was the Nabatean's way to catch the rain water. One sluice-way I noticed came all the way down the mountain into a cistern at the bottom. Some of them are still being used by the Bedouins. The two day tour was over and we single filed on our horses back through the Siq to Wadi Mousa. Here we boarded the bus to our the airplane. Some of the tourists asked if I could fly over the city of Petra after takeoff. They would like to take some aerial photos if possible. I said I would do that, but it would be a bit rough, since it was the middle of the day and the thermal currents would be boiling up from the rocky terrain. After takeoff I stayed low and flew over the Monastery and circled the complete site at about two hundred feet. It certainly was turbulent, yet our guests said they hoped they got some good shots. On the way back, I thought to myself, how fortunate to have been in this ancient land of the scriptures, where Biblical figures once trod.

Margaret finished her contract in London, and cabled that she would be arriving in Beirut towards the end of March. It was great to see her again, At the small apartment Margaret said that she would love to have a baby. So it wasn't long before she was pregnant, or as she called it in her English terminology, "preggis."

For a short time, during the summer months, we moved up to Betmari in the mountains, to escape the heat. That fall, the company had bought a DC-6 from Douglas company in Burbank. A French pilot and myself were asked to pick it up in California and fly it back to Paris for the interior fixings. Margaret was well into her 7th month of pregnancy, but wanted to go along. We took Air France from Paris to New York, and stayed with Geraldine a few days, and to see my mother. The airplane was getting a few

*My son Christian flying the plane to Paris, 1958.*

*Christian a little over a year old, with his friend, Beirut.*

finishing touches, so it was necessary to stay in the Los Angeles for about another ten days in Santa Monica. I called my old friend, Gene Powers, the pilot friend who flew with me in the DC-3 from Miami to Calcutta in 1944, when we poured coffee over him, crossing the equator. Gene was now an office worker for Douglas aircraft factory. We had a chance to reminisce the old CNAC days. Margaret and I did a lot of shopping for our new apartment in Beirut. It was not long before the airplane was ready. Margaret could not go on the plane, since it would only accommodate

the crew. A ticket was arranged on Air France, all the way, and we would meet in Paris. The plane was left at the Le Bourget Airport, where Lindbergh once landed on his solo flight from New York in 1927, with "The Spirit of St. Louis."

We stayed at the Terrace Hotel at Montmartre. Our Air Liban crews usually stayed there, and it was here, that we ran into Moritz Bremer again. He was going to take the flight back to Beirut on Air Liban. At Paris, Margaret was upset about something, and took it out on me. I don't know what it was, but we'd had spats before. But this was the first time I noticed how violent her temper was. I talked to Moritz at the bar, and we thought it was due to her pregnancy. I tried to be aloof, and let her cool down. One good note of this was my dear friend, The Maharajah of Cooch Behar, had arrived in Paris for a couple of days. He, Moritz, Margaret and I had a great time, dining out every night, always at the nicest French restaurants. It seemed to change Margaret and cheer her up, however, once on the flight back to Beirut, I got the cold shoulder. This was not like her, and I was upset. We arrived back and Margaret wasted no time in putting up our new bits and pieces that we had bought in the States, and fixing up the new apartment. The place was big, and everything in it looked new and nice. Margaret came around a bit, but still something was suspicious. I was back on my schedule, and on a trip back from Baghdad early in the morning, Moritz met me at the terminal. "Hurry," he said, "Margaret's been taken to the hospital; the baby is due anytime." When I got to the hospital, I talked to the doctor, an Arab (Dr. Tradd) who had brought Moritz and Ingas' baby, Andreas, into the world. He said all was well, for me to go home, that I would be notified when to come back. I rested that day. It was a terrible early hour in the morning when the hospital messenger knocked on the door. We hurried to the hospital, and Margaret was in the operating room. It was

not long after that the doctor came out all grins. He had what appeared to be a baby in his hands. "Look," he said, "a boy." There was nothing but blood all over him. The baby was a couple of minutes old, a horrible-looking sight; eyes closed, matted, reddish-like hair stuck all over his forehead, nose sort of squished. "Okay," said the doctor, "you can sit down for a while. I'll call you when the baby has been fixed up." It all happened so fast, I hardly knew what to do or to say. I went to the waiting room. It seemed to be forever before the nurse came in and said to follow her. There was Margaret, in bed, smiling, but looking woozy, her eyes glazed. I was able to lean over and kiss her, but not much response. Next to her was the baby, all wrapped up like a cocoon, arms and all, just the little face sticking out. I guess this was probably what you'd call "swaddling clothes." I'd arranged a lot of flowers for the occasion. I took flash pictures, then was told I'd have to leave, that the two needed a rest.

I went back to the Bremers and celebrated. Moritz had champagne ready. In a few days, I had Margaret and the baby home. We had ordered a special crib built for him. Margaret was up and about and busy as a bee. We had bought diapers, bottles, and all the baby things in Los Angeles. We decided the baby was to be called Christian; Christian Joffre Goutiere. Christian was named after some of my relatives in India, who were in the Indigo plantation business, and Joffre was my middle name, after the illustrious and wonderful French General of World War I.

After all this excitement, we settled down to our domestic life. Christian grew fast, he grew a mop of curly, reddish hair, and was a wonderful, healthy boy. For the most part, it was I who would be up at 1 or 2 in the morning. I'd change his diapers, warm the milk, feed him, then would walk the floor, sometimes till 3 or 4 in the morning before he would drop off to sleep. Anyway, I enjoyed it; I was getting to know the rascal. He was turning into an intelligent little fellow and was walking within nine months, and beginning to utter a few words. By the time he was a year-and-a-half, he was a handful of naughtiness, and a great deal of fun.

Christian's first Easter, in 1959, was in the Lebanese mountains, near Betmari. We were joined by the Knemeyers, their children, and the Bremers, also. It was a picnic outing, with an egg hunt for the youngsters. I sat and watched, and at the same time thought of the occasion; that He, Christ, who gave his life for others, and for whom Easter is all about, was born that far away.

On one occasion at the apartment, as naughty boys are wont to do, Christian was able to smear his baby shit all over the crib and parts of himself, same as David did in Maine. Luckily, Christian's crib didn't have wheels to go around the room, or he would have been plastering the walls and windows, as well. Like all babies, he did his share.

One lazy Sunday morning, everything was very quiet...too quiet. I got up and looked in Christian's room - he wasn't there. I looked into the dining room, then the living room. There on the porch, was Christian, on his tip-toes, throwing something over the railing and having a great laugh as he did so. On closer examination, I was shocked to see he had my wallet, and was taking my Lebanese money, one note at a time, and sailing them off the balcony, into the wind. I called to him, and with a shriek, having been caught in the act, he threw the whole lot over. I looked over the railing as Christian took off for the bedroom. There, seven stories below, along the road and off in fields, I could barely make out some of my money, fluttering about. I quickly got dressed and then told Margaret what had happened. She laughed her head off. I was soon scrambling around down-stairs, looking for money. There were not too many souls around at that time, thank good-ness, I retrieved the wallet and some of the cash. When I got back, he was proud as punch, enjoying a bowl of cereal.

On another occasion, Christian was hav-ing a bath in our master bathroom. He loved to dawdle and splash around in the tub and loved to take the sponge and slobber big suds along the tiles. At this particular time, I, too, had to go to the John. I sat on the commode and watched him cleaning the tiles around him with the sponge. I unconsciously made a rude noise. Christian stopped dead, with his back to me. He very slowly turned his head around and, with a sly grin, said, "Daddy, you must put your hand over your mouth when you make a noise like that." He then laughed out loud; I had to join him.

Whenever I had time off, Margaret and I were always trying to take Christian on little picnics, up to the mountains or to the beach. There was a lovely beach called Acapulco, where we spent a lot of time.

During the Haj or pilgrim season, the crews were kept busy not only flying the schedules, but doing a lot of charter work to Jeddah. In the summer of 1958, I was on one of these charters out of Jeddah with the DC-4. I took a load of pilgrims to Khartoum and then returned to Jeddah, then another trip to the island of Comoros, which was via Dar-es-Salaam. It was different and interesting. On the return trip from Dar-es-Salaam to Khartoum, empty, I took the DC-4 up to 14,000 feet and flew close to Mount Kilimanjaro. There was a haze and clouds. The mountain stuck up through it at 18,000 feet, the whole top was snow-covered, some-thing like Fujiyama. It was a beautiful sight. From icy coolness at that point to touchdown at Khartoum was some contrast, at least 112° Fahrenheit.

The Grand Hotel on the Nile where we stayed did not have air conditioning, only ceiling fans, but it was comfortable. The next day, we were back in Jeddah, to take more pilgrims, this time to Fort Lamy, my old place and honeymoon days. At Fort Lamy, we were on stand-by for further instructions. The crew consisted of one Italian First Officer, Berlasi, two Lebanese stewardesses, and a steward. Berlasi was out somewhere that the morn-ing; only the cabin crew and myself were sitting at the dining table at the Hotel du Parc.

*Riding throught the Siq with French passengers, 1956.*

We had finished our lunch and were enjoy-ing coffee, when in rushed Berlasi. He looked white as a sheet, and his eyes bugged out. It took a few seconds for him to catch his breath; then he blurted out that World War III had broken out. We jumped up in surprise. I thought perhaps the U.S. and Russia were at it with their bombs. We asked him to ex-plain what it was all about. He finally said that the American Marines had landed in Lebanon and taken the country. We all sat down and tried to figure out what he was talking about, what in hell were the Marines doing in Lebanon, if what Berlasi said was true. We asked the hotel manager and his wife. They confirmed the radio report from Paris, that the world news in France had defi-nitely stated the U.S. Marines had, in fact, landed in Lebanon and taken the airport and the beaches, and most of south Lebanon. The crew wanted to hop in the plane and head back home; I couldn't blame them, but I said we'd wait for Beirut to tell us. As we sat and sipped our coffee, the Lebanese steward all of a sudden, burst into tears and cried like a baby. One of the stewardesses near him tried to console the fellow, and asked what the problem was.

The steward finally spoke up and said loudly, "The Marines, oh the Marines! They're going to fuck my mother!" There was silence for a few seconds. The two stew-ardesses then burst out laughing and almost fell out of their chairs. I couldn't resist, ei-ther, and had to join them. We all laughed for a few minutes, it struck us so funny. It was sometime before we all got our compo-sure back. The steward, however, couldn't be convinced otherwise. I tried hard to say the Marines are probably all confined to cer-tain areas, but not to worry, everything will be all right. However, he sat there sullenly.

It was late that afternoon when our of-fice sent a message to return to Beirut via Khartoum to pick up some passengers. I told the crew to have a rest, that we would depart around 9 PM. At Khartoum we got our load of passengers for Beirut. The newspapers and everybody were talking about the Marines in Lebanon. It was around 10 AM the next morning when we touched down at Khaldi Airport, Beirut. There was great excitement all around; Marines in all directions. Tanks along the road, the military planes parked at the north end of the airport. They didn't in-terfere with the domestic operations; it was business as usual. The terminal was hum-ming with people. Airline planes came and went. After Customs and on our way out, I wished the steward friend a safe trip home, and not to worry about mother; all would be well.

We saw the U.S. tanks parked at the ar-eas of the pine groves as the crew bus drove to town. The Marine base appeared to be on the east side of the airport away from every-thing; a whole city of drab olive tents dotted that area. There was heavy traffic on the way to town. When I got back to the apartment, Margaret told me all about the sudden inva-sion; she hardly knew it had occurred. It all took place around the airport. Nothing was disturbed north of Beirut, in and around Djouneh. Margaret was nervous, and wanted to return to England till the situation had subsided. This was arranged, as a matter of fact, I flew the flight to Paris and put her on a British European Airways, BEA, flight di-rect to Manchester, with Christian.

After seeing them off from Le Bourget, I caught a train to the town of Blois, on the Loire River. This was where my friend, Raymond and Paulette Poezavara, lived. It was on a weekend, and my birthday; I was now 44. Paulette performed miracles with her French cuisine, and Raymond wasted no time in procuring some very fine champagne. After all, the Loire River is famous wine country. It was back to basics with my French, but we were able to communicate, it was a wonderful birthday with the setting in Blois and the Loire Valley, with its magnifi-cent chateaux and castles. Many have been portrayed in magazines, on calendars, and in movies. I got royally high on the cham-pagne. and the next morning I was suffering

*Tourists tents near Nabataen temple, Petra, Jordan, 1956.*

with a headache. Raymond and I took off into the country and the Loire Valley. He drove into a farmyard to visit some of his friends. I realized the farm was a vineyard, and the gentleman was a winemaker. I was shown around the place, and there, in the middle of a barn, was a structure; it was a huge vat, with a ladder ascending to its top, about fifteen feet high. I was handed a tin mug and ushered up the ladder, where I helped myself to a mug of wine. I still suffered from the headache, and hoped I wouldn't fall off the ladder. Once I was on top, there was no lid or cover over the ten foot wide vat. There was a whole lot of straw floating on top. I moved the straw aside and dipped in. This would be equivalent to about three glasses of wine. It was white wine, cold and delicious. I started down, but Raymond said to stay up there had have a couple mug fulls. I stayed up and sipped the mug empty. The next one I only half-filled. It was good, and started to numb my senses and head. I finally clambered down and congratulated the owner of the super vat and his wine. We left and headed off again.

Raymond then drove to another similar establishment, and again, after introductions, I was up another ladder, and a swig of more delicious wine. Raymond was shrewd; he got his from a small tap barrel nearby. I had now mixed white, red, pink, etc., but no more headache, and no more anything for that matter. It was noon when we drove home, and I decided to have some sleep, this was not for long. Raymond had made up a schedule for the afternoon that took us on a tour of some of the Loire's fancy chateaux. We then stopped out in the country, where Raymond and Paulette said we were going to pick wild mushrooms, Paulette gave me a paper bag and said to go along in a certain area, and showed me the brown mushrooms hidden under the leaves and brambles. There were loads of them. It wasn't long before I had the bag full. I then took out my handkerchief and filled it up. I returned to the car and the two of them were there, waiting for me. I

noticed the smiles on their faces. I gave Paulette the bundle of mushrooms and suggested we get some more. No they said; this was ample. Raymond and Paulette started to laugh. Finally, they confessed that they had sent me onto someone's private estate that was guarded. But they figured if I got caught, I had a good alibi, being an American and not understanding French; they probably would let me go. I enjoyed the prank and I don't mind saying that the mushrooms Paulette cooked up that evening were delicious.

Time just seems to evaporate when having a good time. The next morning, they put me on a train back to Paris, where I caught my flight to Beirut. The Marines seemed to be well-entrenched. I wondered if the steward's Mum ever got laid by a Marine!

I had only been back a few days when I had a caller: my old pilot friend, Bob Bithel, from the Karachi and Crescent Air Transport days. He had been flying for Arab Airways, in Jordan. He had quit and was on his way to England to sign up with Ghana Airways, in Accra, as Chief Pilot. I invited Bob to stay with me for a while. Bob stayed until Margaret arrived a few weeks before Christmas. It was great having Margaret and Christian back in Beirut. The sojourn in England had done her good. She had learned to drive, and with a few more instructions, she was able to get a Lebanese driver's license. We settled down into our routine lifestyle: a few parties, with our wonderful friends, and Christian starting to grow up. It wasn't much longer when the Marines decided the show was over and they would pull out.

As for Christian, his curly hair had been cut; now his hair took on a more reddish tone, and was fairly straight. In February 1959, I had a lot of leave to use up, so Margaret and I decided to take a trip to India. I arranged tickets on Air India to Bombay, Calcutta and Delhi, and back. We were to be gone six weeks. A young German girl would act as governess for Christian, while we were away. She was rec-

ommended by the Bremers; her name was Ursula.

In Bombay, we stayed at the Taj Hotel, and Margaret seemed to enjoy the place, in spite of the filth on the streets. We spent a few days there, seeing everything such as the old gateway to India. Then boarded another flight to Calcutta. Here, we stayed with some friends, relatives of His Highness, the Maharajah of Cooch Behar. His name was Gautham Narayan. It was great seeing him again. Boris was around, gathering supplies to take back to Kathmandu for his restaurant, which he called "The Yak and Yati." Cooch Behar was in town, and suggested we go up to his palace to do some tiger-shooting, or at least ride on some elephants. Margaret was beside herself with excitement. She wanted to go as soon as possible. We were first invited to Bhaiya's estate at Alipore, outside Calcutta, and while at dinner, Margaret asked Cooch Behar, "When we get to the palace, will we have a chance to see your family jewels, Your Highness?" Bhaiya sputtered, and checked himself from laughing. I finally told her the joke, and after turning crimson a few times, she joined in with laughter.

Bhaiya arranged for us to stay at the palace; also for a hunt in Assam, where I had been, back in 1945 and 1946, with CNAC pilots. He had a hunting party there now, and when they were gone, we could take over for a few days. Margaret also knew of my excursions to Darjeeling, and wanted to visit the place to see what the attraction was. I arranged a free trip with an old CNAC pilot who was now running a cargo operation with DC-3s. His name was Eddie Quinn the brother of Babs Huang. He arranged a couple of wicker type seats, bolted up front near the cockpit. The flight was to an airfield at the base of the hills below Darjeeling, and the railroad station called Siliguri. Other than the smell of cargo oil it was a smooth early morning flight to Gauhatti. From there, we found a stray taxi that took us up to the hill station, the weather was clear and cold, the scenery breathtaking. On the way, we took movies of the miniature railroad that traverses up, which I have mentioned before. Margaret agreed that it was a beautiful spot. We stayed at a place called the Windamere Hotel, that was recommended by Bhaiya. I showed Margaret all the sights. We took the tour to Tiger Hill, and witnessed the sunrise on Kanchenjunga, and a glimpse of Everest beyond. I took hundreds of feet of film as we went along, Darjeeling was performing well with the weather, and we got some magnificent movies. We had breakfast at the old Keventers farm. Margaret couldn't stop buying souvenirs and gadgets for the apartment; most of them were Tibetan. She was delighted with the train ride back to Siliguri. Here Cooch Behar had sent his car to drive us back to the palace, about 100 miles southeast. We were met at the Palace by his personal secretary, good old Caju Singh, and his delightful wife, Bhindu, Caju's claim to fame was his peeing in a London taxicab, and having been caught by the same one, who said it was the second time he peed in the same cab. Caju wondered, how, of all the thousands of cabs, did he pick the same one twice?

The French lady, Auntie, was no longer at the palace. She had married and gone to southern India. I missed her, as she was such a lovely person. I was very homesick, being back in my old haunts again, after 10 years. The old servants recognized me and welcomed us back. Caju got us settled in our room. I guess he was quite lonesome taking care of an empty palace, except for the occasional guest, or hunting parties that came from different parts of Europe and the States.

We had a couple of days rest at Cooch Behar. After a hectic trip with an ADC by the name of Naro, we arrived at Katchagon. Nothing had changed at the old forest officers' bungalow where I had stayed before. After unpacking and getting the dust washed off, I took Margaret to meet the elephants and the mahouts. At the Pilkhana the mahouts were delighted to see me, and to meet Margaret. I saw my old elephant and fed her a couple of bananas that I'd brought along. We were to spend a week here and I could have stayed a month. There were a lot of tigers reported in the area and I finally shot one. There was other game, too, I shot a few jungle fowl, which made good curry. All this made Margaret's head swim. She enjoyed it immensely, especially riding the elephants through the jungle, not in howdahs, but only on the pad. I took movies at every opportunity; it might be the last time that I'd come this way. It was hard to say farewell to the mahouts and the elephants, and also Cooch Behar. We took a train this time, back to Calcutta and I still loved the clamor and smell of the stations. Margaret and I spent a couple more days in Calcutta, then flew on to Delhi.

Margaret loved Delhi, too. In fact, I think she was loving the whole trip. For one thing, Delhi was much cleaner and very few beggars. We traveled to Agra to visit the Taj Mahal. By now, Margaret had collected a mountain of souvenirs. I was worried about the overweight, and the cost. I talked to a PanAm station manager in Delhi, who said he could arrange getting the souvenirs onto Air India. The next day he called us at the Ashoka Hotel and said he had arranged everything; there would be no problem about overweight. I was a bit embarrassed when we arrived at the airport with this load of boxes and large brass tray. Air India people didn't blink an eye. It was all tagged, and put on board. At Beirut there was not too much trouble with the customs either. I thought there would be, with the brassware that we had, but all went well. Christian took a couple of minutes to recognize us. Would you believe he came to attention and bowed. The German girl had been teaching him a few German mannerisms. He even spoke a few words of German. Margaret and I were so pleasantly surprised. The girl Ursula was a gem. She had taken good care of Christian and the apartment; I wish we could have kept her on.

In June Christine, my sister, showed up

*Oblsek tomb just before entering the Siq to Petra, 1956.*

from a tour of India. She stayed three weeks with us before returning to Maine. Robert had passed away. She had now married an old friend by the name of Roger Griswold, a downeastern from Maine. They were a good match. Before leaving, Christine had invited us to come and visit her in Maine. Air Liban's workload had dropped off, the Operations Department were encouraging crews to take extra leave, some of it without pay. I decided to take the two weeks without pay. We got our free tickets on Air France all the way to New York via Paris. It was early November when we arrived in New York. The fall weather greeted us, the leaves were still painted their vivid yellows, oranges and browns. I bought an old used car in Manhattan and we drove to Plainfield to visit Geraldine and my mother. The weather held clear, the foliage around Geraldine's home was gorgeous. Christian tried raking leaves and falling into piles of them. If I have not mentioned it before, Geraldine is a great artist, mostly with oils. Her art is normally portrait painting, some landscapes and flowers. She had a lovely skylighted studio on the floor just over the kitchen. Early one Sunday morning, after we'd had a sleep, I felt the covers being pulled at my side of the double bed that Margaret and I were sharing. As I turned over to see what was tugging at me, I was frozen in shock. There stood our little Christian, grinning and squealing at me in delight. If ever there was a miniature Vincent Van Gogh, there he was in front of me. Christian had covered himself not with the usual baby s..., but with every conceivable color of paint from Geraldine's studio. He had removed the lower half of his pajamas, and the top half barely covered to his navel. Christian had done a complete job by daubing himself all the way, literally from top to bottom with a variety of colors from Geraldine's oil paints. Anything he had touched had paint, even our sheets. He looked like something like Van Gogh's sunflowers, and the pile of raked leaves on the back lawn! Margaret was now awake and

when she saw the sight, she was dumbfounded and screamed. Christian stood and let us admire him. Then Margaret started laughing, as only she knows how. We must have created quite a rumpus, because it brought Geraldine and Fred. When they saw Christian, Geraldine let our a shriek and headed for the studio. I decided to follow. The stairs are narrow and steep; I don't know how the little fellow made it. He had left a trail of paint along the way. Christian had not touched the painting on the easel, but sure had dug into the tubes of paint from the large box she had open nearby. When Fred arrived, he had to laugh as well. It was a low, gruff laugh; we all joined in, Christian, too. Before anything else, Geraldine had to take a few photos of him before the process of cleaning up. Geraldine tackled the stairs and everywhere else, while Margaret and I tackled Christian. We used the turpentine diluted, because we knew it would burn and this made Christian cry. It was a while before we succeeded in getting just about all the paint off. I believe I did something like that when my Dad was painting his butterfly collection, back in 1918; I tried to paint over his butterflies. It had happened in the same bungalow where my dog was carried off by the leopard. I guess art just runs in the family!

Our stay with Geraldine and Fred was short, but quite eventful. We spent a lot of time with my mother too, even though she'd get quite nervous when Christian came around the apartment. We soon said "Au Revoir" and departed on our way to Maine and Harrington where Christine and Roger had their home, which they called "The Shack." Margaret and I had a wonderful 10 day visit with them, and then back to New York. I sold the car, and before I knew it we were on our way to Beirut. It always takes a few flights before settling down to our routine schedule again. I was scheduled mostly on the DC-6s, and with the flights to Europe-Rome and Paris. My turn came again for the

*The Bremers, Inga, Moritz and son Andreas. Bet Meri, Lebanon, 1957.*

month's duty in Africa; but now, instead of staying in Fort Lamy, The crew had a new base in Kano, Northern Nigeria. It was much better than Fort Lamy. The weather, for one thing, was cooler, and most everyone spoke English.

A couple of weeks before leaving, Margaret informed me she was pregnant again. I was elated, but Margaret wasn't. She appeared angry, and I couldn't understand that. I suggested that she accompany me to Kano, that the weather would be wonderful that Christian would enjoy it, and there was a swimming pool at the Kano Club where she could "catch the sun." I knew she would enjoy the change. Margaret would have no part of it. She said she didn't want to go. Instead, since I was going there for a month, she wanted a ticket to go back home and see her folks. Well, if that was what she wanted, I couldn't argue differently. I saw her off on one of our flights to Paris, and then take BEA onto Manchester. I couldn't blame her for wanting to see her people, yet there was a strangeness of being pregnant again. With Christian, she was excited, but this time, there was not that feeling. I tried to dispel any thoughts, and looked forward to the trip to Kano.

I got all my paraphernalia, including a shotgun, and was ready to travel. This was now January 1960. At our operations, I met the crew that would be spending the month in Kano. Usually this was to ascertain everyone was in accordance with their responsibilities in Kano. Food was usually brought on the weekly flights from Beirut. There would be no ill feeling before going. For the six days off, the crew could go their ways, but be ready for flight, every Sunday morning. There were no questions, and the seven crew members were happy to be with me. The first Officer was a Romanian; the rest were Lebanese. I noticed that one of the stewardesses was eyeing me during the briefing. She was a very pretty, petite girl. I wondered

if she was 18. As we filed on out to the airplane as deadhead crew, the girl came up to me and introduced herself as Danielle. She stood about 5'2" on her tiptoes. She had dark auburn hair, freckles, and green eyes, and she didn't have to stick out her chest to let me know she was all there. At Kano, I took over command and kept all our belongings with us. The flight stops were the same as we did with the DC-4, but instead of turn around at Abidjan we continue to Dakar Senegal where we would overnight this particular trip. It gave me an opportunity to see a bit of the city. We had a French flight engineer by the name of Descholet. He mentioned that a good place to visit was Goree Island and we could also have a nice dinner at a restaurant he knew on the island. We had quick showers and a change of clothes. The F/E and I took the ferry-boat across to Goree. The place is steeped in the history of slave trade during the 15th through 19th centuries. As we walked along the wharf, I noticed old 18th century canons lying about and very much rusted. There was an old building that looked like a castle, Descholet said it was once known as the "House of The Slaves." The slaves were brought here and kept cramped up in the rooms to await the arrival of the slave-ship that would take them away to some far away land such as the Carolinas or Virginia in the States, or to the Caribbean Isles such as Haiti, Jamaica or South America. They were torn away from their families and native Africa forever. The slave trade was a lucrative business, this caused castles such as this to be built all along the West African coast. They were French, Dutch, English and Portuguese. As I gazed at the building, I could imagine the terrible tortures these poor souls must have endured. They would never see their families or native land again. I told my friend I needed a drink and to think of more pleasant things. He agreed. We had walked most of the Island and I noticed there were no cars, only a

few bicycles. I took pictures of many of the interesting sights on the Island, including a little Mosque hidden away from most of the homes. We finally had our drinks and then a lovely French dinner. I thought this a very quaint place; yet to learn there had been such horrible atrocities that had taken place. I felt sad as I kept thinking of what must have taken place right where we were walking.

Next day we returned back to Kano, all exhausted and happy to reach the apartment. The captains quarters was off to one side of the upstairs apartment. I got my things sorted out, clothes hung up in the closet, and I checked the gun and placed it in the closet that had a lock and key. The locals were noted for their light fingers. I took a quick shower and got into fatigues, then took my bottle of scotch to the main living room. The others were already there, just waiting for me. Most of them preferred beer and Lebanese wine. There was a houseboy assigned to the apartment as well. He produced the ice and soda. Like some things, the first drink was just great. The crew chatted in Arabic. The Romanian pilot and I sat and enjoyed the scotch. Pretty soon, Danielle came over and joined us. She was cute, and talked with a French accent, which made it even more interesting. I don't remember the conversation. Being tired, and the scotch having its effect, I headed for bed. I didn't know a thing until the next morning. There was a lot of hustle and bustle going on outside. I peeked out and saw the girls cleaning up the porch and the steps. I got dressed and joined the group in the dining room. They had cleaned up the whole apartment and made breakfast. When the dishes had been taken care of, by the houseboy, the crew said they were off the Kano Club. I decided to tag along. As mentioned earlier, there were many Lebanese throughout Africa, and Kano had its share. The club was very much on the English style. All of Nigeria was under the British crown. A lot of the people working in Kano were English. The tower operator, customs, etc. The crew and I gathered around a table at the pool. Everyone ordered beer. It was a local beer - I think it was Black Star - but not too bad. It was better than drinking water. When a new bevy of girls show up, the wolves will appear. There were some Lebanese present and it didn't take long before we were invited to their homes for lunch and dinner. When Danielle appeared in her bikini, she was a knockout, and she knew it. Kano still had its charm for me. I remembered being here with Pan Africa in 1942. The old trumpet guy was still there as a symbol at the airport. The club was run by the English. You did not pay cash; you sign a chit, same as you do at the 300 club in Calcutta, Most of the men wore British-type shorts and knee stockings, the bar served Pimms No. 1 and 2 and 3. After meeting some of the Lebanese business people, we were all invited to one of their homes that evening. The local food was done in Lebanese style along with the traditional drink of Arak. It was a fun party and a good get together.

One of the Lebanese was a fellow by the name of Georges. He was a rotund individual, who must have weighed about 280 pounds. He had a petite, attractive wife. The guy liked bird hunting I found out, and he was willing to go anytime, but had to be very early. The partridge, or Francolins, as they are called, were bountiful. He would let me know a day before. I was also told by our host that there were a couple of French people who worked in the town who loved hunting as well, mainly for big game, I'd be introduced to them soon. I knew Kano would be a great station, I was looking forward to the shooting, but wished Margaret was along.

Before turning in that evening, I got out the shotgun, cleaned and oiled it. It was an Italian Beretta make, 12 gauge. Feeling sleepy, I flopped onto the bed and drowsed. I may have gone to sleep, when I was awakened by a knock on the door.

Still half-sleep, I opened it to see if there was anyone there; lo and behold, there stood Danielle in her kimono. She was shivering, as the weather there in the winter is terribly cold at night. I ushered her in and closed the door. She said she couldn't sleep and wanted to talk. I guess Danielle could smell the gun oil from the cleaning rags still on the table and asked what it was. We talked about hunting. Then she said if I went with the Georges, she wanted to go along. I didn't see anything wrong with that. "Sure Danielle; you can come along anytime." Then she said, "You like Mrs. Georges?" She caught me by surprise. I said that Mrs. Georges looked like a nice lady, and she was beautiful, but what did she mean? "Well," Danielle said, "I think she like you. I noticed the way she look at you." "No, Danielle; I'm not interested in Mrs Georges. She's a happily married woman, with children." "No difference; I could tell," she said. "You're jealous!" She looked at me with her big, green eyes, and didn't have to answer. I sat near her on the couch. In her broken French-English style, which was so delightful to hear, Danielle said, "I think there's bugs in my room. My back, it is itching." She said, "Please, Petair, you scratch my back, yes?" Before I could answer, she took off her kimono, under which she wore a flimsy nightie. There was nothing under it, as her beautiful bosoms seemed to push through the nylon. I thought she was delightful, but very young. While I started the backscratching, I asked her how old she was. The answer was "23," that she was part French and part Tunisian and Lebanese, and her Dad worked for Air Liban. The mixture did her well. The scratching slowed down to more of a massaging. It didn't take long for the hands to meander around where they wanted to go all along, without any resistance. We transferred to the bed without any great difficulty. While the performance was progressing, and what had nature planned with my face engulfed in one of her fantastic bosoms, I felt a tapping on my left shoulder. It took some doing to move my head so she could whisper in my ear. What she said was, "Pe-tair, the other one, it is getting jealous!" It took what appeared for-

ever to remove myself from her heaving bosom, I finally did, and obliged the other jealous teat. This was to be an all night session; I don't remember what time she returned to her room. I know I missed breakfast; nearly missed lunch, too. The expression "dragged through the wringer" certainly applied in this case. Going to a football scrimmage was not half as exhausting, but this was a lot more pleasant!

I wandered into the dining room around 12:30. Most of the group had gone to the club. The steward and Danielle were there at the table. She looked shiny and bright. The houseboy seemed to know my wish, and brought a cold beer. Danielle said she had made sandwiches, while the beer brought me back to life. I was still exhausted, and hoped there wouldn't be an afternoon scrimmage. She told me that one of the French guys who worked in town would come over later to discuss hunting.

That afternoon, a jeep drove up, and out hopped a French gentleman. I was introduced to him as Pierre Richleau. He was a young fellow, who spoke excellent English. Pierre and I hit it off right away. We discussed the hunting for a spell. It appeared he knew the area around Kano, and the places to find antelope. He had a rifle, but a limited amount of ammunition. I said I'd bring him some from Europe on my next trip, and anything else he needed. He then insisted that I come over for dinner that evening. Danielle made no bones about her coming along. Pierre arrived about 7 PM and picked us up. It was a nice bungalow that we drove to. His wife was an attractive blonde. They had three children with them, and they all spoke good English. It was great evening, and I liked Pierre. He was just a lot of fun, and full of jokes. It was agreed that Saturday, we would go hunting for the day. His wife would not accompany us; she was more of a home person, and looked after the kids. Danielle and I were dropped back early that evening, after a nice French meal, and Beaujolais wine. Daniel said for me not to lock my door; she would be over. No matter what, I knew I was going to lose a lot of weight. This time, she brought her nightie and toothbrush. there would be no jealous titties around; I'd give them a fair shake! I don't know if it was Lebanese tabbouleh, and arak, that make these young gals so sexy. They just plain love it. Who was I to refuse their desires, being half French myself? But I warned Danielle it was

not to be an all night again; take it easy on me! Besides, we had to get up very, very, very early, to go hunting. She just nodded. We had just dropped off to sleep when the alarm went off. I wasn't sure where I was for a moment. Danielle was up getting ready. She had her shower, etc., and I followed. Prearranged by Danielle, we had coffee and croissants and had just finished our "petite-dejeuner" when Pierre drove up. It was still dark outside, with the usual pariah dogs sniffing around the garbage. We were off in a hurry and it was cold, the breeze blowing on us in an open jeep. Pierre was taking us to a place called Dangura, about 80 miles northwest of Kano. We drove off the main, tar road onto the dirt, which also gave way to trails. We bounced and jounced all the way.

In time, we arrived at a small native thatched-roof village. A tall, thin native came over to us when we stopped at the edge of their town. I think his name was Nitu. He was Pierre's guide, and carried a short spear. Without any further ado, he hopped into the back of the jeep, with me. Once more, we jounced and bounced along a very dusty trail, which came to an abrupt end, where there was a dropoff of rock, on the other side was a slow flowing stream. "This is it", Pierre said, we all bailed out. It was good to get out and stretch, after that cramped ride. The doves were making a racket around the trees and partridge could be heard calling in the distance. Pierre asked not to shoot any birds now; the shooting might disturb any big game that might be nearby. Instead, I loaded up with buckshot. Nitu led the way, with Pierre next, The trail was not thick, and one could see quite a distance.

Every once in a while, Nitu would stop and peer into the distance and check the bare areas for signs of antelope. We saw a few guinea fowl, I was itching to have a go at them.

The walking was easy, as it was flat terrain. But now the sun was getting higher, and the weather warmer. Little Danielle bounced along behind us and was a good sport. At one point, we jumped a young warthog, which took off in a hurry, with its funny tail stuck straight up in the air. No chance for a shot. I suggested to Pierre that the three of us sit here for a period, and let Nitu scout the area. This way, we could get some rest, and not so much noise. We took a drink of water, and relaxed near a tree. We kept quiet and listened to all the strange sounds. It re-

*With my crew at Kuwait, 1956*

*With AirLiban DC-4 in Accra, Ghana, 1956*

*Christian having his mush breakfast on the porch, Beirut.*

minded me of when Margaret and I had gone with Poezavara, in Fort Lamy.

It was a while before Nitu came back. He had seen some antelope, quite a ways off. I told Pierre to go with Nitu. Danielle and I would find our way back to the jeep, and perhaps I'd get a shot at some guinea fowl or partridge. We parted, and I led the way back with Danielle. I did spot a covy of guinea fowl, off to one side in the ravine. I stalked up pretty close. They saw me, and started running in single file. I fired at the lead, knocking it over. The rest took off. Then I knocked down another one, in flight. Danielle was amazed that I could hit a bird in flight. These fowl are pretty good size, and they would make a fine ground-nut stew. Nothing else in sight as we trudged along. We soon came to the stream, which we followed to the jeep. We were not used to all this walking, to say the least. Danielle and I flopped into the jeep and relaxed. There were a few tsetse files around too. They looked a bit like the moose flies in Maine. I had some bugaboo repellent, which I applied on Danielle and myself. It was early afternoon when Pierre returned, empty handed. He said the herd of antelope that they had spotted earlier were hartebeests, they couldn't get close enough for a shot. Danielle spread a cloth and set out the picnic. Nitu was a Moslem and wouldn't join us. He sat apart and ate his flat bread and some sort of dry meat.

The Francolin partridge come out in the late afternoon, and in the mornings, After a rest, I followed a well beaten trail that crossed the stream. I had traversed about half a mile when I heard Francolin calling in a sparsely-treed area. I was always ready for a shot. A partridge got up from a clump of bushes, and I shot it, a covey of them took off, too far to shoot. You have to knock these birds dead, or they will run like hell and be hard to find; winging them is useless, unless you have a dog. I was happy I got this bird, which I gave Nitu; that and some baksheesh would keep

him well. We returned to Kano, dusty and tired. Pierre wanted us to stay for dinner. We apologized, and said we would next week; right now, it was a good bath and an early night. The next day would be our flight to Dakar and back. Rolande said that she would cook a stew of the guinea fowl that we had shot. That evening I took a hot shower and was ready for bed. I told Danielle "No knock knock; no nookie-nookie this night." She was pretty tired and agreed. The trip to Dakar had been routine, but always tiresome.

Monday, Danielle and I visited Pierre and Rolande, and enjoyed the guinea fowl ground-nut stew. The Kano area is famous for its ground nuts (or peanuts). They are harvested and packed into 50 pound gunny-sacks. These are piled into large, almost 50 foot high pyramids, and exported. A stew is made from the freshly ground nuts, hot chilis, and onions; it is eaten with rice, almost like a curry. In fact, the people of Thailand make a curry with ground-nuts. The stew Rolande presented was good, A local doctor was invited over, whom they knew; he was from Malta. Pierre suggested to me that I take his tent, gun and jeep, and stay out at Dangura. Yes, that would be great, as I hated just hanging around the pool and the apartment. Danielle didn't want to be left out either. I wondered if she could stand camp life. "Oh, yes, yes; oui, oui!" she said; "I'll be a good cook." Pierre had a small, one burner cooker. I hoped I could get Nitu to help with the tent and firewood.

Tuesday, Danielle and I shopped for groceries then filled the jeep with gas, the groceries and cooking material. Next day, we were on our way, to Dangura, I found Nitu who was only too happy to get away from his village chores and always ready to help. It didn't take long to put up the make-shift tent under one of the larger trees. There was no worry of anyone stealing, for these people were honest folks, not like those in the city.

That afternoon, we set off, following Nitu and hoped to see some sort of big game. We had taken a different trail this time. After about 15 minutes of walking, Nitu stopped and pointed at something, and I followed the sight of his pointing finger. There, just visible, at quite a distance, I observed something moving under some wild plum bushes. He led the way around to the right, to come up close and upwind. At about 50 yards, on the other side, was a good size warthog, I squatted down and took steady aim. The bullet hit behind the hog's shoulder and knocked him down. It didn't take Nitu long to race up there and put the coup de grace cutting its throat. He then cut down a sapling, and with some special bark peeled from a nearby tree, he was able to tie the hog's legs together. Danielle carried the gun while Nitu and I carried the hog between us. It was quite a haul back to camp. Nitu, though a Moslem, didn't mind dressing the animal, and hung it high in the tree, out of reach of any hungry hyenas. He would camp nearby, after having lit a good, roaring fire. Danielle brought out the drinks, she with a beer and myself with the usual scotch. Nitu politely took a coke. We got the burner going to fry up some hamburgers. It was a simple meal that evening, but so very nice, here in the bush. Various night birds, like owls, made their hoots. In the distance we could hear the hyenas calling. As the fire died down, it made the stars sparkle clearly above us; it was cold and beautiful. The scotch tasted good, and the burgers could have been filet mignon that evening. It was one of those nights one hoped would never end. Nitu had his own bivouac set up, not too far off, with a small fire. Danielle and I crawled into our tent and fastened the tent fly tight. This was the finishing touch to a beautiful evening.

Early morning, I heard a cough, and Nitu was cracking twigs to start the fire. By the time I was up and about, he had a little kettle on the burner for tea. I let Danielle stay in, and had myself a quick sponge bath from a wash basin. The water was cold, but refreshing. Nitu and I made some tea. The dawn was just greying in the east, and one could begin to distinguish the forest and the pathways. Nitu headed off as usual, this time at a fair pace. It was soon broad daylight, and a myriad of birds singing. Nitu spotted warthogs on two occasions, but I said no, I wouldn't shoot another. We had walked a large circle in about two hours, without spotting any other game. By the time we got back, I could smell cooking from quite a distance. Danielle had been busy frying up bacon, and was ready to do the eggs. Instead of toast, we had Lebanese Arab bread, brought from Beirut. We all had our plates ready. I insisted that Nitu join us without the bacon. This late breakfast finished, I relaxed in the tent and dozed. The great outdoors was most enjoyable and I enjoyed the hikes we went on. I didn't care if we scared up any animals or not. The bird shooting was more sporting to me. I had quite a few partridge and guinea fowl for when Pierre and Rolande arrived on Saturday. The hog had been cut up and

I'd made a barbecue. They arrived very early in the morning and caught Danielle and I still tenting! We all had a good laugh. The French are very open about such things. Pierre couldn't wait to get going for a hunt; I guess he was all excited because I had shot the hog. Just Pierre, Nitu and myself took off for another long day. Pierre shot a fine warthog, It was to be another barbecue when we got back. Nitu had fixed a charcoal fire and placed a grate over it. I was surprised how great the food tasted. Rolande had brought her French wine, and it was another great weekend. Pierre took the hog home, and I gave some of the birds that I shot, to Nitu.

One evening, in Kano, Pierre said that he intended to build a small shack, right were we had the tent. He could get hold of wooden packing cases, and with another French friend and a carpenter, the place could be fixed up in a week. I said I was sorry I wouldn't be here to help, but I contributed my share of the money which was gratefully accepted.

The month of January 1960 had flown by, we packed our stuff and deadheaded back to Beirut. Pierre and Rolande saw us off.

Margaret had not returned from England. I sent a cable that I was back. She responded that she and Christian would arrive shortly. I noticed that her message had no ending in love. I finally picked them up at the airport, but there was no warm greeting from her. Christian was just over two, and didn't take long to know me again. He was all boy, and so much fun. I didn't know how to approach Margaret. She was most sensitive, now two months pregnant and beginning to show, and looked awfully cute. I longed to put my arms around her and hug her tight; Margaret would have no part of it. I came back once, from a long night flight from the gulf. It was about 8:30 AM. when I returned to the apartment I heard Christian sobbing in his room. I went in, and Margaret was over him, scolding the little fellow. I asked her what the problem was; before I knew it, she turned around and gave me a hell of slap. I was startled for the moment. Then I noticed a very strange look in her eyes; not just fierce and angry, but strange, almost looking off into the distance and not at me. When I recovered, I asked if she was all right. Margaret just walked past me and entered the bedroom and slammed the door.

Margaret used all the closet space in our room. I had my clothes in the spare room. I took a quick shower and got into some old clothes. Then I got Christian dressed and made breakfast. We sat and played for over an hour before Margaret came out. She called someone on the phone and left by taxi, with not a word to us. I was groggy with sleep, but tried to keep pace with Christian. I bundled him into the car and we went over to the Bremers, not too far away. Christian and the Bremer lad, Andreas, played well together. Moritz came in from his wanderings, and we had a beer. I passed out on their couch and slept soundly. I confided to my friends, who loved Margaret, and hoped it was nothing serious. I took Christian back

*The Dangora camp, 1959.*

*With first officer Abelis, Danielle, and Rolande Richeau and Nitu with wort-hog, 1959.*

for his afternoon snooze. Margaret had not returned. As soon as Christian was asleep, I too flopped on the bed and fell asleep. I woke later when I heard Margaret puttering around in the kitchen. I surfaced and washed up, Christian was already up and playing. She came out with marked change. Margaret asked about the dinner, and did Christian behave. The strange look had gone from her eyes; They were bright and clear. I said I'd help cook steaks, if she would like. That would be great. Slowly, things settled again. Music was turned on, and Margaret had a drink, usually a shandy, a concoction that she'd tried in India: half beer and half lemonade or 7-up. Not too much conversation; I didn't want another flareup. I decided let her do the talking. Once in a while, I thought of that right-hand wallop she gave me; there

was a lot of strength in it. Maybe intuition had told her I had misbehaved in Kano.

Anyway, my flying continued; I made another trip back to Petra. Margaret wouldn't go, so I took a movie camera that I'd purchased in Beirut and took a couple hundred feet of the ancient city. I then had another short vacation, and was able to take Margaret to Jerusalem. Christian was taken care of by the young German girl. It was a lovely, relaxing holiday. Margaret enjoyed all the historic sights; everything appeared to be normal with her. There were parties with all our friends, and Margaret got to know several English couples who were a lot of fun. Christian had his polio shots by a United Nations Relief Association lady doctor. She was one of four English friends, and checked on Christian once in a while. I had some of my pilot friends, who came to visit us. Good old Mitch Mitchell was flying for Middle East Airlines. He and Hopkins now had a bar-restaurant, called The Neptune Bar. Later, they opened another, called the Captain's Cabin. Then Mitch got married to a swell girl, name Ginny that he had met at Margaret-Rose beauty parlor. She was half Lebanese and half Mexican - some combination! There was Bob Mason and Bernice. He flew for TransMediterranian, (TMA), which was all cargo. Then there was Ray Gifford, and Gibby Gibson, from old CNAC. And, of course, Indian Jim Moore and his lovely Chinese wife, Ann. He now had the Commodore Hotel operating, but was not getting along too well with his Lebanese partners. Jack and Cora Brown moved into a new apartment, This was our world, all these old friends from the old days in China and Calcutta, and here we were, living in a fast-moving community from all walks of life. Lebanon, the Paris of the East was a most friendly, tight little country, with scenery to match anywhere. Who the heck would want to fight and be nasty, whether it be political or just family feuds.

That summer, I was assigned to duty in Paris. It was on a charter basis with Air France. The flights were daily - Paris, Nice and Ajaccio, in Corsica, the birthplace of Napoleon. I thought this would be a good change for Margaret, to go with me and Christian; "Yes," with the understanding, though, that she would travel on to Manchester and visit her folks when she wanted.

Our home for the month was at Terrasse Hotel, in Montmarte, the area of the artists colony, and, Sacre Coeur. The DC-6 flights were easy, we used Air France cabin staff. I enjoyed the change of pace, from the night flights in the Persian Gulf area. We had been in Paris a week when Margaret decided to take Christian off to England. This was understandable, since I was gone a lot. On my time off, some of crew and myself went sightseeing and boat rides on the Seine River.

Time hurried by, and before long, the summer had gone and it was time to returned to Beirut. Margaret and Christian joined me in Paris for the last couple of days before departure. Margaret was heavy with child, and I tried to help her all I could. I did a lot of the cooking and looking after Christian in Beirut. He was a young lad now, and well housebroken. In fact, we had a little stool for him, so he could wee-wee into the commode. We had a Lebanese maid who did most of the housework and laundry. This was a great relief for Margaret.

September was upon us, and yet it was still fairly warm, and no rain. Most Lebanese families maintain small homes in the mountains, to get away from the summer heat. They all had little gardens and fruit trees. Dr. Tradd, who delivered Christian and thousands of other babies, had a son who was also a doctor trained in Germany. They had a summer clinic of their own in Aley. Aley was a summer resort in the mountains, just north of Beirut, on the Damascus Highway. Most Arabs from the Persian Gulf countries come to Aley with their families and harems.

*Winging my way across Mont Blanc, Alps in 1960.*

It was a lovely town that overlooked Beirut and the Mediterranean Sea.

One day, as Margaret was feeling her labor pains, I raced her up to the Dr. Tradd's place in Aley. The baby was now due, nothing happened. For precautions, the doctor thought it best for her to remain there while I returned to Beirut with Christian. He was all excited, I explained to him that he would soon have a baby brother or sister to play with. I called the doctor's office the next morning, September 14th, and was informed that nothing had happened yet. After Christian and I had eaten lunch, we were back in Aley, and still nothing. The baby was now a couple of weeks overdue. We sat with Margaret for a little while, I then decided to take Christian for a stroll along the lovely tree-lined road. It was cool and nice. Christian was curious and wanted to examine everything in sight. I guess we walked for about half an hour, and returned to the clinic. I settled Christian down with crayons and paper. He was content with his scribbling. The next thing I knew, there was a commotion going on backstage. A nurse ran in and said, "It's happening!" Would I like to see? "Oh, shit!" I said; I'd not seen anything like that before, I forgot Christian and ran after the nurse, who led the way to the operating room in time for me to see the doctor pull something out of Margaret. It was all bloody and stringy. I don't remembered too much, but he snipped the cord and tied a knot, and presto, it was over. If it was a baby, it certainly didn't look like one; it was a terrible sight. Dr. Tradd was all excited and said, "Look, it's a beautiful baby girl!" I couldn't tell one of end from the other, but I looked at Margaret, who was out cold. I asked if she was all right. "Oh, yes; she'll come around in a few minutes." The baby was carted off, and I was left with Margaret. She finally opened her eyes a little and smiled. I told her I saw the baby, and it was a girl. She asked what color eyes did it have. Hell, I didn't know; they were probably closed, any-

way. I blurted out that they were blue. She relaxed and returned to her drowsy state. The doctor came back and showed me the baby. It now looked like one and, same as Christian was, all wrapped tightly around like a cocoon, with only the head showing, and eyes closed. The doctor suggested that I return home and back first thing in the morning. It was then I thought of Christian. Egad, I hoped he was okay! He was; one of the nurses had taken care of him, he was still scribbling. We finally got home, and I was exhausted. Anyone would have thought that I had the baby! I took care of Christian by giving him his meal and put him into his night things. He played around in the living room with his tricycle. I poured my routine scotch, stood on the porch and looked out at Ras-Beirut, and the Mediterranean. I hoped Margaret would be more happy with the two children; we could lead a happy life together. I loved her a great deal.

Christian was my alarm clock. He woke me up at of dawn for his breakfast. He now had his own bed, and the crib was ready for the Baby girl. Margaret said that if the baby was a girl, she wanted to name her Hannah. Christian and I had our oatmeal in the kitchen, before long we were winding our way back up the Damascus Road for Aley. We had a large bouquet of flowers for the occasion. Margaret was sitting up and looking fresh and pretty as ever. Baby Hannah was with her. Christian was intrigued with his new-found sister. We spent most of the day at the clinic with Margaret. She would return home in a few days. It was still very early evening when we left the clinic, on the spur of the moment, I decided I'd rather have some Lebanese food instead of returning home. I saw a restaurant I had noticed before. The front of the place opened out into a terrace, overlooking Beirut. There were quite a few people already there. Christian, and I sat in a corner. I ordered a small mazza for me, and some grilled chicken: this, Christian could tackle without any trouble. I had wine and watched the beautiful, cool evening. Christian had done pretty with his meal, and was a bit restless to move about. I gave him a clean up, and let him walked around the tables, mostly Lebanese who tried to talked to him. At one table of about four people, one gentleman who had his back to me started stroking Christian head, and asked him his name. Christian said it was "Christian Goutiere." The man looked surprised, and did a double take. He again said to Christian, "Your name is Goutiere?" "Yes," was the answer; "My Daddy is over there," and pointed in my direction. The elderly, fairly bald individual looked around at me and said, "You Mr. Goutiere?" "Yes," I said. "Are you any relation to Alice Goutiere, and are you Vernon Goutiere?" "Good heavens! Yes," I said;" my brother's name is Vernon, and Alice is my mother." He jumped up and said, "You must be Peter." "That's right." "You were in PSC College. Do you remember PSC in Naini-Tal?" I was dumbfounded. He said, "I am Nazi Fetto." We both leaped up and embraced - after all these years! He and his young brother, Sami Fetto, lived in Baghdad, where they owned a pharmacy. He and his family, like so many other people I have mentioned, were escaping the desert heat and were here to enjoy the scenery and coolness. There was so much to talk about! I first had to say I'd become a proud father again, right here in Aley. I said I do fly to Baghdad quite often. My mother was still living, and was in Plainfield, New Jersey, and that Vernon was a doctor in California; that my sister, Geraldine, was also married and lived in New Jersey, that Christine was a well-known writer, living in Maine. What was to be short evening turned into a very lengthy and pleasant one. Christian was about asleep, and I'd had more than my share of wine. I finally took leave, and I said I would write and tell my folks about this meeting, and how it came about, with Christian doing the honors.

Margaret was soon back home, and little Hannah was now the center of attraction. Christian was most excited with his little sister, and watched every moved that went on. Days and weeks went by, and little Hannah grew fast. I nicknamed her "Hannah-Baba," in the manner the ayahs (nursemaids) in India called me, as all babies: I was called "Peter-Baba." I did my flying, and everything seemed well. I was happy, and hoped Margaret would love Lebanon as I did. It had its own special charm. There were so many of my old friends here, and Margaret and I made so many new ones; it was a big, happy family. Alas, it was not to be for long!

It happened when I and another crew took an Air France charter from Beirut to Djibouti and Madagascar. It was a four day trip. It was a good flight all the way and back. However, I could hardly wait to be back with the family. It was late in the afternoon, when I returned and I found no one home. There was no note where Margaret had gone. I called our friends, but none had seen her. I looked about the apartment, and noticed a couple of suitcase missing. I couldn't make myself believe that she would leave without

a note, or discuss it before I went on my trip. The telephone system may not be the greatest, but I was appreciative of the one we had now. It took a while before I finally got through to Margaret's folks in Manchester, in Eccles. Mrs. Miles answered and was surprised to hear me. I asked if Margaret had flown to Manchester. There was a moment of silence. She finally said Margaret was there, she would get her to the phone. When Margaret answered, she acted as though there was nothing wrong. Why did she go without leaving a note, or telling me? It came to her at the last minute, and she'd forgotten to leave a message. Besides, if I was going to be gone all that time, four days, why couldn't she go to England? I asked when she planned to be coming back. She wasn't sure, but would cable me. I was lost for words; I was tired and distraught, confused, upset, and heartbroken. I usually go racing to the Bremers with my troubles, but they had left, and Moritz had signed up with Lufthansa. The only friends I think I had left were the whiskey-drinking ones. I cleaned up and made some cheese and crackers. I got all the makings and sat at the bar with the scotch. I got my music repertoire on the 45-rpm discs, and slowly got inebriated. I said to myself, "Aw, fuck the world! fuck all these crazy women and wives! I'll become a bachelor again, and no more women. I'd cut off my damn cock, and be like prairie dogs. I'll disappear into the Hinterlands of the Himalayas and no one will find me. Shit! All this marriage stuff to hell with them all!" So many thoughts ran through my mind as I sipped my scotch and listened to my favorite tunes. One of them of course, was "Because of You." If Margaret's actions was because I had seen Danielle who Margaret knew, well, good! Then I deserved it! But it wasn't, and she wasn't jealous. There something else that I could not fathom. Something had gone wrong somewhere, but what could it be? I loved Margaret I did everything I knew to make her happy. Whatever she wanted, I would make sure she would get - clothes, travel, whatever it might be! My friends said once that I was spoiling her. Why not, if you love somebody that much? And now with the children, I loved her more, if that were possible. I guess I must have had a snootful. I don't remember too much, but woke up sometime in the morning, with my clothes still on, and a wild headache. I then remembered the evening before, and Margaret and the children. I made a strong cup of tea and took two aspirin, a long hot shower, and made myself presentable. I had a big bowl of yogurt. I enjoyed it with honey; it was cold, and soothed the burning inside.

When in a sad mood, it is not good to be alone, so I went to the Kaneymeyers. They were having lunch, and was asked to join them. I thought the world of these folks, and their two boys. I cried on their shoulders, which made me feel better. Elizabeth was a strikingly good-looking woman, a Marlene Dietrich type, and was most knowledgeable. It was she who said something that began to make sense. It appeared simple and logical.

*With an AirFrance stewardess who served on our AirLiban flights Paris-Ajacio, Corsica.*

She said that perhaps Margaret feels that because of marriage and children, she had been deprived of her theatrical career, that perhaps I am to blame. I pondered this for a long time. I remembered once talking to Margaret about her career, and she had said it did not matter. I remember saying a pilot's life is different from the 9-to-5 variety individual. She had laughed and said the theatrical life was no easy 9-to-5 either. I thought to myself that no budding actress would wish to marry the likes of me, when she could choose from the many handsome actors around. Elizabeth said that Margaret would get over this feeling in time, especially with the children to care for. "Inshallah! (If God wills)," I said.

Then Margaret cabled and said she would be returning. I met them the airport. The cool air of North England had given the kids rosey cheeks, it was the first thing I noticed; I forgot everything else. I was tickled and happy to have the children back. Hannah-Baba was looking cute, and she did have blue eyes; I had guessed right. If there was any difference, with Margaret it was not noticed. Margaret had brought back some new types of lampshades for the ceiling lights, rather tricky to put up, but I was able to figure out the mechanism. I took a few days off and we went to the beach; Margaret wanted to catch the sun. Christian loved playing in the sand, the usual castles. Hannah sat in her pram and seemed to enjoy it all.

One evening, I casually asked Margaret about the theater, and if she missed it. She didn't look right at me, and said, "Not

*Time off and sight-seeing in Paris: The Sacre Coere in the montmartre area.*

really." I let it go at that. On one of my return trips, I got the same strange look of Margaret's; it was that stare through you. She then turned and gave me a tongue-lashing, with a lot of swearing. She made strange accusations I couldn't believe. She said I was purposely planting insects, like cockroaches, around the apartment. I flat out said she was crazy; why in the world would I do a thing like that? Yes! there were roaches around, but I hated them, too. I tried spraying and debugging the place. I'd never dream of anything as crazy as that! She wouldn't let up, rising to a screech. I tried walking away, but she kept at me. I tried to soothe her. I explained that Christian was listening to all of this; think of him. Margaret finally stopped, went into the bedroom and slammed the door again.

My world crumbled around me. I was so upset, I shook. I went to Christian's room, and the little fellow looked up at me with his big blue eyes. He wanted to know why Mommy was crying. I couldn't answer; I just hugged him, and Hannah was playing in her crib. It was Thanksgiving time, and Bob and Bernice Mason had invited us for the traditional dinner. Their boy, Bruce, and Christian got along well together. Margaret didn't want to go. This was the worst I had noted with Margaret; she didn't even wish to talk. I may just as well have been in Africa. There was no Thanksgiving.

I did my annual flight and route checking with the French Chief Pilot, and almost flunked the ride; my mind was not on the job. Then another blow came that damn near blew me out. The American Embassy ( Consulate Section ) wanted to see me; I had forgotten all about that five-year law of natu-

ralized Americans which now raised its ugly head. I visited the Consulate Office and was informed that January was the deadline, that I had better make arrangements to return to the States. I literally begged if there wasn't some way I could remain on. The Consulate thumbed through his regulations and came up with this bright idea: The regulation stated that a naturalized Citizen may remain overseas in a foreign country no longer than the duration of five years, and/or three years in the country of his birth, or commonwealth country. What was being implied was that I may stay another three years in India or some British Commonwealth country; he was not certain if I could get away with it. The only thing I could do was to give it try. He said there was no way I could remain in Lebanon. I asked where did this law come from; why are naturalized citizens regarded as second-class Americans? The reason he gave was that at turn of the century, most naturalized immigrants - Italians, mainly - made all their money in the States and then took off for their homeland and lived happily ever after, and cheaply, they didn't contribute to the country or pay taxes. In 1904 or thereabouts, Congress passed a law that all such citizens could only stay five years in their native country the law was renewed in 1958. I was given an extension through January 1961. I thanked the officer and left. Now to break the news to Margaret! She hadn't got over the roaches yet.

I decided to stop at Mitch's bar, the Neptune, and think things over. This was to be a big decision. On my last tour at Kano, I once stopped at Accra and talked with my old friend, Bob Bethel. He was now Chief Pilot

for Ghana Airways. Bob had mentioned that Ghana Airways were toying with the idea of purchasing two to three Boeing 707s for their Accra-London routes. If it came through, he would like me to join them. Ghana Airways already had a fleet of Russian-Aleutian aircraft, handled entirely by the Russians, Aeroflot people. Bob ran the British section of the Airline. With the Boeings, they probably would have an American section, where I could fit in. We laughed over it then. Now I got a brainstorm. Ghana and Nigeria were still Commonwealth countries. If I got a job in Ghana, I'd have another three years. This would give me time to think over the future. I wondered if Margaret would go for it. After several beers, I picked up enough courage and returned to the apartment.

I sat down and told Margaret about my visit to the Consulate. I said we would have to leave Lebanon in about six months. "Oh, good!" she said, "I'd like to get out of here." I was surprised; I thought she liked Beirut and all it had to offer. "Where are we going?" I told her about Accra, Ghana, that was a possibility of a job there. "Good, I'd like that," she said. She had friends there. I was pleasantly surprised, but dumbstruck. I wasted no time in sending Bob a letter by our airline. Bob came back that the airline had put a down payment on the Boeings, that he would talk to the Managing Director about me, and felt certain I would be hired. Margaret seemed happy again. She asked how we would get all our belongings to Accra. I figured we could send most of the things by Air Liban. Also, Ghana Airways operated a Britania Aircraft that could possibly carry a load of our belongings. I found, too, that I was scheduled for my TDY assignment in Kano, staying for New Years 1961. I suggested to Margaret that she come along on this TDY (temporary duty), that Kano was great, and there were some nice people there. She could also stay over in Accra with the kids, and look the place over with Bob Bethel. Though it was a good idea, she preferred to go back to England and stand by; I didn't argue.

I wrote Bob that I'd be in Kano for a month and would get in touch with him on my way through, that would be on Sunday. Margaret and I had a great Christmas with the children. They were loaded down with toys, Several parties were held, and a lot of our friends, like the Kneymeyers, were sorry that we were leaving Beirut. I saw Margaret, Christian and Hannah-Baba off for England. I think she knew the route well by now. The few days I had before leaving, I sale tagged some of my furniture that we would not need in Accra. I collected a lot of stuff for Pierre and Rolande and their children as a late Christmas. Pierre had written that he and some of his French friends had built a small shack where they said they would, I bought a few dishpans and barbecue gadgets to help. It was the last day of 1960 when we left Beirut for Khartoum and on to Kano, my crew and I deadheading. Yes, Danielle was one of my cabin crew! Oh, what the hell! From Khartoum, we would be flying into the New Year. In fact, the flight would be about over Fort Lamy when 1960 became 1961.

We all had seats up front and after the meal, the cabin lights were out and the passengers asleep. It would be a long day for us to take the flight on to Dakar and back. The flight was smooth, not a ripple. There were no equatorial storms around. I must have dozed off, because, suddenly the DC-6 shook and all the cabin lights came on bright. I thought there was an emergency. I jumped up out of my sleep, as did everyone else in the cabin. The on-duty cabin staff called out "Happy New Year!" with the bullhorn. Everyone woke up. The next moment, champagne corks popped, and the passengers were served "bubble/squeak" in paper cups, and I'll be damned, here arrived Danielle with a cake and a bottle of champagne. "This is for the crew," she said, and gave me a big kiss in front of everyone, and "Happy New Year" I cut the cake, and Danielle poured champagne for the crew soon to be on duty. I might add, this being a French run company, wine is accepted in the cockpit, and always has been. This was a pleasant surprise.

In the midst of this festivity, 18,000 feet or thereabouts over the wilds of central Africa, I was asked to come to the cockpit. The pilot said we were coming up to Fort Lamy in about ten minutes. I contacted the tower and asked to get Raymond Poisevara on the radio, and wish him a "Bonne l'an." It was a clear night, the Southern Cross constellation appeared to be pinned on the horizon. It had taken the tower operators not too long to fetch Raymond, as I remembered, his home was not too far from the airport. With the crew interpreting, Raymond said he was already at a party, but "Happy New Year!" he said he was sipping whiskey as I sipped champagne. We saw the city below, all lit up, and the flashing beacon a top the tower building. In the next few minutes, it was all over. The city had vanished, and Raymond back to his party. I was glad I was able to wish him the season's greetings. We were all awake, and cleaned up for takeover of our flight from Kano. That was quite a New Year's ushering-in that I won't forget. I said to myself, that I wished Margaret and the children a wonderful New Year, and wished they could have been here.

I didn't see Bob on arrival at Accra. I think he was sleeping off a New Year's party. I left word I'd catch up with him on my return from Dakar. "Yep," he looked the worse for wear, but we met, and were able to discuss the job and when could I be there. The Director-General had agreed for me to join Ghana Airways and should sign up by mid March. I gave Bob my U.S. and Lebanese licenses and said he would obtain the Ghanian Air Transport license for me.

Back in Kano, Pierre met me, where I loaded him down with all good things for Christmas and the camp. I also had been able to obtain 100 rounds of cartridges for his rifle. He was absolutely elated. "No rest," said he. "Rolande wants

*Bernice Mason, Ray Gifford, Bob Mason and Annie Gifford at my bar, Beirut 1958.*

you over for dinner." Danielle always seemed to know what was going on; she was standing there with her bag, ready to go. It would be another New Year's party with champagne. They had a few friends over, some of whom I had met before, including the doctor. It was very nice, and I was getting my second wind. Pierre said the jeep was ready, and I was welcome to go at any time to the new camp. Wednesday would be fine; I needed to catch up on myself, Danielle and I were soon shopping for our safari. I had a carton of cigarettes for Nitu as well. Pierre and his friends had done a good job of constructing the camp; Nitu was happy to see us, his eyes popped like circuit-breakers when he saw the cigarettes. Danielle had brought a small battery-operated radio, so we would not be completely shut off from the outside world.

Once inside, the cabin looked quite spacious. They had constructed two double-decker bunks on opposite sides, screened windows, and a long, narrow table off to one side, plus space for storage. I told Nitu I would not be doing any hunting this afternoon, but first thing in the morning, we would try our luck. He had piled a lot of firewood at the fireplace made of stones, Nitu took his leave, and Danielle and I were alone. The weather was cool and very dry. We sat on the edge of the stream and talked. I did not discuss Margaret, but I think she knew there were problems and everyone knew of my pending move to Ghana. She was sad to know I was leaving. I explained the circumstances under which I had to go. Danielle said, "Stupid laws!" Absolutely correct. It was another 5 or 6 years before the law was declared unconstitutional; no more would naturalized citizens be regarded as second-class.

We wiled away the whole afternoon, the sun was a large orange orb, slipping into the west. It got cold, so I decided a fire in the outdoor fireplace would be great. I retrieved two camp chairs as Danielle fixed our drinks. Neither of us was in the mood to cook, so we settled for chicken sandwiches. Night life in the forest had come alive, with varied sounds and cries, But of all the sounds, the weirdest was the hyena's call; it was really eerie it reminded me a bit of the jackals. We finally said good-night to the owls and hyenas. Danielle and I took the lower bunk, which was really for a single person, but when two people tried to wiggle in, I doubt if there would be a comfortable sleep. In other words, it would lay two and sleep one! Somehow, we eventually managed to fall asleep. I don't know what time I awoke, but when I did, I was all aches and pains. My derriere, was ice-cold. Evidently, it had stuck out in the cold while I slept. I heard twigs snapping again, and knew it was Nitu starting the fire. I lit the lantern and started the burner for tea. I stepped out and greeted my friend. It was terribly cold. It reminded me of Darjeeling. I got a basin of water and had a quick wash! Danielle was up and busy making tea. Nitu heated more water, and left the large pot on the wood fire for Danielle. This she took in back of the cabin and had a makeshift bath. Though the early morning was freezing cold, I still loved it: the smell of the fire, the hot tea, the hundreds of birds, mainly doves, that were beginning to make a racket as dawn was beginning to cast its grey streaks out of the east. Time seemed to stand still. I wondered how it would be if one had to live right here and do this routinely the rest of their lives? I only wondered. Nitu was not thinking anything except to get our asses in gear for the hunt. Danielle was all fixed up and was busy cooking breakfast of fried eggs and Arabic bread warmed near the fire.

With everything stashed in the cabin, a water jug for Nitu to carry, we were on our way. I informed him I was not interested in warthogs, only antelope. We walked for over

*Hannah-Baba with Peace in Accra, Ghana. One year old, 1961.*

an hour and rested; nothing in sight. This was no East Africa that abounded with game. There were no lions. Nitu said he had seen leopards, but not for a long time.

We walked some more, and Danielle had to rest more often. Nitu was ranging quite a distance ahead, like a hunting dog, As I mentioned, the bush country was sparse of trees, but a fair amount of underbrush was always there. Nitu came to a stop and signaled for us to come up to him. We were soon by his side. I tried to follow where he was pointing, but could see nothing that resembled game. I kept looking at every tree and shrub. Finally, I saw something; a little movement of white near the ground; it moved again. It was antelope legs; the top part was hidden by the shrubs. We sat and waited. The animal was a good 150 yards away, I would guess. It moved very slowly to our right. I motioned to Nitu that perhaps we could go off to the far right and wait, he nodded. We backed away slowly, then he led us in a wide circle, and back in the direction the antelope was traveling. There was a fairly open space not far ahead of us and from the area where the antelope would have to come out. It was awhile before we spotted the whitish legs moving at the base of the brush. It was now much closer, and I found myself breathing rather heavily. That would not do! I tried relaxing as I sat with the rifle ready. I could see the branches moving near the edge. It seemed ages before I could make out the body, a light brown. There was a small opening, just ahead of him, where the animal was headed. I rested my elbows on my knees and pointed the rifle at the spot. Sure enough, the antelope stepped out in that area and stopped. I took careful aim and fired. The animal dropped, and Nitu bounded out across the open space, and was on the animal. He had his knife and cut its throat, The antelope turned out to be a young reedbuck. I had shot one of these in Fort Lamy. They were good eating. Nitu gutted it, and now began the job of getting it back to camp about 7 or 8 miles

away. Thankfully, it did not weigh more than 80 pounds. Nitu did his masterful trick of obtaining stringing bark and a pole. We had a good rest and a bite to eat, then made the trip back in slow stages. I thought the camp would never show up. I recognized more landmarks as we progressed. Late that afternoon, we were back. Danielle and I were beat. Nitu took charge, skinned, and then wrapped the meat in plastic and hung it up in a tree, as he had done with the hog. Nitu was pleased as punch that he had led us to the first antelope shot at camp. I told him that he would have to eat barbecue with us on Saturday, when Pierre and Rolande showed up. He grinned.

Nitu made enough hot water for both Danielle and myself. She went first around the corner for her bath, then I took my turn. It's amazing how a little something like that can freshen one up and put life into you. I felt clean and ready for scotch. Danielle seemed refreshed too. She went to work and made a makeshift Lebanese mazza. Again, we just relaxed after our long hike, which was enjoyable. We sipped our drinks near the fire, and watched that big golden sun disappear into the western pocket. That's when the temperature dropped sharply and the end of a successful day. We were tired and turned in early, for a good sleep. The next day was spent close to camp, looking for partridge and guinea fowl. Pierre and Rolande arrived very early Saturday, and were excited that we had shot an antelope. Now, just Pierre, Nitu and myself took off for another shoot. No luck at that day. Danielle and I returned to Kano, and Pierre and Rolande would remain Sunday.

I saw Bob Bethel on my next trip, he had my Ghanian pilot's license for me. He said I was all set, that hopefully the next week he would have the contract papers for me to sign. I knew there was an American Consulate in Kaduna, Nigeria. This is where I once landed with Pan Africa in 1942, to pick up the injured crew that had force-

landed a B-26 near there. Through Air Liban I arranged a free ticket on Nigerian Airways from Kano to Kaduna, and return.

I checked in at a little hotel, the Kaduna Inn. It was just a large, rambling, bungalow; one story, with the usual corrugated tin roof, The floors were terazzo. The ceiling fans turned lazily. It reminded me of Calcutta, sans the Indian garden crows. The person at the desk was dark-skinned, tall, husky, and about 50. The minute he spoke, I realized he must be from my part of the world. I asked if he happened to be from India, and his face lit up. Yes; from Calcutta. I said we had a lot in common, that as soon as I finished my business in town, I wanted to talk with him.

An African houseboy showed me my room, a large, clean, and simple one. I got a taxi to the Consulate, and introduced myself to one of the Consulate officers. He was interested in my case, and had me meet his senior. I discussed my problem in detail, and what I had been told by his counterparts in Beirut. They looked up the regulation, it said "and/or." I had to tell them a small white lie, that I was a resident of Kano, that I flew out of there to West Africa. On the basis of this, I was issued an extension on my passport for another year, to January 1962. I was happy, and thanked the Consul very much.

Back at the Inn, I got hold of the Anglo-Indian friend, who was the proprietor, and his wife. There was not much activity at the place, so the couple were able to join me for lunch. We had a great conversation about the old days in Calcutta, especially the war days. These folks had packed up when India got its independence in 1947; As did many others. We even chatted a bit in Hindi. The lunch, or "tiffin" as they called it, had to be good old curry and rice. A cold beer went well. After lunch, we all went our ways for the afternoon rest, which was customary. I lay down and stared at the ceiling, the overhead fan turning. It was cool and pleasant. I felt relieved, the world had been taken off my shoulders, temporarily. Another year to figure the future as I had to provide well for the growing family. I guess I must have dozed off, possibly more from mental fatigue than from the beer and curry. There was a gentle rapping on the door; it was the houseboy. He said my hosts would have afternoon tea on the verandah, about 4:30, they wished that I would join them. I had to settle for a cold shower, as the hot water heater is only turned on at certain hours, namely, in the morning. It woke me up, anyway, and then met my friends, British-Indian style, I thought I was back there. All of a sudden, I missed not having my mother and brother and sisters with me. We always had our afternoon teas in BhimTal and Bhowali.

It was so pleasant and tranquil in Kaduna. I decided to stay one more day. They told me where I could take fairly long walks behind the Inn, along the old, well-worn pathways. They warned me to be on the lookout for snakes, especially spitting cobras. They hang around homes and villages, a barnyard menace. I knew there were cobras, but I had never heard of spitting ones. My host said they were not very large snakes, but their spitting was very accurate and usually aimed at the eyes. The spit was not poisonous, but would blind you for a spell. This is how the snakes can approach and put the finishing touches to their victims. I got a stick and did my walking along the trails. Much of the way was through Kaduna fields that were mainly cassava. The area was loaded with partridge. No one bothered hunting them. What I wouldn't give to have my gun at this point! Maybe I'd have a chance another time. I enjoyed my short stay in Kaduna and talking with some of the villagers. My friends at the inn drove me to the airport the next day. I said I would try to return another time. I haven't made it back yet, but do have wonderful memories of the place. The rest of the month in Kano went fast, I was able to sign my contract with Ghana Airways and was back in Beirut. Margaret and the children were soon to join me. I had started tagging all the things for sale. When Margaret arrived she decided to go over the list with me. It didn't take long to sell the heavy furniture and lot of bric-a-brac. The first week in March I was placing some of my belongings on a Ghana Airways plane, and Bob had a temporary apartment for me where we could store our stuff. A couple of trips had most of our belongings in Accra, but wouldn't you know Margaret took off with the kids back to England. I just didn't understand. I piled the rest of the things onto Air Liban, and on my way to Accra and a new job.

Bob Bithell welcomed me to Accra officially with a few of his English pilot friends. They, too, had been in Burma and Jordan with him. Bob was alone in Accra, and had a nice apartment where he threw a small welcome party for me. Part of the contract included free housing and the company would also buy a car, which was actually theirs, but was for my use, a dry-lease affair. If you wanted to buy the car, they would deduct it from your salary.

The next day Bob took me to the new apartment building that would be my home. It was brand new and still smelled of paint. It was a nice, newly furnished apartment with wide balconies, and I was now able to bring my household things to the apartment.

I then went into town. Egad! it seemed strange that I would be back in Accra to live after almost 20 years! The town had changed. I picked a small car, an Austin A40, a solid hatchback. The company did all the paperwork. I signed the contract and was given the driver's license. Bob had worked fast and before I knew it, I was all set up in the new apartment. A message was sent to Margaret to contact Ghana Airways in London, that a ticket was waiting for her and the children. I arranged the place the best I could, and would let Margaret put in the finishing touches when she arrived. There was a nice English store in town called Kingsway. It was a supermarket. I stocked the refrigerator and was now in

*Plummer funeral home where I met the Mayor of Augusta in his coffin! 1962.*

business. The next project was to obtain a houseboy. I did this by asking the other houseboys to recommend one. It didn't take many days before one was presented to me. He was a young Nigerian. He showed me his papers from a previous employer, which is always necessary to see. The young man's name was Hilary. He looked clean and spoke good English, so I hired him.

Bob held a pilots' meeting officially, and I met most of the people. There were several Ghanian captains and first officers. I made the rounds of the airline facility and the maintenance shops. A lot of the locals were surprised to learn that I was once stationed in Accra with Pan American in 1942. Some remembered the Pan-Africa operation. The Russian counterpart personnel kept aloof from the rest of us. They had their own maintenance schedules and flight personnel. The aircraft were turboprop Aleutians, with Aeroflot pilots, they did not mingle with us. Plus, there was a turnover of their crews every few months. Bithell was to give me my route checks on the DC-3. The routes were to Takaradi, Kumasi, and Tamali. Other routes were to Lagos and to Sierra Leone, Abidjan and back. Bob thought it a bit ridiculous, after all the thousands of hours I had in the plane, and having flown over the West Africa Coast, but we had to go through the motions to satisfy the Civil Aviation authorities and Ghana regulations.

The internal flights were done in one day with an instrument and NDB, non-directional approach to each airport. We would skin the international ones, since I had been flying them with Air Liban. The uniform I was to wear was something else! It was the traditional British shorts and knee stockings all in white. It made me recall the days in India as a lad, and during the snow and cold in Maine. Now it was difficult for me to change to shorts after all the years in long trousers! I went along with their regulations.

I did my scheduled flights almost on a 9-to-5 basis.

I barely had been on the job a couple of weeks when Bob Bithell called me in to discuss something. He said that the Ghana government had canceled the 707 orders; that they would use the Britania turboprops for now, then buy VC-10s; that I was to go with he and several British pilots to receive training on Viscounts in London; that it would be the British-European Airways ground school at Heathrow Airport; Ghana Airways were getting two or three Viscounts for the internal and some of the international routes of Africa. We were to leave in a couple of days, I cabled Margaret the news, that I would be phoning her from London and to stand by!

We hopped on the British Airways flight and wound up at a local hotel, I think it was the Airways Hotel at Heathrow near the airport. Bob obtained a rental car to get back and forth to school. The ground school went well, perhaps a little too dragged-out. Margaret arrived with the children, and they were looking great. When the school was completed we sat for a written test given by the British Civil Air Regulation, or Air Registration Board. When that was completed we went to the Viscount factory and attended a differences course. The ground school we had attended was for the Viscount 700 Series, the ones Ghana bought were the 800 Series. This was another two weeks and then back to Heathrow. Bob informed me I'd have to take yet another course on what was known as a Performance-A Exam by the ARB. It was the performance of complex type aircraft, such as the Britannia. Once this was done we flew to Accra.

It was now July and a lot of tropical rains had arrived. Margaret loved Accra and the new apartment. Christian was tickled to have his old toys again, he hadn't seen them for some time. Hannah-Baba was quite plump and looked awfully cute. There were

*John and Agnes Plummer at their home Augusta, Maine, 1962.*

a lot of English people in Accra, we got to know several families. Most of them were the pilots and their wives, and technicians of the airline.

While in London, I purchase a used Holland and Holland rifle, hopefully to do some more big game hunting up in the northern Volta area of Ghana. Margaret appeared to be enjoying Ghana. She found one of her friends, who was employed now at a diamond field, about 70 miles northwest of Accra whom we visited. I made a butterfly net, and went back to my childhood hobby of collecting butterflies. There were many varieties, some very beautiful. On occasions, we picnicked along beaches. We would have miles of beach to ourselves, Margaret bought a portable barbecue which was great for these occasions. On one occasion, I had one of the Britannia pilots, a fellow whom I'd known in India many years ago, named Bill Jacob; and one of the Viscount instructors by the name of Haley Mills. We drove up to Takaradi, where we rented dugout canoes and paddled a long distance up the Pra River and heavy jungle. It was a fascinating trip.

Margaret located a small kindergarten school for Christian to attend. Would you believe, it was in a section of the barracks we had in 1942, in Pan Africa called Gifford Camp.

Hannah had taken her first steps, which I captured on the movie camera. One day, our houseboy, Hilary, approached us and said he wanted to get married. "Great," I said. "Who is the lucky girl?" Hilary said she lived in Lagos. He would go there for the wedding, but there was one small catch: he had

to buy his wife from her parents; it was the local custom; he didn't have the money. The price was about $50. I gave him the money and sent him on his way and in ten days he returned. The girl he brought back as his wife was 15 years old, her name was Peace. She was great to have with us, and adapted well with the kids, especially Hannah. Peace took over most of the domestic chores, while Hilary did the kitchen and all the other heavy duties. This gave us more freedom to move about.

By the time summer was over, and the tropical rains had diminished, Bob Bethel had left the company and we now had a new Chief Pilot. Evidently, the new guy didn't particularly appreciate having an American in the midst of his British group. He would try and connive ways to aggravate me, with the hope that I would leave. The first few weeks, he wouldn't let me do my final checkout on the Viscount; however, I didn't really mind. I was home more often by flying the DC-3.

On one occasion, I was given a charter to Bathurst. Here, I was to pick up a group of photographers and news people from the British Broadcasting System, for their TV show. One of the gentlemen was a Mr. Tidmarsh. He informed me that the group expected to be dropped off at Takaradi for the State Visit of Her Majesty, Queen Elizabeth, and Prince Philip. Tidmarsh wondered if footage could be taken of them boarding the airplane, of the interior, and of the cockpit in flight. I was happy to oblige. Many of our friends in England later informed me they were pleasantly surprised to see me on the

local "telly." I took Tidmarsh to Takaradi with his group. In so doing, I was able to get a front-row seat when the entourage arrived in a Royal Airforce De Havilland Heron. The Queen and the Prince were met by President Nakruma and his Egyptian wife. I took a lot of color movies of the whole procession and ceremony. Margaret at that time was visiting her friends in the diamond fields, and missed the show. The movies turned out well.

I spent lot of time out in the country, shooting the abundant Francolins. Early in December, I paid a visit to the U.S. Embassy. I wanted to know the status of my passport and citizenship. They told me that the passport would expire on the first of January, 1962. I asked for a reprieve. The Consul gave me an extension to the middle of January, somewhere around the 10th; they also said that if I was a few days overdue on arrival to the States, I would have to pay a fine or penalty of $25. I told the Chief Pilot it would be necessary to leave with Margaret and the kids without pay for six months. Margaret and the children and I went to England for the Christmas holidays and stayed at her sister's place, which was near her folks in Eccles. This is where the famous Eccles Cakes come from. It was a lovely Christmas, with her sister's children as well, but cold, very cold, as there was no central heating in these homes. I almost froze, after the African warmth. I told Margaret we would leave for America about January 10th. She informed me she would stay in Eccles till I had my passport problems resolved. I returned alone to Accra and finished my December flight time.

# PHASE SEVEN: 1962-1963

It was New Year's Eve when I had a few days off and took Hilary in the Austin A-40, with my rifle, and drove to Tamali and the Volta River. Here, I met a South African at a New Year's Party, by the name of Art Chadwick. He was officer in charge of the national park set up by Nakruma. His place was about 80 miles further on, at the edge of the game park reservation, a place called Damongo. He said there was quite a lot of good hunting around the perimeter of the reservation, that I could stay at his bungalow as well. What an offer! In the meantime, I had come down with a cold I caught in Eccles. New Year's Day, about noon, Hilary and I walked about 20 miles to try to get rid of the cold. It worked partially.

Next day, we headed on up to the bungalow at Damongo, in the Volta area. We arrived at a one-story bungalow that Chadwick had, all whitewashed, with corrugated tin roofing. Chadwick met us at the gate, and his boy unloaded the car. Inside the house was bright. The floor was covered with trophy skins, and the walls had mounted heads of all kinds of animals. I could hardly wait to get going, as I didn't have much time. Art made arrangements with a guard to be my guide.

The next morning at dawn, the man showed up. Hilary, the guide and I were on our way by 4:30 or 5 o'clock. The houseboy had made a bunch of sandwiches and a jug of water. We drove through the deserted village onto the dirt road. After a few miles, we came to a ravine. The hills on each side were craggy, and about 200-300 feet high. We made a turn, and as I straightened out, I saw something cross the road. It was too far to know what it was, because it was just beyond the actual beam of light. The guide informed me that the area on the right was the reservation, that we could stop the car in an open area on the left. He pointed up to the top and said that's where we would go. It was now getting light, with the rifle ready I was set. The guide took the knapsack and

his government .303 Enfield Rifle. I said I'd go further along the road and check tracks, to see what had crossed the road. We stopped at the spot, and there were the distinct tracks of a good-sized lion. I strained my eyes and watched for any movement. I hoped I could get a shot, even though it was off limits; I'd worry about that later. Nothing moved. From that point, we turned left and started up the ridge. The guide seemed to know where he was going and we followed. For the first half-mile or so, I was alert, thinking I might see another cat. The craggy steep climb gave way to a plateau-like terrain. The trees were more sparse, and the walking was easier. The man did not hurry. We went wandering along at a slow and easy pace, stopping once in a while. We covered a wide circle of maybe 5 to 8 miles, it had become hot and very dry, not a single animal showed. Only a few flocks of guinea fowl and monkeys. We finally sat in the shade and had our sandwiches. I rested and half dozed from fatigue. We moved on for about another hour. I was tired now, and dehydrated. I finally recognized the area we had climbed up from the car. I was glad we were almost there. I leaned against a tree and stared down at the reddish road. All of a sudden, from nowhere, came a herd of hartebeest. They stampeded from the left, going at an angle down the slope. I had time for a couple of snap shots as they went by. One of them fell ass-over-tea-kettle down the hill, the guide in pursuit. By the time we reached the antelope, the guide had cut its throat. This was no small animal, and would not fit in our little car. The guide covered it with brush, and we headed home. We would attend to bringing it back later.

Art was resting when I told him the news. He had a Land Rover that we piled into and returned to the scene. It took all three of us to hoist the animal onto the top, after it had been gutted and dressed. During the tumble down the rocky pitch, one horn had been broken. This ruined the tro-

phy itself. We unloaded the antelope at the house.

The houseboy brought in a pitcher of ice and placed it on the dining room table. I eyed this for a moment, then took one of my bottles of scotch, which was Vat-69, and poured nearly half the bottle over the ice and filled the rest up with soda water. Art watched me curiously as he nursed his goatee beard. I drank from the pitcher, while some of the cold brew trickled over the edges and down my front. It felt good, inside and out. It didn't take too long to finish. Art grinned and shook his head. I burped and said I was now ready for my siesta. While I rested, Art Chadwick and his guide skinned the antelope and had it hung up and ready for barbecuing. I felt great and relaxed. I had brought along a lot of makings for the barbecue sauce.

I went to work with the cooking while the houseboy had dug a good sized pit and filled it with charcoal. I had a large wire net placed across it. Art had invited some Italian guests over from a small hospital that they were running. Needless to say, the barbecue party was a success, I was congratulated for my efforts. I spent a week in Damango and walked a lot of miles and saw a lot of game. I shot a small cobb antelope for more barbecue. The Italians couldn't get enough of it. The week went fast and it was difficult to tear myself away from my new found friends and the wilderness. But the time had come, Hilary and I drove back to Accra. I packed up my things for my trip to the States, leaving Hilary and Peace in charge of my household. The guns were with a trusted English pilot friend. I planned to leave on the 9th from Accra. The flight on PanAm left on the 10th, my passport read the 10th as the last day of grace. A pilot friend was to take me to the field. He showed up that evening and said that the flight was canceled, due to mechanical problems. The other Britannia was on its way down with spares. So the next flight was not till the 10th. I'd be a day over on my passport.

I was not too worried, since I was advised by the U.S. Consulate that I'd have to pay a penalty of $25 on arrival at New York. I got to PanAm's counter on the 11th; the flight left around 11 AM. Everything went well; the girl checked the ticket, etc., and then looked at my passport. She pointed to the expiration date. I said yes, by one day, but I would pay $25 penalty in New York, as told by the Consulate in Accra. She said OK, but first check with the Embassy in London. Evidently, she was talking to the Consulate. She said that I would pay the fee on arrival in New York. I could hear the guy screaming on the other end of the phone: "No way! Have him report to the office of the Consulate right away." She was sorry, but I had better get on down to the Embassy; that she would book me for tomorrow's flight.

I hopped a cab into town. I no sooner entered the Consulate Office when a grey-haired, hunchbacked individual confronted me, and asked if I was the individual PanAm called about. Yes I was. He didn't even introduce himself when I handed him my passport. He glanced at it and said, "I'll take this, and you'll hear from this office in due time." I said, "Wait a minute; what am I supposed to do now? Why can't I pay the fee, as I was told in Accra?" He looked at me with steely blue eyes and said I had been given the wrong information. He disappeared and slammed the door. I was livid with rage. I asked the secretary, "Who was that guy?" She said he was the Consul General, he was always that way. He was once a Consular in a Communist country someplace, and had a chip on his shoulder ever since. She gave me his name, but I don't remember it now, and the phone number. I went back to the airport and checked in at the Airways Hotel once more. I called my sister Christine, in Maine, and told her the turn of events. She said to sit tight, she would get back to me. Sit tight! What else could I do? No passport, no travel - a man without a country; I guess that's what I was. It was that quick. I don't know why I left it to the last minute to catch my flight. I knew that one cannot rely on aircraft always to be on time. Most airlines in the world have trouble staying on schedule, especially in Third World Countries.

In the meantime, I phoned Bill Jacob to see what was going on. He came by, and we had a few beers. I told him my problem, and he sympathized. I couldn't return to Accra without a passport, or go anywhere. It was a few days before I heard from Christine. She said a friend of hers was in contact with a lawyer friend in Washington; keep standing by! Well, a whole month went by before word came from the Embassy to come and pick up my passport I didn't call Margaret, it would upset her too

much. It was good for one week yet I felt angry; I wanted to see the white-haired bugger, but he didn't show his nose. I was still angry, and the secretary knew it. I finally got myself a reservation for my trip back, and arrived in New York.

I checked in at the old Henry Hudson Hotel, which was somewhere on 57th Street. I called and thanked Christine. Then called my sister Geraldine and said I'd stay a couple of days in New York, before coming to Plainfield.

It was the middle of March of 1962, and John Glenn had orbited the earth - the first American in space. I didn't do much except walk the cold, windblown streets of Manhattan, and have beers at the local pub and try and gather my thoughts. I guess I had been through a bit of hell, having my passport taken away and had no citizenship in the world. For sure, all naturalized citizens were second-class buggers, thanks to the Italians at the turn of the century. "Oh, come on, dammit, Pete; snap out of it!" I told myself.

I finally hopped a bus at Grand Central, and headed for Plainfield. It was great seeing Geraldine and Fred again. When I was settled, Geraldine took me to see my mother. She was now in a nursing home and when I saw her I cried. She seemed to have aged so quickly since 1959. She was happy to see me, we stayed about an hour, then left. Geraldine and I talked of the days in India with Mum, and the wonderful life she must have had, the stories that she used to tell us around the fireplace in Bhowali. It was hard to realize she was now lying in bed, never to get up and walk again. It took me a while to recover.

We sat in Geraldine's large kitchen, and I had several of my scotches. I don't know why, but I feel these scotches help me. I tried to cheer myself up by telling Geraldine and Fred about Ghana, flying and hunting, and the passport nonsense. I needed an automobile, so the next day Geraldine took me to used car dealer, where I bought a second-hand Chevy. I still had an old New Jersey driver's license, that I had renewed by taking a quickie written exam. They wouldn't accept my Ghana one!

I stayed about a week in Plainfield then headed for Washington, D.C., to meet the lawyer who helped me. He personally took me to see people at the State Department, and find out the status of my citizenship, and this second-class nonsense I received from the guy in London. I met with a passport person in Miss Knight's department. Miss Knight was the head of the passport Division. I explained my problem to the individual, a Mr. Curry, all he could do was sympathize. He reiterated that this five-year limit did stem from the time of the Italians back in the 1904 era. He

also emphasized that the Consulate in Accra were partially correct in saying I could pay the $25 penalty in New York; that the individual in London could have issued a day of grace, and allowed me to return home; it was his prerogative. In any case, I felt insulted at being treated as a second class citizen. I felt the five year law should be rescinded. He couldn't have agreed more; perhaps one day, he hoped. As for me, I would be staying awhile in the USA. I said I had a job to return to in Ghana, and hoped I could have my passport renewed within six months. Well, he would try his best. Since I was from Maine, he suggested I try and see Senator Muskie. He obtained Muskie's office phone, and I talked to the Senator's secretary, and was informed he was out of town. I went to my cheap hotel room and fell into one of my doldrums.

Harry Bernard, my old friend from Pan Africa days with our little trip to the House of Mirrors in Ethiopia, was working for Federal Aviation Administration (FAA) in Washington. It had changed from CAA to FAA in 1958. I went downstairs and thumbed through the telephone directory at the public telephone. I had to call several sections of the FAA before I finally tracked him down. He was so surprised to hear from me, and to know I was in town. It was agreed I'd come and stay with him. He would come by and I'd follow him home.

It was great seeing Harry, and talking over the old times. I met his wife, Noreen, and his two children, as well. That evening, I explained my passport problem, and the difficulty I'd had in London. I told Harry all about Accra, how it had changed since we were there in 1942. If he could obtain a movie projector, I promised to show the movies I had taken, and my hunting trip on the Volta. I said I had tried a couple of airlines, including Flying Tigers and CAT in Taiwan for a job. They had offices in D.C., I soon I got the rude awakening that I was not wanted because of my age; I was too old, at the age of 47 to join any airline. Harry then suggested I join the FAA. The FAA? "My God, Harry! After all the barnstorming and bush flying around the world, how could I change over to the other side of the fence and start enforcing the air laws? My goodness - I'd broken so many rules myself, I'd feel like a hypocrite, and now start upholding the law?" "Well," he said, "It doesn't cost anything to fill out the application," he would help me. If I returned to Ghana or another flying job, nothing lost. Harry said you'd never get rich, working for FAA, but it did have some good things going for it. I wasn't too convinced. Anyway, I spent the day in Harry's office, making out a lengthy form called a 171. It was all in the rough. Harry went over it and made a few changes. He chuckled over all the foreign licenses I held, and the international flying I had been doing.

The FAA offices at this time were nothing more than temporary quonset-type buildings, located right in the park area, next to the Washington Memorial. He said a building was underway somewhere on Independence Avenue, for a future office. I wanted to know what kind of salary I would receive, he then explained how the salary system worked. I would start out with a GS-9 and get about $6500. I said, "Is that a month?" he said "No, that's per year!" "That's less than a newly-hired First Officer's first year pay!" He said it wouldn't be for any more than about six months, then I would be a GS-11 for a year, and then a 12, which would put me up to around $9000 or 12,000. It took a few days to finalize the 171 form, which I had printed so it would be presentable.

Harry had introduced me to several of his colleagues in the FAA, such as George Moore, and a Joe Ferrarese. There was another gentleman in the international division. I think his name was John Shaffer (not the Administrator). He was, I think, AIA-1. The international man said he wanted me in the International Division, what with all my overseas flying experience, etc. "No," said Harry; I should get my feet wet with the domestic routine first. They were discussing me as though I was already hired.

In the meantime, I contacted the people that had dealt with my C-46 at Crescent Air Transport, back in 1951. I went over to their offices and said hello to a few friends such as Joe Conasero and George Brinkerhof. During the Howdys, etc., and general conversation, I mentioned about my flying in Ghana, and my passport troubles. One of the gentleman came up with an idea: why didn't I represent their company in West Africa? I would then be working for a U.S. corporation, and the State Department would have to issue me a passport. I thought that quite fantastic; it would not be a bogus deal, but legitimate. It would take awhile to make the arrangements. They would look into the matter, and see what material and aviation equipment might be needed in that area. I thanked my friends, and said I would keep in close touch.

I decided to drive up to Maine, and freeload off my friends there. I thanked Harry for his hospitality, with all he did in making out the forms for the FAA. I loved the drive up to Maine, especially once I left the New York and New Jersey area, into Connecticut. It was a great morning when I packed up and left. I crossed the Tappan-Zee Bridge and headed on 84, I felt relaxed. I had written to Margaret several times, and sent some money as well. As I drove north, I thought of all the fun times I'd had

with her and the kids in Accra. I hoped the deal would work out with the company, so I could continue flying and still represent the company for West Africa. The company's name was Air Carrier Service Corporation, and the Vice President was Ed Lynn. I felt the FAA was not for me, not really my cup of tea; that, and only $6500 a year! I shuddered.

I got tired of driving, and holed up in a motel outside of Boston. I always carried my bottle of scotch (strictly for medicinal purposes!). I relaxed with a couple of drinks and a good sleep. I was off again, early the next morning. It was cold, with snow still piled up on the sides of the highway. I stopped in Augusta and looked up my wonderful old friend, John Plummer and his wife, Agnes. He was my friend from the college days at the University of Maine, and our hunting and fishing trips. During the war, he had been with the Seabees, building runways and so forth, at the various Pacific Islands. John was now with his brother, operating the family funeral home. John was at the office, and when I entered, he almost fell over. He was happy to see me, as I was him. He looked the same, tall, about 6'3", weighing about 250 pounds, a big, blond, husky fellow. I followed him home, and was delighted to see Agnes, too. She was always a charmer, and a fantastic cook, especially with all those New England dishes. They insisted I stay with them. John always loved his bourbon whiskey, and I had my scotch. We had a great afternoon and evening. Agnes had made a chuck roast stew; it was wonderful. I rambled on with all my stories of Lebanon and Africa, and of course, the passport difficulty. John and Agnes came up with an idea. They suggested I stay in a spare apartment that was adjacent to the funeral home. There was a large garage attached to it, where the hearse was kept, Above that area was an apartment. I said I'd give it a try, but I didn't want to inconvenience them. No bother; Agnes would check it out in the morning, clean sheets and all. That was it. I had a great sleep and the three of us checked the apartment next morning. It was necessary to get to the apartment via the garage, and a small hallway, then up the stairs. The place was nice and bright, with its own bathroom. I was shown the light switches in the garage, the hall and the stairwell. I knew I'd be comfortable. There was no phone, so any messages would be taken at John's home.

The Maine weather, hangs on, and still cold. There were snow flurries once in a while. John was a great horse-lover; he rode cowboy style horses, and all the paraphernalia. He usually wound up in the city parades as Grand Marshall and belonged to a riding club which was located between Augusta and Waterville.

Waterville was where I had finished my CPT training in 1941. He and the club members were busy building a big club-house. Not having anything better to do, I joined in and helped hammer the shingles onto the roof, and varnish the maplewood floors. This helped kill the time.

It was a little after mid-April when an amazing incident occurred. It was a Saturday afternoon, when John and I had just about finished the clubhouse. An electrician and plumber had done some of the work on the little kitchen and toilet. The days were still short, we had to turn on the lights. The place was bare, sparkling new and neat, and still smelled of paint and here John hauled out his bourbon. This time, I didn't have my scotch, so I settled for Jim Beam, which was his favorite drink served in paper cups. We toasted the new establishment. After several of these on an empty stomach, I was feeling old Jim Beam, so we decided to head home. Agnes had cooked up a fine supper. We had a couple more drinks, and I felt like bed. John had to drive me home, because I'd already left the car at the garage and it was snowing. I went through the garage door. The place was pitch-dark, and I couldn't find the light switch. I'd made several trips before; I felt I could navigate without the light, but somewhere along the way, I missed the stairs going up. I wandered on in my stupor with my arms outstretched. I felt some curtains that I moved to one side. I went a little further, till my waist came up against something, and I fell over from my waist down, a jackknife effect. I wasn't certain at the moment what it was: It had wheels, casters, and it rolled. I couldn't lift myself up without it rolling, so there I stuck, head and shoulders inside. I tried righting myself by getting a grip on something. When my fingers moved over a head, and then a face, all of a sudden I sobered immediately, the hair on the back of my head raised. I realized I was halfway in an open, occupied coffin. The more I tried to wiggle out, the further in I seemed to go. I was almost rubbing noses with the corpse. I could only just make out a white face. It seemed to be looking at me and smiling. Finally, after what seemed ages, I detached myself from the coffin. Now that I was fairly sober and my eyes a little more accustomed to the darkness, I could make out a doorway to one side. I made a beeline for it. I was in the hall, I saw the stairs, and was able to locate the light switch, I had enough light to find my way back out through the garage and out the door. Luckily, I had left my car, as I mentioned, I got in drove back to John and Agnes in a hurry. They were so surprised to see me. Before they could say a word, I said I needed a drink. I must have looked terrible, ashen. They wanted to know what was going on and what was wrong. We sat in the living room, and John poured me a second shot of scotch. Once I had collected my senses, I told them the story. Before I'd finished, John and Agnes were in stitches of laughter. "It isn't funny," I said. After John got himself a drink, he said, "Do you know who that was?" "How do I know who that was? It was dark and cold in there, and the guy was dead." "That was the Mayor of Augusta. He died last week, and the funeral will be held tomorrow." I said, "You had better check him out again; I think I ruffled his hair and clothes, and his eyes are open!" John almost fell out of the chair with laughter. He said, "If the man only knew what had happened, he would laugh, too." I said he had a smile on his face. John asked if I'd go back there with him. I said, "No, thank you! I'll sleep here on the couch tonight." The two of them had tears running down their cheeks from laughter, I felt tired and ready for sleep, though I think I may have chuckled a little bit, myself. I could hear John and Agnes laughing in their bedroom as I dozed off.

I slept restlessly. When I awoke, Agnes was already making coffee. After a hearty breakfast, which I needed, John and Agnes wanted to know what was next. I decided I'd go up to Bangor for a spell, and see my friends there, such as Horace Chapman and the other people. I thanked John and Agnes; they were still laughing over the coffin episode. I've seen many dead human beings all around the world, some mangled and twisted which I didn't mind, but laid out in a coffin was an eerie effect on me. I gathered all my things and said farewell.

I took the back road - I think it was Route 3, somewhere around China Lakes - and then across the state to Belfast, on the coast. I stopped there to see Bill and his wife, Tina Eldredge. Bill, as you may remember was my partner when we were searching for our lost friend, Bob Burge, on Mount Kathadin. Bill never changed; he was a real "downeaster" from Maine, He was doing commercial art in Bangor, but lived in Belfast, which was about 40 miles distance. Bill suggested that I look into renting a cottage right there in Belfast. It was off season, and I probably could get one cheap. He and I went across the bay, just near Searsport, and talked to the owner of the Colonial Motel. The man was only too eager to let me have a cottage right on the beach for about $60 a month. It was clean and bright, with a pot-bellied, wood-burning stove, and a kitchenette, goodsize living room and bedroom, and full bathroom: perfect! I could drive up to Bangor in just a short period of time. I'd take the old Penobscot Road, right up the river; I could always be back the same day.

Once I settled in my new quarters, I notified Harry Bernard, and my new friends in Air Carrier in Washington of my location. I told Bill that he and his wife Tina would have to come over that evening, we'd celebrate. I loaded up with groceries and drinks, and cooked up some grub; I think it was spaghetti, with Chianti wine. I had the wood stove blasting away, and a lot of good heat was coming out. It was a great evening, we had a good time, they laughed their sides off when I told them about my falling into the coffin.

I visited Horace Chapman at the Bangor House, and also a few friends of mine who worked at the bar. I wrote Margaret and told her of what was developing. Days hurried by, and spring arrived in Maine. It can be very beautiful. John and Agnes came over on occasions, and we had a good time together. I visited my old high school in Brewer, and took a trip up to the University of Maine.

I received word from the FAA that I had been hired, and to report to the Federal Building in Idlewild Airport for an interview by the end of May; I also heard from my Washington Air Carrier Company people, to see them for a briefing, and to work for them in Africa, that my passport would be assured. The time had come, I hated leaving the cottage which I'd become attached to; it had been almost six weeks. I said goodbye to all my wonderful friends, and headed for New York.

I had my interview with the FAA at the New York office, and they wanted to know when I could report to Laguardia Airport for work. I was honest with these folks. One of the interviewers was a Bob Jones. It seemed we had met before, in the Far East, when he flew for Philippine Airlines. I told FAA I was still interested in returning overseas. They said I had time, through the end of September to make up my mind, but be sure to let them know well in advance.

I then headed to Washington, DC. I spent several days being briefed by the aircarrier company, and they gave me a letter to take to the Passport Office. It stated that I would be representing them in sales of aviation equipment. I arranged an appointment, and eventually obtained a new passport. I saw Harry, and gave him the news. I said I'd let FAA know my decision as soon as possible. He wished me well, and hoped I would consider the FAA.

I stayed a couple of days with Geraldine, and saw my mother, though I didn't know it, for the last time. I was heartbroken when I saw her, so frail and delicate. I sent Margaret a telegram that I was on my way to London. When I checked in at London, at the same Airways Hotel at the Airport, I phoned Margaret that I was in town, and I'd re-

port to Ghana Airways office and then call her back.

I went to the operations office at the airport, and the Chief Pilot for the Britannia fleet, who said there was a message for me from the Chief of Operation in Accra. I read the message, and was stunned. The bottom line read that I was no longer needed with the airline, I was not to have any airline privileges, such as tickets. I was livid! I didn't know which way to turn. Bob Bethel had left the company, and Bill Jacob was still a line pilot.

At the Hotel, I called Margaret and told her the news. She suggested I come up to Manchester. I was so happy to see her and the children, they were growing fast. Hannah was almost two, and getting along fine; Christian was almost five. I told Margaret about the FAA alternative. She was all for it, and didn't care about going back to Africa.

I'd been with Margaret and her sister about three or four days when one morning her sister lit into Margaret and me in no uncertain terms. I didn't know what it was all about. At this point, I was so fed up, I could care less. I told Margaret to pack up, that we were leaving. That afternoon we caught the train to London. We checked in at the Airways Motel. A few days later, one of her friends who lived in Wimbledon suggested we could rent a place there quite cheap. Money was getting short now; no pay for a few months.

I went back to the Ghana Airways office in town, and saw a friend I knew. He was the Chief of Sales for the airline, I told him the story. He said not to worry he would arrange a ticket for me. I thanked my friend and headed for Accra. I marched into the Operations Office at the Airport, and told the chief pilot what I thought of him, that I was now going to see the Managing Director of the airline, who was a big, colored Ghanian, and a fine individual. I had to wait, however, about an hour before I was ushered into his office. He was very pleasant mannered and was happy to see me. After introductions, he said he did know of me, that word had come that I had been unofficially training some of the local pilots on the DC-3. I gave the Managing Director a little background about myself, how I was being treated by the Chief of Operations, right here in Accra. The Director said he was sorry to hear this, that if I wished, I could have my job back in full status. I appreciated his offer, but said I could not fly with such a person in charge of operations. I had been offered a job with the FAA in the States. The Managing Director said that was fine, but if at any time I wished to return to Ghana, just to give him the word. In parting, he said he was giving me six months' salary, and tickets on PanAm for me and my family, plus the shipment of my household goods. I thought that was most generous; I thanked him very much. I returned to the Operations Office and told the English pilot to stuff the job up his butt. He never looked up from his desk.

I went to the apartment, where Hilary was still at my service. Peace was there also, plus a fine baby boy. I gave them loads of clothes from me and the kids, and from Margaret. It took a few days of packing to have all the household effects ready, packed in Mahogany crates! That was the local wood of Accra. I also gave Hilary a couple of months' salary, plus the duty time from when I was away. I gave up the apartment, and checked into the Ambassador Hotel. I was able to get a phone call through to the FAA office in New York. It wasn't easy, but once through, I said I would make it back by the end of September, that was fine by them, but to report directly to the LaGuardia office. I asked Bob Jones to please call the people in Washington that the deal was off, that I was returning to the States. "No problem; come on home." I received a check in dollars, and I saw to it that the shipping people had my crates all done, and returned the car to the airline, I was on my way back to London.

It was a long night flight, I had time to think things over. Was I doing the right thing? There was a possibility I could get along with airline operations, if I tried. And what about the Air Carrier sales? There was a possibility I could make quite a bit of money. I felt I was not cut out to be a salesman. A lot of these countries were budding out in aviation; new airports being built, navaids, etc., then I thought of the children, and their future. FAA was a whole new challenge, but could I do it? Oh, what the hell! I guess I could, and do it well.

I got back to Wimbledon and told Margaret all the news. She seemed pleased about the USA. I said it would be difficult at the beginning. Also, there would be no free tickets to fly back and forth to England. It would be a bit disappointing, but we could give it a try. Seemed strange, when I'd worked so hard to obtain a new passport, gone through a lot of problems, being stuck in London, and now I wouldn't need a passport.

I called FAA LaGuardia and spoke to the Chief of the office, a Mr. Dick Kleinert. I said I'd be able to report around Monday, the 24th of September. That would be okay, he said. I already had a desk waiting for me. "A desk! My goodness! I never had one before, except at school." We boarded PanAm, and were on our way to New York.

The FAA would be whole new way of life! I had been a pilot since I received my pilot's license in June of 1940, 22 years of flying in many parts of the world. Then, all of a sudden, my wings seemed to be clipped, I was going to be strapped to a desk. A lump rose in my throat and my eyes swelled with tears. Drifting away, far behind me, was the world I knew and loved, all the flying and everyday challenge. I wondered if I would be able to adjust to this new life. I knew I had to do this for Margaret and the children; I wanted her happy, at all costs.

At Idlewild Airport, New York, the hustle and bustle was on us. I hadn't noticed this so much before. Now it hit me: people scrambling for their luggage, shouting at the top of their lungs, used paper cups and rubbish littering the walkways, taxi drivers trying to squeeze exorbitant amounts of money from unsuspecting passengers. We were treated well by Immigration and Customs officers. I wondered how they were able to keep their tempers, with so many unruly people. However, once through, we got a cab to take us into Manhattan, who tried his fancy tricks, asking almost a double amount. I reminded the driver I was not a tourist, and knew what the fare was, that he'd better get the meter correct, or I may have to call a cop. There was no further problem and we were dropped off at the St. Moritz Hotel

We spent the next day sightseeing along Broadway and Fifth Avenue. I deposited the check into our account at the Chase Manhattan Bank; I think it was on 57th Street, near the Henry Hudson Hotel. It would take a few days for it to clear.

Geraldine and Fred wanted us to come over and stay in Plainfield. We had a few days of grace before I had to report to LaGuardia. I still had my old Chevy at Geraldine's. The children enjoyed staying with her and Fred. The house was big and had spacious grounds. The next task was to find a place to stay, somewhere out on Long Island, and not too far from LaGuardia Airport. I called my old friend, Sam George, from PanAfrica days. Sam and Tish lived in Stony Brook, which was a way out on Long Island, too far to commute. He suggested to come out to their place, and look around the Huntington Station area.

Margaret and I finally found a small house in Huntington Beach, which was semi-furnished, and would do until our belongings arrived from Accra. The owner evidently used the small house as a summer place, when he left, it had not been cleaned up. Margaret took one look at it, and was upset and mad. For this, I couldn't blame her. She said, "Look at the bathroom; the stuff still has black curly hairs in it!" I tried not to laugh, she would have been more angry, so I kept quiet. I agreed to clean up the kitchen and the bathroom areas, if she would go over the other parts of the house. It turned out to be chore. Eventually, it was done, and it looked nice. Christian and Hannah spent the day in the backyard. There was a detached garage, as well, that the kids were interested in. It would be the next day before we were actually ready to move in. It was a nice area, with a kindergarten school close by for Christian. It was our first weekend there, and then early Monday morning, the 24th, I was off to LaGuardia and my first day at the FAA office.

I found the office on the first floor of the TWA Hangar. I entered with an almost foreboding effect. I was greeted by a tall individual who turned out to be Dick Kleinert, the Chief of the office. It was a friendly greeting. He said, "Hiya, Pete! You are our representative from Africa. Welcome to the FAA!" He called all the inspectors, about 8 or 9, and the two secretaries, into his office, I was introduce to the complete staff. Once finished, an inspector by the name of Joe Vacarelli, an Italian, said he would show me around

I sat my briefcase on the desk and followed Joe around. It turned out that Joe had been a part of the China-Burma-India theater and had made several trips across the Hump, so we hit it off well. Kleinert explained there would not be too much to do for now, I should gradually get acquainted. I was told some of the rules, and the do's and don'ts. Lunch would be 30 minutes. There was a TWA cafeteria downstairs, which made it easy. The secretary in charge said she would get the necessary forms that had to be filled out for my health and life insurance, everyone had to have this. I would have to take a driving test, to be issued a Government Driver's License, so I could drive the Government G-cars.

Most of the first week was spent obtaining a license and filling out forms, photographs and IDs for FAA and the airport. Joe and two other inspectors lived in my neighborhood, and asked me to join their carpool. Yes, this would be great.

I was getting a feel for the office routine, and Dick Kleinert was a fine individual. He had a maintenance background. I soon got my ID and Government Driver's License. Joe said he and I would do some airport surveillance. It was done first thing in the morning, and late afternoon. We would check out a G-car with Joe at the wheel. The first stop was around the corner at the Purple Orchid Restaurant and a Catering Outfit. Here, we bought glazed doughnuts, which were new to me, and coffee, not tea! The car had two-way radio with the tower, and a red light on top.

Joe would contact the tower to see there was no traffic, or if there was a lull, we would then drive up and down the runways, looking for any foreign material on the runways, such as nuts and bolts, etc., or even parts of tires, whatever; we would notify the tower when we were clear the runways, and slowly cruise around the perimeter road. Joe normally would park at the area near what I think was runway 31. It was right around the water's edge of Flushing Bay and the sound. Here, Joe turned off the engine, and we would partake of our doughnuts and coffee. I asked the purpose of this vigil. He wasn't sure, but perhaps to see if the landing aircraft made it okay. I smiled to myself. This routine killed about half the morning, and also in the afternoon. I didn't mind, since loads of wild fowl, mainly black ducks, came into this area, and I could watch them. I sat around the office most of the time, answering phones. The weekends were nice. Fall had arrived and the leaves were turning their autumn colors. Though Margaret could drive, she didn't care about doing so here in New York. There were some nice shopping areas that we visited, and a nice beach for the children. Everything was falling into place, and I was adjusting to the different way of life.

One morning at the office, I received a call from Margaret. It was October 14th. Evidently, Geraldine wanted me to call her. This I did, from a pay station downstairs; no long distance on Government phones for personal use. Geraldine informed me that my mother had just passed away. I was grieved and heartbroken. I walked around the ramp outside the hangar, and looked out toward the Long Island Sound, and cried quietly. I soon gathered my composure, and went back up to the office. I saw Kleinert, and told him. He said I could take time off on my own, but couldn't take any Government time, since I hadn't worked long enough to earn any leave. I called Margaret, who knew what Geraldine wanted to tell me.

The next morning, we packed our bags and headed for Plainfield. My sister Christine also came down from Maine. We stayed at Geraldine's, with the funeral service to be held that weekend. In her artistic way, Geraldine had arranged everything at the funeral home where the service was to be held, and not at the church. The decorations were simple, the way I think Mum would have wanted it. She was put to rest in a plot that Fred had for the family, a lovely area, overlooking a small lake. I wondered, though if she would perhaps have been happier if she knew she would be buried in India, near Dad, in Monghyr, or even up in the hills.

I couldn't take too much time, as it was all without pay. When the funeral was completed, Margaret and I headed back to Long Island, and I back to work. Margaret, the kids, and I returned to Geraldine's once in a while, and again for Thanksgiving. It was always a sumptuous meal, and Geraldine was a great cook. Christian and Hannah always enjoyed it there; there was so much room to play around. Christian was shown the room where he had painted himself when he was only two years old. The holiday was over, and then the long journey through the horrendous New York traffic, and out to Long Island.

The sales pitch for Christmas always takes precedence, even over Thanksgiving and Veteran's Day. Christmas was just about on us. The main street of Huntington Beach was beautifully decorated, and all the shops took on that "Christmasy" look. All that was needed was snow. Christine had informed us that she and her husband, Roger, were driving through to Mexico, and that they would like to spend Christmas with us. We all agreed it would be wonderful.

They arrived a few days before, in their International van. It was wonderful Christmas, with the real Christmas spirit. Before we knew it, the Christmas season was over, and Christine and Roger left on their long journey.

By the end of February 1963, Dick Kleinert informed us that the new hires, like myself, would be scheduled to go to Oklahoma City for Indoctrination, and some other flying, to see that we still knew how, and that a couple of us would probably stay over and have our Flight Engineer Ground School and written exam. This would break the monotony of the office life. I told Margaret it would be nice if we all drove out there. It would be at least a two month deal in Oklahoma City. She would see. When the time came, she said no, that Christian was now in school, she didn't wish to change things,

Joe Vaccarelli, another inspector, and myself wound up at Oklahoma for our classes. The indoctrination took a month, and in between, Joe and I saw a bit of the city. I met several fine people in the classes and training. One was a Bill Burnett, who was an instructor on the L-188 Electra. He too, was going to be in the Flight Engineer school, as soon as the rest of us finished the Indoctrination. I had my flight check on the DC-6, Joe took his flight on a DC-3. He had not been in an airplane, or anywhere near one, since WW II, so naturally, he failed. He was really shook up. The word was that Joe would be fired from the FAA because of his poor flying and this was not fair. I talked to several people at training, and said Joe should be given a break. He had not flown in an aircraft for 15 years of more. No, there was no way out. So Joe returned to LaGuardia. Dick Kleinert tried to help. He was told to lay off. So my friend was no longer with the FAA. I thought it brutal.

The Flight Engineer Course was rough for me. It was to last for six weeks. The written test contained a great amount of jet aircraft questions, which I knew nothing about. I thought I would wind up like Joe since I failed the test. I was informed I'd have to stay for some more ground school. I said I'd return home first, and then come back. I had been away for more than two months. It was agreed.

Back at the LaGuardia office, I talked to Kleinert and told him about the test. He called the Region and Oklahoma. They and Oklahoma agreed that I could take another written at the office, but if I failed, I'd have to return to Oklahoma. I studied a little more on my own, and then took the test, this time without any jet questions. I passed. Praise the Lord!

# PHASE EIGHT: 1963-1978

I was now a full-fledge inspector, with a special cockpit authority for riding in the jumpseat on piston aircraft. It's known as a Form 110. Off and on, I flew on Eastern, to Miami and back. It was a nice feeling to be able at least to fly again, even though I was not at the controls. "Backseat driving!" Some of the captains were also from the China-Burma-India Theater; I was still sorry that Joe was not with us. I learned later that he got his old job back, teaching in high school.

By June, Christine and Roger were back in Maine. They did not stop by to see us. They suggested that Margaret and the kids spend the summer with them at the Shack in Harrington. When I had a few days off, I drove them to Maine. The kids were beside themselves with excitement. It had been a year since I left Belfast and the cottage. I pointed it out to Margaret as we drove by the back road to Belfast and Searsport, and showed her the cottage. We stopped at Perry's Nut House, a must for all tourists. It was a curio shop, with all sorts of interesting articles.

I could only stay a couple of days, and was headed back again. I left the family with Christine, who loved the kids. On the way back, I had time only to say hello to the Eldriges, and buy lobsters and clams. By the time I reached home, the old Chevy was showing its wear and tear; too many things going wrong. I decided to try for a new car. I was able to get a loan from the Credit Union, and bought a new Ford station wagon.

In July, Harry Bernard phoned and said he was now Manager of the Flight Standards Districts Office at Washington National Airport. He asked if I would be interested in transferring to his office, to be a Viscount specialist. "Yes," I told him, "I certainly would." The paperwork didn't take long, with a release and travel orders. I also got the OK for packaging all our household goods that had arrived from Accra which were stored in our little garage. I drove down to Washington, and stayed at a nearby YMCA till I could find a place for us. Harry

suggested looking near his home in Springfield, Virginia. I found a small, three-bedroom home for rent, not too far from him. The furniture arrived and I had everything pretty well arranged.

It is a small world. Here, I now was working for our famous "Pagliacci," Harry Bernard. He introduced me to a whole bunch of new faces at the Flight Standards Office in Washington.

It was late August and hot. Harry gave me time off to drive back up to Christine's and bring the family back. Christine had given Margaret bits and pieces of furniture and plants, so it was necessary to rent a small U-Haul trailer. Margaret loved the new car and it was great for the kids. By the time we reached Connecticut, on the way back, Hannah came down with the chicken pox. We holed up at Howard Johnsons so she could rest and be given aspirin or something to lower the fever. The next afternoon, we were back in our new home on Leesville Boulevard, Springfield, VA. I was relieved when Margaret said that she thought the place was just fine with a kindergarten close by for Christian. The only thing now was to get my GS-11 instead of the GS-9 that I presently was. Harry said he would work on that.

We settled down to our new life, and met our neighbors. One couple, the Finches, were wonderful people. Mr. Finch was a gourmet cook, or at least, he thought he was; I thought he was, too and he sure loved his beer. Jean Finch was one who loved animals. She had a Great Dane, and a couple of whippet-like hounds. Hannah soon got over her chicken pox, and spent a lot of her time with the Finches, playing with the animals. Other neighbors had kids who came over and played. My life with the FAA might brighten up, after all.

Fall arrived, and Christian enrolled at the school. When the weather cooled off, we would picnic out on the weekends to the various parts of Virginia. One that always interested us was Manassas Park, the first battlefield of the Civil War.

One thing I should mention; when I finished indoctrination at Oklahoma City, I was issued a new Airline Transport Pilot license, which was endorsed with "All ratings authorized." It meant I could fly jumpseat on any U.S. registered aircraft. This gave me an opportunity to give flight checks in different types of aircraft in Washington, DC. There were several small 135 operators, with DC-3s and Convairs. I was able to break away from the office routine and meet aviation people. I even met a few old cronies I hadn't seen for years. One was an ex-FAAer who had ridden with me on Seaboard World Airlines from New York to Frankfurt, when I was going to join my people in Beirut in 1955. I met another fellow from whom I'd tried to buy a C-46 in Pakistan. He was still in aviation, flying out of New York. I met another pilot whom I had known in Jeddah, back in 1950. I was more content, except for the salary!

The days and weeks hurried by. We saw a lot of Harry and his family. Harry loved music. He enjoyed his piano and singing. This gave Margaret a chance to join in. She hadn't done any of it for as long as I could remember. All of us and Harry hit it off well. Margaret would give her various renditions from *South Pacific* and other stage songs. Everyone enjoyed hearing her sing.

It was office as usual for me. Then one day Harry said I should get a type rating on

*Hannah on coast of Maine, 1964.*

*Learning to drive at Roswell Country Club, 1969.*

*The tent after the rain storm, Flagstaff, 1969.*

the Viscount. "Why do I need that, when I have all ratings?" He said, "Makes no difference; you've gotta get it if I was to conduct orals and flight checks on that airplane." "How about the training I received from British Airways in Ghana?" "It doesn't count." So I attended ground school given by United Airlines for pilots. It was a good class that I enjoyed. Out of the blue, who showed up as one of the instructors but another old CNAC pilot, Ray Hilgert, flying for United. It would take about six weeks for the course to finish.

Right after that, word came in November that President Kennedy had been shot. I was upset and worried. Our class was discontinued. I went back up the hill to the office. The first person I met was one of the secretaries, who was closing up her desk. She said, "Guess what? The President has been shot, so I guess we got the rest of the day off. I'm going home." I was astonished that she should say something like that. Here she was, a regular citizen, and me, a second-class citizen who felt more for the President than

she did. Well, that's the way it goes. I finally received the Viscount rating. Our first Christmas in our new home was wonderful. So many presents for the kids from Christine and Geraldine. It made it even more enjoyable for them. The atmosphere was very Christmasy, with a real Christmas tree and a fire in the fireplace.

1964 was ushered in. That spring, we went to see the cherry blossoms in Washington, DC. The weather was perfect and what a spectacular sight! As soon as school was over Christine wanted Margaret and the kids back up to the Shack. Roger had bought a large trailer which he'd placed behind the Shack and said it would accommodate us. Annual leave was hard to come by, but I had earned enough. On the 4th of July week, I bundled everyone, including bicycles, etc., and drove to Maine. I was dog-tired, by the time I got to Harrington with my eyes bloodshot. The trailer was wonderful and the kids loved it.

I stayed a few days, then headed back alone. I stopped at my favorite lobster pound, and picked up some lobsters. I knew the last time they had lasted all the way, I was sure they would last all the way to Springfield. I promised Harry I'd bring some back for him.

By mid-July, Harry informed me I'd be going to Oklahoma City now to check out on the L-188 Electra and my Flight Engineer practical. In the meantime, I had been doing odd bits of work in the office, mainly violations and incidences at the airport. One of the most common violations was flying over the prohibited area of the White House. This was called a "P-56." Normally, one would have to fly down the Potomac River and then enter the approach. People who didn't know this got caught.

I hardly seemed to have got my breath, and the red out of my eyes, when I drove to Oklahoma. I enjoyed the FAA program, and spent most of my time with Bill Burnett. He was to be one of my instructors. The course was two months, and covered flying and

flight engineer. The aircraft was nice. I got my rating and flight engineer ticket, and returned to Washington. Before I knew it, I was back in Maine to fetch the family down which gave me a few days with Christine and Roger.

The morning of departure, I had everything loaded on the baggage rack on top of the car and well tied down. We said goodbye, and as I backed around the fuel tank, a plastic affair, rammed against an iron grating that stuck out of the fence. It ruptured the tank and most of the fuel spilled out. The kids, of course, were delighted that they would have another day or two in Maine. I was able to get the car to the garage with Roger towing it. The local man did a good job of fixing the tank. Next day, we launched off; this time we were successful. No chicken pox or measles, either.

One morning, the phone at the office rang. It was the airport tower. They said there had been a near midair incident between the checkpoints of Herndon VOR and Washington. A United Viscount, inbound, almost collided with a U.S.. Air Force small twin airplane from Andrews Air Force Base. I told Harry about this, and he said to go ahead and handle it.

On investigation, I learned that one of the cabin attendants on the United States flight was hospitalized with a back injury, due to the evasive action that the pilot took. It was therefore declared an accident. Both flights were on IFR flight plans. The U.S. Air Force plane was visual, and the Viscount was on instruments, letting down through the clouds. As the pilot broke through, he was in a head-on collision path with the Air Force aircraft. The Captain just had time to make an evasive maneuver by pulling up and to the left, a normal reflex action. The NTSB was involved. I received the tapes from ATC, and made transcripts. Using the courses given and flown by the two pilots, I plotted these courses plus the wind drift. It all added up on a collision course. NTSB, with my analysis, showed the ATC at fault for allowing the Viscount to descend in the path of the Air Force plane. I no sooner finished this accident investigation when I was called upon to participate in another accident investigation, of a Flying Tigers L-144 swingtail freighter at Norfolk Airport. The acting and deadheading crew were lucky to escape. On landing, the aircraft's left gear collapsed, breaking the left wing. The right wing was still flying, causing the plane to roll over, skid down the runway, and catch fire. It so happened that the Fire Rescue Squad at Norfolk had been practicing and training off to one side of the airport, and were waiting at the intersection of the runways for the airplane to land before crossing. As the burning aircraft was skidding by, the rescue team was already dousing foam and water on the burning fuselage. The fire was out before the aircraft came to rest. The team then pulled the crew members out to safety. It was determined that the First Officer was at the controls at the time of the accident. He did not have much experience in the aircraft. The Captain, not knowing this, allowed the second pilot to land. The plane leveled out too high above the runway, and dropped in with enough force to push the left main gear through the wing structure, and separate the wing from the fuselage. Fire ensued from the spilled fuel.

These two accident investigations, and numerous other incidents, including the "P-56" overflying the White House, etc., were giving me a good background for my future years with FAA.

During that summer, Margaret's folks decided to come and visit us. They had taken possibly the last trip on the wonderful old Queen Mary of Cunard Steamship Company. We met them in New York, They spent about two months with us, it was wonderful having them, with us. We took a trip to Maine and around Virginia. The time went fast and before long, we were saying goodbye once again. We took them back to the Queen Mary. It was the last trip for the old ship.

That Christmas we decided to spend with Geraldine, in Plainfield. It was always an expedition when we had to go any distance with the children taking along all types of clothing and toys. It had snowed about eight inches that night, so it was necessary to buy some steel linked chains for the rear wheels. The next morning, we were on our way with great excitement, Christmas presents all neatly wrapped in the back, with the luggage on top of the car.

It was a clear, cool morning, but as we headed further north, strangely enough, by late morning, it had warmed up to rid the heavy snow and ice off the highway. The chains made a heck of a racket on the concrete. I was thinking of taking them off when the right rear chainlinks broke. I pulled over to one side, and noticed the fuel gauge was reading zero. I cussed and swore; I thought we had lost it all. I checked the fuel tank with a stick, and found it to half full; it was just the gauge. I got the chains off, and we were on our way once more.

We arrived late in the afternoon, Geraldine came up with the usual drinks to warm us up. It was a wonderful Christmas, as only Geraldine and Fred knew how to arrange. On the return to Springfield, we were still loaded down with gifts, mainly for the kids.

1965 saw me very active giving type ratings on the Viscount and L-188 airplanes. This I enjoyed, as the year flew by Margaret seemed happy. Very seldom was there any disgruntledness or flareup. Our old Ford station wagon had taken quite a beating on our trips back and forth to Maine. The wear and tear had taken its toll. So I talked to the Ford people in Alexandria, and came up with a new Ford station wagon.

That year, we were back up with Geraldine for another Christmas, and 1966 was with us. I returned to Oklahoma City for my recurrent training on the L-188, and for the Viscount I trained locally with United Airlines. It was back to Maine with the family. I finally got my GS-12 and a fair increase in salary. It had taken awhile. I tried once to

*The station wagon loaded down for the return trip to Virginia, 1964.*

quit and join Jordan Airlines. They would take me anytime I wished to return. Harry was always there to talk me out of any wild ideas.

At the office, I saw a bid for an inspector's position in Beirut, Lebanon. As I mentioned before, FAA had a fair sized office there, as part of the FAA Africa-Europe-Middle East geographic area. I sent in my bid for the position. I felt certain I had a good chance, having lived there for so many years and knowing everyone. I got a rude awakening, however, when I learned that they'd selected somebody else. I was upset to say the least. I decided to have a talk with my friend, big John Shaffer of AIA. Our Administrator was Mr. Halaby. Shaffer didn't know I had bid the job. He inquired with the staff who handle these bids. The people in question were unable to answer why I had not been selected, because I had more qualifications than the inspector who they had chosen. Mr. Shaffer then asked if I would be interested in transferring to the International Field Office, or IFO, based in New York; that I would be working on the 707 program. I said yes, if it meant a promotion. Yes, it would be a GS-13. He called New York IFO, and the man who ran it was a Gil Joynt. There was an opening, for me to come up for an interview. I told Harry, who said he was delighted. In fact, he was transferring to the New York office in the Eastern Region. He was to be the Assistant Branch Chief. "See you up there, I hope."

The next day, I enrouted to New York and went to see Gil Joynt. He was out of town, so I talked to the next in charge, a Mr. Jim Moran. It turned out he had been a CAA inspector, before it became FAA in Maine. He knew my old friend, R.A. Thomas, the inspector who gave us our CPT written exams and flight checks. I was given the green light to transfer to the IFO and be a 707 specialist. Margaret had mixed emotions about the move, yet she liked New York City.

She stayed on in Springfield while I went to work in New York in October. I wouldn't be going to Oklahoma to check out in the 707 till around April of 1967. In the meantime, I was Assistant to the Principal Operations Inspector for Pan American, a Dave Switzer. Gil Joynt didn't return to New York. He took another assignment, I think in Seattle. A new man took his place by the name of Bill Huebner. I spent a lot of time getting to know my new colleagues, and one individual was Tommy Thomas. It turned out that I had met Tommy when he was an inspector in our Beirut office, in 1961. The Lead Specialist of the 707 program was a Ray Hirsch. All these people were just great, and I knew I would enjoy working with them. There was also a character by the name of Don Terry. Don was an ex-TWA captain, who was once based in Rome, Italy; quite an outspoken individual, but one who was easy to like. He and Tommy Thomas and myself got along well together.

Dave Switzer did not waste time putting me to work. PAA was experimenting with new navigation system, called Inertial Navigation System, or INS, built by Sperry. They were experimenting with these on their 707s. Don Terry and I were put in charge for getting the INS approved for PanAm. We attended PanAm school for the INS. It was interesting and would revolutionize navigation.

After the ground school, Don and I flew with PanAm on their North Atlantic routes to evaluate the system. It had to prove itself at least 95% correct. The tolerance was small. Both enroute and readouts at destination had to be pretty accurate.

We were kept busy for several months, flying PanAm routes constantly, checking and evaluating their INSs. Eventually, these INSs proved unreliable, and could not be approved.

Whenever there was a lull in our program, I'd race down to Springfield to be with the family. I'd bought another old second-

*Retrieving Hannah and Bhimsa after she peed in Grand Canyon, 1969.*

hand Ford Falcon to get around in. In April of '67 I was on my way to Oklahoma for my first jet experience. At first, I was a bit scared that I might not make it. I studied and worked hard, by the end of May, I was ready for my flight and engineer's check, which I passed successfully. It was a load off my chest. I called Margaret to say I'd passed and was heading home to Springfield before going back up to New York.

Margaret asked if I had done any house-hunting during my time off in New York. I had, but found nothing worthwhile. I asked if she would come on up and look around with me, or on her own. No, she would stay put. She would have to stay there with the children. Margaret further stated that she planned to go to Manchester the coming summer, and hoped I'd find a place by the fall, or she would stay in England. Looked like she was calling the shots.

Back in New York, Switzer and Ray Hirsch kept me busy. I started giving oral exams and simulator flight checks to PanAm and TWA crews on 707's. I was a little weak at the beginning, but soon picked up speed and developed a system for the orals, and how to conduct simulator flight checks. The airplane portion was nothing but the icing on the cake. Something interesting in working for these two companies: a lot of my old friends were flying for PanAm and TWA. It wasn't long before I was meeting the pilots. One of them was a Tom Carroll with TWA. It was Tom who earlier had departed on a flight out of New York with a 707 and collided with an Eastern Airlines Constellation coming the other way. Tom made it back with half a wing torn off. The Connie landed in an open area, I think around Connecticut. The plane caught fire. The Captain, I remember, tried rescuing people from the Connie, and had succeeded in saving a few, until he himself got caught in the fire and died.

I spent several weekends with the Carrolls, Tom and his charming wife, Terry, in Norwalk, Connecticut. They helped me look for a house, with no results. Through a real estate agent on Long Island, I found a nice large home on a corner lot, with a garage and close to schools. I thought it ideal, though it was expensive for an FAA Inspector. However, I thought Margaret would like it. It was in a town called Oceanside. In the meantime, I had been sharing a small dormer apartment with Tommy Thomas, in East Rockaway.

After an enroute flight with PanAm to London, I called Margaret, who was now in Manchester, and said I'd be at the Athenian Hotel. It was in Piccadilly, overlooking Greens Park and for her to meet me there. I got to London ahead of her and arranged a couple of tickets to a show she wished to see, I think it was "The Music Man," with Van Johnson.

Margaret arrived, looking great and most friendly. She didn't wish to discuss housing, only the two of us to have fun. It was an early dinner and then the show. She seemed so happy. The next morning, on Sunday, we had planned a late breakfast and a walk right around Buckingham Palace and Hyde Park. Back at the room Margaret casually asked about the housing and how I was coming along. I told her I had seen several with the real estate agent. I showed her two or three pictures, and the notes. I saved the one I hoped she would like, at Oceanside, for last. The house was almost new. In a matter of seconds, she flared up and started shouting and cussing. She packed up, slammed the door, and was gone. I tried to reason with her, but to no avail. Anything I tried to do to please Margaret was wrong. I just shook my head.

In New York, I went ahead with the house. It was a lovely one, and had a finished basement for the kids to play in, with four bedrooms. There was a train service to Manhattan. I had all the furniture arranged when Margaret and the children showed up; it was late August. I hoped she'd accept the place once she saw it. "It would do," she said.

Work continued at the FAA. I enjoyed my work program that I had on the 707, a lot of certification and surveillance. I did have some other friends from Pan Africa, who had joined PanAm and TWA. In the midst of all this, PanAm had now set up aircraft training at the old Walker Air Force Base in Roswell, New Mexico. I was one of the first to be sent there to give aircraft ratings and proficiency checks. The people, including the Mayor and other VIPs from the banks, laid out the red carpet for PanAm. They wanted PanAm's business badly, since their economy was hurting when the Government had pulled the carpet out by closing the air base. I was regarded as part of the PanAm group, and was invited to all of the functions, such as the rodeo, and Sunday morning brunches given by the VIPs. It was great.

Back at Oceanside, I realized I had to change my Virginia license plates to New York, and obtain a New York driver's license. Margaret and I went to the Motor Vehicle Dept. nearby, and checked in. There was no driver's test, but we did have to fill out forms and take a written exam and eye test. All went well. I had to wear glasses and had that as a limitation on my license. Margaret had good eyesight, so there was no problem.

Back at home, Margaret and I made tea, and sat at the kitchen table with the children. She was looking at her driver's license and said, "Hey! They put 'Must wear eyeglasses.'" I looked, and sure enough, that was on it. I said we should go back and have it changed. There was silence from her for a minute, then suddenly Margaret gave me that strange stare and said that I had told the officers to rig up her license. There was no sense to argue. All I could say was "No, I didn't," that we should go back tomorrow and have the license corrected. There was a tantrum and she started throwing things at me. She was either acting well, or was insane. What in God's name was all this about? I didn't understand. Christian and Hannah had disappeared into their rooms, probably not to get hit by all flying dishes. I took my departure also. There was a nice restaurant-bar in East Rockaway called "The Ship's Inn." I headed for it. Here, it was quiet, and I killed a few scotches and also some hours, to regroup and return home.

At the beginning of our setting up the house in Oceanside, it had been agreed that we'd try and take in a paying guest. I contacted PanAm, and found a fellow by the name of Will Brown, who said he'd like to take a room with us. His home actually was in Connecticut, but he didn't like the drive back and forth every day. He worked in the PanAm Ops office. This would help greatly for our rent. Luckily, the guy was not around when this tantrum had taken place. But the tantrums and the tirades were driving me nuts. I was trying to keep my senses and do my work at the same time. To give oral exams to a pilot applicant needed concentration and clear thinking. My home life was becoming a shambles, yet I loved Margaret and the children very much. Perhaps this was some sort of retribution, who knows?

Strangely, and I really don't know why, but I had always been in touch with Sylvia. She was now a Doctor of Psychology in Manhattan. I never did go to see her, but I did call her once in a while. On this occasion I phoned for advice on how to handle the strange action of Margaret. Not knowing all the facts, she couldn't pass judgment; perhaps Margaret was paranoid.

I continued my job. It was an escape to meet pilots and do some flying. Knowing so many of them, I had an opportunity to fly from the left seat whenever possible, even across the Atlantic. I often flew while the Captain got some shuteye in First Class. I never logged any of this time, but felt well qualified to conduct 707 ratings and proficiencies and these particular enroute inspections. Off and on, I made trips to Roswell and conducted check rides. Then in summer of '68, my immediate supervisor, Ray Hirsch, asked if I'd spend a month in Roswell. There were a lot of checks to be given for PanAm. I said I'd make a deal: I would go to Roswell for all summer, and FAA would have to pay for my car mileage. He agreed.

That evening at dinner, I mentioned my trip to Roswell to Margaret, that I'd like to take the children and the puppy dog. It was a black Labrador Retriever. He was a beautiful pup, and we'd named him Bhimsa, after the book that my sister Christine had written about a black bear in India. Margaret thought it was a good idea. That week, I bought the kids camping gear; we already had a good Sears easy-to-assemble tent. We loaded all the stuff on top of the station wagon, and started our long trip westward to New Mexico. I left the second car for Margaret to do her shopping. I liked to make it out of the New York area before the traffic buildup. Once we crossed the George Washington Bridge onto Route 80, I felt relieved.

Our first stop was to be with my old friend, Bob Burge, the same fellow who got lost on top of Mount Katahdin. He lived on a farm near Cleveland, Ohio. It took a bit of doing, what with having to stop every so often to let the kids and the dog do their things by the side of the road, to stop at Big Macs for hamburgers, The kids loved it. With the seats down, they wiled away the hours in the back, playing with the dog. It was late when we arrived at Bob and Joan Burge's place. It was nice to see and visit them. Their kids were pretty well grown up. Bob was a great horse lover, so Hannah got along very well with him, since she also loved horses. As a matter of fact, one of her pastimes as we drove along was to see how many horses she could count in the fields. Hannah was strictly an outdoor girl, very tomboyish.

We spent a few days at the Burge's. All of us did a little fishing in a pond behind their house. It was loaded with catfish. Hannah caught one every time she threw the line. It was fish fry in the evening. The time came when we said

*Christian and Hannah with Bhimsa on the way to White Sands, New Mexico, 1969.*

farewell. It was an early departure which always gave us a head start on the highways. We drove quite a distance, and holed up before reaching Oklahoma City. The next day, just outside Oklahoma, we saw an attraction place called "Frontier City." Christian and Hannah were beside themselves to stop and visit. We pulled in and made the tour, Bhimsa too. A miniature train ride took us through the badlands, where there was a stage holdup; the bad guys held up the train. Then we took a trip on a little boat through darkened tunnels and spooky canals. Bhimsa barked and yipped; he was as scared as the kids. They also enjoyed riding on the electric motor cars. It was nearly a full day's excursion, before we finally drove on into Oklahoma City, where we stayed at the Howard Johnson's. I don't know where kids get their energy. I no sooner had my suitcases in the room when the two were into the pool for a swim.

I've always loved driving through these midwestern states, so wide open, and the people were nice and no tolls. Next morning early, we stopped at a real rancher's restaurant for a hearty breakfast. We saved some food for Bhimsa. If I recall, we headed west on Route 40 for Amarillo, and then down through Clovis. The kids shouted, "Look!" There was a sign on the highway which said, "Welcome to New Mexico." As we drove down Route 70 from Clovis, we were expecting to see rather arid country. I was pleasantly surprised to see such green vegetation. There had been a lot of rain and all the earth had taken on a green look. I knew this would be a great holiday.

We entered the town; there wasn't that much traffic. At a gas station, I inquired where I'd find the Colony Plantation Apartments. I was given directions, which were easy to follow in Roswell. PAA had arranged a small, ground level apartment for us, it was all very nice. I immediately was giving flight checks, sometimes seven days a week. They

were coming out like a sausage machine. I arranged with PanAm's Chief Pilot at Roswell to get everything done within the first four or five days, with two days off. In this manner I was able to take the children on camping trips, to Lincoln National Park and around Mount Capitan. This was old Apache territory, and also where Billy the Kid shot up the sleepy town of Lincoln in the Hondo Valley and was later tracked down and shot. Once in a while, we would have a dinner at the famous Silver Dollar or Tinnie. The kids enjoyed this immensely.

Then there was a lull in Pan American training. I had almost a week off; I had earned enough compensatory time ("comp time") so I could afford to take time off. The three of us sat down and figured out a tour on our own. First we would visit Alamagordo, then White Sands, then travel on to Flagstaff. We could camp at Flagstaff and take a tour to the Grand Canyon and back. Everything was set, suitcases were packed and placed in the hall; we would have breakfast somewhere on the way. It was an early start. Hannah took Bhimsa for his outing, with Christian getting his last chores done, with me looking around, closing doors and shutting off electricity. We were on our way.

The driving was great. I had my 8-millimeter movie camera, had been taking movies from the beginning, since we left Oceanside. White Sands Park was spectacular; it even rained. The kids and the dog played in the dunes. From here, we continued to Gallup; it was raining hard. I found the campground, but it was too miserable to set up the tent. In fact, the car got stuck in the gooey mud. People pushed us out. I returned to the town and checked in at a motel. We started to unload, and to our amazement, we couldn't find our suitcases. I asked Christian and Hannah if they had placed them anywhere, they weren't in the car. No, they thought I had. They must still be in the hallway at our apartment. Can you imagine? The two kids thought it particularly funny. I was

*With Hannah at Pertified Forest.*

disgusted, wet and tired. I had to buy a couple of sets of underwear for all of us, and some toilet articles. Further along we were able to visit the Petrified Forest. I warned the children not to pick up any of the petrified material lying around, though there was a lot. I guess I should not have mentioned it; as we drove on, I heard a lot of chatter in the back. The two of them had filled their pockets with petrified wood pieces and were comparing their loot. I pretended to be angry. I then devised that when they returned to Oceanside, they would have to research what petrified wood was, by looking it up in the Encyclopedia. I was pleasantly surprised that they would check it out.

Flagstaff was a fair sized city. I was informed there was a real nice campsite at the base of the mountain, with a few campers scattered about. The tent was soon up, and we settled down for a rest before I cooked up a meal. We didn't have to worry about changing clothes. While I rested, Hannah and Christian went exploring. They came back and reported they saw a tent, same as ours, owned by a lady and her daughter who invited us for dinner. The lady was young and cute. She taught art in a school in a northern state, perhaps Ohio. She came here every year and painted the scenery. She was divorced, and I asked her about the weather. She stated the clouds build up in the afternoon, with a few showers. We had planned an all-day affair to the Grand Canyon and back, via the Four Corners, which I think was Utah, Colorado, Arizona and New Mexico. The gal said weather is just like this, always very beautiful, and there was no need to close up the tent. It would be okay.

Next morning, the car hummed smoothly on the way northward toward the Grand Canyon. The weather was clear as a bell. I parked at one of the viewing stations at the edge of the Canyon. I kept busy taking pictures, both slides and movies. I forgot about the children and the dog. When I looked around, I saw Christian, who showed up, but no sign of Hannah. I called several times, but no answer. We were the only people around. Christian and I followed a trail for awhile, calling for her. I looked over the edge to see whether she might have fallen down; all the chasms were deep. Every time I looked, I expected to see Hannah, lying thousands of feet below. I shuddered. At another lookout spot, here comes Hannah, running along a trail with Bhimsa. I scolded her for running off like that. Her retort was, "Well, can't a girl have a little time to take a leak in the Grand Canyon?" I was surprised, but what can you say? I laughed out loud, and hugged her. She was almost eight years old.

Back at the car, after a couples of hours of sightseeing and pictures, I opened up the tailgate and we had our lunch. The whole place was majestic and beautiful as it has always been portrayed. The garbage was dumped in a bin provided by the park. We drove on, toward the Four Corners. Every so often, I would stop and take movies. During one of these stops and picture-taking, Hannah pointed at the camera and casually stated, "Isn't the lid still on the camera?" I looked, the lens cover was on. I don't know how much footage I had taken in this manner. I rearranged the film and removed the lens cover. The kids snickered.

The Four Corners was interesting. Hannah and Christian spread-eagled, so as to be in four states at one time. It was late afternoon when we approached our campsite. I noticed a large cloud had gathered around Flagstaff Mountain; the roads had been soaked with rain, evidently quite heavily. When I drove up to our tent, it looked soaked. We had a small canopy that stretched over the front, supported by the two aluminum poles The poles looked warped. It reminded me of the hind legs of a cow when it's peeing. On closer inspection, I found the canopy had collected at least ten gallons of water; it was this that was weighing on the two poles. No wonder they were bent, like the full bladder of a cow, ready to go. Hannah

and Christian said they would empty the water out. I shouted not to touch it; it was about to collapse. I decided to go under the canopy and just push it forward. Christian and Hannah moved away; they were doubtful about this. As I bent over and got under by the entrance of the tent, I must have brushed the side of the tent with my shoulder. Within a split second, the two poles twisted and collapsed, and doused the ten gallons of water onto me, and into the tent. There I stood, with canopy draped over my head. It must have been a sight! The kids screeched, and laughed like hell. This was not my day, in spite of the beautiful scenery and the good weather we'd had on the trip. What with Hannah missing the Grand Canyon, taking movies with the lens cap on, and now getting myself and the inside of the tent soaked!

It took a while to sop up the inside and get a few things out to dry. I didn't have much choice but to stay wet and shiver. I was able to scrounge some fire logs from the Camp Manager and soon we had a roaring fire going. I sat as close as I could, and began to steam as my clothes warmed up. I sat there with an extra large scotch, feeling miserable. I said I'd take the kids to dinner in town, instead of trying to cook anything. We visited Pizza Hut. I didn't see the lady again, because I was going to tell her about her weather! The next day, we headed back to Roswell.

When we got back to the apartment, there sat our suitcases, ready to go. A couple weekends I took Christian and Hannah to another lovely campsite at Lincoln Park, the original home of Smokey the Bear. My tour was soon at a close, and it was time to pack up and head home. Christian and Hannah had a fantastic holiday, and I know how much they enjoyed it.

We drove into the yard at Oceanside late in the evening. They had phoned their mother earlier, and gave an approximate ETA. She greeted the children with open arms and were gushing with stories to tell her. There were no open arms for me, no hugs; just a cold stare. I unpacked the wagon and placed the tent in the garage. When I came in, Margaret and the kids were having dinner. I noticed there was no place set for me. I didn't say a word. I went into the kitchen and had a scotch... what else? I wasn't that hungry, anyway; if I had been, she took the appetite from me.

I took the suitcases upstairs and thought I'd stretch out for a few moments. I wanted to get that never-ending white dividing line on the highway out of my vision. It had almost been hypnotic, with those thousands of miles of driving. When I got to the bedroom, I noticed a fair-sized letter reposing on my pillow. It was addressed to me, and it had a lawyer's title and address on the envelope. I opened it and found it was an official notice for divorce. This must have been her game right along. I came downstairs and confronted Margaret with this. She shrugged her shoulders and walked away. "Talk to the lawyer." She had also moved a single bed into the lower basement for herself, and Will Brown had left a note that he would no longer be staying here. I surmised that there was something between them and had been for awhile. At this point, I didn't care about Margaret, but only for the children. This Roswell trip had brought us so close together. I knew Margaret would get custody. Well, I'd not give in that easily! I'd get a lawyer and fight. I now felt she had planned this for some time; ultimately, of course, to shack up and marry Will Brown.

This was Sunday. The next day, I was back in the office. I was glum. I cornered my friend, Ray Hirsch, and told him the situation. He sympathized, and said I could get a lawyer friend of his in Manhattan. When I contacted the lawyer, he suggested I move out of the house. I didn't do so until around Thanksgiving, to the little apartment in East Rockaway that I once shared with Tommy Thomas. It was heartbreaking to tear myself away from the children; I loved them so much! Hannah was bewildered. I know she loved her Dad very much. Christian was more understanding, and I think his mother explained things to him, also tried to turn him against me.

Everything seemed futile. All that I had worked so hard for was gone. It was like building a sand castle on the beach, and then the tide rolls in and washes it away. I can understand how husbands and fathers can turn to drink, just to obliterate their memories and try to forget. In my little apartment, I had no TV or radio; just my clothes and my beat up old Ford Falcon parked outside. I spent a lot of evenings at the Ship's Inn, just around the corner. I could not let myself go over the deep end by drinking, yet it was easy to do. I had a responsibility for licensing pilots of two major airlines.

One morning at the office, I must have looked bedraggled and glum and beaten down. I saw the Chief of the office, Bill Huebner. I told him my sad story. He also sympathized with me and knew this was not easy to take. He asked if I'd like to take a vacation, and think about things. I said no, to the contrary. "Give me some chores that no one else wants to do; keep me occupied." Bill thought it over and later that day called me into his office. It had been 6 to 8 months since I had left the house, and it was now early September '68. "Pete," he said, "I have a job for you. See if you like this one: FAA has hired an Ops Inspector for us, he has yet to be interviewed. As you know, normally before hiring, we interview people. How would you like to do that?" "That's fine," I said. "But where, and what's his name?" "Well, his name is Syd Wheatley and he's sitting in Teheran." I did a double-take. "Syd Wheatley! I know that rascal from way back!" I first met Syd in Jeddah, in 1950, back in our Haj days; he flew for Saudi Airlines. I then had him hired to fly for us in Air Liban. He was fine looking guy, and I remember Margaret had her eyes on him. Oh, well! "Yes, I'll go and see him."

*Hannah, Christian and Margaret—cherry blossom time in Washington D.C., 1964.*

Then Bill said, "While you're out there, how about the following: How about continuing on and check PanAm facilities at Karachi and Delhi? From there, I want you to go to Bombay and check TWA facility. Also, TWA wants to use a new alternate airport at Hydrabad, alternate for Bombay. TWA wants a new route to be checked between Ceylon and Bangkok. Check Colombo Airport and their new route." Then he stopped. "How am I doing?" I said, "I lost you Bill, but continue." "Okay," he said. "After checking TWA routes to Bangkok, how about hopping on PanAm? They have special flights that operate Bangkok-Saigon-DaNang, then on to Hong Kong. It's mainly for the R&R troops. Once that is done, do anything you want, come home via PanAm or TWA westbound, or continue over the Pacific."

I hadn't taken any notes, only mentally. Then I thought quickly: "Bill, could I take a week off at Delhi if I do this?" "Yes, of course. Just be sure to state on your voucher when you come back that no pay is requested at that station." I said, "I'll do it, and I'll check with you, to make sure I've got all these chores correctly." I thanked him very much. "No," he said, "We should thank you. This surveillance should have been accomplished long ago. There has been no one to do it. Actually, the inspectors don't want to be away from home that long, nearly six weeks, if it's done correctly."

I returned to my desk, feeling so much better. Since I loved travel, this was right up my alley and I needed it. It would help relieve the hidden pain. I got all the Jeppeson charts for the journey and the letdown approach plates for these various cities, and started making my itinerary. I was given Wheatley's phone number and address.

That weekend, I had Christian and Hannah with me. We went to Jones Beach for a picnic on Saturday, and then movies again, also window shopping at the Valley Stream Mall. They enjoyed it. I explained

*Christian and Hannah with Penny, Jone's Beach, Long Island 1969.*

my trip to them, that I'd be away for some time, but how I'd love to have kidnapped them and taken them with me, hide in some faraway place never to return. I guess I was dreaming. I dropped them back at Oceanside and said I would send cards and see them as soon as I returned.

I called Geraldine in Plainfield and told her I was on my way to India in about a week or so. She was excited and said that she, too, planned to go to India; that she planned to meet a friend of ours, an Audrey Baylis. She used to be a Miss Clay. Audrey and Geraldine were good friends when we were living in India. I remembered Audrey, specially her little blonde-haired sister, Betty, who I think was about eight. I said I'd try and meet them in Naini-Tal, my old school haunt. I gave the approximate dates that I'd be there. Geraldine said she would make sure to arrange it.

*A young Hindu Yogi (Priest) on the way to Naini-Tal. All that is missing is the guitar!*

Instead of taking PanAm Flight 1, that stopped London-Frankfurt-Istanbul, and then to Teheran, I took PanAm Flight 110, direct to Rome and then Istanbul-Beirut-Teheran.

I sent Wheatley a cable before departure, and gave my ETA. The flight left around 1830 in the evening. I checked in with PanAm Ops downstairs at the World Building. The weather was lousy, the flight would be about 30 minutes late. I was informed by dispatch. I had given my FAA Form 160, and looked at a copy of the flight plan. I walked around PAA duty-free shops and drooled. An hour before departure, I walked out to the Boeing 707. The Flight Engineer was already observing the fueling and the walkaround. I went up into the first-class lounge to place my suitcase in the cockpit with the crew's. I was regarded as part of the cockpit crew and listed on their general declaration.

In the first-class section, there was mad confusion, a burly individual detached himself from the group of mechanics and came rushing at me and grabbed me by the arm and ordered me off the plane. "Hold it!" I said. "I'm an FAA inspector, I'm going on this flight." "Oh, no, you're not!" I was taken aback. With all the many, many flights I had accumulated on PanAm to Europe, this was the first time I'd never been accosted or asked to get off a PanAm plane. I was regarded by PanAm Ops personnel as part of PanAm. As I mentioned, I actually did a lot of the flying myself with them. I was taken aback for the moment. I asked the individual who he was, since I didn't see an ID on his coat. As he breathed, I also noticed he smelled of booze. He said he was PAA security and pulled out an ID. Why did he want me off the plane? He mentioned there was a VIP flying to Rome. "So What?" The VIP didn't want any other people in this area except the flight crew. "That's fine," I said. "I'm a part of the flight crew." He was surprised and still reeked. I was getting a little riled up. I flatly told him he was drunk, and if he didn't get himself off the flight, I'd ground the plane myself. His bloodshot eyes bugged out.

"You'll what?" I said, "You heard me. If you think I'm kidding, come with me to Operations." He seemed to sober up in a hurry. "Okay, who's the VIP?" The guy quieted down and said it was the Shah of Iran. Yes, that would be some VIP. I tried not to flinch. "That's fine. He'll be happy to know that he's being looked after by the FAA as well as security."

I never asked what was going on in the first-class, but I went past the individual and had a look myself. I placed my baggage in the lounge. I saw several mechanics putting the finishing touches on a makeshift bed. It was a sloppy, rickety affair. I said it didn't look good and I'd have to call our Airworthiness people over. PanAm had folded a couple of seats, and had tied a box spring mattress over it, as a makeshift bed. So where were the straps, when the Shah decided to lie down? It's the same as the seatbelt. Where was it? "It was not necessary." I said, "Don't fool me. It is necessary, and this is a no-go."

The Chief of PanAm Maintenance was called. He agreed with me that the whole thing was a "no-no." I got dirty looks from all around. I went into the cockpit with the Flight Engineer, and told him that he had better check out the sleeping arrangements. Also, where was the Captain and First Officer? They should be here by now.

While they fussed with the bed, I returned to the Ops Department and learned the Captain had been stuck in some terrible traffic due to the weather. They were contacting a relief Captain. The First Officer had just shown up, and was checking the flight plan. I introduced myself, and said I was glad the flight was delayed because, if it wasn't, I would be delaying it. He laughed and said, "Situation normal." The new Captain arrived, and I was back at the airplane and saw they had set up another, more acceptable sleeping rig for the Shah. The security apologized to me for being so rude. I asked if he was going on the flight. "Yes," he said. I suggested he'd better gargle with some mouthwash, and eat a handful of mints and drink some coffee and stay out of sight.

Once in the cockpit, no one saw the Shah come on board and the first class had been sealed off. The weather was bad when airborne. It was blowing a gale. We were in rough air till we got on top of clouds. We reached altitude and started across the Atlantic. It was clear, with bright stars and a hint of the Aurora Borealis or Northern Lights, giving off streamers of light into the northern skies, most spectacular. By the time we passed latitude 20, the eastern sky started to show early hours of the dawn. This was when everyone's head started to loll, when the orange sun begins to pick up and peek over the horizon.

The stewardess brought us hot wet towels, which smelled of cologne. With these, we washed our face and hands; it did away with the sleepiness. This was followed by coffee and orange juice. The Chief Purser then poked his head into the cockpit and said to the Captain, "His Highness, the Shah, wants to know if he can visit the crew in the cockpit." The Captain looked back at me and said, "Well, what do you think? Your rules say no unauthorized persons may enter the cockpit." I thought for a minute, still trying to be rid of my drowsiness. "Yes, it was okay for him to come on up. The Shah was a qualified pilot, and had just about bought this flight." It was as though it was his own personal airplane. In a few minutes, he was ushered in. The Shah was a slightly built man, with good features, and appeared just as his pictures portrayed him to be. He introduced himself to the Captain and Crew, and when he looked in my direction, I said I was the FAA Inspector checking the crew on this flight. I then offered him my jumpseat. The Shah asked a few questions concerning the Boeing 707. The Captain said that I would be the person to direct the questions to. I discussed the 707 in some detail: the capacity, the cargo and passenger configurations, fuel, and the range. He seemed very interested, and said he was hoping to obtain the right aircraft for his airline, Iran Air. We spent almost an hour talking aviation. I talked about my job function and past experience. He was very easy to talk with and was planning to get off at Rome to meet his wife, Soraya. They were going skiing in the Italian Alps. We were now starting our letdown to Rome. The Shah thanked me very much for all the information concerning the Boeing and returned to the cabin. I feel I may have had some influence in Iran Air obtaining one hell of a lot of Boeings. He wound up with the 707s, 747s, 727s, 737s.

I got off at Beirut for a couple of days' rest, and stayed at the Phoenicia Hotel. I met the FAA fellow who had the position I had hoped for. His name was Argyle Smith. He looked happy with the job. The next couple of days, I was on my way to Teheran. I met Syd Wheatley and his wife, Maria. They insisted I stay at their place though most of their things were already packed. We sat around on crates and drank our scotches. Maria didn't drink. I spent several days with them, and sent a message to Bill Huebner from the Embassy that all was well, to have Syd Wheatley on board FAA as soon as possible. He was hired, and told to report to the IFO in New York.

PanAm Flight 01 arrived at Delhi in the wee hours of the morning and I was exhausted. It was like coming home after almost 10 years: the noise of the early hustle-bustle, and the old taxis, the smell of the burning cow dung, like punk, and the cawing of all the Indian garden crows, the shrieks of the bright green parrots as they flashed by in groups looking like fast-moving arrows.

I took a taxi to the Ashoka Hotel and enjoyed my breakfast at the Semova Coffee Shop, then to the room for a quick nap. There was a lot to do for my trip to Naini-Tal. I hadn't been there in 40 years plus, yet I knew every inch of it because I never let it out my mind, even during all the stay I had in America, especially the old schoolboy haunts. I hadn't been in Delhi or the Ashoka Hotel since I was there with Margaret in 1959. By one o'clock in the afternoon I cleaned up and wandered around the lobby and window shopped in their local arcade. There were always so many things I'd love to have bought: jewelry and brassware and clothes. At the gift shop, I bought a road map of India, and checked the route up to Naini. I then wandered into the main restaurant and ordered a delicious hot curry. This was cooled off by the local beer; I think it was Solon Beer.

Everything closes down in India after lunch: Mexican siesta time, one could call it. Some slang terms called it Charpoy time. Charpoy is a cot or bed. Instead, I wandered on into the gardens at the back of the hotel near the swimming pool where I found a bench and lit up a cigar. I'd taken to smoking cigars in the past few years. I watched the different birds that abound in the garden. There were the black and the white hoopoes, with its topknot that resembles a beak at the back of its head. the mynah birds squabbling and the garden grey seven sisters, with yellowish beaks that looked ugly. There were the ever present crows and the hawks. I sat for about an hour, then returned to the room for an afternoon rest. I dozed off, but could not sleep. I thought of my return to the Kumaon Hills and Naini-Tal. It was now after 4 p.m. and I had my afternoon tea, which was sent to my room. It tasted delicious. I enjoyed this as I looked out of the window, from where I could see the ancient Mogul Emperor Humayan tomb, which resembles the Taj Mahal, only with red stone.

After a shower and cleanup, I sauntered about the arcade till I found the travel agency, which was Mercury Travel Tours. I inquired about a car that could take me to Naini-Tal. "Yes, Sir: of course we can," said the lady, who wore a lovely sari and always-present tika on her forehead. "When do you wish to travel?" I said, "How about tomorrow morning, early?" When I responded like that, she said, "Oh, dear! So soon? I don't have too

*On approaching Kathgodam station; the first welcome view of hills.*

much time, but I will try." "But if I could have gone this afternoon, I would have liked that." "Oh, no, cannot be done; sorry." "We usually need about eight hours, because it is a long drive up there. I will call the head office and let you know in an hour or two. Would you keep the car up there, sir?" "No, just one way, thank you." "Okay. So please call back in an hour."

I wandered into the bar and had a scotch. The local scotch is not that good; however, it would suffice. I killed a little over an hour, and returned to the travel counter. The gal in the sari was all smiles and informed me that the car and the driver would be available, and what time would I like to depart? "The earlier the better, but not later than six a.m." "Yes, that'll be fine," with a little twist of her head. It would cost around 650 rupees, or close to $70, pay in advance. I got to like this little gal; she was really polite. I arranged the money for her.

I also went over to get the headwaiter from the restaurant to make up some cold chicken and Indian chapattees, also orange soda that they call Fanta, enough for two people. I ordered a good breakfast sent to the room, since the coffee shop would not be open that early. When everything was done, I went for a fairly long walk in the park that was adjacent to the hotel. The weather was cool and fresh. I walked for about another hour, and returned for dinner. Jet-Lag or whatever, maybe the local whiskey, was making me drowsy. I was soon fast asleep.

The next moment, there was banging at the door. It took a few seconds to realize where I was. I opened the door, and there stood a bearer with a large tray.

It was 5:30 a.m. I tipped the boy, showered and got ready. Everything was mostly packed. I sat down and had my breakfast of orange juice, fried eggs and bacon with very crispy toast, and wonderful tea. Normally, I couldn't eat this so early, but I forced myself to do so; it would be a long day. I hardly finished when there was another bang on the

door. This time, it was another bearer, with my box of chicken for the trip, and another tip. It was a few minutes past six. I gathered everything and took the lift down to the lobby. It took awhile to have the bills paid. By 6:30, the driver was standing by. He was a large Sikh, with a well-groomed beard. Sikhs never shave or cut their hair; it's part of their religion. All their names are Mr. Singh; it's more of a title. He knew I was his man. He bowed and said, "Mr. Peter." I bowed and said, "Mr. Singh of Mercury Travels." "Yes sir." Then I asked, "You know the way to Naini-Tal?" "Yes sir; been many times." "Well, that's great; let's get going."

The weather was nice and there was not much traffic. We wound our way through the streets, and around the Red Fort, then onto a fairly trafficked bridge that took us across the Ganges. There are no super highways in India, especially in this area; all were two-way roads with a high crown. Along the shoulders were sidewalks made of red brick, lots of which were broken and crumbling. I sat near the driver and watched for scenes that I might photograph. After a few dirty streets and villages, we broke out into more open country. One thing the driver never stopped doing was to keep tooting the horn; it was incessant, yet it was a necessity, since everyone used the road. There were pedestrians with baskets on their heads, people on bicycles; there were bullock carts, and the lorries or trucks. These were a menace, mostly over-laden and top-heavy; they would not give an inch of the road. They took their half in the middle. When two trucks passed, it could be anyone's guess if they would make it or not. Once in awhile, they didn't. They would tip over, spilling everything out, lying on their side and stopping all traffic. We witnessed one such incident. It was necessary to detour through some fields and footpaths to get by; no wonder it would take eight hours and then some! Most of these roads had large trees, mainly banyan, peepal and jamon. These are the main shade trees,

*A group of teapickers in Sri-Linka, 1969.*

they certainly did the job. Here and there, some poor animal had been run over, usually a pariah dog or goat; there were the ever present vultures, either sitting in trees or circling high overhead. They would make quick work of cleaning out a victim, leaving the head, hoofs and bones.

It was noon, and the temperature was getting warm. The driver located a place a short distance off the road, a spot that overlooked some marshy land. Here we sat on a grassy hummock. It had been quite a drive so far, and my Sikh friend had done a good job. The driver and I munched on cold chicken sandwiches and chapattees, and sipped orange soda. It was peaceful and nice. I watched the white egrets and coots and other waterfowl doing their fishing. Once in awhile, there would be an Indian roller, a large, pretty bluejay, and the beautiful white-breasted kingfisher with very bright, iridescent blue wings. Then the bee-eater, which is bright green. These are some of the birds I used to chase as a kid with my slingshot, or take potshots from the train as it sped along. At this moment, Margaret and the children were fond memories, as my thoughts traveled as a youngster in the area we were now in. I relaxed after the meal, and enjoyed my cigar.

Before long, we were on our way. Considerable dust and horn blowing continued. I had the man stop every so often, while I snapped pictures. Then we came to a large town. On entering, there was a railway terminus, and a section where the locomotives were being overhauled, like an enormous garage. There was a turnstile where manually, laboriously, people turned these locomotives around. All the engines were coal-burners. Perhaps one of them had probably drawn our train on one of our trips from Bareilly to Monghyr, or to Hardoi, who knows? The town was called Muradabad. I remember my mother talking of this city where my Dad had chased the Dacoits. It is also located on one of the tributaries of the

Ganges. Close by, there was a burning ghat on the bank of the river. This is one of the sites where the Hindus are cremated and their remains pushed into the river.

The next stop would be the city of Rampur. Rampur was a principality, an estate with a Maharajah. The days of the Maharajah's are finished; they lived there in name only. Those were days gone by. I remember, as a very small boy, my father was a guest here. I think he had helped the Maharajah get rid of some of the Dacoits. I remember there was a parade; I was in the backseat of a touring car with my family. My mother was next to me, and as the parade had progressed, it had passed along a line of elephants that were saluting, with their trunks up on their foreheads. One of them put his trunk out and got hold of the door of the car. There were shouts, and the mahout was able to get the elephant back. Yes, it had happened in this state, and now I was in a closed taxi on the same road. As the car came around the corner, there was a narrow-gauge railway that crossed it. The driver put on his brakes hard; there on the railroad track was a flat car, loaded down with sugar cane, and an elephant was pulling it ever so slowly across the road. I felt sorry for the beast, since that was never the work for elephants. It was a few minutes before we could continue.

Once our car got through, there was a fork in the road. One side said Bareilly, the other pointed to Haldwani, and my heart beat fast for a moment. I had not seen a sign for Bareilly or Haldwani since 1928 - forty years before. The road the driver took was Haldani, leading us through some lovely jungle, with high elephant grass on both sides. It reminded me of the places near Cooch-Behar, where I had hunted. I expected to see tigers leap across the road at any moment. What an imagination - most tigers had been eliminated by poachers and villagers chopping down the forest. From the tall grass, we went through some beautiful sal forests. After a few miles, we were entering the outskirts of

Haldwani. We stopped at the railroad station where I had been so often. I took several pictures and then we continued on.

Approaching Kathgodan, I saw a large mustard field, all bright yellow, and through the haze beyond, I could make out the first ridges of mountains. I had the driver stop a few moments before driving on. I could really see the hills, the slate grey stones, and the landslide pock-marked, just as I had left them. At this moment, I could only think of my mother, and how she would loved to have been here to see the familiar sight.

We drove along, parallel to the old narrow-gauge railway. Soon we entered Kathgodam. I recognized it immediately. I asked the driver to pull over to the railroad station. I got out and walked down a pathway that led me onto the railroad platform. I walked up and down the platform for awhile, I entered the same little Spencer's Restaurant and ordered tea for the driver and myself. I took a lot of pictures before we started ascending the road to Naini, with the Goula River on our right, with its ravine. Here, I stopped by a Hindu temple where a young Hindu priest came out. I asked to take his picture. "Oh, yes." He spoke a little English. As a kid I was scared to death of these fellows. He was happy to have me take his picture, and invited us in for tea. I politely said no.

Halfway up the road again, we stopped, this time at Joelikote, where we once lived right after my Dad's death in 1922, as guests of Mr. Warrick. I went to the little convent and chapel then saw the small room that I once had. I stayed long enough to talk with the Sister in charge. She told me that our Mr. Warrick had died in 1945, and it was learned that Mr. Warrick was, after all, a Miss Warrick. The secret was finally revealed when they lifted her nightie! Another strange chapter had come to an end. Miss Warrick is buried in Joelicote.

I stood outside the premises, overlooking Goula River valley. I could hear a lot of the familiar birds I had known. God! I had returned home! Yet I didn't believe it. Everything I loved; the life in America, flying and the war, was just a faraway memory; perhaps just a dream: Helen, David, Christine, Kim, Kiki, Christian and Hannah, all a vagueness. I guess I must have been standing right here for the past forty years, dreaming. I shook my head and decided I had better get up to Naini-Tal before I make a complete ass of myself standing here gazing into the distance.

I thanked the Sister and the other people in the Mission and continued my drive up , along the steep grade and the hairpin turns of the motor road. I don't know how the old car ever made it. Coming around the last few turns of the road, I could make out St. Joseph's College, far up on my left. On the right, on the opposite mountain, I recognized Philander Smith's College (PSC); beyond that I saw Eagle's Crag with eagles circling over it. In the next moment the driver made the final turn, and straight ahead of us, we entered the town of Tali Tal. I saw the blue water of Naini shimmering in front of me; I had arrived at my old childhood haunt. I will never know why I waited so long to return. All through the war I had many opportunities to do so; I don't know why I didn't take advantage then. Again, I stood and took in the whole panoramic view: the mall around the lake, Cheena Peak towering up at the far end. The church nearby, where my sister Christine and Robert were married in 1923. Coolies were scurrying around trying to pick up my baggage. There were boats, something like the shakaras on Dahl Lake in Kashmir; they wanted to take me across the lake to Mali-Tal. I shook my head to say no. I was going to walk slowly along the mall instead. I gave the driver a well deserved tip and wished him a safe trip back to Delhi. He placed his two hands together to his forehead, as a polite salaam and thank you.

I selected two coolies to carry my bags to the Swiss Hotel in Mali-Tal. I strolled along the mall where I had played as a small boy. I spotted the steep, winding trails and roadway that led up to PSC; I would travel them later. At Mali-Tal, I saw the old horse-stand, where we used to get the horses to take us up to school. There was the Flats, where so many soldiers were buried in the double landslide, back in 1880. The old Hindu Temple was there, by the edge of the lake, and the Cinema House next to it; nothing seemed to have changed. There was the old Naini Yacht Club, still painted green, with its fancy eaves.

I followed my coolies up the steep road till we came to the hotel. There was a shout from Geraldine and Audrey Baylis. They were there to meet me and their driver Indojit Singh. His nickname was Kakar, which means "uncle," even though it does sound rude. He was stockily built, with a big Texas Belly.

Late afternoon tea was served on the verandah. The bearer was in his traditional white gown, maroon cummerbund around his waist, and white pugri. I would have preferred a scotch and soda, after that long wonderful ride from Delhi. The conversation was all reminiscing about the old days. Audrey spoke of her little sister, Betty. Betty and I played together a lot in Naini-Tal, when we were very small. She was a few years younger than me. During the war and the Battle of Britain, Betty had been a nurse, I think she was about 19. She had returned to Naini-Tal to visit Audrey, who was married to Mr. Robbie Baylis, then the judge of Naini-Tal district. (This was before India got its independence. India was still under British rule up through 1947.) In October 1946, when Betty had come to Naini for a visit, Audrey said, one day Betty had gone for a walk on one of the numerous trails behind Cheena Peak, and did not return. Late that afternoon, a search party set out, looking for her. They found her body down a mountainside, where she had evidently slipped and fallen over the edge of a cliff. Most of these mountains are steep and can be treacherous; one has to be surefooted.

Betty had been buried with full military honors, caison and all, at Kaladungi Cemetery. This cemetery I knew well; one of our teachers at PSC was buried there, and as youngster I was present at his funeral.

At the west side of the lake, and above Mali-Tal, two mountains, Cheena Peak and Aiapata, come together, forming a gorge. The main street from the town traverses through this area and then winds down the other side to the little town of Kalabdunghi, where the famed Jim Corbett lived when he hunted the man-eating tigers of Kumaon. I told Geraldine and Audrey I couldn't wait to see the whole lot of my childhood haunts: all those places I tromped about as a boy. Geraldine had been back several times, so she left it up to me to do what I wished. That was fine. I wanted to go up and visit my two schools DBS & PSC. The first one would be the Diocesan Boys School, sometimes called Sherwood.

Geraldine and I walked the old road along the ridge of the mountain that leads to the DBS school. I recognized every turn. Geraldine said for me to go by myself to the school. I took the path that headed up the hill where the school was situated. It was at right angles to the main road, which led to the church and down the hill to the lake. I stopped at the foot of the stairs that led to the compound. It was here that my mother had dropped me off for my first term at school, where I met the tall principal, Mr. Dixon. That was 1923. I walked up the six steps to the small playground in the front of the main building. A long verandah ran the full length. A group of teachers were at the closer end. I introduced myself, and said that I was once a scholar here. Several of them were English; one in particular who was smoking his pipe. He said he was there in the 20's. His name was Thompson. I asked if he had a brother, and did they play the piano? "Good Lord, yes! You remember that?" I said, "That's right; I remember that well." I remember some of the tunes that were taken from "Swanee River," that they had performed little concerts in the auditorium. Yes, he was the one, and his brother was in England. This professor had gone to England and returned to spend his life teaching at DBS.

He took me around the school. I saw the place in the back near the latrines where we settled our differences with bare fisticuffs. I visited the chapel at the far end and looked at the Roll of Honor from WWII, listed on a bronze plaque at the entrance. There were a few names I recognized. Thompson mentioned the ones that died in Europe, and those in Burma and Singapore. The school fellows were now returning to their classes, while Thompson introduced me to a few of the people. The playground was 100 yards down the hill. I walked down by myself, since Mr. Thompson had to return to his class. I lingered on the grounds for a spell before returning to the school and wishing Mr. Thompson farewell.

I met Geraldine at the foot of the hill, and continued down towards the church we school kids attended every Sunday. It was a Church of England, or Episcopal, called Saint Nicholas. It was a beautiful English-style, granite structure building. We went in and looked around. There was no one there. The inside looked as though it needed painting, so we placed some rupees in the alms box with a note, in the hope that they would use it to paint the inside. I've always wondered if they received it. Geraldine and I then walked down the hill where old Smuggler's Rock once jutted out, and now was missing; it was like a tooth having been extracted; there was just a cavity. It had finally fallen from its perch and tumbled down into the lake.

Geraldine and I walked around the lake and back to the hotel. I was out of shape for all this up and down mountain hiking. That, and the high altitude. The three of us had brunch and a rest. Audrey decided not to accompany us to the Kalabdunghi Cemetery. Geraldine and I went through the gorge and the Kalabdunghi Road. About half a mile along, we came to the cemetery on our right. It had a large iron gate. It was very quiet, except for the songbirds. Geraldine said the last time she had visited here, a few years ago, she couldn't find Mr. Fleming's grave.

Mr. Fleming was our assistant principal at PCS. He'd passed away in October of 1927. At that time, I remember the whole school body had to march all the way down for the burial. I told her I knew where the grave was. I stood at the steps halfway down that separated the cemetery in two. I stepped off to one side by another tombstone. I told Geraldine that this was approximately where I stood that day. Then I pointed diagonally off to the left and down about 30 feet. I said, "It should be about the fourth tombstone in that row." Geraldine went along; it was the right one. The tombstone was well covered with lichen and moss; some wild bushes grew around it. I stepped down and scraped off a lot of the moss and lichen and there was a plaque on the stone that said it had been donated by the school children in memory of Mr. Fleming. Geraldine and I cleaned up all around the tombstone before leaving.

Audrey had said that Betty was buried nearby. It took a short while, but we did locate her grave. I placed some wildflowers on it that I had picked along the way. This moment was sad; I remembered Betty, a pretty little blonde girl with pigtails.

We returned to the hotel for afternoon tea, and chatted with Audrey. The next day, Geraldine and I would visit Philander Smith's College, PSC. I suggested we take the long, roundabout way to the gorge near Cheena Peak, then follow the old Upper Mall Road, to a ridge between Cheena Peak and PSC. That whole area was covered with the trees commonly known as the Deodars or Cedars of Lebanon. The ridge was a saddleback, with a lookout site called Snowview. It was here that the terrible landslides occurred that covered the rescue soldiers and formed the Flats.

It was a clear morning with many Cedars that grew on that slope. I was able to take several photos of the lake. At Snowview, we had a beautiful view of the high, snowcapped Himalayas. It was breathtaking; standing out perfectly were the Trisul Mountain and Nanda Davi Peaks, reaching up to 23,000 and 25,000 feet.

We came to the entrance of PSC. There were some changes to the old school. I recognized my haunts and places where I chased butterflies, and beetles. From the main building, where the Principal, Mr. Busher, and Mr. Fleming stayed, then our dormitory and dining hall. Geraldine and I took a covered passageway to the classroom building and the playground further along. It was all there as before. I could almost hear the shouts of my friends as we raced up and down the passage. In a way, it reminded me of a movie I saw later, called *Goodbye, Mr. Chips*, with Robert Donat and Greer Garson. I was filled with nostalgia.

One change was the dining hall being moved down by the classrooms. We talked with the Principal, an Indian who showed us around. I visited my old classroom, and the Physics Lab. The old type bellows were still used.

The Principal said there was still one fellow at the school who might remember us; he had worked at the school all these years. He was the dishwasher (masalchee). The old man was brought out from the kitchen. After talking with him in Hindi, he started to cry. Yes, he remembered Mrs. Goutiere and "Peter-Baba" (that was me). He was so excited to see us! I brought him up to date with all the Goutiere family and our life in America, and that Mrs. Goutiere had passed away. We took several pictures of him.

Geraldine stayed around the school compound. I rushed all over the place, the playground, looking out towards Eagle's Crag. I didn't want to leave. I did tell the masalchee I would be back another time, "Inshallah (if God wills)." It wasn't to be so. I would not return for a couple of years, and when I did, the old masalchee had passed away.

Geraldine and I walked down the pathway to the lake. It was very sheer and very easy to fall and break one's leg or back, or even your neck. This was the old path the school kids had to march, all the way down to the church at Tali-Tal. The walk around the lake was pleasant, and back to the hotel. I had exhausted myself with all the sights I knew I had to see, and taken umpteen photographs. Audrey had to leave for Delhi. We had hoped she would stay but time was pressing. Later, Geraldine and I decided to walk to Bhowali. We told Kakar Singh to drive on ahead and meet us at Bhowali Bazaar. We walked along the upper road, the one we all used to take to Bhowali and BhimTal, where I consumed all those chocolates meant for Geraldine!

We were on our own. It was a wonderful walk. We came out at the Sanitarium where my father had once been, in 1917. It hadn't changed; the yard, as we entered, still had its fountain. We stayed only a few moments, and continued to Bhowali. We rounded the bend and there was the familiar sight of the bazaar and old Applecot as we looked down at it. There was the Cottons' Hotel, his lorry station and restaurant for transients.

As I walked along the main street of the bazaar, the smells of Indian food cooking, I could recognize each one. The pariah dogs still roamed and scavenged in the dirty gutters. The Post Office was no longer in the center of the bazaar. The little stream and bridge just beyond was there where I used to fish for minnows.

We traveled the road that follows the stream, and came to the old Shepherd's Hotel, which was known as the Royal Oak Hotel. It hadn't changed, except it was more weatherbeaten. This was where I'd smoked up a storm with my friend, Eric Thompkins, and got violently ill. Geraldine and I walked up the small path behind the hotel that led up to Shepherd's estate, and also to Applecot. A lot of the garden and rose arbor was gone. The dining room table, solid oak, was put outside on the verandah. The whole place had been taken over by a Catholic mission. The other home, next door, where we'd stayed before going to America, was still there, known as Oak Lodge. It had been bought by an Englishman by the name of Percy Sherred, and his wife, Phyllis. Geraldine had met them before. I was now introduced. I couldn't believe I was back at the old homesite.

I wandered around and noticed the big round rock was no longer in the yard. As a kid, I always tried to climb and shinny up it; at that time I imagined it to be about four feet in diameter. Percy said they had to remove it for the driveway. The building was located on a ledge that looked down into Tirchakhet Valley, and the lower hills beyond. Off to the left was the gorge I always was anxious to see, when returning from the school to BhimTal. BhimTal Lake could be seen, in the distance, far below us; a beautiful sight, four miles away, with Kalias, a sugarloaf mountain just beyond, standing right up as a sentinel. I gazed out at BhimTal and its surroundings. Egad! How often I had looked out on the same scenery. I'd never forgot it, in all the years I had been away. I mentally embraced and loved it all. Just below, on the lower road, I could recognize the songs of the red-vented bulbuls in the wild lantana bushes, and mynah birds,

We decided that we'd spend the night The next day, the Sherreds said, we could drive to their other winter home near Haldwani where Percy had guava orchards. I had a room in the back with Geraldine where our mother used to sleep. The fireplace was lit up. Here Mum used to sit with us and tell all those wonderful stories. The mantelpiece where the silver bowls sat and shone brightly; they were kept polished by the servants. Percy and I drank our scotch while dinner was being cooked, on a makeshift charcoal stove. It was a simple meal but I loved it. I slept like a log that night.

Early in the morning, I was up at dawn, out looking and listening for the familiar birds, when the sun's rays were coming across Kalias mountain and BhimTal; what a sight! I saw all the beautiful birds I loved, including the lovely kastura, a wonderful songbird. No slingshots this time; how could anyone want to shoot this lovely creature, or any of the other birds? I guess all children in India did, once upon a time. I was guilty of it. I looked over to the right, at the side of the mountain. I could see the outcrop of rock where I once saw the leopard; no leopard now.

I walked down the pathway, along the road below, as I used to do, and there in front was the Muslim tomb of Bikanir, still looking ghostlike, with a large wall around it. I walked along the road, past the tomb, and looked through the gorge to BhimTal again. The road forked here, and I took the one to the left that led to the Ghorakhal, which was once a maharajah's summer estate. It was now a private school.

When I got back to the house, breakfast was ready. I didn't say very much; everything had come back to me, as though I had never left. Only one thing: my whole childhood world, which appeared vast then, had now shrunk to half its size. Amazing! Right after breakfast, there was mad hustle with Percy giving orders to the Indian houseboy to get things ready to pack on his old U.S. weapons carrier that he still had, and his 1958 Dodge van. We were on our way. We told Percy to go on ahead; that Geraldine and I would linger awhile in BhimTal, and look at our old house there, that we would meet him back at Haldwani.

There is a motor road that passes through Bhowali down to BhimTal and Kathgodam. It was built by U.S. war funds, and these spots were rest and recuperation (R & R) areas for the troops. Both Geraldine and I decided to walk to BhimTal. It was the same old world once more. We chatted with some of the villagers who were sitting by the wall. They were astounded that we could converse with them. We arrived at the flat area where there had been wheat fields. This was where my brother Vernon and I would come shooting. In those days, there were plenty of rabbits and black partridge. It was too cultivated and grown up now.

We took the side path and climbed up to the old house, which had been purchased by an Indian. Workers were building a wall around it. The yard was a mess. I peeked through the windows and saw some of our old furniture, and steps leading up to the upper floor. The mali (gardener) that we had, had died, and no one knew of Jasma, my little girlfriend. I took a walk behind the house and up a few terraces to the wheatfields. I went to the area where Jasma had taught me all about women! I wondered where she might have gone, and what had happened to her. No doubt she's married, but no one knew.

Perhaps she'd passed away, as most Indians do there at an early age.

We visited the small cemetery nearby, and saw some old familiar names, like Mr. Jones, who owned the estate across from us, and Dekalbera. Geraldine said their hotel had been burnt down, that one sister, Louise Dekalbera, was alive, and living at a place just above the bazaar. We went and visited her. She was still spry, and so delighted when we showed up. She remembered carrying me on her shoulders in Bhowali when I was only three years old. The poor old girl was rather destitute. We bought supplies and necessary items to keep her going, like sugar, tea, powdered milk, and tinned food. Geraldine made arrangements for an allotment of money to be sent to her regularly.

From BhimTal, we drove the rest of the way, down the twisty, windy road to Haldwani, a very dusty back road, to the Sherred's orchards. His home was a lovely place, well-shaded by large trees. The birds were of all varieties, with parrots by the hundreds, all after the guavas. There were the monkeys, all going after a free meal. Percy had a couple of nondescript dogs that tried to keep the monkeys pretty well-checked.

Percy would tell us stories of this place. The place was called Sultan Nagri, named after a Dacoiti who lived in the area years ago. The place was also famous for tigers and wild elephants. It was a part of the famous Terai jungles. Pellibit jungles were famous for tigers, and were also close by. There was no question; this was ideal tiger country. Sultan Nagri was about 800 feet above sea level, smack up against the hill, with streams and lush undergrowth. It reminded me a bit of the Assam jungles where I hunted. Percy said he often would see a tiger walk through the orchards. About ten miles to the west, past the city, was Kaladungi, where Corbett had his home.

I could not sleep. I kept thinking of all the places I'd seen this past week. I was living my childhood again. Next morning, I was up early. I could hear the junglefowl call and black partridge. I took Percy's old shotgun and walked through the orchards and back trails for a shot at a partridge or junglefowl. It was great being able to move through the forest quietly. I came to a stream which was nearly dry, and a haven for pretty butterflies. I walked up the stream bed, hoping to find tiger tracks; there were none. But further on, there were pugmarks of leopard; there were still a few of them in the hills. There was a flurry and a whirr of wings, and two pheasants flew across the draw, too far to shoot.

I returned to the Sherred house. The stay was all too short. They were just lovely people, and so hospitable. I said I would return another time, now that I knew where they lived. Geraldine and I left the next day, bright and early. The traffic is bad, with bicycles and cattle on the thoroughfare. We finally got to Delhi and checked in at the old Imperial Hotel, run by my friend, Tickie Oberoy. I had stayed here often in the old days, with his Highness, Cooch-Behar, and Jaipur. Next day, I checked PanAm Facility and airport inspection with permission from the DGCA.

Geraldine and I spent a few days sightseeing and shopping. It was now time to say bye to Geraldine and be on my way. She would catch her flight back to New York, and I was on my way to Bombay.

At Bombay, I checked in at the Sun-N-Sands Hotel, owned and operated by my ex-brother-in-law, John Voyantsis Jr, the brother of Kiki. We had a great get-together and he brought me up-to-date with all his family. TWA crews stayed at the Sun-N-Sands where I met some of the crew. Next day, I took the flight to Hydrabad on India Airways, to check an airport for TWA. It was to be used as a secondary, or alternate, airport. At Hydrabad, I stayed, believed it or not, at a Holiday Inn, but not like the ones we know. It was an old palace that had been renovated. It was a beautiful spot, with enormous, high-ceilinged rooms. I could have stayed for weeks, but two nights was all I had, and I was back at the Sun-N-Sands.

I met the TWA Captain for the trip to Colombo, Sri Lanka. He was Captain Harry Gaines, a great guy, who had studied Indian yogi and mysticism, and was quite a character. The flight to Colombo was routine. The next day, I did the airport inspection, then caught a train down to south Sri Lanka (Ceylon), called Gali, where I met a friend who took me to his tea estates on the lower hills. The place was lush, and the tea hedges were all bright green and in immaculate straight rows of terraces, where girls in brightly-colored saris wandered amongst the hedges, picking tea. They were Tamals, from South India. It was delightful to see and stay with Pat. There were brightly-colored butterflies going in all directions and I wished I'd had a butterfly net. I could have wound up with a good collection!

In Colombo I checked in at the hotel, which I think was the British (Gullface) Airways Hotel. Next day, I took a tour of the town and saw the old mission where we had stayed before our departure to the States in 1928. It was close to the harbor. My little holiday was up and time to check TWA's desired routes on to Bangkok. From there, I transferred to a PanAm flight that took me on to Da-Nang, in Vietnam, which was loaded with Military Tanks and Aircraft; then to Hong Kong. Good old Hong Kong! It seemed to have shrunk, with all the new skyscrapers, and the runway extending into the sea.

I stayed at the Hilton, on Victoria Island, where I was able to check up on a couple of friends. I contacted a John Shumacher. He took me over to the mainland, Kowloon side, to play golf. I found my old CNAC friends, Bill Newport and Guy Hardin. They were all doing well.

From Hong Kong, I caught PanAm to Singapore, and on to Sydney, Australia. Here, I stayed at the Gazebo Hotel, a roundish-type building. After dumping my suitcase in the room and splashing water on my face, for a needed fresh up, I went down to the bar. I sat at the bar and ordered a cold beer. I was the only one there; it was almost midday. I chatted with the bartender for awhile. I was feeling sleepy and ready to go up to my room and rest. Just then, a lovely looking gal came into the bar and sat down and ordered a beer. The bar-tender, who knew her, introduced us; I don't recall her name, I think something like Crothfeldt. After a couple more beers, she suggested lunch. She said she knew a great restaurant. I was groggy with sleep, having been flying all night, but she kept me awake with her talk and laughter. I noticed her lovely teeth, when she laughed. We had lunch and time was getting on. I finally had to confess that I was beat and needed some sleep. I thought I'd better get back to the hotel. "Nonsense," she said. "I have a great spot for you to rest." We drove out of the city to a nice town with its own harbor, a beautiful spot. She drove along a road next to the beach, and finally turned into a cottage right on the shoreline. "This is my retreat," she said. It was a nice quite place, and she led me to a room with a bed. "Okay, chum stretch out there, I'll be back this evening." I didn't hear the door close; I was asleep.

I don't know what time it was but I was being awakened in a rather friendly manner. The lovely thing had crawled into bed with me. For a moment, I was bewildered, didn't know where I was, and it was dark. The warm body near me didn't take long to bring me back to realization, Wow! What a way to wake up! After a fair rumble-tumble it was time to get up and shower. However, I didn't have any other clothes to change into. That evening we drove to another bar and restaurant, and another great evening, then back to the cottage for the night.

Sometime in the morning we surfaced. I could hear kids laughing and having a great time. The gal got up and pulled the curtains aside. She was nude and stood by the full glass doors that opened onto the beach. Not 50 yards away a whole group of Sea Scouts were rigging their small sailboats. They must have seen the nude figure through the glass doors. I peeked from the bed. It looked as though the scouts were surprised and falling off their boats into the water. I crawled out the other side of the bed and entered the shower. It must have been some sight!

It was noon when this lovely girl dropped me at the hotel. I got to my room and collapsed. After a long snooze and rest, I changed into some fresh clothes. Through the telephone directory, I contacted an old friend from Calcutta, Angela Dekantzow. She was now working at a Travel Agency. Sid had not left her much money, when he died in a car crash. We all knew he had quite a sum when he and Roy Farrell started Cathay Pacific Airlines. He'd sold out in 1952.

I met Angela the next day for lunch. We reminisced a lot about Calcutta, and Cooch-Behar. He had loved Angela. She had asked about Bhaiya; I knew he had

*Our training flight with TWA B-747 stuck in the snow at Tulsa Airport, Oklahoma 1970.*

been in a terrible polo accident, that Jaipur's horse had collided with Bhaiya's knocking him off. The horse had kicked Bhaiya in the head. Cooch-Behar had then been rushed to Delhi, where BOAC took him to London for emergency surgery. He recovered, but lost his memory and became a vegetable. Bhaiya lived another year, then died at his place in Alipore, in Calcutta, April 1970. Jaipur also passed away about the same time in London, after a polo match in May 1970. So ended an era in our lives.

It was nice to see Angela, but a bit sad. She was a lovely person and now to be left high and dry seemed awfully wrong. I said goodbye, and the next day I was winging my way to Honolulu on PanAm.

I was able to get in touch with Jack Brown, in Honolulu the same Jack who had helped me out in Jeddah, back in 1950, when the Haji had run into the spinning propeller. Jack was now working for Aloha Airlines. We had a fine visit together. His wife, Cora, had passed away several years before.

Back in San Francisco, I contacted my brother, Vernon, in Patterson. He came to the airport and took me back to their home. I told him all about my trip to Naini, Bhowali, and BhimTal.

I was soon back in New York, I walked up the creaky stairs to my little dormer apartment in East Rockaway. I had been gone about six weeks, and visited all those friends and places. It was hard to realize I had gone around the world to do so. Here I was now, after all that wonderful trip, in this little dingy apartment on Long Island! I couldn't wait to get all my slides developed; at least, I could live it again on the screen.

Geraldine was back in Plainfield. I told her I had a couple of pine cones I had picked up in Bhowali, from the old pine forest nearby. I planned to placed them at Mummy's grave. She loved India and the hills very much.

188

At the office, I sat with Bill Huebner and thanked him for letting me take the trip. He was glad to know it helped; it certainly did and I couldn't wait for the weekend, to see Christian and Hannah. I'd written cards along the way, now we would have our first weekend together in months.

The kids looked wonderful. We ate at the Ship's Inn, which they always liked and the food was always great. We had a swell weekend, I gave them presents I had brought from India. For Hannah, I had a toy koala bear from Sydney. Its legs were like bracelets that would clamp onto your upper arm. No matter how many times I saw the two of them, my throat swelled up and my eyes blurred when I dropped them home.

Syd Wheatley was now on board and at the office. He and Maria had an apartment not too far from mine. It was nice seeing them and having them close by. Most of the slides that I had taken on my trip had turned out better than expected. I enjoyed just sitting, sipping scotch and letting my mind travel that journey to India.

Christmas had come and gone. Work continued, with some of it in Roswell. Early in the year, I received a phone call in the office. It was my sister Christine. Before I could say hello, she lashed out at me for treating Margaret and the kids cruelly. Evidently Margaret had talked with her. How could this be? I was paying her rent, her car insurance, I'd bought her a new washing machine, took care of the car maintenance; she was charging everything at Sears and Gimbels stores, which I paid for, plus a hefty allowance. Christine wouldn't listen. After calling me a few names as only she knew how, she hung up. I was beside myself with anger. That evening, I went to Sears and Gimbels and canceled all credit cards. I called Margaret and asked what she was trying to prove.

She laughed. Her game was to play the children against me, and now she was turning Christine against me.

About 2:00 a.m., I had a strange feeling in my heart. Physical? The darn thing wouldn't slow down. The heartbeat stopped for a few seconds, then started up at a helluva rate. I thought it must be some sort of a heart attack. I sat up and checked my pulse and timed the surges. I didn't know what to do. I finally got on the phone and called my brother Vernon in Patterson; it would be almost midnight there. I told him the symptoms and what was happening as I was talking. The first thing he said was to sit up, don't lie down. Then he asked if I drank a lot of coffee, or I had been boozing and staying out late? No. Was something worrying me? Did someone say something to upset me? I said "Yes. Your sister Christine had accused me of certain things and had taken up sides with Margaret." "Okay," he said, "don't worry, and don't keep feeling your pulse. Try to sleep sitting up. First thing in the morning, see a doctor, a specialist." He said it wasn't heart attack, but it could develop into one. It was a premature heartbeat, where it would skip a couple of beats and then take off.

In the morning I did as Vernon suggested: I went to see a specialist. The doctor took an electrocardiogram test, the readout was unbelievable. The peaked out areas looked like Mt. Everest! The doctor asked the same questions as Vernon, and gave the same diagnosis. He then dished out some very small white pills which he said I should take as prescribed, not to worry and to keep calm at all times.

At the office, I went back and talked to Bill Huebner and told him what had happened. I hoped all would be well. I was due for my regular FAA physical in a month. I said I'd like to postpone it for a couple of months and have a recheck with the specialist. Bill said there'd be no problem.

I phoned Vernon and said I was on medication. The pills, he said, were probably tranquilizers and not dangerous. They should start showing results before too long. I don't mind telling you, I sweat it out. I went back for another check. The cardiograph showed everything normal. However, the doctor said to keep taking the pills, and gave me another batch. He said, "These should last you for about ten years!" I hoped he was joking.

Next week, I took the second class physical, and no EKG required. I told a couple of lies on the form, regarding any heart problems. There has been no recurrence since (touch wood!).

I briefed Geraldine about the session with Christine, and vowed I never wanted to see or talk with her again.

As the summer holidays approached for Hannah and Christian, Margaret agreed that I could have them for the summer, also the station wagon, since she would probably take off for England for the summer. Not at my cost, though; perhaps Will Brown's, since he was making a cuckold out of me anyway. I am sure she was coining money from me. The office and Ray Hirsch had agreed I could spend July and August in Roswell doing checks for Pan American.

I now knew the route going west, and the best times to be on the highway. It was another great trip. This time we did not stop to see Bob Burge. We went straight to Oklahoma. Here, I did my recurrent on the Boeing 707. And I enjoyed flying it. The FAA instructors were just great people. At one coffee break at the Academy, I sat with several other inspectors, when I noticed a fellow at another table staring at me. He finally came over and asked, "Were you ever with CNAC?" I said "That's correct." He said, "Did you know a George Huang? And a Dick Rossi? And a Pete Goutiere?" I said, "Yes, of course. I'm Pete Goutiere." "Good Lord! What a small world!" "How do you know all this?" "I was the pilot who flew you guys from Calcutta to Delhi, when I landed at the wrong airport, at Gaya." "God, I remember that!" "My name is A.D. Ulsh." He had just joined the FAA as an instructor on the L-188. We had several get-together before I finished my week's program. We would meet often after that.

Hannah and Christian were enjoying the trip. All day was spent at the pool while I flew. Even their ears got green from the chlorine. I had to get alcohol and Q-tips to clear them out.

We finally arrived at Roswell, at the Plantation Inn. The children couldn't wait to go camping. We usually made it to the same area at Lincoln Park. We took many hikes up into the mountains, and explored new areas around Mt. Capitan. These TDYs go fast, when you're enjoying things you like. During the trip, I was introduced to a very attractive, young lady, by the name of Tish Christiansen. She had been divorced, and had four lovely girls. Her Dad, Sil Johnson was a great person. He had a sheep ranch outside of town. Sil's wife, Tish's mother, Gerry, was also a lovely lady. I was immediately accepted into the family. Perhaps it was my background and life in the Far East. I was to meet Tish's inner circle of friends, which she called "My Fan Club." When she knew I could cook such exotic things as special spicy curries and various Arabic dishes, I became a steady visitor to her kitchen. There were to be many parties, both pool and indoor. I was to meet VIPs from the bank, meat packers and artists, and oil people. It was a great association. Tish arranged for me to use the Roswell Country Club. No wonder it was always difficult to depart Roswell for the dreary little apartment on Long Island. Time had come, and I had to leave. The kids found it difficult to say goodbye.

I dropped my two back in Oceanside, and I went back to East Rockaway. Later I was able to find a more decent upstairs apartment, not far away. It was unfurnished, so it was necessary to buy furniture before I could move in. I was much happier here. I got a radio and TV, and Syd Wheatley, who felt

*In the cockpit of TWA B-747.*

he owed me something for having helped him into the FAA and getting the 707 rating, surprised me by buying a small bar for the apartment which I still have.

One day in September, Ray Hirsch called a meeting of the Air Carrier Inspectors. He had good news. PanAm was purchasing a fleet of Boeing 747s, the new Jumbos. Ray and three of us were to go to Seattle to attend Boeing's ground school for 747, that we'd be rated on the aircraft later. It was a fairly long course. I was amazed at the size of the plane, once we had a chance to look it over. On a break in our program, I drove up to Vancouver to visit my nephews I had not seen since 1933 or '34. It was quite a reunion. My namesake, Peter Goutiere, drove me up to a remote place called Lake Anderson, where I also saw another old school friend from Westfield. His name was Paul Hennell.

In November, we were back in Seattle, to give PanAm crews their ratings, and a chance to fly the plane. Altogether, there were to be nine FAA inspectors to check out. In New York, one of the other inspectors and I were assigned to TWA school. This was on Thanksgiving of '69. Bob Lochner and I went through the B-747 simulator training, and after the Christmas holidays, he and I were scheduled to Kansas City to fly the aircraft for our ratings. Bob and I were given twelve hours, including the checkride.

During the A/C training, the weather turned sour. Bob, on one of the flights, was blown off the taxiway at Tulsa Airport, and got mired in the snow and mud. This was a writeup for the news, because the new jumbos were hot, news items. He finished his ride in Indianapolis. I got sick with bronchitis and was laid up for awhile and couldn't talk. The weather continued to be bad, so it was necessary for TWA to take us to Tuc-

son, Arizona for my final check. This was the only area with half-decent weather. Here, I met another old CNAC friend who was in the construction business. His name was Jules Watson. On my checkride, I had to give all instructions with hand signals: gear, flaps, etc., I just couldn't talk. We finally were 747-qualified in January of '70. Though sick, I was glad to have the rating.

In New York, it took a week to recover from the throat infection. From the moment I was qualified on the 747, our office was buzzing with phone calls and work to be done. Needless to say, I was off and running. I barely had time to put my briefcase down, get to the apartment and do the dirty laundry before I was off to PanAm and TWA training centers, giving oral exams and flight checks.

From nowhere, all my old Pan Africa pilot friends seemed to be popping up. The biggest surprise was when Captain Bob Buck of TWA was assigned to me for his oral. As we sat in the 747 simulator, he looked nervous. To break the ice and relax him, I asked if he recognized my name. He frowned and shook his head. I told him to put on his thinking cap and go back to 1932, in Westfield, New Jersey; that there was a Bob Nixon and his sister, Ruth. His face lit up. He said, "I remember them," Ruth was now in Connecticut. Gradually, things began to focus. "Yes, now I remember: the glider behind the garage!" We sat there for about an hour, reminiscing, then of a sudden I realized there was an oral to be conducted. I think I asked Bob half a dozen questions, and that was it. I knew the simulator flight would show his prowess, and it did. He was an expert.

Another TWA applicant was a tawny, tall, dark-haired individual. This time, the tables were turned. He looked at me for a moment and said, "You don't remember me,

*With my CNAC friend Jules Watson after my checkout on TWA 747 Tuscon, Arizona, January 1970.*

do you?" I said, "No, I don't." He gave his name as Horatio Lewis. He said, "Do you remember a kid who came to you one day at Brewer Airport, in November of '41, and asked you for a ride in the Piper Cub? I paid for the fuel, and right after takeoff, about 50 feet, the engine quit? We landed straight ahead in an open pasture, I was amazed at the way you handled the aircraft. That was my first flight ever. You flew back to the field and we tried it again. It was great, and you were my hero. I took up flying, and later joined TWA." I said, "And here you are, in the 747!" That was fantastic.

There were a few of my Pan Africa pilot friends who also came my way. there was Bart Hewitt, Tom Caroll. It was strange being on the other side of the bar.

A lot of the 747 program certification took us into weekends and holidays. Easter found me back in Roswell, New Mexico. PanAm did not have an approved simulator, they did their complete flight ratings in 747 aircraft. This was to prove a little more exciting than the simulator. In the simulator, the pilot could make mistakes and throw his hands up and let it crash, but not so in the aircraft. It was then that I noticed that some of the pilots were not doing that well, I was giving out a few more unsatisfactory (pink slips) than necessary. I learned that PanAm Ops Office had told the pilots they would receive six hours total, including the checkride, which was about two hours. The flight time for one training was four hours. It was on one of these flights, I don't remember the individual's name, but when the pilot who was next, looked drawn and nervous. I took him aside before we entered the cockpit and asked if he was all right, or sick? He shook his head and said, "Yes," that none of the guys were well. He, like the others, instead of taking their nervous pee, were upchucking and getting sick, they were so nervous. I thought he was joking. He said, "No, ask some of them." This was why there

were so many failures. I tried to cheer him up and said I was on his side, and not to be nervous.

We had not been airborne more than fifteen minutes when I knew he couldn't make it. We tried for half an hour, but nothing was going right. I motioned to the instructor, or Safety Pilot, that we should return to the field. At the little room where we had our briefing and debriefing, I started to make out the pink slip, then held off. I had a thought. I told the pilot, in front of the check Pilot, that I wasn't going to issue an unsatisfactorily slip. Instead, I said to him, "I want you to forget flying for the next few days. I want you to buy your special brand of whiskey, find a local whore to keep you company and when you feel like flying, come back." The fellow looked surprised, and so did the check pilot, John Walker. I said I was serious. "Okay," "if you mean it," and he left.

It was about 4 to 6 days when the same pilot reported back and said he was ready for the flight check. Again with John Walker in the right seat, the individual took off. I had John cover all the mandatory maneuvers and emergencies that could be done in the airplane: stalls, steep turns, emergency descents, The pilot flew like one possessed. He did a beautiful job. All flight instruments appeared stuck in their correct positions. John Walker glanced back at me, I gave the thumbs up. He definitely had passed, and well above average.

Back at the little PanAm briefing office, I wrote out the pilot's 747 endorsement on his license. Before handing it to him and giving congratulations, I said, "Before I issue this rating, I want the brand of the whiskey you bought, and the name of the whore!" They both burst out laughing. John Walker said I had been good medicine for this group. Word spread about the repertoire, and the pilots skill improved. For my part, there was much less in the way of pink slips.

I spent the rest of April and all of May and June shuttling between New York and Roswell, doing orals and flight checks for PanAm and TWA. At the end of June, I had returned from Roswell. That morning at the office, the phone rang. It was the Chief of Flight Standards Office in Washington, Joe Ferrarese. Joe told me that PanAm and TWA were pleased with the way I was accomplishing the 747 program. He apologized for the amount of work that was being place at this office. "Well, that's what it's all about, with us public servants." Joe said he didn't know where all the other 747 inspectors had disappeared to, but he had calls from other airlines, wanting their pilots to be given 747 checks. I asked where were we needed? He said if I could go to Salina, Kansas, to cover a group of Northwest Airline pilots, then to Roswell for PanAm. From there to United in San Francisco, and up to Seattle for National Airlines, back to New York for orals and simulators for PanAm and TWA. I thought this over for a moment or two. I said, "Mr. Ferrarese, I'll do it provided that I set up my own schedules with the airlines, secondly, I'll take my car for the complete trip, and get mileage pay." He hesitated. I also added, "I want this so I can take my children with me for the summer." He said, "You've got a deal. When can you get started?" I said I'd like a couple of days, so I could round up my kids.

My ETA to Salina was around July 4th. "They will be there." I think now that Margaret was happy to be free of the children during the summer. I think she was secretly making her move to be Mrs. Brown, and setting up their house in Connecticut. Hannah and Christian told me one day that Margaret had let their dog, Bhimsa, the lovely black retriever, outside, and he had run away and never came back. I'm sure he was picked up by someone. He was a pedigreed dog, and a lovely pet. I knew Hannah was terribly upset, she loved animals dearly. I promised she would have another dog one day.

I gathered up the kids with the usual paraphernalia, tents, etc., and we were off once more on our trip. After a weary drive to Salina, we checked in at the Howard Johnson, where I met some of the Northwest crew. They were delighted to see an FAA inspector. That evening, the kids and I had a great meal of fried catfish. They remembered the ones we had with Bob Burge, a couple of years ago.

I spent a little over a week giving Northwest crews their check flights. They appreciated the fact that I'd come all the way from New York to do so. There was another long haul from there to Roswell, with a layover at Oklahoma City. This time, we stayed at the Roswell Inn, a fine motel, with a pool where Christian and Hannah spent most their time, while I gyrated around Roswell with PanAm. I spent about two weeks here, before we started our long drive to Los Angeles. It was interesting for the children; we saw a lot of the wonderful sights: Indian reservations, and a stop at Tombstone in Arizona, and then on to Los Angeles. We also visited Disneyland, at Anaheim.

I then drove up the valley to Patterson, and a visit with Vernon and Kay. Christian and Hannah behaved well, and found a few neighborhood kids to play with. I kept busy, giving ratings with United Airlines crews. On one particular flight, at Sacramento, which is the alternate airport that we used, I was finishing up a new Captain for his rating. And also evaluating another United Airlines pilot as a Check Airman. The final maneuver was a ADF approach. The applicant had done a good job flying and was doing well on this approach. At 500 feet, the hood was removed, and cleared to land. I told the Check Airman to make a touch-and-go with a full stop at San Francisco. The touchdown was normal with the touch-and-go initiated. After the aircraft had rolled about halfway down the runaway, takeoff power was added by the pilot, the flight engineer trimmed the throttles. The Check Airman was adjusting the flaps and elevator trim when the takeoff warning horn sounded. The aircraft had gained enough flying speed and was approaching the last third of the runaway when the Check Airman said, "I've got it." The pilot gave the controls over to the Check Pilot, who immediately elected to abort the takeoff. The flight Engineer said, "Oh, shit!" and ducked to his right. I didn't have time to say anything. I was dumbfounded, it was too late to tell the guy "No," to continue the takeoff, the result being that all four engines were in reverse thrust with full brakes. The spoiler deployed automatically. The end of the runaway came up fast. This was when I ducked to the left, and made sure I was behind the Captain. We rolled out an overrun which was hard dirt. It was late August, with no rain and the heat making the ground as hard as cement. We kept on rolling, still in reverse, with the debris and cornstalks flying up in front of us. We were unable to see anything. Finally, the plane stopped, the Check Pilot, evidently still in a freeze condition had the engines still reversing. I shouted at him to get the engines back to idle. When the dust debris and cornstalks settled, we saw a large canal just in front. We had overshot the end of the runway by about 500 yards or more. The airport declared an emergency, and the fire rescue trucks were on their way. The Flight Engineer got the auxiliary power unit (APU) turned on, the pilot shut down all engines. I asked the Check Airman why did he abort. He said the flaps did not come up, which caused the takeoff warning. I said, "It takes time, and in any case, the aircraft can fly perfectly with the full flaps, even at takeoff." News media around the world were always watching for any incident involving these new jumbos. If there was a backfiring incident, or one of these monsters coming in with one engine inoperative, it made the TV and front pages. You can imagine what this was going to do! Sure enough, in no time, here they came.

We descended through the hatch, down by the nosewell, and inspected the airplane. For one thing, it was covered with dust and cornstalks. The flaps were in the correct position of 20 degrees for takeoff. The wheels and tires looked fine, but very dusty. The aircraft weighed about 500,000 pounds. Because the ground was so hard and dry, the wheels had not sunk in any more than a couple of inches. The airport rescue people took us back to the terminal and I phoned the Principal Inspector in Denver. He already knew of the incident. I explained briefly what had happened, and said I'd write my report, that I thought the Check Airman should be relieved of that position.

A small plane flew in from 'Frisco, with United maintenance people. On checking it out, they said all that was necessary would be take off some of the fuel, then tow the aircraft back on the runway. The engines, controls, hydraulics, etc., would be checked out. The crew and myself returned to 'Frisco in the small aircraft.

At United Airlines Operations, I told the Chief Pilot my side of the story. I gave the pilot being checked his new 747 rating. I stayed a couple more days in 'Frisco and finished up the remaining flight checks. Somehow, I dodged the news media. They had what they wanted, anyway, and I saw it all on TV that same evening: "Jumbo runs off runway, no injuries; possibly mechanical problems."

I later met another FAA friend who had returned from Bangkok. He said, "Pete, you'll do anything to get on TV!" "What do you mean?" "I saw you on the Bangkok TV with the 747 that ran off the runway at Sacramento."

Back in Patterson with Christian, Hannah and Vernon, I received word to proceed to Seattle, that National Airlines were ready to start their checkrides. I asked Vernon and Kay if I could leave Christian and Hannah with them for about ten days. Yes, it would be okay; they were having a great time; they could care less.

I left the car at the United Airlines employee parking lot and took the flight to Seattle. Here, I rented a car. Reservations had been made at the Renton Airport Inn. First thing next morning, I went to the Boeing Operation Office, to meet the National pilots. I was informed that all of them would be reporting in shortly for a briefing. Perhaps I would start after lunch. I said that would be fine. I was given a list of the crew, and was happy to note that I knew them. I had flown First Officer with them for three years; I had been with National Airlines, 17 years before. I told the Boeing people to tell National that the FAA guy coming from New York office had the reputation of being a mean son-of-a-bitch. He must have done so, because, when I walked into the conference room where they had congregated, they looked somber. Then finally one of them said, "I think I know you! Didn't you fly with us on National Airlines, some time back?" I couldn't hold back my laughter. I laughed aloud and said, "Yes, correct, and it's a good thing you were good to your First Officer and gave him landings once in a while!"

I introduced myself. The leader was a Captain Skeeter Royal. Some of the others I remembered were Captain Ferguson, and Amacan, and Bobby Knox; also several Flight Engineers. The program went well. The checks were given in the aircraft, as I was doing with PanAm. The area was at Moses Lake, the other side of the ridge of Mt. Rainier. For the most part, the pilot performance was good; only two unsatisfactories. They were given an hour or so more training, and rechecked.

Toward the end of the first week, the group held a party at the Inn. There were about 20 stewardesses getting their training in emergency procedures by sliding down the emergency chutes. At the party, I was introduced to them. One of the girls was very attractive. She had once been a "Bunny" at a Playboy Club. What a knockout she must have been at that club, in one of those cute costumes! I had not been interested in girls for an awfully long time, since I had left Oceanside, but this beautiful girl had me revving me up. By the end of the TDY, she satisfied my desires.

The program was now finished, and National Airlines group headed for Miami, and I to Patterson. The kids and I said farewell to Vernon and Kay, and headed East to Roswell. We drove via the Hoover Dam, across Death Valley, into No-Man's Land. It was an exciting sightseeing trip for the three of us. At Roswell, I did a few more flight checks, then returned to New York. I dropped Christian and Hannah off in time for school.

I barely had time to catch my breath and relax when I was told to head for Miami and conduct National Airlines (proving runs) on the 747 Miami-Los Angeles. The same lovely girl was to be on board. I could have fallen in love all over again. I stayed at her home while she operated her scheduled flights. All good things come to an end, though. The flights were completed, and I returned home.

One day my lawyer called and said everything was arranged for the divorce. One problem: in New York State, divorces were for adultery only, and take a year or so to finalize. What should I do? The lawyer said he had arranged with a lawyer in Juarez, Mexico, that I should go there and he'd have the papers finalized immediately. "I guess it's to be a Mexican divorce, then?" "Right." I caught American Airlines to El Paso. From there, I took a taxi over the border. I met the lawyer and signed the papers, and took with me the next day to New York. I was divorced. I was relieved it was finally over, but felt terribly lonesome without Christian and Hannah.

I spent a lot of my time at the Ship's Inn, having my scotch and my meals. One evening, at my new apartment as I watched TV and recovered from my divorce, the phone rang. It was the National Airlines stewardess in Miami. "Hi! How are you doing?" I was happy that she'd phoned, and said I had my divorce. "Well," she said, "that's great! Now hold on to your hat: I think I'm pregnant." I gulped and tried to think what

*Christian and Hannah, Salina Kansas, 1970.*

*Hannah and Christian in nacelle of Boeing 747 engine, 1970.*

let's get it over with." He called the hospital and got me a room somewhere near LaGuardia Airport. It was necessary to be there for one night and he'd do the operation the next morning.

I packed an overnight bag and checked in. I was given a bed in a room with two other patients. Before getting into my bed, a rather large colored nurse said I had to take a shower first, and showed me where the showers were, then gave me a nightgown and that was it. I showered and put on my pajamas and robe and got into bed. I'd just about settled in when here comes the nurse, all chuckles. "OK, sweetie; roll over. I'm going to take your temperature." I pointed to my mouth. She said, "No, too many patients bite the thermometers. This way is safer." I obliged. She shoved the thermometer up my ass. I asked her about my neighbor to my left. She said he had a heart attack. He had tubes going in all directions: up the nose, in his mouth, and a big balloon hanging off the side of his bed. Poor guy! The fellow on the right appeared to be asleep. She informed me that he had the mumps down in his balls; she chuckled, then said, "And wouldn't you know, he got it the day of his honeymoon! Can you imagine?" Poor fellow! I even chuckled.

I was later served a lukewarm dinner. The lights went out at 9 p.m. At the crack of dawn the next morning the same nurse and a male nurse came in and said I had to have an enema. I thought she was joking, but the guy had all kinds of apparatus for the job. "Gee whiz! Is this necessary?" "Yes," she said. So I got the enema. For a moment though, I told the guy to quit pushing that stuff in or to get out of the way, because I might just blow it right back at him. He stopped and I just made it to the John. Good God! I'd never had this before.

I relaxed. There was a hustle on my right side, and two nurses were placing screens around the young fellow with the mumps, then his bride arrived. I guess they wanted a little privacy. There were a few minutes of silence and whispers. Then I heard a racket and cries of agony and pain. The girl started crying. The nurse arrived and the young bride was led away still crying, leaving the poor fellow writhing in pain and agony. The old guy with all the tubes had his eyes bulging out trying to take in the whole scene. What a performance! I wouldn't have missed this for anything. The groom was given a sedative to relax him and put him out of his misery. The honeymooners must have got excited, and he probably got an erection. That did no good for his mumped balls! I just flopped back in my bed waiting for the doctor. But that was not to be. Here came the jolly nurse with the thermometer again. I rolled over, because there was no sense trying to argue.

I was getting comfortable once more when a young colored male nurse arrived. He had a shaving kit with him and after a couple of words, I learned he was a Jamaican, and as queer as a $3 bill. He had come to shave around my crotch. "Oh, no!" I said

to say; my heart pounded and leaped madly. I thought it was another of those silly heart attacks. "Say again?" I said. She said, "I think I'm pregnant. Don't get worried; I'll let you know more in a couple of weeks. Anyway when are you going to come down for another visit? I miss you." "I'm giving check rides like crazy, and a lot of en routes to Europe." "Hey, let me know your schedule, because we fly to Paris and London." "Yes," I said, "it would be great to meet you there. I'll keep you informed." Then she hung up.

I was beside myself. What a fine kettle of fish! And what a birthday present! Of all things; just divorced and now the girl's knocked up! I stomped back and forth in the little apartment and had another hefty scotch, and paraded some more. I thought to myself, "That damned pecker of mine is getting me

into all kinds of trouble! Why not cut the damned thing off? Cut it off? Wow!" I then remembered someone saying, "You ought to get yourself a vasectomy. It's the vogue, you know. Everyone is getting it done. Dutch caps, pills are unreliable." I thought this over as I wore out the carpet walking.

I called my FAA doctor where I took my physicals and asked about getting a vasectomy. He said it would be a problem: I'd have to get the wife's okay, for one thing. I said I didn't have a wife. Well, he wasn't sure. He gave me the address and phone number of a doctor who perhaps could do it. I called the guy and went to see him. He had his office in Flushing and was a Jewish individual. Yes, he said, he could do it, but first I had to fill out a lengthy form and signed statement, etc. "How much?" I asked. He said, "250." I said "OK,

"I can do it." "No, doctor's orders," with a gesture and a flip of his hand. I watched as he deftly manipulated the shaving brush around. Then with a safety razor, he commenced shaving. I might add, he did do a fine job, without a cut. I looked like a plucked chicken. I was a little worried when it came to rinsing off the remaining soap, he tried drying everything with what looked like a hair dryer. He seemed to tarry a little too long. I finally took the towel and finished the job myself, otherwise I may have been able to help the guy's bride out. He packed up and left. I wondered what would be next.

It came. "Not another enema," I said. Oh, no. This was to be an internal anesthetic from the rear. No needle this time. Oh, well; I've come this far - might just as well go along with the charade. I soon felt drowsy after the rectal. The nurses finally brought in a rollabed. They lifted me onto this and rolled it along the corridor and into an elevator, up to another floor. I was not out yet. The nurses kept feeling my pulse and checking my eyes. I was conscious of what was going on, but felt drunk.

In the operating room, I was rolled onto the operating table. The Jewish doctor finally showed up. As I lay on my back, I noticed a large husky fellow. It turned out that he was a German and was standing by with anesthetic. There was also a cute Chinese girl, I think she was Chinese, and the Jamaican nurse, in the background. I said to the doc, "I need a shot of something to knock me out, because I haven't gone yet, as you can see." He was surprised to hear me talk. He gave some orders through the kotex-looking affair he had across his mouth. The big German guy got a needle and punched it in the side of my left arm. It didn't hurt and I was soon out like a light. When I woke up, I was in my bed, back with the other two fellows.

The guy with the mumps was feeling much better, and could talk. He asked me what I was in here for. Was it for hemorrhoids? I said, "Yeah, that was it." I was still groggy, but didn't wish to talk. The fellow with the tubes could only stare at me. I closed my eyes and slept.

It was a little after noon when the big mama nurse came in again, this time without the thermometer. I pointed at my rear and she giggled. "No, not this time, honey. Just came to see how you're doing." I gave her a "thumbs up," and she left, chuckling. Lunch was brought, and I ate a few tidbits. About two p.m. when all was quite, I quietly got up and dressed, packed my few things and headed for the hall. But who did I bump into on the way out but the big jolly nurse. "Where do you think you're going?" she asked. "Home," I said. "No way. You must stay another day." "No, the doctor said I could leave." She told me to wait while she called the doctor. She was surprised when he said I could go. I gave her a kiss, and checked in at the place where I had deposited my watch (Rolex), and billfold. They trust nobody, around here. I asked for the bill, I was astounded to see that the bottom line read $750. The doctor's fee was $275. I dis-

tinctly remember him saying $250. Then came the room for $325. Now I see why they wanted me to stay another night! This included the meals and the nurse with the thermometer. The big German was $75, and $50 for the Chinese nurse who did nothing but look cute; and $25 for the Jamaican shave. I had been robbed. I gave the gal a check and I received my belongings. Then I had to walk nearly half a mile to my car, the walking I did in a rather bowlegged fashion. It's a wonder it wasn't stolen, but it was an old one; probably nobody wanted it.

Next day, I was in the office and told my fellow inspectors about the ripoff. They howled with laughter, and old Tommy Thomas said it only cost him 50 bucks. The doctor did the deed right there in his office. I sent in a voucher to the health insurance that paid me back. In any case, I was relieved that this whole thing was over. Next thing was to see if it had been a successful operation!

One evening not long after, the phone rang, it was my stewardess in Miami, the one who had triggered me to have this operation. "How are you doing?" she asked. "Just fine," I replied. "Good," she said, "I have some news for you; I'm not pregnant." I was silent for a second. I said, "That's great, honey," and I didn't mention the operation. She said, "I'll give you a call when I find out if I'm coming up to New York, and you can give me a call if you get down to Miami." I said I would.

I was extremely busy, with the amount of air carrier work I was doing on the 747. I was getting to know the 747 like the back of my hand. Time was waiting for no one, like clouds rolling by. It was now Christmas of 1970. Margaret had agreed that I would have Christian and Hannah the day after Christmas, and the rest of the holidays. Though the apartment was small, we had loads of fun together. Through a friend, I had bought Hannah another puppy, a fawn-colored Golden Retriever. She called the dog Penny. We took a trip or two to Jones Beach for picnics. The beach was deserted and cold, but the kids and the dog had a wonderful time. It all ended so quickly, and I found myself driving them back. It was that lonely drive back to the little apartment that always left me to a point of despair. It would take a couple of days of work and flying to recover.

Flight checks and more flight checks. PanAm and TWA kept our office busy, but I loved the work. I was with so many of my friends. I had more than my share of flying. I never logged any of this time. By mid-June '71, I must have accumulated nearly 200-300 hours and I don't mean jumpseat observer's time; it was all from the left seat.

Early in July, I took a PanAm flight to Rome, and from there a 707 flight on to Delhi, India. I took along a butterfly net. Can you imagine, an FAA inspector with a butterfly net?! I planned to take a few days off and go chasing butterflies in the Himalayas, After my official duties checking PanAm facilities at Delhi, I journeyed up to Bhowali to be with my English friend, Percy Sherred.

I always made certain to stop by the U.S. Embassy Commissary first. Here, I could buy a lot of American foodstuffs, and whiskey. As Percy always said, I was like Father Christmas every time I came up there, even in July. The monsoons had broken, and the rains were on us. The dry river beds and streams were now roaring torrents of water. My taxi friend, Indrjit Singh, was cautious on the drive up the mountainous roads. We arrived late in the afternoon, it was raining heavily. I was greeted with great hugs and kisses from Percy's wife, Phyllis. They were just a wonderful couple. He had lived there in India all his life, and still tried to live the old English Raj style, though in a humble way. They were not too well off.

I was given a room at the back of the bungalow, the same one my mother used long ago. After a few drinks and a staple dinner, I went to bed. The rain hammered on the roof and windows. The house was very old, and nothing had been renovated in any place or in any form. Consequently, all the rooms leaked. Percy knew where these places were, and strategically had put different sized pots and pans to catch the water. As I lay in bed, I could hear the sound of the dripping water from the leaky roof, hitting the pans. I chuckled to myself. The sound had a musical note, sort of like a Calypso tin drum band tuning up. In fact, it lulled me to sleep.

Early in the morning, the bearer brought me "chota hazari." I loved this spoiled treatment. The rain stopped. It must have been recently, because all the pots and pans were nearly full. It didn't take me long to get dressed. Percy was already up, giving his servants their orders for the day. I stepped out on the verandah and gazed across the valley below. There, in the distance, was my favorite spot, BhimTal, shimmering in the morning sun. I hurriedly got my camera and took a few shots of the scene. It was a gorgeous sight, with the early sun rays beaming across the mountains, and mist drifting off Mt. Kailas, looking majestic in the distance. I stood there for minutes on end as I noticed the different colors and shades as the sun came up over the horizon and the mountain range. Ever since I was a kid, this was my favorite spot. One could never get tired of looking of the scenery; God had done it well.

After breakfast, while the sun was out, Percy let me have one of his servants to accompany me on a jaunt that would take me through a valley to Sat-Tal, where I knew there were a lot of beautiful butterflies as this was the season. I also had a camera to take close up pictures of wildflowers, mainly orchids that my sister Geraldine wanted. She planned to paint them, being a professional artist.

It didn't take long to see beautiful butterflies flashing by. The best of the exotic ones were the green manals, also called peacock manal. They were swift, and not easy to net. The best time was when they settled on a thistle, or lantana flowers. I was excited as a kid. In the next couple of hours, I had a good collection. The servant fellow, Mohan, and I finally came to a hill that we skirted

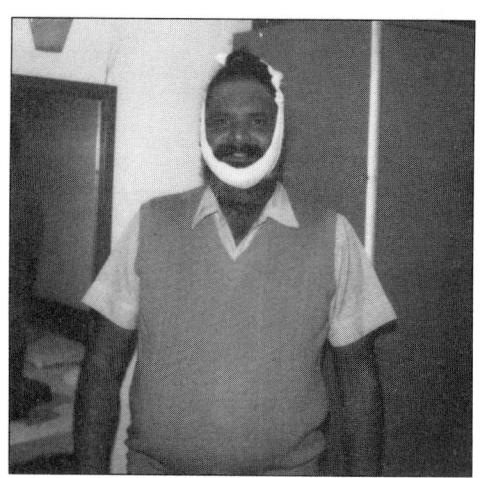

*My taxi friend, Joginder Singh, with beard in rollers, 1982.*

around to the right. The area was dense with rain forest, heavy with lichen and moss. It was slippery on the rocks. The pathway had dwindled away, we had to find our way through some heavy ringal, thin bamboo clumps. Here we saw some fine orchids that I took pictures of. It also necessitated shinnying up a few trees to do so.

We had traversed halfway around the mountain, and could see Sat-Tal far below. It would be about five miles from the Bhowali home. The two of us sat on a ledge and rested. Without warning, the monsoon clouds rolled in and the rain came down. It rained buckets, not just a shower. In an instant, the ground was soggy. The moss and the rocks made the going even more difficult. I tucked the camera away in its case. Mohan spotted an abandoned hut ahead. We crawled in. It did give some relief. Mohan dug out the sandwiches that Phyllis had packed. They'd been preserved in plastic wrap and saved from the torrential rain. I lit up my cigar, the old Dutch Master ones, and Mohan puffed on his Indian cheroot, or what is known as a beerie. I knew we could not wait here for long. The rain would settle in for the rest of the day and into the night.

While we braced ourselves for the rest of the trip, I suddenly froze and the hair on the nape of my neck must have raised up as a thought came to me: we had calmly been walking through Hemadryad Country, a technical name for the King Cobra; we were in their country, and also that of the large rock pythons. The King Cobra was the treacherous one. They grow to about 15 feet and can move like lightning, especially downhill. We were in their habitat, I know. I casually mentioned this to Mohan, and he smiled. Yes, he knew, and the only weapon, was a sickle-type grasscutter Mohan was using to cut the ringal and vines. The only good feature for me was that Mohan was leading the way!

We finally made it to the bungalow. Percy and Phyllis were a little concerned. I gave Mohan a fat tip for his efforts, and he was happy. A hot tub and dry clothes made me feel better. It was fairly cold, and Percy had a fire going in the fireplace. I sat close

to it and nursed a scotch. I showed Percy some of the catch, and he was excited. He said I should mount them on a board before they dried.

That evening, Percy suggested we put a lighted lantern hanging in the verandah. This would attract moths, which I was also interested in. I did catch a few, but nothing exotic. The following night was something else. Mohan came running into the living room and said there was a big moth on the verandah. We went out, and to our delight, there on the wall was a great Atlas moth. It is the largest type of moth family in the world, related to the silk moth. It was a great specimen.

I spent several days with Percy and Phyllis, and had a collection of butterflies and moths. Percy had a long, flat wood box in which I pinned all the trophies, and carefully handled them all the way back to my little apartment on Long Island. The PanAm crews were curious and stared at the collection in the cockpit, and wondered about this FAA Inspector.

In Long Island, I had a picture frame made and arranged the butterflies behind the glass. It was beautiful when hung on the wall.

Early in November, PanAm had been given permission, through a bilateral agreement, to fly their 747s around the world via Delhi and Bangkok. It was called flight 001 Eastbound. The interchange of crews was at Delhi. The New York crew flew the 747 eastbound. A Los Angeles crew brought the flight westbound 002. In Delhi, PanAm changed planes and crews. Our FAA Lead Specialist, Ray Hirsch, asked me if I'd like to make the Inaugural flight on 001 to Delhi. He didn't have to ask twice. It was also agreed that I could take a few days off at Delhi, All the inspectors knew that was my milieu, to fly to Delhi, or anywhere to the far East.

I loaded myself down with rolls of Kodachrome film, and my box of Dutch Master panatella cigars. The first crew would operate to Frankfurt, and that's where I'd pick up the flight, then to Istanbul and Beirut, Teheran, Karachi, and Delhi. I took an early PanAm flight, 707 to Frankfurt, to rest a day, then continue the inaugural on the 747 to Delhi.

Flight 001 was late on arrival at Frankfurt, I think due to the ceremonial hoopla at JFK - champagne and the trimmings. It was necessary for FAA inspectors, as a must, to ride the U.S. airlines' inaugural flights, to ascertain that the crew were familiar with the routes and airports, especially with the handling of a new airplane at the airports. This included the handling of baggage, passenger satisfaction, and security. PanAm had already been flying 001 and 002 with the 707s, and this was a completely new aircraft, handling would be different.

I met the crew at Frankfurt Operations; a crew I had known, and given their ratings at Roswell. At first, there was some difficulty with the loading and unloading of the cargo pallets. The motorized equipment to

handle the pallets had broken down. This was also true, and more so, at Istanbul. It was necessary to do this manually. Another delay ensued. At Beirut, it was more of the same: more confusion in getting the pallets off. The pallets held all the passenger baggage. When all was completed, the pilot had signed the papers, the doors closed and ready for start-up.

As I climbed the spiral stairs to the upstairs lounge and to the cockpit, I noticed a distinguished-looking gentleman sitting in the near front row. I asked a stewardess who was attending that seating, who that person was. She said it was Sir Hilary, of Mt. Everest fame, the first man to climb Mt. Everest. He had got on at London, and was proceeding to Delhi, where he would catch his flight to Kathmandu, Nepal. This person I wanted to meet, as I was greatly interested in Everest expeditions and its history. No time now, however.

The checklist for start-up was being called by the captain. One of the items before starting engines is to have the red rotating beacons on. The ground mechanics called to the captain on the interphone and said the lower belly rotating beacon did not operate, only the one on top of the fuselage was functioning. Everything stopped right there till the Flight Engineer looked up in the Minimum Equipment List (MEL) whether this was a no-go item. They could operate the aircraft to a base repairs could be done. I agreed they could continue.

The start-up was made and we taxiied out for runway 21. Halfway up the taxiway, Operations called and said that a passenger who had got off at Beirut, had left his briefcase on the plane. The pilot called back and said he would not stop now, but they could take the briefcase off at Teheran and send it back on flight 002. It was agreed. About then, the First Officer said to the Captain, "You know, this might be a ruse. Maybe the guy left it on here purposely. It might be a bomb." The Captain slammed on the brakes, all sixteen binders grabbed at once, and the big, more than 500,000 pounds of metal stopped right there, jolting everybody. The Captain called Operation and said, "Negative. We are now turning back."

The Station Manager pulled the ladder up, the briefcase was taken off. That was a lot of excitement. We were soon airborne, for Teheran. On the way up, I excused myself and went to meet Sir Hilary, I introduced myself, and the first thing he said was, "What happened? Why the brake so quick? I almost busted my seatbelt." I told him what it was, and he thought it was a good idea to return. I said, "Oh, yeah; anything like that is a no-go." We chatted for awhile, I said that I would be going to the Himalayas, he was excited. I said we would talk again later, that we didn't have too much time now.

At Teheran, there was more confusion, because the Beirut baggage handlers and pallet handlers had put the respective pallets in backwards: the ones Teheran had been placed in the rear. It meant that all pallets had to be removed before they could reach the ones for Teheran. By now, I had several pages of notes regarding the things going wrong, mainly ground handling. It was at Teheran that I bought some caviar and was able to talk with Sir Hilary. I gave him more details of my functions, that I was checking the Skipper and PanAm. He laughed and said he didn't mind. The cabin staff were giving him all the drinks he could handle and that he had missed his connecting flight to Kathmandu in Nepal anyway.

I told him about Ranikhet and Naini-Tal; that I would be there, taking pictures and hiking. "Oh, yes," "I know that area well. I did some climbing around Trisul Mountain, and Ranikhet." I left again returned to the cockpit. One good thing about the flight: The aircraft was performing well, the weather was excellent. Before reaching Delhi, which would be around noon, eight hours late, I had an opportunity again to talk with Sir Hilary.

At Delhi, Air India's 747 was already there. Nonetheless, the ground staff had rallied and put a red carpet for PanAm 001. I was just interested in getting through Immigration, Customs, and to the hotel. I was staying at the Ashoka which is Government-run and I needed sleep. I joined the deplaning passengers to pick up my luggage. Everyone was getting theirs right away. I waited and waited for mine. The last load was brought in, I figured my suitcase would be on it; it wasn't. I called the ground agent. He scoured the whole area and the aircraft. There was no baggage. Just my luck! Of all the passengers, it had to be mine, and only my luggage that was lost! PanAm was kind enough to supply me with shaving equipment and toothbrush. It would be two days before my suitcase finally showed up.

I saw Sir Hilary at the baggage claim. He already had his associate retrieve his baggage. We talked a few more minutes, while PanAm agents made a last-effort search for mine. then Sir Hilary and I joked about the situation. He said, "Well, in any case, you have reached your destination, I still have a ways to go. I've missed my flight to Kathmandu." We laughed. He wished me well on my stay and trip to Ranikhet and NainiTal. I wished him well, and hoped that we might meet again, one day, perhaps in Kathmandu.

Outside the terminal, I was greeted by Joginder Singh. He placed garlands of marigold flowers around my neck, an Indian custom of "Welcome to India." He drove me to the Ashoka Hotel, where I checked in, all I had was the clothes I was wearing, a sweater, and a mackinaw. It gets cold in Delhi by November. Luckily, I had my camera equipment. My friends said they would come by late afternoon. In India and most of its hotels, the laundry service is exceptional. I don't know how they do it. I was informed at check-in that the laundry would take care of my clothes while I was resting. I gave the roomboy the clothes to be taken care of then I got under the bedsheets in the raw, and tried to catch up on much-needed sleep. It had been more than 24 hours sleep in the jumpseat, which is difficult. I was excited to

be in Delhi and the thought of my coming trip to the mountains. Though this would be my third trip, I was yet to visit Ranikhet, which used to be the R&R for the troops in World War ll. I dozed and slept a while keeping an eye on the time. I guess I finally had dropped off to a deep sleep when I was awakened by a loud knocking on the door. It took a few minutes to figure out where I was. I looked at my watch. It was coming up to 5 p.m. I called out that I'd be there in a minute. After splashing water on my face and wrapping a towel around my waist, I opened the door, and there stood Joginder and Indrojit Singh, and two other friends. Joginder handed me my laundry and drycleaning. He also had brought shaving stuff for me. Sikhs don't shave or cut their hair. It seemed odd to see him with a razor.

I quickly shaved, showered, and put on my newly clean clothes. It was now past teatime; my friends brought a couple of bottles of local Carew's gin. I ordered ice and soda and limes. It was great evening, eating at the famous Indian place in Old Delhi, called MotiMahal, which means "Pearl Palace."

The next day was a relaxing one, just sightseeing, such as the Old Delhi Fort, and the Qutab Minar; The following afternoon, a PAA representative brought me my lost suitcase. Evidently, it had been taken off at Beirut.

I was now ready for my trip. However, Indrojit informed me that I must stay an extra night. One of his close relatives was getting married, and I must attend the wedding. Indeed I would! It was gala event. First, I had obtained real whiskey from the U.S. Commissary. Indrojit had arranged to have a section of a street roped off in Indrojit's neighborhood of Old Delhi. Large tents were set up. As a special favor, I was allowed to witness the official ceremony at the Temple. From there, the procession proceeded to the tents and the festivities. The whole area was now lit up with strings of lights and candles. The tables were laden with all kinds of Indian spicy hot and non-hot food and sweets. After a few scotch-and-sodas, I was ready to dig in. Several of the rice dishes had very thin tinsellike silver paper spread over the goodies; also the sweets. One can eat the tinsel silver, which is pure silver. The wedding celebration lasted into the wee hours of the morning, Indrojit had arranged an elderly Sikh driver to take me on the trip, since he was obligated to stay for the wedding. I arranged to pick up a basket of leftover tandoori chicken and kabab, plus some of the unleavened chapatti bread. Indrojit had supplied an ice chest which I loaded down with coke and beer from the commissary. We also had bacon and cheese.

After three hours rest, the driver was at the hotel entrance at about 6 a.m. to pick me up. It was early enough to dodge the rush-hour traffic. That means bicycles, cars, lorries, bullet-carts, pedestrians. We skirted the old Red Fort of Mutiny fame, and then across the Jamna Bridge, to the Great Trunk Road, and on to Muradabad. Here, we took a junction road, a rather bumpy one, and

headed for Ramnagar, at the base of the mountains. By noon, we had driven approximately halfway to Ramnagar when I called a halt. It was getting warm, and I was caked with dust. After following a canal the driver found a shady spot by a jarmon tree. While he got the food and ice chest out, I washed off some of the dirt. It was good to relax, especially after the wedding party and hangover. After chewing on chicken tandoori, chased down with a nice cold beer, I dozed off for about an hour, when the driver woke me up and suggested we get going, before it got too dark. Driving up in the mountains is dangerous at night. He had everything packed away. Ramnagar was a pleasant town, situated by a fast-moving stream coming down the mountains. I think the river was the Ramganga River.

We stopped long enough for a cup of hot tea, and then started up the mountain. It was a winding road with numerous hairpin turns, much like the other roads in the mountains to the hill stations. I could see why the driver didn't wish to travel here at night, yet we made pretty good time; Even though I had him stop every so often while I took scenic pictures. There were some breathtaking scenes. As we ascended, the foliage gave way to some of the type around NainiTal Road, with large white pines, rhododendrons, and silver oak. The weather was clear and the temperature cold. At about 7000 feet, we made a large circle around the mountain, and there I beheld a wonderful glimpse of the snow-capped mountains in the distance. The driver screeched to a halt. I took several shots of the snows. It was another world.

The driver made it up to the Westview Hotel, where lights were being turned on. The manager, a Mr. Kandpal, had my reservations. It was very cold, near freezing. A bearer took my things out of the car, while I filled out the necessary hotel forms. The driver said he would not stay here. He would make his own arrangements in town.

There was no heat in the hotel, only fireplaces, as all houses in the mountains. I had to order firewood separately. This was done, and the bearer lit a fire in the fireplace. It took forever for the room to warm up. In the meantime, I ordered soda, I sat and enjoyed my scotch. It would be another hour before dinner would be ready. I was prepared for the cold, and had on a heavy sweater and pants. The dinner was meager, but appreciated. It was off-season now and all of the summer people had returned to the plains I was the only guest!

I chatted with the manager and said I had my own special groceries, such as bacon, that I entrusted to the cook. I'd like that with my eggs at breakfast. I also produced a box of Bisquick. I said I would explain to the cook about making pancakes. They were all astonished that I brought these items with me, they do have their own intricate way of conjuring up some fantastic dishes, including pancakes English or French style crepes suzettes.

I arranged with the hotel chokidar who was the guard or caretaker who looked after the premises at night, to wake me before dawn, if he could see the Himalayan range or the snowcapped mountains, if they were clear or cloudy. I wanted to be on the spot to take pictures at sunrise, which gives the snows that blush of pink for which they are famous.

The fire was just about out, when I returned after dinner. It had taken the cold chill out of the air. I must have slept soundly, for I awakened to the knocks on the window close to the bed. I came to and I heard the chokidar calling "Sahib! Sahib!" "Yes," I responded. He informed me that the mountains were clear, he would accompany me to the unused Forest Officer's bungalow. He would show me where it was. This would be the best spot to view of the mountains.

I quickly rinsed my face in ice-cold water and was on my way with the chokidar. Halfway along the road, I spotted two jackals running along ahead. These animals appear to be a little larger than those in the plains, about the size of a coyote, perhaps because they have heavier fur and bushier tails in the mountains. They could have been my pet dogs, running ahead. They were brazen, and made no attempt to run away. The distance from the hotel to the officer's bungalow was about 3/4 of a mile. We walked at a good pace, to keep warm and to reach the destination before sunup. There was also a full moon, which was bright; one could almost read a newspaper by it.

I had my camera ready with a telephoto lens. Just per chance I focused in on the moon, between some pine branches and took a shot. When all pictures were developed back on Long Island, I was surprised to note how well the Pentax captured the moon. But now, we arrived at the officers' bungalow, which was deserted. Here, the chokidar took his leave and returned to the hotel.

In front of the bungalow was a spacious garden, and a gravel path, leading out to a rail fence that jutted out over a steep edge of the hill. From that spot, there was a spectacular view of the mountains. I had a grand view of the full range, where it disappeared in the distance. I adjusted my camera, and waited for the first rays of the sun to pierce the sky. I didn't have long to wait.

As if by magic and by the hand of the Almighty Allah, he painted a blush of pink across the vast range of snow-capped mountains. It was too beautiful and breathtaking! I felt so infinitely small and humble, staring at this vast panorama, I almost forgot about the pictures. I quickly focused in on the nearest peak, which was Trisul Mountain, about 23,000 feet. I kept taking pictures, one after another, with great delight hoping I might have captured the whole visible range, all the way to Mount Nanda Davi. The colors changed fast, as the sun rose higher. In about 40 minutes the peaks were bright shiny white, like the jaws of a young Doberman Pinscher. I guess I finished a roll of 36 exposures in a hurry and had a second one going.

Now, it was too bright, I returned to the hotel for breakfast. I relaxed for awhile,

thinking of that panoramic view, and hoping the pictures would turn out well. The cook did a good job with the bacon I gave him, and with the scrambled eggs; also mixed in were green chilies, chopped up, Indian style. It was good.

I sat and talked more with the manager as I puffed on my cigar. With any kind of luck, the temperature might reached 60 degrees Fahrenheit, but not for long. The days were short, and as soon as the sun would dip toward the west, the temperature would drop to freezing.

With another roll of film, in the camera, I took a long walk along the main road that led to a military barracks about two miles away. I came to a place off the road where I got wonderful views of the snows. At each spot, I sat and wondered at this marvel. Most tourists who come to India never see this sight. They are crammed into a bus on a quickie trip to the Taj Majal, Udipor, Jaipur, and Delhi. Don't get me wrong; it is all worth seeing, but it is only half of it. To visit these hill stations in the Himalayas, and to see the sunrise and sunset on the snows would be the climax! I sat at a spot that protruded out a way from the main road. I wondered about building a small bungalow right here. What a wonderful backyard view I'd have! I felt myself being torn between two words, America and this. They were so vastly different, there was no way that I could make up my mind and say this was it, or America was it. They both were "It;" I loved them both very much.

I had walked for several hours and realized I'd better get back to my lunch. I arranged to have my meal on the hotel terrace. I enjoyed the lunch and returned to my room for a rest. I spent three days in Ranikhet, visiting the bazaar and taking long walks. I paid my bill, and said goodbye to Kandpal and to the servants. I said I would return. My Sikh driver was waiting while I finished and a bearer packed my suitcase into the backseat of the car, after a good baksheesh to all the bearers and the cook. I was on my way to Bhowali, which was 25 miles away and down a sloping road along the Kosi River.

It was, a bright and sunny morning, cold and crisp. The old driver was a fine little fellow for a Sikh. He drove carefully along the winding road. The countryside on the south of the mountain range is sparse of trees. It had been denuded years ago and made into large terraces for wheat, the staple atta flour, for most of the hill people. Far below us, to the right of the motor road, I could see the shimmering blue Kosi River, as we drove along. Though our road was on a slight descending plane leading easterly, the river was running the opposite direction, westerly. The driver must have thought me nuts, as I had him stop at almost every turn to take pictures. The descending drive finally flattened out, and we were now level with the river.

We arrived at a small town called Guram-Pani, literally meaning "Hot Water." I don't know why, and neither did the villagers know why it was called that. Across from the village, at a narrow bridge, a trail

or "pakdundi" was zigzagging up to the opposite mountain. If one followed this trail, it would come to the gorge at the top, where Philander Smith's College is located. As a youngster, when attending the school, I used to come down that trail which follows a small stream. It was a great place for butterflies in spring. Many of the British people who lived and worked at Naini-Tal used to take the same pathway to the River for mahseer fishing. The mahseer in this river have now been fished out, not by sports fishermen, but by a lot of Indians, who would throw dynamite, grenades and even pour lime into the water. This has been done in many of the other famous rivers and lakes. The fishing in the hills is about finished, thanks to this type of carelessness. Not only fish, but all the other game as well.

From Guram-Pani Village, the road starts uphill, and at a particular bend in the road, I stopped. There was a small villager's hut on the right, not occupied. My mind went back to a time long ago, 1927, when my sister Geraldine, the landlord's daughter, Doris Shepherd, and another friend, an ex-military man, had started off on a hike by the mountain opposite the Shepherd estate. When we started down the other side, there were two valleys. We took the one on the left, which turned out to be the wrong one. I think we must have hiked several miles, and eventually came out on the notch of the road that we had originally planned, only to find we had come out further down the road by several miles than expected. It was dark, and the spot where I now stood with the villager's hut is where we had come out. I remember Doris and her friend knocking on that little door. A man finally answered, but would not open the door. From inside, he shouted out that there had been a man-eating tiger reported in the area and we had better get to Bhowali in a hurry! It would be about five or six miles back. I never forgot that. The Shepherds had sent a chokidar with a lantern, to find us. What a welcome sight, but not before we had made it halfway back. I reminisced, at the same spot. I looked up the ravine from where the four of us must have trudged down, oblivious of any dangers at that time.

After a good look, we drove to Bhowali, then through the bazaar. I noticed the same little shops along each side, and the squalid rickety wooden buildings above them. The street was now paved, there were electric lights. There was no electricity in the old days. The Cottons' garage and restaurant were still there, but the name had been changed. It was a going concern once; the British military lorries always stopped here on the way up to Ranikhet, because this was the only road at that time.

It was early afternoon when we arrived at the Sherred's. Percy and Phyllis, always gracious hosts, welcomed me. On this trip, I had also brought fifty rounds of 30.06 ammo for Percy's Winchester rifle. I hoped I could use it myself. We sat and chatted over afternoon tea; I brought them up to date on world events, and my now being qualified on the 747 aircraft.

Later, I went to the edge of the house terrace, and looked down at Therchakhet. The late afternoon sun made the terraces at the bottom of the hill golden, and off to the left, I could see BhimTal, always glistening. It looked like a large, well-cut blue sapphire. The bulbul birds were singing just below, in some lantana shrubs, I could still here the call of the black partridge. I was home, I wished my two kids, Christian and Hannah, could be with me. Perhaps one day, I could bring them to India.

A fire was crackling in the old fireplace. I sat now with Percy and Phyllis. I told Percy I'd be up at dawn, to get some pictures of the pretty birds.

My sleep was erratic, perhaps because I didn't hear the pitpat of the leaky roof into the tins. Perhaps too much nostalgia and thoughts of the past and what I would be doing these next few days. I slept later than I intended as I heard the bearer lightning a fire at the back of the house that was to heat the hot water for a bath and wash up. I quickly dressed and got ready.

I stepped out onto the verandah that faced south. I looked at that lovely view once more. The birds were ahead of me, the mynah birds making a cacophony of noise. The sun was just rising beyond BhimTal, and Mt. Kailas. I took snapshots as though they were going out of style. I also got a picture of two of the bulbuls, and some Rajahlals that were in the trees nearby. I walked over to the edge of the terrace on the right, and looked down at Therchakhet. The sun was now streaming in, giving the whole valley a bright golden hue. The high incline of the mountain just behind the house rose up sharply. My mind shot back to the winter of 1927-28, when I was here and I saw the leopard sitting on the rocks. I remember wondering if he was the fellow that came into our living room in Applecot, or perhaps it's his son. I saw the ledges where I had seen that leopard, now thought the cats were long gone, or shot. There was nothing there, except the sunlight splashing on the hillside.

I turned away and looked toward BhimTal and the valley. I was waiting for any kind of birdlife to settle in at the stunted Oak or lantana bushes, so that I could get closeup photos. Perhaps a few minutes passed, when some inner feeling kept nudging at my subconscious to look back at the hillside on my right. I looked up at the crop of rocks again; there was still nothing. Then my gaze went from the rocks to about 100 feet lower down, and there, lo behold, sat a beautiful, large leopard, staring at me! For a moment, I couldn't believe it; I had to blink a few times, and gradually realized it was true. Slowly I lifted my camera and started taking pictures, I gave it all I had. There was very little breeze, and I was able to hold the camera steady. The leopard was about 200 yards away. Needless to say, I was excited. I wondered if I could get a little closer; I wasn't sure. The leopard, I figured, would probably be the great-grandson of the one

*Ray Gifford, myself and Bob Mason, Meschref 1974.*

that had come to Applecot. He just stared, and I stared right back: it apparently was not frightened. Nonchalantly, I turned away and slowly walked across the compound to the verandan and called Percy. He was just getting up. I told him there was a leopard on the hillside, and to get his camera. Half-dressed, he emerged, excited as myself. Our friend was still sitting, looking at us. Percy suggested that I go around the servant's building and perhaps be able to get a much closer view. He would keep the animal occupied. Once out of view, I raced along the far side of Oak Lodge, to the servants' quarters. I saw one of the men, and told him what was happening, to be quiet, no noise. I passed the building and came to the gorge that opened toward the hillside. I made certain the camera was all set. Cautiously, I made my way through the gap, and peered over the ledge. Just as I located the leopard, he had slowly turned and bounded into some bushes and disappeared. What a shame! This would have been a much closer and better shot.

Next morning I placed myself just above the outcrop of rocks in a blind. I was well hidden and had a vantage spot of the hillside below. To be on the safe side I had brought along the rifle. I made myself comfortable and waited. The sun came up just as Kipling had mentioned in his poem, "The Road to Mandalay." It came up "like thunder across the bay." It was welcome, since it was freezing cold. Nothing moved, it was about this time yesterday that the leopard had sat for me. Birds of all kinds came by and taunted me to take their pictures. I waited another half-hour and still no sign of "Spots." Oh, well; that was that. I got up from my cramped position and returned to the house. Perhaps the old leopard had seen me and was just sitting back waiting for me to go away.

Later that morning, after breakfast, I decided to visit Sat-Tal via the old trail that passed through Thirchakhet; not the one I'd taken when we were after orchids and butterflies, and where the King Cobra's lived. They should be sleeping at this time.

I chatted with one of the villagers. It turned out he owned a small dairy in Bhowali, he had known the Shepherds but could not remember the Goutieres who once lived at the Oak Lodge, He would have been a small boy of about 7 or 8 then.

Another couple of miles took me to the lakes. I came to the main lake, that had a dam. Further along was a small clearing, near the water's edge, and a bench. There had once been a small park. This was a picnic area, where colonials would come when vacationing at BhimTal, or even at Naini, especially retired military people. I now sat and had my sandwich. At the further end of the lake and to the right, was a small village. There were few tree pies (birds). We used to call them long-tailed bluejays. Their tail feathers, about two feet long, with color bars in black and blue, with a white tip on the ends. I tried taking a few pictures of them. After an hour of birdwatching and picture taking, I started up the trail. Not the one I had come on; this was a horseshoe-type trail, around one side of the mountain to the lakes, and then back up the other side. It was steep, at the start, with a small cottage. I recalled that it was here, the same one, that my mother, Vernon, Geraldine and myself came in 1925 for our Christmas lunch, from BhimTal. I climbed along the trail. Halfway along, I stopped. I looked back, I could just see a glimpse of one of the lakes, and decided to take a picture, which would include the trail and, hopefully, the lake.

At the top of the climb, there was a gorge that opened up on Thirchakhet. BhimTal was on the right. A Christian mission had bought the Jones' estate where I now stood. A small church was built at the gorge. In the old days, Vernon and I would come here for pheasant shooting, as long as

*The villa from Ray Gifford home.*

we had Mr. Jones' permission. The rest of the way was easy going.

I stayed a few days longer, and tromped all over the hills around Bhowali, even tried my luck at shooting gurel, the mountain-goat, without success. The day came when I had to say goodbye to Percy and Phyllis. But I would return, because now I'd found another notch in my life.

In Delhi, I met with Juginder and Introjit Singh. I told them, as we sat and talked, about my trip to Roswell, New Mexico, that I had met a lovely lady by the name of Tish Christiansen. They listen intently; that I had once told Tish I came to India often, and she queried me why: "What was the attraction, other than the mountains?" "Oh," I said, "I go to nightclubs with my Sikh friends and watch the Indian bellydancers. When a dancer came close to the table, I'd take the ruby, or whatever jewel she might be wearing in her exposed belly button, and breathe whiskey breath on the stone, give it a good polish with a handkerchief, and place the stone back in the navel." Tish would laugh, so delightfully, then quizzically ask if that were really true. "Of course!" She paused and then said, after a little thought, "I'll make a deal with you. The next time you're back there and you have these dancers gyrating by your table, would you please take the ruby, polish it, but don't put it back in the navel, you keep the girl, and send me the ruby!" Juginder and Indrojit thought it funny. They said Tish must be a great person. The three of us drank a toast to her.

I checked the PanAm crew back to New York. The trip was over, and I was in Long Island. I couldn't wait to see the many slides I had sent for developing. When I did pick them up, I placed the slides into my carousel projector and sat back to enjoy and relive the trip I had just finished. I am happy to say that 90% of the pictures on the screen were perfect; I was elated. Those of the early morning sunrise on the snow-capped Himalayas were exceptional, including the

shot of the moon through the pine trees. The ones of the leopard were clear, but the telephoto didn't bring the animal close enough; one had to use ones imagination to know it was a leopard. His white chest was clear. The rest of him blended into the golden background. Even so, I was pleased to have my friend on the screen. I didn't care if anybody else could see it or not. Then there was one slide, I wasn't certain about. It was the trail, looking back at Sat-Tal. It was the pathway winding down the hill, with a large overhanging oak tree in the foreground. I stared at this for several minutes before I realized I had seen that oak tree before. I raced through my album of old photographs, which were black and white, and some turning a sepia with age. Excitedly, I went through the album and sure enough I found what I was looking for. The picture was one taken in 1925, it showed the footpath going down toward SatTal, On the trail stood my mother, Vernon, and myself. We were on our way to that little cottage I mentioned earlier for our Christmas lunch. In the foreground was the same overhanging oak tree. I had no idea about the old picture when I took this one. You could almost place one over the other, in a stereo-type overlap, It was pure accident. Later, when visiting Fred and Geraldine, I didn't say anything about the coincidence. They oohed and aahed over the beautiful slides. When I came to the one with the overhanging tree, Geraldine didn't know what it was, and I didn't say anything. I asked if she noticed anything familiar, "Yes!" She leaped up and got her album, and came to the same photograph, because we had copies of most of the oldies. "For heaven's sake! This is fantastic!" I told her the story, just plain coincidence, but there must have been something else that made me take shot, same as it was about turning around that early morning and seeing the leopard; all seemed strange. I was happy; I had captured most of the early childhood haunts on slides. I bought a slide editor and rearranged the hundreds of slides and

placed them into several carousels. I would undoubtedly be having my own slide show in the evenings, with my scotch and soda by my side.

Christmas of '71 slipped by, and the cold weather months settled in. Even so, I kept busy with the 747 program. Ray Hirsch kept us going with ratings, and check airman qualifications across the Atlantic with PanAm and TWA. Before I knew it, it was already summer of '72, I never dreamed I'd be doing so much flying. One morning at the office, the phone rang. It was a friend at the FAA office in Washington. He said if I was still interested, the Operations Inspector's job in Beirut was coming up for bid pretty soon. I thanked him, and said I was definitely interested. It was hard to believed it was six years since I first asked for that job and that Mr. Schaffer tried to help me. I didn't waste time making up a Standard Form 171 and other information. All I had to do was wait for the bid and the number. The bid arrived, and all necessary forms were filled out completely and sent to Washington. By the end of August, our secretary, Ana Cruz, excitedly informed me that I was selected for the Beirut position. I think I gave her a big hug and kiss, because I was terribly excited and couldn't wait to get going. The report date, however, was not till January 1, 1973.

Coincidentally, Ray Hirsch asked me to return to Beirut in November, to give 707 ratings to various pilots flying for TransMediterranean Airlines. TMA was operating FAA N-registered 707s on a lease basis.

In doing all this running around, I had bought a new Dodge Dart. I was scheduled to go to Oklahoma City, So I drove the car to OKC. My schooling was to be for General Aviation, and checkout again on small airplanes. There would be a lot of general aviation work in Beirut, I was informed. I enjoyed the change, after being married to the 747 for almost three years. It was a pretty good course and I learned to fly several small planes. I thought I might even kill myself at certain times, with planes such as Cessna 182, Bonanza, Beechcraft, Baron, and the 310, After finishing that program I drove on to Roswell, to visit with my friends, Mr. and Mrs. Johnson and Tish. In fact, I had brought along my treasured silver bowl for her to keep while I was overseas. She was delighted and would take good care of the heirloom.

In Long Island, I started getting things ready for Beirut. The November trip to Beirut would give me a chance to take over a lot of personal items. Though I was eager for the change, I was terribly sad within, since I would not see the children on weekends. I was heartbroken to tell them the news. In the midst of this, Margaret and Will Brown approached me and said they were getting married. I certainly was not surprised. Again, I felt sorry for the children. They moved up to Fairfield, Connecticut. I figured life must go on. I had to keep my senses and do my job.

I arrived in Beirut in November, and visited the FAA office at the U.S. Embassy, and talked with the Chief, Mr. Don

Burlingame. Almost a full day was spent discussing the future assignments, and some of the workload. Don was a fine fellow and a good chief. I knew we would get along well. I was staying at the Phoenicia Hotel, a great luxury place. I remained a week, giving 707 ratings. This also gave me an opportunity to meet a few of my old Air Liban friends. Also in town at that time were my other friends, the Knemeyers, and their two boys, Akhim and Thomas. The boys were strong, goodlooking youths. Everyone was really happy I was returning to Lebanon to stay.

After the checkrides, I flew on to Bangkok, to give a check airman ride to my dear old friend Ray Gifford. He was the fellow I rescued from the shootout back in Karachi, in 1949. We had a great get-together. The flight was to go up to Osaka, Japan, then back to Bangkok, and return to Beirut. At Beirut, I told Ray he had made it as Check Airman. I was able to stay with my friends, the Knemeyers. Being in Beirut after eleven years was almost the same as returning to my childhood haunts in India.

I jumpseated on PanAm 02, right straight through to New York, a long and tiring trip. I even had a problem finding my car in the employees' parking lot. Once back in my little apartment, I made my drink and collapsed on the bed. I guess I slept right through to late the next morning. At the office, I received my travel orders from the Africa, Europe, Middle East Region, (AEU). They were my new bosses. I was given a wonderful send off luncheon by the office at Valley Stream.

New Year's Eve, I arrived via PanAm 01 to London. The flight sneaked in just before the whole country fogged in, like a blanket being dropped over an airport. In a moment, everything was canceled. The hubbub and turmoil at the departure and arrival international areas was terrible; it was utter chaos. Luckily, I had reservations at my old standby hotel, the Airways Motel, where I once spent two months while I waited for my citizenship. I met the BA ground hostess, Sally, who was engaged to a PanAm pilot friend of mine, Jerry Freedman. I gave him his 707 rating in Roswell, in 1969. Sally said that Jerry would be along shortly.

Because of the cancellations, BA and PanAm ground people had now arranged a little winging party for all ground personnel. It turned out to be a good one. I think they commandeered all the catering service goodies off the stranded flights, champagne, caviar et-al. It was held at another hotel nearby. In the wee small hours of New Year's Day 1973 I staggered to my hotel room. That day, nothing stirred. Nobody was flying. The fog hung in there for two days before I could catch a PanAm flight to Beirut.

On approach to Beirut, I asked the pilot if he would notify FAA at the Embassy that I would be in shortly, perhaps half an hour. I was met by Don Burlingame at the Airport. How many times have I been in and out of here, at least a thousand! I would get to know it again. The Knemeyers wanted me to stay

*Three pretty girls stopped by to say hello at the villa, 1974!.*

at their place while they were away in Germany for couple of months which I accepted. Don dropped me off and would pick me up the next morning. The Kneneyers had a Sudanese boy by the name of Ali who took care of my things. I was worn out from the long trip, via Frankfurt and Istanbul. I told Ali I'd like only to have some Arabic bread and homos. I mixed my scotch and made myself comfortable in the living room. I looked out the window onto the Mediterranean; it was a beautiful evening. I lapsed into my own thoughts of Christian and Hannah. This was their home, where they had been born. I hoped I'd have a chance for them to come over, either during the summer or Christmas holidays. I'd also try to call them during the next day or so. I was now relaxed.

At the office Don showed me around, and I settled at the desk and checked where the files were located. I had met the staff last November when I was here.

I had a corner office, with one window that looked over the Mediterranean and Corniche (Boulevard). From the other, the Phoenicia Hotel and the construction of the new Holiday Inn. Don drove me back and forth to the office till my car and belongings arrived. It would be about another six weeks before that would happen.

At the Monday morning Ambassador's meeting, I was introduced to Ambassador Buffum. He announced that all the new Embassy members to be at his office at 10 a.m. the following morning. There were about eight of us. We sat in the spacious office while the Secretary poured out coffee. In this manner, each was asked to introduce themselves and give a brief resume. When I had finished mine, Ambassador Buffum was intrigued. He asked if I had read a book called *Indigo*. I was surprised and stated indeed I had, I'd better have done so, since the book was written by my sister, Christine Weston. The Ambassador was surprised, and laughed. He said he would like to keep the group longer, but we had better get back to our of-

fices. He took me aside and said he'd like to chat again, perhaps at a later date.

I was to meet with Ambassador again, and we had a good talk about India and China, and the war days. He asked if I had read the book *Stillwell and the American Experience in China*. Yes, I had, and had met General Stillwell, once in Calcutta, and in Assam. The Ambassador was just a fine person, whom I thought a great deal of. I was also able to know some of his staff well. Officers like Robert Waring, the Economics Officer. Three years later, in June 1976, when in Rome, I read with great sadness and with anger that my friend Waring, along with Ambassador Malloy, had been assassinated by some Lebanese guerrillas. The world was shocked.

I now settled down to my work program and one of my first assignments was to visit a Cypriot flying club in Nicosia. They had an FAA-approved school and trained student pilots for FAA licensing. I checked in at the Cyprus Hilton and met one of the owners of the club by the name of Paris. He showed me around the school facility and training programs. I also met his flight instructors. The students were from all over the Middle East, such as Pakistan, Iran, and Iraq. There were two Americans from Ankara, and believe it or not, there were three from Israel. I was to be kept busy giving flight checks on these small aircraft, mainly the Cessna 172. I can appreciate the General Aviation course I took back in OK.

I loved Cyprus. One could see it as a tight little island with a great amount of history that dates back to ancient Greek and Roman civilizations. One of Christ's apostles, Barnabas, was to preach Christianity here. He, too, is buried near Nicosia. The little town of Kyrenia, located on the north coast, was a delightful town to visit. It had a perfect, almost enclosed harbor, with a promenade or corniche that followed the shore almost like a circle. Along this corniche were quaint shops and restaurants. Most of the

*The Shah Abbas Hotel in Isphan, Iran. Where I stayed and conducted flight checks, 1974..*

town was occupied by retired British people, unlike Nicosia, which was the main throb of the island. I could see why so many people came to Cyprus to retire, especially the British folk, as it was once a British possession.

The next project was in February, to go to Karachi and represent the FAA at the Pakistan International Airline Engineer Seminar. It was to last a week. There were representatives from many foreign countries: England, France, Turkey, Greece, Afghanistan, Egypt, Saudi Arabia and Singapore, Ethiopia, and several from North Africa. There was a great deal of festivity and sightseeing. I was asked to give a talk on FAA and my duties as an Ops. Inspector. I introduced myself and gave part of the talk in Urdu Hindi. The Pakistanis were greatly pleased,

Right after my return, all hell broke loose with the Lebanese army trying to oust the Palestinians, two to three hundred thousand of them. They had been refugees in the country for some time. Fighting raged in the city, the mountains and the Baaka Valley, which is between Lebanon and Syria. Syria and the other Arab Countries called urgent meetings and finally had Lebanon cease their assault on the poor Palestinians. Syria, mainly, did not wish to have another two to three hundred thousand people pushed into their country. The Palestinians, I might add, were well armed and good fighters.

I was still the guest of the Kneneyers at this point, and for awhile the FAA thought we might have to evacuate. The fighting stopped, and peace was regained. It was the end of March before my household effects and car arrived. Up to now, I had not found an apartment to my liking, and there were not too many. One weekend, I visited Ray and Anne Gifford, who lived in a small community called Meschref almost 20 miles south of Beirut. It was along the coast, and just above the town of Damour. A George Debbas was the owner of the estate, a wealthy individual whose Dad had once been the President of Lebanon. George was married to a young Swiss girl. He had four sons from a previous marriage; an accident had taken the life of their mother. George's idea was to encourage people to build villas in Meschref. No money down, but pay a mortgage, sort of long term financing scheme. The Giffords had one of them. There were many who had also built homes there. A few people, mainly Middle East airlines pilots had reneged on their contracts, figuring it too far from Beirut where the action was. It would be quite a drive back, under the influence of liquor!

Ray and Anne thought it may be a good idea if I talked to George Debbas, perhaps rent one of these villas that he was stuck with. George was a dapper little fellow, about 50. He had a spacious villa, and a couple of German Shepherd dogs caged nearby. I told him of my interest and without any hesitation, he mentioned a villa just up the street from the Giffords. One of the MEA pilots had discontinued his payments and now the place was up for grabs. I said I wouldn't be buying the place, only renting. That was all right, if I changed my mind, my rent would go towards buying the house. The Giffords were tickled that I might be their next door neighbor. I was all for it. It was a large, three bedroom villa, with a spacious kitchen, fireplace, a good sized dining room, and a large living room that opened out onto a gigantic patio. The house was built on a series of steps. The bedrooms were downstairs, and the other rooms were upstairs. Both up and down areas opened out onto large lawns. The grounds were about an acre and it was all walled in. There were giant eucalyptus trees, apricot, fig, and grape vines; a garage, and utility and servants' quarters. The floors were all tile and terrazzo, with large windows and doors. It would be about $600 per month, with a spectacular view of the Mediterranean and a valley to the left. First I would have to get Embassy approval.

I talked to the people at the Embassy, and they okayed the deal. I immediately signed the lease with Debbas, then got the Embassy people to go ahead and have the place completely cleaned. The floors were polished, and it was painted outside and in. It didn't take long to have the furniture put in place. Most places and countries in Europe and in the Middle East have a different electrical system; it is all 220 current with 50 cycle. It was necessary to purchase several transformers so I could use my gas stove, refrigerator, and all the American appliances, such as blender and vacuum cleaner.

I could have used twice the amount of furniture and still rattled around. A local farmer, a Lebanese who lived further down the hill was hired to do my gardening. When everything was all trimmed up, the garden and the house, it was time for a housewarming. This was it. I knew I'd enjoy my sojourn in Lebanon with the FAA, including the horrendous work load ahead of me.

In this community, there was a swimming club and restaurant, tennis courts, and horseback riding. It was a ten-minute drive to the opposite hill, where there was a golf course and club, called the Delamayah Country Club, with an Olympic sized swimming pool and tennis courts. How could anybody want anything more? Maybe girls. Well, they were all over the place including PAA stewardi!

Some of the airport inspections for PanAm and TWA included Karachi, Delhi, Bombay. On a trip to Delhi, I took time to have my curtains made up for the villa. It was done at a place called Cottage Industries Shopping Center. In short order, I had it all in place, including my bar, given me by Syd Wheatley back in 1969, and also my tiger skin, proudly stretched on the wall behind the bar. One could say I was ready for business!

I kept busy, mainly on general aviation assignments. The U.S. military had a flying club in Crete. A group of the Air Force had a flying club on both sides of the island. I was assigned to go to Iraklion, the capital of Crete, which is beautiful. A U.S. Captain who ran the club always found time to have me see various places of interest on Crete. One, of course, was the valley of Windmills, a fantastic place. There were hundreds of them, all drawing water and whirling around in this very green, lush valley.

At Iraklion, I visited the tomb of an author and patriot of Crete. He was a hero of these people, before WWII. However, when the Nazis invaded Crete, they took him, saying he was a spy and a Communist, and shot him. It had created bad feelings toward the Germans. The Greeks had erected a shrine in his memory.

There was a lot of certification work, also, at Addis Ababa, Ethiopia. Ethiopian Airlines had several N-registered Boeing 707s, and a few DC-3s. Their repair station was an FAA-approved one. This was initially a TWA-controlled airline, as was once

Saudi Arabian Airlines. I spent a great deal of time administering written exams, about 70-100 at a time, in all categories: Maintenance, A&P, Dispatchers, Commercial and ATPs. I was busy as a bee.

Iran was something else. Here, the Shah had bought billions of dollars' worth of military equipment, fighter planes, helicopters, you-name-it. All instructions and training were given by ex-U.S. Air Force pilots, mainly from Viet Nam. Their function was to train the Iranian Air Force pilots on these aircraft. At the same time, the U.S. pilots did not have FAA certificates. Therefore, I would come to Iran, to their main base called Isfahan, once the old capital of Persia. There were several other bases in Iran that I would also visit. One of the pilots whom I designated an FAA examiner, Aubrey McLain, was courteous enough to drive me wherever I wanted to go. These adventures could take several weeks at a time.

It was always customary to visit the U.S. Embassy in countries I visited and brief the Economics Officer of my presence and my job functions. From the officer, I'd get permission to use the APO and commissary. Because of these excursions to the foreign countries and the amount of work I was doing, I was getting to be well known. The previous inspector did not have the qualifications to conduct air carrier work and certification on heavy equipment, such as the 707 and 747. The FAA Beirut office geographical area of responsibility officially encompassed from Crete and Greece, to Turkey, parts of North Africa, Egypt, Sudan, Ethiopia, all the Middle East: Pakistan, India, Nepal, Burma, and Sri Lanka. For one Ops Inspector to cover these places, and the major airports operated by PanAm and TWA, which numbered approximately 20, it was necessary to receive permission from the foreign governments first. I'd touch base with our Embassies and the local civil aviation people whom I enjoyed meeting. They appreciated the fact that FAA was around there to enforce air safety for the American flag carriers.

The summer slipped by, and early September of '73 our office received a message from Washington that a TWA Boeing 707 had crashed in the Aegean Sea after takeoff from Athens. "To send Pete Goutiere as FAA Coordinator to Athens immediately." I donned my 7-league boots, and caught an MEA flight, Beirut-Athens.

I checked in with the Greek Civil Aviation authorities and the TWA representatives. At the TWA office, I was introduced to the NTSB officer, a Mr. Doug Dreifus. Meetings had already been taking place with the DGCA, the NTSB and TWA. Preliminary investigations had been set up and I was told that not much else could be done that day. The Greek Navy were at the site where the 707 went in. Evidently, there was considerable flotsam in the area. The Navy was gathering all they could find and would have it at the Athens Airlines hangar in a few days.

Reservations had been made for me at the Hilton, made by the U.S. Embassy. That evening, I was brought up to date by Doug Dreifus and the TWA representatives. The cause was not determined. The only facts available were that the flight departed on schedule for Rome, having come from Tel Aviv. The local CAA had the passenger list, weight and balance. A copy of the tower tape was played and all seemed normal in the cockpit. Clearance calls and checkpoints; no sign of panic or malfunctions of the aircraft system or engine trouble. The last call was the pilot saying they were passing through 28,000 feet on course, then nothing. Coincidentally, at that time, a PanAm flight at 35,000 feet was eastbound to Istanbul on the same route in opposite direction. The PanAm pilot stated to ATC Athens that he saw an aircraft, possibly TWA, passing to his left and below, when he noticed a lot of debris that looked like large pieces of silver tinsel shot out from the rear of the plane, then saw the aircraft pitch nose up and climb almost vertically to near his altitude. Then it winged over and spiraled down towards the sea. He did not see the aircraft hit the water. The pilot gave the location and continued on to Istanbul.

Discussion centered around sabotage, and perhaps an explosion; possibly a bomb on board. The next morning, Dreifus took me to the airport, and at the first meeting of the day, I was introduced to the committee that was involved in the investigation. There were other NTSB people, and an FAA Airworthiness Inspector from Kansas City. Assignments were given to the people present. I was asked to go over the aircraft papers, logbooks, weight and balance, and weather reports, then to take the ATC tape and transcribe it to the best of my ability. This was a tedious task and took most of the day. The airworthiness Inspector was curious about one thing, I think it was the #3 engine. It had trouble before, and the pylons had once been changed in Kansas City. We zeroed in on this aspect. Perhaps the engine came off because of the faulty pylon fittings. This could cause the entire engine to separate, surge forward, then tumble over the wing and crash into the horizontal stabilizer, which in turn could have made the aircraft give that sudden pitch up, and the stall. This was a possibility only. I wrote this up and talked to Dreifus about it. I received the crew history from TWA office at JFK. I knew the Captain. I had given him, a proficiency flight check in the simulator. On the list of the cabin staff, I saw the name of a stewardess that I recognized. She was an Indian girl, from Bombay, based in Hong Kong. She was a lovely person. I had introduced myself to her on a flight from Rome to Tel Aviv and to Bombay when she was a cabin attendant. Since I spoke Hindi, we hit it off very well. At Bombay, we had gone out together and I met her folks. I couldn't believe now that she was on this tragic flight.

The flotsam arrived at the spare hangar and spread out. The few bodies that were taken in were kept separately; I didn't wish to see them. The flotsam was something else. I was surprised to note that a cargo door, intact; a few passenger seats as well; suitcases and baggage of all sizes. The DGCA had requested the services of a British intelligence fellow who knew a great deal about bomb activity. He spent the next day looking over the debris. At the conclusion, he determined that it was a bomb that caused the disaster. He showed us the small foreign bits of metal imbedded in the bottom of the seat cushions. Those seats had been in the section above the aft cargo compartment.

In the meantime, TWA and other security officers had been doing their own sleuthing with the Greek police. They discovered that one of the passengers on board was a young South American, I think Argentinean, who had been with two Arabs at a third class hotel in Athens. The two Arabs turned out to be Lebanese with false passports. They had returned to Beirut the day before the accident. The South American was ticketed to Rome and then on to Nice and Marseille. Security figured that the individual, who had a blue backpack which was placed with the baggage, was unaware that the two Arabs possibly had planted a bomb in it. The baggage was not screened before loading. The PLO later claimed responsibility.

I was almost three weeks in Athens with the investigation team. I had great admiration for the British bomb expert, whose name was Mr. Newton, and the security officials on the case.

I had no sooner finished this when word came that some terrorists had attacked PanAm 707 on the ramp at Leonardo da Vinci Airport in Rome. I was not to investigate it, but go have a look. They already had their own experts and security people there. I did go over and found that when the airplane was parked, with passengers still on board, three terrorists had run through the ramp. One had thrown a hand grenade into the cabin, which rolled down and exploded towards the aft end, and another had been thrown on top. The pilot's wife was killed, with two or three passengers. It was a terrible thing and happily the police caught and shot the terrorists.

In Beirut, before I had gone on my trip to Athens, I had bought several kilos of steaks from a British run grocery store called Spinney's. These I had placed in the freezer compartment. When I had returned, three weeks later, I was tired and only wanted to have a big double scotch and sit on my porch and watch the beautiful sunset over the Mediterranean. I poured the scotch at the bar and went to the kitchen for the ice. I switched on the light, and from the refrigerator, at the bottom, was a long, dark, snake looking trickle. As I got closer, I noticed a rank odor. When I took a real close look, I realized it was blood, coming from the bottom of the refrigerator. I stepped back, and immediately thought perhaps a body had been stuffed in there. One reads of these things in newspapers and can never know what to expect even, in *True Detective* Magazines!

I raced down and got Ray and Ann Gifford to have them have a look. In the

*Myself with Pakistani desert police.*

kitchen, I opened the refrigerator door. The putrefied smell was terrible. The whole inside had this sticky, tar-like blood all down the sides. I then realized the refrigerator must have turned itself off. It was all those wonderful steaks in the freezer section. I was heartbroken, but relieved. Ann said she and her daughters would take care of the kitchen, first thing in the morning. I went back to Ray's for the long-awaited scotch, and told them about my trip to Athens. It turned out to be several scotches and a sandwich.

Next morning, Ann and her daughters cleaned the kitchen. Ray figured that during a very hot spell when I was in Greece, the fridge couldn't cope with the heat, so it shut itself down. What a waste of good expensive meat!

The first Christmas at Meschref was wonderful. A lot of the neighborhood kids came by and sang carols. There were get togethers at various homes, and I had my eggnogs and a small Xmas tree. A few girls came by at the bar. I took pictures of them and the tiger. The pictures came out very well, I had I rush order to make Christmas cards of them for the next Christmas. A PAA crew flew in to town. I had them over for a quickie party. I had a fire going in the fireplace though a bit smoky. New Year's was more of the same. I'd also met a lovely Christian Lebanese girl, an orphan, named Renee. She did a lot to help fix up the house and was great company!

It was the start of 1974. I had my schedules pretty much in order. There was a lot of office work to catch up on. Many violations kept me writing reports. Most of them were private and corporate U.S. aircraft that were overflying countries in our geographical area without any prior permission. It would take months to track down the pilots and owners,

In early February '74, a message from the IFO in New York asked if I would observe the operations of Overseas National Airlines (ONA) that had two DC-8's operating between Karachi and Dacca Bangladesh,(East Pakistan). ONA was con-

tracted to haul refugees and prisoners-of-war to Karachi. It came just at the time of the Muslim Conference, which was also being held in Karachi. It was difficult to obtain a visa for Pakistan. However, through the help of the Embassy, I succeeded.

ONA Chief Pilot handled the operations and gave me all the information about the flights. He also arranged a room for me at the Karachi Intercontinental. I jumpseated ONA's DC-8 that took a 3 1/2 hour flight, almost four hours, from Karachi to Bangladesh. I was sitting and listening to the weather reports from Calcutta. Heavy rains and hurricane force winds were predicted for Dacca. This was the season for the typhoons and cyclones that always caused havoc in the lowlands, especially the eastern part of the country. They generated out of the Bay of Bengal. The wind forces have been known to reach up to 150 miles an hour, causing 50-foot tidal waves that always washed out fishing villages, mainly those along the east coast and around Chittagong. I nudged the Captain and asked if he'd heard the weather forecast. "Yes," he said. He would look see, while making the approach to Dacca. Otherwise, we would divert to Calcutta.

As we approached Dacca, the weather was socking in. The rain pelted the windshield and the aircraft was tossed around like a leaf. Dacca didn't have much in the way navigation equipment, it was necessary to use the radio and VOR of Calcutta. The Flight Engineer picked up Dacca Tower, which reported strong winds and rain. The visibility was anywhere from 2 to 2 1/2 miles. The pilot started his approach, using Calcutta VOR, At about 2,200 feet, he broke out with the field in sight. There was a crosswind at about 30 knots. The pilot stayed visual by making fairly steep banks, 30 degrees plus. Not knowing the DC-8, I still knew it was more than required. The rain was coming down in buckets, but the visibility seemed to hold out. The touchdown was okay, mostly on the left main gear. I noticed the pilot was using all the right rudder and left aileron.

When the nosewheel touched down, there was a shower of water on both sides, like the prow of a boat in rough, heavy seas. All reverses were okay, till the Flight Engineer said that No. 3 had quit. It no doubt was due to water ingestion.

At the terminal, after all passengers were deplaned, the Captain got the okay to start No. 3. It functioned normally. I told the captain he had done a good job, under the circumstances, but I was not happy with the severe bank angles he'd used. He agreed and said normally he wouldn't have. He just wanted to stay visual. I also told him to tell the Chief pilot in Karachi I was staying here to check the airport, that they would have to use high minimums in daylight hours only; that I'd catch the flight the day after tomorrow.

I sloshed through the puddles, way over the ankles, and entered the terminal building, not much had changed in the past 23-odd years since I was there. The name of the airport was Tezgaon; it was a military field during the war, and not much else had been done since then.

A taxi took me to the Holiday Inn in town. I called the Embassy and talked with the commercial officer. I told him my mission and, with time permitting, I hoped to drop by. That would be fine. There was no hope to do any inspection that afternoon, as the rain and wind had picked up. In fact, as I was having tea in the coffee shop, the rain was so heavy, in about 40 minutes the hotel swimming pool filled up and overflowed into the dining room and lobby. All electricity gave out. I had to walk upstairs to my room.

The next morning, the weather had cleared sufficiently so I could do the airport inspection. I met with the airport people and the CAA. I mentioned I had flown here, once upon a time. That was in 1951, with the C-46. These officials were not here then. A whole new group, ex-Indian Air Force and CAA in Calcutta, were now helping the newfound government of Bangladesh, as they had helped fight the East Pakistan military. It was a lot of these Pakistanis that ONA were now evacuating to Karachi.

On checking the runways, I found them to be in sad condition. Nothing had been done to them since WWII; waves and holes all along the runway. No wonder that rainwater was trapped in large puddles! The runway lights were unreliable, half of them not working. The runway markings were obliterated. The manager said a lot of damage had been done during the recent war between East Pakistan and India. It was not for me to say his airfield was in poor condition; I guess he read it in my expression.

As it was an emergency airlift operation, I wouldn't stop ONA operations, but I had to warn the crews to use caution.

That afternoon I inquired about my old cook (Cookie), who was living in Dacca somewhere. I got ahold of a headwaiter who came on duty that evening. He was surprised that I was asking for Rozario. "Yes," he said, "I know him; he is my uncle. My name is also Rozario." This was great. He would contact old Cookie. It would take a while, since he now lived in a village about 25 miles out, and the only way there was by ferryboat. I said I'd be in and out of here for the next couple of weeks.

The third trip back to Dacca, there was my Cookie, waiting for me, still the same spry little fellow. He was tickled to see me as a hound pup. I fixed him up to stay in my room at the Holiday Inn. There was so much to talk about. He was upset about my marriage breakups, especially with Kiki. He was with us then in Calcutta. When I left, I made sure he got a fat check.

Back in Beirut it took a few days to fill out all the required FAA forms, and my voucher. I barely had it done when our office got a couple of messages from New York IFO, and our Frankfurt Office. New York wanted me to certificate a group of Sabena pilots, who were now flying for Air Zaire, which once was Belgian Congo. The company had lease-purchased one of PanAm's Boeing 747s. It was an N-registered airplane, therefore the crews had to have FAA licenses. They had obtained their ATPs, but no 747 ratings. This was where I came in. I was to go to Brussels and meet the Air Zaire people, then proceed with the 747 to Kinshasa, the capital of Zaire.

I was also told that once I finished this project, for me to get off in Rome and proceed to Tripoli, Libya, where I would renew several FAA instructors' licenses, and to give written and flight checks. Also, Airman Certification for a U.S. company flying F-27s for the Libyan Oil Company.

I took PAA to Frankfurt, and Lufthansa to Brussels. I spent almost a week in Brussels giving checkrides and then on to Kinshasa. I administered 747 ratings, and flight checked several pilots for enroute check airmen. The flights were Kinshasa-Rome-Brussels and back. This would take two weeks to accomplish. After a couple of ratings, and another round trip to Brussels; I think it was after the return from Brussels; I had checked in at the Intercontinental Hotel exhausted and after an early dinner, I hit the sack. I must have been very tired and didn't really know it. I was asleep in no time. At first, I didn't know where I was when the phone kept ringing. I turned on the bedside light and looked at my watch, it was just past 3:30 a.m. I figured it had to be morning, but something was wrong when I answered the phone. The person asked if I was Mr. Goutiere. I said "Yes." Then the person stated that he was sorry to disturb me at this hour; that he was from the State Department, and it was very important that he see me immediately in the lobby, and to please bring all my identifications.

I soon came to and dressed. I splashed water over my face and brushed my teeth. In the lobby, I met two well-dressed young men. One of them came forward and said that they were from State Department Security, and showed me their credentials. They apologized again for the hour, but said it was important they see me, that the State Depart-

*My friend Renee from Beirut.*

ment had been trying for a week to locate me. I didn't say anything, just stood and fumbled around for my passport which was the red official one, and my FAA 110 identification. Though they were satisfied with these, they asked what my itinerary was. I said I had just returned from Brussels, that I planned to give a few more flight checks and take another Air Zaire flight to Brussels for a check airman ride. I planned to get off at Rome and catch Alitalia for Tripoli, to do some work with a group of U.S. pilots flying for the Libyan oil company. I guess they were convinced. One of them said, "We have two urgent messages for you; The first one is to forget the rest of the itinerary and return immediately to Beirut. The second message says; "under no circumstances should I go to the Middle East, because my life was in jeopardy." They looked very serious and I knew this was no joke. I asked to see the messages. They said it was all verbal, but rest assured, the messages they gave were fact, and came direct from Washington. I said, "What am I supposed to do?" They just shook their heads. I guess it was up to me. Well, I thanked them and returned to my room.

No question, I was wide awake now! I paced up and down the room, and time just dragged on. At about 7 a.m., when I was getting ready to have a quick breakfast and check out, the phone rang again. I was on edge and startled. The operator said that my call to Tel Aviv was ready. I said I had no call to Tel Aviv. "Sir, the party is waiting to talk." I said there must be a mistake. "Stand by," she said. "No, the party in Tel Aviv said they will talk to you." I was mad and scared. I said I couldn't talk with anyone in Israel, as I lived in an Arab country. She said, "Then you wish to cancel your call?" I said, "Yes," and hung up.

I quickly packed. I had my tea and a couple of fried eggs at the coffee shop, then checked out. At the airport, there appeared to be very little going on. I realized Thursday and Friday were the Zaire weekend. I

checked different airline counters, and Air Zaire was the only one that was active. Most of their flights appeared to be operating within the country. I went over to the PanAm counter which looked deserted. I put my suitcase down to rest, and lit up a cigar. Though nervous, I was getting pretty good with my peripheral vision. I must have been at the counter for almost 10 or 15 minutes when I saw a figure approaching the counter near where I stood. As he got nearer, I thought I knew the individual. When he was right up to me, I said, "Are you Bill Frost?" "Yes." "Well, I'll be dammed! Bill, it's me, Pete Goutiere." "Oh, my God, Pete; what the hell are you doing here?" I told him about my work with Air Zaire. I had not seen Bill Frost since I sold him my furniture and handed him my apartment in Calcutta in 1949. Bill had taken over as Chief Mechanic for PanAm in Calcutta. I couldn't believe it; now he was head man of PanAm in Kinshasa!

I asked Bill if PanAm, by chance, had any flights out of here today, in any direction. He looked at me quizzically. "Yeah," he said, "we have a flight that leaves here this afternoon late, perhaps around 5 p.m., for West Africa, and then to New York. It'll be coming in from Johannesburg." I said, "Put me on the jumpseat to New York." Though it would be a long flight, I was used to these long-winded air safaris by now. He had me check through immigration, and I dumped my things at his office.

Bill raced around, tending to his local chores, and then made some coffee. I tried making out my forms and updating my voucher. I decided to keep quiet and not send messages to FAA Beirut or anywhere else. The time dragged on, but thanks to Bill, we were able to chat and bring ourselves up to date. He arranged with immigration that I could accompany him to the terminal restaurant for lunch. Bill must have noticed that I was worried, and asked if all was okay. I tried to shrug it off by saying that Washington had cut my stay short in Kinshasa, that I planned to go back to the New York office for a couple of days and do some shopping, then return to Beirut. "What a life," he said, "and all for free!" We laughed. I suggested he come and visit me in Beirut some time. He was a great golfer, I told him we had a good golf course in Beirut. He said after this tour, he would return Stateside and retire. His daughter was married to a police officer in Connecticut.

The PanAm flight arrived on schedule from Johannesburg. I met the crew that would be taking me as far as Dakar, Senegal, where there would be a crew change. I said goodbye to Bill Frost and thanked him for everything. Once in the cockpit, I did not get out till the flight arrived at JFK, New York.

Once out of Customs, I took a cab to the FAA office in Valley Stream. I had shaved and cleaned up to look presentable. I went straight to the office of manager Gene Assip. "What the hell are you doing here, Pete? You're supposed to be in Beirut!" I told Gene I had to talk with him privately. He closed the office door, and I briefly explained what was told to me at Kinshasa by the State Department Security Officers. "Holy smoke! Have you been sleeping with some Sheik's wife...or wives?" We chuckled. I said, "No, if that were the case, I'd know what the problem was."

Gene got us some coffee, and decided we had better talk with AIA in Washington, International Affairs; that they may know something. Gene put the phone on loudspeaker, and got through to Mr. Charles Carey. He was AIA-1. Gene told him that he had a Pete Goutiere from Beirut office sitting here, and that he looked worried. "Oh, my goodness!" said Carey. "Tell Pete not to do anything or speak to anyone about what he was told. We have been trying to contact him for over a week." I jumped up and said, "Mr. Carey, this is Pete Goutiere. What in the world is going on? Can I come to Washington and discuss the matter with you," "No, Pete, we will contact you. I don't want you to ride any international flights; do not contact any of your family. You are on administrative leave until further notice. Give Mr. Assip a point of contact. We will be in touch. And one thing: I'm glad you're here in the states." I said, "Thank you, Mr. Carey; I'll do as you say." And that was it. Gene and I sat and looked at each other. I stayed in Gene's office till noon; then lunch. I met some of my friends at the office, and said I was here to do a few errands.

I called Tish Christiansen in Roswell, and said I was coming that way, and needed a room at the Roswell Inn, I'd be there for awhile. She said, "Fine," and that she would meet me as soon as I arrived. I took a TWA flight that stops at Albuquerque. I had to spend the night there and the next day I took Texas Air to Roswell. It was nice seeing Tish. Before I could say anything more, she said that her folks wanted me to stay at their home. There was ample room and I would not be in the way. As I mentioned before, Gerry and Sil Johnson were great people, and welcomed me.

That evening, I had to tell the Johnsons and Tish my real reason for being in Roswell. They were surprised that Washington hadn't briefed me further. I said, "well, that is the way things are in the Government, and I'll just stand by." I called Assip the next day and gave him my whereabouts, and the home numbers of Tish and the Johnsons. It helped me forget the tension and allowed me to enjoy a lot of golf at the country club.

It was the better part of three weeks before I received a call from Gene Assip. He said that Mr. Carey wanted me to go to his office in Washington as soon as possible. I thanked the Johnsons and Tish for all their kindnesses, and left for Dallas. From there, I caught American Airlines to Washington, DC. The FAA had arranged a room at the Marriot across the Potomac on the Virginia side. I checked in late that afternoon, and phoned Mr. Carey's office. His secretary said I was to be at his office at 9 o'clock in the morning. I was anxious to learn what this was all about, yet a bit scared. I really hadn't the foggiest idea why my life was being threatened by someone in the Middle East, or a government in that area. I had been to Israel, only in 1942, when it was Palestine. I had in 1957-58 been to Jerusalem and Ramallah when it was part of Jordan. I tried to clear my mind, if I could know what it was, but the tension was building up. I had an extra scotch that evening, It was a restless sleep.

The wake up call was loud and clear, and startled me out of my sleep. I jogged around the room for a few minutes, and did a few calisthenics. A long, cool shower also helped. A few minutes to nine, I was on the 10th floor of the FAA Building on Independence Avenue. Mr. Carey's secretary greeted me and said that Mr. Carey would be with me shortly. I sat down with my briefcase and tried to look nonchalant. Just about on the dot of nine, Mr. Carey came out of his office and introduced himself. He was a dapper, grey-haired gentleman. He ushered me into his spacious office, and asked his secretary to bring some coffee. That would be fine.

After some conversation, Mr. Carey said that there were other guests who would be along in a few minutes, with the FAA Administrator, Mr. Butterfield. He then said, "Pete, you created a flap in the FAA." I was startled and shrugged. I asked what I had done to upset the FAA? I thought I was doing a fair job at the Beirut office. "Oh," he said, "don't get me wrong, you're doing a bang-up job, from what I hear from our main office in Brussels. No, it's nothing to do with your work, I assure you. Something else has developed concerning you. Mr. Butterfield needed you here to discuss the problem. I guess you know it's for your safety."

I didn't have time to answer. The secretary ushered in Mr. Butterfield, whom I recognized from photographs. The other several people I didn't know, but Mr. Butterfield introduced himself and the others, I don't remember their names or titles. One was from the State Department, I think he was

the 2nd Asst. to Mr. Kissinger; a man from FBI, and one from CIA.

Mr. Butterfield led off the conversation to the people that I was the inspector at Beirut, and was thought a lot of by FAA colleagues and in Brussels. He then reached into his inner coat pocket and took out a strip of paper. "Pete," he said, "I want you to read this message very carefully, but may I suggest you sit down first." This, I did, and then unfolded the paper. It was like a teletype message, at the top were the dates and codes, etc. Then it said: "Subject: - Secret." This is the part I read and read again: "Mr. Peter Goutiere, FAA Representative from the Beirut Office is proceeding to Karachi, Pakistan to assassinate President Gadhafi of Libya." I think I read it again, before I looked up at the people staring me. I guess I was in a state of shock for a moment. Who wouldn't be?

I gulped, and my mouth was dry. Butterfield stated, "We have all read the message. Take your time before any comments you wish to make." I nodded, and took a couple of sips of coffee. I'm not certain of my immediate comments. I did say, "Me? Kill Gadhafi?" The State Department man said, "You were in Karachi when Gadhafi was there, weren't you?" I thought for a moment, and the light came to me. "Yes, that is correct. I was there in February during the Muslim Conference. I was assigned to monitor the ONA operations between Karachi and Dacca. ONA crews and myself were on the first floor of the Intercontinental Hotel. I believe Gadhafi had the whole of the 6th floor. The two weeks or so I was there I never saw him. Some of his staff were in the lobby and lounge once in awhile."

Then jokingly, to break the tension, I said, "Well, while I was downstairs with the crews, chasing stewardesses, Gadhafi was upstairs, chasing greasy boys." It did bring on laughter from everyone. I further pondered the situation. Ridiculous as it may have been, I realized the impact of the message. "Gentlemen, I am dumbfounded, and cannot for the life of me imagine how my name has been implicated in such a bizarre case to knock off Gadhafi. At no time during my stay in Karachi was the name of Gadhafi ever mentioned between the ONA crew and myself at the bar, restaurant, lobby, or airport. If this were really true, why hadn't Gadhafi's henchmen at the hotel done something then?" The FBI man said, "Well, maybe they were just watching you, and waiting for you to make a move." I asked where this message originated. The CIA man said, "It came direct from Tripoli. The Libyan police were waiting for you to arrive from Rome; they knew your schedule. You had a visa for Libya, and the form you filled out stated you would be arriving on a certain date to certificate pilots." "That's correct." Then I said, "When I was at Kinshasa that same morning, I also received a call from Tel Aviv." The CIA guy said, "They probably heard about the message from Tripoli, and were possibly trying to help you come to Tel Aviv as a Safe Haven." I said, "Well, I didn't talk to them, because I was worried."

After an hour's discussion, Mr. Carey, Mr. Butterfield, and the State Department and other officials agreed I had no intention of doing Gadhafi in. Finally, Mr. Butterfield asked me what I wanted to do. Did I wish to return to Beirut? If not, he would arrange any other office for me to relocate. It was a difficult decision, but if I returned, I still must ride on flag carriers. This would give the Arab terrorists and Gadhafi's people an opportunity to try and hijack any plane I was on. Also, if they really intended to kidnap or kill me, they could do so, no matter where I was. With a deep breath, I said I would return to Beirut and take my chances. I then told Mr. Carey I'd like to talk to my Chief, Mr. Burlingame, at the Beirut office. He said he had already arranged that, that Don Burlingame would come to New York, and I would meet him there. I thanked Mr. Carey for his concern, and then said, "What a way to meet all these fine VIP people!" I shook hands and left.

I went to New York, and met Don for a couple of days. He said this had taken him by surprise, when I did not return and no one was giving out any information. He thought I possibly was dead. As for Ambassador Godley, Don said he was highly teed off at the FAA for not informing him of my detour from Zaire. He was responsible for my safety at all times and should have been notified. I told Don I'd take a few days off, and see my children. I then gave a certain date I'd be arriving on PanAm.

I journeyed to Connecticut to meet Christian and Hannah for a few days. It was wonderful to be with them for that weekend. When PanAm departed from Istanbul to Beirut with me in the jumpseat, my stomach started to churn inside. I excused myself from the cockpit and went back to the lounge. The stewardess asked if I was okay. She said I looked ill. She didn't know how ill I really felt. I asked her if she would kindly bring me two nippers of scotch. "You're kidding. You can't drink on duty!" I said, "I've just taken myself off duty. I need the drink; strictly medicinal." "Okay." I finished the double drink on approach to Beirut. Don and his wife, Grace, were waiting for me when I came out of the terminal. I hugged them like long lost friends. Behind them, I noticed two individuals looking in my direction. Before I could say a word, Don said, "They are from Embassy security, just in case." They would escort us to Don's apartment. I planned to go directly home to Meschref. However, Don's idea suited me fine. I stayed a couple of days with Don and Grace. Next, I had a meeting with the Ambassador. He was happy to know I was well, and I filled him in from A to Z on the events. He was happy to know I had decided to return to Lebanon to continue my duties.

I finally made up my mind again to continue on to Meschref. Don drove me to my car, which had been parked at the airport all this time. It was loaded with dust and bird droppings. Amazingly enough, it started right up. I cleaned the windshield, and headed for the 17-mile ride through the PLO camps and Muslim territory. It was clear sailing all the way. I don't mind saying my peripheral vision was getting better and better.

As I drove toward my home, I decided to stop at the Giffords just to say hello. I had been gone almost two months. Annie and Ray were home, and his Australian accent was a treat. The three girls were there, all very cute. As I sipped my scotch, I didn't want any rumors spreading around about myself and Gadhafi. But they were glad I was back.

The first night was hell. I just couldn't get to sleep. The slightest noise woke me. It would take a while to settle down. I remember the CIA fellow in Washington had said that the Libyans would probably forget the incident in about six months. If that were so, I had about four months to go. In the meantime, I caught up with all my reports and vouchers. This voucher was a good one, what with Brussels, Zaire flying, Kinshasa, and the layover in Roswell, it tallied up to a fair amount. My Lebanese girl came by and wanted to know what happened. I had good excuses by now. Besides, I had brought her some presents from the USA., clothes and a Samsonite vanity case.

Before long, I was off and running; this time to Addis Ababa to give some more written exams and flight checks for the local flying club, and for Ethiopian Airlines. I stayed at a friend's house in town. It was not the same anymore. There had been a lot of fighting, and the new Communist takeover by Haile Mariam had disrupted everything. One could not move around freely. At night, I could still hear the static of the machine guns and the odd bomb. It reminded me of the shades of Beirut when I first got there. Anyway, I still did my thing, and I had support from the Embassy and the airline. They escorted me back and forth to the airport. But at night, it was rather tricky. I stayed low, and tried not to have any lights on. Quite often, I could hear the roar of the lions in the zoo down town. They were resentful, I guess, of the takeover! It didn't take long, to finish my work, and then continue to other ports of call, such as Jeddah, and to Iran and all those exciting places. No dull moment.

There had been a few flareups between the Christians and the Muslims in Beirut, but not enough to stop our work. The months hurried by, and I enjoyed my work and my home at Meschref. Early in September, we had a message that an Air France 747 had caught fire on the runway at Bombay, and burned up, no casualties. That was okay, except it was an N-registered aircraft on lease to them. Therefore, Brussels asked that Mr. Goutiere go as the FAA Coordinator.

I arrived at Bombay as soon as I could, and met with the NTSB, people from Boeing and Pratt & Whitney, and Air France. Also present were some CAA officials from Delhi who were in charge. I arrived well after the preliminary investigation had been completed, and crew interrogation. I met the Indian investigator in charge, a Sikh by the name of H.P. Singh. There was not much left of the jumbo; it had burned for nearly ten hours. Both city and airport fire brigades had a tough time with it.

After reading the crew and airport officials' statements, it was determined that the fire was due to brake wheel fires in the right body gear. It was a scheduled night flight from Bombay to Tel Aviv, with about 400 souls on board. While taxiing, there had been a loud bang, heard by one of the cabin attendants. The cockpit crew had heard it but felt nothing. During the takeoff roll, it was normal until reaching about 100 knots, when a vibration set in and the pilot thought it was the nosewheel. At about 115 knots, another bang, and the pilot rejected the takeoff.

According to the tower and fire departments, they said that they saw sparks and fire originating on the right side and under the aircraft. The fire brigade responded to the tower and started down the taxiway. However, the pilot, after stopping, elected to taxi back to the ramp. The tower had the aircraft stop. There was a small fire in the right body gear wheel. The pilot did not know this, with the excitement, and the tower trying to tell the pilot there was a fire on the right side, to shut down the engines, the French pilot misunderstood that the fire was in the right engine, and said, "No, fire. Clear to taxi." The fire engines blocked the taxiway. Because the engines were still running, the firefighters couldn't approach close enough to extinguish the blaze that was now developing higher into the wheelwell and lapping at the underwing area. The cabin crew member came to the cockpit and said there was a fire on the right side. The cockpit crew evidently ignored this, and still wanted to taxi to the ramp. After much conversation between the tower and the cockpit crew, they shut down the engines. At this moment, the cabin staff, on their own, evacuated all 400 passengers from the left side of the plane, via the slides. The fire people were pretty well exhausted and also the fire equipment. They stumbled around with the hoses and could not contain the fire that was now raging in the wheelwell and up the right side of the aircraft. The cockpit crew, unaware of the severity of the fire, calmly went through their shutdown checklist, got their hats and flight bags. As they opened cockpit door and started out, they were greeted by the fire spiraling up the stairway. They had to evacuate through the above hatch, and use the inertia reels. The cause was attributed to an inboard tire on the right body gear that exploded while they were taxiing out. Then on takeoff, it disintegrated, causing vibrations and parts of the tire ruptured the hydraulic line to the brakes. On aborting and using the brakes, there was no anti-skid. The brakes locked and wore down the wheeldrums to the metal, causing excessive heating to the wheel. That, in turn, blew out the tire next to it. When the aircraft stopped, hydraulic lines sprayed fluid on the white-hot wheels. Hydraulic fluid, though not

*Lebanese tanks guarding the U.S. Embassy. The wire mesh is for protection against hand grenades.*

flammable, will burn when in a spray condition.

I stayed a few extra days with Mr. Singh, wrapping up the report. He insisted that any time in the future, when I was in Delhi, to be sure and come to his office.

I now returned to Beirut. Mr. Burlingame had decided he would return to the States on vacation for about six weeks, and put me in charge. I hadn't been in charge long when, in early October, the Embassy called an Emergency meeting. The Ambassador informed us that President Anwar Sadat of Egypt, and Assad of Syria, had attacked Israel during Yom Kippur, the Israeli holy day. The report received was that the Egyptian Army had crossed the Suez Canal and penetrated deep into the Sinai Peninsula. From the north, Syrian forces had retaken the Golan Heights and gone on into Israel. The Israelis had been caught unaware. It had not affected Lebanon, at this time, but they were on alert. The Embassy staff would continue work, but with caution. I messaged our head office in Brussels and Washington.

I then had the other two inspectors and the Lebanese secretary, Joe Nobar, pack up all the classified material, either for shredding or to be sent to Brussels in case of evacuation. Every day now, there were reports of heavy fighting north and south of Israeli borders. Jordan stayed out of it. There were times when, we could witness air battles overhead between Syrian and Israeli planes. One thing the Israelis were not prepared for were the SAM-7 ground-to-air missiles that were knocking off the Israeli aircraft. A few of them fell into the Mediterranean, right outside our front window.

One morning, the phone rang; it was Brussels. They wanted to know where our monthly report was. Just then, there was air battle and some sonic booms. Brussels wanted to know what that was. I said, "There's a war going on." "Yeah, we know that. Are you guys okay?" I said, "Yeah,

we're fine." "Well, forget the monthly report for awhile and just do it when you can."

During this fracas, one early Sunday morning I was sipping my tea on the porch at Meschref. It was a cool, very clear day, about 7 a.m. From the coast to my right, here came a squadron of Israeli fighter bombers. They flew right up the valley, between me and the Delamyah Country Club. I could see the pilots distinctly. The aircraft disappeared over the hill to the left, and then in a few seconds, I heard the bombs exploding. They were striking the Syrians far behind the Golan Heights. There were several of these flights that day. All through the month of October, the battle raged and the flights continued.

It didn't prevent us from playing golf at the Delamayah Golf Club. We cussed whenever there was a sonic boom, which was quite often, it did not help our putting! Egypt and Syria were doing well, until the USA. decided they'd better help Israel by sending hundreds of planeloads of arms and ammunition, and more fighter planes as the Israelis were running short. Soon the Israelis outflanked the Egyptian Army and cornered half their force of about 50,000 on the east of the Sinai. Then they crossed the Suez and headed for Cairo. Egypt capitulated. That left Syria. Israel wasted no time in turning around and sending its forces off to battle Syria. They pushed the Syrian Army back out of the Golan Heights, and were on their way to Damascus. They were now bombing the city itself, and one or two U.N. people were killed in that bombing. The war ended, and Israel returned to keep the Golan Heights, and the Sinai.

I had made several trips to Iran, mainly in Isfahan to check on the operations and licensing of pilots by the FAA Examiner "Mac" MacClain, and to give some written exams that had been requested. Back in Beirut I received a message from the FAA in Frankfurt. The message stated a FAA Ex-

aminer by the name of MacClain had reported to them; that he had received information from reliable authority, that the chief supervisor for the group in Isfahan had copied all the FAA exams which had been kept under lock and key. What no one knew was, the individual had an extra key. At night, when everyone had left the field, he had sneaked back and did the copying of nearly fifty tests. I called Brussels immediately and gave the disturbing news. I followed up with a letter and the number of all the tests. The FBI caught up with the guy back in Ft. Worth, Texas. Oklahoma Office said to disregard destroying the exams, there were too many to replace. I learned a lesson about trusting people overseas, or anywhere for that matter.

I thought we would have to leave Lebanon, but, because of the Israeli victory, peace was restored in the Middle East, temporarily! In the meantime, our office had received a message that a VIP plane, a twin-engine Beechcraft, had disappeared over Pakistan. Of course, would Pete Goutiere go and investigate? It was just about now that Don Burlingame had returned from his vacation. I couldn't leave the office, however, until everything was straightened out here. Further information stated that it was a doctor from Joplin, Missouri who was flying the aircraft to Australia. He was a friend of the U.S Ambassador to Pakistan.

The airplane had been missing for some time, and I was not about to go until further and definite information had been received. Word came from the Embassy in Islamabad, Pakistan, that the plane had been found in the Northeast Pakistan desert, a very remote area. Washington also received the message and said that I should go.

I arrived in Karachi and met with the Civil Aviation people, who would be in charge. At the same time, I also met with the U.S. Consul in Karachi. The Ambassador had asked a U.S. Air Force Captain from the Civil Air Defense in Islamabad to accompany me, plus the Consulate individual from the city of Lahore. He would supply the station wagon and take charge of the body when released by me. I checked, with the Director General of Civil Aviation, he said I was cleared to help his people. Everything had been arranged for me to travel to Multan, where I was to meet the Consulate from Lahore, the U.S. Air Force Captain, and the Pakistan CAA investigators in charge. A Pakistani doctor would also accompany us.

Next day, I took PIA airlines and was met in Multan. I immediately realized there was some dissension, especially with one of the CAA fellows and the U.S Consulate from Lahore. CAA wanted to wait for prearranged Pakistan Air Force helicopter that would take us to the crash site. The Consulate man said it may never arrive, he had the station wagon and the coffin, and was ready to get going to Bhawalpur and then to the accident. The doctor and a couple of his people had a jeep. I agreed that we should start off right away, and not wait for the helicopter. Besides, I didn't like helicopters!

It was getting late, and there was a long way to go. The paved road gave way to a dusty one, and then to nothing more than a track. Thank goodness the weather was cool and clear.

We came to a village and an old fort, probably one from a century ago. We took a breather and dusted ourselves off. The track continued on through the desert, a couple of times the wagon got stuck in the sand. It was necessary for everyone to push. It didn't take long for the night to set in. By 9 p.m., we finally came to a well-established barracks, Ft. Abbas. This was the Pakistan Frontier Police, or Desert Police. The police officer in charge of the barracks said that the crash site was about a mile or so through some rough terrain; the wagon might not make it. We could take camels, if we wished. The Captain and I, next morning, tried the camels. The Embassy van, through a lot of pushing and pulling, made it. I might add that the Consul man thought he was in charge, and started directing orders. The CAA man looked at me, and I winked. I then took the U.S. officer aside, I told him that his only function was to take the body back to Lahore, or Islamabad for shipping to the States, that the CAA was in charge, and I was representing the NTSB/FAA and would assist the team. That was it, period. He was not too pleased.

The sand dunes in the area were about 50 feet high, with deep troughs. The fuselage, when we saw it, was more or less intact and upright. The right wing was gone, and the engines. The CAA man located the engines about 150 yards forward of the plane. I found the battery about another 300 yards beyond that. The body, still in the pilot's seat, with topcoat on, was buckled in. The elements and insects for the past several months had deteriorated the body to almost skeletal. The Captain and I were able to crawl into the fuselage and examine the cockpit, before letting the doctor in. The Captain was familiar with the Beech Baron and the Duke. This aircraft was a new Beechcraft Duke. There appeared to be no indications of emergency. The CAA man had a folder of the accident so far which contained flight plans, etc. The flight had been normal, he had departed from Kuwait to Karachi, with a long-range cabin tank. The doctor had flown all the way that day, and late into the night arrival at Karachi. He should have called a halt and rested. However, he elected to continue on to Delhi. He had made an IFR flight plan that was to take him over the airways to the VOR Rahimyarkhan at 20,000 feet, then direct to Delhi, which is about a 90 degree heading. The weather showed isolated thunderstorms in the area. The right engine appeared to be feathered, and showed indications of having been on fire.

The Pakistani doctor examined the body while it was in the cockpit. He stated the impact had caused a broken neck and back. I then told the Consul officer to have the body

*The same range with "FishTail" at dawn—taken from Pokhara, Nepal, New Years 1976.*

removed and place it in the coffin; it was now his responsibility. The Captain, the CAA Officer, and I, decided to hike from where the wreckage rested and travel west. It was a walk that took us up and down the dunes. Some places were level. We came across parts of the plane, such as the wing ailerons, elevators, and various other sections; It was difficult to know which was which. It must have been a mile that we trudged. The Captain said he'd walked from the other side to about where we now stood. We decided that the aircraft had started coming apart from at least five miles before the fuselage hit with a sudden stop, tearing the engines loose, and projecting them another 100 yards, and the battery beyond that. It must have been going at an excessive speed.

The CAA investigator, the U.S. Captain and I sat and discussed the events. It was thought that after passing RK (Bhawalpur) VOR, and turning due to east to Delhi at 20,000 feet, the pilot possibly experienced engine failure or fire, then feathered the engine. Perhaps while in the severe turbulence, the Joplin doctor lost control and started to spin. At 12,000 feet, where the altimeter had stuck, he recovered and started to pull out. The speed would have been beyond VE speed, or "Never-exceed" speed. At this point, the aircraft started to disintegrate, part of the wing, the elevators and ailerons, it hurtled into the dunes with great velocity, which caused his neck and back to break.

It was late afternoon as we started the long trip back. The jeep got stuck. The Consul wouldn't stop for the jeep, and the Pakistan doctor. At Islamabad, the U.S. Captain and myself reported to the Ambassador. It turned out that he had been in China-Burma-India, or CBI theater, based in Assam, as a civil engineer. We had a great talk of those days, I finally told the Ambassador about the accident and our findings. He was appreciative of the FAA participation. I did mention to him about the strangeness, and

some of the difficulties encountered with the Consulate from Lahore. He would attend to that.

I arrived back in Beirut a few days before Christmas. I told Don Burlingame I was going to take a few days off and finish the report later. A telegraph message in the meantime had been sent to Brussels, NTSB, and AIA-1 in Washington in which I had given most of the facts. I was so glad to be back at Meschref and home. As one might surmise I seemed to spend little time there.

That afternoon at home, I turned my Magnavox record player on, sat at my bar, and poured my favorite drink and felt relaxed. I'd been on the go for so long. I'd eaten so much hot Pakistani curry, and so many wonderful dishes, especially at the 8th floor restaurant of the Karachi Intercontinental, with which I was familiar. Cheese and crackers was all I was interested this evening. My next drink, I enjoyed on the porch, and watched the sunset.

My girlfriend, Renee, showed up the next day, and helped put up the Christmas tree and decorations. It was a great Christmas, but I missed Christian and Hannah. I was able to phone through and talk to them on Christmas of '74. On New Year's there was a wonderful party with the Giffords, George Debbas, the Burlingames, and many other friends in the neighborhood and from Beirut. New Year's Day of '75 shone bright and clear. I did my best to recover from my hang over. It wasn't till we went to the Delamayah Club and had bloody Marys and some Lebanese food that I could shake my head without any pain.

The next week at the office, I soon caught up with my paperwork. Then off and running, visiting the flying clubs in Cyprus and Crete, then to Iran where I gave my usual written tests and some flight checks. I was back in Teheran, with a couple of days to relax. The FAA Examiner, Mac McLean, had driven me up from Isfahan. I remember a special spot he took me to, called "The Cel-

*More destruction. My favorite gas station bombed out, 1976.*

lar," expensive, but definitely first class. Many foreigners patronized the restaurant. It was excellent, U.S. type steaks and good French wine. I would leave the next day on PanAm.

That night, a snowstorm hit the country, especially Teheran, which lies at the foot an 18,000 foot mountain. Flight 02 was on schedule that afternoon. I got a taxi out to the airport. I checked with PanAm operations, and got my usual Caspian Sea caviar. I walked out to the airplane via the terminal building and met the crew. Right after takeoff, PanAm Ops called and said there had been a terrible accident at the terminal. He reported that because of the heavy amount of snow that had accumulated on the roof of the main terminal building, the whole roof had collapsed, killing many people below. I was surprised, so was the crew. "Egad," I said, "I'd only just walked across that same floor, when I went to buy my caviar and back again to go through Immigration!" No PanAm staff were killed. I told the Flight Engineer when he contacted PanAm in Beirut to please have them call Don Burlingame that I was on board and okay, and that I would see him in the morning. He came back later and said the message had been delivered.

At the office, I told Don, if the roof had caved in a short time earlier, I may not have been so lucky. I also briefed the Econ. Officer, my friend, Bob Waring. I asked Don what the heck was I doing wrong, what with getting tangled up with Yom Kippur war and now the Teheran terminal roof collapsing. He said, "Consider yourself real lucky. The Gadhafi one would really have cost you." How true it was?

I never needed an excuse to have a drink, but it sure seemed to happen everytime I returned home. I stopped at the Giffords and had a couple, and a free bowl of soup, before I retired to bed.

The Palestinian camps were scattered in various spots of Lebanon, and around Beirut. While driving to work and passing Khaldi Airport, I had to pass through a large Palestinian camp. I got to know some of the refugees; and on my way home, I'd stop at the small stalls that they had. I'd buy fresh eggs and fruit, and vegetables, I'd buy a lot of candy from the Embassy commissary for their children, and cigarettes for the guys. I felt sorry for these people with no country of their own. Some were well-educated, and spoke good English.

Speaking of buying stuff at the U.S. commissary for all these people, I remember once that Renee had asked me if I could buy some Tampax because she couldn't get any in town. One afternoon after work, while I was buying my usual whiskey and groceries, I remembered the Tampax, so I bought several boxes of them. At the checkout counter, the lady cashier was a redheaded girl, on the husky side and was married to a Marine sergeant; a southern gal. She tallied my articles up, and when she came to the Tampax, she hesitated, then looked me square in the eye while chewing gum a mile a minute. She said, "Ain't you a bachelor?" "That's correct." "Well, what the hell are you doing with Tampax?" She spoke so loud that several Embassy people waiting in line couldn't help but hear. I was taken by surprise for a second, and I presumed they were, too. Then, looking her right back in the eye, I said, "I use them to clean my shotgun!" There was an uproar of laughter. She came back and said, "Well, I've heard it called all sorts of things, but not that!" More uproarious laughter. I said, "Yeah, maybe so, but this one happens to be an over-and-under with a polly choke." That just about did it; she howled, and so did all the other patrons. "Now get your ass out of here, Pete!" I threw her a kiss and left. These little things come to my mind and seem to be a lot of fun.

I enjoyed every minute of my work. I was soon delegated to investigate a heli-

copter accident in Daharan, Saudi Arabia. ARAMCO Oil Company had wet-leased a bunch of helicopters from an outfit in Louisiana. They would take supplies and personnel to the oil rigs and platforms located in the Persian Gulf. This one crashed on landing, killing a couple of passengers. The American pilot was unhurt, and his statement said that the hydraulic section of the controls seemed to jam. I was asked by the Saudi PCA people to take the particular parts to the NTSB in Washington for examination. With Brussels' approval, I was back in the States, I had a chance to see the children, since they couldn't come over to Lebanon because of the political situation, it was still a hotbed of fighting. The NTSB would send their findings to the PCA direct.

Another helicopter accident in Jeddah. There was not enough wharfs for the cargo ships, many lay anchored offshore. An enterprising company hired a copter to hover over the cargo holds. It would lower a cargo net into the holds and, when full, fly goods to shore. This helicopter pilot, while in the process of lowering the net, was so engrossed in what he was doing that he didn't notice the slight drift as the wind had picked up and pushed him into a boom, knocking off a couple of blades. The copter dropped straight into the hold, killing the pilot and several others down below. After furnishing the report to the Saudi PCA, I returned to Beirut. It was business as usual at the office.

One day, like rumbling thunder out of the Lebanese mountains it came: a busload of Muslim people, if my memory serves me right, stopped in the Christian section of Beirut. The Christian military opened fire, killing most of them. That's like poking a beehive with a stick; all hell broke loose. Fighting erupted in several parts of town, then spread north, all the way to the Muslim section of Tripoli, then south to Sidon, just past Meschref, where I lived. The fighting finally stopped, but the atmosphere was tense; anything could start it again I did my commuting as usual through the refugee and PLO camps, without problems. The Palestinian folks were well armed. I used to see them once in a while oiling and pointing their Russian rifles.

Another time there was a loud boom, and immediately the shooting erupted again and went on for several hours. It was necessary to lower the shutters of the office. What caused this outburst, was a British Airways Concorde that had been traveling at 57,000 feet at supersonic speed over the Mediterranean, when it failed to slow down in time to reach the Beirut beacon. The sonic boom went off, thereby setting off all the trigger-happy guys. There was a lot more to come before it stopped. As I say, anything would start a fight; skirmishes kept erupting in different parts of town. There were the Christian faction that fought each other for control, Chamoun's Tigers against Ghamel forces. Then the different Muslim sections.

It grew worse. Various zones were set up. The worst part was near the Beirut museum, which became a no-man's land. There would be a lull, then more fighting. This was also the divider where the St. George's River flowed right through that area. Many people were getting killed. I guess they just wanted to shoot off their rifles and rockets. At times, I was able to talk to my Lebanese Christian friends in Damour at the bottom of the hill, such people as the owner of the Total Gas Station. He supplied my heating oil for the house, and it was also where I gassed up once in awhile. Then there was the guy who did my dry-cleaning, and the local grocer. They all said not to worry. Then there were the caddies, most of them from Damour, who were fine young fellows, some of them could play some pretty good golf. I had given my old golf set of clubs to one of them for Christmas, he was so excited.

By September it was really an all-out war. More people were getting hurt and killed by the scores. At the office, the Lebanese Army had placed three armed tanks at the Embassy. The streets were not too crowded and I still stopped at my Palestinian camp and had my Arabic coffee and chatted with the people.

I asked Don Burlingame about the future here, and whether we should think about evacuating. He had called Brussels several times, and was told that it was considered but only when the State Department gave the word. Well, it didn't come in time and Joe Nobar, the secretary, was worried, his building had been shot up. The area where the Phoenicia and Holiday Inn were located came under fire often. Early in October I was sitting on my porch and could hear the gunfire in Beirut. That same evening, around 11 p.m., when I was getting ready to turn in and had most of the lights turned off with only the record player going, I heard a cannon go off from up the hill where the old Arabic town of Meschref really was located. I heard the whistle of the cannon shell pass overhead, and then saw it land in a banana grove outside of Damour. They fired about six shells that night all landing beyond the town and some in the ocean, one or two right in the banana patch.

I went down and saw the Giffords later. Ray, with his accent, said, "The bastards!" George Debbas called us into his house. There were a few residents still there. He said to be sure to have no lights on after 7 p.m., in the evening, we all agreed. The next day, back at the office, I told Don what was happening back in Meschref. He thought it best to stay in town. That was a good idea I would do so that weekend. I thought I would bring as much as I could fit in the car. The furniture, I hoped could be shipped out. My girl, who lived north of Beirut near Djouneh, was not able to get through. There was heavy fighting between there and Beirut.

At the house that afternoon, I started packing, and I had Bob Mason with me who was still flying for TMA. We packed as much of my valuables into cartons as we could. We took the Magnavox record player

*Entering Damour town with the distruction by Jumblat's forces, January 1976.*

down to the Giffords, and such things as the vacuum cleaner, and the power lawnmower and some of my pictures. That night, there was some more shelling over the house. This time, a couple did hit into the main street. I told Bob we'd make our move on Sunday, but it never happened. On Saturday, my friends from Damour said the main road to the airport had been cut, and that Beirut Airport was closed. All that section was Muslim, all along the mountains above us. We were stuck, stranded. George Debbas said that he would see if he could get a boat to take us to Beirut, but there were none available. The phone lines had gone dead. We still had electricity, because we had our own power at Meschref. The community was cut off completely. No way to go south either. All the area from the golf club to Sidon was Muslim, and they were not about to let any traffic go through. One good thing, I did have my refrigerator loaded with food, and shelves with canned goods. The bar had all the booze for months to come. Another amazing thing. When I ran out of eggs and Arabic bread. So what could I do? I took the mountain road to the old Meschref, where the shooting had been at night. Yeah, that's it, that's where I went! I was greeted just like any of the others for shopping. All the shops were open for business, I could buy most anything. The shopkeeper got to know me, and knew where I lived. I bought my eggs and bread, and a few vegetables, and milk.

All of October, the fighting continued. I'd go down to Damour. It was almost deserted, or so it seemed. Nothing moved. The people were barricaded in their homes and makeshift miniforts made of rock, since most of Lebanon is made of rock, so there was no problem in building material. A lot of my friends here would greet me with large paper bags over their heads, and little peepholes for eyes. All of them were armed with every type of weapon, even shotguns. I couldn't guess who the

caddies were among these young fighters. I'd always ask about the road to Beirut, and the answer was always "La, la," which means, "No, no." The owner of the Total Gas Station promised he would notify me immediately when he knew it was safe to travel. There was absolutely no traffic on the main road through Damour to Beirut. Once it used to be a bustling thoroughfare. There was no chance to play golf. My friends below said it would be dangerous to do that. It was best to stay at home, they were correct.

Bob and I wondered for how long it would last. Once in awhile, we'd have our local friends come and visit us, and Bob introduced them to Salty Dog drinks. They loved it, especially one or two of the English and Australian fellows. The Lebanese were unfamiliar with this drink, but they caught on fast. I thought to myself one day, "What had happened to the Gadafi scare? If ever the Libyans had wanted to get rid of me, this would have been a great opportunity for them." Bob and I did a lot of walking around the community, and swam in the local swimming pool. George Debbas would invite a few of us to his home for sumptuous dinners. He had the three Sechalese girls working for him still. They only spoke French. One was rather cute; I nicknamed her "Cheetah." George was very understanding, and sometimes allowed Cheetah to come and clean up my house, and do the laundry. With my few words of French, and a French dictionary that I still have, we were able to communicate. It reminded me of Fort Lamy, with the Poisevaras.

Thank goodness, the weather was always excellent. I wished so much to get up to the golf club and have a game or two. I knew I'd be stopped by my friends at the bottom of the hill. The Lebanese gardener and his sons came by every Saturday to mow the lawn, trim the hedges, and look after the fruit trees. The month seemed to drag on with no relief. The can-

*My butterfly collection destroyed by Jamblat's people, 1976.*

nons roared at night, and we could hear the shooting beyond Damour, towards the airport.

It was around the 10th of November when my gas station friend showed up, very early in the morning. He said there was a lull in fighting; that there was a truce being negotiated, and that it would be safe to go this morning if I hurried. It was a Monday. I thanked him very much. Bob and I piled all the things possible into the Dodge Dart, a lot of my valuables plus the old tiger skin and also a couple of bottles of whiskey. As I drove by the Giffords, I told them that we were going to try to make it through. They were not worried and would stay on. I saw my friends at Damour and I gave the gardener a few Lebanese pounds to look after the house and belongings that were still there. I hugged his kids, and a group of caddies. I then said goodbye to my friends as we passed through Damour. It was a ghost town, and then into No-Man's Land. There were several burned out cars and trucks along the way. There was no one else in sight, not a dog, or cat, or a mouse. Nothing seemed to move.

We were now going through the Muslim area. A Lebanese tank was parked further along, but no shooting at all. My heart was pounding all the way. We had reached the point of no return. I was elated when we came to the south end of the airport. I passed through the Palestinian camp, and waved to some of the people I knew. There were no smiles. Coming into Ras Beirut area, it was all deserted. Here and there, a car drove along. Usually, there would be a traffic jam. My favorite restaurant, Roc du Pigeon, was closed. I passed on through to the Corniche. That was the last stretch to the Embassy. I could see smoke coming from the Phoenicia and the Holiday Inn. On closer view, we could see they were pockmarked by shellfire.

The three tanks were still parked and guarding the Embassy. Another was now close to the main entrance. I told the guard I would leave the car right on the road next to the Embassy. He nod-ded and said "okay." Bob and I walked into the FAA office, where I saw Don in his fatigues, with a walkie-talkie. "Hi Don," I said. "Hi," he said, then he did a doubletake. "Hey!" With a yell, he dropped the walkie-talkie and greeted me like a long-lost friend, or somebody who's come back from the dead. "Oh, my God! will the Ambassador ever be glad to see you! He was arranging with the PLO to help rescue you, and they might now actually be on their way!" We raced upstairs and saw the DCM, Deputy Chief of Mission, and a security man. The new DCM called Ambassador Godley, to inform him here at the office. The Ambassador said to tie me to my desk, "So we won't lose Pete again!"

I sat down with Bob Mason and made out a power-of-attorney, giving him permission to sell the Dodge to a Lebanese person working at the Embassy. He'd been interested in it before, and was in the process of getting the money from his bank when, if ever, it would open again. Once done, it was witnessed and notarized at the Embassy. Don said I had a room reserved at the Riviera Hotel, just up the street, from our office. I collected my few things that I had in the office, and Bob dropped me at the hotel. I wished him well, he said he would return to his old apartment, if it was still there. Don and his wife were at the hotel, also.

I had a hard time sleeping that first night, mainly due to the gunfire that kept erupting. At the office the next day, we were sweating out the Airworthiness Inspector, who had been on a trip to Teheran. His wife, like me, had been stuck at her apartment in north Beirut near where Renee, my girl, lived. The Embassy somehow had been in contact with her. She was supposed to meet a special launch sent from the harbor around to Djouneh Bay. Word came back that she had refused to take the boat because they would not allow her to bring a whole lot of her belongings, such as her silverware, and a ton of brassware that she had collected. Instead, she took a taxi. They evidently thought it would be clear; she got halfway and was stopped by one of the fighting factions. In fact, they let the taxi go and kidnapped the gal. The inspector nicknamed his wife "Madame Queen." This chain of events, not taking the launch, had infuriated the Ambassador to no end, and rightly so. Luckily, Madame Queen landed in the hands of the Christian fighting force. We later learned, I think it was just fun and games, that she was disappointed that she had not been raped by her captors. Oh well, so it goes. "You can't win 'em all!" Her captors, learning who she was, got her through to the Embassy a few days after I arrived. Coincidentally, so did her husband, who came via Damascus. Don told me that the FAA in Frankfurt was sending a Flight Inspection Convair 340 to pick us up in a couple of days. We had another get together that evening at the hotel, including Joe Nobar, our Administrative Assistant and Secretary. Joe, I learned, had been through hell himself. A shell had exploded in their kitchen. His wife and kids had just been in there a few minutes earlier. Now they had nothing left to cook with. They had to improvise one of their other rooms for cooking. I asked if he and his family could evacuate with us. We could use him when we set our new office, which I understood would be in Rome. But no way could Joe go along right now.

We were having a pretty good time, eating Japanese food, in spite of the war. In the midst of all this food, Madame Queen spoke up and wanted to know if I'd be taking my Lebanese girlfriend. "I'd like to," I said, "but couldn't get in touch with her. I just hope she was safe." The gal then said, "I shouldn't marry a Lebanese, if I were you, but someone else, somebody like me." The husband didn't crack a smile, but Don almost fell off his chair, and so did Joe and myself.

Early morning came with the crackle of gunfire. The so called peace had only lasted a few days. In fact, I heard my road to Damour had just closed, after we had passed by, two days ago. I was packed and ready to leave. Word was received that our plane would arrive about 10 a.m. The sound of machine guns was always there, and pretty heavy up along the mountains and to the northeast, it was all no-man's land.

As we assembled at the Embassy, there were two vans for us that would be led by a Lebanese Army weapons carrier, one in front, and one to the rear. Most of the soldiers, I was told, were from the PLO. It was hard to believe. The DCM, I can't remember his name, had his French wife and two young daughters would also be going. He asked me to look after them. It was truly sad, saying goodbye to my friends at the Embassy, especially the group of Lebanese who worked there, like Joe Nobar. I loaded the boxes and suitcases, and the procession headed for the airport. The whole route was through Muslim areas. The two little girls didn't appear to be scared, I thought they were great. Their French mother was a lovely young person.

At the terminal, the military handled our baggage. Don said he would see to all the passports and customs. I was well known at the airport and had a pass to go through onto the ramp, so I took off. At the ramp, the orange, white and black Convair sat waiting. Across the field, in the lower hills and up around Alley, where my daughter Hannah was born, machinegun fire was nonstop. At the plane, I met the crew. I could see they were scared; they didn't want to get out. They asked me to get the weather and make out the flight plan. I said negative, and coaxed the pilot to accompany me, since he had to sign the flight plan and the papers. Reluctantly he did. While he made out the flight plan, I raced around and got the weather report. At the same time, I said goodbye to the tower operators and the CAA Operations Department. They were fine guys and my friends, yet they had a strange look about them. They saw their country was being torn apart, as though they were saying, "Well, we'll not meet again."

At the plane, the pilot said he needed more fuel. I'd have thought he'd already done that. No, they couldn't fuel where he was parked. It was necessary to taxi a ways off towards the TMA hangar, which was towards the northern section of the airport. The heavy shooting was not too distant from there. Again, after coaxing, we taxiied to the place we were told to go. With full tanks, we were back at the ramp. Don and the entourage were waiting, with the baggage. He and I loaded everything on board. He asked me if everything went okay. I winked. I suggested that we take off from runaway 18, even though it meant a pretty good crosswind. Be sure to bank hard right after the wheels were off the ground, otherwise, we would be flying low over Khaldi, which was Muslim and no-man's land that I knew so well. It was the same old route to Damour and Meschref.

When he taxiied out to the runway, I thought he would take off right there, he was going like hell. I don't think he even checked the engines. Neither would I, I guess, as I did at Jodhpur with the DC-3, many years before. It was a rolling go. I strained my neck over the left side to take a last look at Meschref and my house. I could just see it for a couple of seconds, and then it was gone. I settled down for our trip to Athens.

As I sat there, thinking of what I was leaving behind, and the poor people, as the distance separated us further from Lebanon, I wondered why they were tearing the country apart, and grinding it into little pieces to be thrown into the sea. I could never understand why.

All was routine and we landed safely at Athens. At the ramp, I asked the crew about going back the next day or that afternoon to pick up a lot of our office material and other classified documents, and perhaps a few more evacuees. The pilot looked back at me in shock and said "No way! This is it!" Now I was shocked. The agreement had been, between Brussels and Beirut, that the FAA

*Hannah at Tinello's Restaurant Rome with the "Three dollar Bill" in the middle, 1976.*

plane would make several trips to Beirut, as long as the Embassy could get stuff to the airport.

Late that afternoon, at the Seaview Hotel on the east side near Athens Airport, the pilot informed us they had engine trouble, we would be there an extra day at least. I thought this over myself, "How come? Both engines operated beautifully all the way." The next morning, I took the little girls for a walk along the sandy beach near the hotel. Their Mum thanked me for the care I was taking of the two girls. I told her I had two of my own in the States, and I missed them very much.

The following day, we landed in Frankfurt. I was greeted by some old friends I hadn't seen in quite awhile. I was given a furnished bachelor's apartment in town, a part of the FAA complex. We would set up office at the Frankfurt FAA office at Rhein-Main Airport and have this as our temporary office till our office at Rome was completed. One good thing about Frankfurt: I would have a chance to see my old German pilot friend from Beirut, the Bremers, and one or two other pilots.

I settled into our makeshift office, and the small apartment. We had use of a couple of G-cars. My next-door friend was another inspector. His name was Leo, with a butch haircut. He was a husky individual, of Polish descent. He was one of the Avionics experts with the Air Inspection Group, and married to a German girl who was now in Atlanta. Also, there was an Ops Inspector, Roy Mount, and his wife and daughter. Roy had given me several proficiency checks in Oklahoma, on the Electra airplane. He was now 727 qualified. These folks helped me try to forget a lot of the past events in Lebanon.

There was a commissary nearby to which we had privileges, and the Army Base PX. I finally contacted the Bremers, and said I'd be there hopefully for Thanksgiving, and that I'd be bringing the traditional turkey and

all the trimmings. The Bremers would furnish the wine.

I had quite a time finding the Bremer place in Wiesbaden. It was a lovely city, the Bremers home was delightful. Inga Bremer had to leave that morning to be with her married daughter, but I insisted that she invite the daughter, Gabby, and her husband and young boy, to Thanksgiving dinner, I would do the cooking. Moritz Bremer had brought his Moselle white wine, right from the winery. He normally would get about 24 large bottles filled up. Moritz showed me where everything was in the kitchen, and I started in that morning to cook. We'd have to sample the Moselle wine, it went down smoothly. By the time the turkey was stuffed and in the oven, we were getting stuffed on the wine, and getting "cooked" ourselves! In fact, we were not feeling too much pain. That wine always sneaks up on you.

I think we had finished a couple of his large bottles, and Moritz was getting a laughing jag on. When it came time to baste the bird, which was a pretty good-sized 18-pounder; the two of us got it out, still sizzling hot. We put the pan up on the marbled sink. Moritz held the pan while I basted it, and then I decided to turn it over. That was a mistake. I got the bird halfway over with a couple of forks, when Moritz, still laughing, let go of the pan. The pan went one way and the turkey the other, with very hot grease everywhere. The bird slid along the linoleum floor and slithered right across and bounced against the wall and spun around. We both went after it, slipping in the grease. Moritz picked it up and dropped it again, shouting something in German. I guess it meant it was hot. I tried picking it up, it slipped out of my fingers and skidded back towards the stove. We were both on our hands and knees, trying to catch this damned thing, like a large, hot, greasy football. We were now hilarious with laughter, trying to snare the turkey. By now, there was more grease on us than on the turkey. About then, Inga walked in and

*Percy and Phylis Sherred in Bhowali, 1971.*

gave a shriek. We froze. Then we got a scolding, finally she had to laugh and joined us. She solved the situation by spearing the turkey with a large fork. Before putting it back in the pan, she gave it a bath in the sink, then started the cooking process once more. I'm not too certain, but I think everyone enjoyed the Thanksgiving turkey, American-style, with a little German accent thrown in. Our clothing had to go to the cleaners the next day.

The holiday ended too soon, and I was back at work. I made another trip to Addis Ababa, despite the unpleasant situation there. The crews were not too talkative, and the American pilots were getting ready to pull out. A very fine and wonderful pilot friend who was with me in Maine when we learned to fly together was one of Haile Selassie's favorite people. He planned to retire shortly. The Emperor had given him an honorary citizenship and any land he wished to buy. But now, it was all down the drain, and the old Emperor was dead. So Willie "Babe" Wilder was getting ready to pull out. At night in the hotel, I could still hear the lions in the nearby zoo roaring their disapproval. They were Selassie's pet animals; he called himself "The Lion of Judah." He also stated that he was the descendant of the Queen of Sheba. History has it that the Queen and her entourage sailed across the Red Sea, presumably somewhere near Jeddah, to visit King Solomon, where he promptly knocked her up. She returned to Ethiopia and happily gave birth to Solomon's baby. Yet, Christianity was not to be a part of Ethiopia till around the 4th century A.D., the same time that the Roman Empire, under Constantine, had accepted Christianity. Their proof of Christianity are large, sunken, grotto-stone churches, carved from rock, rooted to the same rock formation. These giant monolithic churches are also wonders of the world, as the Tombs at Petra.

With close coordination from our Embassy, I conducted my work with Ethiopian Airlines. When it was necessary for a Flight

Engineer flight check, usually to Rome and back, it was tricky, because once in the cockpit, I could not leave. The Ethiopian Airlines had the best hard-core security, second to none. Their air guards were military. Their orders were "shoot and kill anyone entering or leaving the cockpit that was not recognized as a crewmember," who usually had to be in uniform, and I was not. Therefore, I was happy to stay put. Crewmembers would tell the guards who I was, and my job function. They would nod, but no smile. This belligerent toughness came about a couple of years earlier, when war was going on between Ethiopia and the attempt to break away of Eriteria, in the northern section of Ethiopia, which was all Muslim. They wanted to have an independent country. Three Eriterians, I believe, tried to hijack an EAL 707. The guards pounced on the hijackers, capturing all three. Their authority of air piracy was final. The three attackers were strapped into the first-class seats with blankets around them. The guards then cut their throats. I guess that's what you call "going first-class!" There had never been another attempt since.

On my last check I deplaned in Rome and came back to Frankfurt. I received a letter from my friend, Percy Sherred. His wife, Phyllis, had died of cancer. He would be in England that winter.

As Christmas rolled around, I took my vacation and went to India anyway. It was always good to break away from this work, and the fighting in Lebanon, to relax in the Himalayas. I would not be in Bhowali this trip. instead, I spent Christmas with my Sikh friends, then took an Air Nepal flight to Kathmandu for a few days. I went to see my old friend, Boris Lissanevitch, the "son-of-a-bitch!" as we called him, and his wife, Inga. They had the famous restaurant, "Yak and Yeti." Boris happened to be away in Europe buying kitchen equipment. I did meet his wife and the two grown-up boys and had lunch, at their restaurant. She brought me up to date with their lives, as I did with mine. It was a great meeting, and yet a little sad because we all missed the wonderful days in Calcutta.

I toured Kathmandu and took loads of pictures. Sometime during the stay, I became violently ill with fever, vomiting and diarrhea, all at the same time. I didn't know which end to put on the pot first. My diet was strictly hot black tea and tangerine oranges. These are the only oranges you get in India. I came to see Nepal, and this was not going to stop me. I didn't even see a doctor.

I arranged for a driver and a car that would take me from the hotel all the way to Pokhara, about 100 miles west of Kathmandu and further down in the valley. The tar road is mostly downhill, and following a river. The scenery was spectacular. In spite of my fever and having to stop to go to the toilet, I'd take pictures. Here and there in a village I would get a cup of black tea.

I checked in at the Crystal Hotel, where there were not many tourists. I noticed only one group of Japanese. They're everywhere.

My driver gave me a tour the next afternoon, of the old sleepy town. Pokhara mainly was a trading area. The town, was picturesque, like a well kept garden. Most prominent of the plants were the poinsettia all in bloom with their red leafy flowers. The town itself was nestled at the base of the mountain range known as Annapurna and another spectacular peak called Machhapuchhare, which means fishtail. The peak rises to about 23,000 feet. Looking up at these snow-covered peaks, which always seem to be in the backyard of Pokhara, I felt dwarfed. The fishtail has been one of the most difficult mountains to climb.

I was feeling miserable by the time I returned to the hotel. I said to myself I would continue sightseeing regardless. I did want to take a small trek around to the base of the mountain, but thought I would never make it. I had a bowl of hot soup and toast and was able to keep it down. I took a couple of aspirin, and told the bearer I didn't want to be disturbed till dinner. The manager said there would be a special New Year's Eve dinner, but I felt I would not make it. I slept like a log, till I was awakened for dinner. I showed up but knew I couldn't join in. I had a large quart bottle of J&B Scotch, which I was hoping to enjoy. It would be great for this occasion.

I came down the stairs and found the party would be outdoors, under the stars, and the silhouette of the great peaks. Some guests were already seated. At one corner were the group of Japanese, who were enjoying themselves. The J&B Scotch was with me in a paper bag, but no way could I indulge. With a deep sigh, I took the bottle over to the Japanese table and plunked it down in their midst. "Happy New Year," I said. They all looked at the whiskey, and then at me. One said, "This scotch?" I said, "Yes." This item, I might add, is hard to come by in India, and in Nepal. The real thing, and if you could find it in the black market, it would at least be about $100. They asked me to join them and enjoy their party. I said I would like that, but for now, I was terribly sick and just couldn't do it. I said, "Just enjoy your 1976." I returned to my room and ordered another bowl of soup with one aspirin and then I turned in. I was awake at 6 a.m. I opened the shutters of the window. The sight was a fantastic surprise. There stood the fishtail mountain; the sun hadn't lassoed the peak as yet. I was feeling a little better, I had my black tea and a couple of oranges. The manager was concerned, and said he'd arrange a doctor. I said, "Later."

The morning air was cool and refreshing. I didn't have to walk far before I was able to take some great pictures of the snow peaks, that almost seemed to fall into the valley. The driver came by, and we toured around the little village of Pokhara. I had my soup for lunch and checked out and back to Kathmandu. I did see a doctor there, but he didn't give me anything special. Yes, I had a fever that wouldn't shake off. I took it easy for a couple of days, then headed for the airport and departed to Delhi on Nepal Airlines.

There were a lot of tourists on the flight, mainly Italian and French. One French couple with three kids got my attention. The guy had bought an Indian sitar, a stringed instrument about 4 feet long. One of the kids was a baby in the crawling stage. They sat two seats in front of me on the 727. The two older ones kept peering over the backs of their seats and stared at me. I was too groggy to make faces at them. The little one kept up an incessant yowling, driving me and the other passengers crazy. Some of the French were kidding these folks. They were oblivious to the din. Finally, at Delhi, I thought that was the end of it. We'd all had to queue up for the immigration. The French family with the sitar were just behind, the guy kept swinging the damned instrument around and banging me on the head. He'd apologize, but kept swinging. I finally moved aside and let this group get ahead of me while they yelled at each other. One asked the sitar fellow where they were going to stay. He said the Imperial Hotel. That was fine by me; I'd be at the good old Ashoka Hotel.

I hurried through Customs. They knew me as the American Hindu-speaking individual. I hopped a cab to the hotel, and after checking in, I told the manager, whom I also knew, that I was sick and probably would need a doctor a little later. First, I was in need of some more good special soup that I knew was very good at their restaurant, and go to bed. It was about 1:30 p.m. The boy took my bags to the room and said he'd bring me the key. The headwaiter greeted me like an old lost friend. "Give me a table," I said, "where no one else would be near me." I wanted a quiet place. "Look," he said, "no one else is in the dining room." True, I was the only one. He escorted me to a table against the wall. "Just a plain nice big bowl of soup, please." The waiter took off. I closed my eyes for a few minutes. Then in the distance, I heard a noise and the chatter of children. Then I heard French being spoken. Oh, God, no! Not again! This can't be true! But sure enough, the first thing coming around the corner into the dining room was the damned sitar, followed by the French family. Wouldn't you know, they were placed right next to me. At the same time, here came my soup. The Frenchman greeted me with a nod of his head, and indicated to my head. I smiled, and acknowledged that he had banged me there with the big Indian banjo. They settled down to study the menu while I started in on my soup. The crawling baby just crawled along the long seat between us. It was yowling, and trying to stand up and stick its fingers into the electric wiring that was for indirect lighting. I was hoping it would give itself a shock, and perhaps they would leave the place in a hurry.

The soup tasted good; in spite of the unwelcome guests, I was relaxed. The waiter asked if I'd have something else. I explained how sick I was, at both ends. He sympathized and said I should now try a bowl of very cold caramel custard. This will settle the stomach. I knew they made it well there. I said, "Okay, we'll give it a try." He raced off like

*Hannah in cottage, Sat-Tal where my family had Christmas picnic in 1925. This picture taken in 1977.*

a good doctor; in no time, the dish was placed in front of me. The baby still yowled and crawled. I watched it from the corner of my eye. No sparks, or its hair would be sticking straight up. However, as I was about to take a good spoonful of the custard, the baby crapped right there on the cushions. The mess oozed out of the small diaper, and the smell permeated the air. Without any to-do, the mother took off its icky diaper and wiped its pink ass and then put on a new nappy.

By this time, I had looked at the diaper mess and at my caramel custard, and I almost upchucked. I called the waiter and explained in detail how it felt, because of the sight. He tried not to laugh, but for me to explain it all in Hindi, he almost doubled over. I apologized for not being able to sit there any longer and finish the pudding. I made a hasty retreat to my room.

The hotel doctor came by that evening. My temperature had risen to a little over 101 degrees. He gave me some powder in a packet, which he mixed with water that I had in a thermos. He thought it might be a slight case of typhoid fever. The symptoms were there. I was to take the powder twice a day. The next morning, I called the Embassy and asked if they would send a message to the FAA in Frankfurt that I was sick and was requesting sick leave, and would return in a few days.

The doctor visited me a few more times, the cost was about $1.70 each visit. When I had more strength in my legs and less dizziness in my head, I caught PanAm Flight 02, off to Karachi. PanOps called to say that if FAA Goutiere was on board, he must get off at Istanbul to investigate an Overseas National Airlines DC-10 that had crashed on the runway with a little over 250 Hajiis on board. I told Pan Ops to relay to the FAA that I was unable to do so because of sickness.

At Istanbul, I saw the wreck, but never left the cockpit. Back in Frankfurt, I went to

the military doctor. He gave me what he called "bung-stoppers." It was for diarrhea. It was more or less gone, since I wasn't eating anything. I guess I lost about 10-15 pounds on that adventure.

When my slides from the trip were mailed back to me from Kodak, I was elated to see how well they had turned out. I received a telegram from my sister Geraldine that her husband, Fred, had passed away, and could I make it to the funeral? It was not possible, having just returned from Nepal. Instead, I telephoned her. I also called Hannah and Christian.

The war in Lebanon had reached a high pitch of hysteria; thousands of people on both sides were being killed. I heard that some of my friends at the airport had been killed. Early in January, the Muslims, led by a fanatic by the name of Jumblat, had destroyed the Delamayah Country Club, and overrun our community at Meschref. They had overrun and destroyed the town of Damour, killing thousands of civilians, a lot of whom were my friends. Some tried to escape and were killed in doing so. Word was also received from Bob Mason, through the Embassy, that my car had been blown up with the Embassy man who was to purchase it. My villa had been ransacked. I had asked the Embassy to try and salvage my things. They informed me they couldn't get there.

I told Don I would return to Beirut at my own risk. He said, "Don't talk to me about your plans. I don't know where you are," which was good enough for me. I caught Trans-Mediterranean Airlines (TMA) cargo flight from Frankfurt, and guess who was flying the airplane? That's right, it was my friend, Ray Gifford. It was evening when we were airborne. I sat in the jumpseat to chat. Ray said my house was okay, but the terrorists had raised hell with the furniture. They were using the place as a stronghold against the Christians in Damour. Ray said

*Rear view of Taj Mahal taken at dawn, 1976.*

he had been able to rescue a few items. The car, he said, had gone. He didn't know about my girl Renee,

It was night as we approached Beirut. We could see sporadic flares and flashes of gunfire. I told Ray he'd better switch off the Nav. lights. "It's okay; we will be over BOD, then fly down the coast to land on runway 18." As we passed the station on descent, with the city on the left, a rocket came flashing right under us. I didn't have to say more. Ray hit the switches and looked at me, and turned them on when we were coming over the threshold of the runway.

We taxiied to the TMA cargo area. Here, a crew car picked us up and took us into the main terminal, and what there was of the immigration staff. It was maintained by the military, which one, I didn't know. Ray introduced me to the colonel in charge, who spoke good English. He suggested we spend the night there and leave in the morning for Ray's house at Meschref. The colonel stated there was a lull in the shooting down south; that Jumblat had control of the whole place. Ray insisted that we go on that same night. I was scared, and tried not to admit it. He got his little Honda Civic, and the colonel said it would be necessary to drive across the airport to a service road, and then down a slight hill to the main road at Khaldi. He would escort us to the service road; then we were on our own.

The colonel led off in a jeep, with another soldier. Before we got going, Ray reached into his flight bag and pulled out a fifth of scotch. "Here," he said; "have a swig. It'll give you courage." We both had a lengthy pull on the bottle and followed the jeep to the service road on the right and down the hill with clumps of tall, bamboo-like reeds, or elephant grass. They were thick and blocked the vision of the main road. The jeep finally came to a cut in the reeds and stopped. At the same time, about 15 or 20 masked people with rifles jumped out from nowhere

and surrounded the jeep, some ran at us. I was about to crap; I'm sure Ray was too. He said, "Oh, shit!" I think we said it together. At this time, we saw the colonel hop out and clasp hands with the leader of the group. He then came over to us. As we got out he said, "Don't be afraid; they are my people, guarding the road." They said the road to Damour was okay, no shooting reported. We thanked the colonel for his help; the guards just evaporated into the darkness.

Ray and I had another couple of swigs from the bottle, then started through the two-tracks in the reeds to the main road. I was expecting to see masked figures jump out at us at any moment. Ray had on his lights and flashers. We hit the main road, the same one that I had traveled often. Ray started doing something odd: he would race along, then slow up, go fast, and then slow. I said, "What the hell are you doing, Ray?" He said, "Well, if the buggers are aiming at us, this fast and slow will make it difficult for them to get a sight on us." He giggled, and we had another pull on the bottle. I was feeling pretty good, no pain. Damour, what little I could see, was deserted. Ray said it was all bombed out. My Total Gas Station was black and ghost like. We pulled up at Ray's house, which was dark. We entered through the kitchen and turned on the lights. His wife, Annie, came in, in her kimono. "What the hell are you doing here at this time of night?" she demanded. "You're not supposed to be on the road at night; damn you Ray Gifford!" I reached over and gave her a big hug and kiss. I said it was my fault. "I only have a few days, so Ray rushed me here." "I know you, too, Pete Goutiere!" she laughed, and then we all had a few more drinks.

The bottle was finished and they gave me a cot in a spare room where I fell asleep. When I awoke, Ray came in and said Annie had tea ready for us. It was a beautiful winter morning, cold and clear. After a good hearty breakfast, Ray and I went up to my house. The walls had Arabic writings all over

them; graffiti, I guess, possibly calling me all sorts of dirty names. My butterflies had been taken out of their frames and crumpled up like cornflakes. My bed and mattress had been shoved up against a window as a shield. There were large, muddy footprints on the mattress; they looked like moon-boot prints. A lot of furniture had been dragged out on the lawn and ripped apart with a knife. I told Ray I still would not let them have it.

After lunch, Ray drove me to the Embassy. The roads were open, and the only shooting was up in the hills, to our right. The security at the Embassy were teed off at me for coming in like this. I said I'd repeatedly asked to have my things shipped out and no one would do so. "There was no problem with the road to Meschref." The security disagreed and said they would report my disobedience. I then saw the DCM, whose kids and wife I had looked after when we evacuated last November. He greeted me and said he would attend to everything, not to worry. I thanked him, and then made the rounds and greeted my friends. I saw Joe, who was still holding the fort as our FAA Rep in Beirut. In spite of his problems, he was jolly and happy to be with the FAA still. I said I would try and get him to Rome on TDY, to help set up our filing system.

Ray then dropped me off at Bob Mason's place. He was okay and made out a true statement that my Dodge car had been blown up. I could not get any word on Renee. He said the rumor was that the terrorists had killed her because she was a girlfriend of a Christian American. I couldn't believe that. Bob then drove me out to Meschref that afternoon where I made an inventory of my things. The stove and refrigerator were perfect, but all the booze I'd stacked up had been destroyed. I stopped in to see George Debbas. He was looking pale and haggard. I saw Cheetah who was still there. We had a drink with George. I suggested that he get out of Meschref. He told me that his family were all-right. He had talked to Jumblat, who had put bodyguards around the estate and a couple for Debbas. He said, "No problem now."

In Beirut, I got a room at the Carlton Hotel overlooking the sea. I remember when it was being built, many years ago. I drove around my old building, where Christian and Hannah had been babies. It was surrounded by other buildings. Most of the structures were pockmarked with bullet holes. I took my list to the Embassy, and they promised to have my things flown out on TMA or Air France, who were still operating. Bob took me to the airport and I hopped on TMA back to Frankfurt.

I talked to Don the next day at the office and told him about what I had seen in Beirut. He shook his head. He said, "What goes on, anyway? They're just destroying themselves." He said he didn't want to go back to Lebanon again; he'd like to remember it the way it was. I agreed.

It was now February, and I had made several excursions to my flying clubs in the Middle East. On my return from one of these,

I had just unpacked my suitcase when there was a knock on my door. When I opened it, there stood my friend, Leo. He looked drawn, and his eyes were bleary. I welcomed him in. We sat for a few minutes and I offered him a drink. He just shook his head. I said, "Is something wrong?" "Yeah; I'm not too sure. Pete. What's the definition of a ferry flight?" I said, "That's when an airplane has been authorized to fly from point A to B, usually to home base for repairs. The plane must carry only the minimum crew and go the most direct route. Why?" "Well, the FAA is ferrying the Sabreliner, one of our flight inspection ones, back to Oklahoma." I said, "So?" He said, "The one they're planning to take has been sitting out at the ramp for over two months, and it's unfit to fly. The rust is getting to it; the fuel tanks leak; it's a plain mess!" I said, "Well, Leo, they probably want to take it back to Oklahoma for repairs, and that's why they're making it a ferry flight. What's the problem?" It should go via London and North Atlantic and Gander to Oklahoma. Leo stated "There won't be a minimum crew, because I have to go along. They plan to fly it via Dakar, West Africa, then to Ascension Island, Recife, Brazil, Panama, and then on to Oklahoma. At each of these places, they will conduct flight inspections. That's why I'm supposed to go along." "Then it's not really a ferry flight, per se. The ferry flight, as I've explained, is when a plane such as 707 or the likes is being taken because one engine is inoperative, or the gears stuck down and will not work, there's no hydraulic fluid, or some mechanical defect, so there would be minimum crew and a direct routing. This sounds like a type of ferry without any emergency." "No, Pete," he said. "This plane is not fit to fly on such a long haul. Now I've told you the problem; this thing will never make it; it will crash for sure!" "Leo, if you think it's that bad, tell the FAA Manager you won't go, because of safety." "Negative. He's okaying it, as well as Brussels."

I said, "The headman from Brussels will be here tomorrow morning, Saturday. He plans to discuss our new office in Rome. I'll talk to him if you like." "No, it won't do, Pete. I know I have to go, and that's that." I said, "Leo, you're crazy to go, if you feel nervous about such a flight. Let someone else go in your place." "There is no one else; it's me, and I'll have to do the avionics work." "Leo, I don't think the FAA would dare take a plane on such a long, roundabout way, if they thought it unsafe. Come on, have a drink, and let's cheer each other up." He agreed. I think he had a stiff bourbon, and I had my usual scotch.

After the drink, he looked me in the eye. He said, "Pete, I want you to do me a great favor." "Sure." He then reached in his jacket and pulled out a sealed envelope. He said, "Please mail this to my wife after I leave tomorrow. It's my last will and testament." "What!?" I almost jumped out of my seat. "Leo, you've got to be crazy. If that's the way you feel, cancel out now! Hell, I'll vouch for you. I'll tell the Brussels chief when he

arrives tomorrow that you're unfit to go on this flight." "Nope," he said, "Pete, I'm sorry; I have no way out." "What can they do to you, if you say no? Nothing!" I was now angry at Leo, but he would have it no other way.

"Let's have another drink; one for the road." I tried to steer his mind clear. "Okay, one more, then I must get some rest; it's a long way to Dakar. But don't forget to mail the letter." No persuasion could alter his decision. Leo left after the drink.

After he'd gone, I pondered his decision, and the new will he'd made for his wife. Did he have some other feeling about the trip, besides the plane being unworthy? I decided to see Don Burlingame first thing in the morning.

I was up early Saturday and raced over to Don with the letter. "Don, I want to discuss a matter with you. It concerns Leo. This letter he's given me is his last will and testament to his wife. He thinks the flight he is going on will not make it." Don said, "He's stupid to go, if that's the way he feels. If he wants to go, that's it." "Rightly so, but this so-called ferry flight: is it legal?" "Probably not a true ferry flight, since all components are working."

I had some coffee with Don, and decided not to pursue the matter any further. Leo's flight left around 9 a.m. Don had his meeting with Brussels people, when they arrived in their Cessna Citation. On Monday, I went down to the APO and sent Leo's letter off, without delay.

Soon after, I took a flight to Rome, to see how the new office was shaping up. I met a Civil Air Attache fellow who was once in Beirut, Lenny Dwor. The office space was a part of the Ambassador Hotel, right across the street from the Embassy. Some of the Embassy offices, such as the Aid program, were also located there. The office that we had looked good. I think each office had a bathroom and shower; you couldn't beat that! Len took me to a place where he said we

could stay. In fact, he was staying there himself. It was called the Aldrovani. They were efficiency apartments, one or two bedrooms. The place was also within walking distance of the office, across a beautiful park, known as Borghese Park. I thought this would be great.

I reported back to Don, and said our offices would be all set in a few days. The next morning at work, Don came in from the front office of the FAA. He was looking glum. He said, "It's about Leo...he's dead." I said, "Oh, my God, no!" He said, "Yeah. The plane crashed in the South Atlantic. He was the only one killed." I sat dumbfounded. "Son-of-a-bitch! Leo was right all along! Does anybody know what happened?" "They have a message up front." I returned with Don to the front office. Everyone was quiet. I read the message. All it said was the flight had left Ascension Island for Recife, they had run out of fuel and ditched about 100 miles short of the destination. The crew were picked up by the Brazilian Navy. Leo was the only casualty. I still couldn't believe it. Leo had some premonition that something would go wrong. I then mentioned to Don that I guessed his wife must have received the letter and the will by then. She could sue the FAA for any amount of money she asked.

A week later, an investigation team arrived from Washington and interrogated me. I told them all that I knew about the conversation, and how I tried to dissuade Leo from going, also the letter and the will which I had mailed. That was it. I later heard that a settlement had been made, out of court. Poor old Leo! Rest in Peace, friend.

The FAA Flight Inspection Convair 340, the same one that flew us and our belongings from Beirut to Frankfurt, was now taking us from Frankfurt to Rome. It was about the end of March '76. We arrived at Fiumicino Airport, Len Dwor and an Embassy station wagon met the flight, then drove us to our apartments at Aldrovani. Spring had arrived, and all the deciduous

*Camels crossing Jumna River at back of Taj Mahal, 1976.*

*Trisul Mountain taken from Ranikhet, Himalayas, India, 1976.*

trees had their new leaves, as well as all the flowers and cherry blossoms in full bloom.

The Embassy wagons had taken all the office material to our new office. When I was in Frankfurt, I had bought a stereo system at the PX. I was anxious to have it set up. I'd never had one like this before; only the Magnavox, that I hoped Ray Gifford now had. There was a lot to be done in setting up the office. We had to obtain Embassy passes, and drivers licenses. Our new G-car had to be diverted from its Beirut destination to the new one in Rome. We had been at our new offices about one week when on a Sunday morning I heard an explosion very early. I knew an explosion when I heard one. A few minutes later, there was a rap on my door, about 7 a.m. it was Len Dwor. "Christ!" he said. He was all bug-eyed. "What's going on?" "Somebody has bombed the Embassy! I just told Don, and he said to wake you. We're going over to see what's happening."

Len had a large, fire-engine red Buick convertible. We all hopped in and drove to the Embassy. There was a lot of activity with the Marines at the gate and several Italian police and military cars with the blue lights flashing. Len and Don asked a Marine close by what had happened. He looked at us and said, "You guys are FAA, aren't you?" We said "Yeah." "Well, somebody bombed the hell out of your office, early this morning." "Oh, shit!" We raced across Via Veneto and around the corner, and sure enough, the side of the building was blackened, plate glass windows smashed. Being a Sunday morning, there was not much traffic or pedestrians, but a crowd had gathered. We entered the building and went to our offices. Len had his adjacent to ours. The place was a mess, mainly broken glass. Don looked at me and said, "I guess Gadafi is still after you, Pete!" That broke the ice, and we had to laugh. Evidently, it had been a nuisance bomb by the leftist Italian Red Brigade, or whatever they called themselves.

"Let's go have some cappucino coffee." We walked to the Via Veneto and sat out-

216

doors and sipped our brew. It would be a few days before the Embassy maintenance people, mainly Italian folks, could get everything cleaned up and new glass windows installed.

I talked to Don about getting Joe over on TDY to set up our files. Up to now we didn't have a regular secretary. There was a strange gal assigned to us; I believe she was Hungarian or Yugoslav. She claimed to be from royalty and called herself "Contessa." She couldn't type worth a damn, but could speak Italian. This was good, since a lot of phone calls were in Italian.

Brussels finally agreed to let us have old Joe come over on TDY, until they could get a secretary named Barbara to come from the Frankfurt office. It would be awhile before they could arrange a permanent girl through the bid system. I greeted Joe at the airport when he arrived. He gave me a Lebanese magazine; it was all in Arabic. There were photos of George Debbas and his family. Joe said some terrorists had shown up at George's house one day, killing him and Cheetah. "Those sons-of-bitches!" I muttered.

Joe fit in well; we were happy to have him. He worked diligently as always, and had our files in good shape. I was sad to see him leave again. I know he didn't want to go, but he had his family back in Lebanon.

Don's household effects had arrived, and were stored at the Coliseum Shipping Company, but there was no news of mine.

On weekends and holidays I walked all over Rome. I got to know the streets well. One of the Italian maintenance people from the Embassy was a buff on radios. He had been in communications for the Italian Army in World War II, based in North Africa. I talked him into helping me put my stereo system together. He came over after work and helped me set it up. It took about an hour before he had everything hooked up. I played my first record and the sound effects were great. Even my friend thought I'd made a good choice. We became good friends after

that. I took him and his wife to Italian restaurants that they knew; in this way, I would know the restaurants, away from tourists. There was one restaurant, however, that I hesitated to visit. It was one near the Boston Hotel, where I had taken Margaret a couple of times, when we met in Rome back in 1955. It was called Tinello's.

Curiosity got the better of me one evening and I decided to pay the restaurant a visit. It was located around the corner from the hotel, in a basement. I walked down the stairs, and was greeted by a waiter who welcomed me. I took a table just about where we had sat before. I was early, as Italians don't dine until around 8 or 9 p.m. I recognized the place immediately. Then I looked at the tables and the ashtrays. The ones they had then were rather flat, and made of copper, with their name. Margaret and I had snitched one; she still had it. The food and wine was excellent. A guitar player came in and sang a couple of songs for the guests. He was joined by a couple more. They did very well. One of the guys appeared a bit odd, and sang tenor; another played the accordion.

When I was leaving, I went to the person managing the bar. I asked if he was here in '55. "No," he said; it had changed hands. He now operated the place. I said I'd be back again, but not as a tourist.

Around July, I received a cable from Margaret to please come to Fairfield, Connecticut. Hannah had run away, and there was no sign of her for two weeks. Don gave me leave, and I went to Fairfield. By then, she had returned. I talked with Hannah. She said she couldn't live with her stepfather, that he was a bastard. She had run off with a dropout boy and he had stolen a car from his sister, and crashed into a tree. Luckily, they had not been hurt, they'd hidden in barns and haystacks to avoid the police. The boy returned to his home. I talked with Hannah for two days.

Don, who was one swell guy, the type like Bill Huebner, asked me if I would get him an exhaust system and muffler for his Camaro, sometime while I was doing my recurrent training in Oklahoma, and try and bring it back. I said I would. I told Margaret I would take Hannah with me to Oklahoma and back to Rome.

On the way to Oklahoma we stopped at Joplin, and I paid my respects to the doctor's wife, the widow of the pilot who crashed in Pakistan in 1974. Hannah was herself again and happy to be with me. I wish I could have had Christian, too, but he was doing well in school, so I let him be. I hoped that Hannah would be happy in Rome. She said she would behave herself.

We did buy an exhaust system for Don, and hauled it all the way back for which he was grateful. In Rome I was able to buy an Italian Fiat from one of the Embassy people who was returning to the States and it still sported diplomatic plates. I was able to drive all over the countryside and show Hannah the sights. I took her out in the country and taught her how to drive the Fiat, which had a stick shift. I had moved into a new apartment about thirty minutes from the office. It was just before Christmas of '76.

We had driven a lot, and weather had turned lousy with sleet and snow. I was up early in the morning to go to work, lo and behold, no car! I checked around where I had parked it just outside the apartment. All I found was some broken glass, and the ignition switch. I called Don and told him the car had been stolen, to please pick me up. At the Embassy I reported the theft. The car still had those diplomatic plates in my name, but once again I was without wheels. The insurance was taking their time about paying me.

It was about this same time that our new secretary arrived, a blonde bombshell. Don was at the airport to meet her, while I set up a party at the apartment. I had everything going when Don showed up with the secretary. It didn't take long to get in the swing. Len Dwor and his wife, with their little silky dogs, were doing fine until our new secretary, MaryAnne, was watching Len feed the little dogs chicken bones. She piped up and said not to feed the dogs chicken bones. Len said, "It's okay; we give them bones all the time." MaryAnne said, "Well, if you don't care about your mutts dying, that's fine." That did it! Len, who worshipped his pets, was highly insulted by her calling his dogs "mutts." He wanted an apology. I think we were all in rather a drunken stupor. They left. I thought Mary Anne was terrific.

Next weekend, I took MaryAnne and Hannah on a trip to the Isle of Capri. The weather was not the greatest. We were on board a hydrofoil boat with several Japanese passengers. The sea was rough; halfway there, the Japanese were getting sick. Then we saw a couple of them swinging on the overhead rails; they looked like chimpanzees swinging in the zoo! Usually I get seasick, but because of the fun the Japs were having, and us watching, I forgot all about it.

Capri was all it was cracked up to be, even in the winter time when there were very few tourists. At one winery, we ran into an Englishman, who still wore his khaki shorts. He joined the three of us, with an eye on MaryAnne. The four of us tried to drink the island dry. In conversation, the Englishman asked where we were from and Hannah said, "Connecticut." He said "Where in Connecticut," and Hannah said, "Fairfield." "Goodness me," he said; "I have a son going to Fairfield University." "Yeah? We know the place well." He rattled off about the place and the college; it was fantastic. We whooped it up some more.

Time for dinner: the Englishman suggested a particular spot where the food was wonderful and cheap. It was a great weekend, hangover and all. Hannah was learning there was a good side to life and thought Capri was great.

In Rome, Hannah stayed in the apartment most of the time. Christian arrived for his Christmas holidays; it was wonderful to have both of them with me! I had a rented car, and for a quickie trip, I was able to take Christian and Hannah to Pisa and see the

*With Christian and Hannah on the way to Sat-Tal. Bhim-Tal in the distance, 1977.*

Leaning Tower, then on to Florence and visit the wonderful historic sites. No sooner were we back than I had arranged a trip to India. It was PanAm to Istanbul, to catch flight 01 to Delhi where Joginder Singh greeted us. I had also hoped to meet my inspector friend Roy Mount's daughter, D'Anne Mount from Frankfurt. She finally showed up with her boyfriend.

Of all my trips to India, this was the most exciting one because I had Christian and Hannah with me. We did our sight seeing in Delhi and to the Taj Mahal. I was taking pictures like crazy. After buying so many nice groceries at the Embassy Commissary, this would be a special for Percy Sherred for Christmas. He had married an old friend, Ruth, who was the Principal at Wellesly College in Naini-Tal, where my mother once taught.

Early in the morning, we were on our way. Hannah brought along a tape recorder for the strange sounds of India. We made it right to the Sherreds at Sultan Nagri. They were excited to see us, and improvised beds for all five. We would spend Christmas with them, before journeying to Ranikat. Percy decided that we should have a Christmas tree. He got his man, Mohan to cut a huge section off a lemon tree, with a lot of yellow lemons still on it. I had brought a lot of decorations from the Embassy. In one box, I had a dozen colored silk-wrap balls for the tree. The kids were all busy fixing up the tree with Percy and Ruth. All of a sudden, when Ruth got hold of the box of these colored balls, she turned to Percy and said, in a clear, loud, English voice, "Percy, why don't we hang Peter's balls right here on the wall?" Needless to say, the kids stifled laughter and ran out of the room. Percy tried to be nonchalant, as well as myself. Ruth was oblivious of anything. It took awhile before the young people could control themselves. Everytime they looked at me, they started to laugh; or even at the colored silk balls that were hanging on the tree.

The home looked very Christmasy. The presents were stacked under the tree. Christmas Eve dinner was something else! For the occasion we had Stateside turkey and Christmas music supplied by Hannah's portable cassette. Christmas morning, after the presents were sorted out, Christian, Hannah, D'Anne, her boyfriend and myself took a long walk along an old jungle trail, then up a slight sloping mountain, at the top of which was a Hindu temple, to worship their deity and their special monkey god. There were about 40 natives present. We were invited to sit at the ritual as long as we had our shoes off, and be very quiet. It was very interesting. I know the kids enjoyed it.

On our return to the bungalow, Percy and Ruth had arranged a picnic luncheon out in the front yard. It was delightful, with all the poinsettia around us. That evening, I had arranged for a maichan (platform) to be placed on a wild plum tree out in Percy's guava orchard. I gave D'Anne's boyfriend the rifle, they were to shoot only at wild boar, if they arrived. This shoot that I had arranged, however, was just to show them the jungle life and there would be a big full moon.

They waited for wild boar, there were a lot in the jungle and raised havoc with the farmers' crops. I stayed at the bungalow with Percy. The wild boar evidently arrived right under the tree, a few shots were fired, but no hits. I was happy that Christian and Hannah were able to sit in a maichan in the Indian jungle.

It had been cold that night, near freezing. There was a hint of frost on the grass and poinsettia. We had an early breakfast on the 26th; then took our leave of the Sherreds and headed for Ranikhet. It would be a long, beautiful ride.

The drive took us through Haldwani, and then on to Kaladungi, where Corbett once lived. His house was now a museum, and showplace. It was closed because it was off-season. We finally came to the town of Ramnagar, where the Ramgunga River flows

*Christian and Hannah at Agra, 1977.*

through. It is also the terminus of the narrow-gauge railroad, the same type as in Kathgodam, that I've mentioned so many times before.

We stopped for tea. The next stop was at Corbett Park. The drive through showed it to be real tiger country. However, we did not spend the night. There were a few herd of sambur deer, and loads of wild boar. The road up to Ranikhet is one familiar to me and I hoped the kids would enjoy the scenery. I took pictures all over again.

It was cold and dark by the time we arrived at the Westview Hotel. The old manager, Mandpal, was still there, and so were the servants and the cook. The rooms were fixed up and heated by the big fires. Hannah drank beer while the rest of us had scotch. It would be up early in the morning I told them that we'd have to walk to the forest officer's bungalow to see the early morning sunrise on the snows. They were up, and had our walk. Once we were there, they had to admit it was beautiful.

We returned and had a good breakfast, but didn't stick around long. We were off again to hike along the main footpaths. Many birds were around, such as the golden-backed woodpeckers and the long-tailed bluejays. The kids were intrigued by the little Hindu temple that had many many Hindu bells and chimes hanging in festoons all around the courtyard.

The third day, we set off for Naini-Tal. I showed the kids where Geraldine, Doris and I hiked down the mountain, back in 1927, and where we had stopped at a hut that was occupied. I said there had been a report of a man-eating tiger in the area. We sat near the hut as I told them the story of our hike of 1927, I mentioned, the book of the Maneaters of Kamaon, and the tiger. That Major Corbett had come to Philander Smith College, (PSC), and the other schools giving warnings that there was a maneater in our vicinity. The tiger had been nicknamed "The Bachelor of Powalgarh." In fact, I told my little group that we had just driven by the village, between Kaladungi and Ramnagar on the way to Ranikhet. Where we sat was only about 15 miles away from that town. "The Bachelor" had rampaged throughout Powalgarh and the surrounding countryside for at least a 20-mile radius, from 1920 to 1930. Up to that

time, the tiger had killed at least 200 people. When I finished the story, I said it was with great delight, back in 1927, when we started walking along this very road, when the four of us saw the watchman that the Shepherds had sent to find us. Christian and Hannah and my two young friends enjoyed hearing the stories I told of myself when I was a kid in Kumaon from a baby until almost 14.

Instead of stopping at Bhowali this time, Juginder took us straight to Naini-Tal. The kids were enthralled with the scenes they saw, when we rounded the last uphill turn into Naini Tal Mall. Without any exception, the shimmering blue lake with the willow trees around the shore, the towering Cheena Peak at the far end, was beautiful. Pictures and more pictures were taken. Juginder drove the car to the Swiss Hotel. I made my group walk about a lengthy mile. This was to show them the places of interest where I walked and played as a kid.

I showed them the church where Christine and Robert were married in 1923. The church was not in use now; it was boarded up. Before walking all the way through to Mali-Tal Bazaar, the last stretch to the hotel, I took them onto the Flats, the playground that was caused by that terrible landslide in 1880. The old Hindu temple was still there. We stopped at the Yacht club and I showed them the pictures that were taken right after the landslide. I was enjoying myself as much as they were, showing Christian and Hannah all these sights. I knew one day I'd bring Christian and Hannah to see all these sights, and here we were.

We checked in at the hotel, and I met the owner whom I had got to know when I first arrived with Geraldine in '69. The staff couldn't do enough to make us comfortable. Fires were lit in the fireplaces to warm up the rooms. Being the off season, as was Ranikhet, we were about the only visitors. Needless to say, little time was spent lounging around.

I arranged ponies for a trip up the hill to PSC. I showed where my dormitory once was, approximately where I had slept; the old covered passageway down to the classrooms and playground. I pointed out the other schools, across the lake, such as St. Joseph's College, Wellesly College, and Sherwood, and Government House. We then walked behind the school to look at a scene of the snowcapped Himalayas. There was the old oak tree, still standing with a gaping hole where I had dug out two large stag beetles. The school was vacant due to the winter holidays. We just rambled all over. The ponies, hill horses, were no easy affair to ride. They were skittish animals who would throw their riders first chance.

As we were riding back, we heard a thump, and saw D'Anne flat on her back. I raised hell with the owner of the pony. D'Anne was okay, a little dusty, but got back on, and we were on our way again. Time came, and we started the walk along the old back trail from Naini to Bhowali, a seven-mile, downhill trudge. it was an interesting walk.

They couldn't believe that, as a youngster, I had to walk all this distance back to school, and then return at the end of the school term.

At Bhowali Percy was waiting. He had the back rooms for the house ready. I showed Christian and Hannah the stomping areas including the place where the leopard hung out. This time, he never showed. We looked around Applecot. We took the back road and went down to Sat-Tal and had our lunch at the lake. Hannah went up the stairs to the old cottage where my mother, Vernon, Geraldine and I had our Christmas picnic in 1925. The old oak tree had been chopped down, the one I took a picture of a couple years before, that could be superimposed on the one we'd taken in 1925.

Christian and Hannah loved every minute. We trekked on down to BhimTal and looked at the old house there. I think we covered about every inch of territory where I played as a kid. Percy and Ruth had returned to Sultan Nagri. The following day our drive would take us via BhimTal, down the back motor road to Khatgodam and on to Sultan Nagri. At BhimTal, I stopped Juginder. I asked the group if they would walk the rest of the way to Sultan Nagri of about 15 miles. Hannah was smart and said no. The rest thought it would be a good idea and we started our hike. It was a beautiful day for it.

I found the old trail that we once used. It was just below the main motor road, mostly grown over. At noon, we arrived at Khatgodam. Here, we stopped at the railroad station and had a small lunch at the old Spencer's Restaurant. I couldn't believe this was happening, that Christian was with me. The terrain had now flattened out, we still had a long ways to go.

It was around 5 p.m. before we staggered onto Percy's verandah. After a bath and clean clothes, we were ready for drinks. Hannah had to say, "What took you so long?" We had another couple of days before leaving. Hannah had a chance, in the meantime, to use the old shotgun and shoot some parrots. These pesky birds were a nuisance and devouring all the guavas, hundreds of them. Time came to say goodbye and we were on our way to Delhi. It would be a long drive, with all the traffic, and Juginder tooting the heck out of the horn.

It was the New Year's that we celebrated at the Ashoka Hotel, a great gathering with a lot of Juginder's friends. He then drove back to Agra to see the Taj. We stayed at the old Holtz Hotel. Early morning, I took the group to the rear of the Taj, where the Jumna River flows by. The sun was just capturing the Taj dome, with a soft hue. We took some wonderful pictures. That afternoon, D'Anne and her friend parted company and took a train to Alahabad to witness a Hindu festival there. In the morning, Christian, Hannah and I returned to Delhi. All of a sudden I was sad; I knew the holiday was over. Juginder had tears in his eyes; he loved the kids.

Christian stayed on PanAm Flight 02 at Teheran; Hannah and I got off to catch another flight to Rome. I was heartbroken to see him go. Hannah and I stayed a couple of days in Teheran and did a little sightseeing, then caught PanAm.

Hannah spent that summer with me. Don Burlingame had bid a position in Seattle and was accepted. He left, and before his replacement arrived, I was acting Chief. Hannah said she would return to school and behave herself. I saw her off. Her mother would meet her at JFK.

I received a letter from Tish in Roswell, that her father, Sil Johnson, had passed away suddenly. It was saddening news. Sil was a wonderful person, who was loved by his friends in Roswell.

Day after day in Rome, FAA work continued. One day, "The Contessa," one of our secretaries, informed me she was having a sumptuous party at her apartment, and I was invited. The party turned out to be a real wingding with a few dignitaries. While I mingled and chatted with the folks, I wandered into the kitchen, as most of the guests normally do. I must have been on my 3rd scotch, when a very lovely blonde lady walked in and started chatting with me. I recognized the accent, but I'm sorry I cannot divulge the country from whence she came. Her husband may one day read this book. I asked where her husband was. He was back at their residence, sick with the flu. He was an Ambassador. EEEK! I thought I'd better behave myself. However, as the evening progressed, she turned to me and said, "You're mine for the rest of the night!" Oh, my goodness! Was I hearing correctly, I thought? I said, "I'd be happy to drop you back home, but I didn't have a car; mine had been stolen a couple of months ago." "Don't worry about that. I have a car and a driver," she said.

As people started to leave, she grabbed my arm and escorted me out. The car was a big, black Mercedes, with her country's flag waving on the front fender. I told her, as we were driving to my place that the apartment building was without electricity, and had been for about a month. I said I'd be happy to escort her up two flights of stairs, offer her warm scotch, and show her my tiger by candle light! That intrigued her no end. She said she'd happy to see the tiger by candle light and drink warm scotch. I asked about the driver. It would be all right, he'd probably go to sleep in the back seat. Who could refuse a pretty blonde lady, even if she was an Ambassador's wife! This turned out to be some evening. The scotch was warm and soothing. The tiger looked even meaner by candle light, where it hung on the wall. She woke me in the morning for a last "quickie" before she had to depart for home. I watched from my balcony as she woke her driver, who had snoozed in the back seat. She waved and was gone. I could see the flag waving as the car rounded a bend in the road. What a gal! I wonder how the Ambassador is now, and how soon he got over the flu.

Don's replacement arrived from the FAA Office in Los Angeles. It was Dave Switcher, an old friend of mine who had been in Brussels when our office was in Beirut. Dave was a natural, and took over without

*The kids at the old administrative building. PSC school, Naini, 1977.*

*The passageway that leads to the PSC classrooms.*

any problem. Well, there was a problem, per se. On arrival, I had Dave set up at the Aldrovani Apartments where we once stayed, the problem being that no pets were allowed. Dave had a daughter who loved animals, mainly cats, and a hamster. I helped Dave smuggle the cats into the apartment. The reason for no cats, I believe, was because the establishment had the apartment wallpapered with Indian raw silk. A previous guest was an actress with her daughter and a cat. The daughter used to throw a tennis ball up against the wall, and the cat would literally climb up the raw silk wall, tearing it all to shreds. The actress had left and paid no damages; now they allowed no cats, period. I told Dave to please take care.

All went well, till one Sunday Dave phoned and said could I help? His daughter was hysterical. Her cat had got loose and climbed a large pine tree in the backyard. I went over, but nothing would budge the cat.

Finally, with his little Italian lingo, Dave called the local fire department. No, they couldn't rescue a cat unless there was a fire. In desperation, Dave called the Embassy and talked with the Marine on duty. The Embassy couldn't help, but the Marine suggested, "Why not do it Italian style?" Dave said, "What's that?" The guy said, "Chop the tree down!" When Dave told me that the next day, I laughed for a long time.

The newspapers and radio were full of the Watergate Scandal. The four conspirators were getting their knuckles rapped. One of them, I think, was Howard Hunt, his wife was on the ill-fated United Airlines flight out of Midway that crashed, killing all on board. His wife was carrying a bundle of money to help Nixon's campaign. It was the FAA Administrator, Butterfield, who blew the final whistle with the tapes that lowered the boom on President Nixon.

*Christian and Hannah at Bikinir Tomb, Bhowali, 1977.*

When the dust had settled, Dave came into the office and said that we had a new Administrator, who had taken Butterfeld's place, a young fellow named Bond. He then said that the guy drove up to the FAA on Independence Avenue, on a Harley Davidson motorcycle. The guard wouldn't let him in the building because he was not dressed well. The man said, "I'm the new FAA Administrator." Bond went up to his office, threw all the papers off the desk and said, "We'll start from scratch!" Dave thought that was quite humorous. He kept on talking about Bond. He then said the man, Langhorne Bond, had been born in China, and his father was with an airline out there. I jumped up and said "I'll be damned! It must be the son of Old Bondie!" Dave said, "You know him?" "Yeah, I know old Bondie. He was the President of China National Aviation Co., CNAC. He was my boss in China. I don't recall his son. He must have been a little fellow when I first arrived in Calcutta in November of 1942. It's got to be Bond's son. Wow! What a coincidence!"

During the summer break from school, Christian came for another visit; this time he wanted to visit Israel as well. I bought him a ticket on TWA, and I would catch up with him in a couple of days at the Ramada Inn. On my arrival at Tel Aviv airport, I was met by a security officer. He wanted to talk to me and asked that I follow him to his office. As we walked across the ramp, my mind raced back to the Gadhafi incident and the mysterious phone call from Tel Aviv to me at the hotel in Kinshasa. What was happening now I wondered. I sat opposite the officer and watched as he thumbed through my official passport. He then took a slip of paper, stamped and signed it; this he attached to the passport. Normally the immigration will not stamp an entry when they know you travel to Arab countries as well. When he had finished, the officer asked me if I had a son named Christian. My heart skipped a couple of beats, and now my mind took a

different tangent. I hesitated a few moments and replied, "Yes, is he all right? Nothing has happened has it?" "No, we detained him on his arrival yesterday. Nothing serious, except his passport showed his place of birth as Lebanon." I took a sigh of relief and nodded. I told the officer a bit of my background and having lived in Lebanon for several years where my two children were born. I was now here on behalf of the FAA to conduct an airport inspection and to discuss some aviation matters with a Mr. Sam Rosenberg of Israel Aviation Corp. Yes he knew Sam and welcomed me to Israel. I then asked about my son. "He is here," and had the assistant bring Christian in. He looked a bit confused and worried. The usual tea was served and Christian became himself once more. I told Christian later, that there never is a dull moment being an FAA inspector in the Middle East! We had a wonderful time together, once I had finished my business and airport inspection. Sam had one of his assistants drive us all over the country. We visited Jaffa, the old ruins of Caesarea, the Dead Sea and Jerusalem. We covered the whole lot, I know Christian enjoyed every moment. Back in Rome and after a rest, we then took the week-end to Naples where I had to conduct a bunch of written and flight tests for the Navy Flying Club. We then went on a sight seeing tour of Pompeii; from there we drove up to the top of Mt. Vesuvius. While we trekked around the crater, our car was vandalized. The bastards had made off with our two briefcases. One had all the exams and completed papers of the Navy applicants, our passports and all my ID cards. "Sons-of-bitches." I was mad. I went to the local police station and got the usual shrug of the shoulders. We then visited the U. S. consulate; here they took down all the information possible, mainly the passport numbers. I telephoned Dave Switzer at home and told him what I thought of our so-called Italian friends. I know one thing, if I had it to do all over again I would do it all over Rome and Naples! I told Dave I'd

had the second generation Italians, they were nothing more than thieving, no good bastards.

Brussels office agreed to my return to the New York office, effective January 1, 1978. I took my last vacation, and traveled back to Delhi, where else? I spent another wonderful holiday with the Sherreds in Sultan Nagri, and a trip to Bhowali, so I could hike around my favorite mountains. I arrived in Rome a few days before Christmas. Dave had taken off on a business trip to visit several countries in the Middle East, so it became my obligation to make out the monthly report for December.

While in the process of this, Mary Ann showed me the latest copy of the FAA World Magazine, which is a monthly publication. In it was an article with pictures of the flight crew that came to evacuate the FAA personnel from Beirut in November of '75. They were being presented with Meritous Awards for the evacuation and bravery. I was peed-off! So I wrote a rebuttal in the Interest Items of my report. Not that any of us at the Beirut office wished medals or meritous awards, because we kept the office open, working our scheduled programs, flying to distant countries, driving through no-man's land everyday, having our cars and homes blown up, while the FAA in Brussels appeared oblivious to what was going on in Lebanon. Ever since 1973, when I arrived in Lebanon, there was the Israeli Arab war of October '74 and during my three years, there was always the chance of being caught in the crossfire of the Muslim-Christian fighting. We never complained, just did our duty and everyday chores.

Right after Christmas, around the 29th, I headed back to my old assignment at the New York Office in Valley Stream. I was to be the Program Manager for the L-1011 aircraft. PanAm had just purchased some of these trimotored aircraft. I felt sad about leaving the International Unit, but couldn't get used to the second Italian generation element in Rome and Italy in general. The country, their history and the food were fabulous, but that's where it ended.

Christian had finished his high school and was now attending General Motors Institute in Flint, Michigan. Hannah had returned to her mother and promised to try and get along and do well in school.

It was the weekend of New Year's when I checked in at the JFK Hilton Hotel. The weather was lousy: cold and windy, with the threat of snow. I had a couple of days to get over the jet lag before reporting to the office, which would be on Tuesday after New Year's. I called Hannah to say I'd arrived back, and would come up to Fairfield the next weekend and would look for an apartment in Fairfield. She was tickled. I also got ahold of Christian in Flint. He hoped to see me on school break in Spring.

I visited the bar and got acquainted with the bartender. The food and Happy Hour were great. I read and watched the TV and the football games. I was eager to see the Bowl Games which would be coming up on

New Year's Day. I hadn't seen any good College football games for a spell. On Monday, New Year's Day, the Rose Bowl Parade, Orange Bowl, etc., were lovely, then the games started. Later in the evening, around 8 p.m. I think the Orange Bowl game came on. I was almost bug-eyed by now. In the midst of the game, a news flash came across the screen, something like, "An Air India Boeing 747 had crashed in Bombay on New Year's Eve." The time was ten hours ahead of us, at least in Standard Time. There were about 225 souls on board, believed to have been killed. I thought, "Oh, no! I'm glad it was not one of our planes, or an N-registered one. I might be one of the investigators."

I sat through the Bowl games, and was mixed up with who played whom, and who won, and what the scores were. By midnight I turned in, bleary-eyed. I'd rented a car through the hotel and the weather had collapsed. It had snowed most of the night. Plows and salt trucks were out doing their thing and I was in no rush.

Parts of the Sunrise Highway had been cleared, but still snowing. I had my breakfast and braved the slippery roads and traffic, which I had not been used to for sometime, Luckily, the office was only about seven miles away. I got there a few minutes past eight and went to the third floor, there was not a soul around. I saw an empty desk, where I placed my briefcase. I sat for a minute or two, then the phone rang. It was the FAA Washington. "Yes," I said, "this is the FAA Valley Stream." "Is Mr. Peter Goutiere there at the office? He was supposed to report there from Rome." I said, "Yes, this is Pete Goutiere speaking." He said, "Hi, Pete. This is Pete Chesney." "I'll be damned! Why the call so darned early?" "Well, did you by chance hear the news of Air India crash at Santa Cruz, Bombay?" "Yeah, I did; why?" "Well, my friend, I hate to do this to you, but we received a message from the Civil Aviation people in Delhi. They specifically asked us to send you over as the FAA Coordinator." "Oh, no!" It's nice to be liked and wanted and all that, but now to pack up and head East again, when I'd barely got over my jet lag! "Well, when do I leave?" "Have you unpacked your things yet?" "No, they're still in storage at the hotel." "Good. Try to catch your favorite flight on PanAm 01 tonight for Delhi, from Delhi to Bombay, you will have to purchase a ticket on the local airline. They want you there as soon as possible. Most of the people that are supposed to be there, like NTSB, Boeing, Pratt & Whitney, are already there." "Okay, Pete Chesney," I said, "I'm on my way! No rest for the wicked."

By now, the office people were arriving. The Chief of the Office, Jim Haight, had just arrived. The storm and slippery roads were causing traffic jams and delays. I introduced myself. "Yes, we were expecting you." "Not right now," I said, and proceeded to tell him about the phone call from Washington. "You seem to be a popular fellow."

We had our morning coffee, and Jim called a general staff meeting. I knew most

*Kids in back of PSC with the Himalayas as back drop.*

of the inspectors and secretaries. I was then shown my desk. After arranging a few things, and getting a bite for lunch, I told Jim I'd see him later in the month. He had his secretary call PanAm Ops and request the jumpseat all the way to Delhi. It would be an ass-aching trip, I knew. The flight left at 8 or 9 p.m., stopping at London, Frankfurt, Istanbul, no more Beirut, but Teheran, Karachi, and then finally Delhi. This would be an all-night, all-next day, and all-next night again.

The flight from JFK was full probably vacationers, I don't mind saying the jumpseat in the 747 is the world's worst! I was up all night, and on to approach to London, I felt my head would roll off my shoulders. At Pan Ops I made out my regular 160 form and met the new crew that would be going to Teheran. I said I'd not bother them; I'd relax in the upstairs lounge. They said that would be okay by them. However; Air India flight to Delhi had a mechanical in London, all their passengers were transferred to PanAm, I couldn't believe it! So this would be full load again, I'd have nowhere to go but sit in the cockpit. Why couldn't they have gone on British Airways? There was no British Airways flight at that time. I don't mind saying it was a killing flight for me. All the way to Delhi, all that day and night in the jumpseat. I was completely exhausted when the flight arrived at Delhi.

I checked in with Air India for an early flight to Bombay. "Yes," the girl said. "However, the flight was delayed by about three hours." This would not be enough time to have a rest at a hotel. I elected to stay in the lounge and sleep on a bench, and sleep I did. Actually, it was near noon before the flight was to take off.

At Bombay, I found my way to Air India office, where the Accident Committee were having their investigation. I met the team people, and the Chief of the Indian CAA, a rotund individual, but a jolly fellow. The NTSB Officer was old Doug Dreyfus the person I was with at the Athens accident. The team was in the process of their afternoon meeting when I collapsed at the table. I was rushed to the Centurion Air India Hotel at the airport; I didn't bother about food or drink. I collapsed again on the bed and slept till next morning. The next day I was able to coordinate and help.

I was asked to get records of the crew and found out that many parts of the physical exam for the Captain were missing. It took several days before I was able to track down his history. The pilot I learned, was diabetic, an alcoholic, overweight, and went on crash diets, and in between was known to have used opium. He had, on New Year's Eve, been to a raucous party, because he was not scheduled to fly, he was on standby and was called for the flight. The flight had been delayed till that evening for its flight from Santa Cruz to Abu-Dabi in the Persian Gulf. Further information showed that while checking out on the Boeing 747 in Seattle, he had failed the night flying portion. How Air India ever checked him out, no one knows!

We were there a little over two weeks when the voice and flight recorder were retrieved from the bay. NTSB took the two black boxes with them to Washington. I took leave and made a quick dash up to Ranikhet and Sultan Nagri to visit the Sherreds. It was a quick and pleasant surprise to see them again, they were unable to believe that I'd been back to the States and here I was again! I joined the NTSB in Washington, and also some of the Civil Aviation people from Delhi, including the Chief Inspector, Mr. Chilappa, the rotund fellow. Then off to Seattle and Boeing who were figuring out the voice recorder. We sat for several days, trying to decipher the conversation. The translation was finally done. The Captain had said that his instruments had spilled, or "toppled," as he put it. The First Officer had then said his, too, had failed. They were at 1500 feet at the time. The flight recorder showed all engines were operating normally.

At the time the pilot said his instruments had "toppled," the heading and bank angle indicated a left turn and a descent and increase of airspeed. These three indicators then showed increases in all parameters. By the time the aircraft hit the water, the bank angle was in excess of 110 degrees. Heading was almost opposite of intended course. Airspeed was 350 knots plus. One can imagine there was not much left of the plane or its passengers when it hit the water. There is an aural warning system and light that will indicate a discrepancy of the gyrohorizon failure. There was no such sound on the voice recorder

*With FAA Administrator, Mr. Langhorne Bond Jr. Son of Bondy our Chief of CNAC, India/China.*

and most unlikely that both horizons could fail at the same time.

I theorized, and told Doug Dreyfus, that the pilot probably had experienced vertigo, a sense of dizziness or seeing his instruments in a different perspective. He probably felt as though his artificial horizon was in a right turn, and therefore was making a left turn to correct what he was imagining. All the time, however, the instruments were in level flight. Vertigo can be caused in different ways, mainly through stress and fatigue. Excessive drinking and lack of sleep is a sure way. I recall, as I mentioned earlier, when flying the Hump for a total of 240 hours in one month, toward the end of 11 round trips I was truly tired. It was all instrument flying during the monsoons. It was nightime, or early morning, about 3 a.m., I was climbing out of Dinjan. I had made my last circle of the field before heading on course. As I leveled out, I experienced a strange sensation that the aircraft was still in a left hand turn. I started to correct and gave it some body English. The more I counteracted for the left turn, the more it seemed to bank in the opposite direction.

Unconsciously, I let go of the yoke. I told the co-pilot to check my horizon, because there was only one in the cockpit. He said it was now correct, straight and level. I closed my eyes for a couple of minutes, and when I opened them again, everything was normal and I continued the flight. I remembered a pilot discussing vertigo and how it was caused, mainly by fatigue. The NTSB took a note of this.

Once again, I was in New York, to continue my normal work program. It was early March when I found a condominium in Fairfield, Connecticut. It was spacious, and I was able to have Hannah stay with me. My household effects had arrived from Rome, including the green Mustang with the Italian plates. I had it all fixed up and gave it to Hannah to commute to school. In the meantime, I had bought a second-hand Ford. Hannah brought her friends over to visit with us once in awhile.

I received a call from the school. It appeared that Hannah had not been attending her regular classes and her grades were down. Hannah confessed to me that she had been skipping classes whenever I was out of town on trips. She was seeing a

dropout student who was nothing but a lout. I told her she had to straighten up, or go back to Will Brown. Things seemed to come along fine after that.

I went to Kansas City and attended TWA's L-1011 course, and was finally checked out as pilot and flight engineer. By now, PanAm had moved its certificate from the New York area to Miami. The L-1011 rating was now not much use to me.

I had no sooner settled in the Fairfield condo and was getting used to the long drive to Valley Stream when one morning I received a call from FAA Washington. The Administrator, Mr. Langhorn Bond wanted to speak to me. First he wanted to know for sure that I flew for CNAC during the war. He then asked if I knew his father, Bond Sr. Yes I did. He said to come on down, that he wanted to meet me and to have an article written about he and myself for the FAA World. The following week I met Langhorn Bond in his office. We had a good talk about the old days of CNAC. He told me his Dad was still alive and living in Virginia. I took my leave and sat with the magazine publisher, who wrote up the resume of me. It was later published in the May issue 1978. I thought it swell of him to have arranged this.

I continued on the 747 program and whenever there was a need for a 1011 rating, I was available.

One night, Hannah's drop out friend tried to sneak into her room which was on the third floor. I was all set to call the police, when Hannah said she would try getting this guy's dad to come over and take care of him, but not before he kicked up quite a rumpus outside. His father finally showed up and took the boy away. The guy looked like he had been on drugs. Next morning, when I was getting ready to go to work the lout had slashed all the tires on Hannah's Mustang and my sedan. This time I did call the police. They asked if I wanted the guy arrested. Hannah begged me not to go through with it. Needless to say I was not able to go to work that day. Instead, I had a taxi take me to Sears and eventually had all eight tires refitted. Luckily the insurance covered the bill.

# PHASE NINE: 1979-1982

It was a simple Christmas for 1978, nothing like the year before at Sultan Nagri with the Sherreds. Christian was home with his mother for the holidays. I was able to have him over for a few days. 1979 rolled around, and I continued 747 check rides. In the middle of May '79 Pan American decided to start a B-747 service to Nairobi, Kenya, via Dakar Senegal, Abidjan Ivory Coast, Accra Ghana and Lagos Nigeria. It would necessitate approving the flight first. I was asked by Ray Hirsch to go on the trip. The pilot of the flight was Captain John Powers. It seemed very strange to be now walking all over these airports checking runways, fire-rescue equipment and security where I once flew DC-3s and 4s. I wanted to revisit Goree Island off the Dakar coast, but couldn't quite fit it into my program. Our meal at Abidjan was at the same restaurant where I had eaten so often with my AirLiban crew. A lot had changed, but the food was still good. In Accra it was like old times where I was able to see several of my Ghanian pilot friends. The airport hadn't changed much. The terminal was new with a lot more curio shops selling their ebony carvings. The Ambassador hotel appeared a bit run down. Lagos also had a new terminal building with more curio shops and a lot more ebony head carvings. At Nairobi I was able to take time off to do a bit of traveling to Amboseli National Park where there was still a lot of wildlife to be seen. It all happened so quickly; the next moment we were winging our way back to New York.

One day I received a call from my fine friend, Bill Huebner. He had retired from the FAA, and was working with the International Civil Aviation Organization (ICAO) in Jeddah, Saudi Arabia. He asked me if I would be interested in joining ICAO and be assigned to the Jeddah group. I said yes I would; I contacted the head office in Montreal to find out more about their program. I was sent a folder of forms to fill out and literature to read. After studying the lot, I filled in all the forms and mailed it back to them. I was accepted, but the date for travel would not be till the end of December and this was only July. Now it was important to figure out something for Hannah. She would never make it on her own at the apartment and school. Reluctantly, I called Margaret and explained the situation. She couldn't take Hannah back because of Will Brown. It was agreed that Hannah should attend a boarding school for which I would pay the bill. There was one located in Vermont, called the Vershire School.

Margaret, Hannah and I sat down and discussed the situation. Hannah cried her eyes out, thinking she was not wanted. I explained the problem, that I needed money to support the two of us. When she consented, Margaret, Hannah and I drove up to Vershire and looked the place over. It didn't appear that wonderful to me, but Hannah thought it great. They had horses and log cabins. I was relieved that she felt good about it.

In September I drove Hannah up to her new school and I was able to talk to the principal. Not to worry, they would take good care of my "Baba." I was heartbroken to say goodbye. It seemed I was always saying goodbye to people I loved most.

During the latter part of October '79, our office asked if I would give another check on Delhi's ILS. PanAm would like to have lower minimums there. Yes, I would go, as long as I could have some of my Compensatory time while in Delhi. Before leaving I had occasion to dine with my friends the Carrolls. At dinner I talked with two of their daughters, TC and Lisa. They were planning an around the world trip and would be in Delhi about the same time. I said that would be fine, I would meet them there.

I checked the approach with the PanAm pilot into Delhi; everything went well till the last five hundred feet. This is where the glide slope dipped down sharply. Had it been actual instruments the plane would have hit the ground short of the runway. This had happened previously with BOAC and Lufthansa. I could not okay the lower minimums at the time.

My taxi friend Joginder Singh met me at the airport and had arranged a room for me at the Ashoka hotel. I was also happy to see my old friend Kakar Singh as well as one of their friends by the name of Doctor Vinyard. He too loved India and came often to visit here from Oregon. A day or so later, as the four of us returned to the hotel, I heard shouts and yells "Peter, Peter." It was TC and Lisa; I had forgotten about them and here they were. They planned to stay in some fleabag place. I told them they could stay here at the Ashoka. They didn't quite have the money for that. I checked them into my room and they could use the extra double bed. They thought it great. Now there are six in our group and the Indian taxis are not that big; they can carry about four. With six, somebody's ass is going to be hanging out of the back door. Somehow we managed to crowd into Joginder's car and headed for Agra to visit the Taj Mahal. We stopped half way and had several beers. Lisa said she was going to drive the rest of the way. In India they still drive on the left side as in England. Lisa decided to drive in the middle of the road dodging lorries bullock carts and bicycles. Somehow we made it.

Back in Delhi, Joginder, the two girls and myself headed up to the hill stations. We stayed in Ranikhet to see the sunrise on the snowy mountains, then to Naini-Tal and Bhowali. They both got Delhi belly; however, that would not deter them. I think they

*Two of Tom Carroll's daughters "TC" and Lisa, whom I intercepted in Delhi. In front of Taj-Mahal.*

223

*About to enjoy the traditional Arab Mensef dish with my Bedouin friend, Wadi Mousa, Jordan.*

enjoyed the ten day tour as much as I did having them with me. Back in Delhi we parted company; Lisa and TC headed East, while I took PanAm West for New York.

On or about November 4th, I was on PanAm 02 making its approach into Teheran; the pilot was letting down to about 10,000 feet. PanAm Ops in Teheran told him to pull up and divert to Istanbul, that the airport was closed. The pilot couldn't figure that out since the weather looked clear. We could all see the field in the distance. PanAm Operations said that there was some sort of trouble in town. Some Iranians were attacking the U.S. Embassy. At Istanbul we heard the story; the long bearded Khomeini had taken over the Embassy and had all the American personnel as hostages. I continued straight through to New York. The news was nothing but the assault on the Embassy. I was too pooped to listen further. I called Hannah in Vershire to say I was home. I went to see the Carrolls and told them of my trip to Delhi and having the kids with me. I even mentioned that they both slept in my room! Tom forgave me.

I put my place up for rent and headed for Jeddah just before Xmas. I took Seaboard World Airlines cargo flight all the way. I was also able to take a great deal of my belongings. At Jeddah I was met by the chief of the ICAO mission who took me to my quarters in a furnished apartment not too far from town. The building was called the China Rose. It had four ICAO families already there, all Americans. Next morning at the office, I met the personnel of flight standards. The chief was a Saudi called Alian-al-Alian, a nice fellow who was quite westernized. His counterpart, was an ex-FAAer by the name of Van Gundy whom I knew.

It didn't take long to get adjusted and learn my job functions. I met with many of Saudi Arabian Airlines VIPs. A number of them I had previously given 707 flight checks and ratings. There were several American old-timers who I had known from the days of my airline back in 1951. I was soon conducting flight checks on the Saudi 707 and 1011 aircraft for ratings. The enroute flight checks presented a problem.

I could not accompany the crew to the aircraft to observe the aircraft walk around by the engineer and the loading of baggage, etc. It was necessary that I accompany and go through the immigrations office with the passengers. This delayed the crew checks.

A few meetings were held with the Vice President of Operations. They highly recommended that I should wear a Saudi Airlines uniform; that this would solve the problem. The chief of our Flight Standards, Mr. Alian also agreed that a uniform should be worn; he said he always did. When Van Gundy was informed of the matter, he resented it.

I had not been in Jeddah long, perhaps two months, when my Saudi Chief Alian informed me that a Prince in Riyadh wanted to renew his FAA license; he also needed a Saudi License be issued on the basis of his American one. He asked me to go to Riyadh and help him out. I arrived in Riyadh and was met by a limousine and driven to the Marriot Hotel where the Prince had arranged my room. It was terribly cold on arrival; I had not come prepared for such freezing weather or to stay any length of time.

Next morning, I was driven to the Palace by two husky, American, football looking guys. I presumed them to be bodyguards. I was ushered into a large living-room and waited for His Royal Highness. In the meantime I was served the traditional Arabic tea in a small glass; almost too hot to handle! It tasted good and took the chill out of me. The Prince arrived in flowing black robe, and in very good English introduced himself. His actual title was, Sultan Ben-Salman-al-Saud. He was a Royal Prince and addressed as His Royal Highness. There was nothing pretentious in the way he talked and acted, I liked him. We went to an office where I set about arranging his Saudi License. Through our conversation, I learned he was attending the University of Denver and owned a Cessna Citation Jet. No wonder he was so Americanized.

I planned to leave the next day for Jeddah. However, His Royal Highness said no, he wanted me to stay another couple of days. I said I hadn't brought any clothes for a long stay. No problem. His two husky bodyguards escorted me to a special clothing store that had all the latest Paris fashions for men. I wound up with suits, sports coats, slacks, sweaters, shirts and odds and ends to last a long time. That evening I was his guest at the Palace. I was led through various corridors and out to a courtyard at the rear. Here the Prince showed me an enormous Bedouin tent all lit up with Bedouin lanterns. The floor was strewn with Persian carpets and large cushions. The Prince said he preferred be-

ing in the tent than in the spacious living and dining rooms of the palace. I think I did too.

There were about thirty of his people sitting in a circle on the floor. I was introduced and then sat crosslegged near His Royal Highness, but not for long. My knees and joints ached; I had to unravel myself and lean against the pillows. Tea and Bedouin coffee was constantly served. The coffee was poured out in small demitasse cups, black with crushed cardamom. It tasted good. The food was also good; it consisted of roast lamb with special fried rice and nuts that we ate with our hands. Nothing could have tasted better. I mentioned to His Royal Highness about the time I was served the sheep's eye by His Majesty King Hussein. He laughed and said that was correct, that it was the normal procedure. It had been a wonderful evening that I spent with His Royal Highness and his friends. I thanked him very much and hoped to see him sometime in Jeddah; that I would arrange a ride in the 707 when on a check flight. He thought it would be great.

The next morning, the bodyguards came by and said that His Royal Highness requested I accompany them to the Suq (bazaar), to buy a souvenir of Riyadh. I picked out an antique Kuwaiti chest, the type which is used by Kuwait seamen on their old dowh boats that plied the Persian Gulf. The chest I chose was studded with brass knobs and a large brass lock.

I thanked the people I was with and was ready to return to the hotel when I was informed there was more to come. I had to choose a pair of old flintlock pistols. Then the guards asked, "How big is your living room?" "Why?" "His Highness wants you to have a carpet to fit it!" "Allah be praised!" The shopkeeper pulled out numerous Persian carpets from a pile that reached the store ceiling. We looked at the largest he had. Thank goodness, there were none larger than 6x10 feet. I tried to refuse the gifts, but was told I would be insulting the Prince if I didn't accept them. The gifts were packed and shipped down to Jeddah on Saudi Airlines. I couldn't take them with me; there was just too much.

Ever since then, His Royal Highness, Prince Saud and I have been in touch. A few years later, in 1985, my friend Prince Sultan Ben-Salman-al-Saud was elected to represent Saudi Arabia as an astronaut on the space shuttle. He made the headlines on that flight and was kind enough to send me several autographed photographs of he and his fellow astronauts.

My work program with ICAO was basically the same as I had been doing with FAA international office. As I mentioned, there were several old friends of mine that go back to 1950-51. One was Captain Sam Biggler. Another was Vic Brozolwski. Vic was a communications technician, that goes back to the old TWA days. Both my friends had been with Saudia for more than 30 years. They were fine people.

There was a club in Jeddah called the Dunes Club. It had a club house, good-sized swimming pool and a 9-hole golf course. You better believe it! There were no green fairways on the course; the greens were oiled down sand and called "browns." On the fairways one was allowed to carry a small mat, like a doormat. You could place the ball on the mat, only if it landed on the fairway. In the rough, one had to play it as it lay.

One day, I was playing golf with Vic and as we approached the second hole, where there were several lovely palm trees that lined part of the fairway, Vic stopped between a couple of these palms and asked me if I remembered a TWA Station Manager by the name of Thomas. He gave me a clue that the fellow was once stationed in Bombay. I vaguely remembered a TWA man there, but wasn't certain if it was Thomas. Vic stated that Tom had transferred to Jeddah and worked for Saudia. TWA in those days ran Saudi Arabian Airlines. In due course Tom discovered that some of the agents were doing some underhanded business in the ticketing department. Tom reported his findings to his American superiors but no action was taken. Tom let the matter drop and forgot the incident. He and Vic decided that Jeddah needed a golf course; so, through their ingenuity the course was born. Shortly, Tom's reporting of the ticketing incident caught up with him. Tom was released and returned to the New York office. He just could not take the city life and make a go of it. He quit, and shortly there after committed suicide. He had sent Vic a letter with a last will and testament. In the will he was going to be cremated and wanted his ashes placed on the golf course. I said, "You've gotta be kidding!" Vic said, "No I'm not, that it is correct. In fact, you're just about standing on him!" That is the way Vic was, you never knew what to expect next.

The religious laws that govern the country through the Muslim Koran are severe; basically tooth for a tooth, and he who liveth by the sword, dieth by the sword. For instance, for robbery a thief may have his hand cut off (or a couple of fingers), usually the hand he eats with. The other hand he uses to cleanse his behind. They use water, not toilet paper; therefore he won't eat with that hand till near starvation, and would be degrading himself to do so. For committing murder, adultery, defamation of the Muslim religion, or treason, you get an automatic death penalty. Justice is swift; no prolonged trials so that shifty lawyers can go laughing to the bank. As I recall, during my stay in Jeddah there were two Koreans who had become violently ill and wound up in the local hospital. They were forced to upchuck some of what they had eaten. On examination, it was discovered that the meat was human. This was secretly reported to the police. The police went to the Korean community and located their apartment. There in the refrigerator were remains of a human body, which turned out to be a missing Pakistani. The two Koreans confessed to having killed the Pakistani and cannibalizing his body (sweet and sour!). Needless to say, justice was swift. There were no lawyers, as in our courts, who can make a mockery of the law and collect large sums of money and publicity. If a crime is committed one day, the execution is the following Friday. The two Koreans were taken to the local Suq (bazaar) and had their heads chopped off. That's all there is to it. The executioner is a hefty guard, usually a Sudanese.

There are no special cemeteries, just a Potter's field, a trench or deep hole in the sand. There are no churches, only Mosques. No holidays as there are in other parts of the world. The only holiday that is recognized is the ten day period right after their Holy Ramadan. All Embassies and business must adhere to these rules. Women are not allowed to work, or be regarded as part of the social life. Their place is in the kitchen and in bed. They are expected to bear children, manage the kitchen and household affairs. They are not allowed to be seen by foreigners in their homes; they are not allowed to drive or work in public businesses. If they come out in public, they must cover their entire person with a black cotton cloth; in India they call it "purdah." One might see these ladies from the harem shopping in the Suq; usually around the gold market! On close examination it is possible to see they are wearing tight jeans underneath, and dainty toes show through the sandals with painted nails. If they look in your direction, you may notice two large brown eyes peering at you through the veil, perhaps seductively!

As mentioned, the jails are for punishment, not for rehabilitation. No air conditioning. The punishment works. Once you have had a taste of that jail, you will not want to go back. Some foreign women can work as nurses in hospitals, stewardesses on the airline. I was aware of the Islamic laws and had no problem.

My Godchild, Louisa Gifford, Ray's daughter came to work for Saudi Airlines as a stewardess. Having been born and raised in Lebanon, she spoke fluent Arabic and French; a beautiful girl and a natural for the job and I promised to look after her. The next thing I knew, Louisa informed me that she had selected a harem for me from the other English stewardesses that were in her group.

One afternoon, there was a knock on the apartment door, and when I opened it, there stood Louisa and four beautiful dolls. They came in and took over. They raided the refrigerator. These English girls were just delightful people. I knew this would enhance my stay in Jeddah. I don't mind saying, I became one of the most popular guys in town. The only problem was escorting these beautiful people back and forth to the Saudi Arabian Airlines compound where they all lived. Another problem was getting the five dolls into my small Japanese Ichibichi car. If ever I was caught with my harem, driving down the highway, I could only think of that mean-looking black Sudanese, about 7 feet tall with his shining 4-foot sword! I shuddered. But then, to have these young giggling females all crammed into the little car, what the hell! I couldn't think of a better way to go.

On one occasion when I had just arrived in Saudi Arabia (it was the end of '79) some terrorists, about a 100 or so, possibly Iranians, tried to take over the Holy City of Mecca and shot up the place and were captured. There was a lot of to-do and publicity around the world. They were condemned and that was it. Normally the executions should take place in Mecca, but the one guy was going to have his work cut out for him, excuse the expression! He would be all worn out trying to whack off 80 to 90 heads. It was agreed that the prisoners be divided up between Riyadh, Jeddah and Mecca. In this way they all got an equal shot at it. On Friday the deed was completed, 90 or more heads rolled on the Suq streets. The Saudis don't mess around and sometimes its a good deterrent against terrorism, hijacking, and cocaine smuggling. Perhaps it should be tried in the States, especially Miami; I'm sure it would work, the only problem being the shifty lawyers would grumble.

When shuttling the girls around I was never stopped, thank goodness! Whenever I was invited to a party, I always had my harem with me. I also had a 26-foot sailboat (sloop) that was kept at the creek about 10 miles up the coast. Every chance, I'd take any or all the girls sailing. They would wear their long robes, and once past the security guards and out in the Red Sea, away from all eyes, whammo! Off would come the robes and there they were in their bikinis! It was about a twelve mile sail to the reefs; here, we could anchor and swim and have a picnic lunch on the boat. Who said Jeddah was a miserable spot. The Saudis say that the Jeddah area was once the Garden of Eden. I have to agree.

There was a great deal of construction going on around the old city of Jeddah. The old wooden buildings were making way for new high rise structures. Very modern hotels were springing up. Super highways were being built leading to a new airport also being constructed. It would be named King Abdul Aziz International Airport, the largest in the country. A wide corniche along the waterfront was built. There were many types of sculptured art at various intersections, depicting the world, ship motifs, and flowers made of metal. There must have been a hundred throughout the area.

I received word from Hannah that she would graduate from Vershire in June. She sounded excited. There was a direct phone system I could use on weekends and with any luck I would try and make it. I also had a friend in Lynbrook, Long Island, who ran the Buick agency and the National Car Rental; his name was Bob Petit. When I was ready to come to New York, I'd call him to pick me up with a rental car. I would drop him off and head for Connecticut.

On one of my trips back to the States, Bob came to pick me up and during the trip back to Lynbrook he asked me a question about China. I said I had lived there. "Why?" Then calmly he said, "I think I read about you the other day. I spend a lot of time in the library and I read a book about the Watergate scandal. One of the guys, I think his name

*The Civil Aviation Assistant Group in Amman, Jordan. Left to right: Frank Day, Lou Clark, Aida (Palestian) Secretary, myself, Jack Kenton and Jim Parnell. A great team accomplished "Mission Impossible."*

*Three of my Harem girls from Saudi Airlines, in Bangkok sightseeing. The girl in the middle is my God child, Luisa Gifford, 1981.*

was Howard Hunt, had written a book about himself as a spy." Bob really had my interest now. He continued, "In the book he speaks of having married a girl who was once married to a Peter Goutiere, who flew in China, for China National Airlines." I was glad Bob was driving, or I would have gone off the road. I said, "Oh my God, no! It couldn't be." I asked if he could get the book for me. "I've done better than that Pete, it so happens I made a copy of that section." At his office he pulled out a folder and some pages clipped together. I read through them, and sure enough there was my name. It all came back to me in a sudden start: the girl in question had been Dorothy Wetzel, who had chased me to Calcutta and ran off with all my loot and evidently kept using my name as her married name, with the bogus marriage certificate. As I read further, it was she who had wound up in that terrible United Airlines crash at the Chicago airport; everyone on board was killed, including Dorothy. I believe she was carrying a lot of money

for the Nixon campaign. I was truly thunderstruck, and dumfounded. I still couldn't believe it, that my name would be tangled up with Howard Hunt and Watergate. There it was in black and white, almost as vivid as when my name was used for the assassination of Gadafi. Good Lord, I was really going through hell now. You try to be a good guy and get someone off your back, and look what happens.

Life goes on. I had to keep doing my thing. I had bought Hannah another car. It was a bright red Ford pickup truck. I had turned the Mustang and sedan in for this. I drove up in the pickup to Hannah's graduation. It was a beautiful day and she looked lovely. Once the ceremonies were over and she received her diploma, it was a happy moment for the both of us. Margaret had shown up, but didn't communicate. Hannah could hardly wait to pack up and drive the pickup back to Fairfield. She would stay with her mother for the time being.

Before I knew it I was back in Jeddah. In August I received word from Margaret that she couldn't cope with Hannah anymore, so I returned to Fairfield to pick her up. We went to the Saudi Consulate near the United Nations building to obtain a visa for Hannah and was informed it would take a couple of weeks. I begged with the people that I needed it today. Not possible, it couldn't be arranged that quick. We went downstairs to have lunch. At the next table I saw a man reading the paper and the headlines stated that a Saudi Airlines L-1011 had crashed in Riyadh, killing all on board. It had burned on the runway. I thought I would be wanted as one of the investigators by the Presidency of Civil Aviation (PCA). I grabbed Hannah and raced back upstairs to the Saudi Consulate. I told them about the accident, which they knew. I explained I had to get back immediately, that very night; to please consider the visa for

my daughter. Lo and behold she had a visa in nothing flat.

We drove back to Fairfield and packed all her things; her boyfriend, John Soboleski, said he would drive us to Kennedy Airport that evening. The Saudia flight left around 9:30 p.m. By the time we finally made it to Jeddah and to the dusty apartment in China Rose, we were pooped out. I had made so many flights across the Atlantic with Saudia, I don't think the jet lag knew which way to go. Sometimes it would catch up with me a couple of days later.

It wasn't long before Hannah made friends with some of the stewardesses and was enjoying Jeddah. She surprised me one day by saying she had a job at the Meridian Hotel as the manager for the swimming pool. I double-checked to make sure it was all okay. I didn't want her winding up in some sheik's harem. It was fine as long as she didn't run around in a bikini. Hannah worked there for a couple of months before she was informed that she would have to quit. No women were allowed to work at the hotel. She was happy with the money she received, enough to buy two large solid 22 karat gold bracelets.

Now that there was nothing to do, Hannah spent considerable time drawing and painting at the apartment. One day, she informed me that she would like to study interior decorating. She had seen an advertisement in a magazine and chose one in Miami called Bauder College. I called them up. "Yes," they would take Hannah, but first they wanted money up front, like $3000. Everything was arranged for her to attend classes, starting the first week of January 1981 and finishing by end of May '82. I was happy she had decided on something like this; I felt she, being artistic, would be good at it. Sitting around in Jeddah was not much fun for a pretty young girl. I thought Hannah may have tried being a stewardess for Saudia; I even inquired on the sly and they would have accepted her. Hannah was not that fond of flying, and the accident in Riyadh didn't help. Interior decorating was the best choice.

Toward the end of November Overseas National Airlines (ONA), who were on wet-lease (airplane plus crew) for Saudi Airlines, was using a B-747. The plane was due for a major maintenance check in San Francisco. I arranged with the captain to let Hannah go along as extra crew, since the flight would be empty. Margaret was visiting my sister Christine in Frisco and I asked her to meet Hannah on arrival. I gave the date and ETA which she said she would do. I later learned Margaret had no intention of meeting the flight; Hannah took a bus into town.

When school was about to start, I came over to make certain everything was all right. Hannah and several other girls shared a couple of rooms at a motel on Brickle Avenue within walking distance to the school in downtown Miami. She was happy with her new found friends and school. A few months previous, I had bought a furnished condo in Stuart. I had made the deal through a PanAm pilot friend of mine who had retired and was in the real estate business. His name was Dick Bohner and quite a character. I told Hannah she could use it on weekends and holidays, but no wild parties.

It was early in '81 that Saudia starting receiving their fleet of B-747s. Again, I was to be a very busy ICAO inspector. It had been agreed that three inspectors would meet the first aircraft at Orly Airport, France. It would be arriving from Seattle, non-stop. The General Manager, Captain Mattar, would be the pilot, along with other dignitaries. From there, we would supervise the flight back to Jeddah, as a proving run.

After the airport inspection at Orly, we found the fueling and ramp section unsatisfactory for the 747 and recommendations were made to get things in order, but that would take some time. The morning for the arrival of the 747, heavy fog had set in and no way could the plane land so it diverted to Rome. When the weather finally cleared, the three of us hopped on Air France to Rome. In spite of the long delay and waiting, Captain Mattar was a perfect gentleman. He knew this was an important part of the flight and approval for the 747 and routing. The weather was clear all the way to Cairo and late that afternoon the flight landed in Jeddah. There was a lot of fanfare at the ramp; many Saudi officials greeted the crew. The three of us vanished in the crowd.

I was now kept busy giving type ratings on the 747 to the Saudi pilots, designating check airmen for the airplane and enroute. Sometimes we would be eight hours in the air, circling around locally, making instrument approaches and landings. There would be four pilots at a time. Flight engineers also had to be checked. When this had been completed, I had to conduct inaugural and approving flights on most of their routes. The important one was the North Atlantic route; here I was checking the route and check airmen. The New York flights were nonstop from Jeddah, 12-13 hours a flight.

It was summer before I had accomplished most of the initial flight checks. Then came the request for Category-II (CAT-II) qualifications, not just for the crew, but for the aircraft as well; this would involve our operations and the Avionics Department. The Saudi people were very cooperative in all departments and all went smoothly, including the emergency ditching and evacuation procedures.

Christian wrote that he would be graduating in a few months from GMI, in the meantime he had a couple weeks leave and wanted to come to Jeddah for a visit. He came via PanAm and I met the flight in Daharan. It was wonderful to see him and he thought Jeddah was intriguing and a great place. He even met some of my harem and Louisa. We had time to do some sailing and a swim off the reefs. Christian became excited when I told him that General Motors had a large facility here in Jeddah. I arranged for him to meet the Americans working for GM, some of the staff had been graduates from GMI. He inquired about the possibility of coming to Jeddah when he graduated. He was told he'd have to wait in line; there were other employees in the States who were also anxious to come over, the extra money being the incentive.

I always hated to see my kids stay for such a short time and then they would be gone. The next moment I was seeing Christian off on his PAA flight from Daharan. In these cases I was glad to be kept busy, I didn't have to sit around the apartment and mope. I still did more exhausting North Atlantic checks. 12 hours to New York, overnight and 12 hours back. Another project came up which was to check and approve all of Saudia airports in the Kingdom, about twenty or so, and then international. It took about ten days to accomplish the ones in Saudi. The company assigned a 737 to take us from one airport to the next. It was interesting to learn that some of these fields were at a high altitude and cold. The airport managers, on learning of our arrival, would lay out the red carpet and give a sumptuous lunch with the usual lamb. I had given many airport inspections with FAA, but never received this kind of red carpet treatment. One of my flights with Saudia took me to Dacca, Bangladesh. I did the airport inspection there at the old Tezgaon base. It was still in miserable condition. The civil aviation authorities said the new airport would be ready in about two months at Camatola. My good old friend Cookie was able to come and visit me for two days. He was still spry and happy in his village. I then covered Saudias' other airports to Delhi, Bombay, Bangkok, Singapore, Kula-Lampur and Manila. I was getting a lot of traveling done at Saudia expense. I even had to do JFK International Airport and found it unsatisfactory! I felt the ATC personnel were lacking in proficiency. After Reagan had fired the original ATC people and filled the gaps with quicky new hires, that were unable to cope with the heavy traffic around New York. I found Runway 31-left did not have the proper markings for displaced thresholds. New taxiways were being made, with large black plastic sheeting to cover the wet cement. The sheeting was not properly tied down, consequently, the wind was blowing plastic onto the runways. A couple of foreign carriers had engines shut down when they ingested the plastic. I believe the Port Authority took a dim view of my report, which I had given to FAA flight standards at Valley Stream.

At Delhi I always found time to contact my friend Joginder Singh. He once played field hockey for the Indian team in the '62 Olympics. He would drive me up the Hills, Naini-Tal and Ranikhet. Another time we drove up to Mussoorie where I located my mother's old home, Whyte-Bank Castle. St. George's college had bought the estate and made additions to accommodate more students. I also visited the old house in Landour further up the mountain. This is where we stayed when I was five years old in 1919. Some of my ICAO friends had their kids attending the American school of Woodstock. I took them to lunch one day and then to tell

*With Elias Aghabi Assistant Director of Civil Aviation for Jordan.*

their folks they were doing fine. One was Teressa MacCarthy. Her dad was maintenance, ex-FAA and was born in Bangor, Maine. I once worked for his uncle Mike at the Bangor House. Small world. His daughter had a nose ring and said not to tell her folks back in Jeddah! I didn't but let them look at some tell tale photos! It was on this trip I learned that my very good friend Percy Sherred from Bhowali had passed away. He was a great naturalist of Indian flora and fauna. It was sad news when I learned this from Joginder Singh.

With all the traveling to the Far East doing airport inspections and other flight checks, time whizzed by. December was on us and Christmas around the corner. Christmas in Saudi Arabia is just another working day. I had already made my plans to return to the States to be with Christian and Hannah for the Holidays. I went to Stuart and my condo where the kids joined me. It was indeed a joyous get together. The two of them seemed happy with their schools. I bought Hannah a second hand car to get around in Miami; the truck had been sold.

It was now 1982 and I was back in Jeddah, enjoying the never ending work program. Our staff began to grow with new ICAO people showing up. Then our American Chief, Van Gundy was starting to act strange, especially toward me. We had been friends; I had shown him around Saudi Airlines and introduced him to all the right people, and spoke highly of him to the PCA officials. Some of my friends said he was jealous of me; my being a bachelor and wearing a Saudi uniform, traveling around the world giving flight checks; and my harem and parties. I tried to just shrug it off.

Hannah wrote that graduation was coming up toward the end of May and hoped I could be there. With the continued Atlantic flight checks, I found time to fly down to Stuart. I phoned Hannah I was home, she would let me know the exact date. Another ICAO friend who had just been released from the Saudi office was coming to Miami and try to obtain his FAA flight engineer certificate on the B-707. I picked Bill Jacob up and brought him back to Stuart and I arranged his written test at the Stuart airport. He planned to take the simulator/aircraft check

*Our first snow storm in Amman Jordan February, 1985.*

*The rock that Moses struck for water. Guard protects the site. The water flows to Petra.*

in Oklahoma City. Bill and I enjoyed the few days playing golf and meeting my friend Dick Bohner. Interestingly enough, while talking to Dick, it turned out that Dick's uncle had founded a college in Lahore, in Pakistan. It was this school that Bill Jacob had attended.

Sunday morning Bill and I relaxed at the apartment. Hannah phoned to say her graduation was the next day, not to come down, that she would drive up that Monday afternoon. Monday morning, Bill and I finished breakfast and cleaned up the mess in the kitchen. About 9 a.m. the phone rang. It was Christian and he sounded choked up. I asked if he was okay and he replied, "Just a second." I gathered something was wrong. Then he said, his voice shaking, "Dad, I have just received word from the police in Fairfield. They just informed me that mother has died in a car crash." I was stunned! We both were silent for a second. I could hear Christian sobbing. I knew how much he loved his mother. That broke me up too. My thoughts of Margaret came rushing back to me; Rome, Beirut, England and Ft. Lamy. I don't recall too much of our conversation at that moment, but I collected my thoughts and asked Christian for some of the story. All he could gather from the police was that Margaret and Will Brown were driving back to Fairfield from New Jersey, where they had been visiting friends. It was late at night, somewhere on the Merritt Parkway. Will Brown went to sleep at the wheel. The car crashed into an abutment of an overhead pass. Margaret died instantly. Brown was still alive, in critical condition at

the Norwalk Hospital. I knew Christian was under strain and I asked if he had called Hannah. He said no; I said I would tell her when she arrived. Christian said he would leave on the first flight from Michigan, where he was now working for the Buick Company. He had called Margaret's sister and had arranged for her to come from Manchester, England. I told him that Hannah and I would leave as soon as she was able and to arrange rooms for us at the Fairfield Inn. Christian said he would handle the whole thing.

I told Bill Jacob what had happened. He said he would go over to the club house when Hannah arrived and I'd contact him there. Hannah drove up about 12:30, bubbling over with excitement and the news that she had passed above average, she had brought along her potted plants for the apartment. I think she saw the expression on my face. She stood for a second and put the plants on the table. How does one break news like this to someone you love so much? I took hold of her and held her tight. Then, half sobbing, I told her that her mother had died in a car accident the night before. Hannah's legs seemed to give away, I had to hold her up. It was several minutes before she could gain her strength. Hannah is a very strong person. There were tears in her eyes, her jaws clenched tight, then she wanted to know what happened. I told her what Christian had mentioned. She wanted to be alone and sat on the porch with a beer and cigarette.

After several hours on the porch Hannah got up and said, "Okay Dad; let's pack up and get started early in the morning." Bill said he would take care of the apartment. Early next morning Hannah insisted on driving in her car. She was fine and we drove straight through. Hannah had her jaw set and golly, how well she drove. We arrived at the Fairfield Inn late the next afternoon. She dropped me off and took off for Brown's house. She wanted to check on her dog Penny. Hannah felt the dog had probably been neglected and left in the garage most of the time. How correct she was!

The poor animal was emaciated with very little food and water.

By the time Christian came for me, I had a shower and felt refreshed. He took me to the house and here I met Margaret's sister, Peggy and brother, Michael, whom I hadn't seen for many years. It was a solemn occasion while Hannah tended to her dog, Christian was very much in charge, making all the funeral arrangements. He was notifying all his mothers friends by phone. I felt strange being in this house and seeing all my belongings that I had gathered in different parts of the world. I hoped that at least the children would be allowed to have them.

The funeral service was held at the Episcopal Church nearby. There were a few PanAm people present. Christine and Geraldine were there too. I could see Christian was feeling the sorrow; Hannah would not let anyone know her own grief. After the service and cremation, which Margaret wanted, the ashes were taken back to England to be placed in a certain spot near her family home in Eccles. Some close friends gathered back at the Browns' house while Christian and I decided we needed a couple of large scotches; he needed it more than me. Brown's layer hovered around and appeared to keep a watchful eye on the household.

The next shock came when Christian mentioned to me that his mother had a new will made, leaving everything to Will Brown and not a damn thing for the kids! I was livid; this had to be a gimmick, some sort of wild scheme of Brown's to arrange a will so that Margaret would leave everything to him, and vice versa. When the final account was made, Brown received all the insurance money, somewhere around $200,000, all her jewelry and other personal effects, plus the furniture that I had collected in the past 20 years. Not one sausage for the children; not a red cent! I tried to get a couple of lawyers to go to bat for us. They informed me it was cut and dry, since the will was made out in the name of Brown, there was nothing that could be done.

I dropped in to see Will Brown in the hospital and in our conversation he admitted he had gone to sleep at the wheel. The last thing he remembered was waking up in a ball on the floor of the tangled car, but I got nothing in writing. His smart ass lawyer was making certain of that. I knew the police had something to that affect; Christian said one of the officers had told him so. We couldn't get to first base with them either.

Penny, Hannah's dog, became very sick, and we took it to the vet. The vet said the dog was riddled with cancer; it was best to put the animal to sleep. I never will forget the moment when I saw Hannah's expression: all her thoughts and love were with the dog now. She even sat in the kennel with Penny. I couldn't bear to see her and walked out. Hannah cried, but she was tough. "Oh God! What a deal!" The whole thing was wearing heavy on me. "Okay, Daddy let's go have a drink." We stopped at the Hi-Ho Restaurant Bar which was located on the Merritt Parkway, not far from where Will Brown crashed the car.

Margaret's relatives returned to England and Christian to the Buick Company in Flint, MI. Hannah got a job doing commercial art for a local company in Danbury, CT and stayed with her boyfriend's folks. I returned to my duties with ICAO in Jeddah.

No sooner was I back to work when I was informed by the American Manager Vangundy in ICAO that my contract would terminate the end of November 1982, because of my age. However, I knew there was more to it than that and I did not wish to pursue the matter.

I sold my yacht and made preparations to leave. I said farewell to the PCA officials and Saudi Airlines. The eventful day arrived and I left Jeddah for New York and the FAA office in Valley Stream. I sold the condo I had in Fairfield. It was to help pay a lot of expenses and I wound up buying another cheaper one in the same area. Hannah was happy in her work in Danbury. Christian decided he was not cut out to be an engineer or mechanic with General Motors and resigned and moved to my condo in Stuart, FL. He soon found a job with a travel agency that he liked very much. I had arranged with him to buy me a car, preferably an Oldsmobile, in Stuart and drive it to Connecticut. He showed up in Danbury with a fine automobile. It felt good to be back from all that horrendous work load that I had in Jeddah. Here I was back home with my two children and a wonderful Thanksgiving. Christian and I then drove back to Stuart for a holiday and to celebrate Christmas and New Year of 1983. Right after that I drove back to Fairfield and my routine air carrier inspector's work.

Although I was assigned to ICAO I still worked for the FAA. Saudia and the PCA made it mandatory that all Saudi cockpit crew members had to obtain United States (FAA) certificates and be rated on the specific aircraft they flew. The crew members were issued Saudi Arabian licenses, based upon their FAA certification. Having flown with most of these crews, I would say they are first class pilots and flight engineers. Therefore, Saudi is an extremely safe airline.

*His Royal Highness, Prince Sultan Bin Salman Al-Saud, of Saudi Arabia, in his astronaut uniform.*

# PHASE TEN: 1983 – 1990

Because of the long distance from Fairfield to Valley Stream, I was able to share a small apartment with a PanAm friend in Jamaica, NY. I stayed with Dave Gober in New York during the weekdays and I'd be back in Fairfield on the weekends. After a couple of weeks of this routine, the Olds was stolen in New York. The police located it after three weeks with not much damage to the car. It had been parked next to a hydrant and was covered with bird droppings and parking tickets. It took a bit of doing to have all the crap and tickets erased. This prompted me to stay in Fairfield. The drive everyday was a bit horrendous. It was an hour and a half, with about $5.50 in tolls everyday. In winter, it was absolute misery.

One day in March of '83 I received a phone call from Christian; he was pretty well shook-up. He told me a growth had formed under his right jaw. The doctor had diagnosed it as cancer of the lymph system. It was necessary to have a major operation to remove a part of his liver for biopsy. I was heartbroken. The poor lad had been through hell with the death of his mother and now this in less than a year. I flew to Stuart to be with him for a few days during the operation. The biopsy was negative and showed the cancer had not penetrated or spread to his abdomen. The doctors recommended that Christian take radiation therapy. In so doing he would lose his hair. I was back in Fairfield when he informed me he was fine except for being bald. I tried to cheer him up by saying that Yul Bryner had been through the same treatment and his trademark was his bald head. I even helped Christian with some of the expenses which the insurance didn't cover. Before long he was back at work and his hair had grown back in. Hannah's friend John was a fine young guy working in the computer programming business with his folks. The Soboleskis had

made a small apartment for Hannah, where she appeared to be happy and had bought another fawn colored Labrador retriever, called Eccles.

On occasions I was scheduled to Miami to conduct B-707 flight checks for the FAA Office. This gave me an opportunity to visit with Christian in Stuart. He was getting along great working at a travel agency nearby.

The year 1983 seemed to slip by. Before I knew it, Christmas had rolled around again. I took some leave and spent the time with Christian. My sister Geraldine also joined us in Stuart.

Early in 1984 I was still chasing PanAm and TWA around on the B-747 program when another company sprang up in New York by the name of People's Express. They operated several B-747s between JFK and Gatwick, England. When not on PAA or TWA, I was flying with People's Express. Then, one day, I received a call from an old FAA friend of mine by the name of Lou

Clark. He and I had been in Jeddah with ICAO. He was now based with the FAA at the Kansas City Office. We had always hit it off together. Lou informed me that the FAA was planning to set up a Civil Aviation Assistance Group (CAAG) in Amman, Jordan. He knew I had once lived there and wanted to know if I was interested in bidding one of the positions? I sure was. The FAA were recruiting a chief, two operations, one avionics and an airworthiness inspector. Lou stated the FAA in Washington were having difficulty in takers for the jobs. They had to rebid the positions. I told Lou I would fill out the usual 171 form and stand by. He said he would call me soon as he obtained further information. Like most government assignments, it's always hurry up and wait. It was late March before the bids and selections were made. Lou Clark was chosen as the airworthiness inspector with two other people and myself. I was to act as the chief and operations inspector (a two hatted job). I called Christian to see if he would like to

*With my FAA colleagues at my retirement party, December, 1990.*

move back to Fairfield into my town house. He thought that would be great. Hannah and a girl friend drove a truck to Stuart and helped Christian move his things back to Fairfield. I was delighted to have my two children with me, even though it was for a very short spell. Brussels then called me and asked that I join their group that was headed for Amman. It was to be a "get to know the lay of the land." I enrouted on TWA 747, a non-stop flight from JFK to Cairo, from there on Royal Jordan Airlines to Amman. Rooms had been arranged at the Marriot Hotel with the rest of the group. Good old Dave Switzer from the Rome office also was there. It was great seeing Dave again and Mr. Phil Swatek, Chief of the Brussels office. Meetings were held with U.S. Embassy officials, the Director of Civil Aviation, General Balqez and his deputy Mr. Elias Aghabi. It was like old home week, being in Jordan after nearly thirty years. I took time to do some apartment hunting with one of the local Jordanians working for the Embassy. Mr. Aghabi showed us where our offices would be. I took a liking to Mr. Aghabi with his frank, gruff ways. Dave and I met on one occasion with General Balqez. He asked us to hold off for about two months, before we all showed up. The DG wanted time to set up the offices and recruit some operations inspectors. The longer we could delay our arrival, the better, at least till after the first week in June. I asked if it would be all right to arrive a week or so in advance to do apartment hunting for the group. That would be fine. Dave sent a message to Brussels and Washington stating the DG's desire for the delay.

Dave and I then took off for Karachi. The Pakistan Director General of Aviation was most interested in having a similar program for their civil aviation. However, the DG hoped that the U.S. Government would foot the entire bill for the program. The FAA would never consider such a deal. We spent two days in Karachi before Dave departed for Rome and I went my way back to New York, enrouting on PanAm.

On my return to Fairfield Christian informed me he had another job at a travel agency in the nearby town of Norwalk. We celebrated these events and he appeared content. One evening he mentioned to me he felt a little strange being back in Fairfield, but hoped to get used to it. One thing he told me and I didn't realize was how much he disliked his step father. Both he and Hannah officially had their names changed back to Goutiere which made me happy. Christian assured me he would take good care of the apartment while I was gone.

In the midst of my move and my plans being made for my departure to Jordan, Hannah and John decided to get married. It was a beautiful wedding held at an inn near CandleWood Lake, Connecticut. Hannah looked stunning in her wedding gown and wide brimmed hat. John was tall and handsome in his tux. What made it all so more wonderful, Christine and Geraldine were able to attend. It was the nicest going away present Hannah and

*Evelyn floating in the Dead Sea, 1986.*

John could have given me, on May 12th, 1984.

The FAA International office in Washington called, advising me that a briefing of the Civil Aviation Assistance Group (CAAG) would be held on the 16th and for all to be present. Christian and I drove down and stayed with my friend and his wife, Pete and Ann Chesney in Annapolis. The first meeting was at the International office (AIA-1). The chief was a Mr. Tom Messier, who in my first impression was a most knowledgeable person. (It was in this same office I had the meeting in 1974, when I was informed my name was being linked in the assassination attempt on Gadhafi.) After the pleasantries and meeting my colleagues who would make up the CAAG team, Mr. Messier discussed our duties in Amman. I was glad that he would be our top advisor when serious questions arose. Our Avionics expert was a Frank Day, a short, robust person. He had been with the FAA flight inspection team in Lebanon for six years. The operations inspector was a Jack Kenton, an unknown quantity. I had met Jack once before when he was with the Eastern Region and had once been a flight engineer with Pan American. After talking with the group, I felt we could accomplish the task. An AIA girl representative gave us a so called overseas briefing, which turned out to be very weak. During another meeting, a call came for me from the Brussels office and wanted to know if we were ready to depart for Amman. Only Clark and his wife Jodi were set to go. Brussels wanted to know what the hold up was, why I wasn't ready. I explained that the Jordan DG was not ready for us. Switzer had sent a message from Amman sometime ago to that effect, and to AIA in Washington. Brussels was not aware of any such message; neither was Washington. Luckily I had a copy. I showed this to AIA and sent a copy to Brussels. This was one of many misunderstandings and lacks of communication between our team and Brussels. Also at the briefing the girl had said we would have to take U.S. carriers as far as possible, then

transfer to Royal Jordan Airlines. I told her negative; that our contract stated we would have free transportation on Royal Jordan Airlines all the way with about four hundred pounds of personal effects. This created a rumpus. To prevent further argument, it was agreed that the others could go on U.S. carrier. I said I would find my own way across. Lou wanted to go as soon as possible to look for apartments. I said I would follow a short while later to help. Again I told Mr. Messier, the DG didn't want us to start work now; but it was okay to do some house hunting. I received my free ticket on RJ and arrived in Amman on the 25th of May. Lou was already setting up the office and meetings with our Jordanian counterparts. The airport (Queen Alia) is fifteen miles south of Amman. I checked in at the Amra Hotel, located on the edge of Amman. The all night jet lag had done me in.

Lou had informed me he had already moved into a fairly nice apartment not far from the Amra hotel. I relaxed that afternoon till Lou came by to pick me up for dinner with them. The other two inspectors arrived ten days later via U.S. carriers with their baggage lost. The extra personal effects of four hundred pounds were also lost some place between Europe and Amman. It would be a couple of months before it showed up. Both Frank and Jack stayed at the Amra hotel till apartments were located. These were just some of the troubles to plague us.

The temporary offices for us were located at the airport Tower building; while arrangements were being made to move to a new location still in the sterile area of the airport. This was yet another mistake. In the meantime Mr. Aghabi was giving us a lot of information and assistance.

Another problem cropped up: no transportation. The Embassy and FAA were supposed to have arranged two cars for our official use before arriving. There was none. The team hitched rides with our Jordanian friends, and to make matters even more difficult, our arrival and office move came at the time of Ramadan, the Muslim Holy

*"Geraldine, myself, Christian, and Hannah and John, at their wedding."*

month. Just to move from the temporary offices to the new one shouldn't have taken more than a day. It took ten days.

On the Embassy notice board I saw a BMW car for sale. It belonged to the Deputy Chief of Mission (DCM), a Mr. Ed Djerejian; I bought it in desperation. A couple years later Mr. Djerejian would be in Damascus, Syria as the new U.S. Ambassador.

The CAAG team was invited to visit with Ambassador Viets and DCM Djerejian. Questions were asked in reference to our mission and our background. I guess this is customary as it was when I had to visit Ambassador's office in Beirut when I was with FAA there in '73. When asked if all was going well and were there any problems, it gave me an opportunity to mention the difficulty of transportation; that it was necessary for me to buy the DCM's car for our wheels to the airport. I said that a vehicle had been bought for us; but due to red tape, the car was still stuck in the Embassy garage. One quick phone call from the Ambassador and a day later CAAG had its first official transportation. In further conversation, the DCM mentioned to the Ambassador that I knew His Majesty King Hussein and had been his friend for more than thirty years. The Ambassador said that was great and to be sure to keep that friendship.

Through the month of July nothing but problems beset our team; though some may have appeared minor, when added up, it was one big can of worms. We had no secretary, no typewriters, no FAA stationary or office supplies, no technical library (a must) to progress with our work. Three of us - Kenton, Day and myself - were still at the Amra hotel with most expenses coming out of our pockets. We were not being perdiemed by FAA as informed at the FAA briefing in Washington. Our perdiem under State Department rules was not more than a few dollars a day, about enough for breakfast. In desperation Day and Kenton accepted apartments that were not that adequate but would suffice. I was more fortunate in obtaining a fairly large villa. I was told I had to have something like that since I would have to entertain important people. I had one problem with the place: it was a heck of a chore to keep clean. I asked one of the officers from the Personnel Department, Mr. Bertolet, if he knew where I could find someone to do my house work. In Jeddah I remember I had a houseboy that worked for me. Mr. Bertolet said he would inquire around.

Through the Embassy I was able to choose a secretary, a local Palestinian girl. She spoke English, Arabic and French; above all, she was a computer expert. Now we had a secretary but no place to put her. The CAA had not provided an office as yet, and no typewriter or computer. It was the Embassy to the rescue again. They agreed to give us office space for the time being and use of one of the word processors. And since we still didn't have FAA stationary we used Embassy letter head. When one problem was alleviated, it seemed to create another. In this case it meant having the secretary fifteen miles away from your office. We would rough draft our correspondence and reports in long hand, then in the afternoon drive to the Embassy, deliver the work for the girl, whose name, by the way was, Aida Qara'een. Her office hours were same as the Embassy, eight to four thirty. Ours were the same as the Jordanian, seven-thirty to two, Saturday through Thursday, Friday being the Muslim sabbath. Aida would type everything the next day; we would check for errors, which were numerous, because aviation lingo was a lot different than normal English. It would be awhile before Aida began to catch on. For now, after corrections, she would have to redo the final typing. In this manner correspondence would take several days. It was better than nothing. Not till February '85 did Aida join us at our office at Queen Alia Airport, without computer or typewriter.

Regardless of our difficulties, the Brussels office said they wanted the Implementation Plan on their desk by mid September. It was a three month project. I gave the Plan to our avionics man, Frank Day. I'll never know how, but Frank accomplished the job, and did it damn well. He literally burned the midnight oil. His apartment was on the fourth floor of a modern apartment house; yet the electrical power was out about fifty percent of the time. We would all help him and his wife Johhanah haul the groceries up four flights of stairs. Frank had bought an oil lamp so he could do some of his work at night. The team presented the Implementation Plan to the new Director General of CAA, General Mohammed Ali. The Deputy Director, Aghabi, called him Cassius Clay, after the boxer! As soon as the plan had been approved and signed, I gave Frank the privilege of hand carrying the package to the FAA office in Brussels. Not only were they surprised that it was on their desk on schedule, they were more surprised at the professionalism of the Plan.

Perhaps this prompted Brussels to assign me permanently as the CAAG manager and a GS-15. I would like to have seen the whole team as GS-15s, since they worked hard against many odds.

At the beginning of August my friend Bob Bertilet called to say he had located a Philippine girl that would like to take care of my villa on a twice a week basis. Her name was Evelyn and would phone me for an appointment. As a parting thought, Bob added, "Pete, don't try to screw her, she is a hell of a nice girl!" "Who, me?" That weekend Evelyn phoned and said she would like to meet me at a place called Sweets Grocery Store located between the sixth and fifth circle on Wadi Sir Road, close to the Amra Hotel. It was on the main drag right into town, on which are also located the American and other embassies, the Zahran Palace and Intercontinental Hotel. On this street there are eight traffic circles. It was the way people explained where certain buildings were located, in conjunction to the appropriate circle, the first circle being near the center of town. I arrived a little early at Sweets and waited in the car and watched for a Philippine girl. There were a lot of Filipino people in Amman; I hoped I'd intercept the right one! The Filipino men were hired mainly for construction work, the women as nurses, waitresses and stewardess for the airlines. In a short time I noticed an oriental girl walking up the street toward Sweets. She looked tall and slender with black wavy hair to her shoulders. The girl walked gracefully with shoulders straight and looked attractive. It was Evelyn. After introductions we headed for the villa. She kept referring to me as "Sir!" Like a lot of people from the Far East countries she had difficulty pronouncing certain words that had "v"; she pronounced it like a "B'. I found it amusing and I liked it. I gave Evelyn a tour of the place. The ground floor had a three bed rooms, two bathrooms, a living room/dining room and a very large kitchen. Downstairs had another bathroom and maids quarters. This I was using as storage and for the washer/dryer. Evelyn wasted no time going to work; she hustle-bussled about the place, setting about making lunch for two! I kept myself occupied writing letters and reports to hand Aida at the Embassy every day. Now that I had Evelyn doing my household chores, a burden had been lifted off my shoulders. Evelyn insisted on doing all the cooking for lunch and left a meal for me in the evening. I agreed to pay her taxi to work.

Not long after working for me, Evelyn came in one morning and seemed upset about something. She finally told me that the people she was staying with were returning to the Philippines and she was unable to take on the apartment by herself. I suggested that she take one of my spare rooms at no cost. This cheered her up. So we drove to the apartment to collect her belongings. I wasn't certain how this would fit in with the Embassy society. Oh well, we would see. Then on September 5th Hannah phoned and said, "How would you like to be a Grand-Daddy?" Wow! She had just had a baby boy, and had decided to call him Miles, her mother's maiden name.

The Director General had a special meeting for CAA and CAAG in early October. There were also members from ATC, Airports and Deputy Aghabi. After several subjects were discussed, Mr. Aghabi stated that it was expected for CAAG members to participate and do some of the flight checks and airport inspections until we had trained our counterparts to a point where they could go on their own. I stated this was not so; we were strictly advisors. "Negative," said Aghabi. "We have a letter from the FAA in Washington stating the CAAG team would do some of the work, check rides, etc., till the Jordanians became competent." I said I had no knowledge of any such agreement. "I'll show it to you." Aghabi took a letter from a folder and handed it to me. Sure enough, there it was, signed by a Mr. Quentin Taylor. I was chagrined and embarrassed. With the FAA, it was a case of one hand not knowing what the other was doing. I later called Brussels regarding Taylor's letter. They were vague about it. No one had seen it; Washington was aware of the letter yet it was not brought up at the briefing. We were informed we were advisors only.

Not only was the CAAG team short one inspector, we were actually trying to do a job that required twice the number we had. According to the Implementation Plan, we were to write all the Jordanian Civil Aviations Regulations, and their Handbooks for inspector's guidance - 20 in all. They expected this to be done in six months. It took three months just to do the Implementation Plan against all odds. We were handicapped as it was. We were now expected to roll up our sleeves and do airman certification, enroutes and airport inspections. My group were ready to throw in the towel and go home. So many things had gone wrong from the start, I could hardly blame them. I had to cajole, humor, wheedle and do everything possible to have them stay. It finally worked out.

Toward the end of November the DG wanted me to qualify a couple of captains as North Atlantic check airmen on the B747. I notified Brussels of the request from Royal Jordanian Airlines. The response I got over the phone was a shock. I was told I was conniving in order to get to the States. For the moment I was lost for words. I explained the situation. "No!" My job was to mind the store; not to go flying around the world. I agreed, but the CAA were holding us to Taylor's letter. Brussels reluctantly gave the okay; however, they needed verification from the DG. He had to send a message to FAA verifying the request. Two days before departure I felt the symptom of a cold coming on; and when I catch one, its usually a grand-daddy. I called Christian to meet me. It was terribly cold and miserable on arrival. It was always wonderful to see my children all grown up. The next day in Fairfield the cold hit me, and I had to see my doctor. Next day was Thanksgiving; cold or no cold we went to visit Hannah and John for a turkey dinner. I was delighted to see my grandson Miles, but didn't dare get too close to him. Friday I decided to venture down to the Eastern Region office. I visited some of my old friends and got permission to raid the supply room for much needed stationary and manuals to start the technical library. These were the essentials that Brussels had yet to furnish. I stayed in bed the next two days and then went back to Amman. The flight back didn't help the cold; my ears had plugged up badly. It was necessary to visit the Embassy clinic. Evelyn had taken good care of the house in my absence and was delighted with the presents I brought her from the States.

Though it's a small area, Jordan boasts unique contrasts in climate; one could say it has four seasons. The weather is characterized by a short cold winter and a short spring, followed by a long summer. Even during the summer, the nights can be extremely cold. The rainy season is in the winter; snow is likely, up to several feet at times. On my arrival back from New York the weather was clear. My colleagues were elated when I unloaded my booty of office supplies from the Eastern Region. I wish I could have brought back a type writer or word processor for Aida. Ours had still not arrived.

One night, not long after my arrival, I guess I had fallen fast asleep, when something woke me. I wasn't too sure in my drowsiness what had happened. I rolled to one side and felt a warm body next to me. It was Evelyn. It took a moment to actually know it was her. It didn't take long to come to my senses. In months to come we were to fall in love. When Christmas was on us, I knew it would be a special one with Evelyn as a part of the household. With direct dial-

*Christian at Mount Nebo where Moses once spoke, Jordan 1987.*

ing I called Christian and Hannah and wished them the Holiday Season. Through the Embassy it was possible to order articles from the special Armed Forces Exchange Catalog (AFES). All purchases were tax and duty exempt. I bought a Hi-Fi set, a camcorder, VCR and television.

The beginning of 1985 was still troublesome as far as getting our work accomplished on schedule. Most immediate information and requests were done over the phone to Brussels and Washington. CAAG finally received the word processor and copy machine in February '85. At last Aida was able to move to our offices at ALIA airport. She was coming along just fine in understanding the strange terminology of aviation.

Work was slow in formulating the aviation civil air rules (CARS) and the handbooks for the CAA inspectors to use as guides. From the beginning, the Ambassador's office was appraised of our difficulties and progress and helped as much as possible. On several occasions our new Ambassador Boeker met the FAA from Brussels and Washington to help iron out some of them.

Another disaster hit us. We had signed a agreement for a tour of three years in Jordan without home leave. At the Embassy we learned that a new order had come out in a FAM-3, stating that a three year tour could be split in eighteen month tours, entitling overseas personnel to home leave. I brought this to the attention of superiors in Washington and Brussels. They would not budge and allow us this privilege. It was a blow that affected my people. Home leave is taken in lieu of annual leave. It appeared the FAA were playing games with us. When perdiem was of concern on our arrival in Amman, they stated we came under State Department rules; when the issue of leave was concerned they stated we came under the FAA rules, and so it went. We just couldn't win.

To cheer us up at the end of February, I woke one morning for work; I looked out of the kitchen window and was surprised to see a blizzard in progress. There was a foot of snow already accumulated on the ground. We always took turns in driving the van to work. I called Frank to see what was on schedule for pick-up. He said he was driving and no problem, that he had lived in Alaska for many years and would be by to pick me up. All

*Evelyn and I enjoying the hot springs that flow to Dead Sea. Roman legions stopped to bathe here when headed north to the city of Damascus, Syria.*

*A view of the Treasury from above.*

offices and schools were closed. The four of us and Aida were the only souls at the office that day.

In June I was scheduled to go to Brussels for the annual conference. Expected were FAA representatives in the AEU geographical area, as well as chiefs from the various CAAGs. It was a good opportunity to meet old acquaintances and make new friends. When my turn came to speak and give my report on our activities, I spoke of the problems that had plagued us since our arrival in Amman. These were aired with recommendations for future CAAG offices that may be established. Back in Amman I briefed the group on what transpired in Brussels. I told them there were no holds barred.

In July Mr. Aghabi informed me there was to be a gala event. The government had purchased a Marconi radar system from England, for their radar control system. There would be a grand opening and presentation to be made. His Majesty, King Hussein would be present and view the station. After that ceremony we would be invited to the radar center to have a look. This was to be followed by a tea reception. It would be an opportunity to meet His Majesty again, and Queen Noor (Najeeb Haliby's daughter). When the DG Mohamed Ali started to introduce us, His Majesty looked at me, then said, "Pete?" "Yes, Your Majesty, its me!" We embraced Arab style. The people watching, particularly the DG, were taken aback. Mr. Ghandour wasn't, he knew that HM and I were old friends. I talked with His Majesty for awhile and reminisced the old days in Jordan. I told him a lot of Holy Water had flowed down the Jordan River since we last met. He hoped we could have another op-

portunity to talk and discuss FAA matters and CAAG at a later date.

By November the team had completed the accident investigation handbook for the DG's approval. The group had worked very hard writing up the handbook; the regulations were coming right along. I arranged with Brussels for most of the CAAG team to return to their homes in the States for Christmas and New Year's. They certainly earned it. It would be annual leave they would have to take. Evelyn and I scanned the AFES catalog to see what we could get ourselves for X-mas presents and for Hannah's kid. We got a artificial Christmas tree and all the decorations. It turned out to be a great Christmas with phone calls back to Connecticut. We invited Mr. and Mrs. Aghabi over for drinks; we became good friends. Quite often Mr. Aghabi took us down to the Dead Sea for picnics. He knew a spot about fifteen miles to the south on the Sea where there were no tourists. The Arab name for the place is Zarqa Ma'in. It is famous for its hot, fresh water springs that gush out of the high barren mountainside. Aghabi showed us how to first plaster oneself with mineral-type mud that oozes from the rocky beach. Let it soak into the skin for a few minutes, then dunk into the Sea, where you float like a cork. The Dead Sea is so heavy with salt, it's impossible to sink. Once mud has been washed off, you sit under one of the hot water falls for a few more minutes. The water pounds on your body like having a massage. One feels invigorated from the treatment. The minerals are said to rid one of any kind of skin infection. This was a famous stop for Roman Legions when they passed along here on their way to Amman and Damascus. Across the Sea are the caves where the Dead Sea Scrolls were discovered. The whole country is steeped in history. Being a history lover, I could stand for hours

and ponder the ancient sea and its biblical surroundings.

On other occasions Evelyn and I would drive north to the ancient city of Jerrash, a Greco-Roman city. It is wonderfully preserved for its time. Hadrian once came to visit the city. The entrance arch, built in his honor, still stands today. I captured a lot of these places on video and with the camera.

Lou Clark and Frank talked about obtaining metal detectors through the AFES catalog. I wasn't to be left out and ordered one myself. It added to the joy of exploring the country and the ruins, searching for coins and other artifacts. Nothing of great value was ever found by us; if they were, I am certain we would turn them over the Department of Antiquities. The coins that I found were mainly of the Byzantine era. There were a few Nabatian coins as well.

The outings cleared our heads from the tremendous work load during the week. It was in October that I had enough time to make my first trip to Petra. Not since the days of AirLiban in Beirut had I been back. This time I took Evelyn. The drive took a little over three hours. I told Evelyn of the times I flew tourists to Ma'an, and then the bus to Petra. The drive was wonderful; the last part I skirted around Ma'an and the scenery was spectacular. After the winding road through pine forests and wheat fields, the descent takes you to Wadi Mousa. I was not able to recognize any of the road till we reached the dry Wadi where the horses were tethered. The horses are for the tourists to ride through the Siq to the ancient city. There are now two hotels near the Siq. One is fairly old and state operated; the other is the Petra Hotel and is run in conjunction with the Amra Hotel in Amman. We were given a room at the Petra Hotel facing toward the ancient city. A large bleak mountain obstructed any view of the city. After a light lunch we took horses and headed for the Siq (narrow gorge). From there on I remembered the trip I took 28 years ago. I had bought a small guide's book that explained the different carved tombs. With this I was able to tell Evelyn some of the history. The horse owners led the ponies along the trail, otherwise the Arab ponies wouldn't budge. I had the fellows stop every so often in order to take pictures. Evelyn was amazed at the structures, especially the first glimpse of the Treasury Tomb through the niche. This particular locale is made famous on Jordanian posters and stamps. Later it was shown in the movie *Indiana Jones and the Last Crusade* (Harrison Ford and Sean Connery). At the ruins we got off and wondered about the rubble and just marveled at the carved tombs that seemed to encompass the whole area. We returned to the Hotel for a shower and a good dinner. As we ate I further told Evelyn of my visits here and how all the tourists and crew had to stay in tents in Petra; the food was camp style. Now here we ate in a fancy hotel.

Next morning Evelyn and I made an early start to get ahead of the tourists. This time we walked instead of taking the ponies. The saddles are hard and rough on the behinds. Evelyn was a good sport and joined me in climbing those myriad of ancient carved steps that lead up to the top of one of the craggy mountains, on which the Nabateans held their sacrificial rites. The spot was called "The High Place." It certainly was just that. From the High Place (a little over 3,000' MSL), there is a magnificent view down over the central part of the rubble-strewn city, and all about one can see serrated peaks glowing in the hot sun. The site of Petra is really appreciated from this bird's eye view, approximately half a mile wide, guarded by towering barren mountains. In the distance it is possible to see the reputed tomb of Aaron on Mount Haroun. We stayed awhile taking in the scenery and photographs. Then, descending down the other side of the mountain was no easy task either. From the bottom of the mountain the trail took us around the base, across the old city. We rested and had a bite to eat. I asked Evelyn if she was ready for the next adventure; it was another myriad of carved ancient steps to the El-Deir tomb, also known as the Monastery from the time of the Byzantines. She was game. This was a horrendous climb. We were not acclimated to long walks and climbing such as this. It just about did us in by the time we arrived back at the hotel. We collapsed on our beds, hot and sweaty. Evelyn had her first shot at the tub. I told her that when she finished, to make a tub for me; good and hot. She came out wrapped in a towel and informed me that the bath was ready and the water steaming hot. I had to ease myself in ever so gently. Once I was in, the water felt great on my aching muscles. I was relaxing half asleep, when Evelyn peeked around the door and asked if the water was hot enough. I said it sure was. Her remark that followed, "Don't hard boil your eggs!" I thought it real cute. This had been a wonderful

*Our wedding: from left, the Greek Bishop, King's pilot Eric Ledger, Evelyn and I, and Ruby Ledger.*

trip to the Ancient City. I have no words of my own to express the wonders of the ancient site. Many people think it nothing more than a dust bowl surrounded by craggy mountains. For me it's not. I regard it as another Wonder of the World. If I may take the liberty of quoting the last two lines from poet Dean Burgon: "Match me such a marvel save in eastern clime. A rose red city, half as old as time." This pretty much sums up my feeling. There is so much to these ruins; one can spend hours and days hiking and exploring miles of ancient trails; and steps wandering and disappearing into the mountains. Many of the areas are never shown by the tour guides. During my three years' stay in Jordan, I knew I would be visiting Petra many, many times.

Beginning of January 1986 my colleagues had returned from their Christmas leave. It was my turn to take off. I arranged for Evelyn to join me. I had called Christian to meet us at Kennedy Airport. Though Jordan was cold, it was nothing to what greeted us on arrival in New York. We thought we would freeze to death. Christian had the car heater going full blast all the way home. It took a couple of days to get adjusted and venture outdoors. I took Evelyn to the fancy malls to do some shopping. Both Christian and Hannah accepted Evelyn as though she was one of the family.

Christian said he wanted to go back to college for his PHD in English literature and hopefully be a professor. I thought it swell. He would be accepted at Washington University in Seattle. In that case, we had better get rid of the condo. I contacted my real estate friend. It only took a couple of days to have it sold at a fair profit. Christian had his things stored with Hannah and my furniture at a storage center. Christian had time off until his school would start early spring. I suggested he take the holiday and come to Jordan for a visit. It was now the end of January with everything packed and ready for our return to Amman. We stayed the last couple days with

Hannah and her growing family. We had just finished our dinner, when the TV news reported an accident had occurred with the space shuttle Challenger. They showed the lift off, then about 30 seconds into the flight, the vivid sight of the shuttle explosion with the fiery debris dropping through the sky. A terrible awesome sight, knowing there were young brave people in that ship. I later wrote to my young friend, Prince Bin Saud, telling him of the disaster. He was aware of the tragedy and was grief stricken.

Christian enjoyed his stay in Jordan. He had an opportunity to visit Aquaba on the red sea, and to take a trip to Greece to visit a cousin on one island. I saved Petra, to be sure we could have a couple of days there. It was a pleasant drive down. We stayed at the Petra Hotel where everyone knew me by now, including the owner of the gift shop. He came from Wadi Mousa and knew the country around Petra like the back of his hand. Christian thought Petra was wonderful and hoped he could come back another time for a visit. His holiday finished all too soon. He had to get back to Fairfield and pack his gear into the car for the long drive to Seattle. He didn't want to miss registering in time. Christian had also arranged a job with Doug Fox Travel agency at Kaitak Intl. Airport of Seattle.

The CAAG work progressed in spite of our built-in problems and as long as I had my diversion of sightseeing with Evelyn, I enjoyed the duty. The year of 1986 hurried by with the occasional trip to Bangkok and Singapore to give check rides and airport inspections for the CAA. It was a shame that my counterparts couldn't go along. They were restricted from travel because of insurance. They would not be insured if they rode in the cockpit. It would be necessary to be issued tickets and the airline wouldn't issue any.

Through our travels, Evelyn and I found another interesting area to visit in the north

*With some of my PAN Africa pilot group (42-A) our 50th reunion, 1991*

part of Jordan: a place called Irbid. It is located on a large plateau that overlooks the Jordan Valley, the Golan Heights and the Sea of Galilee. The Romans had built a large city right at the north tip, called Gedara. Some columns still stand that were once part of a temple. Most of the structures remaining show it was built of lava rock, including the amphitheater. There are remnants where there were hot baths. Recent excavations show burial chambers; some of the granite doors still operate. However, most areas are covered over with olive groves that grow on top of the main city. In another section, the Ottomans had erected their own city using a lot of the old lava blocks. We met two young Jordanian boys who lived in the area of the Ottoman enclave called Um Qeis. They spoke limited English; enough for us to get along. We were invited to their homes that were in the old city. The folks made Arabic dishes that I couldn't resist. I ordered a few things through the AFES catalog for these people. We ordered powerful slingshots for the kids and clothes for the other folks. The two young fellows names were Ahmed and Mohammed. They hoped to go through the Jordan University and perhaps one day to visit the United States.

Early in '87 we realized that all the programs would not be completed on schedule. I asked Brussels office to arrange for three inspectors to come over on TDY for a month to six weeks, to help finish the hand books. This too, turned out to lengthy procedure. A bid system was issued nation-wide without many takers. It would be April before FAA came up with several names. When the three inspectors arrived, I wasted little time in putting them to work.

Christian phoned from Seattle that he was doing well and that he had spring break coming up in mid-May. I arranged his tickets on Royal Jordan Airlines to Amman. It was great having him with me again. Since I was quite busy getting the programs finished, Christian was able to do a lot of touring

around Jordan on his own. On one week end I fixed it for the two of us to drive to Petra again. We walked to many areas where there were no tourists. One evening my Arab friend from the gift shop invited us to his home in Wadi Mousa for dinner. It was the traditional lamb stew with baked rice and almonds. I watched as Christian tried to eat with his hands. He did pretty well considering it was the first time. Where does time go? The next instant Christian was phoning again from Seattle, that he had returned safely and was in the books again. Then Hannah phoned to say I was a Granddaddy again, another boy. They called him Franklin.

Early in June I took a trip by myself to Petra. My Arab friend said he knew a place to look for coins. It was very hot and dry, and also the time of Ramadan. Yet I climbed the ragged mountains. I must have trekked many miles; we collected quite a few coins and pottery. Back in Amman I felt tired and my back ached. Though I soaked in a hot tub several times, the ache persisted.

One morning as Evelyn and I started to go shopping, I began to sneeze and in the midst of this, I felt a piercing pain in my lower back and down the left leg. I couldn't walk. Evelyn helped me to the bed and called the nurse at the Embassy clinic. Mrs. Joan Sarwan arranged an appointment for me at the local hospital. My landlord Jubran (a Palestinian) drove us. Evelyn didn't know how to drive. A fine Jordanian doctor attended to me and administered a pain-killer. The next day I was taken by ambulance to a doctor for X-ray pictures. It was diagnosed that I had a ruptured disc between the fourth and fifth vertebrae. The disc had also pushed against the Siatic Nerve that was causing the terrible pain in my left leg. Back at the hospital I was still in torture. I was placed in a private room and given painkillers. The doctor said I needed an operation. The Embassy was against it. They suggested it be done in the States.

There were a bevy of Filipino nurses to take care of me. When Evelyn found this out, she insisted to take over some of the chores, such as bathing me! She didn't want any of the cuties messing around me! With all the torture and painkillers, I was having difficulty going to the john. I had been given a bed pan for the necessary duty. I found it difficult to manipulate myself with the contraption. I couldn't sit on the metal, it would hit against the nerve and start aching again. They produced a funny looking condom affair with a long tube that was supposed to go into the pan. No way! When I tried it out, the tube couldn't handle the flow; it backed up and blew the condom; pee squirted in all directions. The only way was to be escorted to the toilet across the room. Evelyn was always there to the rescue. I mentioned these problems to the doctor. He would see that I was given something to get rid of the constipation that was developing. At the head of my bed was a telephone with a series of buttons and lights. I remember they were yellow, white and red. Each had a name. I think the white was for the day nurse, yellow for the night and the red was an emergency. That night the nurse placed a bed pan under the bed and left. Sometime I developed stomach cramps and could not sleep, so I pushed the yellow button; instead of a cute Filipino nurse coming in, in came a rather tall Arab guy with a drooping mustache. Egad! I thought, the Gadhafi mob has caught up with me. "Oh well," I might as well go one way or the other. "Speak English?" I asked. "Yes," was the response. "My stomach, it is bad. I need something to go to the toilet." "Yes," he nodded and disappeared through the door. He returned with a rather large, long box. This he opened and produced a large capsule. The guy, who I guess was the night nurse, showed me the capsule. It resembled a bomb, somewhat the shape of the ones dropped by the German Stuka dive bombers. He had me roll over and quickly stuck the projectile up my bum. He stepped back to admire his work. The guy then gave me a big smile that showed his gold tooth, just behind the eyetooth. His smile and look resembled a terrorist; he closed the door behind him when he left. He no sooner had gone when things started to happen. I could have sworn it had a timer on it and the guy had set it to go off in no more than two minutes. After a convulsive feeling and rumbling inside there came an explosion; my whole inside seemed to deluge out and downward. There was no time to reach the bed pan on the other side of the bed; let alone make a hobbled dash to the toilet. It was too late. I think my son David would have enjoyed this moment and shown me how to decorate the walls. I just let it go all over the bed. When I was able, I didn't reach for the yellow button; I felt I needed more than the terrorist nurse. I decided to hit the red button. "What the heck, give 'er a 'go." I pushed hard! Who knows, maybe I'd get the White House of the Kremlin! I could hear a bell ringing off in the distance. Then there were shouts and a lot of scurrying and footsteps running down the hall. The door opened and about four people in white entered, then stopped short, including the terrorist! They took a look at the disaster scene and began to talk in Arabic and Filipino. Finally the guy came over to me; he helped me out of the bed and hobbled me to the toilet. I was given a hot shower and a good clean up. The nurses in the meantime, attended to my bed and the general area. Actually, the terrorist guy turned out to be a pretty good Joe when I got to know him. He came to visit me next day and laughed about the accident. He had been born in Palestine, in the district of Ramallah which was once part of Jordan, before the '67 war. I told him I knew the place well. I had often stayed at the Ramallah Hotel when I flew for AirLiban. The guy was tickled pink when I told him.

I was laid up in the hospital for ten days before I was allowed to return to my house. Evelyn took charge from there on. She was given the rest of the bombs just in case it became necessary. The pain in the back and left leg was not so intense. I was told the disc was now receding back from the nerves; that it would still take time and for me to rest and sleep with my legs propped up. Though confined to the house, I was able to conduct my work and placed Frank Day in charge. I kept in touch with Brussels and Washington by phone.

Early July the Civil Regulations were completed and made into the law for the CAA. We now waited for special binders that the Brussels office had ordered. Though Frank was scheduled home, he politely stayed on till I could function once more.

By the end of July Ambassador Boeker and the DCM were scheduled to depart for the States. Boeker's replacements would not take office till after Labor Day. The new DCM would be acting, a Pat Theros. In the meantime I was able to hobble about. My two young friends Ahmed and Mohammed from Um Qeis came all the way by bus to visit me. They also presented me with a few coins they had found. I wanted to pay for them; they wouldn't accept it. They were swell kids and I hoped they made it to college. Frank drove me to the office every day as my walking progressed and I regained my strength.

I remember once when talking to his Majesty's personal pilot, Eric Ledger, that if he had an opportunity to mention to His Majesty that I would like to take him up on his offer to get together and discuss old times and the roll of the FAA (CAAG); also our connection with the airline and how everything in general was coming along. I had more or less forgotten about it. One morning at work, I was informed by a very excited Aida that His Majesty was on the phone and wished to speak to me. I was surprised as she was. After good wishes, His Majesty's secretary stated that His Majesty wanted to meet me at the Palace right away to discuss some of the problems confronting the airline. Since it was mainly maintenance issues, I brought along Frank Day. I was still in the limping stage when we entered his office.

*Pan Africa reunion, with Geraldine and Evelyn.*

Prime Minister Rafai was also present. I was hoping my friend Ali Ghandour would show up as well, but he was out of town. After introductions, he wanted to know how things were going and to discuss the airline problems. It was a big order. I first gave a run down about the difficulties the team had right along with our offices in Brussels and Washington, and also that of the CAA. I then had Frank discuss the maintenance side. We must have talked for over an hour; all the time the Prime Minister kept taking notes. When the meeting was over, His Majesty said he would take action right away. Indeed he did. The following week there was a shake up of the high echelon in the RJ airline. Meetings were held with the CAA officials and the CAAG team. Ironically, the PM was scheduled to take a Royal Joradanian flight to Geneva for a meeting. There was a delay in his departure: aircraft maintenance. He learned that the maintenance dept. was robbing parts from other aircraft to get his off the ground. The PM queried the mechanics, and learned that what Frank and I had told His Majesty was true. He elected to take another airline to Switzerland and then to Geneva. When the dust had settled, I went to see the new DCM Pat Theros and briefed him on my meeting with His Majesty and what had transpired. I also handed him a written report. It was a copy of the ones sent to Brussels and Washington. When Ali Ghandour returned, I discussed the meeting. He said he arranged the meeting with His Majesty and myself and was glad I had spoken up.

By the end of August Frank Day had left for his station in Seattle. I also received all the fancy binders for the CARS and the handbooks. I had five sets put together immediately. The original was for His Majesty, the next to the Director General, Ali Ghandour, The Ambassador, Brussels and Washington. I was also making plans to pack and leave by October. Brussels had informed me that I may be required to stay another six months.

My back was now healing rapidly and I could get around on my own. One morning Evelyn asked, "What happens to me now that you are leaving? Are you going to throw me out to the wolves?" I asked if she wished to return to the Philippines. "No, I want to marry you." "Wow!" I said I was an old man, that she could do a lot better. I told her I was creeping up to seventy-three! She gave me a dirty look and replied, "Never talk about being old." She loved me and age didn't count.

I talked to Eric Ledger, who was married to a Filipino stewardess. I asked about getting married in Jordan. He and Ruby were excited about our considering marriage. "Don't worry, I can arrange it," said Eric. "It's difficult with the English or American church. I can fix it with the Greek Orthodox Church." Eric contacted the Greek Bishop who told Eric I would have to pay about five hundred bucks, U.S. It meant becoming a Greek for a week! I had just about been everything else; why not a Greek! I told Eric I didn't want the ceremony at the church. "How about at my home?" "Great." So it would be arranged at Eric's place. I had ordered a silk dress from my friend Charles in Bangkok. It fit Evelyn like a glove, Chinese style with slits up the sides to the knees. I had asked that His Majesty be invited, but he was unable to attend as he was going on a state visit to Baghdad. The new Ambassador Suddarth was tied up in opening ceremonies at the Embassy.

The day arrived and a lot of my friends showed up. One of them Jeff Settle elected to capture the wedding on video. The Bishop was all business-like. He had a portable alter with the special candles. Eric was best man and his wife Ruby was Maid of Honor. I was hoping this would be a quicky. I was wrong! The Bishop chanted the whole thing in Greek, Latin and Arabic; with the ending in English so we could all understand. He placed white frilly halos on Evelyn's and my head. The halos were attached with a long

*Christine's tombstone, Mt. Hope Cemetery, Bangor, Maine.*

silky ribbon. Towards the end of the ceremony the two of us had to waltz around the altar three times with the Bishop leading the way. Finally he asked for the rings and then pronounced us man and wife. This was followed with three sips of wine. Evelyn doesn't drink and I thought she was going to get drunk. I, in all this excitement, wound up kissing Ruby instead of Evelyn. Then more friends arrived to help eat the cake. My landlord Jurban, who is Orthodox Greek by religion, remarked to me, "Pete, you are really married this time!" "I guess so, in several different languages." That weekend we took off for a quick honeymoon to Petra, where else! I assure you we didn't do any mountain climbing. We spent the time around the Hotel and a side trip to Little Petra.

Around September 14 I received a call from the Embassy; the Ambassador wanted to see me. I met him in his office with the DCM, Theros. The Ambassador wasted no time in chewing me out for having met with King Hussein without notifying the Embassy first. When someone of that rank tells you off, you have to sit and take it. I'm a hot tempered individual at times; however, I kept my cool! The Ambassador really was teed off. He said I knew nothing of protocol and that I was too old for this job, and had no business talking to the Head of State without the Ambassador's permission. I bit my lip hard so as not to let him have both barrels right back. I was about to say, "His Majesty knows protocol better than both of us. If he wished to go through proper channels he would have called the Embassy first for a request to see me. Instead, His Majesty called me direct and did not want any Embassy people at the meeting." I let it slide. He then stated the contract would end with the CAAG and Jordan government; he would see that it was not renewed and for me to make plans to return to the States. I said "Fine, I'll return home and play golf."

I took my leave from him and left. I was truly peed off too.

In spite of these difficulties, which can happen with any airline, Royal Jordian Airlines continues to be a great airline, and is as safe as any in the aviation world.

Evelyn and I did a lot of packing at home. Then there were the physicals to take, a State Department requirement. To get Evelyn her U.S. resident's visa was to take time. The Embassy had to find out from the U.S. Embassy in Manila whether Evelyn had any bad record there. What a laugh; after all the bandits pouring into Florida from the Caribbean Islands and still pouring in with the State Department's blessing! I phoned Brussels and Washington; I told them about my meeting with the Ambassador, that he had cut off our water.

Evelyn and I arrived in New York on October 14, 1987. I was assigned as an inspector at the Teterboro Airport office in New Jersey. We found an apartment not far from work and settled down to a new way of life. I had called Hannah and Christian and told them of the new assignment and our address. They were happy for me and my marriage to Evelyn. We were able to visit Hannah and John on weekends. Most of my duties involved violations, incidents and complaints about the same as when I joined FAA in LaGuardia 25 years before. Only difference was, the salary was 10 times more.

In mid-December Christian phoned from Seattle to say he and a friend would visit Hannah during his birthday on December 19. Could Evelyn and myself make it? "You bet we could." It was a great get together; we even drove to Avon and got Geraldine. It was a fun week. It was interesting to see Christian handling his nephews. Uncle Christian; I couldn't believe it. There were moments that I noticed he looked drawn; possible from his double duties of work at the travel agency and his classes at school. The party was soon over.

Evelyn and I were back in our Lincoln Park home in New Jersey.

It was not much fun for Evelyn to be on her own. She didn't know how to drive and couldn't get around on her own; the neighbors stayed aloof. Hannah had suggested a trip to Bangor to visit Christine. We drove up from Bethel. On the way we made a stop at the famed L.L. Bean Sporting goods store. It certainly had grown since I first saw it back in 1929. At Bangor I was heart broken when I saw Christine all huddled up on a sofa and couldn't talk. I learned from the day nurse that she was suffering from Lou Gehrig's disease. I always remember her as a tomboyish person who loved walking and the outdoor life, full of fun and conversation. Now this; no communication, no walking. The end would come in this manner. It would be the last time I would see her. She passed away in May 1989.

New Year's Eve Hannah drove in with Christian. He had a few extra days and hoped to see Christine; the weather was lousy and his flight couldn't make it to Bangor. We didn't celebrate New Year's. Christian was tired from all that flying. That afternoon Evelyn and I drove him to Newark Airport for the flight back. To see Christian for just 24 hours was nice. He still looked drawn and tired. Even though I knew he was working hard, I was disturbed.

January 14 was a clear, cold day and the office work had been routine. I was tired when I returned home. The traffic jams would tire anyone. I was relaxing as Evelyn was puttering in the kitchen with dinner. About then the phone rang. Evelyn very seldom would answer the phone when I was home; she was self-conscious about her accent. I was surprised to hear Christian at the other end. His voice sounded muffled and choked. He first asked if I knew Hannah was pregnant again. I said that she had told me a few days earlier. Christian tried to laugh but choked up and I could hear him sob. I asked what was the matter; I could tell he was upset about something. There was silence for a minute; then he came back and said; "Dad, I'm in hospital. I have pneumonia. Dad, the doctors have also diagnosed that I have AIDS." It hit me like a thunderbolt. I was speechless and dazed as I stared at Evelyn, who seemed to grasp the situation and came to me. My knees weakened and I had to sit on the floor. I don't remember too much of my conversation from that point on. Everything was a blur and incoherent. I think Christian and I carried on a conversation; I asked if he wanted me to come to Seattle. "No," he would call back in a few days. He was crying and I wanted to reach out to him. I wanted to hold him as I so often did when he was a little fellow. "I'll call back, later. Bye Dad." The impact of his words left my mind blurred. I heard Evelyn talking; she sounded far away. Gradually I came to. Evelyn helped me up and asked what had happened. I told her it was Christian; that he had AIDS. As I told her this, my heart seemed to be wrenched and I cried like a kid. Without a word Evelyn poured me a scotch and led me to the sofa. It took some time before I was coherent. We sat and talked for awhile as I sipped the scotch. She had noticed Christian when we saw him in December and New Years. When I recovered enough from the shock, I called Hannah. "Yes," she knew. Christian had phoned earlier. Hannah is tough and didn't let her emotions show too easily. At the office next day, I found it difficult to hide my feelings. I took the chief of the office aside and told him about my son. He sympathized and asked if I wanted to take an enroute to Seattle. I thanked him but said I'd wait till I heard further from Christian.

Christian called again around the twenty-sixth. He sounded chipper; as though nothing was ever amiss. He was feeling great and would be back at school. This cheered me up also. Christian kept in touch by phone often. In mid-February he told me he was coming to Miami in March. He and a friend would be taking a cruise ship to the Caribbean and to Cancun, Mexico for ten days. He hoped Evelyn and I could meet them in Miami. He also asked the possibilities of my transferring to the Miami office. He liked Florida and thought it would be neat to come and visit us in Miami every so often. When he finished school and earned his degree, he would try to get a position in one of the schools in Florida. I said I would try and let him know later. I had several friends in Washington office that may be able to assist me in a transfer. I telephoned one of the friends and explained the situation with the possibility of a transfer to the Miami office. I asked that this be kept confidential for the time being. He understood and would get back to me.

By the end of February I received a call from the Washington office that the possibility of a transfer looked pretty good.

It was necessary for me to visit the chief of the office in Miami. This would work out well, since Evelyn and I planned to be there anyway to visit with Christian. We traveled to Florida and I had my interview with the chief of the office, Mr. Reynolds. Evelyn and I had a few days together with Christian before his cruise and again on his return. When Christian and his friend came back from the cruise, they looked fine with their tans; he was also delighted that it was a ninety percent go for my move to Miami. If all went well, I could be here by the middle of July. Christian didn't discuss his problem; I think he wished to keep it to himself. Anyway, what could one discuss? Even if I had a million dollars to search for a cure, we knew it would be futile. Look at Rock Hudson who tried everything possible. We had another day together and then he departed for Seattle.

In June Christian called to say he had another few days off; could I come over for a visit. I hated to leave Evelyn alone for such a long period of time. She said she would be alright.

The weather in Seattle and Washington is usually predicted rain and fog. This time, while I was to be with Christian for the few days, it was clear and beautiful. The camcorder came in handy and I took a lot of wonderful videos. I got the whole Seattle area and the Mount Rainier Park and the mountains while Christian did all the driving. One could never

guess by his attitude that there was anything wrong. The morning came for my departure back to Newark and Christian drove me to the airport to see me off. After a big hug and farewell, I watched him walk away down the full length of the concourse. He never looked back. I didn't know it then, but it was the last time I was to see my son Christian.

All packing and arrangements were made for the move to Florida. Reporting date was July 8. I was given a farewell lunch by the Teterboro office. They were a great bunch of people. The next day we were on our way to Miami. After a couple months of house hunting, Evelyn and I chose a home in Coral Springs; thirty eight miles from the airport office. It was a spacious bungalow with a screened in pool. I knew Hannah and her children would enjoy their vacations here. And one day I prayed Christian too, would be a part of it. God, how I prayed for a miracle and a great break-through in research for a cure.

The FAA Flight Standards Office in Miami is one of the larger, if not the largest office in the Agency. I knew several of the inspectors from past years. Curiosity was aroused as to how I got transferred without a bid. A few were resentful, others ignored me. I could care less. In time I knew I would make friends.

I was assigned as a Principal Inspector on foreign carriers operating U.S. registered (N) aircraft. In the FAA Regulations they come under Part 129. There were sixty to seventy such operators from Central and South America that our office was responsible for. I was given one airworthiness inspector and one operations. Both were fine people that spoke Spanish fluently. From the start our office was deluged with foreign applicants requiring special FAA certificates to operate U.S registered aircraft. It was time consuming and there was no help coming from any of the other sections of Flight Standards. To make it more difficult, the operations inspector, Raul Pomales, was usually on National Guard duty in Puerto Rico, or receiving recurrent training and checking out on new equipment. He was available about fifty percent of the time. The Airworthiness Inspector, Bill Everett, who was slightly crippled in one knee, had to go to the hospital for an operation. He was away from the office for nearly three months. When he returned, it would be for a couple of months. He then was involved in a car accident and was away another two months. I was left to do most of the work solo. I finally was given a secretary on a temporary basis who spoke Spanish. She was a God-send. A little later I was assigned a Air-worthiness man to replace Bill. I never was afraid of work and accepted the challenge. It became necessary to take work home to try and catch up. Keeping the 129 operator's specifications up-dated, licensing crews, attending to violation and incidents, telephone calls and a hundred and one meetings was a mountainous job. Try as I might to recruit more help my requests just fell on deaf ears, like talking to a wall. None the less I enjoyed working in the foreign element. As far as doing any enroute inspections on Pan American or East-

*With John, Hannah and my son Christian.*

*Evelyn and me at my retirement party wearing my CNAC logo.*

ern Airlines to Central or South America, forget it. Nor could my office do any airport inspections where these two carriers operated. Someone said it was not necessary to do these inspections. I had to dig out the regulations and show where it was mandatory. The answer to all this was, "There is not enough manpower or perdiem money." Then how about the numerous repair stations that were FAA approved in the foreign countries. These were long over-due. There was no comment till the U.S Embassies in some countries requested the stations be renewed.

With the endless work, the months flew by and I just kept hanging in there! Almost every weekend I would call Christian and Hannah. Just to hear them on the phone gave me a lift in spirit. Evelyn was a trouper and gave a lot of moral support. I bought her a car and she learned to drive; in this manner she wasn't dependent on me. She kept busy looking after the house and raising orchids. Though all went well in home, there was always the thought of Christian. When would it happen? Hannah had her third baby boy in early September, named Weston.

October arrived with a slight coolness in the weather. Then Christian called one day and said he would be arranging a short leave around the tenth of December. He suggested we all get together at Hannah's in Bethel. He wanted to see the kids; then laughed and said he was looking forward to a couple of Maine lobster meals. "You bet, Christian, Evelyn and I can make it. Be sure to give me your itinerary." "Ya Dad, I'll do that as soon as I arrange the tickets." He then sent a short note with the date of travel. I in turn arranged Evelyn's and my tickets. It was all set.

*Christian and Yvonne Haley, ex-Saudi Airlines stewardess. Taken at Hurricane Ridge.*

*Christian's ashes are scattered on Hurricane Ridge, as he wished.*

It was during Veteran's Day weekend, November 11th when Christian's friend and roommate called. Peter told me he didn't wish to upset me; but thought I better know that Christian's bed had not been slept in. He had checked with Doug Fox where Christian worked. He had not been there either. Peter said not to be alarmed; soon as Christian showed up he would have him call me. Naturally I was terribly upset and called Hannah. A week went by without any news from Christian's friend. Hannah was in contact with Peter as well. She and John asked Peter to get a private detective and notify the police, giving them Christian's car description and license. Two weeks and still no word or trace of Christian. I told Peter to check with Christian's bank, see if he had drawn any money during the interim. He called later to tell me that Christian had drawn fifty bucks on the tenth; and now it was the twenty fourth, Thanksgiving weekend. I told Hannah I would fly out to Seattle right away. She advised me to stay put; that she and John were on their way and would let me know if they find out anything. Hannah and John spent the Thanksgiving week in Seattle. There was no trace of Christian. I was beside myself and found it difficult to do my work. When Hannah and John returned home, they suggested Evelyn and I come to Bethel

as originally planned; that Christian might show up. My mind was going crazy thinking of some foul play or road accident in the mountains where Christian loved to drive. Hannah told the Seattle police to put an alert out nation-wide. All we could do now, was to hope and pray.

Evelyn and I arrived in Bethel on December 8th, and planned to stay through Christmas. Perhaps Christian was driving over to meet us at Hannah and John's. The next afternoon, I think it was Saturday, the phone rang and John answered. It was the Seattle police. They had found Christian's car in a self storage place across Lake Washington in Kirkland. The police said they would call back after further investigation. I knew inside me, the time had come and tried to brace myself for the inevitable news. I could see that Hannah was tense. An hour later the police were on the phone again. They talked with John. As he talked, he looked at Hannah and me. When he hung up I grabbed Hannah as John told us that the police had identified the body in the car as Christian's. He had committed suicide. Hannah and I cried our hearts out. I noticed Evelyn also sobbing. It took some time to recover and then I poured myself that always needed drink. John started making arrangements for our tickets and motel reservations

in Seattle. Sunday afternoon we departed New York. Late that evening we arrived in Seattle and picked up a rental car. Next morning we drove to Peter and Christian's apartment and decided our plan of action. All this time I could hear Christian's voice and laughter. The police informed us it would be best to come to their station, to identify and pick up Christian's belongings that had been on him and in the car. At the police station I identified Christian's wallet and car keys. My guts were in knots. I wanted to shout out to him; my throat was choked and my eyes heavy with tears. He had written three letters for us, had scribbled the names on the envelopes; mine was, "Dad."

Christian's friend Peter had arranged a lawyer by the name of Matt Sayre who was most helpful and understanding and put together the formalities of Christian's estate. His will left everything to Hannah. The car was still at the storage center. I had difficulty looking it over, John did most of that. Christian had done a good job in his preparation; he couldn't have missed. It was terrible to think that the young man had been lying in the car for a whole month. It was only by chance that the storage manager had Christian's phone number and called Peter to say there was rent due for the storage. It was necessary to get a tow truck to get the car out. John then drove it to a special car wash place to have it cleaned inside and out, then we returned to the motel late that afternoon. I ordered drinks and dinner sent to the room. It was then that Hannah and I opened our letter from Christian. I completely broke down after reading his farewell message to me. Hannah did too. He wished to be cremated and the ashes placed on "Hurricane Ridge," located high in the Olympia Mountains overlooking the Pacific Ocean. The service was held at the funeral home. His friends from the travel agency were there. D'Anne Mount, who was with us on the trip to India in 1976; also Mrs. Bernice Mason, Bob's wife from the old days in Beirut when Christian was a small boy. It was not an easy trip to Hurricane Ridge. Half way up the mountain we had to wait for snow plows to clear the road. The weather was still holding out clear and beautiful. We found a lovely secluded spot away from sightseers, here Hannah placed the ashes near a small pine tree. I tried saying a few words of prayer, then it was all done. Christian had known there was no cure and did not wish to wind up in a hospital as a suffering, skeletal being. He had made a living will and took his life. He was a very brave young man; not yet thirty-one. His furniture, car and other belongings were shipped to Bethel, Connecticut. The day before departure I bought two large salmon from the seafood market. Back in Bethel, Hannah planned to celebrate Christian's birthday anyway. It turned out to be a nice party with a lot of Christian's friends from Connecticut. We gave him a rousing toast. Some of the friends tried to cheer me up; but it would take a great deal of cheering. Evelyn and I stayed through Christmas and New Year's. It was a trying time and not really Christmas except for Hannah's three children.

If this was retribution for my sinful ways, why not strike the blow on me? Why take my son to make me suffer? I will never understand the ways of God.

Evelyn and I returned to Coral Springs to start the year of 1989 and pick up the pieces. I thanked my FAA chief for having allowed me to stay away so long. In the meantime the workload had piled up. It helped take my thoughts off Hurricane Ridge, but not completely.

In February 1989 there had been a terrible aircraft accident in the Azores. An airline operator known as Independent Air, based in North Carolina, was operating several B-707s. One of these planes was on a special flight from Italy, enroute to the Dominican Republic with Italian tourists. They were scheduled to make a technical stop at Santa Maria Azores for refueling. It crashed in the mountains of the island, killing all 144 people on board. I was asked by the FAA in Atlanta and Washington to go over as part of the investigating team. I enrouted on TWA to Lisbon; then took a local Portugese airline to Santa Maria. The same airport used to be a major stopover during the war. The last time I was there was when I was on my way to the States from China in March of '44. It hadn't changed. On arrival, I learned that the NTSB and another FAA man from Washington Headquarters were already at the scene of the accident. Some of the old barracks had been made into a hotel and rooms were hard to come by.

An American Consulate Officer, who was officiating the disposition of bodies, was kind enough to let me share his room. After the first day, I could tell there was not much being organized in setting up a proper investigating team. Every one seemed to be just milling around. Once in awhile a group would charge up to the crash site for a look see. All bodies had been removed to a makeshift morgue at the airport. I took my turn and visited the crash site myself to get a first hand picture of the accident. There was not much left of the 707. After hitting the ridge, about three feet from the top, the major part of the plane hurtled over the top and slammed into the large pine trees on the other side. This tore up most of the airplane and the bodies. On the way to the car I met the other FAA man and asked him what was I suppose to do to help. He just shrugged his shoulders. I also noticed that the 707 questions were directed to the chief pilot of the airline. It was quite obvious I was not needed and told the FAA Coordinator guy and the NTSB that I would like to return to Miami. This was a waste of time and money. "Okay, you can leave."

I tried to catch a flight out that day, but all seats were booked solid both ways to Lisbon. Looked like I was stuck. To kill time, I listened to the cockpit voice recorder. The pilot had mistakenly let down to two thousand feet on instruments into the only cloud shrouding the mountain. The minimum altitude in the Santa Maria area is 3000 feet. This is plainly indicated on all the Jepperson charts. It was clearly shown also on the pilot's chart. Why didn't he question the control tower and make certain of the assigned altitude?

I tried the next day to catch a flight to Lisbon; it was still fully booked. In fact, when the NTSB and the FAA man were ready to depart, it was necessary to charter one of the local airline planes. There were other officials that seemed to be stuck and eager to pay extra to ride the charter flight.

The trip eased my mind with a stopover at the major island of Sao Miguel for a sightseeing day. On the island I came to a small, quaint church that Columbus was reputed to have stopped at for water on his historic return trip. I went into the church and said a humble prayer for Christian.

I was happy to return to Coral Springs and my work at the Miami office. The next few months I was trying to play catch-up with the work that had piled up in my absence. Then another sad blow came. Hannah called me to say that my sister Christine had passed away. I felt so sad. I remembered her in Maine with all those hunting and fishing trips we went on with she and Robert. She was a wonderful outdoors person and full of jokes and laughter. I couldn't go up to Maine for the funeral, I was so loaded down with work after the Azores investigation.

It seemed as though the world was closing in on me like flying toward that distant mountain with the controls locked. The mountain keeps approaching, getting closer and closer with no way to make a turn. The closer the mountain approaches, it starts coming at you faster.

Around August Dickie Traube (Sylvia's only son) phoned me; he called to say that his mother was in hospital, unconscious from brain damage. He would keep me informed. Dickie did call again, a few days later to tell me that Sylvia had passed away. It was so hard to believe, my relatives and friends were leaving me. Sylvia, I'll always remember from those wonderful, carefree days in Maine riding in the rumble seat of Tinkle Bell. It couldn't be happening. Had Christine and Sylvia really gone, as all those other wonderful archery friends in Bangor? Perhaps I was just dreaming it. No, it was only too real; real as Christian's departure. All of a sudden I felt old and ready to call it a lifetime. Evelyn, however, had other thoughts about that. She has always been by my side at a time of need and that has been often. She knew the strain I was under and was most compassionate and understanding. She was always there to watch over me. This is one reason I love her so dearly.

John and Hannah and the three children drove down from Bethel to stay with us for three weeks. The kids enjoyed the pool and the sightseeing trips we went on; such as the Parrot Jungle and SeaWorld. Before I knew it they were on their way back to Connecticut. At Christmas Geraldine came to spend a month. These visits gave me a boost and courage to carry on.

Early in 1990, I was able to do several enroutes on American Airlines. They had bought out Eastern Airlines routes to Central and South America. It was strange to be in places like Belize where I once used to stop when I was with United Fruit Co. on the banana boats. And to see Tela and Porto Barios

*Sunset views from our condo in Port Richey where I still dream of the old times in aviation.*

below as we flew over. All this helped me get over the tragedies that had been heaped on me in such a short time.

One evening Evelyn and I sat down and discussed my retirement. I felt I wasn't putting out enough in my daily work. I had the feeling around me that the second generation were wondering, "Why doesn't that old fart retire and let us do our thing!" They probably could be correct. So, let the young guys sit at their desks and play with their computers. I was getting crotchety, grumpy and jumpy. The computer age was over-powering. It was another language with so much going over my head. I told Evelyn the time had come to hang up the wings and call it a day. I set the date for retirement on December 29th, 1990. I had the paper work done and handed in by September. At the end of November I was given a great retirement dinner. Hannah surprised me by sneaking down the night before. I came to the dinner dressed in my CNAC uniform with the Chinese flag on the back of my flight jacket, et al.

I remember once at a party, it may have been at Tish's in Roswell, when one of the guests asked me, "Pete, if you had a chance to live your life over again, would you change any of your past?" I had to conjure this in my mind for a minute before answering. I finally replied, "I once read a famous verse from the Rubaiyat of Omar Khayyam. It goes like this: 'The Moving Finger Writes, and Having Writ, Moves on; nor all the Piety nor wit shall lure it back to cancel half a line; Nor all the tears wash out a word of it.' I have done what I have done and so be it."

I am retired now. I sold the home in Coral Springs and now live quietly in Port Richey, Florida. I often sit on the porch and gaze out over the Mexican Gulf and watch the shrimp boats come and go, and the dolphins play along the channel. These sights and sounds are perhaps alien to me. My mind sometimes drifts to a distant land with high snow-capped mountains called the Himalayas. I can hear the "tonk-tonk-tonk" of the coppersmith bird in the lush green valleys and the brain-fever bird giving the strange hot weather call, "brain fever, brain fever." I'll take another sip of my scotch as my heart beats a little faster; perhaps because this ROGUE is torn between two worlds.

**FINIS**

# EPILOGUE

Where are they now?

JASMA, the little hill girl from Bhim-Tal, probably married and had a bunch of kids. Like most of those people, she probably died fairly young.

ERIC TOMPKINS, my friend in Bhowali, joined the British Indian Army. He was captured in Singapore in World War II and died as a prisoner of war at the infamous prison camp known as Changi. James Clavell wrote a novel based on the prison, *King Rat*.

The Shepherd estate was sold to a Catholic mission. FRANK SHEPHERD and his family moved to Australia in 1947. He later died there. DORIS married and lived in England. She died in 1992.

RICHARD DUNN died in a drowning accident in Maine in 1939.

ROBERT BURGE (lost on Mt. Kathadin) retired and later died of Alzheimer's disease in 1983.

BILL ELDRIDGE is retired from art and still lives in Belfast, Maine.

HORACE CHAPMAN and all of my archery friends have passed away.

The Peacock Room gang, PERCY MORROW, PHIL OSSER, KEN UPTON, and HAROLD WASSEN, have died.

BILL LALIBERTIE has long-since retired from the Navy and lives in Virginia.

PanAmerican Africa Group 42-A have a reunion every year. Some of my good friends from there have folded their wings: BOB BURKE, SAM GEORGE III. Yet my friend HARRY BERNARD, the singer, is getting along well in Myrtle Beach. TOM CAROLL and his brood of ten are enjoying life in Connecticut. BART HEWITT, who was remarried at one of our reunions, lives happily in Colorado.

My CNAC colleagues still have their reunions with Flying Tigers. BOB PRESCOTT and CLIFF GROH both passed away some years ago.

The MAHARAJAHS OF COOCH BEHAR and JAIPUR died in 1970; most of the Calcutta group have as well. Cooch Behar's palace was abandoned. The beautiful gardens have become overgrown with weeds and jungle.

BORIS LISSANEVITCH, of Yak and Yeti, died in Kathmandu, Nepal.

SYD DEKANTZOW and ROY FARRELL, partners in Cathay Pacific Airlines Hong Kong, sold out in 1952. Syd returned to Sydney, Australia. Not long after, he was killed in a car accident. Roy Farrell and I exchange phone calls once in a while. He went into the oil business in Texas. Roy states that the wells keep pumping salt water, and he continues to drink scotch and sodas!

KYLE "MITCH" MITCHELL did well with his bar and restaurant in Lebanon. He is retired from MiddleEast Airlines and lives in Perth, Australia.

RAY GIFFORD retired from TMA and also lives in Perth, Australia.

KIKI remarried and lives in Miami, Florida. Her father JACK died in Bombay years ago.

My good friends, the POEZAVARAS, live happily in Blois, France. We keep exchanging Christmas cards, theirs in French and mine in English!

My nephews, the four sons of my brother GEORGE (who was killed in a bus accident on the island of Jamaica in 1949) and his wife, JESSIE: MARK, the eldest, did well in real estate in Victoria, BC. JUSTIN became a pilot, doing crop-dusting before flying for a charter company. He contracted some ailment from the insecticide he sprayed and died. He managed to write a book called *The Pathless Way*. He leaves his wife ANN and four children. TONY has done well in the jewelry business in Victoria. Then there is my namesake, PETER. He has been in and out of various businesses and resides in Vancouver.

My sister GERALDINE lives alone in Avon, Connecticut. She doesn't do much in the way of painting now; however, she has written a book about her childhood in India. We get to see each other once in a while.

HELEN's husband died. She now lives with our son DAVID and his family at CHRISTINE's old house (Shack) in Harrington. David is now fifty-one. Last year I worked up my courage, feeling it my duty to see my son after forty-nine years, and phoned him while I was in Bangor taking some pictures for this book. We arranged to meet at a restaurant in Ellsworth. Though short, it was a wonderful reunion. I thought David a fine-looking man; I must add, he looks a lot like me! David's wife, MARY-HELEN, is a lovely lady. They have two boys, Scott and Johnathan. Helen looked great and seemed happy to talk about some of the old times. I wanted to talk more to David, but the words wouldn't come. I only hope this has broken the ice, and I can see them more often. I know there is an awful lot to talk about. *Inghallah* - "if God wills!"

We are all placed somewhere on the Good Lord's slide-slope, and someday we all have to make that final touchdown.

PIERRE RICHEAU returned to France from Kano. In 1963 he was looking for a job in Algiers. One weekend he took a girl and his rifle to a desolate stretch of beach. A group of Arabs grabbed them; they tied Pierre to a tree and then raped the girl. They then took the rifle (the same rifle we hunted with in Kano) and shot Pierre. This according to his wife, Rolande.

DANIELLE married an AirFrance guy and lives in Paris, France.

A few of my AirLiban pilot friends still live in Beiruit and want me to visit them someday. My friend BARAKAT has come over to visit me here.

"SOL" SOLINSKI went into the airplane spare-parts business in Los Angeles and later passed away.

WILSON YORK from PanAfrica joined Ozark Airlines, later retiring.

SKIPPY LANE (who was shot in the foot) joined Flying Tiger Airlines and died young.

My good friend HERMAN TOBIN stayed with the American Can Company. He retired and now lives in Los Angeles.

PAUL HENNELL retired from the Canadian AirForce and lives in Vancouver, BC.

JACK RICHARDS (Cactus Jack) wound up at Augusta, GA, working for a fixed based operator. I have tried to contact him, but no one seems to know where he went to. Maybe he's at some local pub, telling his pint-size jokes!

DEMONT EDWARDS has semi-retired and lives near me. I see him and his lovely wife Alfa once in a while.

MORITZ BREMER and INGA have lived in Weisbadden, Germany, since his retirement from Lufthansa Airlines. I recently learned from their son ANDREAS that Moritz has just died of cancer.

My friend AUSTIN YOUNG (CNAC), who helped me with the Haitian airline, was later a prisoner of Castro's in Cuba. He made a daring escape from their prison to Miami, where died a few years ago from cancer.

*Collection of my passports.*

*Silver bowl presented to my father, 1907-1908, for capturing dacoits.*

*Clockwise from top:*

*Down town Karachi in my PanAm uniform, 1942.*

*Naini-Tal looking east with the flats in the foreground.*

*In a ghora-ghari (horse and buggy) Karachi, India, 1942.*

*Rambargh Palace, Jaipur 1948.*

*Clockwise from bottom:*

*Liankiang Mountain around 21,000 feet. On way to Suifu.*

*Pete Peterson and self after successful duck hunt.*

*My father in his Imperial, Indian Police uniform. Age 28, India.*

Clockwise from top:

Elephants wading through tall, tiger grass.

The Monastery Tomb, Petra.

Mt. Ararat, taken from PANAM flight #002 from Teheran to Istanbul, Turkey 1971.

Approaching Jerusalem Airport, Ramallah, Jordan 1956. Occupied by Israel after the '67 war.

*Clockwise from bottom:*

*Roc-du-Pigeon, Beirut, Lebanon 1956.*

*Myself with Jack and Cora Brown, Byblos, Lebanon, 1956.*

*John and Hannah as bride and groom, Connecticut May 12th, 1984.*

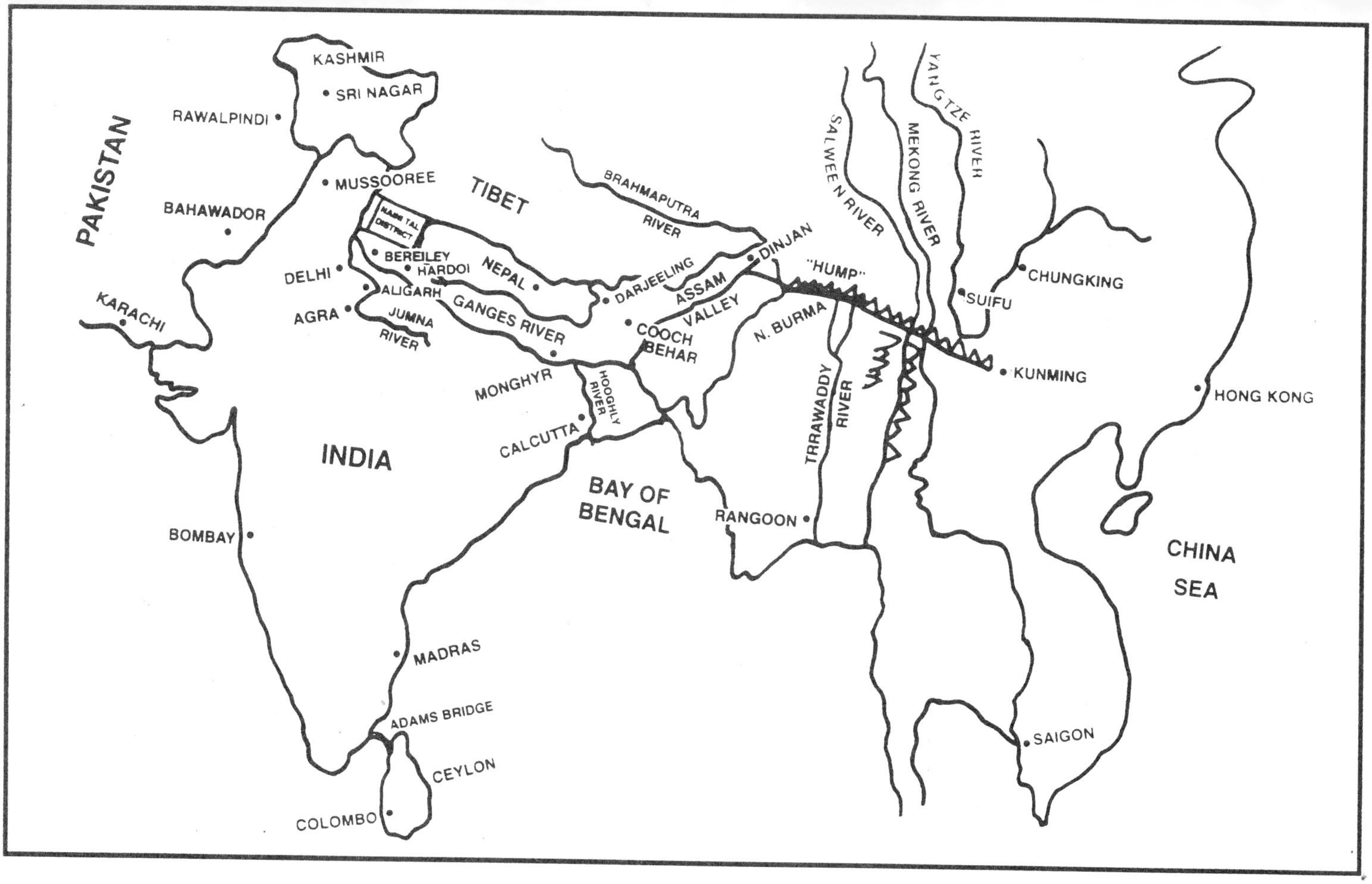

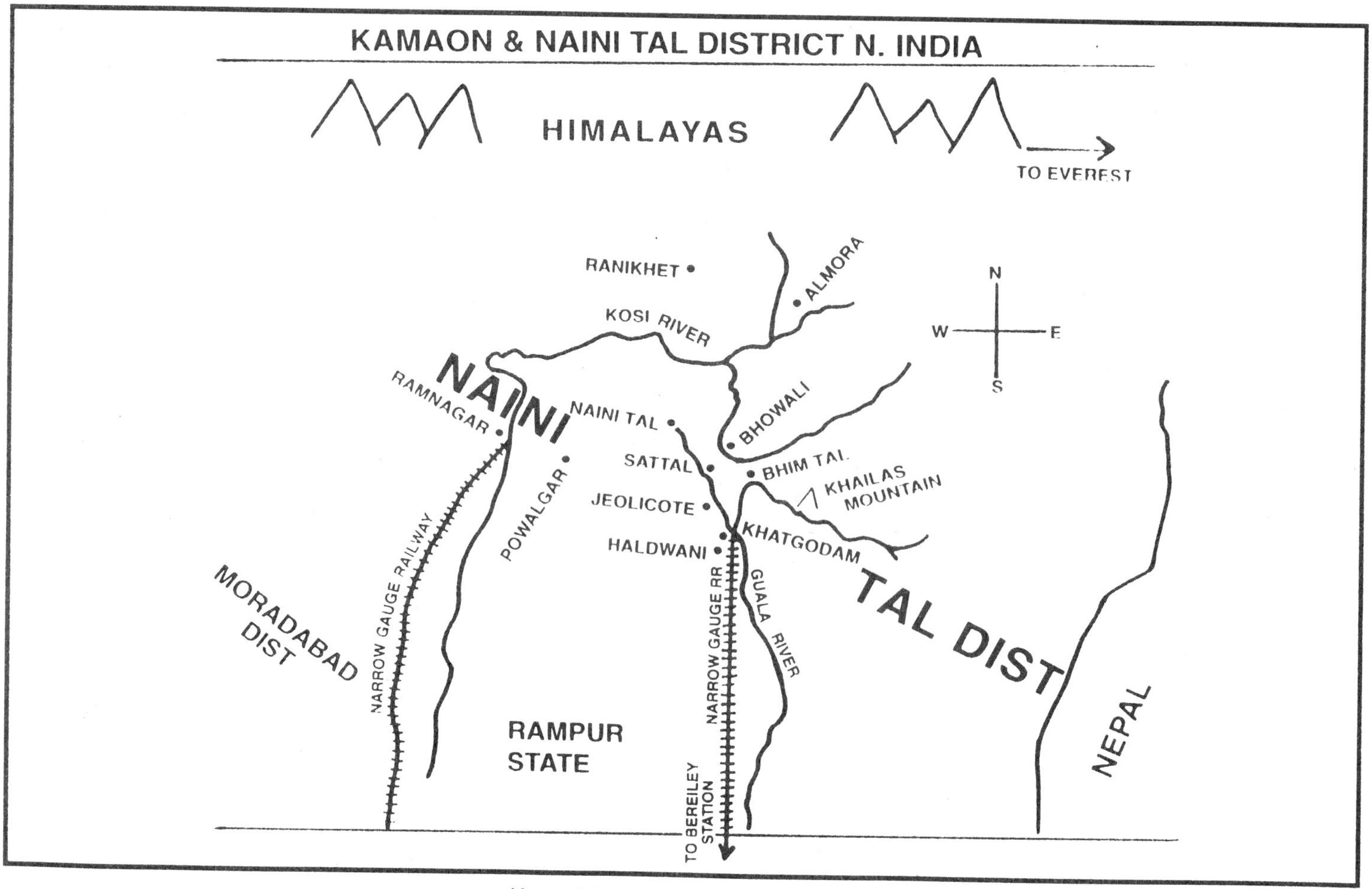

# KAMAON & NAINI TAL DISTRICT N. INDIA

HIMALAYAS

TO EVEREST

*Maps are from sketches by Peter Goutiere*

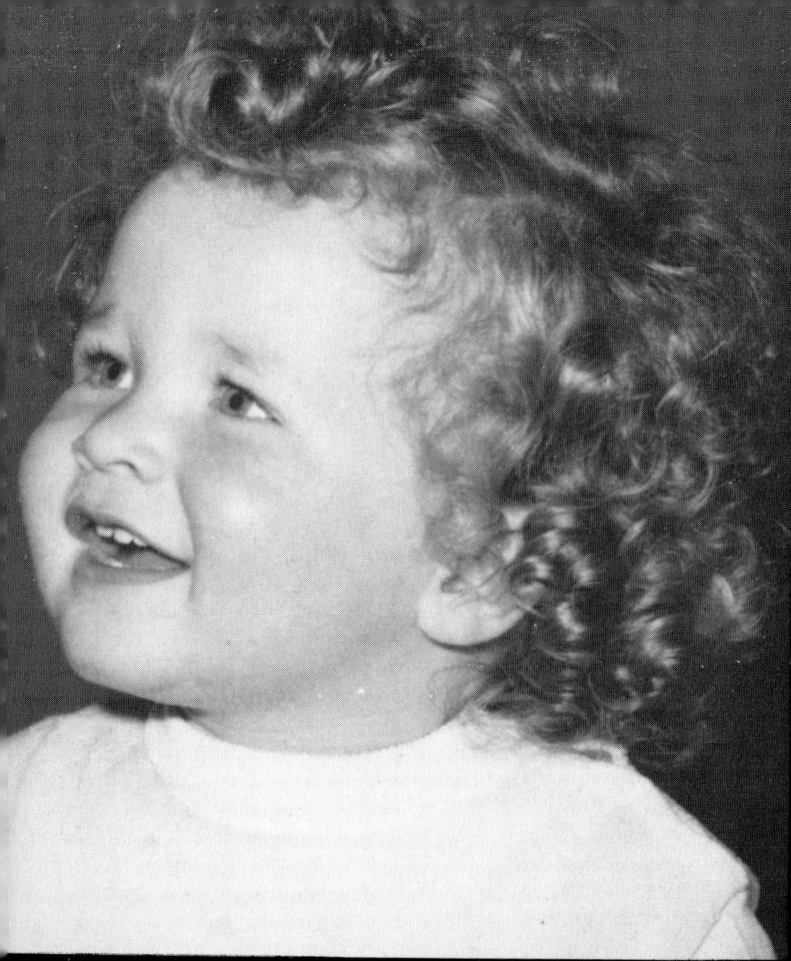

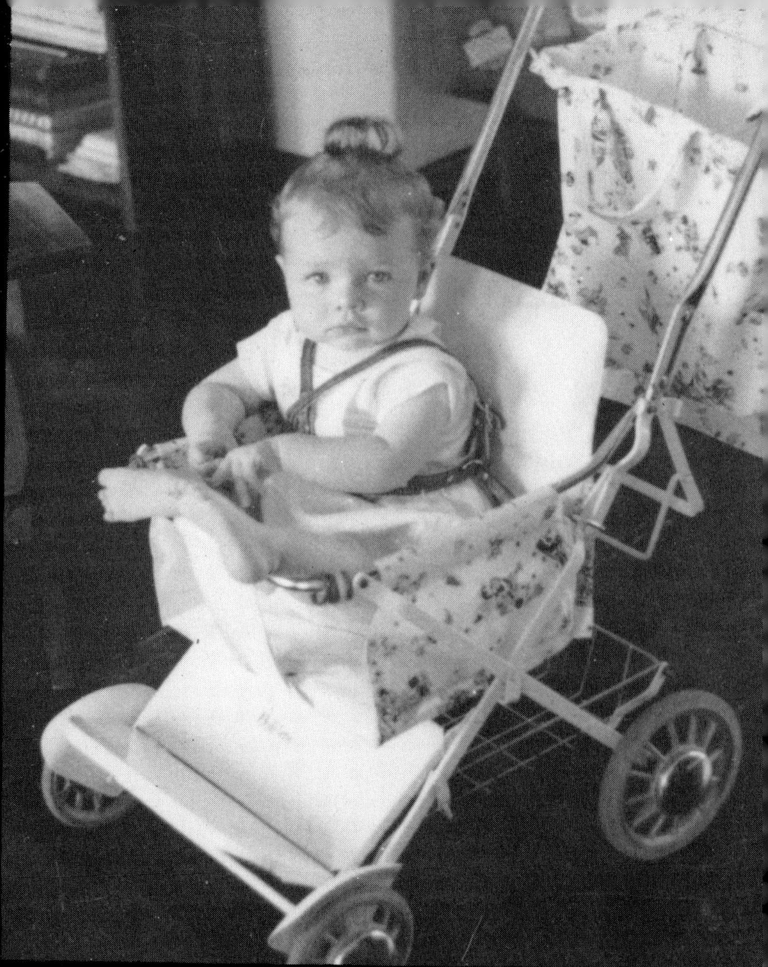